KB262565

Dictionary of Korean Idioms

2013

Idioms
Proverbs
Phrases of Chinese
 derivation
Quotes

한국어 관용어 사전

Kyubyong Park, Michael Elliott

1945

문예림

Authors

• Kyubyong Park

Although my occupation is in the field of natural language, my main personal pursuit has been aiding foreigners in their studies of the Korean language through the many titles I have written on the subject.

My previous publications include:
Tuttle Learner's Korean-English Dictionary (2012), Tuttle Publishing
500 Basic Korean Verbs (2012), Tuttle Publishing
Korean For Beginners (2010), Tuttle Publishing
Teach Yourself Hangul by Video (2010), Sotong
500 Basic Korean Adjectives (2009), Sotong
Survival Korean Vocabulary (2007), Nexus

• Michael Elliott

Michael Elliott is the founder of the popular English study site for Koreans, EnglishinKorean.com, and also runs KoreanChamp.com for advanced students of Korean. His educational podcasts have a weekly audience of more than 50,000.

After relocating to Korea 10 years ago solely to study the language, he passed through the advanced levels at Yonsei University, YBM and Seoul Korean Language Academy. He began working as a professional translator in 2005, and has since been a staff translator for Seoul's largest newspapers, translated scripts and subtitles for some of South Korea's biggest films and been featured regularly on Korean radio.

He has appeared on numerous educational broadcasts teaching English to Koreans and Korean to foreigners and has given lectures on Korean translation and seminars on English education throughout the country.

Michael Elliott is a graduate of the California Institute of the Arts.

Contents

Preface

외국어를 익힐 때 관용어는 가장 어려운 영역에 속한다. 외국인이 한국어를 배울 때도 초·중급에서 중·상급으로 나아가는 단계에서 관용어의 벽에 부딪히게 된다. 한국어를 곧잘 하는 사람도 관용어에 부담을 느끼는 것은 마땅한 교재나 사전이 없기 때문이기도 하다. 국어사전에서 관용어는 단어 표제어의 하위 항목에 속해 있어 검색이 용이하지 않다. 또 그 뜻만 간략하게 나와 있고 예문이 없는 경우도 많다. 해당 관용어의 유래에 대한 설명이 잘 나와 있지 않은 것은 물론이다. 사정이 이러하니 외국인이 국어사전을 통해 관용어를 학습하거나 모르는 관용어를 접했을 때 국어사전에서 찾아 익히기를 기대하기 어렵다. 또 교수자가 관용어 교수를 위해 참고하기에도 국어사전은 적절하지 않다. 이에 우리는 한국어 학습자와 교수자 양쪽 모두가 참고할 수 있는 한국어 관용어 사전을 기획하게 되었다. 우선 주요 국어사전의 관용어를 추출, 비교하여 일반적인 고등교육을 받은 한국인이라면 익히 알고 있을 주요 관용어 목록을 정했다. 이후 각 표제어를 설명하기 위한 표제항 요소를 확정하고 두 사람이 역할을 나누어 작업했다. 대체로 박규병이 먼저 한국어로 원고를 쓰면 마이클이 영어로 번역하고 살을 보태는 방식으로 작업이 이루어졌다.

본 사전의 주요 특징은 아래와 같다.

첫째, 한국어 학습자와 한국어 교습자를 위한 최초의 한국어 관용어 사전이다. 정의나 예문, 참고(note)에 이르기까지 한국어와 영어를 나란히 적어 독자가 한국어와 영어 양쪽을 고두 참고로 할 수 있도록 했다. 만약 한국어로만 서술했다면 외국인 학습자가 참고하기에 불편할 것이고, 영어로만 되어 있다면 한국인 교사에게 부담스러울 수 있음을 감안한 것이다.

둘째, 모든 표제어에는 한 개 이상의 대화문을 용례로 실었다. 관용어 중에는 글보다는 입말에서 자주 쓰이는 것들이 많다. 또 관용어의 정확한 쓰임을 이해하기 위해서는 발화 상황과 맥락을 관찰할 필요가 있다. 여느 사전과 같이 문어에 기반한 단일 문장의 예문이 아닌, A-B(-A-B)의 대화를 보여준 이유가 여기에 있다.

셋째, 참고란을 통해 관용어의 용법이나 유태를 최대한 많이 설명했다. 특히 우리는 관용어의 유래를 설명하는 데 많은 시간을 들였다. 관용어의 유래가 관용어 학습에 크게 도움이 된다는 데는 의심의 여지가 없다. 어떤 관용어는 그 유래가 널리 알려져 있거나 명백하지만 그렇지 않은 것들이 사실 더 많다. 우리는 관용어의 유래를 학술적으로 고증하여 밝히려 하기보다는, 학습자가 그 표현을 보다 쉽게 이해할 수 있도록 하는 합당한 설명을 찾는 쪽에 치중했다. 이를 위해 활자화된 참고문헌뿐 아니라 인터넷 자로와 주변 지인의 지식을 많이 참고했다. 특히 내 친구 조영택은 대단히 뛰어난 직관과 논리로 많은 관용어에 대해 명쾌한 설명을 내놓아 나를 놀라게 했다.

모쪼록 이 사전이 날개 돋친 듯 팔렸으면 좋겠다. 그렇게 된다면 이 책을 수정, 보완하는 등의 후속 작업을 진행하기가 한결 쉬워질 것이기 때문이다.

Kyubyong Park

Many years ago, when I first summoned the courage to pack up my things and move to Korea to begin my full-fledged study of Korean, I arrived in Seoul only to find such a scarcity of resources for learners of the Korean language that I felt like I was blazing my own trail. Bookstore shelves had little more than dry Korean textbooks from the various big universities, and nothing along the lines of conversation practice or idiom books. Across the aisle, however, was an expansive selection of enticing books for Koreans learning English. It was, of course, a less than ideal workaround, but I began taking advantage the array of compelling English-learning materials to learn the Korean phrases I was curious about.

As time passed and the Korean Wave phenomenon has put Korea on the pop culture map, there has been a marked improvement in the offerings for Korean language learners. There has remained, however, a major hole in the literature: a comprehensive dictionary of Korean phrases for learners. It has always been my goal to find a way to help students of Korean so that they would no longer be forced to use English-learning materials in reverse to learn Korean. Through my work at koreanchamp.com and with the publication of this text, I hope that we can make a meaningful contribution.

Today, there are many books out there, but they contain a relatively small amount of phrases and are not organized in a manner that is conducive to use as a reference. My primary hope in this undertaking was to aid learners struggling due to the absence of a comprehensive idiom dictionary and an overall dearth of resources. With this dictionary, we hope to provide you, the students of Korean, with a one-stop resource to look up any unfamiliar phrase you may come across.

Michael Elliott

Guide to the Dictionary

A. Headword

This dictionary contains 2013 essential Korean idiomatic expressions. The entries are organized by alphabetical order in Korean. Spaces and parentheses were not taken into account in determining the order. One hundred twenty-one of the most frequently used expressions were also indicated with an asterisk (*).

가난이 원수 [Lit. Poverty is the enemy.] PROVERB 가난 때문에 억울한 경우나 고통을 당하게 됨 = Poverty at times brings unfair treatment or pain. (*syn.* 가난이 죄다) ▌A: 밤새 내린 폭우로 지하 셋방에 물이 들어와 두 살 된 아기를 잃은 부부의 안타까운 소식을 전해 드리겠습

*가난이 죄다 [Lit. Poverty is a sin.] PROVERB 가난 때문에 억울한 경우나 고통을 당할 때 쓰는 말 = Suggest that being poor brings suffering and unfair treatment. (*equiv.* the sin of being poor / Is being poor such a sin? *syn.* 가난이 원수) ▌A: 어제도 소말리아 해적들한테 우리 선원들이 납

B. Literal Meaning

The most simple and concise definition of an idiom is two or more words combined to create a phrase with a new meaning. To understand the actual meaning of an idiom, it is often helpful to first understand the literal meaning of the words in the phrase. For this reason we have placed the literal meaning directly next to the headword.

가난이 원수 [Lit. Poverty is the enemy.] PROVERB 가난 때문에 억울한 경우나 고통을 당하게 됨 = Poverty at times brings unfair treatment or pain. (*syn.* 가난이 죄다) ▎A: 밤새 내린 폭우로 지하 셋방에 물이 들어와 두 살 된 아기를 잃은 부부의 안타까운 소식을 전해 드리겠습

각양각색 [Lit. 各 each + 樣 shape + 各 each + 色 color → various shapes and colors] QUOTE 다양한 모습을 나타내는 말 = a broad assortment (*equiv.* every color (and shape) under the sun) ▎A: 우와, 정말 모자가 다양하네요. = *Wow, they really have all kinds of hats here.* B: 네. **각양각색**의 모자가 여기 있습니다. 천천히 구경해 보세요. = *That's right. We've got all shapes and sizes. Take your time and check out everything we've got.*

C. Class

Just how much of the Korean language will be classified as an idiom varies from person to person. This book includes idioms (in the narrowest sense of the word), proverbs, phrases of Chinese derivation, and quotes.

가닥을 잡다 [Lit. to catch a strand] IDIOM 1. 대략적인 방향을 결정하다 = to lay down the framework for a decision ▎A: 어떻게 할 거야? 대학원에 갈지, 취직을 할지 결정은 내렸어? = *Have you decided what*

가난이 원수 [Lit. Poverty is the enemy.] PROVERB 가난 때문에 억울한 경우나 고통을 당하게 됨 = Poverty at times brings unfair treatment or pain.

(*syn.* 가난이 죄다) ▌A: 밤새 내린 폭우로 지하 셋방에 물이 들어

각양각색 [Lit. 各 each + 樣 shape + 各 each + 色 color → various shapes and colors] CHINESE-DERIVATION 다양한 모습을 나타내는 말 = a broad assortment (*equiv.* every color (and shape) under the sun) ▌A: 우와, 정말 모자가 다양하네요. = *Wow, they really have all kinds of hats here.* B: 네. 각양각색의 모자가 여기 있습니다. 천천히 구경해 보세요. = *That's*

하루라도 책을 읽지 않으면 입안에 가시가 돋는다 [Lit. Going even a day without reading will make thorns poke out of your mouth.] QUOTE 평소에 독서를 꾸준히 해야 한다는 말 = used to encourage regular reading ▌A: 경희야, 텔레비전 그만 보고 책 좀 읽어라. = *Gyeonghee, turn off the TV and read for a change.* B: 엄마, 책 재미없어요. = *Books are boring, Mom.* A: 너는 학교에서 **하루라도 책을 읽지 않으면 입안에 가시가 돋는다**는 달도 안 배웠니? = *Didn't they teach*

D. Meaning in Korean

This section provides the meaning of each headword in Korean.

가난이 원수 [Lit. Poverty is the enemy.] PROVERB 가난 때문에 억울한 경우나 고통을 당하게 됨 = Poverty at times brings unfair treatment or pain. (*syn.* 가난이 죄다) ▌A: 밤새 내린 폭우르 지하 셋방에 물이 들어

E. Meaning in English

This section provides the meaning of each headword in English.

가난이 원수 [Lit. Poverty is the enemy.] PROVERB 가난 때문에 억울한 경

우나 고통을 당하게 됨 = Poverty at times brings unfair treatment or pain. (*syn.* 가난이 죄다) ▌A: 밤새 내린 폭우로 지하 셋방에 물이 들어

F. Related Words

The following four related expressions are provided in parentheses.

a. *equiv.* (equivalents): English expressions that can be substituted for the provided headword

b. *syn.* (synonyms): Expressions that are similar to the headword

c. *ant.* (antonyms): Expressions that have the opposite meaning of the headword

d. *cf.* (confer): Reference expressions

*눈이 높다 [Lit. to have high eyes] IDIOM 1. 이성이나 어떤 대상에 대한 기대 수준이 높고 까다롭다 = to have high standards pertaining to members of the opposite sex or other matters (*equiv.* to have high standards / to set one's sights very high *syn.* 눈높이가 높다 *ant.* 눈이 낮다 *cf.* 눈을 높이다) ▌A: 눈이 높으신가 봐요. 아직까지 결혼을 안 하신 걸 보니. = *Considering the fact that you still haven't gotten married, it looks like your standards must be pretty high.* B: 아니에요. 그냥 아직 짝을 못 만

G. Example Dialogue

We have provided a minimum of one sample dialogue per expression to allow learners to familiarize themselves with the precise usage of each phrase. The headword has been written in bold within each sample dialogue.

가난이 원수 [Lit. Poverty is the enemy.] PROVERB 가난 때문에 억울한 경

우나 고통을 당하게 됨 = Poverty at times brings unfair treatment or pain. (*syn.* 가난이 죄다) █ A: 밤새 내린 폭우로 지하 셋방에 물이 들어와 두 살 된 아기를 잃은 부부의 안타까운 소식을 전해 드리겠습니다. = *Next, the devastating news of parents who lost their two-year-old as their room was deluged last night in the severe rainfall.* B: 부부는 **가난이 원수**라며 오열해 주위를 안타깝게 했습니다. = *The couple tearfully denounced poverty as the true great enemy and the story of their plight brought grief to many.*

H. Cross-reference

One way of using this reference would be to look up any unknown expressions within these pages whenever one encounters them. This book, however, can also serve as a textbook for learning idioms. Our inclusion of other idioms within the dialogues of this book was a deliberate attempt to promote exposure to a greater number of useful expressions. To enable readers to quickly find the other idioms used in the dialogues, we have included their page numbers as well.

어안이 벙벙하다 [Lit. for one's tongue to be dumbfounded] IDIOM 놀랍거나 기막힌 일을 당하여 얼떨떨하다 = to be bewildered because of a surprising or perplexing happening (*equiv.* to be wide-eyed in astonishment / to be dumbstruck) █ A: 수상 소감 부탁드립니다. = *How do you feel about winning this award?* B: 제가 대상을 받게 될 줄은 꿈에도 몰랐어요. ➡p.113 그래서 지금 좀 **어안이 벙벙합니다**. = *I never in my wildest dreams imagined I would be holding this prize in my hands. That's why my jaw is still hanging wide open.*

I. Note

The note section contains comments in Korean and English on the usage or origin of each phrase. The exact origin of the majority of Korean idioms is unknown. In instances where the origin was unknown or there existed contrary ideas on the origin of the phrase, we have strived to include a comprehensive list of the possible origins of the phrase and a logical explanation on its derivation.

가는 날이 장날 [Lit. The day one goes is the market day.] PROVERB 어떤 일을 하려고 하자 마침 예상하지 못한 일이 발생함 = One sets out to complete a certain task and is met with an unexpected happening. (*equiv.* as luck would have it / just my luck) ▌A: 오늘 목욕탕 갔다 왔어? = *You stopped by the sauna today?* B: **가는 날이 장날**이라고, 오늘이 한 달에 한 번 있는 휴일이지 뭐야. = *Just my luck, today was their monthly day off.*

NOTE: 과거에는 장이 서는 날, 즉 장날이 정해져 있어 이날에는 마을 사람들이 모두 나와 물건을 사고팔았다. 따라서 이날에는 집이 비어 있는 경우가 많았다. '가는 날이 장날'이라는 말은 아는 사람 집에 놀러 갔는데 그날이 마침 장날이라 집에 사람이 없더라는 뜻이다. 보통은 공교롭게 부정적인 상황에 놓였을 때 쓰지만, 때로는 마침 운이 좋았을 때 쓰기도 한다.

In the Korea of yore, markets were not held every day, but only on certain days. Such days were called 장날, or market days, and the whole town would likely turn out to take part. Accordingly, most houses were left empty when the market was open. This phrase means that of all days one could choose to visit a friend's house, one happened to choose a market day, thus finding a deserted house. It is most often used when referring to an undesirable outcome, but can sometimes be employed to describe a positive twist of fate as well.

ㄱ

가난이 원수 [Lit. Poverty is the enemy.] PROVERB 가난 때문에 억울한 경우나 고통을 당하게 됨 = Poverty at times brings unfair treatment or pain. (*syn.* 가난이 죄다) ▌A: 밤새 내린 폭우로 지하 셋방에 물이 들어와 두 살 된 아기를 잃은 부부의 안타까운 소식을 전해 드리겠습니다. = *Next, the devastating news of parents who lost their two-year-old as their room was deluged last night in the severe rainfall.* B: 부부는 **가난이 원수**라며 오열해 주위를 안타깝게 했습니다. = *The couple tearfully denounced poverty as the true great enemy and the story of their plight brought grief to many.*

가난이 죄다 [Lit. Poverty is a sin.] PROVERB 가난 때문에 억울한 경우나 고통을 당할 때 쓰는 말 = suggests that being poor brings suffering and unfair treatment (*equiv.* the sin of being poor / Is being poor such a sin? *syn.* 가난이 원수) ▌A: 어제도 소말리아 해적들한테 우리 선원들이 납치됐대요. 참 큰일이에요. = *I heard that some Korean sailors were kidnapped yesterday by Somalian pirates. What a big mess!* B: 맞아요. 그 사람들도 좀 안됐어요. **가난이 죄**라고 먹고살 길이 없어서 해적이 된 거 아닐까요? = *That's right. Their situation is pitiable as well. Their poverty probably led them to life as pirates. I guess that's why they say poverty is a sin.*

가는 날이 장날 [Lit. The day one goes is the market day.] PROVERB 어떤 일을 하려고 하자 마침 예상하지 못한 일이 발생함 = One sets out to complete a certain task and is met with an unexpected happening. (*equiv.* as luck would have it / just my luck) ▌A: 오늘 목욕탕 갔다 왔어? = *You stopped by the sauna today?* B: **가는 날이 장날**이라고, 오늘이 한 달

에 한 번 있는 휴일이지 뭐야. =*Just my luck, today was their monthly day off.*

NOTE: 과거에는 장이 서는 날, 즉 장날이 정해져 있어 이날에는 마을 사람들이 모두 나와 물건을 사고팔았다. 따라서 이날에는 집이 비어 있는 경우가 많았다. '가는 날이 장날'이라는 말은 아는 사람 집에 놀러 갔는데 그날이 마침 장날이라 집에 사람이 없더라는 뜻이다. 보통은 공교롭게 부정적인 상황에 놓였을 때 쓰지만, 때로는 마침 운이 좋았을 때 쓰기도 한다.

In the Korea of yore, markets were not held every day, but only on certain days. Such days were called 장날, or market days, and the whole town would likely turn out to take part. Accordingly, most houses were left empty when the market was open. This phrase means that of all days one could choose to visit a friend's house, one happened to choose a market day, thus finding a deserted house. It is most often used when referring to an undesirable outcome, but can sometimes be employed to describe a positive twist of fate as well.

가는 말이 고와야 오는 말이 곱다 [Lit. Outgoing words have to be pretty for the incoming words to be pretty.] PROVERB 다른 사람을 잘 대해야 그 사람도 자신에게 좋게 한다는 말 =One must treat others well if one wants to be treated well in return. (*equiv.* What goes around comes around. / Do unto others as you would have them do unto you. *syn.* 가는 정이 있어야 오는 정이 있다) ▌A: 너나 잘 해! =*Mind your own business!* B: 뭐? 어떻게 나한테 그렇게 말할 수 있어? =*How can you talk to me like that?* A: 가는 말이 고와야 오는 말이 고운 법이야. 네가 먼저 나한테 심한 말을 했잖아. =*It's the Golden Rule—you went overboard first with what you said to me.*

가는 정이 있어야 오는 정이 있다 [Lit. There must be outgoing compassion for there to be incoming compassion.] PROVERB 다른 사람을 잘 대해야 그 사람도 자신에게 좋게 한다는 말 =One must treat others with compassion if one wishes to be treated with compassion. (*equiv.* You scratch my back, I'll scratch yours. *syn.* 가는 말이 고와야 오는 말이 곱

다) ▌A: 오늘 내 생일인데, 선물 없어? = *Today's my birthday. Don't you have anything for me?* B: 너는 내 생일에 선물 안 줬으면서, 지금 선물 달라는 거야? **가는 정이 있어야 오는 정이 있지.** = *You didn't get me a present on my birthday and you're asking for one from me? You take care of me and I'll take care of you back.*

가닥을 잡다 [Lit. to catch a strand] IDIOM **1.** 대략적인 방향을 결정하다 = to lay down the framework for a decision ▌A: 어떻게 할 거야? 대학원에 갈지, 취직을 할지 결정은 내렸어? = *Have you decided what you're going to do: go to grad. school or get a job?* B: 어. 대학원에 가는 쪽으로 **가닥을 잡았어.** = *Yep. I've decided to go with grad. school.* **2.** 상황을 파악하다 = to understand the situation (*equiv.* to get a handle on something / to begin to grasp something) ▌A: 아, 취직하기가 너무 어려워. = *Finding a job is so tough.* B: 뭐 우리나라만의 문제겠어? 전 세계적으로 불황이잖아. 경제 전문가들도 경제 위기의 **가닥을 못 잡고 있는 것 같아.** = *Do you think Korea's the only country like that? The whole world is going through a recession right now. It seems like even the experts on the economy have no idea what's going on.*

NOTE: 가닥은 한 곳에서 갈려 나간 낱개의 줄을 말한다. 가닥을 잡고 그 가닥을 따라 올라가면 줄이 시작된 지점에 자연스럽게 도착할 것이다. 이 지점에서부터 전체적인 방향이나 흐름이 결정된다.
A 가닥 is a strand of thread that has frayed. Following the thread will naturally lead one to the starting point of the string. Once this starting point has been established, one can determine the proper course of action in a given situation.

가닥이 잡히다 [Lit. for the strand to be caught] IDIOM **1.** 결정의 대략적인 방향이 결정되다 = for the framework of a decision to be made (*equiv.* to lay a framework) ▌A: 이번 학기 등록금은 결정되었습니까? = *Has the tuition been set for next semester?* B: 아직 논의 중입니다. **가닥이 잡히지 않은 상황입니다.** = *It's still under discussion. The framework is yet to be set.* **2.** 상황이 파악되다 = to grasp a situation (*equiv.* to get a handle on something) ▌A: 김 형사, 이번 실종 사건은 좀 **가닥이 잡**

히는 것 같아? =*Detective Kim, do you feel like you are starting to get a handle on this missing-person case.* B: 좀 더 수사를 해 봐야 할 것 같아요. =*A little more investigation and I think we'll be at that point.*

가랑비에 옷 젖는 줄 모른다 [Lit. In a light drizzle, one doesn't notice one's clothes are getting drenched.] PROVERB 대단치 않은 것도 반복되면 심각한 결과를 초래할 수 있음 = Small things in large volume can be of great consequence. (*equiv.* Big trouble comes in small packages. / the straw that breaks the camel's back / Many drops make a flood.) ▌A: 엄마, 용돈 떨어졌어요. 용돈 좀 주세요. =*Mom, I'm all out of spending money. Please give me a little more.* B: 용돈 받은 지 얼마 안 됐잖아? =*It's only been a few days since I gave you money last time.* A: 매일 과자 사 먹느라고 조금씩 썼더니 벌써 다 없어졌어요. =*I just spent a little every day on snacks and stuff and then all of a sudden it was gone.* B: 그러게, **가랑비에 옷 젖는 줄 모르는** 법이지. =*That's the way it goes: many drops make a flood.*

가려운 곳을 긁어 주다 [Lit. to scratch the spot that itches] IDIOM 다른 사람이 꼭 필요로 하는 것을 만족시켜 주다 = to satisfy people exactly in the way they wish (*equiv.* to hit the spot / to scratch an itch / to satisfy someone's hunger) ▌A: 새로 온 수학 선생님 정말 잘 가르치시는 것 같아. =*The new math teacher is really great.* B: 내 생각도 그래. 학생들이 뭘 모르는지 잘 아시는 것 같아. =*That's exactly what I was thinking. He really seems to know exactly what the students need to know.* A: 가려운 곳을 긁어 주시는 기분이야. =*Yeah, his teaching really scratches an itch.*

가만있자 [Lit. Let's be still.] IDIOM 생각이 얼른 떠오르지 않을 때 쓰는 말 = used when one cannot immediately think of what to say (*equiv.* Hold on (just a second). / Let me think just a moment.) ▌A: **가만있자** ……. 내가 여권을 어디에 뒀더라? =*Hold on just a second ... Now where did I set down my passport again?* B: 안방 서랍 속에 넣어 뒀잖아요. =*You put it in the drawer in the master bedroom.*

가만히 앉아 있다 [Lit. to sit still] ɪᴅɪᴏᴍ 적극적인 행동을 하지 않고 방관하고 있다 = to not take an aggressive approach to an issue and instead stand idly by (*equiv.* to sit idly by / to sit still / to stand at the sidelines *syn.* 뒷짐만 지고 있다, 팔짱(을) 끼고 구경만 하다, 앉아서 보고만 있다) ▌A: 이 문제를 어떻게 해결하면 좋을까? = *How do you think we can address this problem?* B: 글쎄, 우리가 할 수 있는 일이 있을까? = *Well, do you really think there is anything we can do about it?* A: 지금 **가만히 앉아만 있자**는 말이야? 그럴 수는 없어! = *Are you suggesting that we just sit idly by and do nothing? That is not an option!*

가면을 벗다 [Lit. to shed a mask] ɪᴅɪᴏᴍ 정체나 속마음을 드러내다 = to bring out into the light one's true identity or intentions (*equiv.* to drop the facade / to shed one's mask *ant.* 가면을 쓰다) ▌A: 김 이사가 이번에 사장님 몰아내는 데 앞장선 거 알아? = *Did you know that Director Kim headed up the charge to drive out the boss?* B: 나도 들었어. 그동안 되게 친해 보이더니. 드디어 **가면을 벗은** 거로군. = *Yeah, I heard that too. But they looked so close. I guess he finally showed his true self.*

가면을 쓰다 [Lit. to wear a mask] ɪᴅɪᴏᴍ 속마음을 감추고 거짓으로 행동하다 = to conceal one's true emotions and act in an affected way (*equiv.* to wear a mask *syn.* 탈을 쓰다 *ant.* 가면을 벗다) ▌A: 길거리에서 모르는 사람이 과자 사 줄 테니 같이 가자고 해도 절대 따라가면 안 된다. = *Never go with a stranger who promises to buy you something to eat.* B: 착해 보이는 아저씨라도? = *Even if they look like a nice person?* A: 그럼. 나쁜 사람도 착한 척 **가면을 쓰고** 있을 때가 많거든. = *Of course not. Bad people often pretend to be kind.*

가물에 단비 [Lit. a welcome rain during a drought] ᴘʀᴏᴠᴇʀʙ 오랫동안 기다려 온 일이 마침내 이루어짐 = a long-awaited event finally taking place (*equiv.* like rain after a long drought) ▌A: 어제 우리 학교 야구부가 오랜만에 이겼다지? = *Our baseball team finally won a game yesterday, huh?* B: 정말 얼마만의 승리야? 올해 첫 승이지? **가물에 단비** 같은 첫 승이네. = *Yeah, how long has it been? It's the first time this year, huh? It's like a cool rain after a long drought.*

가물에 콩 나듯 PROVERB = 가뭄에 콩 나듯

가뭄에 콩 나듯 [Lit. like beans sprouting in a drought] PROVERB 드물게 = rarely (*equiv.* once in a blue moon / few and far between *syn.* 가물에 콩 나듯) ▌A: 장사는 좀 돼? = *How's business these days?* B: 처음에는 손님이 있었는데, 겨울이 되니까 **가뭄에 콩 나듯** 있어. 큰일이야. = *We had a lot of customers at first, but now that winter has come, they're few and far between. It's a serious problem.*

NOTE: 콩은 물이 충분히 공급되어야 잘 자란다. 그런데 가뭄에는 비가 오지 않으니 콩이 잘 자랄 수가 없다. '가뭄에 콩 나듯'이라는 속담은 가뭄에 어쩌다 한번 콩이 자라나듯이 어떤 일이 드물게 발생할 때 쓰는 표현이다. '가물에 콩 나듯'이라고도 한다.

Beans take plenty of water to properly sprout. But during a drought, the scarcity of water means that no beans will be sprouting anytime soon. To say that it's "like a bean sprouting in a drought," is to say that a certain occurrence is extremely rare. The expression is also sometimes used with 가물 instead of 가뭄.

*가방끈이 길다 [Lit. to have a bag with long straps] IDIOM 학력이 높다 = to have an impressive academic background (*ant.* 가방끈이 짧다) ▌A: 이번 회사 창립기념일 행사 때 퀴즈 대결을 한다는데, 우리 팀 대표로는 누가 제일 좋을까요? = *They're saying there's going to be a quiz at the company's foundation day party. Who should we choose to represent us?* B: 김 대리가 제일 낫지 않을까요? 그래도 우리 중에서는 제일 **가방끈이 길잖아요**. = *Don't you think Mr. Kim would be the best choice? He is the most educated among us.*

NOTE: 학생은 가방을 들고 학교에 다니게 마련이니 가방과 학생은 상징적으로 관련이 깊다. 이 표현에서 가방끈은 가방을 들고 다닌 기간을 상징하는데, 가방끈이 길다는 것은 그만큼 학생이었던 기간이 길다는 뜻이므로 곧 학력이 높다는 말이다. 가방끈이 짧다는 표현은 그 반대의 의미를 지닌다.

Students head off for school with a bag slung over their shoulder. Therefore, the idea of a bag or backpack is closely linked to the learned world in Korean allegory. The straps represent the amount of time one shouldered a book bag, so saying that someone's bag has long straps is a way of saying that they spent a lot of time within the walls of academia. On the flip-side, saying 가방끈이 짧다 is a way of saying that someone is not quite up to snuff in terms of schooling

***가방끈이 짧다** [Lit. to have a bag with short straps] IDIOM 학력이 낮다 = to not be well educated (*ant.* 가방끈이 길다) ▌A: 제가 **가방끈이 짧아서** 아는 것이 많지 않습니다. =*I'm rather uneducated, so I don't know very much.* B: 무슨 겸손의 말씀이십니까? 선생님처럼 대단하신 분이 어디 있다고요. =*Why are you being so modest? There's no one out there at your level.*

NOTE: See the note on 가방끈이 길다.

가슴에 멍이 들다 [Lit. to have a bruised heart] IDIOM 마음에 상처를 입다 = to have one's feelings hurt (*equiv.* to be emotionally scarred / It really hurts me (when you say that).) ▌A: 소영아, 제발 엄마 말 좀 들어라. =*Soyoung, just listen to what I'm saying.* B: 엄마, 잔소리 좀 그만 하세요. 귀찮아요. =*Stop nagging me, Mom. It's annoying.* A: 네가 그렇게 말하면 엄마는 **가슴에 멍이 들잖니**. =*When you talk like that, it really hurts my feelings.*

가슴에 못(을) 박다 [Lit. to hammer a nail into someone's heart] IDIOM 다른 사람의 마음에 깊은 상처를 주다 = to hurt someone emotionally (*equiv.* to stab someone in the heart / to shoot someone through the heart *cf.* 못(을) 박다) ▌A: 난 이제 네가 싫어졌어. 우리 그만 헤어지자. =*I'm really starting to hate you. Let's end this.* B: 어떻게 너는 남의 **가슴에 못 박는** 말을 그렇게 쉽게 할 수 있니? =*How can you just shoot me through the heart like it's nothing?*

가슴에 못이 박히다 [Lit. to get nailed in the heart] IDIOM 마음에 깊은 상처를 입다 = to be deeply hurt (emotionally) (*equiv.* to get stabbed in the heart / to be shot through the heart) ▌A: 저는 아빠하고 말 안 한 지 일 년이 넘었어요. = *It's been a year since I've spoken to my father.* B: 저런! 무슨 일이 있었어요? = *What? What happened between you two?* A: 저희 결혼을 반대하시면서 하신 말씀 때문에 **가슴에 못이 박혔거든요.** = *The things he said while opposing my marriage were like a knife in my heart.*

가슴에 새기다 [Lit. to engrave something on one's heart] IDIOM 기억하다
= to bear in mind (*equiv.* to sear something into one's memory / to keep something at the front of one's mind) ▌A: 두 사람은 항상 서로를 사랑하고 존중하며 살아가기 바랍니다. = *I hope you two will always love and respect each other.* B: 네, 그 말씀 **가슴에 새기고** 살겠습니다. = *Yes. We will live by those words.*

가슴에 손(을) 얹다 [Lit. to place a hand on your heart] IDIOM 양심에 의거하다
= to listen to one's conscience (*equiv.* I cross my heart.) ▌A: **가슴에 손을 얹고** 다시 말해 봐. 정말 넌 몰라? = *Put your hand on your heart and tell me again. Are you sure you don't know anything about this?* B: 몇 번이나 말했잖아. 정말 난 모르는 일이야. = *I've already told you a hundred times. I don't know anything about it.*

NOTE: 미국이나 다른 서양 여러 나라에서 오른손을 가슴에 대는 행위는 경의나 엄숙함을 상징한다. 선서나 맹세를 할 때 흔히 이런 몸짓이 수반된다.
Just as in the US and many western nations, placing your right hand on your heart is considered to be a sign of reverence or solemnity. It is also associated with taking an oath or swearing by one's words.

*가슴에 와 닿다 [Lit. to touch one's heart] IDIOM 감동을 일으키다 = to
give rise to emotions (*equiv.* (That movie etc.) really hit close to home / It was touching. / I could really relate to it.) ▌A: 오늘 강연은 어땠어요? = *How was the talk today?* B: 교수님의 유학 시절 경험담이 **가슴에 와 닿았어요.** = *I could really relate to the professor's account of his experiences studying abroad.*

가슴에 칼을 품다 [Lit. to carry a knife in one's heart] IDIOM 누군가에게 원한을 갖다 = to hold unresolved malice towards someone (*equiv.* to have it out for someone / to hold a grudge) ▌A: 요즘 뉴스를 보면 원한 살인이 참 많은 것 같아요. = *There seems to be so many stories of revenge killings in the news recently.* B: 세상이 각박해져서 **가슴에 칼을 품고** 사는 사람이 많아서겠죠. = *With the world becoming as heartless and cold as it has, many people have it out for their fellow man.*

가슴을 쓸어내리다 [Lit. to stroke down one's heart] IDIOM 안심하다 = to regain one's composure (*equiv.* to pull oneself together) ▌A: 옆집 사람들 많이 놀랐겠네. 애 잃어버린 줄 알고. = *The neighbors must've had quite the shock—thinking they had lost their child like that.* B: 네. 곧 찾았으니 다행이죠. 그제서야 **가슴을 쓸어내리**더라고요. = *Yeah, it's just lucky that they found him as soon as they did. It wasn't until then that they were finally able to regain their composure.*

가슴을 열다 [Lit. to open one's heart] IDIOM 속마음을 보이다 = to show one's inner thoughts (*equiv.* to open up to someone) ▌A: 나 요즘 고민이 많아서 너무 답답해. = *I have so many worries all pent up inside me.* B: 무슨 일인데. **가슴을 열고** 시원하게 말해 봐. = *What's going on? You can open up to me. It'll be a big relief.*

가슴을 울리다 [Lit. to make someone's heart ring out] IDIOM 감동을 주다 = to give someone a deep impression (*equiv.* to touch someone / to resonate with (the listeners) / to strike a chord (with the audience) *syn.* 가슴을 적시다) ▌A: 참 훌륭한 연설이었습니다. = *That really was a remarkable speech.* B: 뭘요, 부끄럽습니다. = *Oh, you're making me blush.* A: 아닙니다. 정말 많은 사람들 **가슴을 울렸어요**. = *No, really. Your remarks really resonated with the audience.*

가슴을 적시다 [Lit. to wet someone's heart] IDIOM 감동을 주다 = to give someone a deep impression (*equiv.* to touch (someone) / to leave someone with a deep impression / to get to (someone) *syn.* 가슴을 울리다) ▌A: 영화 참 감동적이지 않아? = *That movie was really touching, wasn't it?* B: 응, 맞

아. 보는 사람의 **가슴을 적시는** 영화는 참 오랜만인 것 같아. = *Yeah, it was. It had been a long time since I had seen a movie that really got to the audience like that.*

가슴(을) 치다 [Lit. to strike oneself in the chest] IDIOM 안타까워하거나 후회하다 = to lament (*equiv.* to beat one's chest in grief) ▌A: 부모님 살아 계실 때 효도하세요. 돌아가신 후에 **가슴을 치고** 후회해도 소용없어요. = *You have to be a loving son to your parents while they are still here on Earth. There's no use beating your chest in regret once they're gone.* B: 오늘 부모님께 전화나 드려야겠네요. = *I'd better give them a call today.*

NOTE: 일이 마음대로 되지 않아 억울하거나 답답해서 가슴을 두드리는 행동을 형상화한 말이다.
This expression paints an image of a man striking his chest in frustration out of vexation or when he thinks he has been treated unfairly by the world.

가슴(을) 태우다 [Lit. to burn one's heart] IDIOM 무엇인가에 대한 걱정으로 초조해하다 = to be vexatious with worry (*equiv.* to burn with worry *syn.* 속(을) 태우다, 속(을) 끓이다, 애(를)태우다) ▌A: 너무 **가슴 태우지** 마세요. 그냥 마음을 비우세요. = *Don't fret about it too much. Just let it go.* B: 저도 그러고 싶은데, 잘 안 되네요. = *I wish I could, but it's not really working out.*

가슴(을) 펴다 [Lit. to stretch one's chest] IDIOM 당당하다 = to assume a confident air (*equiv.* to straighten one's shoulders / to keep your head held high / to keep one's chin up *syn.* 어깨(를) 펴다) ▌A: 요즘 왜 그렇게 힘이 없어? = *Why are you looking so worn out recently?* B: 이번에 또 시험에 떨어져서 가족들 볼 면목이 없어요. = *I failed the test again and now I can't face my family.* A: 뭘 그걸 갖고 그래? 괜찮아, 다음에 붙으면 되지. **가슴 펴고** 다녀. = *Why are you making such a big deal out of it? It'll be fine. Just make sure you pass next time. Keep your chin up.*

➡ p.242

가슴이 내려앉다 [Lit. for one's chest to collapse] IDIOM 몹시 놀라다 = to be very shocked (*equiv.* to be scared out of one's wits / to experience heart-stopping fright *syn.* 가슴이 철렁하다) ▌A: 야, 넌 무슨 그런 장난을 쳐? 너 때문에 **가슴이 내려앉는** 줄 알았어. = *Hey! What do you think you're doing playing that kind of prank? You almost gave me a heart attack.* B: 그랬어? 미안 미안. = *Really? Sorry. Sorry.*

가슴이 넓다 [Lit. to have a broad heart] IDICM 이해심이 많다 = to be magnanimous (*equiv.* to have a big heart *syn.* 속이 넓다 *ant.* 속(이) 좁다) ▌A: 철수야, 정말 미안해. 네가 빌려 준 책을 잃어버렸어. = *Cheolsu, I'm so sorry. I lost that book that you lent to me.* B: 괜찮아. 잃어버릴 수도 있지. = *That's OK. Sometimes those things just happen.* A: 넌 역시 **가슴이 넓은** 친구야. = *That's my Cheolsu—always so understanding.*

가슴이 덜컹하다 IDIOM = 가슴이 철렁하다

가슴이 따뜻하다 [Lit. to have a warm heart] IDIOM 인간적이다 = to be warm-hearted ▌A: 우리 반 담임 선생님은 매달 한 번씩 저희들에게 편지를 써서 주세요. = *Our homeroom teacher writes us a letter every month.* B: 우와, 정말 **가슴이 따뜻한** 분이시구나! = *Wow, she sounds like a really warm-hearted person.*

가슴이 떨리다 [Lit. for one's heart to tremble] IDIOM 긴장되다 = to be nervous (*equiv.* for one's heart to skip a beat / for one's heart to palpitate) ▌A: 너, 그 애랑 사귄 지 얼마나 됐어? = *How long have you two been going out?* B: 좀 있으면 백 일이야. 아직 얼굴만 봐도 **가슴이 떨려.** = *We're almost at 100 days now. My heart still skips a beat every time I see her face.*

가슴이 뜨겁다 [Lit. to have a hot heart] IDIOM **1.** 열정적이다 = to be passionate (*equiv.* to have a fire in the belly) ▌A: 아직 **가슴이 뜨거운데,** 벌써 제 나이가 쉰이네요. = *I still have the burning heart of my youth but I'm already fifty years old.* B: 그래서 그런지 나이보다 훨씬 젊어 보이세요. = *Maybe that's the reason that you look so young for your age.* **2.** 감동을 받다 = to be moved ▌A: 어제 TV에서 30년 전에 잃어버린 딸하고 만난 엄마 봤어? = *Did you see that mother get reunited with her* *daughter after 30 years on TV yesterday?* B: 응. 그것 보고 나도 **가슴이 뜨거워져서** 울었어. = *Yeah, I saw that and was moved to tears myself.*

가슴이 뜨끔하다 [Lit. to have a prickly sensation in one's heart] IDIOM 어떤 일로 인해 양심의 가책을 느끼다 = to feel the pang of guilt (*equiv.* to have something eating at one's conscience) ▌A: 아빠가 아끼시는 도자기를 실수로 깨뜨렸는데 사실대로 말을 안 했어요. 그런데 어제 갑자기 아빠가 그 도자기가 어디 갔냐고 물으시더라고요. = *I broke a piece of pottery that was really precious to my father by accident and still haven't been able to tell him what really happened. Now he's asking me if I know what happened to it.* B: 정말 **가슴이 뜨끔했겠군요** = *That must be eating at your conscience.*

가슴이 철렁 내려앉다 IDIOM = 가슴이 철렁하다

가슴이 철렁하다 [Lit. to have one's heart struck] IDIOM 몹시 놀라거나 충격을 받다 = to be very surprised or shocked (*equiv.* I almost had a heart attack. *syn.* 가슴이 내려앉다, 가슴이 철렁 내려앉다, 가슴이 덜컹하다) ▌A: 어제 할머니를 흔들어 깨워도 안 일어나셔서 **가슴이 철렁했어요**. = *Yesterday I couldn't wake up Grandma at first, even when I tried to shake her awake. I was so shocked.* B: 왜요? = *Why?* A: 나이가 아주 많으시고 자주 편찮으시거든요. = *She's really getting on in the years and has been sick a lot lately.*

가슴이 타다 [Lit. for one's heart to be on fire] IDIOM 긴장이나 걱정으로 초조해지다 = to be fretful with nerves or worries (*syn.* 속(이) 타다, 애(가)타다) ▌A: 도대체 어디 간 거니? 엄마 걱정하는 거 몰라? = *Where on Earth were you? Do you know how worried I was?* B: 죄송해요. 전화하는 걸 깜빡했어요. = *I'm so sorry. I just forgot to call.* A: 정말이지 **가슴이 타는** 줄 알았다. 다음부터는 전화하는 거 잊지 마라. = *I was so worried I really thought I was going to die. Don't forget to call next time*

가시(가) 돋치다 [Lit. to sprout thorns] IDIOM 공격의 의도나 불만이 있

다 = to harbor intentions of aggression or to be dissatisfied ▌A: 왜 울어? 무슨 일 있어? = *Why are you crying? What's wrong?* B: 미영이 이것이 엄마한테 어찌나 **가시 돋친** 소리를 해 대는지. 아무리 철이 없어도 그렇지 말이야. = *Miyoung let her sharp tongue get the best of her again. No matter how immature she still may be, she went way too far.*

가시(가) 박히다 [Lit. to contain a thorn] IDIOM 말에 다른 사람을 공격하려는 의도가 있다 = to target someone with one's words (*equiv.* (to make) pointed remarks / (to make) biting remarks *syn.* 가시가 있다) ▌A: 소영아, 왜 울어? = *Soyoung, why are you crying?* B: 민호가 내 글을 보더니 초등학생이 쓴 글 같다고 했어. = *Minho read something that I wrote and said that it seemed like something an elementary school student had written.* A: 걔는 사람 앞에서 꼭 그렇게 **가시 박힌** 말을 잘하더라. = *He always makes those kind of biting remarks.*

가시가 있다 [Lit. to have a thorn] IDIOM 말에 다른 사람을 공격하려는 의도가 있다 = to target someone with one's words (*syn.* 가시(가) 박히다 *cf.* 뼈(가) 있다) ▌A: 방금 철민이가 한 얘기에는 **가시가 있는 것 같아.** = *I think there was a dagger hidden in Cheolmin's remarks.* B: 신경 쓰지 마. 별 뜻 없이 한 얘기일 거야. = *Don't worry about it. I'm sure there was no deeper meaning to what he said.*

***가시방석에 앉다** [Lit. to sit on a cushion of thorns] IDIOM 마음이 불편한 상황에 처하다 = to be faced with a very uncomfortable situation (*equiv.* to be in the hot seat *syn.* 바늘방석에 앉다) ▌A: 시부모님이 올라오셨다고요? = *So, your in-laws are in town?* B: 네. 저희 시어머님은 우리 부부 문제에 너무 참견을 하세요. 계신 동안은 하루하루가 **가시방석에 앉은** 기분이에요. = *Yeah. My mother-in-law is always meddling in our private life. It's like I'm perpetually in the hot seat when they're around.*

가시밭길을 가다 [Lit. to walk a road of thorns] IDIOM 힘겹고 험한 삶을 살다 = to live a difficult and fraught-filled life (*equiv.* (to walk) a difficult path) ▌A: 왜 편한 길 놔 두고 굳이 **가시밭길을 가려고** 합니까? = *Why do you turn away from the easy path and purposely walk a path of* *thorns?* B: 제가 하고 싶은 일이라면 가시밭길이라도 각오가 되어 있습니다. = *When it comes to doing what I love, I'm always ready to walk the more treacherous road.*

가위질(을)하다 [Lit. to do scissor work] IDIOM 영화, 방송, 문서 등의 일부를 삭제하여 편집하다 = to delete parts of a movie, broadcast or document etc. to censor it (*equiv.* to take the scissors to (a work)) ▌A: 영화가 편집이 좀 이상해. = *The editing of the film seemed a little strange.* B: 못 들었어? 사전에 심의위원회에서 엄청 **가위질을 했다고** 하던데. 아마 그래서일 거야. = *Didn't you hear? The Film Standards Commission went to town on it with the scissors. That's probably why it felt a little off.*

가재는 게 편 [Lit. The crayfish sides with the crab.] PROVERB 입장이 같거나 잘 아는 사람들끼리 서로서로 감싸 줌 = Among people of the same ilk or opinion, there is a tendency to protect one another. (*equiv.* There's honor among thieves. / People stick up for their own kind. *syn.* 팔이 안으로 굽는다, 초록은 동색) ▌A: 너 내 동생하고 싸웠다며? 얘기 들어 보니 네가 잘못한 거야. = *I heard you got in a fight with my little brother. From what I heard, it sounds like it was your fault.* B: 지금 네 동생 편 드는 거니? **가재는 게 편**이라더니. = *You're just going to take his side like that? I guess people really do watch out for their own kind.*

NOTE: 가재와 게는 생김새도 비슷하고 생물학적으로도 같은 갑각류에 속한다. 이처럼 비슷한 일에 종사하는 사람이나 관계가 있는 사람들이 서로 사정을 봐 줄 때 '가재는 게 편'이라는 표현을 쓴다.
Crayfish and crabs look similar and are roughly the same type of creature. It's not clear if they'd back each other up in a street fight on the seafloor, but people who hail from the same town or belong to the same groups certainly look out for each other. That's why this expression is often employed to describe a situation where people involved in the same business have each other's back.

가지고 놀다 [Lit. to play with] IDIOM 다른 사람을 만만하게 보고 마구 부리다 = to think little of a person and treat them carelessly (*equiv.* to play games with someone) ▌A: 왜 이랬다 저랬다 해? 지금 나를 **가지고 노는 거야?** = *Why do you keep changing your attitude. Are you just playing games with me?* B: 아, 죄송해요. 갑자기 사정이 생겨서요. = *I'm really sorry. Something just came up.*

가지(를) 치다 [Lit. to grow a branch / to trim off the extra branches] IDIOM
1. 원래 있던 것에서 부차적인 것을 만들다 = for a supplemental thing to appear where something already was (*equiv.* to grow legs / to branch out) ▌
A: 소문이 **가지를 치기** 전에 사람들 입을 막아야 합니다. = *We'd better stop this rumor before it grows legs.* B: 네, 맞습니다. 안 그러면 일이 어떻게 될지 모릅니다. = *That's right. If we don't, there's no telling how this could turn out.* 2. 불필요하거나 중요하지 않은 부분을 제거하다 = to clear away unnecessary parts (*equiv.* to cut to the chase / to write to the heart of the matter) ▌A: 글에 불필요한 부분이 좀 있네요. **가지를 쳐** 내고 핵심만 쓰세요. = *There are some superfluous parts to this composition. Eliminate the extras and just write to the heart of the matter.* B: 네, 알겠습니다. 감사합니다. = *All right. I understand. Thank you.*

가지 많은 나무에 바람 잘 날 없다 [Lit. A tree with many branches will never be still.] PROVERB 자식이 많으면 걱정이 많다 = Having many children leads to many worries. (*equiv.* A mother with a large brood never has a peaceful day. / There is no rest for a mother with many children.) ▌A: 그 집 큰아들이 어제 사고로 병원에 입원했대요. = *The eldest of that household got in an accident yesterday and had to go to the hospital.* B: 둘째랑 셋째는 만날 싸움만 하고 돌아다녀서 부모 속을 썩이더니. 하여튼 **가지 많은 나무에 바람 잘 날 없네요.** = *Their second and third children are always prowling around and getting into fights. I guess there's no rest in a crowded household.*

각광(을)받다 [Lit. to be in the footlight] IDIOM 많은 사람들의 관심이나 인기를 끌다 = to garner attention (*equiv.* to get spotlight / to be in the spotlight / to be in the limelight) ▌A: 김치 안 매워요? = *Isn't the kimchi too spicy?* B: 미국에서도 가끔 김치를 먹었어요. 요즘에는 김치가 외국에서도 **각광받고** 있거든요. = *I used to eat kimchi back in the US* *sometimes too. Kimchi has been getting the spotlight recently all over the world.*

각방을 쓰다 [Lit. to use separate rooms] IDIOM 부부가 서로 다른 방에서 자다 = for a couple to sleep in different rooms ▌A: 우리 부부는 **각방을 쓴** 지 벌써 일 년이 넘었어. = *It's already been a year since we started sleeping in separate rooms.* B: 야, 그래도 잠은 한 방에서 자야지. = *What? I think you've got to at least try to sleep in the same room.*

각양각색 [Lit. 各 each + 樣 shape + 各 each + 色 color → various shapes and colors] CHINESE-DERIVATION 다양한 모습을 나타내는 말 = a broad assortment (*equiv.* every color (and shape) under the sun) ▌A: 우와, 정말 모자가 다양하네요. = *Wow, they really have all kinds of hats here.* B: 네. **각양각색**의 모자가 여기 있습니다. 천천히 구경해 보세요. = *That's right. We've got all shapes and sizes. Take your time and check out everything we've got.*

간담이 서늘하다 [Lit. to have one's liver and gallbladder shudder] IDIOM 몹시 놀라고 섬뜩하다 = to be very scared or terrified (*equiv.* to be struck with terror / It gave me the creeps. *syn.* 등골이 서늘하다) ▌A: 오늘 보니까 우리 선생님도 화 내실 때는 정말 무서운 것 같아. = *Today I saw just how scary our teacher can be when he's mad.* B: 내 생각도 그래. 오늘은 정말 **간담이 서늘했어**. = *That's just what I was thinking. He really struck terror into our hearts today.*

NOTE: See the note on 간도 쓸개도 없다.

간도 쓸개도 없다 [Lit. to have neither liver nor gallbladder] IDIOM 자존심이 없이 비굴하다 = to lack confidence and act in an obsequious manner (*equiv.* to have no guts / to be a pushover) ▌A: 오늘 민주한테 가서 다시 만나 달라고 사정할 거야. = *Today, I'm going to ask Minju to take me back.* B: 뭐? 너는 **간도 쓸개도 없어**? 어떻게 너를 버린 애한테 그렇게까지 할 수가 있어? = *Do you have no self-respect at all? How can you go to those lengths for someone who's already once tossed you aside?*

NOTE: 간과 쓸개는 위아래로 인접해 있을 뿐만 아니라 기능적인 면에서도 관련이 깊다. 옛 사람들도 이 둘의 관련성에 더해서 인지하고 있었던 것 같다. '간담이 서늘하다', '간에 붙었다 쓸개에 붙었다 하다' 등 간과 쓸개가 들어간 관용어를 찾아볼 수 있다.
The liver and gallbladder are not only similar in function but also are located within close proximity in the body. People have long known of their similarity. In addition to this phrase these organs can be found in the idioms 간담이 서늘하다 and 간에 붙었다 쓸개에 붙었다 하다.

간발의 차이 [Lit. the difference of a hair] IDIOM 아주 작은 차이 = an extremely small margin (*equiv.* (to win etc.) by a hair) ▌A: 지금 건 세이프 아니야? = *Wasn't he safe just now?* B: 해설자 말로는 **간발의 차이로** 아웃이라는데? = *The commentator is saying that he was out by a hair.*

간에 기별도 안 가다 [Lit. The message won't even reach one's liver.] IDIOM 양이 차지 않다 = The portions are not enough to satisfy. (*equiv.* I hardly felt like I had eaten.) ▌A: 몇 인분 주문할까? = *How much should we order?* B: 한 3인분이면 되지 않을까? = *Three portions should probably do it.* A: 에이, 3인분으로는 **간에 기별도 안 갈걸.** 5인분은 시켜야지. = *Huh? My stomach won't even notice three portions. We'd better order five.*

간에 붙었다 쓸개에 붙었다 하다 [Lit. to be attached to the liver and then to the gallbladder] PROVERB 자신에게 유리한 쪽을 좇아 가볍게 입장을 바꾸다 = to switch sides according to what benefits oneself (*equiv.* to keep changing sides / to flip-flop) ▌A: 김희철 씨 말이야, 얼마 전까지 그렇게 과장님한테 잘 보이려고 하더니, 요새는 또 부장님만 졸졸 따라다니네? = *You know Kim Heecheol? Up until recently he was trying so hard to give the section head a good impression, but now he's always following the department head around.* B: 사람이 왜 그런지 모르겠어요. **간에 붙었다 쓸개에 붙었다 하고** 말이에요. = *Yeah, I don't know why he's like that. He always just latches onto whoever he thinks will benefit him.*

NOTE: See the note on 간도 쓸개도 없다.

간(을) 졸이다 [Lit. to boil down one's liver] IDIOM 초조해하다 = to be fretful (*equiv.* to be on pins and needles) ▌A: 동생이랑 싸워서 동생이 엄마한테 심하게 혼났어. = *I got in a fight with my little brother and he got in big trouble.* B: 너는 혼나지 않았어? = *You didn't get into any trouble?* A: 저도 혼날 줄 알고 **간을 졸였는데요**, 다행히 저는 별로 안 혼났어요. = *I was really on edge too but luckily I hardly got punished at all.*

NOTE: 전통적으로 간은 신체 내부의 에너지를 조절하는 장기로 이해되어 왔다. 그 때문에 한국 속담에서 간이 용기와 관련되어 쓰이는 예가 많다. The liver is traditionally understood to regulate energy in the body. Therefore, it is also closely associated with courage in the world of Korean proverbs.

간(이) 떨리다 [Lit. for one's liver to quiver] IDIOM 초조해하다 = to fret (*equiv.* to tremble with fright) ▌A: 다음이 네 차례야. = *Next it's your turn.* B: 아, **간 떨려** 죽겠어! = *I'm so nervous I'm shaking like a leaf.*

***간(이) 떨어질 뻔하다** [Lit. to almost have one's liver drop] IDIOM 순간적으로 몹시 놀라다 = to be suddenly shocked (*equiv.* You scared the crap out of me. *syn.* 애 떨어질 뻔하다) ▌A: 왜 사람을 놀래고 그래? **간 떨어질 뻔했네.** = *Why'd you sneak up on me like that? You scared the crap out of me!* B: 사람 오는 줄도 모르고 무슨 생각을 그렇게 해? = *How could you be so lost in thought that you don't even notice someone coming up behind you?*

간이라도 빼 줄 듯이 [Lit. as if one is ready to offer up one's liver for another] IDIOM 자신에게 아주 소중한 것도 내어 줄 정도로 = as if one is willing to make any sacrifice for someone (*equiv.* to be willing to give one's firstborn child) ▌A: 아무도 돈을 안 빌려 준다고? 평소에는 서로 **간이라도 빼 줄 듯이** 친한 척하더니. = *No one is willing to lend you any money? But everyone always carried on as if they would give up their firstborn if you did so much as ask.* B: 친한 사이일수록 돈 거래는 안 하는 게 좋잖아. = *Well, it's true that the closer people are, the more they should* *avoid business deals with each other.*

***간이 붓다** [Lit. to have a swollen liver] IDIOM 처지에 맞지 않게 배짱을 부리다 = to have confidence beyond one's lot (*equiv.* to be (too) cocky / to be too sure of oneself) ▌A: 사장님 앞에서 그런 말을 하다니, 네가 **간이 부었구나!** = *How could you say that in front of the boss? Aren't you getting just a little too sure of yourself?* B: 나도 모르게 그 말이 튀어나왔어. 나 이제 어떡하지? = *I don't know what happened. It just slipped out. Now what do I do?*

***간이 작다** [Lit. to have a small liver] IDIOM 겁이 많다 = to have many fears (*equiv.* to be a chicken / to be yellow *ant.* 간(이) 크다) ▌A: 어디서 오는 길이야? = *Where are you coming back from?* B: 은행에서 돈 찾아오는 길이야. 큰 돈을 갖고 있으니까 떨려 죽겠어 = *I just swung by the bank to pick up some cash. Carrying around all this money is making me really tense.* A: 남자가 그렇게 **간이 작아서** 어떡하려고 그러니? = *How can a man be so timid?*

***간이 콩알만 해지다** [Lit. for one's liver to become as small as a bean] IDIOM 몹시 겁이 나다 = to be in a very frightened state (*equiv.* to be scared out of one's wits / I almost had a heart attack.) ▌A: 여기 있던 내 지갑 못 봤어? = *Did you see my wallet that was just right here?* B: 그거 바닥에 떨어진 걸 내가 주워서 갖고 있어. = *It fell on the ground so I picked it up.* A: 휴우, 다행이다. **간이 콩알만 해졌어.** = *Phew, that's good news. I was just about scared out of my wits.*

***간(이) 크다** [Lit. to have a big liver] IDIOM 대범하고 용기가 있다 = to be bold and courageous (*equiv.* to have guts *ant.* 간이 작다) ▌A: 혼자 밤에 돌아다니면 안 무서워요? = *Aren't you afraid to wander around by yourself at night like that?* B: 아니요, 하나도 안 무서워요. = *Nope, not scared at all.* A: 우와! 정말 **간이 크시네요.** = *Wow, you're a brave man.*

간판으로 내세우다 [Lit. to set forth as a sign] IDIOM 표면에 내세우다 = to put to the fore (*equiv.* to showcase / to headline (a show etc.)) ▌A: 이번에

새로 시작하는 드라마 재밌을까? = *Do you think this show will be good?*
B: 응, 재밌을 거 같아. 한류 스타를 **간판으로 내세웠다던데?** =
Sure. They've got a lot of Korean Wave stars headlining it.

간판을 걸다 [Lit. to hang up a sign] IDIOM 영업을 처음 시작하거나 단체
가 활동을 시작하다 = to start a new enterprise (*equiv.* to hang up one's
shingle *syn.* 문(을) 열다 *ant.* 간판을 내리다) ▌A: 여기서 장사하신 지
는 얼마나 되셨어요? = *How long have you been running this business?* B:
저희가 **간판을 건** 지가 벌써 20년이 넘었네요. = *Well, it's already
been more than 20 years since we hung up our shingle.*

간판을 내리다 [Lit. to take down one's sign] IDIOM 사업을 접거나 단체
가 활동을 중지하다 = to conclude one's business operations (*equiv.* to
shutter a business / to close down *syn.* 문(을) 닫다 *ant.* 간판을 걸다) ▌A:
오늘 점심은 학교 옆 식당에서 먹을까? = *Want to grab lunch at the
restaurant next to the school?* B: 거기 손님이 없어서 어제 **간판 내렸
어**. = *That place wasn't getting enough customers, so they closed down
yesterday.* A: 거기 김밥 맛있었는데. = *But that place had really good
gimbap.*

간판을 따다 [Lit. to pluck a sign] IDIOM 겉으로 내세우기 위해 학력이
나 명분을 갖추다 = to attain academic credentials or justification ▌A: 솔
직히 **간판을 따려고** 대학원에 오는 학생들도 많아요. = *Honestly,
there are many students come to graduate school just to be able to list an
advanced degree under their accomplishments.* B: 그렇죠. 아직 우리나라
에서는 사회에서 간판이 중요하니까요. = *Of course. Such accolades
are still very important in Korean society.*

***갈 길이 멀다** [Lit. to have a long way to go] IDIOM 앞으로도 해결해야
할 과제나 고비가 많다 = to still have much to do and many problems to
resolve (*equiv.* We still have a long way to go. *syn.* 넘어야 할 산이 많다)
▌A: 여러분들 덕분에 무사히 제품을 출시했습니다 = *Thanks to
everyone here, we pulled off a successful launch of this product.* B: 수고하셨
어요, 팀장님. = *You've really outdone yourself, boss.* A: 하지만, 이제부

터가 중요합니다. 아직 **갈 길이 멀다**는 거 다들 알고 있죠?=*But what we do from here on out is even more important. You all realize that we still have a long way to go, right?*

갈 데까지 가다 [Lit. to go as far as one can] IDIOM 극도로 부정적인 상태가 되다=to have gone to extremes in a negative direction (*equiv.* to have gone way too far / to hit rock bottom *syn.* 막장까지 가다) ▌A: 요즘 철민이는 어떻게 지내?=*How is Cheolmin doing these days?* B: 못 들었어? 매일 술 마시고 게임만 하다가 학사 경고 받았잖아.=*You didn't hear? He kept getting drunk every day and playing video games so they put him on academic warning.* A: 정말? **갈 데까지 갔구나**.=*I guess he went too far this time.*

갈림길에 서다 [Lit. to stand at a fork in the road] IDIOM 선택을 해야 하는 상황에 처하다=to be faced with a decision (*equiv.* to stand at a fork in the road / to stand at a crossroads) ▌A: 철민 씨, 요즘 어떻게 지내?=*Cheolmin, how have you been?* B: 취업이냐, 유학이냐 **갈림길에 서** 있습니다.=*I'm standing at a crossroads right now: finding a job or studying abroad.*

****갈수록 태산** [Lit. With time it becomes a huge mountain.] PROVERB 갈수록 더욱 어려운 상황에 처함=to grow worse with time (*equiv.* Things keep getting worse and worse. / Things have gone from bad to worse. / out of the frying pan into the fire *syn.* 산 넘어 산이다) ▌A: 감독님, 갑자기 남자 주인공이 아파서 오늘 못 온답니다.=*Mr. Director, the male lead says he's sick and won't be able to make it today.* B: 이거 큰일이군. 어떡하지?=*That's going to be a major problem. What should we do?* A: 그리고 여자 주인공도 오는 길에 사고가 나서 지금 병원에 있다고 연락이 왔어요.=*We also just got a call that our female lead was in an accident on the way and is now in the hospital.* B: **갈수록 태산이네**.=*Things have just gone from bad to worse.*

갈지자를 그리다 [Lit. to draw the Chinese character for *ji*] IDIOM **1.** 이리저리 비틀거리며 걷다=to totter along (*equiv.* to walk to and fro) ▌A: 정신

좀 차려요. 자꾸 **갈지자 그리지** 말고요. = *Snap out of it! Stop stumbling along like that.* B: 나도 그러고 싶은데, 내 마음대로 안 되네요. = *I'd like to, trust me. I can't exactly control my body right now.* **2.** 중심을 잡지 못하고 주위에 휘둘려 이리저리 왔다갔다하다 = to waiver back and forth (*equiv.* to be wishy-washy) ▌A: 감세 정책이 결국 무산됐네. = *The tax-reduction policy has come to naught.* B: 정치권의 입김에 **갈지자를 그리더니** 결국 그렇게 됐네. = *After being tossed around in the political arena, that's just the way it turned out.*

NOTE: '갈지자'란 '가다'를 뜻하는 한자 '지(之)'를 가리킨다. 이 글자를 보면 좌우로 획이 왔다갔다하는 것을 알 수 있다. '갈지자를 그리다'라는 표현은 사람의 우유부단한 행동이나 태도를 갈지자의 이러한 특성에 비유한 말이다.
The Chinese character 之(지) means "to go." As you can see, the strokes of the character go back and forth. This expression is used when someone moves in a manner akin to the strokes of this character.

갈피를 못 잡다 [Lit. to not be able to catch a niche] IDIOM 헷갈리다 = to not have any idea (about something) (*equiv.* to not be able to make heads or tails of / to have no idea (about what to do) / I don't get it.) ▌A: 아까 그 사람은 왼쪽으로 가라고 했는데. = *Earlier that guy told us to go left.* B: 그러게 말이야. 이 사람은 오른쪽으로 가라고 하니, 이거 원 **갈피를 못 잡겠네.** = *That's what I'm saying. Now this guy is telling us to go right. I have no idea what to do.*

NOTE: 갈피는 겹쳐 있거나 포개져 있는 것들의 사이를 말한다. 책을 어디까지 읽었는지 표시하기 위해 끼워 놓는 작은 물건을 책갈피라고 한다.
The word 갈피 refers to the space between two things that are stacked on top of one another. A place-keeper or bookmark that goes between pages of a book is called 책갈피.

감개무량하다 [Lit. 感 feel + 慨 feel + 無 no + 量 amount + 하다 adjectival suffix → to experience feelings beyond measure] CHINESE-DERIVATION 오랜만에 하는 경험으로 인해 깊은 감동을 받다 = to be overwhelmed with emotion (*equiv.* to overflow with emotions) ▌A: 얼마 만에 한국에 돌아오신 거죠? = *How many years has it been since you were in Korea last?* B: 십 년 만이네요. 정말 **감개무량합니다**. = *It's been ten years. I'm so overwhelmed with emotion right now.*

감언이설 [Lit. 甘sweet + 言word + 利benefit + 說say → sweet words for one's benefit] CHINESE-DERIVATION 상대방을 속이거나 자신이 원하는 바를 이루기 위해 꾸며 내는 말 = words used to deceive the listener or to achieve one's aims (*equiv.* sweet-talk) ▌A: 그러지 말고 같이 가자. 모임에 네가 좋아하는 요리도 많이 나올 거야. = *Come on. Let's go together. There'll be a lot of the kind of food you like at the meeting.* B: 그런 **감언이설**로 나를 유혹하지 마. 나 다이어트 중이란 말이야. = *Don't try to tempt me like that. You know I'm on a diet.*

감지덕지(하다) [Lit. 感feel + 之particle + 德thanks + 之particle → feelings of gratitude] CHINESE-DERIVATION 대단히 고맙게 여기다 = to feel gratitude ▌A: 늦게 와서 미안해. = *Sorry for being late.* B: 아니야. 와 준 것만 해도 **감지덕지지**. = *No bother. I'm happy just to have you.*

감투를 쓰다 [Lit. to wear an old-fashioned hat] IDIOM 높은 직위에 오르다 = to attain a high position (*equiv.* to move up in the world) ▌A: 왜 당신이 그런 것까지 하고 있어? = *Why are you doing that?* B: 나밖에 할 사람이 더 있어? 회장 **감투를 쓴** 덕분에 이런 일까지 내 차지가 된 거지. = *Who else is going to do it? Now that I'm wearing the title of president, this is part of the job.*

NOTE: 감투는 조선 시대에 관리들이 머리에 쓰던 관을 가리킨다. 지금은 더 이상 아무도 감투를 쓰지 않지만, 어떤 직책을 맡았을 때 아직 이 표현을 쓴다.
A 감투 was a piece of headgear that signified rank and was worn by government officials during the Joseon Dynasty. This piece of headwear can no longer be found adorning the heads of Korean officials, but the phrase is still part of the lexicon.

갑론을박(하다) [Lit. 甲 the first + 論 argue + 乙 the second + 駁 argue against → arguments for and against] CHINESE-DERIVATION 자신의 의견을 내세우고 다른 사람의 의견을 반박하다 = to put forth one's opinion and refute another's (*equiv.* to discuss the pros and cons) ▌A: 왜 그렇게 싸우고들 있어? = *Why are you two fighting?* B: 싸우는 게 아니라 이 사람을 뽑을지 말지에 대해 **갑론을박하고** 있는 거예요. = *We're not fighting. We're just discussing the pros and cons of hiring this applicant.*

강 건너 불구경 [Lit. watching a fire across the river] IDIOM 자신과 상관없는 일이라 여겨 적극적으로 참여하지 않음 = to not actively participate in an affair after having judged oneself disinterested (*equiv.* to stand by with one's arms folded *syn.* 강 건너 불 보듯 *cf.* 나 몰라라 하다) ▌A: 그렇게 **강 건너 불구경**하고 있지 말고 너도 좀 도와. = *Don't just stand there with your arms folded like that. Help me.* B: 나도 그러고 싶은데, 다리를 다쳐서 움직일 수가 없어. = *I'd like to help out, but I hurt my leg and I can't move.*

강 건너 불 보듯 [Lit. as if one is watching a fire burn across the river] IDIOM 자신과 상관없는 일이라 여겨 적극적으로 참여하지 않는 모양을 가리키는 말 = the air of a disinterested party (*equiv.* to stand at the sidelines *syn.* 강 건너 불구경 *cf.* 나 몰라라 하다) ▌A: 네 일 아니라고 **강 건너 불 보듯** 지켜만 보고 있기야? = *You're just going to stand at the sidelines because you think this doesn't have anything to do with you, huh?* B: 아, 미안. 내가 뭘 도와주면 돼? = *Oh, sorry. Is there anything I can do to help?*

강단에 서다 [Lit. to stand at the lectern] IDIOM 대학에서 학생들을 가르치다 = to teach at a university (*equiv.* to ascend to the rostrum *cf.* 교단에 서다) ▌A: 교수님, 올해로 **강단에 서신** 지 몇 년 되셨습니까? = *Professor, how many years has it been since you first ascended the rostrum?* B: 올해로 딱 30년 되었습니다. = *This year is exactly my 30th year.*

같은 값이면 다홍치마 [Lit. If it's the same price, go for the crimson skirt.] PROVERB 다른 조건이 동일하다면 품질이 좋거나 예쁜 것을 택

한다 = If all the conditions are the same, one's better off choosing a product of high quality or esthetic beauty. (*equiv.* You might as well spring for the (best one). *syn.* 기왕이면 다홍치마, 이왕이면 다홍치마) ▌A: 아무 옷이나 입지 뭘 그렇게 브랜드에 신경을 써? = *You can just wear anything. Why are you so concerned with brand names?* B: 그래도 **같은 값이면 다홍치마**라고 좋은 거 입고 싶어서요. = *I know but it's just that if the price is about the same, I'd rather wear nice clothes.*

NOTE: 고려가 중국 원나라의 간섭을 받던 시기, 원에서는 매년 고려의 여자들을 데려갔다. 이때 그들은 가급적 결혼하지 않은 여자를 뽑고 싶어했다. 당시 고려는 결혼한 여자는 푸른색 치마를, 결혼하지 않은 여자는 다홍색 치마를 입는 관례가 있었다. 이 때문에 당시 원나라 관리들이 다홍색 치마를 입은 여인을 선호했던 데서 이 표현이 나왔다. 기왕이면 다홍치마, 이왕이면 다홍치마라는 말을 쓰기도 한다.

There was a time during the Goryeo Era that the Yuan Dynasty of China meddled in Korean affairs. Every year, Yuan took women from Goryeo back to China. There was a custom at the time for unmarried women to wear skirts of crimson and married women to wear skirts of blue. It was thought that if one were about the business of choosing a woman, one might as well go for the unmarried one. This phrase is also iterated as 기왕이면 다홍치마, 이왕이면 다홍치마.

개같이 벌어서 정승같이 쓴다 [Lit. to work like a dog and spend like the prime minister] PROVERB

악착같이 돈을 벌어 여유 있게 살면 된다는 말 = to work tirelessly and spend lavishly (*equiv.* to work like a dog and live like a king) ▌A: 왜 그렇게 힘들게 일해서 번 돈을 다 기부하셨습니까? = *Why would you just donate that money that you worked so hard to earn?* B: **개같이 벌어서 정승같이 쓰라는** 말이 있잖아요. 힘들게 번 만큼 좋은 일에 쓰고 싶었습니다. = *Haven't you ever heard the expression, work like a dog and spend like a king? I wanted to put my money towards something that was worthy of how hard I worked for it.*

NOTE: 한국의 속담이나 관용어에서 개는 부정적인 것을 상징할 때가 많다.
In the world of Korean proverbs, dogs usually carry a negative connotation.

개과천선하다 [Lit. 改 change + 過 fault + 遷 move + 善 good + 하다 verbal suffix → to correct one's faults and improve] CHINESE-DERIVATION 지난날의 잘못을 뉘우쳐 착하게 되다 = to reform oneself (*equiv.* to be a new man) ▋A: 네가 어쩐 일이야? 나한테 밥을 다 사고. = *You're buying me dinner? What's gotten into you?* B: 만날 얻어먹기만 해서 미안해서. = *I started to feel bad about how you are always buying me food.* A: 우와, 너 개과천선했구나! = *Wow, you're like a new man.*

***개구리 올챙이 적 생각 못한다** [Lit. The frog doesn't remember his tadpole days.] PROVERB 성공하고 나서 어려웠던 때의 일을 잊어버림 = to forget about one's lesser days after becoming successful (*equiv.* Hard times are soon forgotten. / How soon we forget the bad old days. / Danger past, God forgotten.) ▋A: 요즘 그 사람 좀 변한 것 같지 않아요? = *Doesn't it seem like he has really changed?* B: 맞아요. **개구리 올챙이 적 생각 못한다더니**, 돈 좀 벌었다고 너무 목에 힘을 주고 다니는 것 같아요. ▶p.250 = *Yeah. I guess that's why they say hard times are soon forgotten. People earn a little money and then start prancing around with their chin high up in the air.*

개똥도 약에 쓰려면 없다 [Lit. You can't even find dog poop when you need it for medicine.] PROVERB 평소 흔히 접할 수 있는 물건도 꼭 필요한 상황이 되면 눈에 잘 보이지 않음 = Even things that are readily available normally are no where to be found when you need them most. (*equiv.* How come I can never find it when I need it?) ▋A: 뭐 찾아? = *What are you looking for?* B: 빈 박스 찾아요. 택배 보낼 게 있어서요. 그런데, 눈을 씻고 봐도 없네요. **개똥도 약에 쓰려면 없다니까요**. ▶p.147 = *An empty box. I need to send something by home delivery, but no matter where I look, I can't find a single box. I guess it's true: something's always right there in plain sight until the moment you need it.*

NOTE: 옛날에 정말로 개똥이 약에 쓰였는지는 모르겠다. 그러나 예나 지금이나 개는 우리 주변에서 가장 흔하게 볼 수 있는 동물이며 개똥도 흔히 볼 수 있었다. '개똥도 약에 쓰려면 없다'는 말은 평소에는 쉽게 접할 수 있는 물건도 꼭 필요해서 찾으면 눈에 잘 띄지 않는다는 뜻이다. 때로는 개똥 대신 소똥을 넣어 말하기도 한다.

It is unclear if dog feces was really used to produce medicine in days of yore. But today, as in the past, dogs are all over the place, and thus, so is dog poop. This phrase means that even things that seem to be everywhere you look when you don't need them, become suspiciously hard to find when you do need them. Cow feces, 소똥, is sometimes substituted in this expression.

개똥밭에 굴러도 이승이 좋다

[Lit. Even if you have to roll around in a field of dog poop, this life is the best.] PROVERB 아무리 사는 게 힘들어도 죽는 것보다 낫다는 말 = No matter how hard you're life is, it's better than being dead. (*equiv.* Even still, you're better off being alive. / At least you're not dead. / It's the best of all possible worlds) ▌A: 요즘에는 먹고살기가 정말 힘드네. 사는 재미도 없고. = *It's so hard to make a living these days. And life is such a bore.* B: 무슨 말이야! **개똥밭에 굴러도 이승이 좋다**는 말 몰라? = *What are you talking about? Don't you know this is the best of all possible worlds?*

개미새끼 하나(도) 얼씬 못하다

[Lit. Even baby ants couldn't come close.] IDIOM 아무것도 접근할 수가 없다 = No one or nothing can get through. (*equiv.* Not even a cockroach could get past (me).) ▌A: 별일 없나요? = *Anything going on?* B: 네. 아두 이상 없습니다. **개미 새끼 하나도 얼씬 못하게** 철통같이 경비를 서고 있습니다. = *No. Nothing out of the ordinary. I'm like an impenetrable fortress that not even a cockroach could get past.*

개미새끼 하나 볼 수 없다

[Lit. One couldn't even see a baby ant.] IDIOM 아무것도 보이지 않음 = Nothing is visible. (*equiv.* No one showed up. / Not even a single soul (made it).) ▌A: 누구누구 왔어? = *Who all came?* B: 사람은커녕 **개미 새끼 하나 안 보인다**, 얘. = *Who? Not even a single soul.*

개발에 편자

[Lit. a horseshoe on a dog] PROVERB 물건은 좋으나 그 소유자가 그 물건의 격에 어울리지 않음 = An certain item is of high quality, but the bearer isn't worthy of it. (*equiv.* (to be like) lipstick on a pig *syn.* 돼지 (목)에 진주 (목걸이)) ▌A: 우와, 시계 정말 좋은 거 차셨네요. =

Wow, that's a really nice watch you've got on. B: 그래 봤자 **개발에 편자**죠 뭐. 아내가 사 줬는데 저한테 안 어울리게 비싼 물건이에요. = *Well, it may be nice, but it's just lipstick on a pig. My wife bought it for me but it's way too flashy for me.*

NOTE: 편자란 말의 발굽을 보호하기 위해 말의 발바닥에 대는 쇳조각을 가리킨다. 편자는 만들기가 까다로와서 귀한 물건이지만 개발에는 아무 쓸모가 없다. '개발에 편자'란 가치 있는 물건이 그에 어울리지 않는 대상과 있다는 말이다. 한국 속담에서 개는 평범한 것, 값어치가 낮은 물건을 상징하는 예가 많다.

편자 is the word for a the metal piece, or horseshoe, nailed to a horse's hoof to protect it. In the olden days, the craft of fashioning horseshoes was very involved and required special skills, meaning that horseshoes were precious items. 개발에 편자 denotes something precious in a context unbefitting its worth. In Korean proverbs, dogs usually represent something ordinary or of low value.

개밥에 도토리 [Lit. an acorn in the dog food] PROVERB 따돌림을 받는 사람 = someone who is not accepted by a group (*equiv.* to be left out / to be the odd man out *syn.* 낙동강 오리알) ▌A: 새로 옮긴 부서에서는 잘 적응하고 있나요? = *Are you getting used to your new department?* B: 새 팀에서 나만 다른 일을 하다 보니 **개밥에 도토리**가 된 기분이야. = *Since I'm the only one there working on other things, I feel like the odd man out.*

NOTE: 개는 도토리를 먹지 않는다고 한다. 따라서 개밥 속에 도토리가 끼어 있으면 마지막에 도토리만 남을 것이다. 무리 속에서 다른 사람과 어울리지 못할 때 흔히 개밥에 도토리 신세라고 말한다.

They say that dogs don't eat acorns. So if an acorn does happen to find its way into the dog's dish, it will be the only thing remaining after the dog has eaten its fill. This is the perfect expression for describing someone who just seems to stick out.

개뿔도 모르다 IDIOM = 쥐뿔도 모르다

개뿔도 아니다 IDIOM = 쥐뿔도 아니다

개뿔도 없다 IDIOM = 쥐뿔도 없다

개천에서 용(이) 나다 [Lit. a dragon born from the gutter] PROVERB 좋지 않은 환경에서 뛰어난 인물이 나올 때 쓰는 말 = used to describe an outstanding individual who has emerged from a less than ideal environment or home life (*equiv.* It is a case of a kite breeding a hawk. / a lion born in the humblest of places / like a phoenix born from the ashes *cf.* (미꾸라지) 용 됐다) ▌A: 우리 마을 이장님 큰아들이 시장이 됐대요. = *The eldest son of our town manager became the mayor of a city.* B: 그래? 이렇게 작은 마을에서 출세했네. **개천에서 용 났군**. = *Really? Someone found the path to success in our little town. I guess a lion can be born in even the humblest of places.*

개 팔자가 상팔자 [Lit. A dog's fate is a desirable one.] PROVERB 일이 고생스러워 푸념을 늘어놓을 때 하는 말 = used when complaining about one's circumstances (*equiv.* A dog's life would be an enviable lot. *cf.* 오뉴월 개 팔자) ▌A: 애견 호텔이라고 들어 봤어? 거기에서 개들이 먹고 자고 목욕도 한대. = *Have you heard of dog hotels? Dogs eat, sleep and bathe there.* B: 나도 들었어. 하룻밤에 10만 원이라며? = *Yeah, I've heard of those. They cost about 100,000 won per night, right?* A: 요즘은 **개 팔자가 상팔자야**. 가끔은 개들이 부러워. = *It must be nice to be a dog these days. It's an enviable life indeed.*

NOTE: See the note on 오뉴월 개팔자.

거기서 거기 [Lit. That's there.] IDIOM 크게 차이가 없음 = to be mostly the same (*equiv.* six of one, half dozen of the other *syn.* 대동소이하다, 그 나물에 그 밥, 그놈이 그놈이다, 오십보백보) ▌A: 눈에 들어오는 지원자가 있나요? = *Have any of the applicants caught your eye?* B: 아뇨. 별로 눈에 띄는 사람이 없네요. 모두 **거기서 거기**인 것 같아요. = *No one is really standing out. It's six on one side, half dozen on the other.*

거두절미하다 [Lit. 去 get rid of + 頭 head + 截 cut + 尾 tail + 하다 verbal suffix → to cut off the head and tail] CHINESE-DERIVATION 부차적인 부분은 모두 빼고 요점만 말하다 = to cut out any superfluous talk and just state the salient points (*equiv.* to dispense with the pleasantries / to cut to the chase / to get to the point *cf.* 단도직입(적)) ▌A: 안녕하세요? 그동안 어떻게 지내셨습니까? = *Hi. How have you been?* B: 죄송하지만, **거두절미하고** 용건만 말씀하시죠. = *I'm really sorry, but would you mind just getting down to business?*

***거리가 멀다** [Lit. for the distance to be far] IDIOM 관련이 거의 없다 = to be almost entirely unrelated (*equiv.* for A to be a long way from B *syn.* 거리가 있다) ▌A: 운동 좋아하세요? = *Do you enjoy working out?* B: 사실 저는 움직이는 걸 별로 안 좋아해요. 운동하고는 **거리가 먼** 생활이죠. = *I actually don't like moving around very much. My life is far from being centered on exercise.*

거리가 생기다 [Lit. for a space (between people) to come into existence] IDIOM 사이가 나쁘게 되거나 멀어지게 되다 = for a relationship to become strained (*equiv.* to become distant / to grow apart *cf.* 금(이) 가다) ▌A: 요즘도 명희랑 잘 지내? = *Are things going well these days with Myeonghee?* B: 아니, 바빠서 한동안 못 만났더니 **거리가 생긴** 것 같아. = *Nope, I've been too busy to meet her for a while and now it seems like we've kind of grown apart.*

거리가 있다 [Lit. to have distance] IDIOM 차이가 나다 = to be far from (something) (*syn.* 거리가 멀다) ▌A: 텔레비전에 나오는 연예인들 보면 정말 생활이 화려할 것 같아요. = *From what I've seen on TV, it really looks like celebrities have lavish lifestyles.* B: 아니야. 사실 대부분의 연예인들의 생활은 화려함과는 **거리가 있어**. = *Actually, most celebrities have lives that are far from lavish.*

거리로 나앉다 IDIOM = 길거리로 나앉다

거리를 두다 [Lit. to put space (between oneself and another)] IDIOM 관계를

가까이 하지 않다 = to not maintain a close relationship with someone (*equiv.* to keep one's distance) ▌A: 뭐라고? 너가 마음에 두고 있는 사람이 네 형 예전 여자 친구였다고? = *What are you saying? The girl you've kept in your heart all this time is your older brother's ex-girlfriend?* B: 응. 그래서 그런지 그 사람이 자꾸만 나하고 **거리를 두는** 것 같아. = *Yeah, so that's why I think she keeps trying to keep her distance from me.*

거울(로)삼다 [Lit. to consider something a mirror] IDIOM 모범이나 본보기로 여기다 = to take something as an opportunity for reflection (*equiv.* to use (this) as a learning experience / to learn one's lesson *cf.* 타산지석) ▌A: 이번 일을 **거울삼아** 더 열심히 하겠습니다. = *I'll learn my lesson from this and try harder from now on.* B: 그래, 좋은 경험이었다고 생각해. = *Yeah, I think you should consider this a learning experience.*

거짓말을 밥 먹듯 하다 [Lit. to tell lies like one eats rice] IDIOM 거짓말을 자주 하다 = to often tell lies (*equiv.* Every second word (out of someone's mouth) is a lie.) ▌A: 김학선 씨 또 지각 아니야? = *Is Kim Hakseon going to be late again?* B: 왜 아니겠어요? 오늘은 또 무슨 핑계를 댈지 모르겠어요. = *Why not? I'm curious what excuse he'll use this time.* A: **거짓말을 밥 먹듯 하니,** 이제 학선 씨 말은 믿을 수가 없어. = *Every second word out of his mouth is a lie. I don't believe anything he says anymore.*

***걱정도 팔자다** [Lit. Even worries can be one's fate.] PROVERB 하지 않아도 될 걱정을 하다 = to worry unnecessarily (*equiv.* to worry over nothing *syn.* 걱정을 사서 하다) ▌A: 늦잠 자서 못 일어나면 어떡하지? = *What if I oversleep tomorrow?* B: 참, **걱정도 팔자다** 알람 맞춰 놓고 자면 되지. 마음 놓고 어서 자. = *Don't worry over nothing. All you have to do is make sure you set your alarm. Just relax and try to get some sleep.*

걱정을 사서 하다 [Lit. to buy one's worries] IDIOM 하지 않아도 될 걱정을 하다 = to worry about things unnecessarily (*equiv.* to get all worked up about nothing *syn.* 걱정도 팔자다) ▌A: 아빠, 저 키가 안 자라서 어른

이 돼서도 키가 작으면 어떡하죠? =*Dad, I'm not getting any taller. What if I'm an adult and still just this tall?* B: 녀석아, 별 소리를 다하네. 밥 잘 먹고 시간 가면 키가 크지, 왜 안 커? 왜 **걱정을 사서 해**? =*Hey, kiddo, you sure say the darndest things. If you just eat right, you'll grow tall soon enough. Why wouldn't you? Why are you getting all worked up about nothing?*

걱정이 태산이다 [Lit. for one's worries to be a huge mountain] IDIOM 걱정이 아주 크다 =to have a great many worries (*equiv.* to have a mountain of worries / to have a million things to worry about) ▌A: 남편이 회사 그만뒀다며? 이제 어떡할 거야? =*I heard your husband quit his job. Now what are you going to do?* B: 안 그래도 **걱정이 태산이야**. =*Yeah, I've already got a million things to worry about.*

걷기도 전에 뛰려 한다 [Lit. to try to run before one can walk] PROVERB 쉽고 기초적인 과정을 건너뛰고 어려운 것부터 하려고 할 때 쓰는 말 =to skip over the fundamentals in a certain process and immediately attempt the hardest things (*equiv.* to try to run before one walks) ▌A: 오늘은 첫날이니까 라켓을 쥐는 법부터 배우겠습니다. =*Since today is your first day, let's learn how to hold onto the racket* B: 선생님, 바로 코트에 가서 게임하면 안 되나요? 선수들처럼 해 보고 싶어요. =*Can't I just go to the court and play a game? I want to do it like a real pro.* A: **걷기도 전에 뛰려 하니**? 차근차근 배워야지. =*Are you trying to run before you can walk? You have to learn step by step.*

걸고넘어지다 [Lit. to (make someone) trip and fall] IDIOM 관련이 없는 사람이나 일을 언급하며 트집을 잡다 =to blame someone or something for something they didn't do (*equiv.* to be made scapegoat for something / to be made someone's patsy) ▌A: 경찰은 이번 사건의 책임이 네티즌에게 있대. =*The police are saying the responsible party in this affair was the Netizens.* B: 경찰은 왜 툭하면 네티즌을 **걸고넘어지는지** 모르겠어. =*I don't understand why the police are always trying to blame the Netizens for everything.*

걸신(이)들리다 [Lit. to be possessed by a hunger spirit] IDIOM 몹시 굶주려 음식을 지나치게 탐하다 = to have a ravenous hunger (*equiv.* to have a bottomless pit for a stomach) ▌A: 엄마, 나 배고파. 통닭 한 마리 시켜 먹자. = *Mom, I'm hungry. Let's order some chicken.* B: 애가 **걸신이 들렸나**. 밥 먹은 지 얼마나 됐다고. = *Do you have a bottomless pit for a stomach? It hasn't even been very long since we ate.*

NOTE: 걸신은 구걸하여 얻어먹는 귀신이다. 제대로 먹지 못해 늘 먹을 것에 집착하는 거지처럼 식탐을 보이는 사람에게 하는 표현이다.
A 걸신 is a kind of spirit that subsists by begging its food. This expression is used to describe those who always seem to fixate on their next meal and beg for food like a beggar begs for money.

걸음마를 떼다 [Lit. to toddle] IDIOM 이제 막 무엇을 시작하다 = to have just begun a new undertaking (*equiv.* to take one's first steps *syn.* 첫걸음마를 떼다) ▌A: 한국말 잘하세요? = *Are you good at Korean?* B: 아니요, 이제 막 **걸음마를 뗀** 정도예요. = *No, I'm just taking my first steps in Korean now.*

걸음아 날 살려라 [Lit. Steps, save me!] IDIOM 있는 힘을 다해 빨리 도망침을 이르는 말 = to use one's last bit of energy to make an escape (*equiv.* to get away as fast as one's legs will carry you / Feet, don't fail me now! *syn.* 다리야 날 살려라 *cf.* 삼십육계) ▌A: 어젯밤에 놀이터 앞에서 깡패를 만났어요. = *I came across some gangsters at the playground last night.* B: 그래서 어떻게 했어요? = *So, what did you do?* A: **걸음아 날 살려라** 도망갔죠. = *I got out of there as fast as my legs could carry me, of course.*

검은 머리 파뿌리 되도록 [Lit. until one's black hair turns into the root of a green onion] PROVERB 아주 늙을 때까지 = until one is very old (*equiv.* until one is old and gray) ▌A: 신랑과 신부는 **검은 머리가 파뿌리가** 될 때까지 서로 사랑하고 존중하겠습니까? = *Do you promise to love and respect each other as long as you both shall live?* B: 네! = *I do.* A: 이제 두 사람은 부부가 되었음을 선언합니다. = *I now pronounce you man and wife.*

NOTE: 파뿌리는 백발을 비유적으로 일컫는 말이다.
파뿌리, the roots of a green onion, is a metaphor for gray hair.

겉 다르고 속 다르다 [Lit. for one's interior and exterior to be different]

PROVERB 겉으로 드러나는 행동과 마음속으로 갖고 있는 생각이 서로 다를 때 쓰는 말 = used to describe a situation in which the actions one takes and one's true intentions differ (*equiv.* Appearances can be deceiving. / to say one thing and mean another / to speak with tongue in cheek) █ A: 엊그제 순희네 집에 도둑 들었잖아요? 글쎄 이웃집 남자가 범인이었대요. = *The other day someone broke into Soonhui's house, huh? They say it was the guy who lives next door.* B: 그래? 그 사람 평소에는 얌전하고 성실해 보이더니. **겉 다르고 속 다른** 사람이었나 보군. = *Really? But he looked so normal and trustworthy. I guess appearances can be deceiving.*

겉보리 서 말만 있으면 처가살이하랴 [Lit. If I had even three *mal*

(around 54 liters) of unhulled barley, would I be living with my wife's family?] PROVERB 처가살이의 힘듦을 비유적으로 하는 말 = used to compare one's difficulties to the hardships of a man who lives with his in-laws (*equiv.* It's better to starve than live with your wife's parents. / I'd rather starve than live with my in-laws.) █ A: 결혼해서 살 집은 구했어? = *Have you found the house you'll be living in once you get married?* B: 그냥 처가에 들어가서 살 생각이에요. = *We're thinking about just moving in with my wife's parents.* A: **겉보리 서 말만 있으면 처가살이하지 말라는** 말도 있는데 웬만하면 다시 생각해 보는 게 어때? = *They say it's better to starve than to live with your wife's parents. Don't you think you'd better give that a second thought?*

NOTE: 한국은 전통적으로 가부장 사회여서 결혼을 하면 대개 남자의 집에서 살았다. 결혼 후 여자의 집에서 산다는 것은 좀처럼 보기 드문 경우였고 수치스럽게 여겼다. 지금은 여자의 부모와 같이 사는 경우를 예전에 비해 흔히 찾아볼 수 있지만, 아직도 떳떳하게 생각하지 않는 사람들이 있는 것 같다.

As a traditionally patriarchal society, after marriage, couples lived with the man's family. As such, it was exceedingly rare, to see a married couple living with the woman's relatives and was considered shameful. Nowadays, it is not unheard of for couples to live under the same roof as the wife's family, but those with a conservative bent still consider it improper.

격세지감 [Lit. 隔 apart + 世 world + 之 of + 感 feel → the feeling of being worlds apart] CHINESE-DERIVATION 많은 것기 달라져 다른 세상에 온 것과 같은 느낌 = the feeling one gets when so much has changed in one's absence that returning is like entering a new world (*equiv.* a sea change / night and day / worlds apart) ▮ A: 요즘에는 휴대전화 안 갖고 있는 사람이 없군요. = *There really isn't anyone left who doesn't have a cell phone.* B: 제가 어릴 때만 해도 집에 전화가 없는 사람도 많았는데 말이죠. = *When I was young, a lot of people didn't even have phones in the house.* A: 참 **격세지감**을 느끼네요. = *It really is a different world we're living in today.*

견물생심 [Lit. 見 see + 物 thing + 生 grow + 心 heart] CHINESE-DERIVATION 어떤 물건을 실제로 보면 갖고 싶은 마음이 생김 = the desire to possess something after seeing it (*equiv.* To see (it) is to want (it).) ▮ A: 어제 백화점에 갔다 온 이후로 애가 장난감 사 달라고 자꾸 떼를 써요. = *Since we went to the department store yesterday, my kid has been pestering me to buy him a toy.* B: **견물생심**이라고 물건을 봤더니 더 사고 싶은가 보네요. = *Well, of course seeing those things is going to make him want to have one.*

결자해지(하다) [Lit. 結 tie + 者 person + 解 untie + 之 that → He who tied the knot must untie it.] CHINESE-DERIVATION 일을 벌인 사람이 그 일을 해결해야 한다 = One must deal with the problems of their own creation. (*equiv.* You've made your bed, now lie in it. / You invited this. / You asked for it.) ▮ A: 제가 일을 벌였으니 **결자해지** 차원에서 제가 해결을 하겠습니다. = *Since I'm the one who caused this incident, I must be the one to repair it.* B: 역시 경태 씨는 책임감이 강해. = *That's the Gyeongtae I know! Always with a sense of responsibility.*

결초보은(하다) [Lit. 結 tie + 草 grass + 報 repay + 恩 favor → repaying a favor by tying grass] CHINESE-DERIVATION 은혜를 잊지 않고 반드시 갚다 = to return a favor at all costs ▌A: 제발 이번 한 번만 도와주십시오. 그러면 정말 평생 **결초보은**의 마음으로 살겠습니다. = *Please, just help me out this one time. If you do, I'll live the rest of my life with the goal of repaying you.* B: 그렇게까지 말씀하시니 이번 한 번만 도와드리죠. = *Well, if you're going that far, I suppose I can help you out this once.*

NOTE: 중국 춘추시대 때 한 남자에게 첩이 있었다. 그가 병이 들어 죽으면서 아들에게 그 여인을 자신과 함께 묻으라는 유언을 남겼다. 그러나 아들은 유언을 할 때 아버지의 정신이 온전하지 않았다며 그 유언을 따르지 않고, 대신 그녀를 다른 사람에게 시집 보냈다. 얼마 후 전쟁이 터져 그도 전장에 나가 적군과 싸우게 되었다. 그런데 마침 상대편 장수가 풀에 걸려 넘어져 그 장수를 사로잡게 되었다. 그날 밤 아들의 꿈에 한 노인이 나타나 이렇게 말했다. "나는 당신이 시집 보내 준 여인의 아버지다. 당신이 내 딸을 도와준 데 대한 보답으로 풀을 묶어 그 장수가 넘어지게 만든 것이다."

Long ago in China, there lived a man and his concubine. The man grew ill and died. In his will, he instructed his son to bury his concubine at his side. The son, however, judged that his father's mental state was not sound at the time of his testament, and decided not to abide by his instructions, instead marrying the woman off to another man. Not too long after war broke out and the man was engaged in battle with enemy forces when the opposing commander's horse was entangled in weeds and fell to the ground. The man captured the enemy general. That night a ghost appeared in the man's dream. The ghost said that he was the father of the concubine that the man had spared and had knotted the weeds to repay his debt of gratitude.

겸사겸사(해서) [Lit. 兼 double as + 事 work + 兼 double as + 事 work] CHINESE-DERIVATION 여러 가지 일을 한꺼번에 = in a way that fulfills two functions (*equiv.* to do double duty / to kill two birds with one stone) ▌A: 여기는 어쩐 일이야? = *What brings you here?* B: 볼일도 있고, 네 얼굴도 볼 겸 해서 **겸사겸사** 왔지 뭐. = *I had some work to take care of, so I thought I'd see you too on the way and kill two birds with one stone.*

경거망동하다 [Lit. 輕 light + 擧 elect + 妄 unreasonable + 動 move + 하다 verbal suffix] CHINESE-DERIVATION 생각 없이 경솔하게 행동하다 = to choose a thoughtless course of action ▮ A: 사장님이 바뀐 이후로 회사 분위기가 좀 이상해요. = *After we got the new boss, the mood around here has been a little strange.* B: 이럴 때일수록 **경거망동하지** 말고 일만 해야 돼요. = *That's precisely why now is not the time for any rash decisions. Just focus on your work.*

경종을 울리다 [Lit. to sound the alarm bell] IDIOM 잘못이나 위험을 경계하여 주의를 환기시키다 = to rouse one's surroundings to a threat or danger (*equiv.* to sound the alarm / to set off alarm bells / to wake up the masses to a certain threat) ▮ A: 어떻게 운동 선수가 승부 조작에 개입할 수가 있지? = *How could a player be involved in throwing games like that?* B: 어제오늘 일이 아니라던데. 이번 사건이 우리나라 스포츠계에 **경종을 울리는** 계기가 되어야 할 텐데. = *It's not a new thing. I hope this finally wakes people up to this practice.*

계란으로 바위 치기 [Lit. (it's like) hitting a boulder with an egg] PROVERB 도저히 이길 수 없는 상대나 성공할 수 없는 과제에 무모하게 도전할 때 쓰는 말 = taking on an unbeatable opponent or an unwinnable challenge (*equiv.* like a flea biting an elephant / like hitting one's head against a brick wall / to make no noticeable difference / step into the ring against an unbeatable foe *syn.* 달걀로 바위 치기) ▮ A: 우리 둘이서 뭘 하겠니? **계란으로 바위 치기야.** = *What can we do about it? Get into a fight we stand no chance of winning?* B: 해 보기 전에는 알 수가 없는 거잖아. = *We won't know until we've tried.*

계산기(를) 두드리다 [Lit. to tap on the calculator] IDIOM 이익과 손해를 따져 보다 = to weigh the costs and benefits (of a proposal etc.) (*syn.* 주판알(을) 튀기다) ▮ A: 이번에 제10구단 유치와 관련해서 왜 각 구단들이 입장을 발표하지 않는 걸까요? = *Why aren't the other teams announcing their stance on the establishment of a tenth team?* B: 저마다 속으로 **계산기를 두드리고** 있겠죠. = *I'm sure they're just weighing the issue silently.*

계산에 넣다 [Lit. to put (something) in the calculations] IDIOM 고려하다 =
to consider (*equiv.* to take something into account / to plan for something) ▌
A: 왜 이렇게 늦었어요? = *Why are you so late?* B: 죄송합니다. 차가
너무 막히더라고요. = *I'm so sorry. The traffic was so bad today.* A: 그것
도 **계산에 넣었어야죠**. = *Well, you should have taken that into*
consideration.

고개가 수그러지다 [Lit. One's head bends.] IDIOM 존경하는 마음이 생
겨나다 = to respect somebody (*equiv.* to bow one's head (before someone) /
to bow down) ▌A: 김 교수님만 생각하면 **고개가 저절로 수그러져**
요. = *When I think about Prof. Kim, I can't help but respect him.* B: 저도 그
래요. 일흔이 넘으셨는데도 매일 연구에 몰두하시잖아요. = *Same*
here. Even though he is well into his 70s, he keeps at his research every day.

고개를 갸웃거리다 [Lit. to cock one's head to the side] IDIOM 어떤 일에
대하여 의심스러워하다 = to be suspicious (*equiv.* to tilt one's head in
suspicion) ▌A: 그 외국인에게 길 설명은 잘 해 줬나요? = *Did you*
give that foreigner good directions? B: 설명을 듣고서 **고개를 몇 번 갸**
웃거리더니 그냥 저 쪽으로 가던데요. = *He cocked his head a few times*
after listening to what I said and then just went off in that direction.

고개를 내밀다 [Lit. to stick out one's head] IDIOM 세력이나 감정 따위가
생겨나다 = for a certain force or emotion to emerge (*equiv.* (for an emotion
or force) to rear its head *syn.* 고개를 들다, 머리를 들다) ▌A: 어제 현
장에서 김 씨가 크게 다칠 뻔했다죠? = *I heard Mr. Kim was almost*
gravely injured on the site yesterday. B: 한동안 사고가 없었는데. 또 안
전 불감증이 서서히 **고개를 내미나** 봅니다. 직원들한테 다시 한
번 주의를 줄 필요가 있겠네요. = *For a while we hadn't had any*
accidents. I guess apathy towards safety is again starting to rear its ugly head.
It looks like it's time to emphasize the importance of caution once again.

고개를 들다 [Lit. to raise (its) head] IDIOM 눌렸던 감정이나 일, 세력 등
이 일어나다 = for an emotion or force that was oppressed to emerge (*equiv.* to
rear its head / to raise its head *syn.* 고개를 내밀다, 머리를 들다) ▌A: 이러

다 정말 전쟁 터지는 거 아닌지 걱정이에요. = *I'm worried that If things continue like this, war will break out once again.* B: 맞아요. 북한에 강경하게 나가야 한다는 주장이 또다시 **고개를 들고** 있잖아요. = *That's true. The idea of no compromise with North Korea is again rearing its head.*

고개를 못 들다 [Lit. to be unable to raise one's head] IDIOM 떳떳하지 못하여 행동이나 태도가 움츠러들다 = to lower one's head in shame because of a dishonorable action (*equiv* to not be able to look someone in the eye / to not be able to face someone) █ A: 내가 요즘 너 때문에 동네 사람들 보기 부끄러워 **고개를 못 들고** 다닌다. = *Thanks to you I can't even look our neighbors in the eye.* B: 엄마, 죄송해요. 그렇지만 이혼하고 친정에 온 게 죄는 아니잖아요. = *Sorry, Mom. But getting a divorce and coming back home is not a sin.*

고개(를) 숙이다 [Lit. to bow one's head] IDIOM 기세가 꺾이거나 굴복하다 = to be dispirited or to be obsequious (*equiv.* to lower one's head / to be cowed) █ A: 정말 이번 여름은 너무 더웠어. 그렇지 않아? = *This summer was really hot, am I right?* B: 그러게. 이제 선선한 바람도 불고 더위도 한풀 **고개를 숙인** 것 같아. = *It sure was. Now the chilly winds are blowing and even the heat has been cowed.*

고군분투(하다) [Lit. 孤 lonely + 軍 military + 奮 vigorous + 鬪 fight → a fierce fight put up by a small number of troops] CHINESE-DERIVATION 다른 사람의 도움 없이 홀로 힘든 일을 잘해 나가다 = for a small number of isolated troops to fight with more ferocity (*equiv.* to fight with one's back up against the wall / to fight like one has nothing to lose) █ A: 아빠가 회사 운영하시느라 밤낮으로 **고군분투하시는** 거 보면 마음이 안쓰러워요. = *It's hard to watch my father work night and day with his back up against the wall.* B: 우리나라에서 중소기업을 운영하는 게 정말 쉬운 일이 아니죠. = *In Korea, running a small business is no easy task.*

고기는 씹어야 맛이고 말은 해야 맛이다 [Lit. You have to chew meat for it to taste good and you have to speak words for them to have flavor.] PROVERB 하고 싶은 말은 해야 한다는 말 = You have to say what you want to say. (*equiv.* Words are for saying. / Feelings are meant to be expressed. / Speak what's on your mind. / Don't hold back.) ▌A: 재은이한테 할 말이 있는데, 걔가 기분 나빠할까 봐 말을 못 꺼내겠어. =*I have something to tell Jaeun, but I can't bring it up because I'm afraid she'll feel bad.* B: **고기는 씹어야 맛이요, 말은 해야 맛이라는** 말도 있잖아. 조심스럽게 애기를 해 봐. =*Don't hold back. Just be careful how you say it.*

고기도 먹어 본 사람이 많이 먹는다 [Lit. People who have eaten meat before eat more of it.] PROVERB 무슨 일이든지 경험이 있는 사람이 더 잘할 수 있다는 말 =No matter what it is, people with experience do it better. (*equiv.* Experience makes the difference.) ▌A: 이번 한국시리즈는 누가 이길까? =*Who do you think is going to win the Korean Series this time?* B: 우승을 많이 해 본 SK가 유리하지 않을까? **고기도 먹어 본 사람이 많이 먹는** 법이잖아. =*Don't you think it'll be SK, with their history of victories? Experience makes the difference.*

고래(를) 잡다 [Lit. to catch a whale] IDIOM (속된 말로) 포경 수술하다 =(slang) to get circumcised (*equiv.* to get cut) ▌A: 너 왜 그렇게 걷는 게 어정쩡해? 어디 불편한 데 있어? =*Why are you walking like that? Are you injured or something?* B: 이거 비밀인데, 어제 병원에 가서 **고래 잡았거든**. =*This is a secret, but, I went to the hospital and got circumcised yesterday.*

NOTE: 포경(包茎)의 발음이 고래잡이를 뜻하는 포경(捕鯨)과 같은 데서 나온 익살스러운 표현이다. '고래를 잡았다'는 말은 곧 '포경을 했다'는 말이다. 나라마다 포경수술에 대한 인식이나 시행률이 다 다른데, 한국에서는 대체로 부모들이 남자아이가 어릴 때 포경수술을 시켜주는 사람이 많다. Circumcision is called 포경(包茎) in Korean but as fate would have it, its pronunciation is exactly the same as the word for whaling, 포경(捕鯨). This led to the wordplay of "catching a whale" being used as a sly way of saying "I got circumcised." As circumcisions are performed within a few days of birth in most western countries, one rarely gets the opportunity for clever repartee when discussing one's recent circumcision. In Korea, however, the average age at which males "get cut" is 12. Thus enabling colorful Moby Dick tales to be told in the nation's elementary school classrooms.

고래 싸움에 새우 등 터진다 [Lit. A shrimp is easily squished in a fight between whales.] PROVERB 강한 무리의 싸움으로 인해 공연히 약자가 피해를 입게 될 때 쓰는 말 = used when a weaker bystander is unnecessarily injured during a fight between two powerful foes (*equiv.* A clash of titans is no place for a dwarf.) ▮ A: 김 과장님하고 이 과장님이 어제 사람들 앞에서 크게 싸웠다면서요? = *I heard that the two section heads, Kim and Lee, got into a big fight in front of everyone yesterday.* B: 네. 그 바람에 제 입장이 난처해졌어요. 완전히 **고래 싸움에 새우 등 터지는** 격이죠. = *That made my position pretty awkward. A fight between whales is no place for a shrimp like me.*

*****고무신(을) 거꾸로 신다** [Lit. to put on rubber shoes backwards] IDIOM 여자가 사귀던 남자와 일방적으로 헤어지다 = for a woman to leave a man (*equiv.* to send someone a Dear John letter / to put on one's walking boots / to have a change of heart) ▮ A: 오랜만이다. 소영 씨도 잘 지내지? = *It's been so long. How's Soyoung doing?* B: 걔 얘기는 하지 마. 나 군대 간 사이에 **고무신 거꾸로 신었어**. = *Don't bring her up. She walked out on me while I was doing my military service.*

> NOTE: 오래 전에 한 여자가 바람을 피우고 있었다. 어느 날 딴 남자와 집에 있는데 남편이 갑작스레 들이닥치자 그 여자는 놀란 나머지 고무신을 거꾸로 신고 도망을 쳤다. 그때부터 여자가 남자에게 이별을 선언하고 딴 남자에게 갈 때 이 표현을 쓰게 됐다. 요즘은 주로 남자가 군대에 간 사이 여자가 변심했을 경우에 쓰인다.
>
> Long ago, there was a woman carrying on an affair. She was at home with another man when her husband suddenly burst in. The woman was so scared, so put on her rubber shoes backwards and escaped. Since then, putting on one's shoes backwards has been the expression used to describe a women who chooses another man. Of late, the expression is most often used to describe women that have a change of heart when their boyfriends are off serving in the military.

고배를 들다 [Lit. to drink from a bitter cup] IDIOM 패배나 실패 따위의 쓰라린 경험을 하다 = to experience the bitterness that follows a defeat

(*equiv.* to swallow the bitter pill of defeat / to eat humble pie / to experience a sore defeat *syn.* 고배를 마시다, 쓴잔을 마시다, 쓴잔을 들다)

▌A: 벌써 세 번째예요. 번번이 우승 문턱에서 **고배를 든** 게요. = *This is the third time already. Every time I've stood at the threshold of victory I've been forced to eat humble pie.* B: 너무 실망하지 마세요. 다음 기회가 있잖아요. = *Don't be too disappointed. There will be more opportunities.*

NOTE: 고배는 쓴 술잔을 말한다. 승리를 한 자는 기뻐하며 술을 마시지만, 패배한 자가 마시는 술은 쓴 법이다.
A 고배 is a glass of bitter drink. When the victor raises his glass in celebration, it is a sweet wine, but the drink of the vanquished is always bitter.

고배를 마시다 IDIOM = 고배를 들다

고삐가 풀리다 [Lit. for the reins to come undone] IDIOM 통제에서 벗어나다 = to break free of restraint or oppression (*equiv.* to break free of the reins of control / to break free of someone's spell) ▌A: 철수는 요즘 어때요? = *How's Cheolsu been doing?* B: 당신 없으니 완전히 **고삐가 풀려서** 항상 늦게 들어와요. 당신이 전화해서 한마디해 주세요. = *Since you're not around, I've completely lost control over him and now he almost always comes home late. Say something to him over the phone, please.*

NOTE: 고삐는 한 끝을 말이나 소의 재갈에 잡아매어 몰거나 부릴 때에 쓰는 줄이다. 아직 길들여지지 않은 말이 고삐가 풀리면 어떻게 되겠는가? 그래서 제멋대로 행동하는 사람을 보고 '고삐 풀린 망아지 같다'라고 말한다.
고삐 is the word for the reins that are attached to an animals muzzle or bit. What is a horse likely to do if it breaks free of the reins? Go on a wild romp, of course. A person who does as he pleases and lacks restraint is often referred to as a 고삐 풀린 망아지 (a colt that has broken free of the reins).

고삐를 늦추다 [Lit. to let up on the reins] IDIOM 경계나 긴장을 누그러뜨리다 = to lessen one's boundaries or tension level (*equiv.* to let up / to ease up on the gas / to slacken the pace) ▌A: 아, 하루만 푹 쉬고 싶어.＝*I just want to take it easy for a day.* B: 네 마음 알아. 하지만 시험이 얼마 안 남았는데 지금 **고삐를 늦추면** 안 돼.＝*I know where you're coming from, but the test is coming up soon. We can't let up now.*

NOTE: See the note on 고삐가 풀리다.

고사(를) 지내다 [Lit. to carry out a religious rite] IDIOM **1.** 따라 놓은 술을 오랫동안 마시지 않다＝to not drink liquor that has been poured in front of one (*equiv.* to abstain *syn.* 제사(를) 지내다) ▌A: 뭐 해? **고사 지내는 거야?** 어서 한 잔 해.＝*What's with you? Are you abstaining from alcohol? Hurry up and drink.* B: 네. 부장님도 한 잔 더 하시죠.＝*All right. Why don't you have another glass with me?* **2.** 어떤 일이 이루어지기를 간절히 바라다＝to earnestly hope for something (*syn.* 제사(를) 지내다) ▌A: 또 떨어졌어? 도대체 이번이 몇 번째야?＝*You failed again? Just how many times has it been now?* B: 다섯 번째예요. **고사라도 지내야** 할까 봐요.＝*Five times. I guess maybe I'll have to pray harder.*

NOTE: 고사는 어떤 일이 무사히 이루어지기를 기원하며 드리는 의식이다. 요즘도 어떤 사업을 시작할 때 상 위에 돼지머리나 과일 등을 올려 놓고 절을 하며 사업의 번창을 기원하는 모습을 흔히 볼 수 있다. 술이나 음식을 앞에 두고 멀뚱멀뚱 보며 먹지 않는 사람에게 '고사 지내냐?'며 핀잔을 준다.

A 고사 is a ceremony carried out to pray for smooth execution of a certain endeavor. Even today many shop owners mark the launch of their new store with a pig's head, fruit and a few deep bows. When someone inexplicably leaves a meal or drink sitting before them untouched, this would be the perfect expression to hurl at them.

고사리 같은 손 [Lit. a hand like bracken] IDIOM 어린아이의 작고 여린 손을 비유적으로 이르는 말＝a metaphor for the small and delicate hand of a child ▌A: 유치원 선생님이시라고 들었어요. 아이들을 좋아하시나 봐요.＝*I heard that you're a kindergarten teacher. You must really love children.* B: 네. 아이들이 **고사리 같은 손**을 흔들면서 인사할 때는

정말 행복해요. = *Yes. Just seeing their little hands wave hello to me is enough to bring me happiness.*

NOTE: 고사리의 모양이 마치 아기가 손가락을 말아쥔 것과 비슷한 데서 나온 표현이다. 또 고사리는 솜털이 있고 그 촉감이 매우 부드럽기 때문에 꼭 아기 손의 느낌과 비슷하다.
The shape of bracken closely resembles that of a clenched baby's fist. With its fleece and softness to the touch, it is often compared to the hand of a child.

고생 끝에 낙이 온다 [Lit. Merriment follows hardships.] PROVERB 어려운 일을 겪고 나면 즐거운 일이 생긴다는 말 = Good things come after many hardships. (*equiv.* No pain, no gain. / Hard work pays off. / April showers bring May flowers. / After the storm comes the calm.) ▌A: 낮에 일하고 밤에 학원 다니면서 시험 준비 하더니 결국 해냈군요. **고생 끝에 낙이 온다고,** 그동안 수고 많았어요. = *I guess working all day and taking classes at night really paid off in the end. Hard work pays dividends. Good job.* B: 감사합니다. 다 선생님 덕분이에요. = *Thanks. It really was all thanks to you.*

고생을 사서 하다 [Lit. to buy your own hardships] IDIOM 자신의 현명하지 못한 판단이나 행동으로 인해 괜히 고생을 하게 될 때 쓰는 말 = to carry out a difficult task for no particular reason (*equiv.* to make things hard on oneself *syn.* 사서 고생(을)하다 *cf.* 젊어서 고생은 사서도 한다) ▌A: 힘들지 않니? 안 해도 된다는데, 왜 **고생을 사서 하니**? = *Isn't that a hassle? You really don't have to do that. Why are you making things harder on yourself?* B: 안 힘들어요. 제가 하고 싶어 하는 건데요 뭘. = *It's no problem. I'm really just doing it because I want to.*

고성방가(하다) [Lit. 高 high + 聲 sound + 放 release + 歌 song] CHINESE-DERIVATION 크게 소리를 지르거나 노래를 불러 주변을 시끄럽게 하다 = to cause a clamor by singing loudly or shouting (*equiv.* to cause a clamor / to be uproarious) ▌A: 이 동네는 밤만 되면 너무 시끄러워 못 살겠어. = *This neighborhood is so noisy at night. I can't take it anymore.* B: 술 취해서 **고성방가하는** 사람은 왜 이리 많은지. = *Why does everyone* *have to get drunk and cause a clamor on the streets?*

고슴도치도 제 새끼는 예쁘다고 한다 [Lit. Even the hedgehog thinks its offspring is beautiful.] PROVERB 부모의 눈에는 제 자식이 다 잘나고 귀여워 보인다는 말 = Every parent thinks their child is especially smart or cute. (*equiv.* He thinks all his geese are swans. / The beetle is a beauty in the eyes of its mother.) ▌A: 네 딸이야? = *Is this your daughter?* B: 응, 예쁘지? **고슴도치도 자기 새끼는 예쁘다고** 하는데 우리 딸은 뭘 해도 예뻐 보여. = *Yeah, isn't she pretty? Everyone thinks their child is special, but my daughter really does stand out.*

NOTE: 이 속담은 '고슴도치도 제 새끼는 함함하다고 한다'가 원래 표현이다. '함함하다'는 '보드랍고 윤기가 있다'라는 뜻이다. 온몸이 가시로 덮인 고슴도치도 제 새끼는 보드랍다고 느끼는 법이다.
The original form of this expression is "고슴도치도 제 새끼는 함함하다고 한다." The adjective 함함하다 means soft and shiny. Accordingly, this phrase means that despite the fact that the hedgehog's entire body is covered with quills, in the eye's of his mother, he is soft.

고양이 목에 방울 달기 [Lit. attaching a bell to a cat's neck] PROVERB 이론적으로는 쉬우나 실제 행동으로 옮기기는 어려운 해결책 = a great idea that no one can carry out (*equiv.* to bell the cat) ▌A: 우리 월급이 너무 적은 것 같지 않아요? 사장님한테 월급 올려 달라고 얘기합시다. = *Doesn't our salary seem a little low? Let's ask the boss for a raise.* B: 좋아요. 그런데 누가 대표로 말을 꺼내죠? = *All right. Who's going to speak for us?* A: **고양이 목에 방울 달기**군요. = *Good idea, but who's going to bell the cat?*

NOTE: 이 표현은 다음 설화에서 비롯되었다. 고양이가 쥐들을 쫓아다니자 쥐들이 모여 대책을 의논하였다. 오랜 논의 끝에 마침내 고양이 목에 방울을 달면 고양이가 오는 것을 알 수 있지 않겠냐는 의견이 나와 모두 좋은 생각이라고 했다. 그때 늙은 쥐가 그럼 누가 하겠냐고 물으니 아무도 나서지 못했다. 말은 쉽지만 실행하기는 어려운 것을 가리켜 이 표현을 쓴다. 공교롭게도 이솝우화에도 동일한 내용의 이야기가 실려 있다.

This expression comes from the following old tale. Mice were sick of being chased around by a cat, so they got together to discuss what could be done. After much discussion, the idea of attaching a bell to the cat's neck was proposed. All the mice agreed that it was a capital idea until an elderly mouse asked who would be willing to carry out the plan. No one stepped forward. This expression is used to point out that, no matter how clever a plan, if it's too dangerous to carry out, it is of no use. Surprisingly, the very same story exists in the fables of Aesop.

고양이 세수 [Lit. the washing of a cat] IDIOM 대충 물만 묻히는 세수＝ washing up by just splashing a little water on one's face ▌A: 연진아, 얼른 가서 세수하고 와. ＝*Yeonjin, hurry and wash up.* B: 아까 세수했어요, 엄마. ＝*I washed up earlier, Mom.* A: 원, 애는 **고양이 세수**를 했나. 눈곱이 그대로 있잖아. ＝*Well, it looks like you didn't do a very good job of it. You still have sleep in your eyes.*

NOTE: 고양이는 앞발을 혀로 핥아 침을 묻혀서 얼굴을 문댄다. 그 모습이 마치 세수를 하기 싫어 대충 물만 손에 적셔 얼굴 부분 부분을 씻는 동작과 닮아 이런 표현이 생겼다.
Cats moisten up their paws by licking them and then rubbing them against their face. This expression comes from that behavior, which seems to look like someone who hates washing up and instead just splashes a little water over their face.

고양이 앞의 쥐 [Lit. a mouse in front of a cat] PROVERB 무서운 상대를 만나 잔뜩 움츠린 상황＝inability to take action against an intimidating person (*equiv.* a deer in the headlights) ▌A: 영호 씨는 참 남자다운 분 같아요. 아마 집에서도 큰소리치면서 사실 거 같아요. ＝*You truly are a manly man. I bet you run the show at home too.* B: 어휴. 밖에서만 그래요. 아내랑 있으면 저는 완전히 **고양이 앞의 쥐**예요. ＝*I just act that way when I'm out. When I'm with my wife, it's like watching a mouse next to a cat.*

고양이에게 생선 가게 맡긴 격 [Lit. (It is as if) you've left the cat in charge of the fish shop] PROVERB 어떤 일이나 물건을 믿지 못할 사람에게 맡겼을 때 쓰는 말＝used to describe a situation in which the most unreliable party has been left in charge (*equiv.* to let the fox guard the henhouse) ▌A: 큰일이야. 회사에서 경리 보던 직원이 회사 장부를 다 들고 사라져 버렸어.＝*We've got a major problem. The employee in charge of accounting for the company absconded with the books.* B: 그래? 정말 야단났네. **고양이에게 생선 가게를 맡긴 격**이었네.＝*Really? What a mess. I guess you really did leave the fox guarding the henhouse.*

고양이 쥐 생각 [Lit. the way a cat thinks about a mouse] PROVERB 속마음과 달리 다른 사람을 위하는 척할 때 쓰는 말＝used to describe the act of feigning consideration of another (*equiv.* to soften somebody up for the kill) ▌A: 난 다 당신 힘들까 봐 당신 생각해서 하는 얘기야.＝*I'm just saying all of this out of consideration for you.* B: **고양이 쥐 생각**해 주시네요. 고맙지만, 난 괜찮아요.＝*Wow, the cat is really considerate of the mouse. Thanks, but no thanks.*

고육지책 [Lit. 苦 bitter + 肉 flesh + 之 cf + 策 plan] CHINESE-DERIVATION 어려운 상황에서 벗어나기 위해 자신의 피해를 무릅쓰고 내놓은 대책＝plans made through agonizing (*equiv.* a desperate attempt / a last-ditch effort) ▌A: 요즘 동네 슈퍼들이 할인 행사를 많이 하는 것 같아요.＝*These days, mom-and-pop stores often have bargain sale events.* B: 대형 마트들이 들어서면서 경쟁이 심해지니까 **고육지책**이겠죠.＝*That might be a desperate attempt to compete with all the big-box retailers that have sprung up.*

NOTE: 이 말은 중국의 삼국지연의에서 온 표현이다. 유비와 주유의 연합부대가 조조에 맞서 적벽대전을 준비하고 있을 때였다. 주유가 가까운 부하인 황개와 짜고 일부러 사람들 앞에서 황개에게 곤장 100대를 때리는 벌을 내렸다. 황개는 이에 조조에게 거짓 투항했다. 조조는 황개를 의심했지만 그가 곤장을 100대나 맞은 것을 알고는 그를 믿게 되었다. 황개는 조조 진영에 가 조조 군의 배를 다 태워버렸다. 고육지책은 이처럼 자기 몸을 희생하면서 낸 계책을 가리킨다.

This expression comes from the Romance of the Three Kingdoms. It was just as the combined forces of Liu Bei and Zhou Yu prepared to go up against Cao Cao in the Battle of Red Cliffs. Zhou Yu conspired with his subject Huang Gai and as part of their plan, lashed him 100 times. Huang Gai then feigned his surrender to Cao Cao. At first Cao Cao was suspicious, but once he saw that Huang Gai had been lashed, he believed him. Huang Gai went to the Cao Cao camp and burned all of their ships. His scheme and the sacrifice of his own life was successful. Now 고육지책 is used to describe a desperate and painful plan.

고주망태 [Lit. 苦 bitter + 酒 alcohol + 망태 basket → a basket of bitter drink] CHINESE-DERIVATION 감당을 못할 정도로 술을 많이 마셔서 정신을 차리지 못하는 상태 = extreme drunkenness and inability to regain one's senses (*equiv.* (slang) to be wasted *cf.* 떡(이) 되다) ▌A: 어머님 오셨어요? = *Mother, is that you?* B: 그래, 경수는 뭐하냐? = *Yes, what is Gyeongsu doing?* A: 어젯밤에 **고주망태**가 되어 들어오더니 아직 자고 있어요. = *He came home very drunk last night and is still sleeping it off.*

NOTE: 고주망태의 유래에 대해서는 정확히 알려진 바가 없다. 그러나 고주가 쓴 술(苦酒)을, 망태가 술을 담는 망태기를 뜻하여, 쓴 술을 담는 망태기에서 유래했다고 보는 설명이 그럴듯해 보인다.
There is no consensus on the origin of this phrase. 고주 means a bitter liquor and 망태 is the word for a basket of liquor, so that seems to be its fundamental origin.

고진감래 [Lit. 苦 bitter + 盡 to the end + 甘 sweet + 來 come → Sweet life comes after suffering through hardships.] CHINESE-DERIVATION 고통이 다하면 행복이 찾아옴 = After many hardships one will find happiness. (*equiv.* sweet after bitter / No pain, no gain.) ▌A: 아드님이 국회의원이 됐으니 얼마나 좋으세요? = *Now that your son made it all the way to the National Assembly, you must be so proud.* B: 네, 감사합니다. = *Yes, we are. Thank you.* A: **고진감래**라고 그동안 고생 많이 하셨으니 이제 좋은 일만 있으실 거예요. = *After all those long years of hardship, things are now finally going his way. The road to success is fraught with hardship.*

고춧가루(를) 뿌리다 [Lit. to sprinkle chili powder (around)] IDIOM 훼방을 놓거나 일을 망치다 = to ruin the plans (*equiv.* to be a wet blanket / (slang) to be a Debbie Downer / to throw a monkey wrench into the plans *syn.* 소금(을) 뿌리다, 재(를) 뿌리다, 초(를) 치다, 찬물(을) 끼얹다) ▌A: 한 잔 더 하자. = *Let's have another drink.* B: 안 돼. 오늘은 일찍 들어가 봐야 해. = *No way. I've got to get home early tonight.* A: 너는 꼭 분위기 좋을 때 **고춧가루를 뿌리더라**. = *Whenever things start getting good, you're always such a wet blanket.*

NOTE: 적당히 양념이 된 완성된 음식에 누군가가 매운 고춧가루를 확 뿌리는 장면을 상상해 보라.
Imagine someone sprinkling too much pepper powder on a perfectly seasoned dish and you will grasp the meaning of this phrase.

곧 죽어도 [Lit. even if one were about to die] IDIOM 무슨 일이 있어도 = no matter what happens (*equiv.* would it kill you to (admit, recognize etc. something)) ▌A: 내가 부상만 안 입었어도 너한테 지지는 않았을 거야. = *If I weren't injured, I definitely would have beaten you.* B: **곧 죽어도** 실력이 없어서 졌다는 얘기는 안 하는군. = *Would it kill you to admit that your lack of skills cost you the victory?*

골때리다 [Lit. to hit the brain] IDIOM (속된 말로) 말이나 행동이 어이없다 = (slang) for words or actions to be shocking or appalling (*equiv.* to be mind-blowing) ▌A: 어제 텔레비전에 여자 옷만 입는 남자가 나왔어. = *There was a guy on TV yesterday who only wears women's clothing.* B: 정말? 진짜 **골때리는** 사람이네. = *Really? There really are some shocking people out there.*

골로 가다 [Lit. to go to one's grave] IDIOM (속된 말로) 죽다 = (slang) to die (*equiv.* to be six feet under / to kick the bucket) ▌A: 당신, 그렇게 지금 좀 잘나간다고 까불다가 **골로 가는** 수가 있어. = *Talking like that because things are going well for you now might get you put six feet under.* B: 지금 나를 협박하는 건가요? = *Are you threatening me?*

NOTE: 이 말은 조선 시대 공동묘지가 있던 지역인 고태골에서 유래했다고 전해진다. 사람이 죽으면 고태골로 옮겨지기 때문에 '고태골로 갔다'는 말이 '죽었다'라는 뜻으로 통했고, 세월이 지나면서 '골로 가다'라는 형태가 되었다는 것이다. 혹은 관(棺)을 뜻하는 옛말 '골'에서 유래했다는 설도 있다. 이 표현은 속된 표현으로 다른 사람에게 쓰지 않는 편이 안전하다.

This phrase dates back to the Joseon Dynasty, when a public cemetery was located at 고태골 (Gotae valley). At the time, the expression "He went to the Gotae Valley" sprang up as a euphemism for someone's death. As time passed, the expression was shortened to simply 골로 가다. There are also some who say that the phrase originates from the old word for 관 (coffin), which was also pronounced "골." This expression is informal and would be extremely offensive if used to describe someone's death.

골머리(를) 썩이다 [Lit. to let one's brain rot] IDIOM 해결하기 어려운 문제 때문에 생각에 몰두하다 = to be racking one's brain to solve a certain problem (*equiv.* to rack one's brain *syn.* 골머리(를) 앓다) ▌A: 요즘 새로 들어온 사람들 때문에 **골머리를 썩이고** 있어. = *I'm racking my mind over what to do with all these new hires.* B: 나도 소문 들었어. 완전히 제멋대로라며? = *I heard the rumors. So, they just do as they please?*

골머리(를) 앓다 [Lit. to make yourself sick in the head] IDIOM 해결하기 어려운 문제 때문에 생각에 몰두하다 = to trouble oneself over an issue till you get a headache (*equiv.* to give yourself a headache *syn.* 골머리(를) 썩이다) ▌A: 이번에 새로 입사한 정우 씨는 어때요? = *How's that guy Jeongu who just started?* B: 안 그래도 정우 씨 때문에 다들 **골머리를 앓고** 있어요. 적응을 잘 못하는 것 같아요. = *That guy's been a major headache for everyone. I don't think he's fitting in very well.*

골이 깊다 [Lit. for the valley to be deep] IDIOM 사이가 나쁘다 = for a relationship to be on bad terms (*equiv.* to be on bad terms / to be on the outs / There's a vast gulf between two parties.) ▌A: 이번 파업이 원만하게 해결될 수 있을까요? = *Do you think this strike can be resolved amicably?* B: 글쎄요. 워낙 노사 간에 갈등의 **골이 깊어서** 쉽지는 않을 것

ㄱ

같아요. = *Well ... considering the vast gulf between management and labor, the outlook is not good.*

골(이) 비다 [Lit. to have an empty head] IDIOM (속된 말로) 배운 것이 없어 무식하다 = (slang) to be void of opinion due to lack of education (*equiv.* to be empty-headed) ▌A: 넌 어떤 여자가 좋아? = *What kind of women do you like?* B: 난 솔직히 예쁜 여자가 좋아. = *Honestly, I'm really into pretty women.* A: 예쁘기만 하고 **골이 비었**으면 어떻게 할 거야? = *So, what if she's pretty but completely empty-headed?*

***골탕(을) 먹다** [Lit. to eat *goltang*] IDIOM 손해를 입거나 난처한 입장이 되다 = to suffer a loss or find oneself in an untenable situation (*equiv.* to lose out / to have a hard time / to pay dearly for) ▌A: 왜 이렇게 늦었어요? = *Why were you so late?* B: 내비게이션이 엉뚱한 길을 알려 줘서 **골탕 먹었어요.** = *The navigation gave me ridiculous directions and I paid dearly for believing them.*

> NOTE: 골탕이란 원래 소의 머릿골과 등골을 맑은 장국에 넣어 끓여 익힌 국물을 가리키는 말이었다. 그러던 것이 골탕의 '골'자가 '곯다', '골리다' 등과 발음이 유사해 오늘날과 같이 쓰이게 되었다.
> 골탕 is a tasty soup made from the head of a cow and its spine but its pronunciation sounds similar to the word 곯다 (to go bad) or 골리다 (to tease), so the word settled into its current use.

***골탕(을) 먹이다** [Lit. to feed someone *goltang*] IDIOM 남에게 손해를 입히거나 난처하게 만들다 = to cause someone to suffer a loss or hardship (*equiv.* to pester / to give someone a hard time) ▌A: 하하, 또 속았지, 누나? = *Ha, fooled you again, huh?* B: 너는 누나 **골탕 먹이는** 게 그렇게 좋니? = *Is it so fun to pester me?*

> NOTE: See the note on 골탕(을) 먹다.

공든 탑이 무너지랴 [Lit. Can a well-built tower collapse?] PROVERB 정성을 다한 일은 헛되지 않는다는 말 = *Something well done will not come to naught.* (*equiv.* A solid foundation will hold the building straight. / Your hard work will carry you. / Hard work always pays off.) ▌A: 이제 시험이 코앞이야. 이번에 시험 잘 못 보면 또 1년 더 고생해야 하는데, 걱정이야 = *The test is just around the corner now. If I don't do well, I'll have another year of hard work ahead of me. I'm worried.* B: 그동안 열심히 했잖아. **공든 탑이 무너지겠어?** = *You've been working hard for a while now. All that hard work will carry you through.*

공명정대하다 [Lit. 公 fair + 明 clear + 正 straight + 大 big + 하다 adjectival suffix] CHINESE-DERIVATION 일이나 태도가 정당하고 떳떳하다 = for an affair or one's actions to be just and honorable (*equiv.* fair and square) ▌A: 너희 반 담임 선생님은 되게 엄하신 분 같은데, 왜 아이들한테 인기가 좋아? = *Your teacher seems to be very strict, but why does everybody like him?* B: 모두한테 똑같이 대하시니까. **공명정대하신** 분이야. = *Because he treats everybody impartially. He is a good man.*

공사다망하다 [Lit. 公 public + 私 private + 多 much + 忙 busy + 하다 adjectival suffix] CHINESE-DERIVATION 공적인 일과 사적인 일이 모두 매우 바쁘다 = to carry out a hectic work and private life (*equiv.* for one's life to be in disarray) ▌A: 야, 조용히 하자. 앞에서 사회자가 얘기하려나 봐. = *Let's keep it down. I think the MC is trying to say something.* B: **공사다망하신** 가운데 이 자리에 참석해 주신 여러분께 진심으로 감사드립니다. = *In spite of your hectic schedules, thank you for all managing to be here today.*

공수래공수거 [Lit. 空 empty + 手 hand + 來 come + 空 empty + 手 hand + 去 go → how we all come with nothing and leave with nothing] CHINESE-DERIVATION 인생의 무상함과 덧없음을 가리키는 말 = used to describe the vanity and fleeting nature of life (*equiv.* ashes to ashes, dust to dust / the vanity of life) ▌A: 왜 힘들게 번 돈을 다 기부하셨어요? = *Why would you just give away all that money you worked so hard for?* B: 어차피 인생은 **공수래공수거** 아닙니까. 죽을 때 돈을 가지고 갈 것도 아니고 좋은 데 쓰고 싶었습니다. = *Because one thing's for sure, you come into this world empty-handed and that's how you leave it. Since I'm not taking this money with me, I thought I'd use it for good.*

공수표(를) 날리다 [Lit. to write blank checks] IDIOM 거짓 약속을 하다=to make empty promises

▌A: 이번에도 **공수표 날리는** 거 아니에요? 저번에도 약속해 놓고 안 지켰잖아요. =*Is this just another empty promise? Last time you didn't keep your word either.* B: 이번에는 진짜예요. 믿어 주세요. =*This time it's for real. Please, believe me.*

공은 공이고 사는 사다 [Lit. Public is public, private is private.] PROVERB 공적인 일과 사적인 일은 엄격히 구분해야 한다는 말=One must differentiate between one's work and private life.

▌A: 교수님, 제가 교통사고를 당해서 지난주에 시험을 못 봤는데요, 오늘 저 혼자 시험을 볼 수 없을까요?=*Professor, I got into a car accident last week and wasn't able to take the test. Is there any way I could take it today?* B: 아, 저런. 사정은 딱하네만, **공은 공이고 사는 사니** 그건 안 되겠네. =*That's terrible and all, but you can't let what you do outside of school get in the way of your work here. I don't think there's anything I can do for you.*

공자 앞에서 문자 쓴다 [Lit. to elaborate in front in Confucius] PROVERB 지식이나 실력이 부족한 사람이 자신보다 나은 사람 앞에서 가소롭게 잘난 체할 때 쓰는 말=used to describe someone's attempts to show off in front of a true expert (*syn.* 번데기 앞에서 주름 잡다 *cf.* 문자(를) 쓰다)

▌A: 어때요? 저 운전 잘하죠?=*How am I? Don't you think I'm a good driver?* B: 너 지금 **공자 앞에서 문자 쓰냐?** 나는 20년 무사고야. =*I think you're showing off in front of the wrong person. I've gone 20 years without a single accident.*

> NOTE: 공자는 중국 춘추전국시대의 대표적인 학자이자 성현이다. 그 앞에서 학문에 대해 논하는 것은 아인슈타인에게 상대성 이론을 설명하는 격이다.
>
> Confucius was the representative scholar and sage of the Warring Lu period of China. Discussing scholarship in front of Confucius would be like discussing the Theory of Relativity in front of Einstein.

공중에 뜨다 [Lit. to float in midair] IDIOM 어정쩡한 상태가 되다=to remain unresolved (*equiv.* to hang in the balance)

▌A: 마을회관 짓는 문

제는 어떻게 되었나요? = *How did the issue of building a cultural center for the town get resolved?* B: 그 문제를 앞장서 추진하던 사람이 갑자기 이사를 가면서 **공중에 떠** 버렸어요. = *The person who led the charge for the project suddenly moved away and left the issue unresolved.*

과거(가) 있다 [Lit. to have history] IDIOM 예전에 깊은 이성 관계가 있었다 = to have had a deep relationship with a member of the opposite sex (*equiv.* to have history) ▌A: 남편이 결혼 전에 사귀었던 사람들에 대해 알아요? = *Do you know about the people your husband dated before you two got married?* B: 아니요. 저희 부부는 서로에게 **과거가 있는지** 관심 없어요. = *No, we don't worry about each other's past.*

과대망상 [Lit. 誇 boast + 大 big + 妄 false + 想 think → exaggerated, false thinking] CHINESE-DERIVATION 자신이 현재 가진 것을 실제보다 부풀려 평가하고 이것을 사실이라고 믿는 생각 = thinking of oneself in terms and scale that are far beyond one's actual lot (*equiv.* (to suffer from) delusions of grandeur) ▌A: 넌 커서 어떤 사람이랑 결혼하고 싶어? = *What type of person do you want to marry?* B: 외국의 공주하고 결혼해서 국왕이 될 거예요. = *I'm going to marry a princess from a foreign land and become a king.* A: 동화를 너무 많이 봤구먼. **과대망상**이 심한걸. = *You've been reading too many fairy tales. I think you may be suffering from delusions of grandeur.*

과부 사정은 홀아비가 안다 [Lit. The widower understands the plight of the widow.] PROVERB 다른 사람의 어려움은 비슷한 처지에 있는 사람이 잘 알 수 있다는 말 = It's easy to sympathize with those in a similar plight. (*equiv.* Misery loves company.) ▌A: 중국에 있는 가족 생각이 나서 요즘 잠을 못 자겠어요. = *Thoughts of my family back in China are keeping me up lately.* B: 저도 그 마음 알아요. 지금 아내가 아이들하고 캐나다에 가 있거든요. = *I know what you mean. My wife is with the kids in Canada right now, you know.* A: **과부 사정은 홀아비가 아는 법**이죠. = *Misery loves company.*

과유불급 [Lit. 過 pass + 猶 same + 不 no + 及 reach] CHINESE-DERIVATION 지나

친 것은 모자란 것보다 오히려 모자람 = Too much is as bad as too little. (*equiv.* Overdoing it is just as bad as not doing enough.) ▌A: 어쩌다 몸살이 났어요? = *Why do you think you're coming down with a cold?* B: 갑자기 무리해서 운동을 했더니 온몸이 쑤시네요. = *I overdid it with the exercise yesterday and now I ache all over.* A: 뭐든지 **과유불급**이죠. = *That's why they say overdoing it is just as bad as not doing it enough.*

광에서 인심 난다 [Lit. Generosity comes from the pantry.] PROVERB 자신의 살림이 넉넉해야 다른 사람을 도울 여유가 생긴다는 말 = One's own life must first be comfortable before one can help others. (*equiv.* When you have a lot, you can give a lot. *syn.* 쌀독에서 인심 난다) ▌A: 연말인데 우리도 남들도 돕고 그래야 되지 않을까? = *What with it being the end of the year and all, don't you think we ought to make a donation somewhere?* B: 글쎄, 맞는 말이긴 한데, **광에서 인심 난다고** 우리 먹고살기 빠듯하니 남 돕기도 쉽지 않네. = *That's a good point but they say you have to get your own life in order before helping others. We aren't that well-off ourselves.*

교단에 서다 [Lit. to stand on the teaching platform] IDIOM 교사로 일하다 = to work as a teacher (*equiv.* to ascend the rostrum *syn.* 교편을 잡다 *cf.* 강단에 서다) ▌A: 퇴임이 멀지 않았는데 기분이 어떠세요? = *It isn't long now until your retirement. How do you feel?* B: 많이 아쉽네요. 저는 **교단에 서** 있을 때가 가장 행복한 사람이거든요. = *It's a real shame. When I'm at the podium, I'm the happiest man alive.*

교편을 놓다 [Lit. to put down the rod] IDIOM 교사 생활을 그만두다 = to quit teaching (*ant.* 교편을 잡다) ▌A: 정년퇴임이 내년이시죠? **교편을 놓으시면** 뭘 제일 먼저 하고 싶으세요? = *You'll be hitting retirement age next year, right? After you put down the rod for the last time, what is it you most look forward to doing?* B: 글쎄요, 우선 가족들과 여행을 가고 싶어요. = *Well, I guess the first thing I'd want to do is take a vacation with my family.*

NOTE: See the note on 교편을 잡다.

***교편을 잡다** [Lit. to hold the rod] IDIOM 교사로 일하다 = to work as a teacher (*syn.* 교단에 서다 *ant.* 교편을 놓다) ▌A: 직업이 어떻게 되세요? = *What line of work are you in?* B: 중학교에서 **교편을 잡고** 있습니다. = *I'm a teacher at a middle school.*

NOTE: 교편은 수업이나 강의를 할 때 교사가 사용하는 회초리를 말한다. 요즘은 학교에서 체벌이 금지되었지만 전통적으로 한국은 교사가 학생들을 지도하기 위해 매를 드는 것에 관대했다. 그래서 그 매를 사랑의 매라고 부르며 교사의 상징처럼 여겼다.
A 교편 is the rod that teachers used to carry when they conducted class. Corporal punishment has been banned now in Korean schools but traditionally teachers were given wide leeway to use the rod in their instruction of pupils. The rod was referred to as the "whip of love" and become a representative implement of the teaching profession.

구관이 명관이다 [Lit. The former official is an honored official.] PROVERB 바뀌기 이전의 것이 바뀌고 난 이후의 것보다 더 좋을 때 쓰는 말 = After changing or great loss one comes to long for the original state or thing that one has lost. (*equiv.* You don't know what you've got until it's gone.) ▌A: 새로 온 팀장님은 어때? 예전 팀장님하고는 잘 안 맞았잖아. = *How's the new team leader? You never got along well with the old guy.* B: 그랬지. 그런데 새로 온 분은 더 심해. = *That's true, but the new guy is even worse.* A: 그러니까 **구관이 명관이라잖아**. = *That's why they say you never know you've got until it's gone.*

구김살(이) 없다 [Lit. to not have any wrinkles] IDIOM 성격이나 표정이 밝고 명랑하다 = for one's expression or personality to be bright (*equiv.* to not have a crease (of worry) on one's face) ▌A: 진희 어디가 그렇게 좋니? = *What do you like so much about Jinhee?* B: 다 좋지만 무엇보다 **구김살 없는** 모습이 참 마음에 들어. = *I like everything about her, but I guess my favorite thing is how bright her personality is.*

구더기 무서워 장 못 담글까 [Lit. Will fear of maggots keep you from making sauce?] PROVERB 약간의 어려움이 있어도 해야 할 일은 해야

한다는 말 = You can't let a little difficulty stop us from doing what we need to do. (*equiv.* You can't be afraid of getting your hands dirty. / You can't succeed if you are afraid of failure. / If you don't make mistakes, you don't make anything.) ▌A: 관광산업을 활성화시키기 위해 무비자 정책을 확대할 예정입니다. = *There are plans to invigorate the tourist industry by expanding the visa-waiver policy.* B: 그러다 불법 체류 문제가 발생하면 어떻게 합니까? = *Then what happens if there's an illegal alien problem?* A: **구더기 무서워 장 못 담글까**라는 속담도 있지 않습니까? 여러 가지 문제는 해결책을 마련하겠습니다. = *We can't let a fear of what might happen stop us from doing what needs to be done. We will prepare for all contingencies.*

NOTE: 한국의 전통 양념인 장은 발효 식품이기 때문에 오래 두면 구더기와 같은 벌레가 생기는 수도 있었다. 그러나 벌레가 생기지 않게 관리를 잘 할 궁리를 해야지, 그것이 무서워 장을 담그지 않는다면 그것은 어리석은 일이다.
The traditional seasoning, soy, is fermented and therefore can grow maggots and other pests when left for a long time. It would be ridiculous, however, to not make soy for fear of maggots. Instead of abandoning a course of action out of fear, one must seek a safer way to implement that plan.

구렁이 담 넘어가듯이 [Lit. like a snake passes over a wall] PROVERB 남이 눈치채지 못하게 은근슬쩍 넘어가려는 모양을 가리키는 말 = with a smooth prowess that evades the detection of others ▌A: 어제는 또 왜 늦게 들어 온 거야? = *Why were you late getting home again last night?* B: 어제는 또 그럴 만한 일이 있었어. = *I had my reasons.* A: 매번 **구렁이 담 넘어 가듯이** 얼렁뚱땅 넘어갔지만 이번에는 그렇게 못해. = *You always smooth talk your way around the issue with no real answers, but not this time.*

구르는 돌에는 이끼가 끼지 않는다 [Lit. A rolling stone gathers no moss.] PROVERB 끊임없이 노력을 해야 침체기가 찾아오지 않는다는 말 = Continued hard work keeps one from slipping into a period of stagnation. (*equiv.* A rolling stone gathers no moss. *cf.* 흐르는 물은 썩지 않는다)

▌A: 요즘 사는 게 너무 재미없고 따분해. = *Life is such a pleasure-less bore these days.* B: **구르는 돌에는 이끼가 끼지 않는다는데,** 넌 변화를 싫어하니까 그런 거야. 뭘 좀 배워 보는 건 어때? = *Don't forget that a rolling stone gathers no moss. Maybe it's because you dislike change so much. What about learning something new?*

NOTE: 이 표현은 A rolling stone gathers no moss.라는 영국 속담을 번역한 말이다. 저 영국 속담이 자주 직장이나 사는 곳 따위를 옮기면 좋지 않다는 뜻을 가지는 데 반해, '구르는 돌에는 이끼가 끼지 않는다'는 한국 표현은 노력을 하지 않거나 변화를 두려워하여 정체돼 있는 것을 경계하라는 의미를 갖는다. 그러나 근래에 들어서는 영국 속담과 같은 뜻으로 쓰일 때도 많다.

There are two interpretations of the old English proverb, "a rolling stone gathers no moss," where this Korean expression comes from. One equates the "moss" with roots and implies that someone who is constantly moving never puts down deep roots or takes on any meaningful responsibilities. Another interpretation—the meaning most often used in Korea—equates the "moss" with stagnation and suggests that staying in one place too long can atrophy one's intellect. As of late, the Korean version too, is sometimes used with the original intent of the phrase.

구사일생 [Lit. 九nine + 死die + 一one + 生live → nine fatalities and a sole survivor] CHINESE-DERIVATION 죽을 고비에서 가까스로 살아남 = to narrowly survive (*equiv.* a narrow escape / an evasion by the skin of one's teeth / a close call) ▌A: 지난 일요일에 등산을 갔다가 산속에서 길을 잃어서 큰일날 뻔했어요. = *I almost got into serious trouble last week when I got off the path while hiking.* B: 저런. 그래서 어떻게 했어요? = *Gosh, what did you do?* A: 한참을 헤매다 간신히 길을 찾아서 **구사일생**으로 살아났어요. = *After wondering around for a while, I finally found the path and managed to get out of there by the skin of my teeth.*

구석에 몰리다 [Lit. to be driven into a corner] IDIOM 어려운 처지가 되다 = to be faced with a difficult situation (*equiv.* to have one's back up against the wall *syn.* 코너에 몰리다) ▌A: 결국 그 국회의원 사퇴하겠다고

발표했어요. = *That lawmaker finally announced that he would be resigning.* B: 어제까지만 해도 절대 자기 발로 물러나는 일은 없을 거라고 했잖아요. = *Only just yesterday he was saying how he would never step down.* A: 네. **구석에 몰리니** 어쩔 수 없었나 봐요. = *That's right. I guess he had his back up against the wall with no other way out.*

구슬이 서 말이라도 꿰어야 보배다 [Lit. Even with three barrels of beads, you don't have jewelry until the beads are strung.] PROVERB

아무리 좋은 것이라도 실제로 사용할 수 있게 잘 정리해 놓아야 제 가치를 인정받을 수 있다는 말 = Nothing is complete until the final touches have been applied. (*equiv.* It takes more than pearls to make a necklace. / It's not over till the fat lady sings. / It's not over till it's over.) ▌A: 강의 준비는 다 됐어요? = *Are you all prepared for the lecture?* B: 자료 수집은 일단 끝났어요. 그런데 **구슬이 서 말이라도 꿰어야 보배**라고, 학생들이 이해할 수 있게 잘 정리하는 일이 큰일이네요. = *I'm done assembling materials, but it takes more than pearls to make a necklace. Organizing it in a way that the students can grasp is a big job.*

구워삶다 [Lit. to bake and boil] IDIOM

어떤 수단과 방법을 써서 상대편이 자신의 생각에 따르도록 만들다 = to use every method at one's disposal to bring a person into agreement (*equiv.* to talk someone into doing something / to make someone come around) ▌A: 다른 사람들은 다 설득했는데 손철민 씨만 버티고 있습니다. = *I was able to convince everyone else, but Son Cheolmin is still holding out.* B: 시간이 얼마 없는데. 어떻게든 **구워삶아** 봐. = *We don't have much time. Do whatever it takes to make him come around.*

*구태의연하다 [Lit. 舊 old + 態 state + 依 depend on + 然 so + 하다 adjectival suffix → to rely on the old ways] CHINESE-DERIVATION

발전하지 않고 낡은 옛것을 그대로 따르는 모습을 비판적으로 일컫는 말 = used to pejoratively describe someone who adheres to the old ways (*equiv.* to be stuck in the past) ▌A: 신입사원 기획안은 어땠어요? = *How was the proposal from the new employee?* B: 실망스러워. 젊은 사람이라 참신할 줄 알았는데 내용이 너무 **구태의연해**. = *It was disappointing. He's pretty* *young, so I was expecting something innovative, but his approach was way too old-fashioned.*

***국물도 없다** [Lit. to lack even broth] IDIOM **1.** 돌아오는 몫이나 이익이 없다 = to be left without even the slightest gains (*equiv.* to have nothing coming / to be left high and dry *syn.* 콩고물도 없다) ▌A: 정말 어떻게 삼촌이 나한테 그럴 수가 있지? 이번에 삼촌 가게 공사할 때 내가 얼마나 열심히 도왔는지 당신도 알지? = *How could my uncle do this to me? You saw how much I helped him out while the store was under construction.* B: 그러게. 장사도 잘 된다는데, 당신한테는 **국물도 없**네. = *That's right. And now they saw the store is doing well, but you're left high and dry.* **2.** 사정을 봐 주지 않다 = to not take someone's excuse into consideration (*equiv.* to show no mercy) ▌A: 정말 죄송해요. 차가 너무 막히는 바람에 ……. = *I'm terribly sorry. It's just that traffic was so backed up ...* B: 오늘은 그냥 넘어가지만 내일도 또 지각하면 정말 **국물도 없을** 줄 알아. = *Today we can let it slide but if this happens again tomorrow, there'll be no mercy.*

NOTE: 한국의 전통 밥상에는 보통 밥과 마른 반찬, 국이 올라간다. 이 국에서 중요한 것은 국물보다 건더기이다. 국에서 (건더기는커녕) 국물도 없으니 결국 먹을 게 전혀 없는 셈이다. 돌아오는 몫이나 이득이 전혀 없을 때 이 표현을 쓴다.
Traditionally, a Korean meal consists of rice, a dry dish, and broth. The most important element to the broth however, is not the broth itself, but the stock, or bits of food within the broth. If not only the food is missing, but the bowl even lacks broth, there truly is nothing to eat at all. When one's share turns out to be next to nothing or one's exertions are left without compensation, this is the phrase to use.

***국수(를) 먹게 해 주다** [Lit. to feed others noodles] IDIOM 결혼식을 올리다 = to throw a wedding (*equiv.* to tie the knot / to get hitched) ▌A: 언제 국수 먹게 해 줄 거예요? = *When are you two walking down the aisle?* B: 그게 뭐 생각대로 돼야 말이죠. 좀 기다려 보세요. = *Well, things have got to go according to plan first. Hold on for a little while longer.*

NOTE: 전통 결혼식에서 손님들에게 국수를 대접한 데서 비롯됐다.
This phrase is rooted in the Korean custom of providing 국수, long thin noodles, to wedding attendees.

군계일학 [Lit. 群 crowd + 鷄 chicken + 一 one + 鶴 crane → a crane among chickens] CHINESE-DERIVATION 많은 사람 가운데 가장 뛰어난 인물 = a person that excels within a group (*equiv.* to be head and shoulders above the rest / a triton among minnows / a giant among men) ▌A: 솔직히 눈에 띄는 선수가 없네요. 저 한 선수만 빼고요. = *Honestly, none of the players really stand out. Well, except for that one over there.* B: 그렇습니까? = *Is that so?* A: 네. 저 선수가 **군계일학**이네요. = *Yes, he's a triton among minnows.*

군침(을) 삼키다 [Lit. to swallow when one's mouth is watering] IDIOM 이익이나 재물을 보고 탐을 내다 = to covet a material gain or treasure (*syn.* 군침(을) 흘리다) ▌A: 이 계약 어떻게 따 내셨어요? **군침을 삼키는** 업체가 한둘이 아니었던 걸로 아는데요. = *How did you manage to win this contract? More than just a few other companies were lusting for it.* B: 저희 측이 제시한 조건이 마음에 들었나 봐요. = *I guess they just liked the conditions we set forth.*

군침(을) 흘리다 IDIOM = 군침(을) 삼키다

군침(이) 돌다 [Lit. for one's mouth to water] IDIOM 이익이나 재물을 보고 탐이 나다 = to covet a material gain or treasure ▌A: 오늘 재형이 만났는데, 이 회사 주식을 사면 얼마 안 있어 엄청나게 오를 거래. = *I met with Jaehyeong today and he was telling me that if I buy stock in this company, it won't be long until the value goes up a lot.* B: 그렇게 **군침 도**는 이야기만 믿고 주식에 손댔다가 망한 사람이 내 주변에 한둘인 줄 알아요? = *I've known more than just a few people who have believed that kind of mouthwatering spiel and tried their hands in stocks only to fail miserably.*

▶p.373

***굴뚝같다** [Lit. to look like a chimney] IDIOM 무엇을 하고 싶은 마음이 간

절하다＝to be anxious (to do something) (*equiv.* to crane one's neck out in anticipation / to be waiting in earnest anticipation) ▌A: 이번 주말에 영화 보러 갈까?＝*Do you want to go see a movie this weekend?* B: 마음은 **굴뚝같은데** 이번 주말에는 회사에 나가 봐야 할 것 같아. 일이 잔뜩 밀렸거든.＝*I'd like that more than anything, but it looks like I'll have to work this weekend. Things have really piled up at the office.*

NOTE: 약속한 사람을 간절히 기다리며 그 사람이 나타날 방향으로 목을 길게 빼고 있는 모습이 굴뚝의 모양과 닮은 데서 비롯된 표현이다.
This phrase literally means "to be like a chimney." For English speakers, this may bring to mind the image of a man smoking away like a chimney, but the Korean phrase comes from the way people tend to crane their necks high and to the left and right when they are anxiously awaiting someone's arrival.

굴러 온 돌이 박힌 돌 뺀다 [Lit. A rolling stone knocks a fixed stone out of place.] PROVERB 새로 들어온 사람이 원래 그 자리에 있던 사람을 내쫓거나 그 권리를 빼앗을 때 쓰는 말＝used when a newcomer wins out over the person who was originally in that position, or takes away some of their authority (*equiv.* Bad money drives out good.) ▌A: 요즘에 우리 모임의 멤버들이 자꾸 탈퇴를 해서 큰일이에요.＝*Members continuing to drop out like this is a real problem.* B: 왜요? 무슨 일 있어요?＝*Why? What's the problem with that?* A: 새로 들어온 사람 하나가 설쳐 대서 다른 사람들이 불편해하는 것 같아요.＝*Well, the newcomer rampaging around seems to have made the others uncomfortable.* B: **굴러 온 돌이 박힌 돌 빼고 있군요.**＝*I guess the new is pushing out the old.*

굴러 온 호박 [Lit. a pumpkin that came rolling along] IDIOM 뜻밖에 생긴 좋은 물건이나 행운＝a stroke of unexpected good luck (*equiv.* a windfall *cf.* 호박이 넝쿨째 굴러 들어오다, 웬 떡이냐) ▌A: 이번에 며느리 얻으셨다면서요? 어때요?＝*I heard you have a new daughter-in-law. How is she?* B: 정말로 **굴러 온 호박**이에요. 어른들한테는 깍듯하고 남편한테도 잘하고, 아주 복덩어리예요.＝*Things just all fell into*

place. She's polite to her elders and good to her husband—a true stroke of good fortune.

NOTE: 호박은 즙을 내어 먹기도 하고 얼굴이나 몸이 부은 환자에게 달여 주면 붓기를 가라앉히기도 한다. 또 단맛이 나고 향기가 좋기 때문에 엿을 만드는 재료로도 많이 쓰이는 인기 식품이다 그런 호박이 저절로 굴러 왔으니 뜻밖의 선물이 아닐 수 없다.

In Korea, pumpkin is used to make pumpkin porridge, of course, but it is also boiled down and given to patients to reduce swelling. With its fragrant smell and good taste, it is always a popular food That's why a pumpkin that just came rolling along is nothing less than a windfall.

굴레를 벗다 [Lit. to break free of the bridle] IDIOM 구속이나 통제에서 벗어나다 = to break free from the fetters of restriction or oppression (*equiv.* to cast off the fetters / to break the chains *syn.* 멍에를 벗다 *ant.* 굴레를 쓰다)

▌A: 아, 어떻게 하면 이 지긋지긋한 가난의 **굴레를 벗을** 수 있을까요? = *How can I break free from this yoke of abominable poverty?* B: 글쎄요. 복권에 당첨되는 수밖에 없지 않을까요? = *Well, don't you think a winning lottery ticket would be your only way out?*

NOTE: 굴레는 말이나 소의 목에서 고삐에 걸쳐 얽어매는 줄이다. 멍에는 수레나 쟁기를 끌기 위해 말이나 소의 목에 얹는 구부러진 막대를 가리킨다. 굴레는 소가 평생 쓰고 있어야 하는 것이지만, 멍에는 일을 할 때만 쓰는 것이다. 이 둘은 속박이나 구속을 상징하는 것으로 서로 바꿔 쓸 수 있는 경우가 많지만, 그런 맥락에서 미세한 어감 차이가 있다. 굴레는 벗어나기 힘든 선천적인 것이나 반복되는 것에, 멍에는 살면서 경험하는 아픔이나 고비에 주로 쓰인다.

The word for "bridle" in Korean is 굴레 and this is the part that connects to the reins that go around the animal's neck. On the other hand, 멍에 is a yoke, or a wooden brace that is put over an animal's neck when pulling a cart or plow. While the 굴레 is worn for a lifetime, the 멍에 is only worn at work time. Therefore, there is a subtle difference in their usage when used metaphorically to denote restaint or oppression. 굴레 implies being born into a life of inescapable servitude, whereas 멍에 suggests a period of hardship.

굴레를 쓰다 [Lit. to wear the bridle] IDIOM 구속에 얽매이다 = to be oppressed or restricted (*equiv.* to be tied down / to be chained up / to be bridled / to wear the yoke *syn.* 멍에를 쓰다 *ant.* 굴레를 벗다) ▌A: 오랜만이다. 결혼은 했어? = *It's been so long. Did you get married?* B: 다음 주 토요일이 결혼식이야. = *I'm getting married next Saturday.* A: 아, 그래? 축하한다! 너도 드디어 결혼이라는 **굴레를 쓰는구나**. = *Oh, really? Congratulations! Finally, even you'll be wearing the yoke of marriage.*

NOTE: See the note on 굴레를 벗다.

굼벵이도 구르는 재주가 있다 [Lit. Even the cicada larva has the talent of crawling along.] PROVERB 아무리 무능한 사람도 잘하는 것이 하나는 있다는 말 = Everybody has a talent to offer. (*equiv.* There is no tree but bears some fruit.) ▌A: 난 왜 이렇게 잘하는 게 없을까? **굼벵이도 구르는 재주가 있다는데**. = *Why is there nothing I can do well? Even worms are good at digging.* B: 네가 왜 잘하는 게 없어? 숨쉬는 것도 잘하고, 밥 먹는 것도 잘하잖아. = *What do you mean you can't do anything well? You're good at breathing, and eating too.*

NOTE: 높은 나무에 사는 다른 애벌레와는 달리 굼벵이는 썩은 짚이나 땅속에서 살기 때문에 걸을 일이 별로 없어 다리가 퇴화했다. 그래서 이동을 할 때 옆으로 굴러 몸을 뒤집은 뒤 등으로 이동한다. 동작이 굼떠서 할 줄 아는 일이 없는 것처럼 보이는 굼벵이도 정말로 구르는 재주가 있는 것이다.
Unlike other insects of the caterpillar variety that live in trees, the cicada larva calls rotting houses and earthen canals its home. It gets around by squirming and wiggling. So, despite it's lackluster appearance, even the lowly 굼벵이, or cicada larva is quite gifted when it comes to squirming.

굿이나 보고 떡이나 먹으면 된다 [Lit. It's enough to just watch a shamanic ritual and eat some *tteok*.] PROVERB 남의 일에 쓸데없이 간섭하지 말고 가만히 있다가 그 이익을 취하라는 말 = Do not unnecessarily interfere with another's doings and instead just enjoy the free benefit of another's labors. (*equiv.* Sit back and enjoy the free ride.) ▌A: 요즘 통 정

신이 없어서 상황이 어떻게 돌아가는지 모르겠어요. = *I've been so busy recently, I don't even know what's going on* B: 너는 신경 쓸 필요 없어. 너는 **굿이나 보고 떡이나 먹으면 돼**. = *You don't need to know. Just sit back and enjoy the ride.*

NOTE: 굿은 누군가에게 좋지 않은 일이 있을 때 그것을 치유해 달라고 신에게 기원하며 행하는 무속 의식이다. 고민거리가 있어 굿을 하고 있는 사람에게 이래라저래라 말해 봤자 도움이 되지 않는다. 제3자는 그냥 굿이나 보고 차려진 음식이나 먹으면 될 일이다.
A 굿 is a shamanistic ritual that appeals to the gods for aid when some tragedy has befallen a household. If someone is carrying out this ritual, things have already deteriorated past the point where some friendly advice will do the trick. For a disinterested party, simply watching the ceremony and eating some of the food is all that needs to be done.

궁여지책 [Lit. 窮 poor + 餘 extra + 之 of + 策 plan] CHINESE-DERIVATION 아주 입장이 난처하고 어려워 어쩔 수 없이 짜낸 대책 = the emergency measures one may assume when left with no other choice (*equiv.* the last resort / a last-ditch effort) ▌A: 회사에서 머그컵을 나누어 주는 이유가 뭘까요? = *Why do you think they are giving out mugs at work?* B: 사람들이 일회용 컵을 너무 많이 쓰니까 **궁여지책**을 낸 거겠죠. = *They're doing it as a last resort because people keep using too many of the paper cups.*

권모술수 [Lit. 權 power + 謀 plan + 術 skill + 數 trick → designs on power using skills and trickery] CHINESE-DERIVATION 원하는 것을 이루기 위한 온갖 꾀와 방법들을 다소 부정적으로 표현한 말 = used to pejoratively describe all sorts of trickery one resorts to in order to achieve one's aims (*equiv.* to use every trick in the book) ▌A: 난 정치가 싫어. 온갖 **권모술수**가 난무하잖아. = *I hate politics. It's rampant with scheming and dirty tricks.* B: 개중에는 깨끗한 사람도 많이 있을 거야. = *I'm sure there are plenty of politicians who aren't like that.*

권선징악 [Lit. 勸 recommend + 善 good + 懲 punish + 惡 evil] CHINESE-DERIVATION 착한 일을 권장하고 악한 일을 벌함 = encouragement of good, punishment of evil (*equiv.* good triumphing over evil / Good wins out in the end.) ▌A: 옛날 동화들은 주제가 거의 **권선징악**인 것 같아요. = *It seems like the plots of all the old children's books were good winning out over evil.* B: 네. 아이들에게 착한 사람이 상을 받고 나쁜 사람이 벌을 받는다는 생각을 심어 주기 위해서겠죠. = *Yeah, they were probably trying to instill the idea in children's heads that evil is punished and good is rewarded.*

궤도에 들어서다 IDIOM = 궤도에 오르다

궤도에 오르다 [Lit. to get on track] IDIOM 어떠한 일이나 사업 등의 성과가 일정 수준에 이르다 = to achieve a certain measure of success in a business or project (*equiv.* to get on track / to get underway / to get into the swing of things *syn.* 궤도에 들어서다) ▌A: 사업은 좀 어떠세요? = *How's your business going?* B: 아직 힘들어요. **궤도에 오르려면** 시간이 좀 더 걸릴 것 같아요. = *We're still having trouble. It looks like it'll take some time for us to get on track.*

귀가 가렵다 [Lit. to have itchy ears] IDIOM 남이 제 말을 하는 것 같이 느끼다 = to feel like someone is talking about you (*syn.* 귀가 간지럽다) ▌A: 누가 제 말 하고 있나 봐요. = *I think someone must be talking about me.* B: 왜요? = *Why?* A: 갑자기 **귀가 가려워서요**. = *Because my ears are suddenly feeling itchy.*

NOTE: 오른쪽 귀가 가려우면 남이 내 칭찬을, 왼쪽 귀가 가려우면 남이 내 욕을 하는 것이라는 속설이 있다.
It is commonly said that if one's right ear is itchy, someone somewhere is saying something good about you and if one's left ear is itchy, someone is saying something bad about you.

귀가 간지럽다 IDIOM = 귀가 가렵다

*귀가 닳다 [Lit. to wear out one's ears] IDIOM 어떠한 이야기를 지겹도록 많이 듣다 = to wear out one's ears by hearing something too many times.

(*equiv.* to be sick of hearing something / to have heard something a thousand times *syn.* 귀가 따갑다 *cf.* 귀에 딱지가 앉다, 귀에 못이 박히다) █ A: 제발 좀 치우고 살아. 집 꼴이 이게 뭐니? = *Could you please pick up after yourself? How can you live like this?* B: 너까지 잔소리야? 우리 엄마한테 벌써 **귀가 닳도록** 그 얘기 들었다고. = *Now even you're nagging me? My mom has already told me a thousand times.*

***귀가 따갑다** [Lit. to have aching ears] IDIOM 어떠한 이야기를 너무 많이 들어 듣기가 싫다 = to have heard something too many times (*syn.* 귀가 닳다 *cf.* 귀에 딱지가 앉다, 귀에 못이 박히다) █ A: 집에서 엄마가 제일 많이 하는 얘기가 뭐예요? = *What's the one thing that your mom talks to you about the most?* B: 공부하라는 말이요. 정말 **귀가 따갑게** 들었어요. = *She's always telling me to study. It's really starting to give me a headache.*

귀가 뚫리다 [Lit. to have one's ears penetrated] IDIOM 외국어를 알아듣게 되다 = to grow familiar with a foreign language (*equiv.* to make a breakthrough (with a language)) █ A: 한국에 온 지 1년쯤 되었을 때 **귀가 뚫렸어요**. = *I started really making breakthroughs with my Korean after I had lived here for a year.* B: 우와, 정말 한국어 공부를 열심히 하셨나 봐요. = *Wow, I guess you really studied hard.*

귀(가)빠지다 [Lit. for one's ears to drop off] IDIOM 태어나다 = to be born █ A: 오늘은 제 **귀빠진 날**이에요. = *Today is the day I was born.* B: 아, 그래요? 축하해요! 미역국은 먹었어요? = *Oh, really? Congratulations. Did you have seaweed soup?*

NOTE: 아기가 태어날 때 보통 머리가 먼저 나온다. 그래서 신체 부위 중 가장 먼저 보이는 곳이 귀라고 한다. 생일을 귀 빠진 날이라고 한다.
In the birthing process, it is usually the head a newborn that emerges first. Therefore, it is the ears that are the first part of a newborn seen by the parents. A birthday is thus referred to as 귀 빠진 날, the day one's ears popped out.

귀가 얇다 [Lit. to have thin ears] IDIOM 남의 말을 쉽게 잘 믿다 = to be easily swayed by the words of others (*equiv.* to be gullible / to be a sheep / to be a sucker) ▌A: 너 핸드폰 또 바꿨어? = *You changed cell phones again?* B: 응. 사람들 말이 요즘은 다들 이걸 쓴대. = *Yeah, I heard that everyone is using this one now.* A: 넌 참 **귀가 얇구나**. = *You're a real sucker.*

NOTE: 가볍고 얇은 종이가 바람에 이리저리 흩날리는 모습을 생각해 보라. 다른 사람의 말이나 여러 가지 주변 상황에 쉽게 휘둘리는 사람을 두고 흔히 '팔랑귀를 가졌다'고 한다. 여기서 '팔랑'은 '바람에 가볍고 힘차게 나부끼는 모양'을 가리키는 부사에서 왔다.

Envision a light, thin sheet of paper that flutters in the wind to and fro. If a person has ears like that, they too will be easily swayed by the environment and the things people say. Such gullible individuals were originally described as 팔랑귀를 가졌다. In this expression, 팔랑 describes the image of something flapping in the wind.

귀를 의심하다 [Lit. to doubt one's ears] IDIOM 믿기 어려운 이야기를 들어 잘못 들은 것이 아닌가 생각하다 = to think one has misheard something because it is so hard to believe (*equiv.* to not believe one's ears *cf.* 눈을 의심하다) ▌A: 얼마나 좋으세요? 민수가 그 어렵다는 대학에 척 붙었으니. = *You must be so happy right now. Minsu made it into a school that everyone knows is so competitive.* B: 사실 합격 소식을 들었을 때 제 **귀를 의심했었어요**. 믿기지가 않더라고요. = *I actually couldn't believe my ears when I first heard the news. It was just unbelievable.*

귀신같다 [Lit. to be like a ghost] IDIOM 솜씨나 재주, 추측이 놀랄 정도로 대단하다 = to have an amazing ability to do a certain thing ▌A: 왜 이렇게 추운데 밖에 오래 서 계세요? = *Why are you standing out in the cold like that?* B: 담배 냄새 없애려고요. 제 아내는 제가 내가 담배 핀 것을 **귀신같이** 알아낸다니까요. = *I'm trying to get rid of the smell of cigarette smoke. My wife has an uncanny ability to figure out whenever I've smoked.*

귀신이 곡하다 [Lit. for a ghost to let out a wail] IDIOM 기가 막힐 정도로 신기하고 기묘하다 = to be vexed by something queer or inexplicable (*equiv.* to be uncanny) ▮ A: 정말 **귀신이 곡할** 일이네. 여기 있던 반지가 어디로 갔지? = *It really is inexplicable. Where did my ring that was just right here go?* B: 여기에 벗어 둔 거 맞아요? 세면대 위에 벗어 둔 거 아니에요? = *Are you sure you left it here? Didn't you take it off over by the sink?* A: 아, 맞다! 역시 당신이야! = *That's right! You're the best!*

NOTE: 곡이란 사람이 죽었을 때 장례식장에서 살아 있는 사람들이 우는 것을 말한다. 그런데 이미 죽은 영혼인 귀신이 곡을 한다는 것은 말이 되지 않는다. 상식적으로 이해가 되지 않는 희한한 상황일 때 '귀신이 곡할 노릇'이라는 말을 자주 쓴다.
The 곡 in this idiom refers to the wailing of the bereaved at a funeral. It doesn't make sense, however, that a ghost would be wailing for the dead. 귀신이 곡할 노릇 is often used when a situation defies understanding.

귀에 거슬리다 [Lit. to be offensive to the ears] IDIOM 듣기 불쾌하다 = to be offensive ▮ A: 표정이 왜 그래? 내 말이 **귀에 거슬려**? = *Why are you making that face? Is what I'm saying offensive to you?* B: 솔직히 기분이 그리 좋지는 않네. 그 얘기를 지금 꼭 해야겠니? = *Honestly, I'm just not feeling that well. Do we really have to have this talk now?*

귀에 걸면 귀걸이 코에 걸면 코걸이 [Lit. Hanging on the ears, it's an earring; on the nose, it's a nose ring.] PROVERB 일정한 원칙이 없이 경우에 따라 이쪽도 되고 저쪽도 될 수 있는 상황을 비판적으로 표현한 말 = used to critically describe a situation that lacks a clear set of standards and could go any which way (*equiv.* to be open to interpretation / It's all things to all men. / It's a matter of how you see it. / It all depends on how you look at it.) ▮ A: 우리 학교 교칙은 **귀에 걸면 귀걸이 코에 걸면 코걸이**인 것 같아. = *Our school's regulations seem a little too open to interpretation.* B: 맞아. 그때그때 말이 달라지니 종잡을 수가 없어. = *You're right. They are always telling us something different so it's hard to get the gist.*

귀에 딱지가 앉다 [Lit. to have a scab on the ears] IDIOM 어떠한 말을 너무 많이 들어 지겹다 = to have heard something to the point of being sick of it (*equiv.* to be sick of hearing something *syn.* 귀에 못이 박히다 *cf.* 귀가 따갑다, 귀가 닳다, 한 번만 더 들으면 백 번이다) ▌A: 이 안 닦고 자면 충치 생긴다고 엄마가 말했잖니? = *I've told you that you'll get cavities if you go to bed without brushing your teeth.* B: 엄마, 그 얘긴 **귀에 딱지가 앉을** 만큼 들었어요. = *You've already told me that a thousand times.*

***귀에 못이 박히다** [Lit. to have calluses in one's ears] IDIOM 어떠한 말을 너무 많이 들어 지겹다 = be sick and tired of hearing something (*syn.* 귀에 딱지가 앉다 *cf.* 귀가 따갑다, 귀가 닳다, 한 번만 더 들으면 백 번이다) ▌A: 철수야, 텔레비전 그만 보고 숙제부터 해라. = *Turn off the TV and do your homework first.* B: 아빠, **귀에 못이 박히겠어요.** 공부하라는 말씀 좀 그만하세요. = *You're like a broken record. Please stop telling me to study all the time.*

NOTE: 많은 사람들이 이 표현에 나오는 못을 나무를 박을 때 쓰는 못이라고 생각하지만 실제로는 굳은 살을 뜻한다. 손바닥에 계속해서 압력을 가해질 때 못이 박히듯, 어떤 사람이 같은 얘기를 계속해서 듣는다면 귀에 못이 생길지도 모른다.
In the most common usage of this phrase, most people think that the 못 in the sentence is a nail. It is actually a callus. Just as calluses develop on one's hands from doing the same work over and over again. This idiom plays with the idea that hearing something over and over can cause calluses to develop in one's ears.

귀에 익다 [Lit. to be familiar to the ears] IDIOM 들어 본 기억이 있다 = to sound familiar (*equiv.* to ring a bell) ▌A: 이 멜로디 **귀에 익은데.** 어디서 들었더라 ……. = *This melody sounds familiar. Where was it that I heard it again?* B: 어제 우리 커피숍에 있을 때 나온 노래 아냐? = *Isn't this the song that we heard at the coffee shop yesterday?*

귓가에 맴돌다 [Lit. to spin around one's ears] IDIOM 어떤 소리가 더 이

상 들리지 않는데도 마음에 남아 여전히 들리는 듯하다 = for a certain sound to seemingly still be audible even after the sound has stopped (*equiv.* (for a sound or melody) to keep running through one's head *syn.* 귓전을 울리다) ▌A: 왜 그래? 무슨 걱정 있어? = *What's wrong? Do you have something on your mind?* B: 그건 아닌데 ……. 어제 들은 얘기가 **귓가에 맴돌아서**. = *No, that's not it. It's just ... what was said yesterday keeps running through my mind.*

귓등으로도 안 듣다 IDIOM = 귓등으로 듣다

귓등으로 듣다 [Lit. to hear with the back of the ears] IDIOM 남의 말을 주의해서 듣지 않고 건성으로 듣다 = to listen in a distracted or desultory way (*equiv.* to half hear / to half listen *syn.* 귓등으로도 안 듣다, 귓전으로 듣다) ▌A: 내가 어제 분명히 말했잖아. 오늘 다섯 시까지 오라고. = *I told you clearly yesterday to be home by five today.* B: 네가? 난 기억에 없는데? = *You said that? I don't remember that.* A: 사람 말을 **귓등으로 들으니까** 그렇지. = *That's because you're always just half-listening to everything I say.*

귓전으로 듣다 IDIOM = 귓등으로 듣다

귓전을 때리다 [Lit. to smack the ears] IDIOM 시끄러운 소리 따위가 들려오다 = to hear a loud sound (*equiv.* to be hit with a loud sound) ▌A: 이거 이사를 가든지 해야지 원. = *We've got no choice left but to move.* B: 왜요? = *Why?* A: 어제 윗집 부부가 부부싸움을 하는 바람에 잠을 한숨도 못 잤어. 그 부부 고함소리가 밤새 **귓전을 때려서** 잠을 잘 수가 있어야지. = *I couldn't get a wink of sleep last night because of the couple fighting upstairs. Their shouting was like a jackhammer to the head all night long.*

귓전을 울리다 [Lit. to ring the area around one's ears] IDIOM 어떤 소리가 마음속에 잊혀지지 않다 = to not forget a certain sound (*equiv.* for one's ears to keep ringing with the sound (of something) *syn.* 귓가에 맴돌다) ▌A: 인도네시아 여행은 어땠어요? = *How was your trip to Indonesia?*

B: 그런데 거기는 새벽에 사원에서 기도하는 소리가 온 동네에 다 들리더라고요. 아직도 **귓전을 울리는** 느낌이에요. = *Well, the sound of praying at the temples was audible throughout the whole neighborhood starting at the crack of dawn. It's still ringing in my ears now.*

그 나물에 그 밥 [Lit. the same vegetables, the same rice] PROVERB 서로 수준이 비슷하여 큰 차이가 없다는 말 = to be of the same level or almost indistinguishable (*equiv.* They're two of a kind. / They're like peas in a pod. *syn.* 그놈이 그놈이다, 거기서 거기, 오십보백보, 대동소이하다)
▌A: 모레가 드디어 대통령 선거 날이네. 누구 뽑을 거야? = *The presidential election is finally coming up the day after tomorrow. Who are you going to vote for?* B: 아직 고민 중이야. **그 나물에 그 밥** 같아서. = *I'm still thinking that over. They seem to be hardly indistinguishable from each other.*

NOTE: 먹을 것이 풍족하지 않던 시절 주된 반찬은 나물이었다. 그나마 매번 다른 나물을 풍족하게 먹을 수 있는 것은 아니었으므로 매번 밥상 위에 올라오는 나물은 크게 차이가 나지 않았다. 밥도 어제 먹었던 것과 같은 밥, 나물도 어제 먹었던 것과 같은 나물이 올라오는 밥상을 받는 것처럼 큰 차이를 느끼지 못할 때 쓰는 말이다.
Back in the days when there wasn't enough food to go around, the most common side dish was wild greens. It wasn't as if the herbs would be varied every day, however, and most days would see the same assortment gracing the table. Just as one may be underwhelmed by the same old herbs and the same old rice day after day, this phrase can be used to describe an utter lack of variety.

그놈이 그놈이다 [Lit. That guy is that guy.] IDIOM 서로 수준이 비슷하여 큰 차이가 없다는 말 = to be of the same level or almost indistinguishable (*equiv.* to be identical *syn.* 그 나물에 그 밥, 거기서 거기, 오십보백보, 대동소이하다) ▌A: 이번 선거에서 누구 찍을 거예요? = *Who are you going to vote for in this election?* B: 글쎄요. 좀 심하게 말하면, **그놈이 그놈이라** 누구를 찍어야 할지 모르겠어요. = *Well, to put it frankly, they all seem about the same to me. I don't know who to*

vote for.

그늘에 가리다 [Lit. to be covered in the shadows] IDIOM 도드라지는 다른 무엇 때문에 드러나지 않다 = to be concealed by something that stands out (*equiv.* to be overshadowed / to hide in the shadows *ant.* 빛을 보다) ▌A: 이 그림은 상당히 좋네요. = *This drawing is quite good.* B: 이 그림을 그린 분의 형이 유명한 화가예요. 이분은 형의 **그늘에 가려서** 빛을 못 보고 있죠. = *The older brother of the person who painted this is a famous artist. He's kind of been overshadowed by his older brother.* A: 형 때문에 동생이 제대로 평가를 받지 못하고 있군요. = *Ah, so his brother is the reason he hasn't been getting the recognition he deserves.*

NOTE: '그늘'은 비유적으로 정반대의 두 가지 뜻을 모두 지니고 있다. 즉, 내가 의지하고 있는 대상의 보호나 혜택을 의기할 수도 있고, 나의 능력을 발휘하지 못하게 하는 제약이나 환경을 의미할 수도 있다. '~의 그늘에 가리다'라는 표현에서의 '그늘'은 후자에 해당한다. 반면, '부모의 그늘에서 벗어나다'라는 말에서의 '그늘'은 전자의 의미에 해당한다.
The concept of shade, has two opposite meanings in the world of Korean idioms. One meaning is that of the protection or favorable treatment one can receive from a benefactor. The other meaning is pressure or external factors that can prevent someone from achieving to the fullest of their abilities. In this expression, shade plays the role of the latter. This phrase is most often used in the following form, "~의 그늘에 가리다." If 그늘 appears in the phrase, "부모의 그늘에서 벗어나다," then the meaning is that of the former example from above.

그도 그럴 것이 [Lit. that's because] IDIOM 앞에서 얘기한 사실에 대한 이유를 언급하려고 할 때 쓰는 말 = used when referencing the reason for the aforementioned fact ▌A: 엄마, 오빠가 므슨 밥을 걸신들린 사람처럼 먹어요. = *Mom, he is eating like a wild man.* B: 배가 많이 고프겠지. **그도 그럴 것이** 하루 종일 한 끼도 안 먹었거든. = *Well, he must be really hungry. It's probably because he hasn't had anything to eat all day long.*

그러면 그렇지 [Lit. That's what happens when you do that.] IDIOM 어떤 일이 생각한 대로 되었을 때 하는 말 = used when something turns out as one had expected (*equiv.* Of course. / That's what I thought.) ▌A: 시험은 어떻게 됐어? = *How did the test go?* B: 가볍게 통과했어요. = *I passed it easily.* A: **그러면 그렇지.** 역시 내 아들이야. = *Of course you did. That's my boy.*

그렇고 그렇다 [Lit. just like that and that] IDIOM 특별할 것이 없다 = to not be anything special (*equiv.* nothing special / just normal) ▌A: 이번에 새로 온 인턴은 좀 어때요? 일 잘해요? = *How's the new intern? Is he good at the job?* B: **그렇고 그런** 편이에요. 특별히 열심히 하는 것 같지는 않아요. = *Just normal. It doesn't really seem like he's working especially hard.*

그릇이 작다 [Lit. to have a small bowl] IDIOM 어떤 일을 해 나갈 만한 능력이 되지 않다 = to lack the capability or wherewithal to carry out a certain task (*equiv.* to not be up to the task / to fall short *ant.* 그릇이 크다) ▌A: 이번 시장 선거 후보로 나온 김인철 씨를 어떻게 생각하세요? = *How do you feel about the candidate for mayor, Kim Incheol?* B: 인상은 좋은데 시장이 되기에는 **그릇이 좀 작은** 것 같아요. = *He gives a good impression but seems a little too inept for a mayor.*

NOTE: 그릇의 크기에 따라 담을 수 있는 음식의 양이 결정되듯, 사람이 감당할 수 있는 일의 크기는 사람의 능력에 달려 있다. '그릇이 작다', '그릇이 크다'라는 표현에서 '그릇'은 그러한 사람의 능력을 비유한 것이다.

Just as the amount that a bowl can hold depends on its size, the amount and scale of work that a person can handle depends on the person. The "bowl" in this expression is a metaphorical representation of a person's ability, or more precisely, capacity.

그릇이 크다 [Lit. to have a large bowl] IDIOM 능력이나 잠재력이 크다 = to have great potential or capability (*equiv.* to be a person of means / to be a go-getter *ant.* 그릇이 작다) ▌A: 민수 씨는 사람이 참 괜찮은 것 같

아요. 마음 씀씀이도 크고 성격도 대범하고요. = *I think that Minsu is a really fine guy. He has a big heart and a forgiving personality.* B: 그러게요. 평범한 사람은 아닌 것 같아요. **그릇이 큰** 사람이죠. = *That's true. He's not just an ordinary man. He has a big heart.*

NOTE: See the note on 그릇이 작다.

***그림의 떡** [Lit. *tteok* in a painting] IDIOM 탐이 나지만 실제로 가질 수 없는 물건 = something unattainable (*equiv.* a pie in the sky / a pipe dream) ▌ A: 저런 근사한 집에서 한번 살아 보고 싶지 않아? = *Wouldn't you like to live in a splendid house like that just once?* B: 살아 보고 싶지. 하지만 나한테는 **그림의 떡**이야. = *Of course I'd like that, but to me it's a pie in the sky.*

그림(이) 좋다 [Lit. to be a good picture] IDIOM 함께 있는 남녀가 잘 어울림을 비꼬아서 하는 말 = used as a sarcastic way of saying that a couple looks good together (*equiv.* Aw, what a pretty picture.) ▌ A: 어이, **그림 좋은데**! = *Oh, how sweet! What a pretty picture you two make.* B: 어디서 시비야? 좋게 말할 때 꺼져! = *Are you picking a fight? You'd better get out of here while I'm still asking nicely.*

그림자도 안 보이다 [Lit. to not even cast a shadow] IDIOM 흔적이나 자취가 없다 = to leave no trace behind (*equiv.* to leave not a trace / to see neither hide nor hair of someone) ▌ A: 형민이는 어디 갔어? = *Where'd Hyungmin go?* B: 몰라, 오늘 하루 종일 **그림자도 안 보이는데**? = *I don't know. I haven't seen hide nor hair of him all day long.*

그물에 든 고기 [Lit. a fish in the net] PROVERB 잡혀서 꼼짝하지 못하는 신세 = the state of being caught and unable to move (*equiv.* to be a fish on the line / a hatched egg / for one's goose to be cooked *syn.* 독 안에 든 쥐) ▌ A: 어떻게 하지? 경찰이 쫙 깔렸는데 더 이상 도망갈 데가 없어. = *What do we do now? The police have got us. We've got nowhere left to run.* B: **그물에 든 고기** 신세군. 이제 다 끝이야. = *We're like fish on the line. I guess this is it.*

그 아버지에 그 아들 [Lit. the father, the son] PROVERB 아들이 여러 면에서 아버지를 닮았을 때 쓰는 말 = used when a son resemble one's father in terms of personality or physical characteristics (*equiv.* like father, like son / The apple doesn't fall far from the tree. / a chip off the old block *syn.* 부전자전) ▌A: 우리 아들 녀석은 아침잠이 많아서 큰일이야. = *My son really enjoys sleeping in. I think we may have a problem.* B: **그 아버지에 그 아들**이네. = *Like father, like son.*

그저 그만이다 [Lit. That alone is more than enough.] IDIOM 아주 좋다 = to be very good ▌A: 이 공원 잘 꾸며 놓았군. 넓고 공기도 좋고. = *They sure fixed this park up nicely. It's so big and the air is nice too.* B: 그렇지? 아이들 데리고 오면 **그저 그만일** 것 같아. = *Yeah, if I bring my kids next time it'll be perfect.*

극악무도하다 [Lit. 極 extreme + 惡 evil + 無 no + 道 Tao + 하다 adjectival suffix] CHINESE-DERIVATION 매우 악하다 = to be very evil (*equiv.* evil itself) ▌A: 어떻게 어린애한테 이런 짓을 할 수가 있지? = *How could someone commit such an act against a child?* B: 그런 **극악무도한** 범죄 뉴스를 볼 때마다 애 키우기가 겁이 나요. = *Every time I hear about that kind of pure evil on the news it makes me scared to raise a child.*

근처도 못 가다 [Lit. to not even be able to go close] IDIOM 비교할 수 없을 정도로 뒤떨어지다 = to be so far behind that it's beyond compare (*equiv.* to not even come close) ▌A: 너는 어쩌면 그리 농구를 잘하니? 부럽다 애. = *How'd you get so good at basketball? I'm jealous.* B: 내가 무슨. 나는 우리 형에 비하면 아무것도 아니야. 나는 우리 형 **근처도 못 가**. = *Who, me? Compared to my older brother I'm nothing. I don't even come close to his level.*

근하신년 [Lit. 謹 solemnly + 賀 congratulate + 新 new + 年 year → solemn congratulations for the coming year] CHINESE-DERIVATION 삼가 새해를 축하한다는 인사말 = a polite New Year's greeting (*equiv.* Happy New Year! *cf.* 송구영신) ▌A: 연하장에 쓰여 있는 **근하신년**이라는 말이 무슨 뜻이죠? = *What's the meaning of 'geunhashinnyeon' written here on this New*

Year's card? B: 새해를 축하한다는 뜻이에요. =*It is just a common New Year's greeting.*

글자 그대로 IDIOM =문자 그대로

긁어 부스럼(을) 만들다 [Lit. to scratch an itch into a rash] PROVERB 아무 것도 아닌 일을 공연히 크게 만들어 화를 자초하다 =to needlessly make a small issue into a major affair (*equiv.* to make a big deal out of nothing / Just let sleeping dogs lie. / to make a mountain out of a mole hill) ▌A: 이 일을 선생님한테 말씀드려야 할까? =*Don't you think we have to tell the teacher about this?* B: 괜히 **긁어 부스럼 만들지** 말고 가만히 있어. =*Don't make such a big deal of it. Let's hold off on that.*

***금강산도 식후경** [Lit. Even at Mt. Geumgang, it's food and then sightseeing.] PROVERB 배가 부른 후에야 다른 여러 가지 놀거리의 재미 를 느낄 수 있다는 말 =Other amusements can be best enjoyed with a full stomach. (*equiv.* Everything goes better on a full stomach. / A good meal trumps all else.) ▌A: 시간 없어! 빨리 구경하지 않으면 오늘 내로 다 못 볼지도 몰라. =*We don't have time. If we don't hurry up and start sightseeing, we won't be able to see everything today.* B: 잠깐만. 나 배가 너무 고파. **금강산도 식후경**이잖아. =*Hold on a second. I'm really hungry. Food always comes first.*

금배지를 달다 [Lit. to attach a golden badge] IDIOM 국회의원이 되다 =to become a member of the National Assembly ▌A: 인철 씨는 꿈이 뭐예 요? =*Incheol, what's your goal in life?* B: 일단 이 길로 들어섰으면 **금 배지는 한번 달아** 봐야 하지 않겠어요? =*Since I've already chosen this path, I'd better go for a golden badge, hadn't I?*

NOTE: 금배지는 국회의원의 상징이다. 오래전 한 국회의원이 금광을 갖고 있었는데, 자신의 금광에서 난 금으로 배지를 만들어 동료 의원들에게 선물을 했다. 이후부터 모든 국회의원들에게 금배지가 지급되었는데, 군부 정권에서 이것이 지나치다고 하여 은배지로 바꾼 이후 현재까지 계속되고 있다. 그러나 아직 관용표현 속에서는 은배지가 아닌 금배지 가 국회의원의 상징으로 남아 있다.

The golden badge is a symbol for the lawmakers of the National Assembly. Long ago a lawmaker in the assembly gave out badges made of gold from his own mine to other representatives. After that, gold badges were presented to those who attained Korea's most illustrious post, but during the times of military rule, it was determined that this was excessive and the badges were then on produced from silver. The golden badge, however, still lives on as a symbol for the nation's legislators.

금상첨화 [Lit. 錦 silk + 上 over + 添 add + 花 flower → flowers on top of silk] CHINESE-DERIVATION 좋은 일 위에 또 좋은 일이 더하여짐 = for one good thing to happen right after another good thing (*equiv.* the icing on the cake) ▌A: 어때? 마음에 들어? = *How is it? Do you like it?* B: 괜찮기는 한데. 조금만 더 길이가 길면 **금상첨화**일 텐데, 그게 좀 아쉽네. = *It's fine, but if it were just a little bit longer, it would be like icing on the cake. It's a shame.*

금수강산 [Lit. 錦 silk + 繡 embroider + 江 river + 山 mountain → landscape of silk embroidered rivers and mountains] CHINESE-DERIVATION 매우 아름다운 산천 = very beautiful scenery ▌A: 외국에 나가 보니 우리나라만큼 자연이 아름다운 나라도 많지 않을 것 같아요. = *Traveling abroad, I realized that there aren't many other countries with natural landscape that's as beautiful as Korea.* B: 예부터 우리나라를 **금수강산**이라고 했잖아요. = *That's why it's been called a land of great natural beauty since long ago.*

NOTE: 우리나라 산천을 비유적으로 이르는 말이다.
금수강산 is a metaphorical description of the beauty of Korea.

금시초문 [Lit. 今 now + 始 first + 初 first + 聞 hear → news that one is just hearing] CHINESE-DERIVATION 바로 지금 처음으로 들음 = to be hearing something now for the first time (*equiv.* That's new to me.) ▌A: 우리 담임 선생님이 학교를 그만두신다는 얘기 들었어? = *Did you hear that our teacher is quitting?* B: 뭐? 그게 사실이야? 나는 **금시초문**인데. =

What? Is that true? That's news to me.

금(을) 굿다 [Lit. to draw a line] IDIOM 한계를 정하거나 구분을 명확히 하다＝to set a limit or clarify something (*equiv.* to draw a line / to delineate *syn.* 선(을) 굿다) ▌A: 당신은 왜 늘 회사 일을 집에 가져와? 회사랑 집에 **금을 분명히 그어야지**. ＝*Why are you always taking work home with you? You have to clearly delineate your work and home life.* B: 나도 그러고 싶은데, 일이 너무 많은 걸 어떡해?＝*I'd love to do that, but what about all the work I have to get done?*

금의환향(하다) [Lit. 錦 silk + 衣 clothes + 還 return + 鄕 hometown → a silk-clad homecoming] CHINESE-DERIVATION 출세를 하거나 성공해서 고향에 돌아오다＝to return home after much success away (*equiv.* a triumphant homecoming) ▌A: 아드님은 언제 왔어요?＝*When is your son getting back?* B: 네. 어젯밤에 와서 아직 자고 있어요. ＝*He got back last night and he's still asleep.* A: 그 어렵다는 사법시험에 합격하고 고향에 왔으니, **금의환향이네요**. ＝*Well, after passing a hard test like the judicial examinations, he sure is making a triumphant homecoming.*

금(이) 가다 [Lit. for a crack to grow longer] IDIOM 사이가 멀어지다＝to grow distant from someone (*equiv.* to grow apart *syn.* 틈이 벌어지다, 틈이 생기다 *cf.* 거리가 생기다) ▌A: 야, 여자 때문에 우리 십 년 우정에 **금이 가면** 되겠냐? 너도 민정이 좋아한다니까 내가 양보할게. ＝*Hey, are we really just going to let our ten years of friendship dissolve over a woman? Since you say you like Minjeong too, I'll give her up.* B: 고맙다. 그럼 이제 민정이 곁에 얼씬도 하지 마라. ＝*Thanks. Now don't even show your face near her again.*

금이야 옥이야 [Lit. It is gold, it is jade.] IDIOM 크게 정성을 들여 자식을 기르는 것을 가리키는 말＝used to describe the action of putting one's all into raising one's children ▌A: **금이야 옥이야** 기르신 딸을 시집 보내는 마음이 어떠세요?＝*How do you feel about marrying off a daughter whom you loved so dearly?* B: 기쁜 동시에 좀 서운하기도 하고 그렇네요. ＝*Well, I guess I'm feeling happy and sad at the same time.*

금지옥엽 [Lit. 金 gold + 枝 branch + 玉 jade + 葉 leaf → branches of gold and leaves of jade] CHINESE-DERIVATION 귀한 자손을 가리키는 말 = used to describe a beloved offspring (*equiv.* the apple of someone's eye *cf.* 불면 꺼질까 쥐면 터질까) ▌A: 재민이 이제 어떡하냐? 하나밖에 없는 아들을 사고로 잃었으니 ……. = *What's Jaemin to do now ... losing his only son in an accident like that?* B: 그러게, 정말 걱정이야. **금지옥엽** 같은 아들이었는데. = *I'm worried about him myself. His son was the apple of his eye.*

급물살을 타다 [Lit. to ride a fast current] IDIOM 일의 진행이 빨라지다 = to the speed of work to pick up (*equiv.* to pick up the pace) ▌A: 전국을 떠들썩하게 했던 여대생 실종 사건의 수사가 **급물살을 타고** 있습니다. = *The investigation into that missing college girl case that the whole nation has been talking about is starting to pick up.* B: 네. 경찰은 실종된 여대생이 마지막으로 찍힌 CCTV를 확보하여 분석 중이라고 밝혔습니다. = *Yeah, police secured the last security camera footage of the girl and have begun analyzing it.*

급한 불을 끄다 [Lit. to put out an urgent flame] IDIOM 급한 문제를 해결하다 = to solve an urgent problem (*equiv.* to put out the fire) ▌A: 문제는 잘 해결했어? = *Did you get it solved?* B: 일단 **급한 불은 껐는데**, 그 다음이 걱정이야. = *We took care of the most urgent issues. It's the next step I'm worried about.*

급할수록 돌아가라 [Lit. The more urgent it is, the more you should go around.] PROVERB 다급한 상황일수록 더 여유를 가져야 한다는 말 = The more urgent your work is, the more carefully you should do it. (*equiv.* Haste makes waste.) ▌A: 뛰어! 10분밖에 안 남았어. = *Hurry up! We've only got 10 minutes left.* B: 우리 천천히 가자. **급할수록 돌아가라고** 하잖아. = *Let's take it slow. Haste makes waste.*

급히 먹는 밥이 체한다 [Lit. Food consumed in haste leads to indigestion.] PROVERB 너무 급히 서두르면 일을 그르치게 된다는 말 = Working too hastily leads to sloppy results. (*equiv.* Haste makes waste. /

Measure twice cut once.) ▌A: 우리 민수도 남들처럼 여러 학원에 보내야 하는 거 아닐까요? 남들은 벌써부터 영어에, 미술에, 태권도까지 가르친다는데 ……. = *Should we send Minsu to a bunch of different institutes like everyone else? All the other kids are already learning English, art, and even taekwondo.* B: **급히 먹는 밥이 체한다잖아요**. 천천히 합시다. = *Too much too fast isn't a good idea. Let's just take it slow.*

기가 꺾이다 [Lit. to lose energy] IDIOM 기세가 꺾이다 = to lose energy

(*equiv.* to lose heart / to lose faith *syn.* 기(가)죽다 *cf.* 코가 납작해지다) ▌A: 저 팀은 너무 강해 보여요. 우리가 이길 수 있을까요? = *That team just looks too strong. Do you think we have any chance of winning?* B: 아직 시작도 안 했는데, 벌써부터 **기가 꺾이면** 어떡해요? = *We haven't even started yet. How can you already be losing faith in us?*

*기(가)막히다 [Lit. to have one's energy flow blocked] IDIOM 1. 무슨 말을

해야 할지 모를 정도로 너무 놀랍거나 황당하다 = to be so surprised that one doesn't know how to respond (*equiv.* This really takes the cake. / to be appalled / to be taken aback *syn.* 기(가)차다, 어처구니(가)없다) ▌A: 왜 그렇게 씩씩거려? 무슨 일 있어? = *Why are you panting like that? Is something wrong?* B: 우리 팀장 말이야. 내가 한 일을 가지고 자기가 한 것처럼 발표하더라니까. **기가 막혀서**! = *It's our team leader. He took my work and presented it as if it were his own. I was flabbergasted.* 2. 무어라고 말할 수 없을 만큼 대단하다 = to be great beyond words (*syn.* 기(가)차다) ▌A: 와! 정말 이 차 디자인 **기가 막히게** 멋지다! = *Wow, the design of this car is really jaw-dropping.* B: 그렇지? 나도 디자인 때문에 이 차를 골랐어. = *Yeah, the design is what made me choose it.*

기(가) 살다 [Lit. for one's energy to be alive] IDIOM 기세가 오르다 = to be

reinvigorated (*equiv.* to get a second wind / to get too cocky *ant.* 기(가)죽다) ▌A: 민우 녀석 때문에 골치가 아파요. 아빠만 오면 **기가 살아서** 자기 마음대로라니까요. = *That Minoo is giving me a headache. Whenever his dad gets home, he gets too cocky and just does as he pleases.* B: 아빠가 늘 자기 편을 들어 주나 봐요? = *I guess his father is always on his side?*

기가 세다 [Lit. to have strong energy] IDIOM 행동에 거침이 없고 주장이 강하다 = to be unreserved and have strong opinions (*equiv.* to be strong-willed / to be thick-headed) ▌A: 저 여자는 말만 하면 소리 지르고 꼭 이기려고 해. = *No matter what I say, she always yells and tries to win.* B: 맞아. 너무 **기가 세서** 무서워. = *Yeah, she's so strong-willed, it's scary.*

***기(가)죽다** [Lit. for one's energy to die] IDIOM 기세가 꺾이다 = to lose one's energy or will (*equiv.* to have the wind taken out of one's sails. *syn.* 기가 꺾이다 *ant.* 기(가) 살다 *cf.* 코가 납작해지다) ▌A: 오늘 발표 잘했어? = *Did you do well on your presentation today?* B: 아니요. 제 앞 사람이 발표를 너무 잘하더라고요. 그 바람에 **기가 죽어서** 잘 못했어요. = *No, the person before me did so well, it took the wind right out of my sails.*

기가 질리다 [Lit. to have one's energy overwhelmed] IDIOM 겁이 나서 용기가 없어지다 = to lose one's courage out of fright (*equiv.* to lose one's nerve) ▌A: 그렇게 가만히 앉아만 있으면 어떡해? 얼른 시작해야지. = *How come you're just sitting there like that? We'd better hurry up and get to work.* B: 나도 알아. 산더미처럼 쌓인 서류를 보니까 **기가 질려서** 그래. = *I know. I just lost my nerve when I saw that mountain of documents over there.*

기(가)차다 IDIOM = 기(가)막히다

기고만장(하다) [Lit. 氣 spirit + 高 high + 萬 ten thousand + 丈 unit of length] CHINESE-DERIVATION 우쭐하여 잘난 체하는 기세가 대단하다 = to be gloating and in high spirits (*equiv.* to be elated / to be in high spirits / to gloat) ▌A: 우승팀 맞히기 내기한 거 어떻게 됐어? = *How did your bet on the championship go?* B: 기영이 녀석이 이겼어. 녀석 지금 완전히 **기고만장해** 있다니까. = *Giyeong won. Now he's walking on air because of it.*

NOTE: '장'은 길이의 단위로 사람의 키 정도에 해당한다. 어떤 사람의 기가 만 장에 달한다면 그 기세가 얼마나 대단할 것인가!

A 장 is a measure of height that is approximately that of a person. If one's zeal reaches the lofty height equal to 10,000 men, that is being truly enthused.

기둥뿌리(가) 뽑히다 [Lit. to have the foundation of a pillar plucked away] IDIOM 근본이 위태롭다 = to have a shaky foundation (*equiv.* to pull the rug out of under someone) ▌A: 대학등록금이 단만치 않을 텐데 대학생 두 명 뒷바라지하기 힘들지 않아? = *College tuition these days is no joke. Isn't it tough to support two kids in college?* B: 안 그래도 등록금 때문에 집안 **기둥뿌리가 뽑힐** 지경이야. = *That's right, it's like they're going to pull the rug out from under us with these educational expenses.*

기둥뿌리(를) 뽑다 [Lit. to pluck out the foundation of a pillar] IDIOM 근본을 망하게 하다 = to ruin the foundation (*equiv.* to take the shirt off of someone's back / to pull the rug from under someone) ▌A: 엄마, 나 이 밥솥하고 청소기 내가 가져가도 돼? = *Mom, can I have this rice cooker and the vacuum cleaner?* B: 애가 친정 와서 살림을 챙겨 가려고 하네. 왜 **기둥뿌리를 뽑아** 가지 그러니? = *You come back to your parent's home to get all your necessities for life, huh? Fine, go ahead and take the shirts off of our backs too, why don't you?*

기(를) 쓰다 [Lit. to use one's energy] IDIOM 있는 힘을 다하다 = to use up all of one's energy (*equiv.* to give one's all / to use every last ounce of one's energy) ▌A: 윗집 아기가 울어 대는 통에 잠을 제대로 못 잤어요. 아주 **기를 쓰고** 울더라니까요. = *The kid upstairs kept crying and crying so I wasn't able to sleep well. He really cries his little heart out.* B: 어떡해요? 아기가 말을 알아들을 리도 없고. = *What is there to do? It's not like he can understand what we're saying.*

기(를) 펴다 [Lit. to flatten out one's energy] IDIOM 억눌려 있던 상황에서 벗어나 자유롭게 되다 = to break free of an oppressive situation (*equiv.* like a breathe of fresh air) ▌A: 집 샀다면서? 축하해! = *I hear you bought a house. Congratulations!* B: 고마워. 집주인 눈치 안 보고 살아서 참 좋아. 이제 좀 **기 펴고** 사는 기분이야. = *Thanks. It's so nice not to have to worry about the landlord. It's like I've been set free.*

기름을 끼얹다 [Lit. to pour oil (on something)] IDIOM 감정이나 행동을 부추겨 문제를 더 심각하게 만들다 = to exacerbate a situation by encouraging someone else (*equiv.* to fan the flames *syn.* 기름을 붓다) █ A: 어제 TV 봤어? 농민들이 화가 나서 국회 앞에서 소를 풀어 놓고 농성을 했잖아. = *Did you see it on TV yesterday? The farmers let a cow run loose in front of the National Assembly as part of their protests.* B: 안 그래도 솟값이 떨어져서 난리인데, 이번 정부의 안일한 대처가 **기름을 끼얹은 거지 뭐**. = *Well, the prices of cattle were already dropping and the government's overly complacent response just fanned the flames.*

기름을 붓다 IDIOM = 기름을 끼얹다

기사회생(하다) [Lit. 起 rise + 死 die + 回 return + 生 life → returning to life from death] CHINESE-DERIVATION 죽을 고비에서 간신히 살아나다 = to survive almost certain death (*equiv.* to barely make it / to survive by the skin of one's teeth) █ A: 이 드라마는 어떤 내용이야? = *What is this drama about?* B: 남편이 아내를 죽이려고 일부러 교통사고를 내는데, 그 여자가 **기사회생해서** 복수하는 내용이야. = *A guy tries to kill his wife in a car accident, but the wife survives and is out for revenge.*

기상천외(하다) [Lit. 奇 unusual + 想 think + 天 heaven + 外 outside → an unusual idea that comes from outside this world] CHINESE-DERIVATION 생각이나 행동이 아주 기이하다 = to have a very peculiar thought or take such an action (*equiv.* out of this world / extraordinary) █ A: 내일 서커스 보러 갈래? = *Do you want to go to see a circus tomorrow?* B: 와, 그거 재밌겠다. = *Wow, that sounds fun!* A: 응. **기상천외한** 묘기들을 볼 수 있대. = *Yeah, you can see stunts that are out of this world.*

기세등등하다 [Lit. 氣 spirit + 勢 force + 騰 rise + 騰 rise + 하다 adjectival suffix → to be bold in force and spirit] CHINESE-DERIVATION 기운이 넘쳐 보는 이를 압도할 만하다 = to overflow with vigor and confidence (*equiv.* to walk around with starch in one's collar / to have one's head held high) █ A: 김 대리 말이야, 어제 회의에서 사장님께 칭찬 들었다고 오늘 아주 **기세등등한데**? = *You know Mr. Kim? Yesterday the boss said a few nice things about him and today he's walking around with his head held high.* B: 하하, 젊은 친구니까 너그럽게 봐주자고요. = *Well, he's still young.*

Let's just go easy on him this time.

기염을 토하다 [Lit. to throw up flames] IDIOM 기세가 높다 = to be in high spirits █ A: 오늘 열린 테니스 결승에서 조코비치 선수가 승리했습니다. = *Jocovitch won today's tennis finals.* B: 이로써 조코비치 선수는 올해 열린 대회에서 모두 우승하는 **기염을 토했습니다**. = *With this latest victory, he has now pulled off the amazing feat of winning all of the year's events.*

기왕이면 다홍치마 PROVERB = 같은 값이면 다홍치마

기지개를 켜다 [Lit. to stretch out one's body] IDIOM 어떤 활동이나 현상이 시작되다 = to slowly begin to move again (*equiv.* to come back to life / to reawaken *syn.* 기지개를 펴다) █ A: 침체되어 있던 부동산 시장이 서서히 **기지개를 켜는** 것 같아요. = *It seems like the stagnate real estate market may be slowly coming back to life.* B: 그것 참 다행이네요. = *That would sure be a fortunate turn.*

기지개를 펴다 IDIOM = 기지개를 켜다

기진맥진하다 [Lit. 氣 energy + 盡 to the end + 脈 pulse + 盡 to the end + 하다 adjectival suffix → to be out of energy and lose one's pulse] CHINESE-DERIVATION 몹시 지치고 기운이 다하다 = to be completely worn out █ A: 겨우 세 바퀴 뛰고 **기진맥진한** 거예요? = *You're exhausted after just three laps?* B: 어제 술을 많이 마셨더니 오늘 유달리 더 힘드네. = *Well, I had a lot to drink last night, so I'm having a harder time than usual.*

긴말할 것 없다 [Lit. There's nothing to talk long about.] IDIOM 더 논할 필요가 없다 = for further discussion to be unnecessary (*equiv.* I've heard enough. / Enough said. / Say no more.) █ A: 정말 죄송합니다. = *I'm so very sorry.* B: **긴말할 것 없이**, 환불해 주세요. = *I've heard enough. Please, just give me a refund.*

길거리로 나앉다 [Lit. to be out on the streets] IDIOM 머물 곳이 마땅하지

않을 정도로 가난해지다 = to be so poor that one even lacks a place to live (*equiv.* to be out of house and home / to be kicked out on the streets *syn.* 거리로 나앉다 *cf.* 깡통(을) 차다, 바가지(를) 차다, 쪽박(을) 차다) ▌A: 살면서 가장 힘들었던 때가 언제인가요? = *What was the hardest moment of your life?* B: 고등학교 때 아버지의 사업 실패로 가족들이 **길거리로 나앉게** 되었던 때가 아닌가 싶어요. = *Well, it was probably when my whole family was without house and home after my father's business collapsed.*

***길고 짧은 것은 대 보아야 안다** [Lit. To be certain of the length of something, you have to measure it.] PROVERB 실제로 겨루어 보기 전에는 승부를 알 수 없다는 말 = Before you've seen it for yourself, it's impossible to say who has won and lost. (*equiv.* It isn't over till it's over. / It isn't over until the fat lady sings.) ▌A: 너희 팀 주전 선수 두 명이 부상인데 너희가 우리를 이길 수 있을까? = *Your team's best players are both injured. Do you really think you'll be able to win?* B: **길고 짧은 건 대 봐야 알지.** = *It isn't over till it's over.*

길이 아니면 가지 말고, 말이 아니면 듣지 말라 [Lit. If it's not a road, don't walk it; if it's not speech (worth listening to), don't listen to it.] PROVERB 항상 바르게 생활하라는 말 = used to encourage people to live in an upright manner (*equiv.* See no evil, hear no evil, speak no evil.) ▌A: 저 사람은 어쩌다 저렇게 사기꾼이 되었을까? = *How did he get to be such a swindler?* B: 뉴스에서 보니까 어릴 때 나쁜 친구들이랑 어울리다 그렇게 됐다던데. = *From what I saw on the news, hanging around with a bad crowd when he was young did it to him.* A: 그래서, **길이 아니면 가지를 말고 말이 아니거든 듣지를 말라고** 했지. = *That's why they say you've got to choose your path wisely.*

김(이)빠지다 IDIOM = 김(이)새다

김(이)새다 [Lit. to leak steam] IDIOM 의욕이나 흥미가 사라지다 = to lose interest or zeal (*equiv.* to be a spoilsport / to lose steam *syn.* 김(이)빠지다) ▌A: 저는 오늘은 빠질게요. 몸이 좀 안 좋아서요. = *I won't be* *able to make it today. I'm not feeling well.* B: 김 대리, 왜 이래? **김새게.** 오늘 김 대리가 주인공이잖아. = *Why are you being such a spoilsport? You're the star of the show today.*

***김칫국부터 마신다** IDIOM = 떡 줄 사람은 생각도 없는데 김칫국부터 마신다

ㄲ

까마귀가 아저씨 하겠다 [Lit. A crow might call you uncle.] PROVERB 몸이 몹시 더러운 사람을 놀리는 말 = used teasingly to refer to someone in an unclean state (*equiv.* to be dressed in rags / to be a ragamuffin) ▌A: 야, 좀 씻고 다녀. **까마귀가 아저씨 하겠다**. = *Hey, don't you ever take showers? You look like a ragamuffin.* B: 씻는 게 귀찮은 걸 어떡해요. = *Staying clean is too much of a hassle. What am I supposed to do?*

NOTE: 까마귀의 까만 몸 색깔에서 온 표현이다.
This expression comes from the crow's stark black appearance.

까마귀 고기를 먹었나 [Lit. Did you have crow meat?] PROVERB 잊어버리기를 잘하는 사람을 놀리는 말 = used teasingly to refer to someone who is forgetful (*equiv.* Is your Alzheimer's acting up again?) ▌A: **까마귀 고기를 먹었어**? 왜 만날 핸드폰을 놓고 다녀? = *Did you really forget again? Why are you always leaving your cellphone everywhere?* B: 내가 원래 건망증이 심하잖아. 그래도 찾아서 다행이네. = *You know how forgetful I am. Lucky I found it, though.*

NOTE: 무엇인가를 완전히 잊어버렸을 때 '까맣게 잊어버리다'라고 하는 데서 알 수 있듯 기억을 상실하는 것은 까만색과 관련이 있다. 또한 '잊어버리다'를 속된 말로 흔히 '까먹다'라고도 하는데, 까마귀의 까만 몸 색깔과 발음의 유사성(까마귀–까먹다) 때문에 이 표현이 생긴 것으로 보인다.
The idea of forgetting is often associated with the color black. Even in English there is the expression "I blacked out" etc. When something is completely forgotten, the phrase 까맣게 잊어버리다 is often used. There is

also the slang expression, 까먹다, which has a similar meaning. It seems that this phrase came into existence because of the bird's stark black color and the similarity of the pronunciation between 까마귀 and 까먹다.

까마귀 날자 배 떨어진다 [Lit. A pear drops as soon as the crow flies.]

PROVERB 아무 관련이 없는 일들이 공교롭게 동시에 일어나 관계가 있는 것처럼 의심을 받게 될 때 쓰는 말 = used to describe a situation in which seemingly unrelated events happen simultaneously in a manner that seems suspicious (*equiv.* to be at the wrong place at the wrong time / an unfortunate coincidence / an unlucky confluence of events) ▌ A: 이러다 민수한테 오해를 사는 건 아닌지 걱정이어요. = *As things stand, I'm worried that Minsu might have misunderstood something.* B: 왜요? = *Why?* A: 민수 집에 놀러 갔었는데, 제가 간 그날 중요한 물건이 없어졌대요. = *The day I went over to Minsu's house, something important turned up missing.* B: **까마귀 날자 배 떨어진** 셈이군요. 친구 사이에 그런 일로 오해하겠어요? = *Wow, you really were at the wrong place at the wrong time. Do you really think a friend would misunderstand something like that?*

NOTE: 배나무 숲에서 까마귀 한 마리가 까마귀가 '까악'하고 날아올랐다. 그런데 하필 그 순간 배나무의 배가 뚝 떨어졌다. 농부는 까마귀가 배나무를 건드려 배를 떨어뜨린 줄 알고 화를 냈다. 우연의 일치가 오해를 불러올 때 쓰는 표현이다.
A farmer was in his fields tending to his pear tree. Suddenly a crow flew by and cawed. Right at that moment, a pear dropped from high in the tree. The farmer was angry because he thought that the pear fell because the crow had disturbed the tree. Just as the wrongly accused crow of this story, this expression is used to describe an unfortunate confluence of events that leaves someone blamed for something that they didn't do.

깡통(을) 차다 [Lit. to wear a can (around one's waist)]

IDIOM 거지가 되다 = to become a beggar (*equiv.* to go bust / to be out on the streets *syn.* 바가지(를) 차다, 쪽박(을) 차다 *cf.* 길거리로 나앉다) ▌ A: 돈 좀 있어? 있으면 좀 빌려 줘. = *Do you have any money? If you do, lend me some, please.* B: 엊그제 월급 받았잖아. 그건 어쩌고? = *You just got paid the other day. What about that?* A: 말도 마. 이것저것 사다 보니 다 써 버렸어. **깡통 차게** 생겼어. = *Don't even ask. I bought this and that, and pretty soon it was all gone. It looks like I'll be out on the streets pretty soon.*

NOTE: 한국전쟁 이후로 많이 생겨난 전쟁 고아나 난민들은 깡통을 들고 구걸을 했다.
This phrase was born in the period following the Korean War when a great number of war orphans and refugees begged with cans.

***깨가 쏟아지다** [Lit. (for it) to rain sesame seeds] IDIOM 주로 신혼부부가 사이가 좋고 다정하여 재미가 나다 = used to describe newlyweds who get along well and enjoy each other's company (*equiv.* to be in the honeymoon stage (of a relationship) / to be like two lovebirds / to be wearing rose-tinted glasses.) ▌A: 소영 씨는 요즘 어떻게 지내요? = *How's Soyoung been doing recently?* B: 이제 결혼한 지 두 달밖에 안 됐으니 남편이랑 **깨가 쏟아지겠죠**. = *It's only been two months since she got married. I'm sure they're still in the honeymoon stage.*

껌뻑 죽다 [Lit. to suddenly die] IDIOM 몹시 좋아하다 = to like very much (*syn.* 사족을 못 쓰다, 오금을 못 쓰다, 자다가도 벌떡 일어난다) ▌A: 저 친구 또 바둑 얘기가 나오니까 좋아하는 것 좀 봐. = *Look at how excited he is that someone's talking about playing baduk.* B: 원래 바둑이라면 **껌뻑 죽는** 친구잖아. = *He always gets that way when someone brings it up.*

꼬리가 길다 [Lit. to have a long tail] IDIOM 방문을 닫지 않고 드나들다 = to not close the door when coming and going (*syn.* 꽁무니가 길다) ▌A: 누구야, **꼬리가 긴** 사람이. = *Who keeps leaving the door open?* B: 아까 민수 녀석 나가면서 문을 안 닫았나 보네요. 제가 닫고 올게요. = *It looks like Minsu must've left the door open. I'll close it.*

꼬리가 길면 밟힌다 [Lit. If a tail is long, it gets stepped on.] PROVERB 나쁜 일을 여러 번 반복하다 보면 언젠가는 들키고 만다는 말 = suggests that one's misdeeds will always be found out if one repeats them (*equiv.* Crime doesn't pay. / An evil deed will be discovered. / Misbehavior eventually catches up with one.) █A: 그 두 사람 사귀는 거 아니라고 그렇게 부인하더니, 손 잡고 같이 있는 사진이 찍혔네. = *They always maintained that they weren't together and now we have a picture of them holding hands.* B: **꼬리가 길면 밟히는** 법이잖아. = *Misdeeds always catch up with you in the end.*

꼬리가 잡히다 [Lit. to have one's tail caught] ᴅɪᴏᴍ 있는 곳이나 실체가 탄로나다 = for one's whereabouts or identity to be found out █A: 선배님, 드디어 **범인의 꼬리가 잡혔습니다.** CCTV에 모습이 찍혔어요. = *Sir, we finally have something on the criminal. He was captured on security camera footage.* B: 아, 그래? 이제 녀석을 잡는 건 시간 문제군. = *Really? Now catching him is just a matter of time.*

꼬리를 감추다 [Lit. to hide one's tail] ᴅɪᴏᴍ 슬그머니 사라져 자취를 감추다 = to slip away and hide one's tracks (*equiv.* to slip away into the night / to vanish without a trace) █A: 아까까지 여기 있던 친구 어디 갔어? = *What happened to the person who was here just a few minutes ago?* B: 사람들이 몰려드니까 **꼬리를 감추었네.** = *He slipped away as people started to crowd in.*

꼬리(를) 내리다 [Lit. to put down one's tail] ᴅɪᴏᴍ 상대편에게 기가 꺾여 움츠러들다 = to feel overpowered and give in to the opposition (*equiv.* to back down / to throw in the towel / to change one's tune) █A: 내가 얼마 전에 산 핸드폰이 고장 나서 매장에 찾아갔었는데, 내 잘못이라고 막 우기지 뭐야. = *The phone I bought a few days ago broke, so I took it back to the store and they're claiming it's my fault.* B: 뭐, 정말? 그래서 어떻게 했어? = *So what did you do?* A: 회사 홈페이지에 신고하겠다고 하니까 바로 **꼬리 내리던데.** = *I said I would report them on the company's webpage and they backed down right away.*

꼬리를 밟다 [Lit. to step on someone's tail] ᴅɪᴏᴍ 미행하다 = to follow someone (*equiv.* to tail someone) █A: 그런데, 성호가 바람 피우는 건 어떻게 알았어? = *But how did you find out Seongho was cheating on you?*

B: 전화도 잘 안 받고 만날 바쁘다고 하길래 수상해서 **꼬리를 밟았지**. = *It was suspicious how he was always saying that he was busy and not taking my calls, so I tailed him.*

꼬리를 빼다 [Lit. to pull off one's tail] IDIOM 뒤로 물러나거나 달아나다 = to run away (*equiv.* to make a mad dash / to leave behind neither hide nor hair *syn.* 꽁무니(를) 빼다) ▌A: 너 만날 귀찮게 하던 남자 오늘은 안 보인다? = *What happened to that guy who was always bugging you?* B: 며칠 전에 내가 크게 화를 내니까 **꼬리를 빼더라고요**. = *I really let him have it a few days ago and he hit the road.*

꼬리(를) 치다 [Lit. to wag one's tail] IDIOM (여자가 남자에게) 잘 보이려고 아양을 떨다 = to act in a seductive manner to draw the attentions of another (most often describes the actions of a female) (*equiv.* to flirt around *syn.* 꼬리를 흔들다) ▌A: 그 여자가 우리 남편한테 **꼬리를 친** 게 분명해요. 안 그러면 우리 남편이 바람을 피울 사람이 아니에요. = *I'm sure she did something to catch his eye. Otherwise, my husband is not the type of man to cheat.* B: 아니, 이 상황에서 남편 편 드는 거야? = *Huh? In this situation you are taking his side?*

> **NOTE:** 개가 반가운 손님이나 주인이 왔을 때 꼬리를 흔드는 모습을 상상해 보라.
> If you imagine a dog excitedly wagging its tail at the sight of a friendly face, you'll grasp what this expression is all about.

꼬리를 흔들다 IDIOM = 꼬리(를) 치다

(꼬리에) 꼬리를 물다 [Lit. to bite someone's tail.] IDIOM 연이어 나타나다 = to be continuous (*equiv.* to be caught in a whirlpool / to spiral out of control) ▌A: 왜 그렇게 피곤해 보여? 잠 못 잤어? = *Why do you look so tired? Weren't you able to sleep?* B: 어. 생각이 **꼬리를 물어서** 통 못 잤어. = *My thoughts just kept spiraling out of control all night long and I couldn't get a wink of sleep.*

꼬리표가 붙다 [Lit. to have a tag attached (to oneself)] IDIOM 어떤 사람에게 나쁜 평가나 평판이 내려지다 = to have a bad reputation (*equiv.* for one's reputation to follow one around *syn.* 딱지가 붙다) ▌A: 학창 시절에 김예슬 씨는 어떤 학생이었습니까? = *What was Kim Yeseul like back in her school days?* B: 골치 아픈 아이였습니다. 중학교 때 한 번 가출을 했었는데, 그 이후로 문제아라는 **꼬리표가 붙어** 늘 따라다녔지요. = *She was definitely a headache. She ran away once in middle school and after that, her bad reputation just followed her wherever she went.*

꼬리표(를) 떼다 [Lit. to remove one's tag] IDIOM 좋지 않은 평가나 상황에서 벗어나다 = to shake off one's bad reputation or to escape from a bad situation (*equiv.* to shine up one's reputation *syn.* 딱지(를) 떼다) ▌A: 아, 저는 언제쯤 막내라는 **꼬리표를 뗄** 수 있을까요? = *When will people stop treating me like a fresh-faced beginner here?* B: 때가 되면 자네도 후임을 받고 막내 신세를 면하게 될 거야. = *When the time comes, someone new will come along and then you'll no longer be the newest hire.*

꼬집어 말하다 [Lit. to pinch something and speak of it] IDIOM 어떤 사건이나 현상 등에 대해 분명하고 정확하게 말하다 = to speak in a clear and precise manner about an incident or phenomenon (*equiv.* to pinpoint something / to put one's finger on it) ▌A: 새로 이사 온 사람들은 어때요? = *How's the person who just moved in?* B: 첫인상이 그렇게 좋지는 않았어요. **꼬집어 말할** 수는 없는데 왠지 좀 그렇더라고요. = *Well, the first impression they gave us wasn't that great. I can't pinpoint exactly what it is, but there is just something about them.*

꼬투리(를) 잡다 [Lit. to grab a husk] IDIOM 공연히 남의 작은 약점을 들추어 시비를 걸다 = to unnecessarily point out another's weaknesses and quarrel over it (*equiv.* to nitpick / to find fault *syn.* 트집(을) 잡다 *cf.* 꼬투리(를) 잡히다) ▌A: 이 물건은 다 좋은데 색깔이 좀 마음에 안 들어요. = *Everything else about this product is great, but I'm just not pleased with the color.* B: **꼬투리 잡을** 생각이라면 사지 마세요. = *If you're just going to nitpick it, you don't have to buy it.*

NOTE: '꼬투리'는 원래 콩, 팥, 완두 등 콩과 식물의 씨가 들어 있는 껍질을 가리킨다. 알맹이가 꼬투리에서 나오므로 어떤 일의 단서나 빌미라는 비유적 의미를 갖게 되었다. '꼬투리를 잡다', '꼬투리를 잡히다'라는 표현의 '꼬투리'는 남을 해코지할 만한 빌미라는 뜻으로 쓰인 것이다. 꼬투리 is the husk that holds beans of all varieties or the similar husks that contain the seeds of plants. As seeds come from these husks, the 꼬투리 came to have a metaphorical meaning of a "pretext" or "clue." The 꼬투리 in the expressions 꼬투리를 잡다 or 꼬투리를 잡히다 seems to denote a small weakness that can be used to tease or harass someone.

꼬투리(를) 잡히다 [Lit. for a husk to be caught] IDIOM 다른 사람에게 약점을 노출하거나 시비 거리를 제공하다 = to expose one's flaws to another or provide them with someone to hassle you about (*syn.* 트집(을) 잡히다 *cf.* 꼬투리(를) 잡다) ▌A: 그거 알아? 접촉 사고가 나면 절대로 먼저 사과하면 안 돼. = *Do you know that when you're in a car accident, you should never apologize first.* B: 왜? = *Why?* A: 나중에 **꼬투리 잡힐** 수 있거든. = *Because they can use it against you later.*

NOTE: See the note on 꼬투리(를) 잡다.

꽁무니가 길다 IDIOM = 꼬리가 길다

꽁무니(를) 빼다 [Lit. to pluck off one's tail] IDIOM 뒤로 물러나거나 달아나다 = to retreat or to back off (*equiv.* to cop out / to chicken out / to turn and run / to hightail it out of there *syn.* 꼬리를 빼다) ▌A: 자, 다들 어제 약속한 거 잊지 않았죠? 다같이 팀장님한테 얘기하러 갑시다. = *So, everyone remembers the promise we made yesterday, right? Let's all go and talk to our team leader.* B: 저, 그게 저는 아무래도 좀 힘들 것 같아요. 저는 회사에 들어온 지 얼마 되지도 않았고요. = *I've been thinking about it, and I really don't think I'll be able to do that. I haven't been with the company for very long and all.* A: 영식 씨, 오늘 와서 혼자 **꽁무니 빼는** 거예요? = *Youngsik, you're really going to be the only one who cops out today?*

꽃(을)피우다 [Lit. to make the flowers bloom] IDIOM 어떤 일이나 현상 이 왕성하게 일어나게 하다 = to make an enterprise or endeavor thrive (*equiv.* to make it / to be a rainmaker / to (make things) come up roses) ▎A: 장래가 유망한 선수 중에 부상 때문에 **꽃을 피우지** 못하는 선 수들이 많습니다. = *A lot of athletes with bright futures didn't make it because of injuries.* B: 네. 역시 운동 선수들은 부상을 제일 조심해 야 합니다. = *Yeah, injuries really are what athletes need to be most careful about.*

꽃(이)피다 [Lit. for flowers to bloom] IDIOM 어떤 일이나 현상이 한창 일어나다 = for an undertaking or phenomenon to reach its zenith (*equiv.* (for something) to peak / to reach its climax) ▎A: 이제 아프리카 여러 나라 에도 민주주의의 **꽃이 피려나** 봐. = *It looks like the rose of democracy will finally be blooming across Africa.* B: 요즘 연이어 독재 정권이 물 러나는 걸 보면 아무래도 그런가 봐. = *Seeing the dictatorships crumble one after the other certainly makes it seem that way.*

꽉 잡고 있다 [Lit. to have a tight grasp on something] IDIOM 무엇인가에 대해 잘 알거나 영향력을 갖고 있다 = to exercise influence over or have a firm grasp of something (*equiv.* to know something like the back of one's hand / to have a handle on *syn.* 쥐고 흔들다, 쥐었다 폈다 하다) ▎A: 이 근처에서 밥 먹고 가자. 어디 갖있는 집 없을까? = *Let's eat something around here before we go. Are there any good restaurants around?* B: 민우한테 물어보자. 민우가 이 동네 음식점은 **꽉 잡고 있거 든**. = *Let's ask Minoo. He knows this area like the back of his hand.*

***꿀 먹은 벙어리** [Lit. a mute who has eaten honey] PROVERB 속에 있는 생 각을 겉으로 나타내지 못하는 사람 = a person who is for whatever reason unable to express themselves (*equiv.* Cat got your tongue? / to be dumbstruck) ▎A: 어제 사장님한테 가서 연봉 올려 달라고 얘기한다더니 어떻게 됐어? = *How did it go when you asked the boss for a raise yesterday?* B: 그 게 말이야. 사장님 앞에 가니까 **꿀 먹은 벙어리**처럼 말이 안 나오 더라고. = *Well ... once I got in front of the boss, I lost all powers of speech.*

NOTE: 옛날에 한 학생이 선생님이 꿀 단지를 감추고 있다는 사실을 알게 되었다. 학생은 그 꿀을 맛보고 싶어 선생님의 허락도 없이 몰래 꿀 단지를 찾아 한 숟가락 퍼 먹었다. 그런데 그때 선생님이 나타나 뭐하고 있었냐고 물었다. 그러나 그 학생은 입에 꿀이 들어 있어 아무말도 하지 못했다. 그 이후로 '꿀 먹은 벙어리'는 어떠한 이유로 진실을 얘기할 수 없는 사람을 뜻하게 되었다.

Long ago, a student found out that his teacher was hiding a pot of honey. He so wished to taste the honey, that he went, without his teacher's permission, to the pot and lifted a spoonful to his mouth. At that instant, the teacher suddenly showed up and demanded to know what the child was doing. The lad's mouth was filled with honey, however, and he couldn't manage a reply. Ever since, a 꿀 먹은 벙어리 has meant a person, who for some reason, is concealing the truth.

***꿈 깨라** [Lit. Wake up from your dreams.] IDIOM 허황된 생각을 하는 상대에게 하는 말 = used in the imperative to tell someone to wake from their fantasies (*equiv.* Snap out of it. / Wake up. / Dream on.) ▌A: 와, 이효리는 정말 예뻐. 이효리랑 하루만 데이트해도 소원이 없겠다. = *Wow, Lee Hyori really is beautiful. If I could spend just one day with her, I wouldn't wish for anything more.* B: **꿈 깨라**. 이효리가 왜 너랑 데이트를 하냐? = *Wake up! Why would she ever go on a date with you?*

꿈도 야무지다 [Lit. for even one's dreams to be shrewd] IDIOM 실현 가능성이 없는 것을 기대하는 사람에게 냉소적으로 하는 말 = used to sarcastically refer to someone who harbors overblown dreams (*equiv.* to have a pipe dream / to have fanciful ideas) ▌A: 나 결심했어. 이제 하루에 잠은 세 시간만 자고 나머지 시간에는 공부할 거야. = *I've made up my mind. I'm only going to sleep three hours a day and study the rest of the time.* B: 참 **꿈도 야무지구나**. 그러다 병 난다. = *Don't you think that's biting off more than you can chew? You're going to make yourself sick.*

꿈보다 해몽이 좋다 [Lit. The dream analysis is better than the dream.] PROVERB 어떠한 현상에 대해 자신에게 유리한 쪽으로 해석할 때 쓰

는 말 = to interpret something in a way that is favorable to oneself (*equiv.* to read (a lot) into something) ▌A: 영화 마지막 부분에서 주인공이 옷을 갈아입는 건 새롭게 태어나겠다는 의지를 나타낸 거라고 나는 생각해. = *I think that the way the main character changed his clothes in the final scene represented his will to be reborn.* B: **꿈보다 해몽이 좋다.** 내가 보기에는 그냥 아무 생각 없이 옷 갈아입는 것 같던데? = *Don't you think you're reading a little too much into that? To me, it looked like he was just changing his clothes.*

***꿈에도 몰랐다** [Lit. to not have known ever in one's dreams] IDIOM 전혀 예상하지 못했음 = to not have had any idea something would take place (*equiv.* never in my wildest dreams / I never would have dreamed it. *syn.* 꿈에도 생각하지 못하다) ▌A: 지현이드 너를 좋아하고 있었다는 거 알고 있었어? = *Did you know that Jihyun liked you too?* B: 아니. 나한테 늘 퉁명스러워서 나를 좋아하는 줄은 **꿈에도 몰랐지.** = *No. She's been so short with me I never in my wildest dreams thought that she was into me.*

꿈에도 생각하지 못하다 IDIOM = 꿈에도 몰랐다

꿈이냐 생시냐 [Lit. Is this a dream or reality?] IDIOM 너무나 뜻밖의 일이라 믿기지 않을 때 쓰는 말 = used when one is presented with unbelievable occurrence (*equiv.* Pinch me. I must be dreaming. / I can't believe my eyes.) ▌A: 이게 **꿈이냐 생시냐!** 도대체 몇 년 만이야! = *Am I dreaming? How many years has it been?* B: 거의 이십 년 만이지? = *It's been about 20 years now, hasn't it?*

꿍짝이 맞다 [Lit. for the rhythm to be a match] IDIOM 서로 뜻이 맞다 = for the aims of two people to be a good match (*equiv.* to be on the same page / to be on the same wavelength *syn.* 쿵짝이 맞다, 죽이 맞다) ▌A: 영택이와 너는 처음부터 그렇게 친했니? = *Were you that close with Youngtaek from the start?* B: 네. 처음부터 **꿍짝이 잘 맞아서** 금세 친해졌어요. = *Yeah, we've always been on the same wavelength, so we got close right away*

NOTE: 꿍짝은 북이나 장구, 드럼 따위가 리듬에 맞추어 내는 소리를 가리킨다. 서로 잘 어울리는 악기들처럼 사람들 사이에 서로 뜻이 맞을 때 꿍짝이 맞다고 한다.

The onomatopoeia 꿍짝 is a verbal representation of the sound made when a 북 (traditional bass drum), 장구 (hourglass-shaped drum) or any other drums sound in rhythm. If the 꿍짝 matches, two parties are in perferct sync.

꿔다 놓은 보릿자루 [Lit. a bag of borrowed barley] PROVERB 여럿이 모여 이야기하는 자리에서 말없이 있는 사람을 가리키는 말 = used to describe a person who stands quietly and awkwardly at a gathering (*equiv.* like a fish out of water / to stand out) ▌A: 어제 회식은 어땠어요? = *How was the staff party yesterday?* B: 친한 사람이 없어서 저는 좀 그랬어요. **꿔다 놓은 보릿자루**처럼 혼자 멍하니 술만 마셨어요. = *I'm not really close to anyone there so it wasn't all that great. I was like a fish out of water, so I just drank and zoned out.*

NOTE: 지난 가을에 수확한 양식이 떨어지고 보리가 여물려면 아직 기다려야 하는 음력 4~5월을 보릿고개라고 불렀다. 보릿고개에는 보리가 얼마 없어 보릿자루가 많이 필요하지 않지만 얼마 안 있어 보리를 수확할 때를 생각해 빈 자루를 빌려 방안에 두는 경우도 있었다. 그러면 이 자루는 지금 당장은 쓸모가 없는데도 자리만 차지하게 된다. 이처럼 무리에서 잘 어울리지 못하고 혼자 겉도는 사람을 일컬어 '꿔다 놓은 보릿자루'라고 부른다.

There was a time in the farming villages of yore when the existing food supply was depleted, around the forth and fifth month of the lunar calander, and people were forced to wait for the next barley harvest. This period was referred to as 보릿고개 (the barley hump). Borrowing a sack during this period to harvest the barley a few months later, would not only be of no use, but would simply be taking up space. That is why people who don't fit in will with a group, and those who seem out of place, are often called 꿔다 놓은 보릿자루 (a borrowed barley sack).

꿩 대신 닭 [Lit. a chicken instead of a pheasant] PROVERB 적당한 것이 없

어 비슷한 것으로 대신할 때 쓰는 말＝used to describe use of a lesser item in the absence of the preferred item (*equiv.* Half a loaf is better than none. / At least it's better than nothing.) █A: 내가 얘기한 화장품 사 왔어?＝*Did you buy the cosmetics I asked for?* Ɜ: 그거 마침 다 나갔다고 해서 대신 다른 것 사 왔어. 직원이 이것도 좋은 거라고 하던데?＝*They said they were out of that so I bought this instead. The employee said that this was just as good.* A: 어쩔 수 없지 뭐. **꿩 대신 닭**이라고 이걸로 만족해야겠네.＝*Well I guess there's nothing to be done. Something is always better than nothing.*

NOTE: 한국의 전통 음식인 떡국은 원래 꿩고기를 넣어 만들어야 제맛이라고 한다. 그런데 꿩고기는 구하기가 힘들기 때문에 실제로는 그 대신 닭고기를 넣는 경우가 많았다. '꿩 대신 닭'은 적당한 것이 없어 그보다 좀 못하지만 비슷한 것으로 대신할 때 쓰는 말이다.
According to the tenets of Korean cooking, pheasant meat should be used in 떡국 to achieve the proper taste. As pheasant can be hard to come by, however, chicken is a common substitute. In this way, this phrase is used to describe the substitution of something of lesser quality for that which was originally called for.

꿩 먹고 알 먹기 [Lit. eating a pheasant and its eggs too] PROVERB 한 가지 일로 두 가지 이상의 이익을 보게 될 때 쓰는 말＝used to describe the situation in which one action is met with two rewards (*equiv.* to have one's cake and eat it too / to kill two birds with one stone *syn.* 도랑 치고 가재 잡기, 임도 보고 뽕도 딴다, 일거양득, 일석이조) █A: 요즘 살이 많이 쪄서 고민이야.＝*I'm really worried about how much weight I've been gaining recently.* B: 차만 타고 다니면서 걷지를 않으니까 그렇지. 걸어 다니면 살도 빠지고 돈도 안 들고, 이게 바로 **꿩 먹고 알 먹기** 아니겠어?＝*That's because you always drive and never walk anywhere. Walking doesn't cost anything and it helps you lose weight. It's having your cake and eating it too.*

NOTE: 꿩은 모성 본능이 강한 동물로 알려져 있다. 옛날에 산불이 난 후 산에 가 보면 끝까지 알을 품고 있다가 타 죽은 꿩이 자주 발견되었다고 한다. 그래서 꿩과 함께 그 알도 가져올 수가 있었기 때문에 이 표현이 생겨나게 된 것 같다.

The pheasant is an animal known for its strong maternal instinct. There are tales of finding mother pheasants burnt to a crisp after forest fires because they had guarded their nest to the bitter end. Being able to take the pheasant and its eggs as well, was the genesis of this expression.

끙끙 앓다 [Lit. to groan with pain] IDIOM 고민을 겉으로 드러내지 못하고 혼자 속으로 삭이다 = to not reveal one's worries to others (*equiv.* to keep problems to oneself) ▌A: 너는 그게 문제야. 왜 무슨 일이 생기면 다른 사람하고 의논을 안 하고 혼자 **끙끙 앓는** 거야? = *That's what your problem is. Why do you always keep things to yourself instead of talking with someone.* B: 타고난 성격이 그런 걸 어떡해. = *I can't help it. That's just the personality I was born with.*

ㄴ

나 먹기는 싫어도 남 주기는 아깝다 [Lit. Even though one won't eat it, one resents giving it to others.] PROVERB 자기에게 쓸모가 없는 줄 알면서도 다른 사람에게 주기는 싫은 심리를 꼬집은 말 = used to describe a situation in which even though something is of no use to you, you have no intention of giving it to someone else ▌A: 진희야, 너 옷장에 왜 이리 안 입는 옷들이 많니? 이 옷들 안 입을 거면 동생 줘라. = *Jinhee, why do you have so many clothes in your closet that you never wear? If you're not going to wear them, just give them to your sister.* B: 싫어요, 안 입어도 제 옷인데, 왜 영희를 줘요? = *No! Even if I don't wear them, they are still my clothes. Why would I give them to Younghee?* A: **나 먹기는 싫어도 남 주기는 아깝다더니, 무슨 옷 욕심이 그리 많니?** = *You should give them to someone who will use them. Don't be such a hoarder.*

나 몰라라 하다 [Lit. to say I don't know] IDIOM 무관심한 태도로 간섭하지 않다 = to exhibit a lack of interest and not involve oneself (*equiv.* to turn someone away *cf.* 강 건너 불구경, 강 건너 불 보듯) ▌A: 도와주셔서 감사합니다. = *Thank you for helping me.* B: 제가 당연히 도와야죠. 제가 어떻게 **나 몰라라 할** 수 있겠습니까? = *Of course I have to help you. How could I ever just turn you away?*

나무를 보고 숲을 보지 못한다 [Lit. to see the tree and not see the forest] PROVERB 큰 틀에서 생각하지 못하고 작은 일부분에만 집착하는 모습을 비판할 때 쓰는 말 = used to criticize someone who focuses on a small or irrelevant matter and misses the more important parts of an issue (*equiv.* to not see the forest for the trees / You're not seeing the whole picture. / to miss the bigger picture) ▌A: 그 사람은 꼼꼼하기는 한데 그것 때문

에 좀 더 중요한 부분을 놓칠 때가 가끔 있어. = *He is very thorough, but that sometimes causes him to miss the more important points.* B: **나무만 보고 숲을 보지 못하는** 경우군. = *It's a case of missing the forest for the trees.*

나발(을) 불다 [Lit. to blow the trumpet] IDIOM **1.** 당치않은 말을 함부로 하다 = to say something inappropriate or thoughtless (*equiv.* to spread something (a rumor etc.) all around / to blab) ▌A: 이 얘기 나 말고 아는 사람 있어? = *Does anyone else know about this besides me?* B: 어. 어제 영희한테 얘기했는데? = *Yeah, I told Younghee yesterday.* A: 큰일났다. 영희가 알았으면 동네방네 **나발을 불고** 다닐 텐데. = *What a mess! If she knows, she'll spread it all over the place.* **2.** 술이나 음료수 등을 병째로 마시다 = to drink liquor etc. out of the bottle ▌A: 너는 대낮부터 또 소주로 **나발을 부냐**? = *It's the middle of the day and you are already drinking soju out of the bottle again?* B: 제가 무슨 낙이 있나요? 헤헤. = *What other pleasure have I in life? Ha ha.*

NOTE: 나발은 쇠붙이로 만든 한국의 전통 관악기다. 나발은 농악에 쓰여 서민들에게 친숙한 악기였는데, 그 소리가 익살스럽고 수다스럽게 들린다. 그런 성격 때문에 오늘날 '나발(을) 불다'라는 표현이 생긴 듯하다. The 나발 is a traditional wind instrument. As it was used in farming music, it was a familiar sound to the commoners. The instrument has a humorous and boisterous sound. This timbre is what led to the current proverbial meanings.

나사가 빠지다 [Lit. for the screws to fall out] IDIOM 긴장이 풀려 정신 상태가 해이해지다 = to relax after the lessening of tension (*equiv.* to let up / to slack off *syn.* 나사가 풀리다) ▌A: 김 병장은 어디 갔어? = *Where did Sergeant Kim go?* B: 아마 PX에 간 것 같습니다. = *I think he's probably over at the PX.* A: 일과 시간에 PX를? 제대 얼마 안 남았다고 **나사가 빠졌구먼**. = *While he's on duty? He's really slacking off now that his discharge is coming up.*

나사가 풀리다 IDIOM = 나사가 빠지다

나이는 못 속인다 [Lit. One cannot deceive (others) about one's age.] PROVERB 말이나 행동, 외모에서 제 나이에 걸맞은 흔적이 묻어날 때 쓰는 말 = used when one's behavior or appearance makes one's age known (*equiv.* to feel one's age / You can't hide your age.) ▌A: 엄마, 어서 바닷가로 가요. = *Mom, hurry up! Let's go to the beach.* B: 너희끼리 가라. **나이는 못 속인다고**, 엄마는 비행기를 오래 탔더니 좀 피곤하구나. 일단 방에서 좀 쉬어야겠다. = *You just go ahead without me. I'm feeling my age today. After being on the plane for so long, I'm really worn out. I'll have to stay here and take it easy for a while.*

낙동강 오리알 [Lit. a duck egg from the Nakdong River] IDIOM 무리에서 떨어져 나오거나 혼자 쓸쓸히 지내는 처지 = the state of being ostracized from a group or passing time alone (*equiv.* to be left behind / to be left out *syn.* 개밥에 도토리) ▌A: 나 아프다고 친구들이 나만 빼고 다 제주도로 놀러 갔대요. = *I was sick so my friends all left me behind and went to Jeju Island.* B: **낙동강 오리알** 신세구나. = *I guess they just ditched you, huh?*

NOTE: 이 표현의 정확한 유래는 알려져 있지 않다. 낙동강 주변에 을숙도라는 섬이 있는데, 이 섬에는 매해 여러 종류의 철새가 들러 알을 낳고 간다. 그런데 그 중에서도 오리알은 상대적으로 크기가 큰 편이기 때문에 눈에 쉽게 띄고 이질적이다. 이러한 연유로 '낙동강 오리알'이라는 표현이 생겨난 게 아닌가 싶다.
The exact origin of this phrase is unknown. In the Nakdong River sits Eulsook Island. Every year hundreds of migratory birds of all varieties lay their eggs here and move on. Amongst those, however, a duck's egg is larger and catches the eye. This may have given rise to this expression.

낙타가 바늘 구멍 들어가기 [Lit. a camel's walking through the hole in a needle] IDIOM 매우 어려운 일 = a very difficult task (*equiv.* for a camel to pass through the eye of a needle) ▌A: 한국에서는 공무원 시험 준비하는 사람이 많죠? = *There are a lot of people studying for the civil service exam in Korea, right?* B: 그래서 공무원 되기가 **낙타가 바늘 구멍 들어가기**예요. = *Yes, that's why becoming a civil servant is like a camel* *passing through the eye of a needle.*

NOTE: "낙타가 바늘귀를 통과하는 것이 부자가 하늘나라에 들어가는 것보다 쉽다"라는 성경 마태복음 19장 24절에서 나온 표현이다. 알렉산드리아의 키릴로스를 비롯해 많은 사람들이 이 구절이 낙타와 밧줄을 혼동한 번역 실수라고 주장했다. 한편 바늘귀는 예루살렘의 성문이 닫히고 난 뒤에 통행하는 좁은 문을 가리키는 것이라는 해석도 있다. 여러 다양한 해석이 있지만 결국 중심 의미는 매우 어려운 일을 비유한 것이라는 점에는 이견이 없다.

This expression and its English equivalent come from the well-known bible verse, "Again I tell you, it is easier for a camel to go through the eye of a needle than for a rich man to enter the kingdom of God." Matthew 19:24. Some, including Cyril of Alexandria, have claimed that this form of the verse is a mistranslation and instead of "kamêlos" (camel) the text should have read, "kamilos," meaning "rope." The "eye of a needle" has also been thought to refer to a narrow after-hours gate in Jerusalem as opposed to the actual eye of a needle. The jury is still out the exact metaphor Jesus was using, but the meaning is clear and the above form of the verse is in broad use.

난다 긴다 하다 [Lit. for people to say (someone is) flying or crawling] IDIOM 능력이 남들보다 뛰어나다 = to be more capable than others (*syn.* 날고 기다) ▌A: 국가대표에 뽑히다니 정말 대단하다! 합숙 훈련은 언제부터야? = *To be chosen for the Korean team like that—you really are amazing. When do you start training together?* B: 내일부터야. 거기 가면 **난다 긴다 하는** 사람들이 다 모여 있을 텐데 좀 걱정이야. = *We start tomorrow. Everybody there will be tops at what they do. I'm starting to worry a bit.*

날개(가) 돋치다 [Lit. to sprout wings] IDIOM 상품이 빠른 속도로 팔려 나가다 = for a product to sell quickly (*equiv.* to sell like hotcakes / to fly off the shelves) ▌A: 요즘 학생들 졸업 선물로 인기 있는 기종이 뭔가요? = *What product is popular as a graduation present?* B: 이 제품입니다. 요즘 정말 **날개 돋친** 듯 팔리고 있는 모델입니다. = *That would* *be this item. It's really been flying off the shelves recently.*

날고 기다 IDIOM = 난다 긴다 하다

날(이) 새다 [Lit. for day to break] IDIOM 일이 성사될 가망이 없다 = for things to have no chance of success (*equiv.* It's all over now. *syn.* 종(이) 치다) ▌A: 시험이 코앞인데 영희가 공부는 안 하고 잠만 자요. = *The test is just around the corner and Yeonghee just sleeps all day and never studies.* B: **날 샜다**, 애. 남들은 밤에 잠도 안 자고 공부하는데, 그런 자세로 합격할 수 있겠어? = *It's over for her now. The other kids don't even sleep at night they are so busy studying. How is she going to pass with that kind of approach.*

남의 눈에 눈물 내면 제 눈에는 피눈물이 난다 [Lit. If you make others shed tears, you will shed tears of blood.] PROVERB 남에게 나쁜 짓을 하면 자신은 더 큰 해를 입게 된다는 말 = If you harm others, an even worse happening will soon befall you. (*equiv.* That's bad karma. / That will come back to haunt you.) ▌A: 너 미선이한테 어쩌면 그런 말을 할 수가 있니? **남의 눈에 눈물 내면 제 눈에는 피눈물이 난다**는 걸 알아야지. = *How could you say that kind of thing to Miseon? You know that'll come back to haunt you, right?* B: 나도 후회하고 있어. 사과할 거야. = *I regret what I said. I'm going to apologize.*

남의 눈의 티는 보면서 내 눈의 들보는 보지 못한다 [Lit. to notice a speck of dust in another's eye but fail to see the timber in one's own eye] PROVERB 남이 가진 작은 흉이나 문제는 잘 알지만 정작 자신의 큰 흉이나 문제는 잘 모를 때 쓰는 말 = used to describe a person who notices even the smallest fault in others but fails to notice their own more significant problems (*equiv.* to be hypocritical / to assume a holier-than-thou attitude *cf.* 똥 묻은 개가 겨 묻은 개 나무란다) ▌A: 어제 맞선은 어땠어? = *How was the meeting yesterday?* B: 다 좋은데 이혼을 한 게 마음에 걸리더라고요. = *Everything was fine about her, but her former marriage gets to me a little.* A: 너도 이혼했잖아. 애도 있고. **남의 눈의 티는 보면서 내 눈의 들보는 못 보는** 격이구먼. = *But you're*

divorced too, with a child. Don't you think you're being a little hypocritical?

남의 떡이 더 커 보인다 [Lit. The other man's *tteok* always looks bigger.] PROVERB 자기가 가진 것보다 다른 사람의 물건이 더 대단해 보이는 심리를 표현한 말 = used to describe how one always perceives another's circumstance to be better than one's own (*equiv.* The grass is always greener (on the other side of the fence).) ▌A: 우와, 네 핸드폰 되게 좋다! 내 것보다 가볍고 디자인도 좋고. = *Wow, that's an awesome phone! It's lighter than mine and the design is nice too.* B: 나는 네 거가 더 좋은 것 같은데? 원래 남의 떡이 더 커 보이는 법이잖아. = *Yours looks better to me. Well, the grass is always greener on the other side of the fence.*

남의 잔치에 감 놓아라 배 놓아라 한다 [Lit. to tell people whether they should set out persimmons or pears at somebody else's feast.] PROVERB 남의 일에 공연히 간섭하고 나설 때 하는 말 = used when someone meddles in other people's business unnecessarily (*equiv.* to stick one's nose into other people's business / to meddle in other people's affairs / It's none of your business. / Mind your own business. / Stay out of my business.) ▌A: 에이, 그게 아니잖아. 왼쪽이 아니라 오른쪽이야. = *Hey, that's not how you do that. Not the left, the right.* B: 넌 왜 남 게임하는데 와서 참견이니? 남의 잔치에 감 놓아라 배 놓아라 하지 말고 네 할 일이나 해. = *Why are you butting in on someone else's game? Why don't you just mind your own business?*

NOTE: 한국 전통적인 조상 숭배 의식인 제사의 상을 차릴 때는 정해진 규칙이 있었다. 그러나 그 규칙이 지역이나 집안에 따라 약간의 차이가 있었는데, 특히나 과일을 놓는 순서에서 감과 배의 순서가 지역마다 달랐다. 그래서 마을 잔치 등 여러 집안이 모이는 자리에 가면 감과 배를 놓는 순서를 두고 입씨름이 흔히 있었다. 오늘날 남의 일에 지나치게 간섭한다는 의미로 이 표현을 쓴다.

When setting the ritual feast to carry out the ancestral worship, 제사, there are many rules that must be adhered to. Especially concerning the placement of persimmons and pears, there was much regional variation. These varying understandings of the proper placement of the ceremonial food, led to many an argument at the village rites or other instances where the ritual was carried out with a mixed crowd of people with different regional backgrounds. These disagreements gave rise to this phrase.

남존여비 [Lit. 男 man + 尊 superior + 女 woman + 卑 inferior] CHINESE-DERIVATION 남자를 여자보다 우대하고 존중하는 일 = the idea of male superiority ▌A: 아버님은 왜 내가 일하는 걸 그리 못마땅하게 여기실까? = *Why won't Dad approve of the idea of me working?* B: 당신이 이해해. 그 세대 분들은 **남존여비** 사상을 갖고 계시는 경우가 많잖아. = *You should understand. Most people of his generation still believe in the idea of male superiority.*

낫 놓고 기역자도 모른다 [Lit. to not know *giyeok* in front of the scythe] PROVERB 아주 무식하다 = to be utterly ignorant (*equiv.* to not know A from B) ▌A: 아버지는 사실 초등학교도 안 다니셔서 한글도 모르셨습니다. ➡p.219 말 그대로 **낫 놓고 기역자도 모르신** 분이죠. = *My dad never even went to elementary school, so he didn't even know how to read Korean. He was not a learned man.* B: 그래도 이렇게 자네가 성공해서 대학교수가 되었으니 저승에서도 흐뭇해하시겠구먼. = *Even so, to see his son become a college professor—I'm sure he is smiling down on you from heaven.*

NOTE: 낫의 모양이 한글의 첫 자음 'ㄱ'과 유사한 데서 온 속담이다.
This proverb comes from the way the first letter of the Korean alphabet, *giyeok* (ㄱ), resembles the scythe.

낮말은 새가 듣고 밤말은 쥐가 듣는다 [Lit. The birds hear what is said during the day and the mice hear what is said at night.] PRCVERB 아무도 안 듣는 데서라도 말조심해야 한다는 말 = used to urge caution in one's speech as someone else may be listening (*equiv.* Birds may hear you during the day and rats at night. *syn.* 벽에도 귀가 있다) ▌A: 왜 그렇게 목소리를 낮춰요? 어차피 여기 우리 둘밖에 없는데. = *Why are you lowering your voice like that? There's nobody here but us.* B: **낮말은 새가 듣고 밤**

말은 쥐가 듣는다는 말도 있잖아요. 조심해야죠. = *You never know when someone is listening. We have to be careful.*

NOTE: 이 속담은 과학적으로도 근거가 있다. 소리의 파장은 낮에는 기온이 낮은 위쪽으로 휘어지고, 밤에는 반대로 지면 쪽으로 휘어진다. 따라서 낮에는 공중에 있는 새가, 밤에는 지면에 있는 쥐가 소리를 더 잘 듣게 된다.
There is a scientific basis for this proverb. During the day, sound waves bend upwards, where the temperature is lower. At night, on the other hand, sound waves bend down towards the earth. That's why, during the day, you've got to watch out for those eavesdropping birds and be mindful of the rats hearing you at night.

낮이나 밤이나 IDIOM = 밤이나 낮이나

낮가죽이 두껍다 IDIOM = 낮(이) 두껍다

***낯을 가리다** [Lit. to distinguish faces] IDIOM 낯선 사람과 선뜻 얘기를 나누지 못하고 불편해하다 = to be shy in front of strangers and at a loss for words ▌A: 지선 씨는 오늘따라 왜 그리 말이 없어요? = *Jisun, why are you so quiet today?* B: 제가 원래 처음 보는 사람 앞에서는 **낯을 좀 가려요**. = *I'm just a little shy with strangers.*

낯을 들지 못하다 [Lit. to not be able to lift one's face] IDIOM 창피하여 다른 사람 앞에서 떳떳하게 행동하지 못하다 = to be too ashamed to act with confidence in front of others (*equiv.* to not be able to look someone in the eye *syn.* 얼굴을 들지 못하다) ▌A: 다 늙어서 가출이라니 ……. 자식들 앞에서 **낯을 들지 못하겠어요**. = *To run away like that at her age ... I won't be able to face my children.* B: 그러게 왜 엄마한테 그러게 심한 말씀을 하셨어요? = *That's right. Why would you ever talk to mother that way?*

낯(이)간지럽다 [Lit. to have an itchy face] IDIOM 몹시 어색하고 부끄럽다 = to feel awkward and ashamed (*equiv.* to blush *syn.* 얼굴(이) 간지럽다)

▌A: 나한테는 당신밖에 없어. 당신은 나만의 천사야. = *There's no one else for me but you. You're my angel.* B: 아니 **낯간지럽게** 왜 이래요? = *Oh, why are you making me blush like that?*

낯(이) 두껍다 [Lit. to have a thick face] IDIOM 뻔뻔하다 = to be very brazen (*equiv.* to have thick skin *syn.* 얼굴(이) 두껍다, 낯가죽이 두껍다) ▌A: 지금 전국에 물난리가 났는데, 국회의원 몇 명이 해외로 휴가를 떠났대요. = *The nation is in the midst of a flood disaster now, but some lawmakers have left for vacations abroad.* B: 참 **낯이 두꺼운** 사람들이네요. = *They really do have thick skin.*

낯(이)뜨겁다 [Lit. for one's face to be hot] IDIOM 부끄러워하다 = to be ashamed (*equiv.* for one's face to be red with shame) ▌A: 얘, 너는 대낮에 그런 **낯뜨거운** 옷차림으로 어딜 가려는 거니? = *Don't you feel ashamed wearing something like that out in broad daylight?* B: 아빠는 이 옷이 어디가 어때서요? 다들 요즘 이렇게 입어요. = *What's the problem with this outfit, Dad? Everybody dresses like this these days.*

낯이 없다 [Lit. to not have a face] IDIOM 미안하거나 부끄러워 얼굴을 대하기 어렵다 = to be so sorry or ashamed (*equiv.* to not be able to face (someone or something) / to not be able to show one's face *syn.* 면목(이) 없다) ▌A: 어제는 왜 안 왔어? 기다렸는데. = *Why didn't you show up yesterday? I was waiting.* B: 너 볼 **낯이 없어서** 못 갔어. 내가 어떻게 거길 가겠니? = *I didn't have the courage to face you, so I didn't go. How could I have gone there?*

***내 코가 석 자** [Lit. My nose is running three ja (90 cm).] PROVERB 내 문제가 급해 다른 사람을 도와줄 여유가 없을 때 쓰는 말 = used when one is facing urgent problems and is therefore not at liberty to help others (*equiv.* I've got my own problems to deal with. / I've got my hands full.) ▌A: 이번에 불우 이웃 돕기 성금 냈어요? = *Did you make a donation for the needy?* B: 내고 싶었는데, **내 코가 석 자**여요. 이번 달 카드 대금도 어떻게 낼지 고민이에요. = *I wanted to, but I have troubles of my own. I don't even know how I'll be able to pay my credit card bill this month.*

NOTE: 이 표현에서의 코를 실제 코로 이해하는 사람도 있지만, 그보다는 콧물로 해석하는 편이 더 타당할 것이다. 한 자는 30cm에 해당하는데, 콧물이 90cm에 이를 정도라면 얼마나 다급한 상황이겠는가! Normally the word 코 just means nose. But in this idiom, it means "runny nose." If one's nose is running so much that 90 centimeters, worth has passed through one's nostrils, that is indeed a major problem.

냄새(가) 나다 [Lit. to (give off a) smell] IDIOM 수상한 낌새를 느끼다 = to detect something suspicious (*equiv.* to smell of something / to reek of something / to smell something fishy) ▌A: 와, 그 사람이 범인인 걸 어떻게 알았어? = *Wow, how did you know that he was the culprit?* B: 처음에 등장할 때부터 딱 **냄새가 나던데** 뭐. = *He smelled fishy from the beginning.*

냄새(를) 맡다 [Lit. to smell a scent] IDIOM 감추려고 하는 일의 낌새를 알아차리다 = to notice something that others are trying to hide (*equiv.* to get wind of (a plan, or cover-up)) ▌A: 야, 얼른 짐 챙겨서 튀어! = *Hey! Pick up these bags and get going.* B: 왜 그래? = *What's wrong with you?* A: 경찰이 **냄새를 맡은** 거 같아. 서둘러! = *I think the police are onto us. Hurry up!*

냉수 먹고 속 차려라 [Lit. You should drink some cold water and pull yourself together.] PROVERB 정신 차려라 = Pull yourself together! (*equiv.* Wake up and smell the coffee. / Snap out of it. *cf.* 속(을) 차리다) ▌A: 너는 공부를 그렇게 안 해서 뭐 되려고 그러니? = *What do you plan to do later on life if you don't study?* B: 엄마, 공부는 해서 뭐 해요? 저는 그냥 돈 많은 남자 만나서 호강하면서 살 거예요. = *What is studying going to do for me? I'll just marry a rich man and live a life of luxury.* A: 쯧쯧, 언제 정신 차릴래? **냉수 먹고 속 차려라.** = *Tsk, tsk. When are you going to wake up and smell the coffee? Snap out of it!*

너 나 할 것 없이 [Lit. not to mention you or me] IDIOM 모두 = everyone ▌A: 요즘 동아리방에 왜 아무도 안 나와? = *Why isn't anyone showing up to the clubhouse anymore?* B: **너 나 할 것 없이** 취직 준비에 바쁘

잖아요. = *Everyone is busy trying to find a job, just like you and me.*

너 죽고 나 죽자 [Lit. Let's die.] IDIOM 죽을 각오로 임할 때 쓰는 말 = said when one undertakes a task with the conviction to die if necessary (*cf.* 이판사판, 사생결단) ▌A: 오늘 경기는 누가 이길까? = *Who do you think is going to win today's match?* B: 글쎄. 실력은 미국 선수가 앞서지만, 일본 선수도 이번에는 **너 죽고 나 죽자**는 각오로 덤빌 테니, 뚜껑을 열기 전에는 알 수가 없네. = *Well, in terms of skill, the American athlete is better but the Japanese player is going to come after him with a do-or-die mindset, so there's no way to tell.*

넋(을) 놓다 IDIOM = 넋(을) 잃다

넋(을) 잃다 [Lit. to lose one's soul] IDIOM **1.** 멍한 상태가 되거나 정신을 잃다 = to be vacant psychologically or lose one's mind (*equiv.* to grow absentminded / to be vacant / to be an empty shell *syn.* 넋(을) 놓다) ▌A: 하선이는 좀 어때? = *How is Haseon doing?* B: 완전히 **넋을 잃고** 앉아 있더라고. 안쓰러워 혼났어. = *She just sits there all day with a blank stare. She's pitiful. It's hard to deal with.* **2.** 다른 것을 보지 못할 정도로 어떤 사물을 보는 데 열중하다 = to be so enthralled in one thing that one looks at nothing else (*syn.* 넋(을) 놓다) ▌A: 완전히 **넋을 잃고** 보는구먼. 그렇게 재밌어? = *You're totally wrapped up in that. Is it that interesting?* B: 너도 한번 봐 봐. 눈을 뗄 수가 없다니까. = *You give it a try. I can't look away.*

넋(이) 나가다 [Lit. for one's soul to leave] IDIOM 멍한 상태가 되거나 정신을 잃다 = to be vacant or lose one's mind (*equiv.* to be lost in one's thoughts) ▌A: 얘가 **넋 나간** 사람처럼 왜 이러고 있어? = *Why are you just sitting there with a blank stare on your face?* B: 아, 언제 왔어? 잠시 딴 생각 좀 하고 있었어. = *Oh, when did you get here? I was just lost in my thoughts for a moment.*

널뛰기를 하다 IDIOM = 널(을)뛰다

널(을)뛰다 [Lit. to jump on the seesaw] IDIOM 오르고 내리기를 반복하거나 그 차이가 크다 = to repeat a path of ups and downs (*equiv.* to seesaw / to go up and down *syn.* 널뛰기를 하다) ▌A: 오늘 하루 환율이 **널을 뛰었습니다**. = *The won has been up and down a lot today.* B: 원−달러 환율이 1100원에서 출발해 오후 한때 1400원까지 치솟았다가 결국 1200원으로 마감했습니다. = *The won-dollar exchange rate started the day at 1,100, skyrocketed all the way to 1,400, and was back at 1,200 by the close.*

NOTE: 널뛰기는 긴 널빤지의 가운데를 괴어 놓고 양쪽 끝에 한 사람씩 올라서서 번갈아 뛰어오르는 우리나라 고유의 놀이다. 주로 음력 정월이나 단오, 추석에 여자들이 널뛰기를 했다. 널을 뛸 때 사람이 올라갔다 내려갔다를 번갈아 반복하는 모습을 연상하면 이 표현이 이해가 될 것이다. The traditional Korean seesaw is a long plank with a support in the middle. People take turns jumping on each end. This game is most often enjoyed by women on *Chuseok*, Lunar New Year's Day or on the fifth day of the fifth lunar month, known as 단오. If you imagine people on two ends of a seesaw bouncing up and down repeatedly, you'll undestand what this expression is all about.

넘어야 할 산이 많다 [Lit. There are many hills to pass over.] IDIOM 앞으로도 해결해야 할 과제나 고비가 많다 = There is still much hard work to be done. (*equiv.* There is still a long way to go. / I've still got a long way to go. *syn.* 갈 길이 멀다) ▌A: 휴우, 겨우 다 했다. = *Phew, I'm done now.* B: 벌써 다 끝낸 거야? = *Are you already finished with it all?* A: 헤헤, 실은 열 개 중에 한 개 다 한 거야. 아직 **넘어야 할 산이 많아**. = *Ha. No, I actually just did one tenth of it so far. I've still got a long way to go.*

노래를 하다 [Lit. to sing a song] IDIOM 같은 말을 되풀이하며 졸라 대다 = to beg for something by repeating the same words (*equiv.* to carry on about something / to be singing that song again) ▌A: 가희 엄마는 반찬 뭐 샀어요? = *What did you buy for appetizers?* B: 햄 샀어요. 애들이 어제부터 햄 먹고 싶다고 **노래를 해서요**. = *I bought ham, because the kids haven't let up about ham since yesterday.*

노발대발하다 [Lit. 怒anger + 發occur + 大big + 發occur + 하다verbal suffix] CHINESE-DERIVATION 크게 화를 내다 = to be very angry (*equiv.* to lose it / to go crazy / to fly into a fit of rage) ▌A: 할아버지한테 너 국제결혼 하겠다고 말씀 드렸니? = *Did you tell Grandpa about your plans to marry a foreigner?* B: 네. 예상대로 **노발대발하시더라고요**. = *Yes, he lost it, just like we predicted.*

노심초사하다 [Lit. 勞worry + 心heart + 焦burn + 思think + 하다verbal suffix] CHINESE-DERIVATION 몹시 마음을 졸이며 걱정을 하다 = to be worried or vexed about something (*equiv.* to be on pins and needles) ▌A: 아직 발표 안 났어? = *The results still haven't be posted?* B: 모르겠어. 발표 나면 전화 준다고 해서 기다리고 있어. = *I don't know. They said they would call me, so I've just been waiting.* A: 그렇게 앉아서 **노심초사하지** 말고 전화를 먼저 해 보지 그래? = *Don't just sit there on pins and needles about it. Call them up first, why don't you?*

***녹(이)슬다** [Lit. to rust] IDIOM 기능이나 솜씨가 무뎌지다 = for an ability or talent to fade with disuse (*equiv.* to be rusty (at something)) ▌A: 내 결혼식 때 네가 피아노 쳐 줄래? = *Would you mind playing a little piano for my wedding?* B: 음, 글쎄. 그러고 싶기는 한데, 내가 피아노를 안 친 지 오래 돼서 손이 **녹슬었을** 텐데. = *Hmm, well … I'd like to of course, but it's been so long since I've played. I'm sure I'm going to be quite rusty.*

***녹초가 되다** [Lit. to become a melted candle] IDIOM 몹시 지쳐 축 늘어지다 = to be worn out or exhausted (*equiv.* to be worn out / to be spent / to be all used up) ▌A: 왜 오늘 같이 날씨 좋은 날 집에 있는 거예요? = *Why are you staying home with the weather as good as it is?* B: 어제 하루 종일 집안일을 했더니 **녹초가 되어** 버려서 손도 꼼짝 못 하겠어요. = *I did chores all day yesterday so I'm worn out. I can't even move.*

NOTE: 녹초는 녹은 초를 말한다. 초가 녹아내리면 흐물흐물해진다. 사람이 피곤해서 힘이 빠진 상태를 그 모습에 비유한 표현이다.
The word 녹초 means a candle that has melted down to almost nothing. Melted candles are soft and mushy. This phrase is used to describe a person who is in such a worn-down state.

놀고 있다 [Lit. to be messing around] IDIOM 마음에 들지 않게 행동하는 것을 비꼬아 하는 말 = used to sarcastically describe someone's cavalier actions ▌A: 언니, 이것 봐. 나 그림 잘 그리지? 이참에 나 공부 때려치우고 미술 할까? = *Look. I'm good at drawing, huh? Should I take this to mean that I should quit studying and be an artist?* B: 놀고 있네. 공부나 열심히 해. = *Stop messing around. Keep studying.*

놀랄 노 자 [Lit. the letter no for "surprised"] IDIOM 몹시 놀라운 일이나 상황 = a very surprising situation or turn of events (*equiv.* That's surprising with a capital s. *cf.* 뻔할 뻔 자) ▌A: 네가 웬일로 아침에 이렇게 일찍 일어났니? 놀랄 노 자네. = *How unlike you to be up so early in the morning. What a shock!* B: 배가 고파서 깼어요. = *I was hungry so I got up.*

NOTE: 실제로 한자 중에 '놀랄 노'라는 글자가 있는 것이 아니라 단순한 언어유희에 불과하다. 비슷한 것으로 '뻔할 뻔 자'라는 표현이 있다.
You may have guessed it, but there is no Chinese character 노 for 놀랍다. It's simple wordplay. There is another expression along the same lines: 뻔할 뻔 자.

높이 나는 새가 멀리 본다 [Lit. The bird that flies high sees far.] QUOTE 꿈을 크게 가지라는 말 = used to encourage the setting of high goals (*equiv.* The bird that flies high sees the farthest.) ▌A: 한국에서 공부할 수도 있잖아. 왜 굳이 외국으로 유학을 가려고 해? = *You can study right here in Korea. Why do you have to go abroad to study?* B: 높이 나는 새가 멀리 보는 법이잖아. 더 넓은 세상을 보고 싶어. = *The bird that flies the highest sees the farthest. I want to see the whole wide world.*

NOTE: 리처드 바크가 쓴 '갈매기의 꿈'에 나오는 유명한 구절이다.
This is a line from Richard Bach's "Jonathan Livingston Seagull."

높이 사다 [Lit. to buy highly] IDIOM 다른 사람의 태도나 어떤 일의 가치를 인정하다 = to acknowledge someone's behavior or the value of a certain action (*equiv.* to appreciate / to recognize (one's merits or achievements))

A: 이런 상을 저에게 주셔서 감사합니다. = *Thanks so much for giving me such an award.* B: 회사에서 박 부장의 업무 능력을 **높이 산** 거겠지요. = *The company just recognizes your capabilities, Director Park.*

뇌리를 스치다 [Lit. to graze one's consciousness] IDIOM 갑자기 어떠한 생각이 들다 = for a thought to suddenly occur to one (*equiv.* (for an idea) to cross one's mind) **A**: 어제 보이스 피싱을 당했다면서요? = *I heard you were a victim of telephone fraud yesterday.* B: 네. 하마터면 당할 뻔했는데 갑자기 불길한 예감이 **뇌리를 스쳐서** 재차 확인한 덕분에 간신히 위기를 넘겼어요. = *Yeah, but right when I was about to fall for it, I suddenly had this bad feeling. I gave it a second thought and narrowly evaded disaster.*

NOTE: 뇌리는 사람의 의식이나 기억, 사고 따위가 작용하거나 이루어지는 영역을 의미한다.
The 뇌리 describes the part of one's conscious that deals with one's awareness, memory, or thought process.

뇌리에 박히다 [Lit. to be stuck in one's mind] IDIOM 말이나 감정이 마음속에 뚜렷한 흔적을 남겨 쉽게 잊혀지지 않다 = for words or emotions to leave a deep impression and not easily be forgotten (*equiv.* to be seared into one's memory *ant.* 뇌리에서 사라지다) **A**: 이제 아버님하고 화해할 때 되지 않았어요? = *Don't you think it's time for you to make up with Dad?* B: 그래야 되는데, 이상하게 그때 그 안 좋은 감정이 **뇌리에 박혀서** 사라지지를 않네요. = *Yeah, but the bad feelings of that day are still seared into my mind. I can't seem to forget about it.*

뇌리에서 사라지다 [Lit. to disappear from one's mind] IDIOM 잊혀지다 = to be forgotten (*ant.* 뇌리에 박히다) **A**: 이번이 한국 첫 방문이세요? = *Is this your first time visiting Korea?* B: 아니요. 작년에 왔었는데, 그때 본 불꽃 축제가 **뇌리에서 사라지지를** 않아서 올해 또 왔어요. = *No, I came here last year. But memories of the fireworks festival never left my mind, so I came back again this year.*

누가 ~ 아니랄까 봐 [Lit. to be worried someone wouldn't call you a ...] IDIOM 상대의 말이나 행동이 그 사람의 평소 성격이나 신분 등에 딱 어울릴 때 쓰는 말 = used when one's counterpart says something that perfectly fits their normal personality, or role in life (*equiv.* How just like you to say that.) ▌A: 이 두 문서는 내용이 틀린데? = *The content of these two documents is "wrong."* B: 틀린 게 아니라 다른 거겠지. = *They are not "wrong" they are "different."* A: **누가 국어 선생 아니랄까 봐** 우리 말 지적이야? = *How just like you to correct my Korean. Were you worried I had forgotten you're a Korean teacher?*

누구 코에 바르겠는가 [Lit. Who could put this on a nose?] IDIOM 어떤 물건을 여러 사람에게 나누어 주어야 하는데 그 양이 너무 적을 때 쓰는 말 = used when an insufficient quantity of food must be divided up amongst many (*syn.* 누구 코에 붙일까) ▌A: 돈이 좀 남네. 사람 수대로 나눌까? = *We have a little money left. Should we split it up between us all?* B: 얼마 되지도 않는 돈 나누면 **누구 코에 바르겠어?** 그냥 좋은 일에 쓰자. = *That's too little to even bother with. Let's just spend it wisely.*

NOTE: 물론 음식을 코에 직접 바르지는 않지만 먹기 전에 냄새를 맡기 위해 코 앞에 가져가는 예는 흔하다. 음식 양이 너무 적어 냄새를 확인해 봐야 할 정도라는 표현이다. '누구 코에 붙이나'라고도 말한다.
Food is not usually wiped on the nose, however, the practice of bending in close to get a good whiff of a meal before you enjoy it is quite common. This expression depicts an amount of food so small that it's not even enough to smell. This expression is also sometimes expressed as, 누구 코에 붙이나.

누구 코에 붙일까 IDIOM = 누구 코에 바르겠는가

누울 자리 봐 가며 발을 뻗어라 [Lit. You should stretch your legs to make sure there is room.] PROVERB 결과를 미리 생각하고 일을 시작하라는 말 = Consider the outcome before beginning something. (*equiv.* Stretch your arm no further than your sleeve will reach.) ▌A: 미안하지만 나 돈 좀 빌려 줄 수 있어? = *I'm sorry but can you lend me some money?* B:

야, **누울 자리 봐 가며 발을 뻗어야지**. 나 지금 백수인 거 몰라?＝
You'd better think about my situation first. Don't you know I'm out of a job right now.

***누워서 떡 먹기** [Lit. lying down and eating *tteok*] PROVERB 아주 쉬운 일＝an easy task (*equiv.* a piece of cake / a walk in the park *syn.* 땅 짚고 헤엄치기, 식은 죽 먹기 *ant.* 하늘의 별 따기) ▌A: 이렇게 넓은데 어느 세월에 다 치우죠?＝*How on earth can I clean such a large place?* B: 이 청소기만 있으면 **누워서 떡 먹기**예요.＝*If you have this vacuum, it will be a piece of cake.*

NOTE: 사실 누운 채로 무엇인가를 먹는다는 게 그리 쉬운 일은 아니다. '누워서 떡 먹기'는 누운 채로 떡을 먹는다는 뜻이 아니라, 아무 노력도 하지 않은 채 다른 사람이 가져다주는 음식을 덕는다는 뜻이다. 한국은 전통적으로 행사나 축제가 있을 때 마을 사람들끼리 서로서로 돕는 풍습이 있었다. 만약 아파서 일을 도울 수 없는 사람이 있으면 이웃들이 잔치 음식을 싸다가 가져다 주었다. 바로 이와 같은 상황을 가리키는 표현이다.

Most people have at some point attempted to eat something in a reclining position. It's not that easy. This phrase does not literally mean to eat 떡 while lying down but rather means to enjoy the food someone else has brought with no effort exerted on one's own part. It was common for the entire village to come together to prepare for a feast or ceremony in the past. When the festival was concluded, people would carry the food that they had prepared to the beds of those who were too sick to have helped in the festival preparation. This phrase connotes such a situation.

***누워서 침 뱉기** [Lit. lying down and spitting] PROVERB 자기 자신에게 해가 돌아오는 행동＝doing something that hurts oneself (*equiv.* to shoot oneself in the foot / to sabotage oneself *syn.* 하늘 보고 침 뱉기) ▌A: 영미는 왜 동창회만 나오면 남편 흉을 그렇게 볼까?＝*I don't understand why Youngmi always find fault with her husband.* B: **그래 봐야 누워서 침 뱉기**라는 걸 모르나 봐.＝*I guess she doesn't realize that she's just shooting herself in the foot.*

누이 좋고 매부 좋다 [Lit. What is good for one's sister is good for one's sister's husband.] PROVERB 서로에게 다 이롭고 좋다 = to be mutually beneficial (*equiv.* a win-win situation / What's good for the goose is good for the gander.) ▌A: 저는 잘 안 입는 옷은 자선 단체에 갖다 줘요. 그럼 저는 옷장이 정리되어서 좋고, 어려운 사람은 옷이 생겨서 좋으니까요. = *I usually donate clothes that I no longer wear to charity centers. It's good for me because I can get rid of clothes that I don't wear, and those in need can be clothed.* B: 그것 참 **누이 좋고 매부 좋은** 일이네요. = *It really is a win-win.*

눈 가리고 아웅 [Lit. to cover someone's eyes and make an "aung" sound] PROVERB 얕은수로 남을 속이려 애쓸 때 쓰는 말 = to try to deceive by transparent guile (*equiv.* to bury one's head in the sand) ▌A: 저 집에서 과일 사면 안 되겠어요. = *I'd better not buy fruit in that store again.* B: 왜요? = *Why?* A: 요전에 귤 한 상자를 샀는데 눈에 보이는 부분만 싱싱하고 아래쪽에 있는 건 모두 썩어 있었어요. **눈 가리고 아웅하기지** 뭐예요. = *A few days ago, I bought a box of mandarin oranges there and the ones on top looked great but ones on the bottom were rotten. And they thought they'd get away with that?*

NOTE: 아웅은 얼굴을 가렸다가 떼면서 아이를 어르는 장난을 말한다. 아이들은 물론 이런 놀이에 재미있어 하지만, 얼굴을 가렸다가 뗀다고 해서 사람이 사라졌다 다시 나타나는 거라고 생각하는 어른은 없을 것이다. 이처럼 얕은 꾀나 어설픈 행동으로 남을 속이려 하는 것을 가리켜 '눈 가리고 아웅한다'라고 말한다.

아웅 is the practice of covering up and uncovering one's face to entertain a child. Young children, of course, enjoy this game but one would be hard-pressed to find an adult that actually thought the person standing in front of them had disappeared and then reappeared once they uncovered their face. This phrase depicts attempts to deceive others with obvious fraud or a transparent scheming.

눈곱만큼도 [Lit. (not) even a grain of sand in the eye] IDIOM 전혀 = not even a little bit (*equiv.* not even one modicum) ▌A: 네 문제에 참견하고 싶은

생각은 **눈곱만큼도** 없지만, 너도 이제 결혼을 생각해야 되지 않겠니? = *I have not even the slightest interest in meddling in your affairs, but don't you think it's about time you thought about marriage?* B: 저도 결혼할 마음이 없는 건 아니에요. = *It's not that I'm not interested in marriage.*

> **NOTE:** 눈곱은 아주 적거나 작은 것을 비유할 때 쓰인다. 더 과장해서 말할 때는 '개미 눈곱'이라는 표현도 쓴다. 개미의 눈곱을 본 적이 있는가? Sleep or sand in the eyes, is usually a small quantity and therefore is used in the world of proverbs to refer to a very small amount. Taking it one step further, one may also use the expression, 개미 눈곱 (a grain of sand in the eye of an ant). The perfect expression for some sarcastic belittling.

눈길을 끌다 IDIOM = 눈길을 모으다

눈길을 모으다 [Lit. to attract glances] IDIOM 관심을 끌다 = to garner attention (*equiv.* to be eye-catching *syn.* 눈길을 끌다) ▌A: 이 핸드폰이 인기를 끄는 이유가 뭘까요? = *Why do you think this phone is so popular?* B: 깔끔한 디자인이 사람들의 **눈길을 모으는** 것 같아요. = *Its clean look seems to have caught the eyes of consumers.*

눈길(을) 주다 [Lit. to give (something or someone) glances] IDIOM 주의와 관심을 기울이다 = to pay attention or show interest ▌A: 아, 외롭다 외로워. = *I'm lonely. Lonely, I'm telling you.* B: 너 좋다는 남자 없어? = *No guy is interested in you?* A: 없어. **눈길 주는** 남자도 하나 없는걸. = *Nope. I don't think anyone even looks at me.*

눈 깜빡할 사이 IDIOM = 눈 깜짝할 사이

눈 깜짝할 사이 [Lit. in the moment an eye blinks] IDIOM 매우 짧은 순간 = in an instant (*equiv.* in the blink of an eye *syn.* 눈 깜빡할 사이) ▌A: 여보, 일어나. 다 왔어. = *Honey, wake up. We're here.* B: 벌써? **눈 깜짝할 사이**에 왔네. = *Already? Wow, we got here in the blink of an eye.*

눈꼴(이)사납다 [Lit. to be vicious on the eyes] IDIOM 하는 행동이 밉살 맞고 눈에 거슬리다＝for behavior to be offensive to the eye (*equiv.* The site of something makes one sick. / Oh, my eyes! *syn.* 눈꼴(이)시다) ▌A: 요즘 젊은 사람들은 부끄러운 줄도 모르고 저렇게 길거리에서 뽀뽀를 한다니까.＝*Kids today have no shame—just kissing like that on the street.* B: **눈꼴 사나울** 때가 많아요, 그죠?＝*It's enough to just make you sick sometimes, isn't it?*

NOTE: 눈꼴은 눈의 생김새나 눈의 움직이는 형태를 얕잡아 이르는 말이다. 눈꼴 is a disparaging word for the shape or movement of the eyes.

눈꼴(이)시다 [Lit. for one's eyes to be sour] IDIOM 하는 행동이 밉살맞고 눈에 거슬리다＝for someone's behavior to be offensive or abominable (*syn.* 눈꼴(이)사납다) ▌A: 어제는 왜 먼저 갔어?＝*Why did you leave before everyone else like that yesterday?* B: 정수 녀석 시험 붙었다고 어찌나 잘난 척을 하던지 **눈꼴이 시어서** 못 봐 주겠더라고.＝*Jeongsu kept bragging about how he had passed the test. I just couldn't take it anymore.*

눈높이가 낮다 IDIOM＝눈이 낮다

눈높이가 높다 IDIOM＝눈이 높다

눈높이를 낮추다 IDIOM＝눈을 낮추다

눈높이를 높이다 IDIOM＝눈을 높이다

눈높이를 맞추다 [Lit. to match (someone's) eye level] IDIOM 자신의 수준이나 인식, 입장을 다른 사람과 같게 만들다＝to match someone's cognition level or adjust one's standing to match that of others (*equiv.* to lower oneself (to their level)) ▌A: 요즘 전 세계적으로 뽀로로가 인기인데요, 어떻게 이런 캐릭터를 생각하게 되셨나요?＝*I heard that Pororo is popular all over the world now. How did you think of such a character in the first place?* B: 아이들과 **눈높이를 맞추어서** 생각한 것이 주효한 것

같습니다. = *Thinking at the level of the children is what brought me the idea I'd say.*

눈도 깜짝 안 하다 [Lit. to not blink one's eyes] IDIOM 조금도 놀라지 않고 태연하게 행동하다 = to remain calm and not even show a hint of surprise (*equiv.* to not bat an eye / to not even blink / to not even flinch *syn.* 눈 하나 깜짝 안 하다, 눈썹도 까딱 안 하다) ▌A: 아버지가 계속 우리 결혼을 반대하시면 집을 나가겠다고 했어. = *I told my father that if he continues to oppose our marriage, I'll move out.* B: 그랬더니 뭐라셔? = *And what did he say in response?* A: 눈도 깜짝 안 하시던데. = *He didn't even bat an eye.*

눈독(을) 들이다 [Lit. to give the poison from one's eyes] IDIOM 욕심을 내어 눈여겨보다 = to greedily desire something (*equiv.* to have one's eye on (something) / to have one's eyes fixed on (something)) ▌A: 경미야, 이번에 너 결혼하면서 네 물건들 처분한다고 했지? 이 의자 나 주면 안 돼? = *Gyeongmi, you said you were going to get rid of your stuff when you got married, right? What about giving me this chair?* B: 얘, 그거 경미가 나 주기로 했어. 눈독 들이지 마. = *Hold up. She said she was going to give that to me. Don't get too attached to it.*

눈 딱 감고 [Lit. with one's eyes closed] IDIOM 다음에 벌어질 일이나 주위 형편을 생각하지 않고 = without considering what might happen next or thinking about the circumstances (*equiv.* to look the other way / to look something over *syn.* 두 눈 딱 감고) ▌A: 그러지 말고 이번 한 번만 눈 딱 감고 도와줘. = *Come on. Look the other way just this once and help me out.* B: 이번이 마지막이다! = *This is the last time!*

눈뜨고 코 베어 가다 [Lit. to have one's nose cut off while one's eyes are open] PROVERB 뻔히 알면서 피해를 당할 만큼 험하다 = to be so dangerous that one will be victimized despite knowing of the danger (*equiv.* It's a dog-eat-dog world out there.) ▌A: 서울 생활은 좀 어때? 적응은 좀 됐어? = *How's life in Seoul? Are you getting used to it?* B: 웬걸요. 서울은 눈뜨고 코 베어 가는 곳이라더니, 정말 시골하고는 많이 다

른 것 같아요. = *No way! Seoul is a dog-eat-dog city. It really is nothing like the countryside.*

눈뜬장님 [Lit. a blind person who opened their eyes] IDIOM **1.** 무엇을 보고도 알지 못하는 사람 = somebody who fails to notice something even when they are staring right at it (*equiv.* (You're a) blind fool) █ A: 실례지만 이혼하신 지는 얼마나 되셨어요? = *Forgive me, but how long has it been since you got divorced?* B: 일 년 됐어요. 그 사람하고 헤어지고 나서야 그 사람의 소중함을 깨달았어요. 저는 완전히 **눈뜬장님**이었어요. = *One year. It wasn't until after we split up, that I realized how important she was to me. I was a blind fool.* **2.** 글을 모르는 사람 = an illiterate person █ A: 한국에 처음 오셨을 때 느낌이 어떠셨어요? = *What was it like when you first came to Korea?* B: 다른 건 다 좋았는데, 한글을 몰라서 **눈뜬장님** 신세였죠. 그게 좀 힘들었어요. = *Well, everything else was fine, but since I couldn't read Hangul, I was like a blind person trying to get around. That was a little hard to deal with.*

눈만 뜨면 [Lit. if one just opens one's eyes] IDIOM 항상 = always █ A: 경진이는 뭐 해? = *What is Gyeongjin up to?* B: 아침부터 지금까지 계속 컴퓨터 게임하고 있어. 요즘에 **눈만 뜨면** 컴퓨터 앞에 앉는다니까. = *He's been playing video games since he got up this morning. I'm telling you, as soon as he opens his eyes, he heads straight for the computer.*

눈먼 돈 [Lit. blind money] IDIOM 주인 없는 돈 = money that belongs to no one (*equiv.* money that is up for grabs / money that is yours for the taking) █ A: 이번에 정부가 부실 은행에 돈을 지원하기로 했대. = *I heard that the government is planning to aid banks that are in distress.* B: 예나 지금이나 국민이 봉인 줄 아나 봐. 세금을 **눈먼 돈** 취급하는 거 보니. = *It's just like it's always been, the government treats the public like a pushover. It looks like they think our tax money is just up for grabs.*

NOTE: 돈이 눈이 멀어 자기 주인을 찾지 못한다면 가져가는 사람이 곧 임자이다.
If money is "blind" and cannot find its owner, the person who snatches it up first may claim it as their own.

눈물이 앞을 가리다 [Lit. One's tears obscure what lies ahead.] IDIOM 슬퍼서 눈물이 흐르다＝to shed many tears due to extreme sadness (*equiv.* to be drowning in tears) ▍A: 어제 텔레비전에서 장애인 남편을 돌보는 여자 얘기를 봤는데 정말 감동적이었어.＝*Yesterday I saw a very moving story on TV about a woman who was taking care of her disabled husband.* B: 나도 봤는데, **눈물이 앞을 가리더라**.＝*I saw that too and ended up drowning in my own tears.*

눈 밖에 나다 [Lit. to be outside of someone's eyes] IDIOM 신뢰를 잃고 미움을 받게 되다＝to lose reputability and be the object of scorn (*equiv.* to get on someone's bad side / to fall out of (someone's) favor *ant.* 눈에 들다) ▍A: 팀장님이 왜 김 대리님한테 그렇게 쌀쌀맞게 대하시죠?＝*Why is the team leader always so hard on you?* B: 내가 옛날에 말대꾸하다 팀장님 **눈 밖에 났거든**.＝*A long time ago, I talked back to him, and got on his bad side.*

눈살(을) 찌푸리다 [Lit. to furrow one's brow] IDIOM 못마땅해하다＝to be displeased (*equiv.* to furrow one's brow *syn.* 이맛살을 찌푸리다) ▍A: 길거리에서 담배를 못 피우게 했으면 좋겠어요.＝*I wish they would make it so people couldn't smoke on the streets.* B: 특히 정류장에서 담배 피우는 사람들은 **눈살을 찌푸리게** 하죠.＝*Yeah, I especially can't stand those people who smoke at the bus stops.*

눈썹도 까딱 안 하다 IDIOM＝눈도 감짝 안 하다

눈썹이 휘날리게 달려오다 [Lit. to run so fast that one's eyebrows flap in the wind] IDIOM 몹시 서둘러서 달려오다＝to run very quickly (*equiv.* to run as if one's pants are on fire / to make a mad dash) ▍A: 경기 시간에 딱 맞게 왔네?＝*You got here just in time for the game.* B: 응. 안 늦으려고 **눈썹이 휘날리게 달려왔지**.＝*I didn't want to be late, so I made a mad dash.*

눈앞에 선하다 IDIOM＝눈에 선하다

눈앞에 아른거리다 IDIOM ＝ 눈에 아른거리다

눈앞이 깜깜하다 IDIOM ＝ 눈앞이 캄캄하다

눈앞이 캄캄하다 [Lit. for it to be dark in front of one's eyes] IDIOM 절망스러워 어찌할 바를 모르다 ＝ to be in despair to the point of not knowing what to do (*equiv.* The outlook is bleak. / to be at a loss / to feel like it's the end of the world *syn.* 눈앞이 깜깜하다, 하늘이 노랗다) ▍A: 어제 지갑을 잃어버렸어요. ＝ *I lost my wallet yesterday.* B: 저런. 중요한 게 많이 들었어요? ＝ *Oh, no. Did you have a lot of important stuff in it?* A: 현금은 없지만, 카드하고 신분증이 다 들어 있었어요. 어떡해야 할지 **눈앞이 캄캄해요.** ＝ *I didn't have any cash, but my credit cards and my ID were in it. I don't really know what to do. The outlook is bleak.*

눈에 거슬리다 [Lit. to be offensive to the eyes] IDIOM 보고 있으면 마음에 들지 않아 불쾌한 느낌이 있다 ＝ to feel displeasure at the sight of something (*equiv.* to be offensive to the eyes / to be an eyesore) ▍A: 수미야, 옷 좀 얌전하게 입어라. ＝ *Sumi, why don't you dress a little more modestly?* B: 아빠는 제가 그렇게 **눈에 거슬리세요?** 왜 저만 보면 그렇게 야단만 치세요? ＝ *Is what I'm wearing really that offensive to your eyes, Dad? Why do you always criticize everything I do?*

눈에 넣어도 아프지 않다 [Lit. to not be painful even when put in one's eye] IDIOM 귀엽고 사랑스럽다 ＝ to be very cute and lovable (*equiv.* to be the apple of one's eye) ▍A: 요즘 박 부장님 기운이 없고 말씀이 별로 없으세요. ＝ *Director Park seems lethargic and hasn't said very much recently.* B: **눈에 넣어도 아프지 않을** 아들을 사고로 잃었으니 그러실 만도 하죠. ＝ *He lost his son, the apple of his eye, in an accident. It's only natural for him to be that way now.*

눈에는 눈 이에는 이 [Lit. an eye for an eye, a tooth for a tooth] PROVERB 해를 입은 만큼 되갚는 것을 가리키는 말 ＝ used to promote payment or punishment equal to one's transgressions (*equiv.* an eye for an eye (a tooth for a tooth)) ▍A: 뭐 해? ＝ *What are you doing?* B: 철민이 녀석 의자에 앉

을 때 골탕 먹이려고 껌 붙이는 중이야. 어제 녀석이 내 의자에 똑같은 짓을 했었거든. =*I'm putting gum on this seat to play a trick on Cheolmin when he sits down here. He did the same thing to me yesterday.* A: 눈에는 눈 이에는 이라는 거지? =*So it's an eye for an eye, huh?*

NOTE: 가장 오래된 법전인 '함무라비 법전'에 이와 같은 법 규정이 있으며 성경에도 이와 비슷한 구절이 있다. 이처럼 가해자에게 똑같은 복수를 하게 한다는 보복의 법칙을 탈리오법칙(lex talionis)이라고 한다.
Just as its English cousin, this expression is taken from the oldest extant code of laws, the Code of Hammurabi. The tenet of doling out the identical punishment to the transgressor is also called lex talionis, or mirror punishment.

눈에 들다 [Lit. (for something) to be taken by one's eyes] IDIOM 마음에 들다 =to be fond of (*equiv.* to catch one's eye *ant.* 눈 밖에 나다) ▌A: 우리 동기 수민 씨 말이야, 이번에 제일 먼저 대리로 승진했잖아. 능력이 뛰어난가 봐. =*You know that girl Sumin, who started at the same time we did? She was the first one of us to get promoted. It looks like she's got talent.* B: 그런 것도 있지만, 저번 프로젝트 때 사장님 **눈에 들었나** 봐. =*Yeah, there's that. Plus, I think she caught the eye of the boss when she did her last project.*

눈에 뭐가 씌다 [Lit. to put something on one's eyes] IDIOM 어떤 사람이나 대상을 몹시 좋아하게 되어 다른 것을 신경쓰지 않다 =to be so interested in something or someone that one lacks interest in anything else (*equiv.* to only have eyes for (someone, something) / to have blinders on) ▌A: 아니 그 옷 버리려고? 당신이 아끼는 옷 아니야? 그 옷 사려고 몇 달 동안 돈 모았었잖아. =*You're really going to throw those clothes away? Aren't these some of your most precious outfits? You saved up to buy these for months.* B: 그때 내가 **눈에 뭐가 씌었었나** 봐. 지금 보니까 영 별로야. =*I guess I wasn't seeing straight then or something. I can see now that they are totally not my style.*

눈에 밟히다 [Lit. to be stepped on by one's eyes] IDIOM 전에 보았던 광경

이나 대상이 자꾸 떠오르다＝for something one has witnessed to keep popping into one's consciousness (*equiv.* to always be on one's mind *syn.* 눈에 아른거리다, 눈에 어리다) █A: 제일 보고 싶은 사람이 누구예요?＝*Who do you miss the most?* B: 고국에 두고 온 아이들이 **눈에 밟혀요.**＝*Well, the children I left behind back home in the mother country are always on my mind.*

NOTE: 어떠한 물건이 바닥에 흩어져 있다면 쉽게 발에 밟힐 것이다. '눈에 밟히다'에서 '눈'은 '생각'을 의미한다. 어떠한 대상이 눈에 밟힌다는 말은 머릿속에 온통 그것과 관련된 생각뿐이어서 그 생각을 떨쳐 버릴 수 없다는 뜻이다.
If something is scattered all over the floor, it will soon be stepped on. In this idiom, "eyes" are a stand-in for the mind. Therefore, 눈에 밟히다 means someone or something that is occupying one's whole mind, rendering it impossible to think about anything else.

눈에 보이는 것이 없다 [Lit. to see nothing in front of one's eyes] IDIOM

사리 분별을 못하다＝to be senseless or fearless (*equiv.* You don't know what's good for you.) █A: 네가 감히 나한테 그런 식으로 말하다니. 눈에 보이는 것이 없는 모양이구나!＝*How dare you speak to me that way? I guess you're not afraid of anything.* B: 저도 참을 만큼 참았어요. 이제는 할 말은 해야겠어요.＝*I've taken all I can stand. Now I'm going to say my piece.*

눈에 불을 켜다 [Lit. to turn on the light in one's eyes] IDIOM

1. 몹시 욕심을 내거나 열중하다＝to possess great avarice or interest in something (*equiv.* to have fire in the belly / to have a fire in one's eyes (for something)) █A: 우와! 한 학기도 안 놓치고 매번 장학금을 받는 비결이 뭐야?＝*What's your secret to getting scholarship money every semester?* B: 그냥 **눈에 불을 켜고** 공부하는 거지 뭐.＝*It's nothing more than having a fire in my belly and studying hard.* 2. 화가 나서 눈을 부릅뜨다＝to look with fierce eyes (*equiv.* for one's eyes to flash in anger / to glare at) █A: 난 이제 민희한테 죽었다.＝*I'm so dead right now.* B: 왜?＝*Why?* A: 걔가 아끼는 목걸이를 빌렸는데 잃어버렸거든. 아마 **눈**

에 불을 켜고 달려들걸. = *Minhee lent me a necklace that's really precious to her and I lost it. I can already imagine the fire that's going to be in her eyes when she pounces on me.*

눈에(서) 불이 나다 [Lit. to have a fire in one's eyes] IDIOM

1. 몹시 화가 나다 = for one's emotions to grow intense (*equiv.* to see red) ▌A: 요즘 젊은 사람들이 아무 데서나 막 안고 뽀뽀하는 거 보면 어떨 때는 **눈에서 불이 나요.** = *The way youngsters today just hug and kiss anywhere they like—sometimes it makes me see red.* B: 우리 때랑은 시대가 많이 달라졌으니까요. = *These are just different times from what we know.* **2.** 어떤 일에 몹시 열중하다 = to be very passionate (about something) ▌A: 영철이는 뭐 해? = *What's Yeongcheol up to?* B: 자기 방에서 공부해. 시험이 얼마 안 남아서 요즘 **눈에서 불이 날** 정도로 열심이야. = *He's studying in his room. He's been studying with a fire in his eyes recently since his tests are just around the corner.*

눈에 선하다 [Lit. to be vivid in one's eyes] IDIOM

잊히지 않고 기억에 생생하다 = to be vivid in one's memory (*equiv.* It's as if I can still see it. / to clearly remember something *syn.* 눈앞에 선하다) ▌A: 지금의 부인을 대학교 때 만나셨다고요? = *You said you met your current wife when you were in college?* B: 네. 소개팅에서 처음 봤는데요, 문 열고 들어오던 그 모습이 지금도 **눈에 선해요.** = *Yes, it was a blind date. The image of her walking through that door is still so vivid in my mind.*

눈에 쌍심지를 켜다 [Lit. to light two wicks in one's eyes] IDIOM

몹시 화가 나서 눈에 핏대를 올리다 = to be so angry that the veins in one's eyes bulge out (*equiv.* for one's eyes to bulge in anger / for one's eyes to flash in anger) ▌A: 아까 봤어? 사장님한테 **눈에 쌍심지를 켜고** 대드는데, 내가 다 민망하더라니까. = *Did you see what happened earlier? His eyes flashed in anger and he kept talking back to the boss. It was such an awkward situation.* B: 김 과장님 그렇게 안 봤는데, 참 무서운 사람 같아요. = *I never would've thought Mr. Kim was that type of guy. I guess he's a scary guy.*

눈에 아른거리다 [Lit. to glimmer in one's eyes] IDIOM 전에 보았던 광경이나 대상이 자꾸 떠오르다 = for visions of something one has seen to continue to haunt one (*equiv.* for something to still haunt you / for an image to dance in one's head *syn.* 눈에 밟히다, 눈에 어리다, 눈앞에 아른거리다) ▌A: 얼마 전에 아빠가 되셨다죠? 축하합니다. = *I heard you're a new father. Congratulations.* B: 네, 감사합니다. 요즘에 아기 얼굴이 **눈에 아른거려서** 얼른 집에 가고 싶어 죽겠어요. = *Yeah, thanks. When I'm away from home, visions of my kids keep dancing in my head. I'm always dying to get home.*

눈에 안 차다 [Lit. to not fill one's eyes] IDIOM 흡족할 만큼 마음에 들지 않다 = to not be enough to satisfy someone (*equiv.* not suit one's fancy / to be less than satisfying / to not be up to snuff) ▌A: 아직도 못 골랐어? = *You still haven't decided?* B: 네. 이것저것 보기는 했는데, 다 **눈에 안 차네요**. = *I saw a few things, but nothing was really up to snuff.*

눈에 어리다 [Lit. to flicker in one's eyes] IDIOM 전에 보았던 광경이나 대상이 자꾸 떠오르다 = for images of something one has seen to keep popping into one's mind (*equiv.* (for images/thoughts) to keep popping into one's mind *syn.* 눈에 밟히다, 눈에 아른거리다) ▌A: 무슨 일 있어요? 눈가가 촉촉한 것 같은데. = *What's wrong? I see a little moisture around your eyes.* B: 오늘이 돌아가신 어머니 기일이에요. 어머니 생전의 모습이 **눈에 어리네요**. = *Today is the anniversary of my mother's death. I keep seeing her face in my mind.*

눈에 익다 [Lit. to be familiar to the eyes] IDIOM 많이 보아 친근하다 = for something to seem familiar because one has seen it many times (*equiv.* to be a familiar sight / to look familiar) ▌A: 이 편지는 누가 쓴 거야? 글씨가 **눈에 익은데**. = *Who wrote this letter? The handwriting looks so familiar.* B: 당신이 연애할 때 나한테 쓴 편지잖아요. 자기 글씨도 못 알아봐요? = *It's the letter you wrote to me back when we first fell in love. You can't even recognize your own handwriting?*

눈에 콩깍지가 씌다 [Lit. to wear bean pods (on one's eyes)] IDIOM 어떤

사람을 몹시 좋아하게 되어 다른 것은 신경쓰지 않다 = to like someone so much that one loses interest in all else (*equiv.* to be blinded by love / to see the world through rose-tinted glasses) ▌A: 우리 지호 씨 탤런트 장동건 닮지 않았니? = *Don't you think my Jiho looks just like the actor, Jang Donggeon.* B: 네가 **눈에 콩깍지가 단단히 씌었구나!** = *Wow, you really are seeing things through rose-tinted glasses.*

NOTE: 콩깍지를 벗기기 전에는 안에 들어 있는 콩이 잘 익었는지 알 수가 없다. 눈에 콩깍지가 씌면 상대를 객관적으로 보지 못하게 된다는 말이다. '콩깍지가 벗겨지다'라는 반대 표현도 쓴다.

Before removing the shell of a bean, it is impossible to know if the bean it contains is ripe or not. If someone's eyes are blinded by bean shells, it is impossible to gain an objective look at one's counterpart. The phrase 콩깍지가 벗겨지다 is also used to describe the removal of the proverbial "tinted glasses."

눈에 흙이 들어가다 [Lit. for dirt to go in one's eyes] IDIOM 죽다 = to die (*equiv.* to bite the dust / Over my dead body!) ▌A: 아빠가 뭐라고 하셔도 저는 그 사람하고 결혼할 거예요. = *Dad, I'm going to marry him no matter what you say!* B: 내 **눈에 흙이 들어가기** 전에는 절대로 안 된다. = *Over my dead body!*

NOTE: 주로 '내 눈에 흙이 들어가기 전에는'의 꼴로 쓰인다.

As seen in the example sentences, this phrase is often used like the expression "over my dead body" and is most commonly seen in the 내 눈에 흙이 들어가기 전에는 form.

눈엣가시 [Lit. a thorn in one's eye] IDIOM 몹시 미워 보기 싫은 사람 = a person that one dislikes to the point of feeling disgust at their sight (*equiv.* a thorn in one's side / a pain in the behind / an eyesore) ▌A: 김 상무님 퇴사하시는 거 알아요? = *Did you hear that Deputy Director Kim is leaving the company?* B: 그래요? 왜요? = *Really? Why?* A: 뻔하죠. 사장님하고 김 상무님 사이 안 좋은 건 유명하잖아요. 사장님으로서는 상무님이 **눈엣가시**였을 거예요. = *It's obvious, isn't it? He and the boss are on* *famously bad terms. Kim was like a thorn in the boss's side.*

***눈(을)감다** [Lit. to close one's eyes] IDIOM 1. 죽다 = to die (*equiv.* to close one's eyes for the final time) ▌A: 마음이 많이 아프시죠? = *You must be so sad.* B: 네. 하지만 할머니가 마음 편히 **눈을 감으셔서** 그래도 다행이에요. = *Yes, I am. But at least Grandma went peacefully.* 2. 남의 잘못을 모르는 체하다 = to pretend not to have seen the mistake of someone else (*equiv.* to look the other way / to overlook something) ▌A: 신호 위반하셨네요. 면허증 제시해 주세요. = *You failed to observe the traffic signal. Please hand me your driver's license.* B: 제발 한 번만 **눈감아** 주세요. 신호를 못 봤어요. = *Please overlook it just this once. I didn't see the signal.*

눈을 낮추다 [Lit. to lower one's eyes] IDIOM 이성이나 어떤 대상에 대한 기대 수준을 낮추다 = to lower one's expectations (*equiv.* to lower one's standards / to lower the bar *syn.* 눈높이를 낮추다 *ant.* 눈을 높이다 *cf.* 눈이 낮다) ▌A: 취직은 했니? = *Did you find a job?* B: 아직이요. 계속 원서 쓰고 있어요. = *No, not yet. I'm still filling out applications.* A: **눈을 좀 낮춰** 보는 건 어떠니? 중소기업도 좋은 데 많은데. = *What about lowering your expectations a little? There are a lot of great smaller companies out there too.*

눈을 높이다 [Lit. to raise one's eyes] IDIOM 이성이나 어떤 대상에 대한 기대 수준을 높이다 = to raise one's expectations (*equiv.* to raise one's standards / to raise the bar *syn.* 눈높이를 높이다 *ant.* 눈을 낮추다 *cf.* 눈이 높다) ▌A: 요즘에는 영화에서 신기한 장면이 나와도 별로 놀랍지가 않아요. = *I'm rarely amazed by movies anymore.* B: 아바타 같이 특수효과가 화려한 영화가 사람들 **눈을 높여** 놓은 때문이겠죠. = *That's because movies like "Avatar" really raised the bar for special effects.*

눈(을) 돌리다 [Lit. to turn one's eyes] IDIOM 관심을 옮기다 = to shift one's interest (*equiv.* to shift one's gaze) ▌A: 왜 너는 만날 돈 버는 거밖에 관심이 없니? 다른 문제에도 **눈을 돌려** 봐. = *Why are you only interested in making money? It's time you shifted your gaze to other matters.* B: 그럴 시간이 어딨어? 먹고살기도 바쁜데. = *Where I would find the* *time to do that? I'm already busy enough just trying to make a living.*

눈(을) 뜨고 볼 수(가) 없다 [Lit. to not be able to open one's eyes and watch] IDIOM 참혹하거나 민망하여 차마 볼 수가 없다＝to not be able to look at something because it is too tragic or embarrassing (*equiv.* to not be able to look at (something) / I can't look.) ▌A: 내일 동창회 나올 거지?＝*Are you going to the alumni meeting tomorrow?* B: 내가 거길 왜 나가?＝*Why would I go there?* A: 왜? 오랜만에 애들 얼굴 보고 좋잖아?＝*Why? To see everybody again, after so many years.* B: 야, 저번에 나가 보니까 애들 잘난 척하는 꼴 **눈을 뜨고 볼 수가 없더라**.＝*Hey, last time everyone was bragging about themselves so much it was hard to even watch.*

눈(을)뜨다 [Lit. to open one's eyes] IDIOM 잘 알지 못했던 분야의 이치를 깨닫다＝to realize a new concept or idea (*equiv.* to open one's eyes to (a new idea or concept) / to wake up to (a new idea)) ▌A: 우리 애 요즘 사춘기인가 봐. 말도 잘 안 듣고 외모에 신경을 부쩍 많이 써.＝*I think my kid has hit puberty. He doesn't listen to me and is awfully concerned with his appearance.* B: 원래 그 나이 때는 다 그래. 이성에 **눈을 뜨는** 시기잖아.＝*That's normal at his age. That's the time when their eyes are opened to the opposite sex.*

눈(을) 붙이다 [Lit. to shut one's eyes] IDIOM 자다＝to sleep (*equiv.* to get some shuteye) ▌A: 한두 시간이라도 잠깐 **눈 좀 붙이지** 그러니?＝*Why don't you at least get a few hours of shuteye.* B: 안 돼. 내일 시험인데 아직 책을 다 못 봤어.＝*No way. I've got a test tomorrow and I still haven't finished the book.*

눈(을) 씻고 보다 [Lit. to wash one's eyes and see] IDIOM 여러 차례 주의 깊게 보다＝to look at something carefully and many times over ▌A: 내 시계 찾았어?＝*Did you find my watch?* B: 아니, 못 찾았어. **눈을 씻고 봐도** 없던데.＝*No. No matter how hard I look, I just can't find it.*

눈을 의심하다 [Lit. to doubt one's eyes] IDIOM 믿어지지 않다＝to not be

able to believe something (*equiv.* to not be able to believe one's eyes / I can't believe my eyes. *cf.* 귀를 의심하다) ▌A: 오늘 수진 씨 봤어요?=*Did you see Sujin today?* B: 네, 정말 오늘은 딴 사람인 줄 알았어요.=*Yeah, I thought she was someone else.* A: 그러게요. 저도 처음 보는 순간 제 **눈을 의심했다니까요**.=*Me too. I couldn't believe my eyes at first.*

눈(을) 피하다 [Lit. to avoid someone's eyes] IDIOM 다른 사람이 보는 것을 피하다=to avoid being seen by others (*equiv.* to avoid someone) ▌A: 재석아, 나하고 얘기 좀 하자. 너 왜 요즘 내 **눈을 자꾸만 피해**?=*Jaeseok, let's have a little chat. It seems like you've been avoiding me recently.* B: 내가 그랬어? 아니야. 내가 왜 널 피하겠어?=*I did what? No way. Why would I avoid you?*

***눈이 낮다** [Lit. to have low eyes] IDIOM 이성이나 어떤 대상에 대한 기대 수준이 높거나 까다롭지 않다=to not have high standards pertaining to members of the opposite sex or other matters (*equiv.* to have low standards *syn.* 눈높이가 낮다 *ant.* 눈이 높다 *cf.* 눈을 낮추다) ▌A: 소연이는 왜 맨날 그런 놈들만 데려오는 거야?=*Why is Soyeon bringing those types around?* B: 아무래도 우리 딸이 **눈이 낮은가** 봐요.=*I guess our daughter just has low standards.*

***눈이 높다** [Lit. to have high eyes] IDIOM **1.** 이성이나 어떤 대상에 대한 기대 수준이 높고 까다롭다=to have high standards pertaining to members of the opposite sex or other matters (*equiv.* to have high standards / to set one's sights very high *syn.* 눈높이가 높다 *ant.* 눈이 낮다 *cf.* 눈을 높이다) ▌A: **눈이 높으신가** 봐요. 아직까지 결혼을 안 하신 걸 보니.=*Considering the fact that you still haven't gotten married, it looks like your standards must be pretty high.* B: 아니에요. 그냥 아직 짝을 못 만난 것뿐이에요.=*No, that's not it. I just haven't found my perfect match yet.* **2.** 안목이 높다=to have good taste (*equiv.* to have an eye (for luxury etc.) / to have expensive tastes *syn.* 보는 눈이 있다) ▌A: 이 옷 밍크인가요?=*Is this fur mink?* B: 네. 역시 사모님은 **눈이 높으시네요**. 저희 매장에서 제일 잘나가는 제품이에요.=*Yes, ma'am. You really do have quite the eye for luxury. This is one of our most popular items.*

눈(이) 뒤집히다 [Lit. to have one's eyes turned upside down] IDIOM 이성을 잃다 = to lose rationality at a shocking happening (*equiv.* to lose it / to lose one's temper) █ A: 아니, 어떻게 하다가 길거리에서 싸움을 하게 된 겁니까? = *How did you end up getting into a fight on the street like that?* B: 지나가다가 그 사람하고 살짝 부딪혔는데요, 그 사람이 먼저 욕을 하잖아요. 순간적으로 **눈이 뒤집혀서** 티격태격하게 됐습니다. = *I lightly grazed a man as I passed by and he just started cussing at me. I lost my temper and we exchanged blows.*

눈이 많다 [Lit. There are many eyes.] IDIOM 보는 사람이 많다 = for there to be many people watching (*equiv.* There are eyes everywhere.) █ A: 연예 인들은 사실 굉장히 피곤할 거야. = *Life must be very tiring for celebrities.* B: 맞아. 보는 **눈이 많으니까** 행동도 자유롭게 못 할 거 야, 아마. = *That's right, with people always watching, they must never be able to act freely.*

눈(이) 맞다 [Lit. for one's eyes to meet another's] IDIOM 이성 간에 사랑 하는 마음이 생긴 것을 속되게 표현하는 말 = a slang expression for falling in love (*equiv.* to fall for someone / to fall in love with someone *cf.* 전 기가 통하다) █ A: 내 사촌 영식이 알지? 얼마 전에 이혼했대. = *You know my cousin, Yeongshik, right? I heard he got divorced not too long ago.* B: 그래? 왜? 금슬 되게 좋았잖아. = *Really? Why? They seemed to have such a happy marriage.* A: 영식이 아내가 바람이 났대. 다른 남 자랑 **눈이 맞았다나** 봐. = *They're saying his wife had an affair. I guess she fell for some other guy.*

눈(이)멀다 [Lit. to have far-off eyes] IDIOM 어떤 것에 마음을 빼앗겨 판단력을 잃다 = to lose one's rationality due to avarice or lust (*equiv.* to lose oneself in something *syn.* 눈이 어둡다) █ A: 그런데 영호 왜 이번에 시 험 보러 안 왔어? = *But why didn't Youngho come to take the test this time?* B: 몰랐어? 걔 요즘 연애한다고 학교 거의 안 나와. = *You didn't hear? He's in the middle of a steamy romance, and he barely makes it to school anymore.* A: 완전히 사랑에 **눈이 멀었구먼**. = *He's really losing himself in that girl.*

눈이 벌겋다 [Lit. to have red eyes] IDIOM 자신의 이익을 좇아 열중하고 있는 모습을 묘사할 때 쓰는 말＝used to depict an intense passion in chasing after profit (*equiv.* till one's blue in the face / for one's eyes to be bloodshot (from overwork etc.) *syn.* 혈안이 되다) ▌A: 요즘 한솔이는 뭐 해?＝*What's Hansol up to lately?* B: 말도 마. 이번에 둘째 태어났잖아. 아기 분유 값 번다고 **눈이 벌게** 가지고 밤낮으로 일해.＝*Don't even ask. He just had his second kid. And now he's working night and day to come up with the money for baby formula.*

눈이 빠지도록 기다리다 [Lit. to wait until one's eyes pop out] IDIOM 몹시 애태우며 오랫동안 기다리다＝to wait for someone eagerly for a long time (*equiv.* to wait and wait / to wait in suspense / I've been waiting and waiting for you. *syn.* 목이 빠지도록 기다리다) ▌A: 뭐 때문에 이렇게 늦은 거야? **눈이 빠지도록 기다렸어**.＝*What kept you this late? I was waiting and waiting for you.* B: 미안, 미안. 눈 때문에 길이 너무 미끄러워서 뛸 수가 없었어.＝*Sorry. Sorry. The roads were slippery because of the snow and I couldn't run.*

눈이 삐다 [Lit. to twist one's eyes] IDIOM 어떤 대상에 대해 잘못된 판단을 내리다＝to make an erroneous judgment about someone (*equiv.* to not be seeing straight / What was I thinking?) ▌A: 야, 저기 저 여자 참 괜찮지 않냐?＝*Don't you think that girl over there is pretty all right?* B: 네가 **눈이 삐었구나**. 내가 보기에는 외모는 영 아닌데.＝*Are you not seeing straight? She sure doesn't look like much to me.*

눈이 어둡다 [Lit. to have dark eyes] IDIOM 어떤 것에 마음을 빼앗겨 판단력을 잃다＝to lose one's judgment because one is too deeply engrossed in a certain pursuit (*equiv.* to get lost in (a certain pursuit) *syn.* 눈(이)멀다) ▌A: 무엇 때문에 도둑질을 하게 되었습니까?＝*What was it that made you become a thief?* B: 제가 돈에 **눈이 어두워** 죄를 짓게 되었습니다. 죄송합니다.＝*I lost myself in my desire for money. I'm so very sorry.*

눈이 오나 비가 오나 IDIOM＝비가 오나 눈이 오나

눈총(을) 맞다 IDIOM = 눈총(을) 받다

눈총(을) 받다 [Lit. to be hit with eye guns] IDIOM 다른 사람에게 미움을 받다 = to be despised by others (*equiv.* to be glared at *syn.* 눈총(을) 맞다 *ant.* 눈총(을) 주다) ▌A: 야 딱 한잔만 더 하자. 내가 살게. = *Hey, let's just have one more drink. I'll buy.* B: 벌써 많이 마셨어. 괜히 늦게 들어가서 마누라한테 **눈총 받지** 말고 이만 들어가자. = *We've already had a lot. There's no need to head back late and get glared at by the wives. Let's just head home.*

눈총(을) 주다 [Lit. to give someone an eye gun] IDIOM 노려보아 미워하는 마음을 전하다 = to express distaste with a venomous look (*equiv.* to look daggers at someone / to glare at someone / to give someone a dirty look *ant.* 눈총(을) 받다) ▌A: 오늘 지하철에서 어떤 사람이 큰 소리로 통화를 하는 거야. 사람들이 **눈총을 주는데도** 모르는 체하고. = *Someone was talking really loudly on his cell phone on the subway today. People were giving him dirty looks, but he just pretended not to notice.* B: 예의가 없는 사람들이 너무 많아. = *There are so many rude people out there.*

눈칫밥(을) 먹다 [Lit. to eat while watching out of the corner of one's eyes] IDIOM 다른 집에 얹혀 살면서 기를 펴지 못하다 = to be awkwardly dependent on another for a place to live (*equiv.* to dine on someone else's dime) ▌A: 역시 영찬 씨는 눈치가 빨라. = *That's the Yeongchan I know—always very tactful.* B: 제가 어려서부터 **눈칫밥을 많이 먹어서** 눈치 하나는 빨라요. = *Ever since I was a child, I survived on the kindness of others, so I got used to being conscious of the feelings of others.*

*눈코 뜰 새(가) 없다 [Lit. to lack the time to open one's eyes and nose] IDIOM 아주 바쁘다 = to be too busy to do anything (*equiv.* to be as busy as a bee) ▌A: 요즘 많이 바쁘지? = *You're really busy these days, aren't you?* B: 네. 이번 주까지 끝내야 할 일이 있어서 **눈코 뜰 새가 없어요.** = *I have something I need to finish by this week, so I'm feeling a little overwhelmed.*

NOTE: 눈은 뜨고 감기를 반복하지만 코는 그럴 수 없다. 중심 의미는 눈에 있고 코는 단지 그 의미를 강조하기 위해 덧붙인 것에 불과하다. 코는 눈과 가장 위치가 가까운 감각기관이기 때문에 둘을 묶어서 생각한 것이다.

The eyes can be readily opened and closed again in repetition, but this is not the case for the nose. The original phrase was built around the eyes, i.e., "to lack even a moment to blink," and the nose part was just tacked on for good measure. The nose was probably chosen for the job because it is the closest sensory organ to the eyes.

눈 하나 깜짝 안 하다 IDIOM = 눈도 깜짝 안 하다

늦게 배운 도둑질에 날 새는 줄 모른다 [Lit. to not even notice the days go by as one (is lost in) belatedly learned thievery] PROVERB 뒤늦게 시작한 일에 크게 열중하다 = to be absorbed in a pursuit one has only recently begun ▌A: 아버지는 어디 가셨어요? = *Where did Dad go?* B: 네 아빠 요즘 등산 다니느라 얼굴 보기 힘들다. **늦게 배운 도둑질에 날 새는 줄 모른다더니** 뒤늦게 웬 등산이람. = *Your dad is out hiking so often I barely get to see him. I guess that's why they say it's easy to get wrapped up in a hobby picked up late in life. But what's with the hiking?*

늪에 빠지다 [Lit. to get lost in a swamp] IDIOM 헤어 나오기 어려운 상황에 처하다 = to find oneself in a situation that is hard to get out of (*equiv.* to be in a quagmire / to be stuck in a morass) ▌A: 아 언제쯤이면 경기가 좀 풀릴까? = *When is this economy going to get better?* B: 우리가 졸업할 때쯤이면 좀 상황이 나아져야 할 텐데. 일본처럼 불황의 **늪에 오래도록 빠지는** 건 아니겠지? = *I hope things will get better by the time we graduate. We're not going to end up stuck in a economic morass for the long term, are we?*

다다익선 [Lit. 多many + 多many + 益increasingly + 善good] CHINESE-DERIVATION 많으면 많을수록 좋다 = for more and more to be better (*equiv.* the more the better / the more the merrier) ▌A: 2세 계획은 어떻게 되세요? = *What are your plans for having kids?* B: 힘 닿는 데까지 낳으려고요. 자식은 **다다익선** 아니겠어요? = *I'll have as many as I can bear. When it comes to offspring, it's the more the merrier, isn't it?*

다람쥐 쳇바퀴 돌듯 [Lit. like a squirrel running in circles in a tread wheel] PROVERB 늘 같은 일을 되풀이하며 앞으로 나아가지 못하는 상황을 비유하는 말 = a metaphor for continuous quotidian repetition with no real advancement (*equiv.* like a hamster in a wheel) ▌A: **다람쥐 쳇바퀴 돌듯** 하루하루가 너무 똑같아. = *Every day is exactly the same. It's like I'm a hamster in a wheel.* B: 나도 그래. 어떤 때는 어제 일이 오늘 일 같다니까. = *Same here. Sometimes I can't even remember if something happened yesterday or today.*

다른 게 아니라 [Lit. It's not something else.] IDIOM 말의 용건이나 이유를 본격적으로 설명하기 전에 하는 말 = used right before getting to the point (*equiv.* The reason I'm calling is ... / I'm here to ... *syn.* 다름(이) 아니라) ▌A: 무슨 용건으로 오셨습니까? = *What business brings you here today?* B: **다른 게 아니라** 뭐 좀 여쭤 볼 게 있어서 왔습니다. = *I'm actually here to ask a few questions.*

다름(이) 아니라 IDIOM = 다른 게 아니라

다름(이) 아닌 [Lit. It's not something else.] IDIOM 뒤이어 설명하는 대상

을 강조하기 위한 말＝used to emphasize the object of the following explanation (*equiv.* none other than / no other than) ▌A: 얼마 전 세상을 충격에 빠뜨린 살인 사건의 범인이 **다름 아닌** 피해자의 아들로 밝혀져 다시 한번 충격을 주고 있습니다.＝*The murder that shocked the world has dealt the public yet another shock as it was revealed this morning that the perpetrator was none other than the victim's son.* B: 범인은 오늘 아침 경찰서에 출두해 자백을 했습니다.＝*The son visited a police station today to confess to the crime.*

다리(를) 놓다 [Lit. to put (down) a bridge] IDIOM 중간에 끼여서 두 대상에 관계를 맺어 주다＝to build a connection between two parties (*equiv.* to build a bridge between two people / to hook up two people) ▌A: 우와, 저 아가씨는 누구냐?＝*Wow, who's that girl over there?* B: 응, 내 사촌 영미야.＝*That's my cousin, Yeongmi.* A: 아, 그래? 정말 괜찮네. **다리 좀 놓아 줘.**＝*Oh, really? She's really all right. Could you hook us up?*

다리야 날 살려라 IDIOM＝걸음아 날 살려라

다반사 [Lit. 茶tea + 飯meal + 事work → the act of drinking tea and eating] CHINESE-DERIVATION 늘 있는 일＝the quotidian events of daily life (*equiv.* one's everyday life) ▌A: 여보, 민식이가 오늘 또 싸웠어요. 뭐 되려고 맨날 싸움질인지 모르겠어요.＝*Honey, Minshik got into another fight today. I don't know what he's going to do with himself, fighting every day like that.* B: 사내 아이들이야 싸움쯤이야 **다반사**지 뭐. 그러면서 크는 거 아니겠어요?＝*They are young men. It's commonplace. Isn't that part of growing up?*

다사다난하다 [Lit. 多much + 事work + 多much + 難difficult + 하다 adjectival suffix] CHINESE-DERIVATION 여러 가지 일도 많고 어려움도 많다＝to have much work and many difficulties (*equiv.* to be overwhelmed / to be under great strain) ▌A: 벌써 한 해가 다 끝나 가네.＝*One more year is already drawing to a close.* B: 시간 정말 빠르지? 참 **다사다난한** 한 해였는데.＝*Time sure flies, huh? But it was an eventful year for sure.*

다재다능하다 [Lit. 多many + 才gift + 多many + 能ability + 하다adjectival suffix → to have many gifts and many abilities] CHINESE-DERIVATION 재주가 많고 능력이 뛰어나다 = to be very capable and have many talents (*equiv.* to be gifted) ▌A: 제가 교편을 잡은 지 20년이 됐는데, 영진이만큼 **다재다능한** 아이는 처음입니다. = *I've been a teacher now for 20 years and I've never seen a child as gifted as Yeongjin.* B: 선생님께서 잘 좀 지도해 주세요. = *Please teach her well.*

다정다감하다 [Lit. 多much + 情affection + 多much + 感feel + 하다 adjectival suffix → to feel much affection and deep feelings] CHINESE-DERIVATION 정이 많고 감성도 풍부하다 = to have deep compassion and an abundance of emotions (*equiv.* to be a person of sentiment / to be passionate) ▌A: 이상형이 어떻게 되세요? = *Tell me about your ideal mate.* B: 저는 **다정다감한** 사람이 좋아요. = *I really like deep, passionate people.*

단도직입(적) [Lit. 單single + 刀knife + 直straight + 入enter → a stab with a single knife] CHINESE-DERIVATION 에둘러 표현하지 않고 요점을 곧바로 말하는 것 = getting quickly to one's main point (*equiv.* to get right to the heart of the matter / to cut to the chase / to be frank *cf.* 말(을) 돌리다) ▌A: **단도직입적**으로 말씀드리겠습니다. 김성수 씨는 이번 일에 어울리지 않는 분 같습니다. = *I'm just going to be frank with you, this job doesn't seem to be a good fit for you.* B: 네, 무슨 말씀이신지 알겠습니다. 그동안 감사했습니다. = *Yes, I understand what you're saying. It was a pleasure working with you.*

단맛 쓴맛 다 보다 IDIOM = 쓴맛 단맛 다 보다

달걀로 바위 치기 PROVERB = 계란으로 바위 치기

달달 볶다 [Lit. to roast] IDIOM 괴롭히다 = to bother someone (*equiv.* to nag someone / to be on someone's back (about something) *syn.* 들들 볶다) ▌A: 주말에는 잘 쉬셨어요? = *Did you have a restful weekend?* B: 주말 내내 아내가 **달달 볶아** 대서 쉬어도 쉰 것 같지가 않아요. = *The whole weekend, my wife kept nagging me about this and that. So it doesn't really* *seem like I rested at all.*

NOTE: 콩을 볶듯 사람을 불 위에 올려 놓았다고 생각해 보라. Envisioning a fully roasted bean will give you an idea of what this expression is all about.

달도 차면 기운다 [Lit. Even the moon wanes when it is full.] PROVERB 무엇이나 흥할 때가 있으면 쇠할 때가 있기 마련이라는 말 = Everything has its ups and downs. (*equiv.* Every flow has its ebb. / just as the moon waxes and wanes *syn.* 오르막이 있으면 내리막이 있다) ▌A: 천하를 호령하던 선수가 이제 저런 신인 선수한테도 지다니. 참 나이는 속일 수가 없네요. = *An athlete who once brought the world to its knees now is beaten by a rookie like that? Everyone really does get old.* B: 달도 차면 기우는 법이죠. = *Even the moon waxes and wanes.*

⬧p.119

달면 삼키고 쓰면 뱉는다 [Lit. if it's sweet it gets swallowed; if it's bitter it gets spit out] PROVERB 다른 사람을 대함에 있어 자신의 이익만을 생각하는 야비한 태도를 비난하는 말 = a pejorative for people who only seek their own benefit in relationships with others (*equiv.* to chew someone up and spit them out) ▌A: 정치인들 참 무섭지 않아? 간이라도 빼 줄 것처럼 굴 때는 언제고 지금은 저렇게 모질게 돌아서다니. = *Politicians sure are a scary bunch of people, aren't they? They always act as if they'd give up their first born if you so much as asked but now look at how heartless they can be.* B: 원래 정치라는 게 달면 삼키고 쓰면 뱉는 그런 거잖아. = *Politics is a game of chewing people up and spitting them out.*

⬧p.34

달밤에 체조하다 [Lit. to do gymnastics on a moonlit night] IDIOM 상황에 어울리지 않는 행동을 하다 = to do something that does not match the setting (*equiv.* to do something that's out of left field / to do something that is out of place) ▌A: 야, 우리 잠도 안 오는데 노래방이나 갈까? = *Hey, since we can't sleep, what about going out for karaoke?* B: 얘가 갑자기 달밤에 체조를 하고 그래? 내일 나 일찍 출근해야 해. = *That's out of leftfield. I have to get up early tomorrow morning and go to work.*

닭 잡아먹고 오리발 내민다 [Lit. to catch and eat a chicken and then present a duck foot] PROVERB 자신의 잘못을 인정하지 않고 엉뚱한 수작으로 넘어 가려는 얄팍한 태도를 비판하는 말 = to not admit to one's own mistakes and try instead to move past the issue with a transparent trick (*equiv.* to play innocent / to play dumb / to put on an act *cf.* 오리발(을) 내밀다) ▌A: 하여튼 정치인들은 믿을 수가 없어. 선거 때는 지키지도 못할 약속을 해 놓고 당선되고 나던 시치미를 뗀다니까. = *Anyhow, you just can't trust politicians They go around campaigning with promises they can never keep and then when they get elected, they just play dumb.* B: 그러게. **닭 잡아먹고 오리발 내미**는 격이지. = *That's right. They just put on an act and pretend like they don't remember.*

NOTE: 다른 사람이 자신의 닭을 잡아먹은 것을 알고는 찾아가 따지자, 엉뚱하게도 내가 먹은 것은 닭이 아니라 오리라며 그 증거로 미리 준비한 오리발을 내미는 상황이다. 상대가 거짓말을 하고 있다는 것을 알지만 상대가 작정하고 자신을 속이려고 할 때는 증명하기가 쉽지 않은 법이다. This expression depicts a scenario in which a man's chicken has been stolen and eaten by another. When the owner of the chicken finds the culprit, the accused presents a duck foot as proof that the bird he recently consumed was not a chicken but a duck. When you know someone is lying, but they have it in mind to deceive you, proving one's case is never easy.

닭 쫓던 개 지붕 쳐다본다 [Lit. A dog that was chasing a rooster is left gazing at the roof.] PROVERB 애써 하던 일이 실패로 돌아가다 = to feel frustration after finding out one's efforts were futile (*equiv.* It was an exercise in futility.) ▌A: 최정희 씨, 영업팀 김 대리랑 결혼한대요. = *I heard Ms. Choi Junghee is going to get married to Mr. Kim from the sales division.* B: 허허, 우리 팀 박 대리가 그렇게 쫓아다녔는데. **닭 쫓던 개 지붕 쳐다보**는 신세가 돼 버렸네. = *Oh, Mr. Park from our team worked so hard to win her over. What a colossal waste of time that turned out to be for him.*

NOTE: 개에게 쫓기던 닭이 지붕 위로 올라가 버렸다. 닭처럼 날 수 없는 개는 어쩔 수 없이 지붕만 쳐다볼 뿐 어떻게 할 방법이 없다.

A chicken ran up on the roof to escape a dog that was chasing it. Being unable to leap as high as the wing-aided chicken, the dog is left with no choice but to stare helplessly at the bird from below.

담(을)쌓다 [Lit. to build a wall] IDIOM 전혀 관계하지 않다 = to have no relationship or connection (to a person or field) (*equiv.* to be cut off from something or someone / to steer clear of something *syn.* 벽(을) 쌓다) ▌A: 혹시 이 문제 아시겠어요? = *Do you happen to know the answer to this question?* B: 아, 저는 고등학교 이후로 영어하고는 **담을 쌓고** 살아서요. = *Oh, I'm afraid I've steered clear of English since high school.*

당근과 채찍 [Lit. a carrot and a stick] IDIOM 회유책과 강경책 = a policy of threats and reward (*equiv.* the carrot and the stick) ▌A: 김 선생, 김 선생 반 아이들 성적이 그렇게 좋은 비결이 뭐야? = *Mr. Kim, what's your secret for getting your students to get such good grades?* B: 잘하면 상을 주고 못하면 혼내는 거죠 뭐. = *I just give rewards to those who perform and scold those who don't.* A: **당근과 채찍**, 이거군. = *Sounds like the old carrot-and-stick policy to me.*

NOTE: carrot and stick이라는 영어 표현에서 유래했다.
This phrase originates in the English expression "carrot and stick."

대가리에 피도 안 마르다 IDIOM = 머리에 피도 안 마르다

대기만성 [Lit. 大big + 器vessel + 晩late + 成accomplish → The big vessel takes long to complete.] CHINESE-DERIVATION 남들보다 더 오랜 시간이 흐른 뒤에 능력을 발휘함 = to finally exhibit one's abilities long after others (*equiv.* to be a late bloomer) ▶p.327 ▌A: 저 가수는 오랫동안 빛을 못 보다가 이제야 인기를 얻는군. = *That singer is just now getting popular after being a no-name singer for so long.* B: **대기만성**인 거지 뭐. = *I guess he was a late bloomer.*

대동소이하다 [Lit. 大big + 同same + 小small + 異different + 하다

adjectival suffix → to be mostly similar with few differences] CHINESE-DERIVATION 전체적으로는 같고 작은 차이가 있다 = to be almost completely the same with just some small differences (*equiv.* to be practically identical *syn.* 거기서 거기, 그놈이 그놈이다, 오십보백보, 그 나물에 그 밥) █A: 이것보다 좀 밝은 색은 없나요? = *Don't you have anything brighter than this?* B: 그럼 여기 이 색깔은 어떠세요? = *Well, what about this?* A: 음 ……. **대동소이하네요**. = *Well ... it seems just about the same to me.*

***대박(을) 터뜨리다** [Lit. to blow up the jackpot] IDIOM 어떤 일이 크게 성공하다 = to achieve a major success (*equiv.* to hit the jackpot) █A: 이 영화 완전히 **대박 터뜨린** 셈이지? 벌써 관객이 100만이 넘었으니까 말이야. = *They really hit the jackpot with this movie, huh? I mean, since they've already topped more than a million viewers.* B: 그럼, 이런 기세면 얼마 안 있어 200만도 넘길 것 같아. = *That's right, if this level of intensity keeps up, it won't be long until they've hit two million.*

NOTE: 대박은 어떤 일이 크게 이루어짐을 비유적으로 이르는 말이다. 이 말의 어원은 정확하게 알려져 있지 않고 몇 가지 설이 있다. 먼저, 큰 배를 의미하는 대박(大舶)에서 왔다는 설이 있다. 큰 배가 항구에 들어온다는 것은 물고기나 교역을 위한 물건들이 대거 들어오는 것을 의미하므로 큰 이득과 관련이 있을 수 있다. 또 노름 용어인 박과 관련이 있다고 보는 설도 있다. 노름에서 박은 판돈을 배팅한 횟수를 세는 단위이다. 대박은 여러 번 배팅이 오고 가 판돈이 커진 것을 말하고 대박이 터졌다는 것은 그 판돈을 누군가가 가져갔다는 의미가 된다는 것이다. 재미있는 것은 최근 젊은 층에서 '대박'이라는 말이 아주 황당한 일을 묘사할 때도 쓰인다는 점이다. 예를 들어, "소정이 있잖아, 남자 친구랑 헤어진 지 두 달만에 다른 남자랑 결혼한대. 완전 대박이야."와 같이 쓸 수 있다.
대박 is used as a metaphor for a major success. The precise origin of the phrase is unclear, but there are two stories on how it came to be. One says that the phrase came from 대박(大舶), or "large ship." When a large ship came into the port, there was much money to be made with all the fish and other commodities to trade that it would bring. There is also the story that it came from gambling terminology. In gambling, a 박 is a word used to count

the rounds of betting that have gone into building the pot. A 대박 therefore, would be a large pot that had been built up through many rounds of betting. 대박 터지다 would then mean that someone had taken the pot. An interesting thing about this expression is how the youngsters have, as of late, coopted this word and transformed its usage to include happenings that are more surprising than positive. Here's an example: "소정이 있잖아, 남자 친구랑 헤어진 지 두 달만에 다른 남자랑 결혼한대. 완전 대박이야." (You know, Sojeong? I heard she's marrying some guy just two months after breaking up with her last boyfriend. That's crazy.)

***대박(이) 나다** [Lit. for a jackpot to happen] IDIOM 어떤 일이 크게 성공하다 = for an endeavor to be met with major success (*equiv.* to hit the jackpot / (slang) to blow up *syn.* 대박(이) 터지다) ▌A: 가게 오픈하셨다죠? 얘기 들었습니다. **대박 나시길** 바랍니다. = *I heard you started up a business, right? I heard all about it. I hope it's a major success.* B: 감사합니다. 잘돼야 될 텐데 걱정이네요. = *Thanks. I've really got to succeed this time. I'm feeling a little worried.*

NOTE: See the note on 대박(을) 터뜨리다.

***대박(이) 터지다** IDIOM = 대박(이) 나다

대성통곡(하다) [Lit. 大 big + 聲 sound + 痛 painful + 哭 cry] CHINESE-DERIVATION 큰소리를 내어 슬프게 울다 = to cry out with sadness (*equiv.* to wail) ▌A: 선희한테 갔다 왔어? = *Did you go see Seonhee?* B: 응, 어제. 선희 어머님이 **대성통곡을 하시더라**. 나까지 눈물이 나와서 참느라 혼났어. = *Yeah, yesterday. Her mom was wailing so much it was hard to stop myself from crying too.*

대어를 건지다 IDIOM = 대어를 낚다

대어를 낚다 [Lit. to catch a big fish] IDIOM 큰 성과를 올리거나 중요한 사람을 데려오다 = to accomplish big projects or to gain great items or persons (*equiv.* to land a whale / to catch a big one *syn.* 대어를 건지다, 월척을 낚다, 월척을 건지다) ▮A: 이번에 우리 팀에 김현주 선수가 들어왔대. =*Kim Hyeonju will be joining our team.* B: 정말? 이번 시즌 최고의 유망주잖아. =*Really? He is the most promising player this season.* A: 그렇지. **대어를 낚은** 셈이네. =*That's right. We've really landed a whale this time.*

NOTE: 대어는 큰 물고기를 말한다. 여기에서는 큰 인물이나 일을 비유하는 말로 쓰였다.

대어 is the Korean word for "big fish." Its role here is that of a stand-in for a very important person or business venture.

더도 덜도 말고 [Lit. neither more nor less] IDIOM 딱 이 정도만 =just the proper amount (*equiv.* no more, no less / to be just right) ▮A: 오늘 정말 날씨 좋네요. 어디 놀러 가기 딱 좋겠어요. =*It's nice weather. It would be a perfect day to get out of the house.* B: **더도 말고 덜도 말고,** 늘 날씨가 오늘만 같았으면 좋겠어요. =*It's just right. I wish it was always like this.*

*더위(를) 먹다 [Lit. to eat the heat] IDIOM 더위에 지쳐서 몸에 기운이 없거나 정신이 없다 =to feel sick and exhausted due to the heat (*equiv.* to suffer from heatstroke) ▮A: 왜 음식을 이렇게 많이 남기셨어요? =*Why did you leave so much food on your plate?* B: 어젯밤 열대야였잖아요. 밤새 **더위 먹었나** 봐요. 입맛이 별로 없어요. =*Last night was another one of those "tropical nights." I think I've got heatstroke. I don't have much of an appetite.*

덜미(를) 잡다 [Lit. to grab (someone) by] IDIOM 꼼짝 못하게 하다 =to not allow someone to move (*equiv.* to paralyze someone / to render someone impotent *cf.* 덜미(를) 잡히다) ▮A: 정말 이 후보는 이번 선거에서 아깝게 됐어. =*This election sure turned out badly for that candidate.* B: 누가 아니래? 아들 병역 문제가 **덜미를 잡을** 줄 생각이나 했겠어? =*That's what I'm talking about. How could anyone have known that the issue of his son's military service was going to paralyze him like that?*

덜미(를) 잡히다 [Lit. to be seized by the back of one's neck] IDIOM 못된 일을 꾸미다 들키다 = to be found out in the midst of a bad deed (*equiv.* to be caught red-handed / to be caught by the scruff of one's neck *cf.* 덜미(를) 잡다) ▌A: 네 지갑 훔쳐 간 사람 잡았다며? = *Did they catch the person who stole your wallet?* B: 응. 내 신용카드로 물건을 사다가 **덜미를 잡혔어**. = *Yeah, he was caught red-handed when he tried to buy something with my credit card.*

덤터기(를) 쓰다 [Lit. to take on the burden] IDIOM 남에게서 누명이나 큰 걱정거리를 얻게 되다 = to have a false charge leveled at one or to be burdened with a major concern (*equiv.* to take the blame / to take the fall / to get stuck with something *cf.* 바가지(를) 쓰다, 덤터기(를) 씌우다) ▌A: 아, 괜히 총무는 맡아서 이 고생이네. = *Taking on the role of treasurer has been nothing but trouble.* B: 그러게 말이야. 당신이 **덤터기 쓴 거야**. = *That's what I'm saying. It's too bad they stuck you with it.*

NOTE: '덤터기'의 '덤'은 '두엄(거름)'을 가리키는 방언으로 보인다. 뜻하지 않은 사고로 인해 거름을 머리에 뒤집어썼으니 얼마나 재수가 없는 일인가!

The 덤 in this expression appears to be a regionalism for 두엄 or 거름 (manure). It goes without saying that ending up with manure on one's head due to someone else's accident would be an unforgettably bad experience.

덤터기(를) 씌우다 [Lit. to place the burden on someone else] IDIOM 다른 사람에게 누명이나 큰 걱정거리를 떠넘기다 = to level a false charge at someone else or place a major burden on them (*equiv.* to stick someone (with a burden, blame or undesirable task) *cf.* 바가지(를) 씌우다, 덤터기(를) 쓰다) ^{→p.192} ▌A: 어제 수업 땡땡이치자고 한 건 너였잖아! = *You're the one who suggested we skip out on class yesterday!* B: 아니, 얘가 지금 누구한테 **덤터기 씌우는 거야**? = *Just who are you trying to stick with the blame right now?*

NOTE: See the note on 덤터기(를) 쓰다.

덫에 걸리다 [Lit. to be caught in a trap] IDIOM 함정에 빠지거나 어려운 상황에 처하다 = to fall into a trap or face a difficult situation (*equiv.* to be ensnared / to be entrapped / to hit a snag *syn.* 덫에 빠지다) ▌A: 놈이 우리가 쳐 놓은 **덫에 걸렸으니** 이제 놈을 잡는 건 시간 문제입니다. = *He has fallen into our trap. Now it's just a matter of time before we catch him.* B: 그래, 이제 됐어. 그래도 마음 놓지 말자고. = *That's right. It's almost done. But it's still too soon to let down your guard.*

덫에 빠지다 IDIOM = 덫에 걸리다

도가 트다 [Lit. for one's Tao to be clear] IDIOM 어느 방면에 매우 뛰어나다 = to excel in a certain area ▌A: 경민이 손 좀 봐. 손이 안 보여. 완전히 **도가 텄어**. = *Look at Gyeongmin's hands. They're a complete blur. He's achieved enlightenment.* B: 밤낮으로 게임만 했으니 그럴 법도 하지. = *Playing games all day and night will do that to you.*

도둑이 제 발 저리다 [for the thief to have numb feet] PROVERB 잘못을 숨기고 있는 사람이 공연히 남이 자신을 책망하는 듯한 생각이 들어 지레 발끈할 때 쓰는 말 = Somebody who commits a wrong feels pangs of guilt. (*equiv.* A guilty conscience needs no accuser. *cf.* 오금이 저리다) ▌A: 명호야, 여기 있던 내 돈 네가 가져갔니? = *Myeongho, did you take the money that was here?* B: 우와, 누나는 왜 무턱대고 날 의심해? 내가 안 가져갔어! = *Ha! Why do you always start by accusing me? I didn't take it!* A: 그냥 물어본 건데 왜 화는 내니? **도둑이 제 발 저리는** 거 아냐? = *I'm just asking. Why are you freaking out like that? Is your conscience getting to you?*

NOTE: 불편한 자세로 오래 앉아 있으면 발이 저린 법이다. 죄를 지어 마음이 불편한 도둑이 시간이 지나면서 마치 몸이 불편한 것처럼 발이 저리게 된다는 뜻이다.
Sitting for a long time in an awkward position is bound to put your feet to sleep. A thief who commits a crime is likely to feel pangs of guilt and this idiom suggests that his discomfort may cause his feet to fall asleep.

도둑질을 해도 손발이 맞아야 한다 [Lit. Even in thievery feet and hands have to line up.] PROVERB 무슨 일이든 하는 사람끼리 서로 뜻이 맞아야 쉽게 할 수 있다는 말 = No matter what the task is, the people doing it must be in sync. (*cf.* 손발이 맞다) ▌A: 아, 그런데 방금 그게 무슨 말이야? = *Oh, but what was that you just said?* B: 이거 원, **도둑질을 해도 손발이 맞아야 하는** 건데 척하면 알아들어야지. = *Hey, if we're going to work together, we have to be in sync. You've got to understand what I say, when I say it.*

도랑 치고 가재 잡기 [Lit. clearing the creek and (still) catching a crawfish] PROVERB 한 가지 일로 두 가지 이상의 이익을 보게 될 때 쓰는 말 = used when one achieves two positive outcomes by way of a single effort (*equiv.* to have one's cake and eat it too / to kill two birds with one stone *syn.* 꿩 먹고 알 먹기, 임도 보고 뽕도 딴다, 일거양득, 일석이조) ▌A: 악! 이게 뭐야? 너는 왜 집에서 지렁이를 키워? = *Yuck! What's this? Why are you raising worms at home?* B: 아, 지렁이가 음식쓰레기 분해해 주잖아. 쓰레기 문제도 해결하고 거기에 비료까지 만들어지니 이거야말로 **도랑 치고 가재 잡기야**. = *Ah, worms help the food trash decompose. They solve the trash problem and make fertilizer too. It's like having your cake and eating it too.*

NOTE: 도랑이란 작고 좁은 개울을 말한다. 논농사에서는 물을 대고 빼는 것이 중요하기 때문에 물이 잘 흐르도록 도랑을 쳐서 물길을 만든다. 도랑을 친다는 것은 이렇게 도랑을 파서 물길을 내는 것을 말한다. 도랑을 치면 돌멩이 밑이나 진흙 속에 몸을 숨기고 있던 가재들이 눈에 쉽게 드러나게 된다. 그래서 도랑을 치면서 동시에 눈에 띄는 가재도 잡아 부가적인 성과를 거둔다는 표현이 생겨났다.

A 도랑 is a small creek. In rice farming, filling up the paddy with water and then lowering the water level is very important. That's why the creek had to be cleared out in order for the water to flow smoothly. 도랑 치다 means to clear our the creek bed of any obstructions. In this process, crawfish that were hiding under rocks on the creek floor can suddenly be seen scurrying away. That's why this phrase is used to describe a single action that yields two positive outcomes.

도로 아미타불 IDIOM = 십년공부 도르 아미타불

도마 위에 오르다 [Lit. to be put on the cutting board] IDIOM 어떤 사람이 다른 사람들로부터 비판의 대상이 되다 = to become a target of negative talk or criticism (*equiv.* to be in the hot seat / to be in hot water / to be on the chopping block) ▌A: 그 가수 말이야. 이번에 발표한 곡이 또 표절 문제로 **도마 위에 올랐다며**? = *You know that one singer? Did you hear that a plagiarism controversy surrounding his latest song has him in hot water again?* B: 응. 벌써 몇 번째야? 아직 정신을 못 차렸나 봐. = *Yeah. How many times has it been? I guess he still hasn't wised up.*

NOTE: 도마는 생선 따위를 올려놓고 칼로 손질하는 도구이다. 사람이 도마 위에 올랐다는 것은 마치 칼질을 기다리는 생선처럼 다른 사람들의 비판의 대상이 되었다는 뜻이다.
A 도마, is the chopping block that butchers use to prepare meat. Like a fish being sliced up on the cutting board, people who are on the receiving end of stinging criticism can be described with this phrase.

도매금으로 넘기다 [Lit. to sell (something) at a wholesale price] IDIOM 각각이 차이가 있음에도 같은 무리로 취급 받을 때 쓰는 말 = used when an entire group is treated alike despite clear differences among them (*equiv.* to be lumped together) ▌A: 이 물건 또 말썽이야. 이 회사 제품들은 하나같이 문제야. = *There's a problem with this product again. Everything that this company makes is a problem.* B: 너무 **도매금으로 넘기는** 거 아니니? 나는 그 회사 물건 괜찮던데. = *Aren't you kind of lumping it all together there? I've found their merchandise to be just fine.*

도시락 싸 가지고 다니면서 말린다 [Lit. to wrap up a lunch and attempt to dissuade someone] IDIOM 기를 쓰고 하지 못하게 말린다는 말 = to put great effort into dissuading someone from a certain course of action ▌A: 요 앞에 새로 생긴 식당 가 봤어? 오늘 거기서 점심 먹을까? = *Have you been to that new restaurant over there? What about eating lunch over there today?* B: 내가 그저께 가 봤는데, 정말로 맛없어. 누가 간다고 하면 **도시락 싸 갖고 다니면서 말리고** 싶을 정도야. = *I tried*

it out the other day, and it's terrible. It's so bad, whenever anyone says they're going there, I try to dissuade them till I'm blue in the face.

도장(을) 찍다 [Lit. to stamp with one's seal] IDIOM **1.** 계약하다 = to sign a contract (*equiv.* to ink a contract) ▮A: 박찬호 선수가 결국 연봉 10억 원에 **도장을 찍었대**. = *I heard Park Chanho finally signed a deal for a 1 billion won per year.* B: 우와, 10억 원 구경이라도 해 봤으면 좋겠다. = *Wow, I'd be satisfied just to see what one billion won looks like.* **2.** 이혼하다 = to divorce (*equiv.* to make it official) ▮A: 옆집 부부 결국 이혼한대요. = *I heard the couple next door finally got a divorce.* B: 매일같이 싸우더니 결국 **도장을 찍는구먼**. = *Well, they were constantly fighting. I guess they finally made it official.* **3.** 마음에 드는 물건이나 사람을 제 것이라고 마음속으로 정하여 두다 = to make something one's own (*equiv.* to call (something, someone) / to claim) ▮A: 이번 신입생 중에 신애 말이야. 정말 예쁘지 않아? 어떻게 번호 좀 알 수 없을까? = *You know that new freshman girl, Shinae? Isn't she pretty? How do you think I can get her number?* B: 야, 꿈도 꾸지 마. 내가 벌써 **도장 찍어 놨어**. = *Dream on. I've already claimed her.*

도토리 키 재기 [Lit. (it's like) measuring the height of an acorn] PROVERB 능력이나 크기 따위가 대단하지 않고 비슷비슷한 사람들끼리 서로 다툴 때 쓰는 말 = used when two contenders of no remarkable skill or size vie for position. (*equiv.* No one really stands out. / to be underwhelming) ▮A: 이번에 괜찮은 신인이 들어왔나요? = *Did we get anyone good this time?* B: 한 선수만 빼고는 다 **도토리 키 재기**예요. = *One's all right, but the rest are certainly underwhelming.*

NOTE: See the note on 막상막하.

독불장군 [Lit. 獨alone + 不no + 將general + 軍military] CHINESE-DERIVATION **1.** 무슨 일이든 자기 멋대로 처리하는 사람 = someone who does what they wish in all endeavors (*equiv.* to be as stubborn as a mule / to be a maverick) ▮A: 아버지도 늙으셨나 봐. 젊었을 때는 **독불장군**처럼 엄마한테 큰소리치셨는데, 언제부터인가 엄마 입김이 더 세졌

➡p.459

어. = *It looks like Dad's getting old. In his younger days, he would stand up to Mom with the stubbornness of a mule. But then one day, hers became the louder voice.* B: 맞아. 우리 아빠 좀 안돼 보여. = *You're right. He's starting to look a little pitiful.* **2.** 따돌림을 받는 외로운 사람 = ostracization from a group (*equiv.* to be an outcast) █A: 이 사람은 참 말년이 비참하군. = *This man's final days sure were pitiful.* B: 병원에서 찾아 주는 사람 하나 없이 **독불장군**으로 지내다 죽었다지? = *They say no one visited him in the hospital and he died a loner, huh?*

독수공방하다 [Lit. 獨alone + 守keep + 空empty + 房room + 하다verbal suffix ⟶ to keep an empty home] CHINESE-DERIVATION 아내가 남편이 없이 혼자 지내다 = for a wife to be home alone without her husband (*equiv.* to be home alone / to keep an empty nest) █A: 영자야, 내일 우리 집에 놀러 와. = *Yeongja, come over to our place tomorrow.* B: 내일? 네 남편 있지 않아? = *Tomorrow? Isn't your husband going to be there?* A: 그 사람 해외 출장 가서 요즘 나 **독수공방하고** 있어. = *He's overseas on business so I'm home alone for a while.*

독 안에 든 쥐 [Lit. a mouse in a pot] IDIOM 궁지에서 벗어날 수 없는 처지 = isolation or being caught in a circumstance impossible to escape (*equiv.* to be a mouse in a trap *syn.* 그물에 든 고기) █A: 이 근방을 철통같이 지키고 있으니 범인이 달아날 곳은 없습니다. = *With the wall of defense we have put up in this area, it is impossible that the perpetrator will evade us.* B: 그렇다면 녀석은 이제 **독 안에 든 쥐**군. = *If that's true, he's just like a mouse in a trap now.*

NOTE: 우리나라의 시골집들은 마당에 장독이나 쌀독 등 독 안에 음식을 보관해 둔다. 그 때문에 쥐가 몰래 독 안에 들어가 음식을 먹는 수가 많았다. 가끔은 쥐가 독 안에 들어가 있는 상태에서 갇혀 나오지 못해 봄에 독을 열었을 때 발견되는 경우도 있었다.
In the Korea of old, food was stored in large crocks. Many mice often ventured into the pots trying to get a bite to eat. If the lid was put back while the mouse was still inside, the mouse would be trapped until people again opened the pots in the spring and discovered its lifeless body.

독을 품다 [Lit. to hold poison] IDIOM 모진 마음을 먹다 = for one's heart to harden with purpose (*equiv.* (to carry out a certain action) like crazy *syn.* 칼을 갈다) ▌A: 강철이 정말 대단하지 않아? 어떻게 그 시험을 준비한 지 3개월 만에 합격할 수가 있지? = *Gangcheol sure is something, huh? How was he able to pass that test with only three months' preparation?* B: 걔 가 좀 독한 구석이 있잖아. 이번에도 **독을 품고** 공부하더니 기어 이 해내는 거 봐. = *He has an intense side to him. Once again, his relentless approach to studying made it possible for him in the end.*

독(이) 오르다 [Lit. for the poison to rise] IDIOM 모질고 사나운 기운이 돌다 = to bear a mood of severity and intensity (*equiv.* to become venomous / to be spiteful) ▌A: 네가 먼저 화해하자고 해. 지는 게 이기는 거잖 아. = *Why don't you just suggest a reconciliation first? Losing in this case is actually a win.* B: 나도 그러고 싶은데, 정희가 잔뜩 **독이 올라** 있어 서 말을 붙일 수가 있어야지. = *That's what I'd like to do but Jeonghee is so filled with spite right now, I can't even talk to her.*

돈방석에 앉다 [Lit. to sit on a cushion of money] IDIOM 큰 돈을 갖게 되 다 = to grow wealthy and comfortable (*equiv.* to be sitting on a mountain of money *syn.* 돈벼락(을) 맞다) ▌A: 제 친구 하나가 이번에 주식이 대박 나서 **돈방석에 앉았어요**. = *One of my friends made a killing in stocks recently and is sitting on a mountain of money.* B: 우와, 부럽네요. 어떤 주식이었어요? = *Wow, I'm so jealous. What stock was it?*

➡ p.160

돈벼락(을) 맞다 [Lit. to be struck with a lightening bolt of money] IDIOM 갑 자기 많은 돈이 생기다 = to suddenly earn a lot of money (*equiv.* to strike it rich *syn.* 돈방석에 앉다) ▌A: 착하게 살 생각을 해야지. 너 계속 그러다 벼락 맞는다. = *You have to live in an upstanding way. If you keep on like that, you'll be struck down by a bolt of lightening.* B: 벼락? **돈벼락** 이라면 맞고 싶은데 말이야. = *Well if it's gold-laced bolt of lightening, that'd be fine with me.*

돈을 물쓰듯 하다 [Lit. to use money like it's water] IDIOM 돈을 함부로 아무렇게나 쓰다 = to spend money in a reckless manner (*equiv.* to throw one's money around) ▌A: **돈을 물쓰듯 하면** 아무리 부자라도 당해 낼 수가 없는 법이죠. =*Even the wealthy can't just throw their money around like that forever.* B: 그럴 돈이라도 있어 봤으면 좋겠네요. =*I wish I had that kind of money.*

돈이 나오냐 밥이 나오냐? [Lit. Does it bring money or food?] IDIOM 무슨 소용이 있느냐? =What purpose does it serve? (*equiv.* What does it get you? / What good does it do?) ▌A: 왜 밤낮으로 책만 읽어요? 그런다고 **돈이 나와요, 밥이 나와요?** =*Why do you read all day and night? What does it get you?* B: 책 읽을 때가 제일 행복한 걸 어떡해요? =*I'm at my happiest when I'm reading. What else would you have me do?*

돈이 썩어 나다 [Lit. for one's money to rot] IDIOM 다 쓰지도 못할 정도로 돈이 많은 경우를 부정적으로 일컫는 말 =used to describe the state of having so much money that one does not know what to do with it (*equiv.* to have more money than you can spend / (to have so much money it is as if) money grows on trees) ▌A: 제발 부탁드려요. 사정이 너무 급해서 그럽니다. =*Please, I beg of you. I'm just in such urgent circumstances.* B: 내가 **돈이 썩어 나는** 줄 아냐? 너 빌려 줄 돈 없다. =*Do you think money just grows on trees? I don't have the money to lend you.*

돌다리도 두드려 보고 건너라 [Lit. Even if it's a stone bridge, one should tap it before crossing.] PROVERB 잘 아는 것을 할 때도 주의를 하라는 말 =used to promote caution even in endeavors you are familiar with (*equiv.* Look before you leap. / Better safe than sorry. *syn.* 아는 길도 물어가라) ▌A: 어? 뭔가 저번이랑 달라진 것 같은데. =*Hmm. Something seems different about it this time.* B: 그래? 뭐 상관없잖아. 그냥 하자. =*What does it matter? Let's just do it.* A: 잠깐만 기다려 봐. **돌다리도 두드려 보고 건너라**고 했잖아. 신중해서 나쁠 건 없잖아. =*You've always got to look before you leap. There's nothing wrong with being prudent.*

돌(을) 던지다 [Lit. to throw rocks] IDIOM **1.** 비난하다 =to show contempt / to scorn (*equiv.* to throw rocks *syn.* 손가락질(을)하다, 침(을) 뱉다) ▌A: 인터넷 악플 문제가 정말 심각해요. =*The issue of people leaving* *malicious comments on the Internet is getting serious.* B: 그러게요. 그 사람들은 자신이 하는 짓이 죄 없는 사람에게 **돌을 던지는** 행위라는 걸 모르나 봐요. = *That's what I'm saying. It's as if they don't know what they're doing is hurting innocent people.* **2.** 바둑에서 패배를 인정하고 승부를 포기하다 = to give up a match (in the game of go) (*equiv.* to throw in the towel *cf.* 수건(을) 던지다) █ A: 언제쯤 자신의 승리를 예감하셨습니까? = *At what point did you start to predict that you would be victorious?* B: 사실 상대가 **돌을 던지기** 전까지 제가 이기리라고 확신하지 못했습니다. = *I actually wasn't sure of anything until my opponent threw down his stones.*

동거동락하다 CHINESE-DERIVATION = '동고동락하다'의 잘못된 말 = an incorrect form of 동고동락하다

동고동락하다 [Lit. 同together + 苦bitter + 同together + 樂enjoy + 하다 verbal suffix ⟶ to be together during bitter times and enjoyment] CHINESE-DERIVATION 괴로움도 즐거움도 함께하다 = to be together through hardship and joy (*equiv.* to stick together through thick and thin) █ A: 지난 일 년간 **동고동락한** 동료들과 헤어질 생각을 하니 마음이 안 좋네요. = *It's hard to think that soon I'll have to say goodbye to all these colleagues that I've shared so many ups and downs with.* B: 그래도 더 좋은 곳으로 가는 거니까 잘된 일이죠. = *Even still, you're moving on to a better position. That's a good thing.*

동문서답(하다) [Lit. 東east + 問ask + 西west + 答answer ⟶ a question about the east and a reply about the west] CHINESE-DERIVATION 질문에 대해 엉뚱한 대답을 하다 = to give an answer that doesn't fit the question (*equiv.* a non sequitur / to talk at cross purposes) █ A: 고기는 많이 잡았어? = *Did you catch a lot of fish?* B: 한 두어 시간 됐어. = *It's been about two hours.* A: 고기 많이 잡았냐니까, 왜 **동문서답을 하고** 그래? = *I asked if you'd caught any fish. What's with the non-sequiturs?*

동병상련 [Lit. 同same + 病illness + 相mutual + 憐pity ⟶ feeling among fellow sufferers] CHINESE-DERIVATION 어려운 처지에 있는 사람끼리 서로

를 불쌍하게 여김 = People in a similar plight understand and pity each other. (*equiv.* Misery loves company.) ▌A: 많이 힘드시죠? 다른 사람들은 잘 이해를 못 해 줘서 더 힘드실 거예요. = *You're having a hard time aren't you? The others not understanding you must make it even worse.* B: 네. 역시 **동병상련**이라고 같은 처지에 있는 분을 만나니 제 마음을 알아 주시네요. = *Yes, it's easier to understand people when you're in the same boat so I do feel a little better.*

동분서주하다 [Lit. 東east + 奔hurry + 西west + 走run + 하다verbal suffix → to scurry from east to west] CHINESE-DERIVATION 사방으로 몹시 바쁘게 돌아다니다 = to be running busily in all directions (*equiv.* to be crisscrossing the country / to be running all around town) ▌A: 요즘 사업 힘들다며? = *I heard business is bad.* B: 말도 마. 애 엄마가 여기저기 돈 빌리러 다니느라 **동분서주하고** 있어. = *Don't even bring it up. My wife is running all around the city trying to get people to lend us money.*

동상이몽(하다) [Lit. 同same + 牀bed + 異different + 夢dream → sleeping in the same bed but having different dreams] CHINESE-DERIVATION 겉으로는 같은 입장인 듯하지만 실제로는 다른 생각을 하다 = to appear to have the same aims but actually be at odds ▌A: 참 홍철 씨 경쟁사로 옮겼다며? = *I heard Hongcheol is working for the competition now, huh?* B: 네. 어제가 마지막 출근이었어요. = *Yeah, yesterday was his last day.* A: 전혀 눈치 못 챘었는데, **동상이몽을** 하고 있었구먼. = *I sure had no idea. Even as he worked alongside us, he had his heart set on something else all along.*

동서고금 [Lit. 東east + 西west + 古old + 今present → east and west, old and new] CHINESE-DERIVATION 인간의 역사 전체를 가리키는 말 = the whole history and entirety of humankind (*equiv.* across the ages and around the world) ▌A: **동서고금**을 통틀어 남자들이 예쁜 여자를 좋아하는 건 똑같은 것 같아. = *It's a universal truism: men like beautiful women.* B: 그러는 너도 잘생긴 남자 좋아하잖아. = *You say that, but you too are into handsome men.*

동에 번쩍 서에 번쩍 [Lit. with a flash in the east and a flash in the west]

PROVERB 종잡을 수 없을 정도로 여기저기 나타나는 모양＝springing up here and there (*equiv.* to be popping up everywhere / to really get around *cf.* 신출귀몰하다) ▋A: 너는 아까까지만 해도 여기 있더니 언제 거기 갔대? **동에 번쩍 서에 번쩍** 하네.＝*When I last checked a minute ago, you were right here. When did you get all the way over there? You're really bouncing around today.* B: 그래서 제 별명이 홍길동이잖아요.＝*That's why they call me Hong Gildong (a legendary teleporter from Korean literature).*

돼지 멱 따는 소리 [Lit. a pig's death squeal] IDIOM 아주 듣기 싫은 시끄러운 소리＝a loud voice (*equiv.* a screech) ▋A: 도대체 아침부터 누가 이렇게 **돼지 멱 따는 소리**로 노래를 하는 거야?＝*Who on earth would sing in that pig squeal of a voice so early in the morning?* B: 그러게. 시끄러워 죽겠네.＝*I know. It's driving me crazy too.*

NOTE: 도살장에서 돼지를 잡을 때는 돼지의 목을 땄다고 한다. 그때 돼지가 죽으면서 내는 소리가 듣는 이를 몹시 고통스럽게 하기 때문에 생겨난 표현이다.

In slaughterhouses, they used to cut the throats of pigs. The sound of the pigs was said to be very painful to the ears.

돼지(목)에 진주 (목걸이) [Lit. a pearl necklace on a pig] PROVERB 가치를 모르는 사람에게는 아무리 좋은 물건도 소용이 없다는 말＝a thing of value that is wasted on those that do not know its value (*equiv.* to cast pearls before swine *syn.* 개발에 편자) ▋A: 우와, 이 핸드폰 최신 기종인데, 좋으시겠어요.＝*Wow, that handset is the latest model out. I'm so jealous.* B: 그래 봤자, **돼지 목에 진주 목걸이**예요. 저는 통화밖에 안 하거든요.＝*Well, for me, it is like casting pearls before swine, because I only use it to make phone calls.*

NOTE: 마태복음 7장 6절 "거룩한 것을 개에게 주지 말며 너희 진주를 돼지 앞에 던지지 말라. 그들이 그것을 발로 밟고 돌이켜 너희를 찢어 상하게 할까 염려하라"에서 온 표현이다.

This phrase comes from Matthew 7:6, that states, "Do not give dogs what is sacred; do not throw your pearls to pigs. If you do, they may trample them under their feet, and then turn and tear you to pieces."

되로 주고 말로 받다 [Lit. to give a *doe* (a dry measure) of something and receive a *mal* (a larger dry measure) of something back] PROVERB 남을 조금 건드렸다가 그보다 훨씬 크게 당할 때 쓰는 말=to mistreat another slightly and be severely mistreated in return (*equiv.* to sow the wind and reap the whirlwind / to give a peck and get a bushel) ▮A: 어쩌다 개한테 물린 거야?=*How did you end up being bitten by a dog?* B: 그냥 ……. 장난삼아 개를 발로 찼더니 그 개가 갑자기 나를 물잖아.=*Well ... I just kicked it in a playful way, and the dog suddenly bit me.* A: **되로 주고 말로 받았구나**.=*Sow the wind and reap the whirlwind.*

NOTE: '되'와 '말'은 곡식이나 가루 따위의 부피를 잴 때 쓰는 단위다. 한 되는 약 1.8리터에 해당한다. 한 말은 한 되의 열 배로 약 18리터에 해당한다.

A 되 and a 말 are dry measures used to measure flour or grains. One 되 is approximately equal to 1.8 liters and a 말 is ten times greater than that, or approximately 18 liters.

된서리를 맞다 [Lit. to be hit with a hard frost] IDIOM 큰 타격이나 억압을 받다=to be dealt a major blow or be oppressed (*equiv.* to suffer a bitter blow / to suffer a major setback *syn.* 철퇴를 맞다) ▮A: 피곤해 보이네. 일이 많아?=*You look tired. Have you been busy?* B: 요즘에 감사 기간이잖아. 우리같이 작은 정부 기관일수록 이대 ▶p.541 트집 잡히면 **된서리를 맞는** 수가 있거든. 그것 때문에 요즘 좀 정신이 없어.=*It's audit time at work and a small government agency like ours will be dealt a major blow if they find any faults with us. That's why I've been a little stressed out recently.*

될성부른 나무는 떡잎부터 알아본다 [Lit. A promising tree shows it from the first bud.] PROVERB 잘될 사람은 어려서부터 장래성이 엿보인다=People who will be successful later in life show promise from a young age. (*equiv.* As the twig is bent, so grows the tree. *ant.* 싹수가 노랗다) ▮A: 경태는 아직 어린데도 참 어른스럽고 믿음직스러워요.=*Gyeongtae is still young but sure acts very responsible and adult-like.* B: **될성부른 나무는 떡잎부터 알아본다더니**, 녀석 나중에 큰 인물 되겠네.=*Yep,* *you can tell who the special ones are, even at a young age.*

두각을 나타내다 [Lit. to grow horns] IDIOM 재능이나 실력이 남보다 뛰어나 두드러지다 = to have talents or abilities that exceed others (*equiv.* to shine / to stand out / to be head and shoulders above the rest *cf.* 두각이 나타나다) ▌A: 저 친구는 입사한 지 얼마 안 됐는데 벌써 혼자 **두각을 나타내는군요**. = *That guy hasn't even been working here that long and he's already showing his abilities on his own.* B: 그러게요. 단연 군계일학이에요. = *That's what I'm saying. He's head and shoulders above the rest.*

NOTE: See the note on 두각이 나타나다.

두각을 보이다 IDIOM = 두각을 나타내다

두각이 나타나다 [Lit. to sprout horns] IDIOM 재능이나 실력이 남보다 뛰어나 두드러지다 = to have talents or abilities beyond that of others (*equiv.* to shine / to stand out from the crowd *cf.* 두각을 나타내다) ▌A: 저런 선수가 어떻게 고등학교 때까지는 **두각이 나타나지** 않았던 건지 모르겠군요. = *I don't know why it took him all the way to the end of high school before he started to show his athletic abilities.* B: 부상 때문에 고등학교 때는 이름이 알려지지 않았었죠. = *An injury early on in high school kept him from becoming better known.*

NOTE: 두각(頭角)은 짐승의 머리에 난 뿔을 의미한다. 무리 속에서 뿔이 보인다는 것은 그만큼 두드러진다는 말이다.
두각 is the Sino-Korean word for horns. Just as a beast with horns stands out in a group, this phrase is a metaphor for people whose abilities make them stand out from the crowd.

두 눈 딱 감고 IDIOM = 눈 딱 감고

두 눈(을) 시퍼렇게 뜨고 있다 [Lit. to have both eyes wide open] IDIOM 죽지 않고 멀쩡하게 살아 있다 = to have not died and be alive and well (*equiv.* to be alive and well *syn.* 시퍼렇게 살아 있다) ▌A: 시어머님은

정정하세요? = *Is your mother-in-law still in good health?* B: 아직 **두 눈 시퍼렇게 뜨고 계세요.** 내일 모레면 연세가 아흔이에요. = *She's still alive and ticking. She's going to be 90 pretty soon.*

NOTE: '시퍼렇다'의 1차적 의미는 물론 색깔이 짙게 파랗다는 뜻이다. 하지만 더 나아가 몹시 날카로운 도구나 기세가 무서운 것을 보고도 시퍼렇다고 표현한다. 예를 들어 '칼의 날이 시퍼렇게 섰다'나 '살기가 시퍼렇다'라고 말할 수 있다.
The word 시퍼렇다 originally means a deep shade of blue but is also used to describe a very sharp tool or something with a scary aura. For example, 칼의 날이 시퍼렇게 섰다 means to that a blade is extremely sharp and 살기가 시퍼렇다 means that someone has deep malice and homicidal thoughts.

두 다리(를) 쭉 뻗고 자다 [Lit. to stretch out one's legs and sleep] IDIOM 마음 편히 자다 = to relax / to be relieved (*equiv.* I can finally have a good night's sleep. / I can finally let out a sigh of relief.) ▌A: 드디어 수능이 끝났네. 뭐 하고 싶어? = *The college entrance exam is finally over. What do you want to do?* B: 그냥 잠이나 자고 싶어요. 이제 **두 다리 쭉 뻗고** 잘 수 있을 것 같아요. = *I just want to sleep. Now I'll finally be able to get a good night's rest.*

두 마리 토끼를 잡으려다가 둘 다 놓친다 [Lit. Chasing after two rabbits will mean missing them both.] PROVERB 여러 가지 일을 동시에 잘 하려고 하면 어느 하나도 잘할 수 없다는 말 = Trying to do too many things will only ensure that you do nothing well. (*equiv.* If you run after two hares, you will catch neither. / to spread oneself too thin / to bite off more than one can chew / Between two stools, one falls to the ground. / You can't have your cake and eat it too.) ▌A: 이제 스페인어 공부도 하는 거야? = *Are you studying Spanish now too?* B: 응. 요즘 세상에 외국어는 영어 말고도 하나쯤 할 줄 알아야 될 것 같아서. = *Yeah, because I think it takes more than just English these days.* A: 하지만 넌 영어도 잘 못하잖아. **두 마리 토끼를 잡으려다가 둘 다 놓치는 거 아냐?** = *But you're not even good at English yet. Don't bite off more than you can chew.*

두말하면 잔소리 [Lit. Saying it twice would be nagging.] IDIOM 이미 말한 내용이 틀림없으므로 다시 언급할 필요가 없다는 말 =used when you are so sure of what you've just said there's no need to repeat it (*equiv.* needless to say / It goes without saying. / You bet your life.) ▌A: 상금 타면 반씩 나누기다? =*If we win, we're splitting the winnings, right?* B: **두말하면 잔소리**지! =*You bet your life we are.*

두문불출하다 [Lit. 杜shut + 門door + 不no + 出come out + 하다verbal suffix → to seal the doors and stay inside] CHINESE-DERIVATION 외출을 하지 않고 집에만 있다 =to confine oneself indoors (*equiv.* to be cooped up at home / to confine oneself to home) ▌A: 이지은 씨 아직까지 **두문불출**하고 있어요? =*Lee Jieun is still cooped up at home?* B: 네. 남자 친구하고 헤어진 이후로 줄곧 그러고 있어요. =*Yeah, ever since she broke up with her boyfriend she's been like that.*

두 손(을) 들다 [Lit. to raise both hands] IDIOM 자기 능력에서 벗어나 포기하다 =to give up when a certain task is beyond one's abilities (*equiv.* to throw up one's hands in defeat / to throw in the towel / to give up *syn.* 손(을) 들다, 백기(를) 들다, 수건(을) 던지다) ▌A: 오토바이는 위험해서 안 된다고 엄마가 몇 번이나 말했잖니? =*How many times have I told you, riding motorcycles is too dangerous?* B: 조심해서 타면 괜찮아요, 엄마. 제발요. =*But I'll be fine if I ride carefully. Please, Mom.* A: 참, 네 고집에는 **두 손 들었다**. 네 마음대로 해. =*Fine then. I give in. Do whatever you want.*

둘도 없다 [Lit. There is no second.] IDIOM 오직 하나뿐이다 =to be the only one (*equiv.* (there's) no one like someone / to have no equal / to be unmatched) ▌A: 순자네 아들은 참 부모한테 잘하지 않아? 순자가 아들을 참 잘 키웠어. =*Doesn't Sunja's son treat his parents well? Sunja raised him right.* B: 맞아. 세상에 **둘도 없는** 효자지. =*You're right. There's no one quite like him out there.*

둘러치나 메어치나 (매한가지) [Lit. to throw someone to the ground or toss someone to the ground] PROVERB 이렇게 하나 저렇게 하나 결과는

같다는 말＝No matter how you do it, the result will be the same. (*equiv.* It makes no difference. / It'll be the same either way.) ▋A: 늦었는데 지하철 말고 택시 탈까?＝*Since it's late, why don't we take a taxi instead of the subway?* B: 어차피 지금은 막히는 시간이라 **둘러치나 메어치나 매한가지야**.＝*But since there's going to be a lot of traffic at this hour it's pretty much the same either way.*

둘이 먹다가 하나(가) 죽어도 모른다 [Lit. Even if your fellow diner died mid-meal, you wouldn't notice.] PROVERB 음식이 아주 맛있을 때 하는 말＝used to describe a very tasty meal (*equiv.* It's to die for.) ▋A: 이 된장찌개 정말 **둘이 먹다 하나 죽어도 모르겠어요**.＝*This dwenjang-jjigae is to die for.* B: 이 집이 음식 잘하기로 유명한 집이에요.＝*Yeah, this place is famous for good food.*

둘째가라면 서럽다 [Lit. to be sad if called second place] IDIOM 누구나 인정하는 첫째이다＝to be clearly the best (in a certain field) (*equiv.* to be second to none / to be unrivaled) ▋A: 안 힘들어요? 벌써 다섯 바퀴째인데.＝*Aren't you tired? You've already done five laps.* B: 전혀요. 제가 원래 체력이라면 **둘째가라면 서러울** 정도로 자신 있거든요.＝*Not at all. I'm second to none when it comes to stamina.*

둘째(로) 치다 [Lit. to consider (something) second place] IDIOM 그보다 중요하거나 급한 일이 있어 일단은 고려하지 않다＝to have more urgent tasks to attend to (*equiv.* It's not one's main problem. / to have bigger fish to fry) ▋A: 내일 검사 받으려면 오늘 저녁 여섯 시 이후로 아무것도 먹으면 안 되겠네? 배고프겠다.＝*If you're planning to have a checkup tomorrow, I guess you can't eat anything after six, right? You must be hungry.* B: 배고픈 건 **둘째 치고** 겁이 나 죽겠어.＝*I've got bigger things to worry about than being hungry right now. I'm scared to death of the procedure.*

둥지(를) 틀다 [Lit. to build a nest] IDIOM 살 곳을 마련하다＝to find a place to live (*equiv.* to build a nest) ▋A: 서울에 처음 올라오셔서는 어디에 사셨어요?＝*Where did you live when you first came to Seoul?* B: 제

가 열아홉 살 때 처음 서울에 와서는 학교 근처 하숙집에 처음 **둥지를 틀었지요**. = *Back then, I was only 19 years old, and I lived in a boarding house near my school in Seoul.*

뒤가 구리다 [Lit. for one's rear to stink] ɪᴅɪᴏᴍ 숨겨 둔 약점이나 잘못이 있다 = to have a hidden weak point or flaw (*equiv.* Something smells fishy (about him).) ▌A: 보아 하니 이번 비리도 또 수사가 흐지부지되나 봐. = *It looks like this corruption investigation too is going to come to naught.* B: 검찰도 **뒤가 구리니** 적극적으로 수사를 하지 않는 거야. = *Something smells fishy with the prosecutors. They're never aggressive in their investigations.*

뒤가 꿀리다 ɪᴅɪᴏᴍ = 뒤가 켕기다

뒤가 드러나다 [Lit. to have one's back exposed] ɪᴅɪᴏᴍ 비밀로 하던 일이 알려지다 = for doings that one had carried out in secret to be made public (*equiv.* to have one's backstory exposed / to have light shed on one's doings / to have one's dirty laundry aired) ▌A: 이것 봐. 김인애 교수 **뒤가 드러났대**. = *Take a look at this. Prof. Kim Inae's darker side has been brought into the light.* B: 신문에 뭐라고 나와 있어요? = *What does the article say?* A: 학부모들한테 뇌물을 받았다네. = *They're saying she took bribes from the parents of her students.*

뒤가 든든하다 [Lit. to have a strong back] ɪᴅɪᴏᴍ 믿고 의지하는 사람이나 세력이 있다 = to have many people supporting and believing in you (*equiv.* to have strong backing / to have strong support / to have someone powerful in your corner) ▌A: 저 사람은 왜 일도 안 하고 놀기만 하지? = *Why does he get to never work and just mess around all the time?* B: 사장님 아들이잖아. **뒤가 든든하니까** 그런가 보지. = *He's the boss's son. He's got good backup.*

뒤가 켕기다 [Lit. for one's back to be stiff] ɪᴅɪᴏᴍ 잘못이나 마음에 걸리는 것이 있어 마음이 편하지 않다 = to have guilt or other worries on your mind that prevent your from relaxing (*equiv.* to have a guilty conscience *syn.* 뒤가 꿀리다) ▌A: 야, 왜 갑자기 차를 돌려?＝*Hey, why did you suddenly turn the car around like that?* B: 저기 경찰이 있어서. 나는 잘 못한 것도 없는데 경찰만 보면 왜 **뒤가 켕기는지** 모르겠어. ＝ *Because there's a cop over there. I didn't do anything wrong, but for some reason, I get nervous whenever I see police.*

뒤끝이 없다 [Lit. to not hold a grudge] IDIOM 기분 나쁜 일을 마음속에 담아 두지 않다 ＝to not hold anger in one's heart for long (*equiv.* to not hold a grudge / to let things go / to get over things quickly) ▌A: 사장님 화내실 때 보면 정말 무서워요. ＝*The boss is really scary when he gets angry.* B: 하지만 **뒤끝은 없는** 분 같아요. 금세 또 웃으시잖아요. ＝*Yeah, but he doesn't seem to hold a grudge. He's laughing again the next minute.*

뒤로 호박씨(를) 까다 [Lit. to be peeling pumpkin seeds with one's anus] IDIOM 겉으로는 안 그러는 척하면서 몰래 나쁜 짓을 하다 ＝to pretend to be innocent while carrying out bad deeds in secret (*equiv.* to be leading a double life / to have a darker side *syn.* 호박씨(를) 까다) ▌A: 내 친구 영숙이 남편 알지? 바람 났대. ＝*You know my friend Yeongsuk's husband, right? I heard he had an affair.* B: 그 사람 참 순진하게 생겨 가지고, **뒤로 호박씨를 까고** 있었구먼. ＝*But he looked so trustworthy. I guess he had a darker side to him.*

NOTE: 여기서의 뒤는 뒤쪽이 아니라 항문을 가리킨다고 알려져 있다. 그러나 말 그대로 자기 혼자 몰래 호박씨를 먹기 위해 손을 뒤로 한 채 호박의 껍질을 까고 있는 행위를 연상해도 될 것이다.

It is understood that the 뒤 in this expression is not "behind" or "back," but the anus. It may be more desirable to envision someone with their hands behind their backs to conceal that they are cracking pumpkin seeds.

뒤를 노리다 [Lit. to stalk someone's back] IDIOM 남의 약점을 찾아내려고 기회를 엿보다 ＝to try to find someone else's weaknesses (*equiv.* to be out to get someone) ▌A: 조심하십시오, 회장님. 회장님 **뒤를 노리는** 사람이 있습니다. ＝*Be careful, Mr. Chairman. There are many people out to get you.* B: 걱정 말게. 나 아직 죽지 않았어. 쉽게 당하지는 않

아. = *Don't worry. I'm not dead yet. I'm not a pushover.*

뒤를 밀어 주다 IDIOM = 뒤를 보아 주다

뒤를 밟다 [Lit. to step on someone's back] IDIOM 몰래 쫓다 = to follow someone without their knowledge (*equiv.* to tail someone / to track someone) ▎A: 저기가 내가 말한 그 아가씨 집이야. = *That's where that girl I was telling you about lives.* B: 매일 버스 정류장에서만 보는 사이라면서 집은 어떻게 알았어? = *You said she was just someone you bumped into every day at the bus stop. How do you know where she lives?* A: 하루는 버스에서 내려서 **뒤를 밟았지**. = *I tailed her one day after we got off the bus.* B: 야, 너 스토커냐? = *What are you, some kind of a stalker?*

뒤를 보아 주다 [Lit. to support someone's back] IDIOM 도와주고 돌보아 주다 = to help and watch out for a person (*equiv.* to support / to prop up / to have someone's back *syn.* 뒤를 밀어 주다) ▎A: 저 가수는 노래도 못하고 인기도 별로 없는데 어떻게 TV에 저렇게 자주 나올까? = *That singer can't really sing and isn't very popular either. Why do you think she's on TV so often?* B: **뒤를 보아 주는** 사람이 있나 보지 뭐. = *I guess someone important has her back.*

뒤를 잇다 [Lit. to be linked (at the back)] IDIOM 대를 잇다 = to carry on a family line (*equiv.* to carry the family name) ▎A: 옛날 사람들은 왜 그렇게 아들에 집착했을까? = *Why do you think people used to be so obsessed with having sons?* B: 그때 사람들은 아들을 낳아야만 **뒤를 이을 수** 있다고 생각했으니까. = *Because at that time they thought the only way to carry on the family line was to have a son.*

뒤를 캐다 [Lit. to dig into someone's past] IDIOM 은밀하게 뒷조사를 하다 = to carry out a thorough investigation into someone (*equiv.* to delve into someone's past / to dig up dirt on someone *syn.* 뒤를 파다) ▎A: 아무래도 아이들 아빠가 요즘 좀 수상해. 여자가 생긴 것 같아. = *My husband has been acting so suspicious lately. I think he may be seeing someone.* B: 정 의심스러우면 **뒤를 캐 봐**. = *If you're that suspicious, start digging into*

what he's been doing.

뒤를 파다 IDIOM = 뒤를 캐다

뒤통수(를) 때리다 [Lit. to hit someone in the back of the head] IDIOM 믿고 있던 사람에게 해를 입히다 = to hurt someone who believed in you (*equiv.* to let someone down / to stab someone in the back *syn.* 뒤통수(를) 치다 *ant.* 뒤통수(를) 맞다) ▌A: 경아가 내 **뒤통수를 때릴** 줄은 정말 몰랐어. = *I never imagined that Gyeongah would stab me in the back like this.* B: 왜, 무슨 일 있어? = *What? What happened?* A: 아는 사람이 그러는데 경아가 뒤에서 내 욕을 하고 다닌대. = *I heard that she's talking trash about me.*

뒤통수(를) 맞다 [Lit. to be hit in the back of the head] IDIOM 믿고 있던 사람에게서 해를 입다 = to be blindsided / to be stabbed in the back (*equiv.* to be stabbed in the back) ▌A: 나 완전히 **뒤통수 맞았어**. = *I got totally blindsided by my girlfriend.* B: 왜? 무슨 일 있어? = *Why? What happened?* A: 엊그제 여자 친구한테 비싼 가방을 선물해 줬는데, 오늘 이제 그만 만나재. = *I bought her an expensive purse just a few days ago, but today she's saying she wants to break up.*

뒤통수(를)치다 IDIOM = 뒤통수(를) 때리다

뒷구멍으로 들어가다 IDIOM = 뒷문으로 들어가다

뒷맛이 개운치 못하다 [Lit. to not have a refreshing aftertaste] IDIOM 일이 끝났지만 마음에 걸리는 게 있어 느낌이 좋지 않다 = A certain happening has been concluded, but the unpleasant heaviness remains in one's heart. (*equiv.* to leave a bad taste in one's mouth / to be unfulfilling *syn.* 뒷맛이 쓰다) ▌A: 이 영화 참 재미있지 않았어? = *Did you think that movie was great?* B: 응, 볼만했어. 그런데 결말이 너무 황당해서 **뒷맛이** 좀 개운치 못하더라고. = *Yeah, it was worth seeing, but the conclusion was less than fulfilling.*

뒷맛이 쓰다 [Lit. to have a bitter aftertaste] IDIOM 일이 끝났지만 마음에 걸리는 게 있어 느낌이 좋지 않다 = to experience a lingering bad feeling after an undesirable outcome (*equiv.* to have a bitter aftertaste *syn.* 뒷맛이 개운치 못하다) ▮A: 오늘 경기는 이겼지만 판정 시비 때문에 **뒷맛이 써요**. = *We won the game today, but the dispute over the referee's call sure left a bad taste in my mouth.* B: 다음 번에는 더 확실히 눌러 줍시다. = *Next time we'll have to beat 'em down even more.*

뒷문으로 들어가다 [Lit. to come in through the back door] IDIOM 정당하지 못한 방법으로 어떤 무리에 끼다 = to enter into a certain group by unjust means (*equiv.* to be admitted by nefarious means / to be a backdoor admission / to have someone pull some strings *syn.* 뒷구멍으로 들어가다) ▮A: 저 사람이 어떻게 우리 회사에 들어왔는지 모르겠어요. 실력도 경험도 없는 것 같은데 말이에요. = *I don't know how that guy got a job here. It seems like he's got neither talent nor experience.* B: 쉿! 실은, **뒷문으로 들어왔다는** 얘기가 있어요. = *Shh! The word is that someone pulled some strings for him.*

***뒷북치다** [Lit. to hit the drum too late] IDIOM 뒤늦게 어떤 일을 하다 = to carry out a belated action (*equiv.* jump on the bandwagon / to be a Johnny come lately / Get with the program!) ▮A: 참, 이번에 연봉이 안 오른다는 얘기 있던데, 들으셨어요? = *Hey, I heard that they aren't going to give us raises this time around. Did you hear that?* B: 지금까지 그 얘기하고 있었어요. 명수 씨는 꼭 다른 사람 말을 잘 안 듣고 있다가 **뒷북치더라**. = *That's what we've all been saying for a while. You always ignore what everybody else is saying and then jump on the bandwagon way too late.*

NOTE: 과거에는 높은 사람들이 길을 지나갈 때 북이나 나팔 등을 불면서 사람들에게 길을 비킬 것을 알렸다. 그런데 행차가 다 지나간 다음에 북을 쳐 봤자 무슨 소용이겠는가. 일이 이미 끝난 후에 뒤늦은 행동을 할 때 뒷북친다고 말한다.

Long ago, the passage of an important personage was indicated by the striking of a drum or the sounding of a trumpet. Striking the drum after the VIP has passed, however, is just wasting everyone's time. When you see someone partake in an exercise in futility, or do after the fact what should have been done beforehand, this is the perfect expression to use when you give them a hard time.

뒷짐만 지고 있다 [Lit. to clasp one's hands behind one's back] IDIOM 적극적인 행동을 하지 않고 방관하고 있다 = to not behave in a proactive way but instead stand idly by (*equiv.* to stand idly by / to stand around / to stand on the sidelines *syn.* 가만히 앉아 있다, 팔짱(을) 끼고 구경만 하다, 앉아서 보고만 있다) ▌A: **뒷짐만 지고 있지** 말고 이리 와서 좀 도와줘. = *Don't just stand around. Hurry up and help me.* B: 아, 나도 그러고 싶은데 나 급한 일이 생각났어. 먼저 가 볼게. = *Oh, yeah, I'd really like to help you but I just remembered something urgent that I have to take care of. I'd better get out of here.*

든 자리는 몰라도 난 자리는 안다 [Lit. You can notice someone's absence, even though you failed to notice their presence.] PROVERB 어떤 사람의 가치는 그 사람이 없을 때야 비로소 드러난다는 갈 = describes only noticing the value of a person once they are gone (*equiv.* You don't know what you've got till it's gone.) ▌A: 정 대리가 오래 자리를 비우니 여러 가지로 곤란하구먼. = *With Jeong gone for so long, all of our lives have been made a little bit harder.* B: 그러게 **든 자리는 몰라도 난 자리는 안다잖아요**. = *That's right. We never know what we've got till it's gone.*

듣기 좋은 꽃노래도 한두 번이지 [Lit. Even an enjoyable song about flowers is just (nice to hear) once or twice] PROVERB 좋은 이야기도 너무 많이 들으면 싫다 = It's even possible to get sick of hearing good things. ▌A: 지영 씨는 우리 팀 최고의 미녀야! = *Jiyoung, the most beautiful woman on our team!* B: 부장님, **듣기 좋은 꽃노래도 한두 번이죠**. 자꾸 그러시니까 저 놀리시는 거 같잖아요. = *Thanks for the compliment, but it's starting to get a little old. The way you say that all the time makes it seem like you're teasing me.*

듣도 보도 못하다 [Lit. to not hear or see (something)] IDICM 아는 것이

전혀 없다＝to have never heard anything about (something) (*equiv.* I've never heard of such a thing!) ▌A: 세상에 이런 법이 어디 있습니까? 한복을 입으면 호텔 식당에 출입할 수 없다는 규정은 **듣도 보도 못했어요**. ＝*How on earth could there be such a rule? I've never heard of something as ridiculous as not letting people in dressed in a hanbok into hotel restaurants.* B: 죄송합니다. 저희 호텔만의 방침이라 어쩔 수 없습니다. ＝*I'm very sorry, but it is just our hotel's policy. There's nothing else I can do.*

들들 볶다 IDIOM＝달달 볶다

들러리(를) 서다 [Lit. to serve as bridesmaid or groomsman] IDIOM 다른 사람을 보조하는 역할을 하다＝to aid or support someone else (*equiv.* to play second fiddle / always the bridesmaid, never the bride) ▌A: 왜 갑자기 회사를 그만두셨어요? ＝*Why did you quit so suddenly like that?* B: 남들 **들러리 서는** 데 지쳤어요. 이제는 저도 제 사업을 하고 싶습니다. ＝*I was sick of playing second fiddle to everyone else. I want to run my own business now.*

등골(을) 빼먹다 [Lit. to pluck out and eat someone's spine] IDIOM 남의 재물을 착취하다＝to exploit the fortune of another (*syn.* 등골(을) 뽑다) ▌A: 돈이 좀 모자라네. 어디 빌릴 데 없을까? ＝*We're a little short here. Don't you have anyone you can borrow from?* B: 부모님한테 손을 좀 벌리면 어떨까? ＝*What about getting a handout from the parents.* A: 어떻게 그래 ……. 부모 **등골 빼먹는** 것도 정도가 있지. ＝*How could we do that? There's a limit to how much we can ask for from our own parents.*

▶p.373

등골(을) 뽑다 IDIOM＝등골(을) 빼먹다

등골(이) 빠지다 [Lit. for one's back bone to fall out] IDIOM 몹시 고생하다＝to have a very hard time (*equiv.* to be worked to the bone) ▌A: 요즘 부모들도 참 힘들겠어. 사교육비로 한 달에 백만 원이 넘게 나간대. ＝*It must be really hard for parents today. I heard they spend more than one million won per month on private education.* B: 부모 **등골이 빠지는**

거지 뭐. = *They're being worked to the bone.*

등골이 서늘하다 [Lit. to have a chill in one's spine] IDIOM 몹시 놀라고 섬뜩하다 = to be very surprised or horrified (*equiv.* to have a chill run down one's spine / for one's heart to stop in fright / to get the chills *syn.* 간담이 서늘하다) ▌A: 어제 인터넷뱅킹을 하다 실수로 계좌번호를 잘못 입력하고 이체를 누른 거야. = *Yesterday, when I was doing some Internet banking, I typed in the wrong account number and then accidently pressed "transfer."* B: 저런, 어떻게 됐어? = *Oh, no. What happened?* A: 순간적으로 **등골이 서늘했는데**, 다행히 번호가 틀리니까 이체가 안 되더라고. = *Well, I almost had a heart attack, but luckily, since it was the wrong number, it didn't go through.*

등골이 오싹하다 [Lit. to have a chill in one's spine] IDIOM 공포감을 느끼다 = to be horrified (*equiv.* to experience something spine-chilling / to get the chills) ▌A: 어제 TV에서 '여고괴담' 봤어? = *Did you see "Girl's School Ghost Story" on TV yesterday?* B: 집에서 혼자 보는데 **등골이 오싹해서** 끝까지 볼 수가 없었어. = *I was watching it at home by myself, and it sent chills right up my spine. I couldn't even watch the whole thing.*

등에 업다 [Lit. to carry on one's bag] IDIOM 남의 세력에 의지하다 = to depend on the power of another (*equiv.* to ride a wave (of support)) ▌A: 이번 대통령 선거에서 누가 이길까? = *Who do you think is going to win the presidential election?* B: 안 교수가 되지 않을까? 서민들의 열렬한 지지를 **등에 업고** 여기까지 왔으니까. = *Don't you think it'll be Prof. Ahn? He's been riding a wave of popular support that's brought him this far.*

*****등(을) 돌리다** [Lit. to turn away] IDICM 관계를 끊다 = to end a relationship (*equiv.* to turn one's back on someone) ▌A: 민정이는 애가 완전히 변했어. 대기업에 취직하더니 친구들을 너무 무시해. = *Minjeong has completely changed. Now that she works at a big company, she completely ignores her friends.* B: 그래서 친구들 전부 민정이한테서 **등을 돌렸잖아**. = *Yeah, that's why all of her friends have turned their backs* *on her.*

등(을) 떠밀다 [Lit. to push someone's back] IDIOM 일을 억지로 시키다 = to compel someone to do something (*equiv.* to push someone into something) ▌A: 어쩌자고 당신이 동창회 회장직을 맡았어요? 그거 여간 골치 아픈 게 아닌데. = *What were you thinking, taking on the job as alumni association president? It's more than just a little small hassle to be in charge.* B: 하도 애들이 내 **등을 떠밀어서** ……. 휴우. = *Everyone just kept pushing me into it ... (sigh).*

등이 휘다 [Lit. for one's back to bend] IDIOM 고생을 하여 힘이 부치다 = to face much hardship (*equiv.* to be hunched over from overwork / to be worked to the bone *syn.* 허리가 휘다) ▌A: 아빠, 아빠는 왜 이리 흰머리가 많아? = *Dad, why do you have so much gray hair?* B: 너희들 먹여 살리려고 **등이 휘도록** 일하다 보니 이렇게 흰머리가 많아졌지. = *I worked till my back was hunched over trying to keep you kids fed. That's why I have so much gray hair.*

등잔 밑이 어둡다 [Lit. for it to be dark right under the lantern] PROVERB 가까이 곳에서 생긴 일을 오히려 잘 모른다는 말 = used to describe how people are often most ignorant of what is going on right around them (*equiv.* (for what one is looking for to be) right under one's nose) ▌A: 우리 팀 김경민 씨하고 고경란 씨가 사귄다면서요? = *Did you hear that two employees on our team, Kim Gyeongmin and Go Gyeongran, are seeing each other?* B: 어, 나도 어제 들었어. **등잔 밑이 어둡다더니**, 팀 내에서 연애를 하는 줄은 꿈에도 몰랐네. = *Yeah, I just found out yesterday. It was right under our noses and none of us even dreamed they were together.*

➡ p.113

따끔한 맛을 보다 [Lit. to taste bitterness] IDIOM 호된 고통이나 어려움을 겪다 = to receive a bitter reproach or scolding (*equiv.* to be put in one's place *syn.* 뜨거운 맛을 보다, 매운 맛을 보다) █A: 이번 일은 제 잘못이 아니에요. = *What happened this time wasn't my fault.* B: 네가 **따끔한 맛을 봐야** 정신을 차리겠니? = *Is it going to take a bitter scolding for you to shape up?*

따 놓은 당상 PROVERB = 떼어 놓은 당상

딱 잡아떼다 [Lit. to clutch something and tear it off] IDIOM 아는 것을 모른다고 하거나 한 것을 하지 않았다고 하다 = for one to feign ignorance or disavow one's actions (*equiv.* lie through one's teeth / to tell a boldface lie / to play dumb *syn.* 시치미(를) 떼다, 오리발(을) 내밀다) █A: 민수 녀석 말이야, 어제 나한테서 돈 빌려 가 놓고 오늘 그런 적 없다고 **딱 잡아떼는** 거 있지? = *You know Minsu? So last night that guy comes and borrows money from me and today he's lying through his teeth that it never happened.* B: 정말? 설마. 기억이 안 나서 그랬겠지. = *Really? No way. He must've just forgotten about it.*

딱지가 붙다 [Lit. to affix a ticket] IDIOM 어떤 사람에게 나쁜 평가나 평판이 내려지다 = to be judged in a negative way (*equiv.* to be labeled something negatively *syn.* 꼬리표가 붙다) █A: 전과자라는 **딱지가 붙어서** 힘드신 점이 많으셨을 것 같은데 어떻게 극복하셨나요? = *With people labeling you as an ex-con you must have had a hard time. How did you overcome that?* B: 취직은 꿈도 못 꿨습니다. 뭐든지 열심히 하자는 각오로 일하다 보니 사람들의 색안경 낀 시선도 조금씩 바

뀌더군요. = *I couldn't even dream of getting a job. But doing everything to the best of my abilities and has done a little to change the light in which people see me.*

NOTE: See the note on 딱지(를) 떼다.

딱지(를) 놓다 IDIOM = 퇴짜(를) 놓다

딱지(를) 떼다 [Lit. to rip off a label] IDIOM **1.** 좋지 못한 상황이나 미숙한 단계에서 벗어나다 = to break free of a bad situation or advance out of an unskilled state (*equiv.* to break free of a label) ▌A: 와, 수정이가 언제 이렇게 컸니? 완전 아가씨가 다 됐네! 아이 **딱지를 완전히 뗐는데**? = *Wow, Sujeong, when did you get that big? You're a young woman now! You're not a kid anymore.* B: 아저씨도. 저도 이제 스무 살이라고요. = *Oh you. I'm 20 years old now.* **2.** 교통 법규를 위반하여 경찰에게 단속 당한 뒤 벌금형을 받다 = to be caught for a traffic violation and have to pay a fine (*equiv.* to get a ticket) ▌A: 왜 이렇게 늦었어? = *Why are you so late?* B: 안 그래도 늦어서 서두르다가 교통 경찰한테 걸려서 **딱지 뗐어.** = *I was worried I would be late, so I was speeding and got a ticket.*

NOTE: 딱지는 우표나 상표처럼 무엇인가를 표시하게 위해 쓰는 종이를 의미한다. 그것이 추상적인 의미로 발전하여 어떤 사물에 대한 평가나 인정이라는 의미를 갖게 되었다. '딱지를 떼다'가 1번의 의미로 쓰일 때나 '딱지가 붙다'라는 표현은 이 의미와 관련이 깊다. '딱지를 떼다'가 2번의 의미로 쓰일 때, 딱지는 교통 경찰이 교통 법규를 어긴 사람에게 주는 벌금 고지서를 의미한다. 벌금 고지서는 수첩처럼 수십 장이 묶여 있고, 낱장을 쉽게 뗄 수 있도록 되어 있어 실제로 경찰이 이 수첩에서 한 장을 떼어 운전자에게 준다. 실제로 딱지를 떼는 주체는 경찰이므로 운전자의 입장에서는 '딱지를 떼이다'라고 해야 맞지만 관용적으로 '딱지를 떼다'라고도 많이들 얘기한다.

A 딱지 is a piece of paper similar to a stamp or ticket that is used to display information on a product. The usage of this word evolved into the more abstract sense akin to the way the word "label" has morphed in English. If 딱지 is used in the sense of the first definition or 딱지 붙다, 딱지 denotes such a "label." The ticket in the second usage is the kind of ticket that the policeman rips of his pad and gives to you when you've been caught breaking a traffic law. The party that's actually doing the tearing of the ticket in this sense is the cop and not the driver. Accordingly, the expression should be in the passive form, or 딱지 떼이다, but the expression is almost exclusively used in the form listed here.

딱지(를) 맞다 IDIOM = 퇴짜(를) 맞다

딴 주머니를 차다 [Lit. to attach another pocket] IDIOM 돈을 빼서 따로 보관하다 = to put aside money (*equiv.* to squirrel away money / to hold out on someone) ▌A: 당신 요즘 왜 이렇게 월급이 적어? 혹시 나 몰래 딴 주머니 찬 거 아냐? = *Why has your paycheck been so small recently? Are you holding out on me?* B: 보험이다 뭐다 해서 떼 가는 게 많으니까 그렇지 딴 주머니는 무슨 …….= *Well, there's insurance and this and that that get taken out. Holding out on you? No way ...*

딴죽(을) 걸다 [Lit. to sweep (someone's leg)] IDIOM 다른 사람의 말이나 행동에 공연히 트집을 잡거나 이의를 제기하다 = to unnecessarily find fault with the actions of others or raise an object needlessly (*equiv.* to rock the boat / to stir the pot) ▌A: 이 부분은 재검토해 봐야 할 것 같은데요.= *I think you'd better recheck this part.* B: 그 부분은 어제 다 얘기 끝났잖아요. 왜 이제 와서 또 딴죽을 거세요?= *We finished dealing with that part yesterday. Why are you rocking the boat now?*

> NOTE: 딴죽은 씨름에서 상대의 다리를 옆으로 걸어 넘어뜨리는 기술을 말한다.
>
> In the world of traditional Korean wrestling, 씨름, sweeping the opponent's foot with one's leg or grappling at their feet to pull them off balance is called 딴죽.

딴지(를) 걸다 IDIOM '딴죽(을) 걸다'의 잘못된 말 = an incorrect but often used way of saying 딴죽(을) 걸다

땅에 떨어지다 [Lit. to fall to the ground] IDIOM 명예나 권위 따위가 회복하기 힘들 정도로 손상되다 = to lose reputation or authority to the point where a recovery is almost impossible (*equiv.* to hit rock bottom) ▌A: 이 빵집 빵에서 벌레가 나왔다는 뉴스 봤지? = *Did you hear the news that someone found a bug in the bread they sell here.* B: 어. 신용이 **땅에 떨어졌으니** 앞으로 장사하기는 틀렸을 거야. = *Yep. With customer trust at rock bottom, I don't know how they ever expect to run the business from here on out.*

땅을 치다 [Lit. to strike the ground] IDIOM 몹시 분하고 애통해하다 = to be filled with rage and lamentation (*equiv.* to lament / to feel unfairly treated) ▌A: 너 내 말 안 들은 거 나중에 **땅을 치고** 후회할걸. = *Later on you'll rue the day you didn't listen to what I said.* B: 글쎄, 두고 보면 알겠지. = *Only time will tell.*

땅(을) 파 봐라 [Lit. (Go ahead and) try to dig in the ground.] IDIOM 돈을 벌기가 쉽지 않음을 강조하는 말 = used to emphasize the difficulty of earning money ▌A: 잔돈 받았어? = *Did you get your change?* B: 아니. 귀찮아서 그냥 안 받았어. = *Nope. It's a bother so I didn't take it.* A: 애 좀 보게. **땅을 파 봐라.** 10원 한 장 나오나. = *Wow, look at you. Money doesn't grow on trees, boy.*

땅(을) 파서 장사하다 [Lit. to dig in the ground and run a business] IDIOM 밑천을 들이지 않고 장사를 하다 = to start a business without capital (*syn.* 흙(을) 파서 장사하다) ▌A: 천 원만 깎아 주세요. = *Could you just cut 1,000 won off the price.* B: 아, 누구는 **땅 파서 장사하는** 줄 아세요? 여기서 천 원 깎으면 남는 것도 없어요. = *Hey, I'm trying to run a business here. If I slash 1,000 won off the price, that'll leave me with nothing.*

NOTE: 흔히 '땅 파서 장사하는 줄 아나?' 와 같이 쓰인다.
    Often used with the phrase, 땅 파서 장사하는 줄 아나?

땅 짚고 헤엄치기 [Lit. swimming with one's hands in the dirt] PROVERB 아

주 쉬운 일＝a very easy task (*equiv.* easy as pie / It's a piece of cake. / child's play / a cinch / no sweat *syn.* 누워서 떡 먹기, 식은 죽 먹기 *ant.* 하늘의 별 따기) ▌A: 컴퓨터 설치 좀 해 줄래? 나는 뭐가 뭔지 모르겠어.＝*Could you help me set up my computer for me? I don't know what's what.* B: 그거야, **땅 짚고 헤엄치기**지.＝*No sweat!*

NOTE: 실제로는 땅에 손을 짚고 헤엄을 칠 수는 없다. 따라서 이 표현은 발이 바닥에 닿는 곳에서 수영을 한다는 것으로 이해하는 것이 맞을 것 같다. 수영을 할 줄 모른다고 해도 발이 닿는 얕은 물에서 팔로 헤엄치는 시늉을 하는 것은 누구나 할 수 있다.

It is impossible to actually swim anywhere with one's hands planted in the dirt. Accordingly, this expression means swimming in water so shallow that one's feet touch the ground. Even people who don't know how to swim can easily mimic the motions of swimming with their feet planted in shallow water.

때(가)묻다 [Lit. to be dirtied] IDIOM 세상 물정을 알게 되어 순수함을 잃다＝to learn the ways of the world and lose one's innocence (*equiv.* to know what's what) ▌A: 오랜만에 아들 보니까 어땠어?＝*How was it seeing the kids after so long?* B: 좋았어. 그런데 다들 세상의 **때가 많이 묻었더라**. 어릴 때의 순수한 기억하고는 좀 다르더라고.＝*It was good. But they're so worldly now. They are a far cry from the innocent little ones I remember.*

때(를) 벗다 [Lit. to shed dirt] IDIOM 시골티나 어린 티를 벗다＝to no longer show signs of being from the country or of being young ▌A: 너는 언제쯤 **때를 벗을래**? 벌써 서울 온 지도 몇 년이나 되었잖아.＝*When are you going to shed your country nature? You've been in Seoul for how many years now?* B: 삼촌, 제가 아직도 시골티가 난다는 말씀이세요? 다들 제가 서울 사람인 줄 아는데요.＝*Are you saying, Uncle, that it still shows that I'm from the country? Everyone I meet thinks I'm from Seoul.*

때리는 시어머니보다 말리는 시누이가 더 밉다 [Lit. The mother-in-law that beats you is less detestable than the sister-in-law who tries to stop her.] PROVERB 아예 드러내 놓고 나를 해하는 사람보다, 겉으로 나를 위하는 척하지만 속으로 나쁜 마음을 품고 있는 사람이 더 밉다 = *I more deeply despise those who pretend to care about me than those who openly dislike me.* ▌A: 시부모님하고 같이 산다며? 힘들지? = *So, you're living with the in-laws? That's tough, huh?* B: 말도 마. 시부모님도 시부모님이지만 시누이가 보통이 아니야. 어머님이 한마디하시면 옆에서 열 마디를 거들어. = *Don't bring it up. The in-laws are just what you'd expect, but the sister-in-law is really something else. Whenever my mother-in-law says anything, she says ten times more.* A: 그러니까 **때리는 시어머니보다 말리는 시누이가 더 밉다는** 말이 생겼지. = *That's why they say that a sister-in-law can be even ten times worse than a mother-in-law.*

때 빼고 광내다 [Lit. to clean off the dirt and shine something up] IDIOM 몸치장을 하고 멋을 내다 = to get spiffed up / to get dolled up / to clean up nicely (*equiv.* all dressed up) ▌A: 어디를 가는데 그렇게 **때 빼고 광내**는 거야? = *What are you all spiffed up for?* B: 간만에 소개팅이 있어. 이번에는 좀 잘해 봐야지. = *I'm finally going on a blind date again. I've got to give it my best this time.*

땡땡이치다 [Lit. to ring the bell] IDIOM 수업이나 업무를 빼먹거나 주어진 일을 열심히 하지 않다 = to neglect one's duties or to carry out one's work in a shipshod manner (*equiv.* to ditch class / to play hooky) ▌A: 너 이번 달에 수업 **땡땡이친** 게 몇 번째야? 이러다가 낙제하면 어떡하려고 그래? = *How many times have you ditched class this month? What are you going to do if you flunk?* B: 나도 알아. 이제 마음 잡고 공부할 거야. = *I know. I've made up my mind to study hard from now on.*

▶p.208

NOTE: 이 표현의 기원은 정확하게 알려져 있지 않다. 다만 학교에서 수업이 시작하고 끝났음을 알리는 종소리에서 왔다는 설명이 가장 그럴듯해 보인다. 즉, '땡땡'하고 종이 울리면 수업이 끝났음을 의미하는데 시간이 흐르면서 현재와 같이 '수업을 빼먹다'는 뜻이 생겨났을 것이라는 설명이다.

The origin of this ubiquitous phrase is unclear. The idea of it being related to the ringing of the bell at the start and end of class, however, seems most likely. The ringing of the school bell meant that classes were brought to an end and it was time to relax. It is possible that the current meaning of skipping class came from this practice.

땡(을)잡다 [Lit. to get a good hand in the game *go-stop*] IDIOM 뜻밖에 좋은 일이 생기다 = to receive an unexpected profit or boon (*equiv.* to be the beneficiary of a windfall) ▌A: 이 핸드크림 너 가질래? 나는 여러 개 있어서. = *Do you want this hand cream? I already have a lot so much.* B: 야호, **땡잡았다**! 안 그래도 핸드크림 사려고 했는데. = *Nice, what a score. I was just planning to go buy some.*

NOTE: 화투로 하는 노름 중에 '땡'이라는 패가 있다. 이는 같은 카드 두 장을 가지는 것을 말하는데 상당히 높은 패에 해당한다.
In Korean traditional card playing there is a certain hand known as the 땡. It is a relatively powerful hand, so this expression means that the likelihood of success is very high.

떠오르는 별 [Lit. a rising star] IDIOM 어떤 분야에 새롭게 등장하여 주목을 받는 사람 = a newcomer in a field that is causing a stir (*equiv.* a rising star / a promising talent / the subject of much anticipation) ▌A: 저 선수는 누구야? 눈에 단연 띄는데? = *Who is that athlete? She really stands out.* B: 김연하라고 전국대회 고등부에서 우승한 애야. **떠오르는 별**이지. = *That's Kim Yeonha, the kid who won the national high school division. She's definitely a rising star.*

떡고물이 떨어지다 [Lit. for the crumbs of *tteok* to fall] IDIOM 어떤 일에서 부수적인 이익을 얻다 = to be the beneficiary of a secondary profit from a certain enterprise (*equiv.* to eat the crumbs (off of someone's table) / to get the table scraps / to get a slice of the pie *syn.* 콩고물이 떨어지다) ▌A: 이번에 사우회장 선거에 우리 팀 지영 씨가 나가는데 꼭 됐으면 좋겠어요. = *In the employee election I really hope Jiyoung from our team wins.* B: 왜요? 되면 한턱 낸대요? = *Why? Did she say she'd take you* *out for dinner if she won?* A: 아니요. 그래도 **떡고물이 떨어질지도** 모르잖아요. = *No. But I'm sure I could get a slice of the pie.*

NOTE: 떡고물은 떡의 겉에 묻히는 가루를 말한다. 비유적으로 어떤 일에 대한 부수적인 이득을 의미하는데, 떳떳하지 못한 일에 대한 대가를 의미할 때가 많다.

떡고물 refers to the sprinkles of flour etc. that is found on the traditional treat, 떡. Metaphorically it is used to describe any secondary benefits. It is most commonly used to refer to a unwarranted boon or perk.

떡 벌어지게 차리다 [Lit. to set the table broadly] IDIOM 여러 가지 좋은 음식을 많이 차리다 = to create a feast of many delectable treats (*equiv.* to lay out quite a spread *syn.* 상다리가 부러지다, 상다리가 휘어지다)

▌A: 미진이 아이 돌잔치는 어땠어? 많이 차렸어? = *How was Mijin's kid's first birthday? Was there a lot of food?* B: **떡 벌어지게 차렸더라.** 아주 정성을 많이 들인 것 같았어. = *It was quite a spread. It looked like they put a lot into it.*

떡 본 김에 제사 지낸다 [Lit. Now that one sees *tteok*, one holds a memorial service for ancestors.] PROVERB 마침 좋은 기회가 와 하려던 일을 해치운다는 말 = to go ahead with something that needed doing when one is met with a fortunate opportunity to do so (*equiv.* since we are here, we might as well ... / while we are at it / since it was mentioned)

▌A: 컴퓨터가 오래 돼서 너무 느리네. 이번에 업그레이드할까? = *The computer is so old and slow. Is it time for an upgrade?* B: 그래요. 그리고 **떡 본 김에 제사 지낸다고,** 텔레비전도 새로 사요. = *Let's do it. And while we're at it, let's buy a new TV too.*

떡(을) 치다 [Lit. to pound the *tteok*] IDIOM 1. 어떤 일을 하는 데 양이 충분하다 = to have enough of what is necessary for a given task (*equiv.* to be more than enough)

▌A: 이걸로 될까? 손님이 열 명도 넘게 올 텐데. = *Is this going to be enough? There's probably going to be more than ten people coming.* B: 스무 명도 먹겠어요. 이 정도면 **떡을 치고도** 남아요. = *This could feed twenty people. This is more than enough.* 2. (속된 말

로) 성관계를 갖다=(slang) to have sex (*equiv.* to hit it / to go at it *syn.* 만리장성을 쌓다, 몸을 섞다, 살을 섞다) ▍A: 아니, 저것들은 어떻게 된 게 하루 종일 **떡을 치냐**?=*All I'm saying is, how could they be going at it all day long like that?* B: 엄마, 딸 앞에서 **떡을 치냐**가 뭐야?=*Mom, I can't believe you just said, "going at it" in front of your daughter.*

NOTE: 옛날에는 떡을 만들 때 두껍고 큰 나무판에 찹쌀을 올려 놓고 큰 나무 망치로 여러 번 내려쳐 짓이겼다. 그렇게 해야 쫀득한 떡이 되기 때문이다. '성관계하다'를 뜻하는 '떡을 치다'라는 말은 남녀간에 관계를 할 때 살끼리 부딪치면서 나는 소리가 떡을 치는 소리와 비슷하고, 섹스의 동작이 떡을 치는 행위를 연상시키기 때문에 생긴 표현이다. 한편, '떡을 치다'가 '양이 충분하다'라는 뜻을 갖게 된 것은 가난했던 시절, 밥을 해서 먹고도 쌀이 남아 떡까지 칠 수 있다는 의미에서 온 것으로 이해할 수 있다.

Making *tteok* in the olden days involved putting a large quantity of sticky rice on a thick, broad piece of wood and hitting hit continuously with a large wooden hammer. That was the only way to get the rice properly mashed made into chewy *tteok*. As far as the phrase's sexual connotation, that seems to have arisen because the slapping together of two bodies makes a sound similar to that heard in the *tteok* smacking process and the actions themselves are not dissimilar. The meaning of being sufficient comes from the fact that in Korea's poorer days, most people didn't have enough rice to eat, let alone make *tteok* with. If one had enough to even "pound the *tteok*," it meant that there was plenty to go around.

떡(이) 되다 [Lit. to become *tteok*] IDIOM **1.** 크게 곤욕을 당하거나 매를 맞다=to be berated or beaten (*equiv.* to get pulverized *syn.* 묵사발(이) 되다) ▍A: 야, 지금 야구 경기 어떻게 돼 가고 있어?=*Hey, how's the game?* B: 벌써 끝났어. 롯데가 기아한테 **떡이 됐어**.=*It's already over. Kia pulverized Lotte.* A: 그래? 안 보기를 잘했구나.=*Really? I guess I'm lucky I didn't watch it.* **2.** 술을 많이 마셔 엉망진창이 되다=to be out of sorts from drinking too much (*equiv.* to be wasted / to be smashed *cf.* 고주망태) ▍A: 엄마, 우리 집 대문 앞에 웬 남자가 쓰러져 있

어, 술이 **떡이 된** 것 같던데. = *Mom, some guy is passed out in front of our house. It looks like he's wasted.* B: 혹시 네 아빠 아니니? = *Are you sure it's not your father?* A: 아, 그런가? 어쩐지 낯이 익더라니. = *Oh, is that who it is? I thought he looked familiar.* **3.** 머리가 한데 뭉치다 = for one's hair to stick up (*equiv.* to have a cowlick) █ A: 너 머리가 왜 그래? 완전히 **떡이 됐는데**? = *What's up with your hair? You've got quite the cowlick going on.* B: 아까 졸려서 잠깐 엎드려 잤더니 그렇게 됐네요. = *I was tired earlier so I put down my head and slept for a while and this is what happened.*

NOTE: 떡은 찹쌀을 반복해서 때려 만들었다. 그래서 심하게 맞았을 때 '떡이 되었다'라는 말을 쓰게 되었다. 술을 많이 마시면 마치 많이 맞은 사람처럼 몸을 가누지 못한다는 점에서 2번 뜻도 1번 뜻과 관련이 있다. 이때는 흔히 '술이 떡이 되다'라고 말하지만 실제로는 술이 떡이 된 것이 아니라, 술을 마신 사람이 떡이 되었다고 이해해야 한다. 떡은 쌀이 뭉쳐서 된 것이기 때문에 머리가 한데 뭉쳐 있을 때 비유적으로 '떡이 되었다', '떡(이) 졌다'라고 말한다.

As the process of making *tteok* involved striking rice dough repeatedly with a hammer, being beaten up badly was also referred to as "becoming *tteok*." When one has been drinking heavily and loses control over one's body, the effect is similar to what experiences after being knocked about a few times, so the first two meanings are clearly related. In these instances, people often say 술이 떡이 되다 (the alcohol has become *tteok*), but it would be more accurate to interpret that drink has made *tteok* of those that drank it. Because *tteok* is made of rice that is mashed together, someone's hair, when clumped together and sticking up, it is said that their hair "has become *tteok*."

떡 주무르듯 하다 [Lit. to do (something) as if one were kneading *tteok*] IDIOM 하고 싶은 대로 마음대로 하다 = to do as one wishes (*equiv.* (to manipulate people like) clay in one's hands / to have one's way / to deal with (something) as if it's nothing) █ A: 김 사장은 역시 손이 커. 지금 여기 밥값이 수십만 원은 나올 텐데 자기가 사겠대. = *Just as I thought, Mr. Kim is very generous. The food here is going to run into the 100,000s.* B: 하루에도 수억을 **떡 주무르듯 하는** 사람이니 그깟 수십만 원이야 아

무엇도 아닌 게지. = *For a man that deals with hundreds of millions of won every day like it's nothing, I don't think it's that big of a deal.*

떡 줄 사람은 생각도 없는데 김칫국부터 마신다 [Lit. to start by drinking the kimchi soup even though nobody has offered you *tteok*] PROVERB

일이 이루어지기도 전에 마치 이미 실현된 것처럼 섣부르게 행동한다는 말 = to take a premature action under a certain assumption (*equiv.* to count one's chickens before they're hatched *syn.* 김칫국부터 마신다) ▌A: 뭐하세요? = *What are you up to?* B: 파티에 초대받으면 입을 옷 고르고 있어요. = *I'm choosing the clothes I'll wear if I get invited to the party.* A: 아직 초대받을지 않을지도 모르잖아요. **떡 줄 사람은 생각도 없는데 김칫국부터 마시는** 거 아니에요? = *You don't even know if you'll get invited to the party yet. Don't you think you're counting your chickens before they're hatched?*

> NOTE: 떡을 먹다 보면 자칫 목이 막혀 사레가 들 수도 있다. 그래서 떡과 함께 마실 것을 마시면 좋은데, 전통적으로 김칫국은 떡과 아주 잘 어울리는 마실 것이다. 누군가 당신에게 떡을 주겠다고 하지도 않았는데, 벌써 그것을 기대하며 김칫국을 마시고 있다면 얼마나 우스꽝스럽겠는가.
> When eating 떡, it is sometimes possible to choke. That's why it's important to have something to drink as well. Traditionally what is thought to complement 떡 the best, is kimchi soup. If someone has yet to even offer you 떡 and you are already wolfing down the kimchi soup, you've clearly gotten a little ahead of yourself.

떼어 놓은 당상 [Lit. an already picked court official] IDIOM

틀림없이 될 것이 확실한 것 = something that is certain to happen or someone who will certainly be chosen for a position (*equiv.* to be a shoo-in (for a certain position) *syn.* 따 놓은 당상) ▌A: 올해에는 우리나라가 우승할 수 있을까요? = *Do you think Korea will take the championship this year?* B: 이번에 좋은 선수들이 많으니까 우승은 **떼어 놓은 당상**이에요. = *Well, we've got a lot of great athletes this year, so I'd say it's a done deal.* A: 그래도 길고 짧은 건 대 봐야 아는 거죠. = *Even so, it's not over till it's over.*

p.102

NOTE: 당상은 조선 시대의 꽤 높은 벼슬을 가리킨다. 떼어 놓은 당상은 당상 자리를 맡아 놓은 것이나 다름없다는 뜻으로, 어떤 일이 확실할 때 쓰는 표현이다. '따 놓은 당상'이라고도 한다.

A 당상 was a very high-ranking government official during the Joseon period. A 떼어 놓은 당상 is someone who is a shoo-in for the job, but the meaning of this phrase is something that is a done deal. It is used to describe something with a extremely high likelihood of occurring. This phrase is also iterated as 따 놓은 당상.

똑소리(가) 나다 [Lit. to make a *ttok* sound] IDIOM 말이나 행동, 일처리 등이 야무지다 = to be shrewd in one's speech, comportment and business

▌A: 김지연 씨는 일 하나는 정말 **똑소리가 나게** 해. = *Kim Jiyeon sure knows what she's doing when it comes to business.* B: 정말이에요. 이제 좋은 남자만 만나면 되는데. = *Yeah she does. Now all she needs to do is find a good man.*

NOTE: '똑'은 '조금도 틀림없이'를 뜻하는 부사이다. 예를 들어 "영희는 무슨 일이든 똑 부러지게 한다."라고 하면 일을 확실하게 처리한다는 뜻이다. 똑소리는 실제 소리를 가리키는 것이 아니라 조금의 빈틈도 없이 똑 부러지게 하는 일을 의미한다.

똑 is an adverb used similarly to "certainly" or "precisely." "영희는 무슨 일이든 똑 부러지게 한다," would mean something like, "Yeonghee always gets it done." It's a way of saying that someone always takes care of business in a reliable and precise manner. The 똑 in this case is not replicating any actually sound but rather depicts the way someone handles business in a 똑 부러지게 way.

똥끝(이) 타다 IDIOM = 똥줄(이) 타다

똥 묻은 개가 겨 묻은 개 나무란다 [Lit. A dog with excrement stuck to it finds fault with a dog covered with chaff.] PROVERB 자신의 큰 흉은 생각하지 못하고 도리어 남의 작은 흉을 본다는 말 = used to describe the tendency of some to fail to notice their own major flaws while pointing out

the relatively minor faults of others (*equiv.* The pot calls the kettle black. / to make hypocritical statements *cf.* 남의 눈의 티는 보면서 내 눈의 들보는 보지 못한다) ▌A: 너는 어쩌면 운전면허시험에 다섯 번이나 떨어지니? = *How could you fail your driving test five times?* B: **똥 묻은 개가 겨 묻은 개 나무란다더니, 너는 여섯 번이나 떨어졌잖아.** = *Is the pot calling the kettle black? You failed it six times*

NOTE: 겨는 벼의 껍질을 말한다. 똥이 묻은 개와 겨가 묻은 개, 어느 쪽이 더 더러운가?
겨 is the word for rice husks or chaff. Between a dog smeared with feces and one smeared with chaff, who is the dirtier dog?

똥오줌(을) 못 가리다 [Lit. to be unable to urinate or defecate] IDIOM (속된 말로) 사리 분별을 못하다 = to not be able to distinguish right and wrong (*equiv.* He doesn't know what's good for him.) ▌A: 명진 씨네 신입 사원 말이에요, 어제 보니 사장님을 보고도 인사도 안 하던데요. = *You know Myeongjin, the new hire? He didn't even say hi to the boss yesterday.* B: 그 친구 누가 신입 아니랄까 봐 **똥오줌을 못 가리는군.** = *How just like a new hire to not know what's good for him.*

똥(을) 밟다 [Lit. to step on poop] IDIOM 재수가 없다 = to have no luck ▌A: 누가 버스 좌석에 껌을 붙여 놓아서 옷이 엉망이 되어 버렸어. 아침부터 재수가 없으려니. = *My clothes got messed up because someone left gum on the bus seat. Is today going to be another unlucky day?* B: 그냥 **똥 밟았다** 생각해. = *Just think of it as a moment of bad luck.*

똥줄(이) 타다 [Lit. to have burning poop] IDIOM 몹시 마음을 졸이다 = to be extremely anxious (*equiv.* to crap oneself with fear / to be shaking in one's boots / to have the fear of God *syn.* 똥끝(이) 타다) ▌A: 영수 시험이 며칠 안 남았죠? = *Yeongsu's only got a few more days till the test, huh?* B: 네. 녀석도 이제야 **똥줄이 타는지** 방에 틀어 박혀서 공부하네요. = *Yeah, he's so nervous he's about to crap himself. He never comes out of his room anymore.*

똥칠(을)하다 [Lit. to paint with feces] IDIOM 체면이나 명예를 더럽히다 = to dirty someone's honor or reputation (*equiv.* to smear (someone's reputation) / to besmirch *syn.* 먹칠(을)하다) ▌A: 네가 이 아비 얼굴에 **똥칠을 하는구나**. = *It's like your smearing shit on our family name.* B: 아버지, 제가 시험에 떨어진 게 그렇게 부끄러우세요? = *Dad, are you really that ashamed of me for failing the test?*

***뚜껑을 열다** [Lit. to open the lid] IDIOM 사물의 내용이나 결과를 보다 = to peer inside and see the content or see the results of an undertaking (*equiv.* to unveil / to disclose) ▌A: 이번 경기에서 누가 이길까요? = *Who is going to win the game?* B: **뚜껑을 열기** 전에는 아무도 모르죠. = *There's no way to know until it's all over.*

뚜껑(이) 열리다 [Lit. for the lid to be opened] IDIOM **1.** 사물의 내용이나 결과가 드러나다 = for the contents of an item to be revealed or for the outcome to be made known (*equiv.* I guess we will just have to wait and see.) ▌A: 올해 노벨 문학상은 고은 시인이 받을 수 있을까요? = *Do you think the poet Go eun will win the Nobel Prize for Literature this year?* B: 글쎄요. 매해 소문만 무성하니 ……. **뚜껑이 열려** 봐야 알겠죠. = *Well, every year so far, there's just been a lot of rumors. I guess we'll just have to wait and see.* **2.** (속된 말로) 화가 나다 = (slang) to be angry (*equiv.* to blow one's lid / to go through the roof) ▌A: 아, 어떻게 저런 상황에서 골을 못 넣지? 나라도 넣겠다 저건. **뚜껑 열리네**. = *How could he not make a goal in that situation? Even I could've done it. I'm gonna blow my lid over here.* B: 기다려 봐. 또 좋은 기회가 있겠지. = *Hold on. He'll get another chance.*

뚝배기보다 장맛이다 [Lit. the sauce more than the pot] PROVERB 겉모습은 별로지만 내용이 훌륭할 때 쓰는 말 = used when the appearance of something is less than stellar, but it turns out to have great value (*equiv.* Don't judge a book by its cover. / Appearances can be deceiving. *ant.* 보기 좋은 떡이 먹기도 좋다 *cf.* 빛 좋은 개살구) ▌A: 이번에 새로 들어온 현주 씨 말이야, 일 참 잘하지 않아? = *You know Hyunju, that girl who just started? Isn't she a good worker?* B: 맞아. 솔직히 첫인상은 좀 무뚝뚝

해 보였는데. 역시 **뚝배기보다 장맛이야**. = *Yeah. Honestly, her first impression was a little stiff. I guess that's why they say appearances can be deceiving.*

NOTE: 뚝배기는 찌개 따위를 끓일 때 사용하는 그릇으로 모양이나 빛깔이 곱지 않다. 찌개를 끓일 때 뚝배기에 다른 재료와 함께 장을 넣게 되는데, 이때 결국 중요한 것은 뚝배기의 고양이나 빛깔이 아니라 장이 얼마나 맛있느냐다. 겉은 별로지만 실속이 있는 경우에 이 표현을 쓴다.
The 뚝배기 is a earthenware pot used for boiling Korean soups and the like, but its color and shape is rather drab. 장 is the word for a traditional Korean spice. When preparing Korean stews in this pot, 장 is mixed with other spices, but it's not the space or color of the pot that is important, but the taste of the food that makes the difference. That's why this expression is used to describe something with valuable content, or insides, but an underwhelming appearance.

뛰는 놈 위에 나는 놈 있다 [Lit. Above one who runs is one who flies.] PROVERB 아무리 재주가 뛰어나도 그보다 더 뛰어난 사람이 어딘가에 있게 마련이라는 말 = No matter how outstanding one's skills may be, there is always someone else who is better. (*equiv.* There's always someone better.) ▌A: 와, 중학교 때는 달리기하면 내가 항상 1등이었는데 고등학교 오니까 나보다 빠른 대가 많아. = *Wow, back in middle school I was always the fastest runner. But here in high school, a lot of kids are faster than me.* B: **뛰는 놈 위에 나는 놈 있는** 법이잖아. = *There's always going to be someone better out there.*

뛰어 봤자 부처님 손바닥 [Lit. Even though one jumps, one will still be on the palm of Buddha.] PROVERB 도망쳐 봤자 크게 벗어날 수 없다는 말 = Even though you try to escape, you won't make it far. (*equiv.* I can read you like the back of my hand. / Nothing gets past me. *syn.* 뛰어야 벼룩 *cf.* 손바닥 (들여다)보듯 훤하다) ▌A: 당신 담배 피웠죠? = *You smoked, didn't you?* B: 어? 어떻게 알았어? 양치질 했는데. = *Huh? How did you know? I brushed my teeth and everything.* A: 당신이 **뛰어 봤자 부처님 손바닥**이죠. = *Nothing gets past me.*

NOTE: 중국의 4대 기서 가운데 하나인 '서유기'에서 온 표현이다. 서유기의 주인공 손오공은 속박이 싫어 있는 힘껏 달아나지만 결국 그것이 부처님의 손바닥 위였다는 걸 알게 된다. 한편 이 표현에서 파생된 것으로, '손바닥 (들여다)보듯 훤하다'라는 표현도 있다. 손오공이 달아나려고 자신의 손바닥 위에서 애쓰는 모습을 다 지켜보고 있는 부처님처럼 속속들이 모든 것을 잘 알고 있을 때 쓰는 표현이다.

This expression comes from "Journey to the West," one of the Four Great Classical Novels of China. The protagonist of the book, Sun Wukong, so despised being tied down, that he leapt with all his might, only to find that he was still within the palm of Buddha. He thus realized his own limitations. From this story also comes the expression 손바닥 (들여다)보듯 훤하다. This expression is used when one, like the Buddha gazing down at the hapless Sun Wukong, sees the overarching implications of everything that is taking place.

뛰어야 벼룩 [Lit. It can run, but it's just a flea.] PROVERB 도망쳐 봤자 크게 벗어날 수 없다는 말 = used primarily to threaten the listener by pointing out that they won't get far even if they do attempt to escape (*equiv.* You can run, but you can't hide. *syn.* 뛰어 봤자 부처님 손바닥) ▌A: 놈이 어디로 갔을까? 순식간에 사라졌네. = *Where did he go? He vanished in a flash.* B: 그래 봤자 **뛰어야 벼룩**이지. 이 근처에 있을 테니 다시 찾아보자고. = *He couldn't have gone far. He's sure to be right around here. Look again.*

***뜨거운 감자** [Lit. hot potato] IDIOM 이러지도 저러지도 못하는 문제나 미묘해서 다루기 힘든 사안 = an issue that is hard to deal with or one that requires finesse ▌A: 이 영화는 실화를 바탕으로 했다죠? = *This movie was based on a true story, right?* B: 네. 이 영화 덕분에 요즘 파병 문제가 다시 **뜨거운 감자**로 떠올랐잖아요. = *Yes. And thanks to this film, the issue of troop deployments has once again become a hot potato.*

NOTE: 영어의 hot potato에서 온 표현이다.

This expression comes from the English expression, "hot potato."

뜨거운 맛을 보다 IDIOM = 따끔한 맛을 보다

뜬구름 잡다 [Lit. to catch a floating cloud] IDIOM 막연하거나 허황된 것을 좇다 = to chase after something vague or absurd (*equiv.* to have one's head in the clouds / to be full of hot air / to be on a wild-goose chase) █ A: 오늘 회의는 정말 시간 낭비였어. = *Today's meeting was such a waste of time.* B: 맞아요. 두 시간 동안 **뜬구름 잡는** 얘기만 한 것 같아요. = *You're right. It was pie in the sky talk for two straight hours.*

뜸(을) 들이다 [Lit. to steam thoroughly] IDIOM 본격적으로 일이나 말을 하기 전 잠시 가만히 있다 = to wait around before getting to one's main point (*equiv.* to beat around the bush) █ A: 음 ……. 제 생각에는요 ……. 그러니까 ……. = *Well ... I think ... um ...* B: 아, 뭔데 그래요? **뜸 들이**지 말고 속 시원히 말해 봐요. = *Oh, what? Don't beat around the bush, just spit it out.*

뜻이 있는 곳에 길이 있다 [Lit. There is a way where you have a will.] PROVERB 어떤 일을 이루고자 하는 의지가 있으면 그 방법도 찾을 수 있게 마련이라는 말 = suggests that when one has the desire to accomplish something, one will always find a way to realize that desire (*equiv.* Where there is a will, there is a way. / Nothing is impossible to a willing mind.) █ A: 저는 키가 작은데 농구 선수가 될 수 있을까요? = *Do you think I can be a basketball player even though I'm short?* B: **뜻이 있는 곳에 길이 있어.** 열심히 하면 키가 작아도 훌륭한 농구 선수가 될 수 있어. = *Where there's a will, there's a way. You can be a great basketball player if you work hard at it.*

마각을 드러내다 [Lit. to lay bare one's horse legs] IDIOM 숨기고 있던 일이나 정체를 드러내다 = to expose a happening or identity that one had been concealing (*equiv.* to betray one's identity or intentions / to give oneself up *cf.* 마각이 드러나다) ▌A: 어제 보이스 피싱 전화가 걸려 왔었어. = *Yesterday someone tried to scam me over the phone.* B: 저런, 당한 건 아니지? = *Oh, my. You didn't get taken, did you?* A: 어. 내가 수상해서 캐물으니까 나중에 가서야 **마각을 드러내더라고.** = *Something seemed suspicious, so I kept asking a lot of questions and he finally slipped up.*

NOTE: 이 표현에는 다음과 같은 설들이 있다. 첫째로 연극에서 왔다는 설명이 있다. 말이 등장하는 연극에서는 보통 말의 모습을 만든 다음 그 위를 천으로 씌우고 그 속에 사람이 들어가 연기를 한다. 어쩌다 연기자가 실수하여 천이 벗겨지면 말의 다리[馬脚]가 사실은 사람의 팔이라는 것이 드러난다. 또 중국 주원장의 부인인 마씨 부인의 일화에서 왔다는 설도 있다. 중국 주원장의 부인이 마(馬)씨였는데 전족을 하지 않아 발이 컸다고 한다. 당시는 작은 발을 미인의 조건으로 여겼기 때문에 마씨는 늘 자신의 발을 부끄럽게 여겨 감추고 다녔다. 그러던 어느 날 수레에서 내리다 실수로 발이 드러나고 말았다. 즉 마각(馬脚: 마씨의 발)이 드러난 것이다. 또는 영어의 show the cloven hoof(갈라진 발굽을 드러내다 → 본성을 드러내다)라는 표현과 관련이 있는 것이 아닌가 싶기도 하다. 영어 문화권에서는 갈라진 말의 발굽이 악마의 상징으로 여겨진다. 그러한 상징이 변형된 것일 수도 있다.

There is an assortment of stories relating to the origin of this phrase. When horses appear on the stage, the effect is usually pulled off by creating the shape of a horse, covering it with cloth and placing actors underneath the costume. But if the actors let the cloth hanging down slide too much to one side and expose their legs, the audience will immediately see that the legs of the animal are far from being that of a horse's. The other story dates back to ancient China. The emperor Zhu Yuanzhang had a wife whose last name was 마(馬), which means horse. As she had not bound her feet, they were quite large. At the time, having small feet was an absolute must if a woman wanted to be considered beautiful. Ashamed of her relatively large feet, she kept them hidden whenever she could. As she was alighting a carriage one day, however, she made a misstep and her feet were laid bare. That precisely could have been described as 마각을 드러내다, or "laying bare Ma's feet." The expression may also be rooted in English, which has the expression "to show the cloven hoof," and in which "cloven foot" or "hoof" have long denoted devils and demons. As often happens, the meaning of the phrase may have been shifted as it entered the Korean lexicon.

마각이 드러나다 [Lit. for one's horse legs to be exposed] IDIOM 숨기고 있던 일이나 정체가 드러나다 = to lay bare a happening or identity one had sought to keep hidden (*equiv.* to be found out / to be unmasked *cf.* 마각을 드러내다) ▌A: 되려 그쪽에서 나한테 막 욕을 하는 거야. 참 기가 막혀서. = *They have been saying all kinds of terrible things about me. It's really getting to me.* B: **마각이 드러나니까** 자기도 화가 난 게지. = *He's just mad because he's been found out.*

NOTE: See the note on 마각을 드러내다.

마른하늘에 날벼락 [Lit. a bolt of lightning in a dry sky] PROVERB 예상하지 못한 상황에서 닥친 재난 = a disaster that one had absolutely not anticipated (*equiv.* It came out of the clear blue. / lightning on a clear day / a bolt from the blue *syn.* 청천벽력) ▌A: 왜 집안 분위기가 이렇게 어두워요? = *Why is the mood so down in here?* B: 정수 말이야, 대학 합격자 발표가 났는데, 또 떨어졌어. = *It's Jeongsu. The admissions were announced today and he didn't make it into college again.* A: 아니, 이번에는 시험 잘 봤다면서요. 이게 무슨 **마른하늘에 날벼락**이에요? = *What? I thought he did well on the test this time. What a bolt from the blue!*

마음에 걸리다 [Lit. Something hangs in one's heart.] IDIOM 마음에 꺼림칙한 느낌이 있다 = for one to have an uneasiness in one's heart (*equiv.* Something is eating me. / I can't get over the fact that ... / to have qualms about something) ▌A: 어젯밤 남편하고 싸우다 한 말이 **마음에 걸려요**. 내가 너무 심했던 것 같아요. = *Last night, I fought with my husband, and what I said is still eating me. I think I went too far.* B: 오늘 집에 들어가서 미안하다고 먼저 말하는 게 어때요? = *Then why don't you be the first to say you're sorry as soon as you get home tonight?*

마음에 없는 말(을) 하다 [Lit. to say something that is not in one's heart] IDIOM 실제 마음은 그렇지 않은데 남의 비위를 맞추기 위해 괜히 빈말을 하다 = to say things that one doesn't actually feel in order to please others (*equiv.* to pay lip-service to someone) ▌A: 우와, 머리 스타일을 그렇게 하니까 부장님 십 년은 젊어 보이세요. = *Wow, that new hairstyle makes you look 10 years younger.* B: 이 대리 괜히 **마음에 없는 말 하는** 거야? 그래도 기분은 좋네. 고마워. = *Are you just saying that, Ms. Lee? Well, no matter. It still makes me feel good.*

마음에 와 닿다 [Lit. to touch one's heart] IDIOM 깊이 공감이 되다 = to feel a deep sympathy for something (*equiv.* (Those remarks etc.) really resonated with me / It really hit close to home.) ▌A: 아빠는 맨날 나보고 집에 일찍 들어오라고 잔소리야. = *Dad is always nagging me to come home early.* B: 뭐 틀린 말씀은 아니잖니? = *Well, it's not like he's exactly wrong, is he?* A: 그렇기는 한데, 아빠도 자주 늦게 들어오면서 나한테만 그러니까 그 말이 **마음에 와 닿지를** 않아. = *That's true, but since he's always coming home late too, it's hard to take him too seriously.*

마음에 차다 [Lit. to fill one's heart] IDIOM 만족스럽다 = to be satisfied (*equiv.* to feel fulfilled) ▌A: 저 녀석, 내 아들이지만 커서 뭐가 될지 모르겠어. = *That boy is my son and all, but I sure don't know what's going to become of him when he grows up.* B: 좀 너그럽게 봐 줘요. 병완이 어디가 그렇게 **마음에 안 차는** 거예요? = *Cut the kid some slack. What about our Byeongwan do you find so unfulfilling?*

마음을 굳히다 [Lit. to harden one's heart] IDIOM 결심을 확고히 하다＝to resolve oneself to do something (*equiv.* to make up one's mind / to be set in one's course of action) ▌A: 나 그 사람이랑 헤어지기로 **마음을 굳혔어**.＝*I've made up my mind to break up with him.* B: 정말? 후회하지 않겠어?＝*Really? Are you sure you won't regret it?*

마음(을) 놓다 [Lit. to lay down one's heart] IDIOM 안심하다＝to be at ease (*equiv.* to let down one's guard / to breathe a sigh of relief) ▌A: 일본에 또 지진이 났대요. 참 큰일이에요.＝*I heard another earthquake hit Japan. What a disaster!* B: 우리나라도 **마음을 놓을** 수는 없어요.＝*Even Korea shouldn't let down its guard when it comes to earthquakes.*

마음을 돌리다 [Lit. to turn one's heart around] IDIOM 생각을 바꾸다＝to change one's thoughts on a matter (*equiv.* to have a change of heart / to change one's mind) ▌A: 정민이 결국 자퇴했다며?＝*I heard that Jungmin ultimately dropped out of school.* B: 응. 가족들 모두가 걔 **마음을 돌리려고** 했지만, 걔 고집을 누가 꺾어?＝*Yeah, his family tried to change his mind, but no one can get through to him.*

***마음(을)먹다** [Lit. to eat one's heart] IDIOM 결심하다＝to resolve oneself to a course of action (*equiv.* to make up one's mind) ▌A: 내가 먼저 아내에게 사과하기로 **마음먹었어요**.＝*I made up my mind to apologize to my wife.* B: 잘 생각했어요. 지는 게 이기는 거잖아요.＝*That's good. Sometimes losing is really winning.*

마음을 비우다 [Lit. to empty one's mind] IDIOM 욕심을 버리다＝to abandon one's greed or avarice (*equiv.* to let go one's desires / to cast one's greed away) ▌A: 아, 꼭 이기고 싶은데, 시간이 얼마 안 남았어.＝*Oh, I've really got to win. But there's not much time left.* B: 그냥 **마음을 비워**. 다음에 이기면 되지.＝*Just let it go. You can win next time.*

마음을 사다 [Lit. to buy someone's heart] IDIOM 누구의 마음에 들다＝to win someone's favor (*equiv.* to win somebody's heart / to win somebody over) ▌A: 처음에는 장인 어른이 저희 결혼을 반대하셨어요.＝*At first, my* *father-in-law opposed our marriage.* B: 그런데 어떻게 장인 어른의 **마음을 산 거야?** = *Then, how did you win him over?* A: 그냥 자주 찾아뵈니까 좋아하시더라고요. = *I just went to see him often, and he started to like me.*

마음을 사로잡다 [Lit. to capture someone's heart] IDIOM 마음을 한곳으로 쏠리게 하다 = to draw rapt attention (*equiv.* to captivate somebody / to win someone's heart) ▌A: 저 가수는 목소리가 참 매력적이야. = *That singer has such a beautiful voice.* B: 맞아. 듣는 사람의 **마음을 사로잡는** 힘이 있어. = *You're right. He is very captivating.*

마음(을) 쓰다 [Lit. to use one's heart] IDIOM 관심을 기울이고 신경을 써 주다 = to show interest or caring ▌A: 몸이 안 좋다면서요? 정 안 좋으면 오늘 일찍 퇴근해요. = *I heard you haven't been feeling well. If you aren't up to it, just go ahead and go on home.* B: **마음 써** 주셔서 감사합니다. 그 정도까지는 아니에요. 괜찮습니다. = *Thanks so much for caring, but it's really not that big of a deal. I'll be fine.*

마음을 읽다 [Lit. to read someone's heart] IDIOM 생각이나 마음을 알아차리다 = to grasp someone's thoughts or feelings (*equiv.* to read somebody's mind) ▌A: 당신은 어쩌면 그렇게 내 **마음을 잘 읽어?** 마치 내 속에 들어갔다 나온 사람처럼. = *How are you always able to read my mind like that? It's like you know what I'm thinking before I even think it.* B: 내가 당신하고 산 세월이 얼마야? = *It's only natural considering how long we've lived together.*

마음(을)잡다 [Lit. to catch one's heart] IDIOM 마음을 바로 가지거나 새롭게 결심하다 = to make up one's mind or make a resolution to live in a more upright manner (*equiv.* to turn over a new leaf / to straighten up / to be right-minded) ▌A: 자네 아직도 남의 물건에 손대는 옛 버릇 못 고친 건 아니지? = *Have you still been unable to fix your habit of laying your hands on other people's belongings?* B: 김 형사님, 저 완전히 손 씻었어요. 요즘은 **마음잡고** 기술 배우고 있어요. = *Detective Kim, I've completely cleaned up my act. I've turned over a new leaf and now I'm* *learning a trade.*

마음(을) 졸이다 [Lit. to boil down one's heart] IDIOM 긴장하여 초조해하다 = to be in a state of nervous agitation (*equiv.* to be on edge / to be in suspense) ▌A: 왜 이제 왔어? 누가 올까 봐 얼마나 **마음을 졸였다고**. = *Why are you just getting here now? I was so worried that someone was going to show up.* B: 미안, 갑자기 급한 일이 생겨서 늦었어. = *Sorry, something urgent came up.*

마음을 주다 [Lit. to give one's heart] IDIOM 이성을 좋아하다 = to like a member of the opposite sex (*equiv.* to give one's heart away / to grow fond of someone) ▌A: 넌 하여튼 사람한테 너무 쉽게 **마음을 주는** 게 탈이야. 그러니까 자주 상처를 받지. = *The way you just give your heart away so easily is a major problem. That's why you're always getting hurt.* B: 내 마음이 내 뜻대로 안 되는 걸 어떡해. = *I can't control the way I feel.*

마음을 터놓다 [Lit. to open up one's heart] IDIOM 속마음을 숨기지 않고 드러내다 = to keep nothing concealed and make one's feelings known (*equiv.* to open up (to someone) / to lay one's heart bare to someone) ▌A: 회사에서 **마음을 터놓고** 얘기할 사람이 있어요? = *Is there anybody you can open up to at work?* B: 글쎄요. 깊은 얘기를 나누는 사람은 없는 것 같아요. = *Well ... There's no one who I can really have any deep talks with.*

마음(을) 풀다 [Lit. to undo one's heart] IDIOM 화를 풀다 = to get over anger (*equiv.* to let it go / to get over something) ▌A: 내가 잘못했어. 그러니까 이거 먹고 **마음 풀어**. = *It was my fault. So just eat this and calm down.* B: 내가 이번 한 번만 참는 거야. 절대 먹을 거 얻어먹어서 화 푸는 거 아니야. = *OK, but I'm just letting it slide this once. I'm not the type to just let things go when someone takes me out for dinner.*

마음(의 문)을 닫다 [Lit. to close the door to one's heart] IDIOM 자기의 마음을 다른 사람에게 보이지 않거나 다른 사람의 마음을 받아들이지 않다 = to not allow others even a glimpse into your heart and not allow others to draw close (*equiv.* to build a wall around one's heart / to be closed off) ▌A: 민진이가 웃는 걸 마지막으로 본 게 언제인지 기억도 안 나. = *I don't even remember when the last time I saw Minjin laugh was.* B: 작년 봄, 남자 친구랑 헤어지고는 **마음의 문을 닫은** 이후로 죽 저 상태네. = *Yeah, after she broke up with her boyfriend last spring she's been like that continuously.*

마음(의 문)을 열다 [Lit. to open the doors to one's heart] IDIOM 자기의 마음을 다른 사람에게 터놓거나 다른 사람의 마음을 받아들이다 = to open up emotionally to another or accept another into one's heart (*equiv.* to open up) ▌A: 민진이가 **마음을 열려면** 어떻게 해야 할까? = *What do you think it'll take to get Minjin to open up again?* B: 소개팅이라도 시켜 줄까? = *Should we set her up on a date?*

마음의 준비 [Lit. preparation of one's heart] IDIOM 어떤 일을 하기 위한 계획이나 각오 = planning or readiness for a certain task (*equiv.* emotional preparation) ▌A: 민진아, 내일 소개팅할래? = *Minjin, do you want me to set you up on a blind date tomorrow?* B: 고맙지만, 아직 새로운 사람을 만날 **마음의 준비**가 안 됐어. 나 아직 그 사람 못 잊었어. = *Thank you, but I'm not still ready emotionally. I still haven't been able to get over my ex.*

마음이 가다 [Lit. for one's heart to go] IDIOM 관심이 쏠리다 = to feel interest ▌A: 너는 어느 쪽이 마음에 들어? = *Which one do you like?* B: 저는 이쪽에 **마음이 가요**. = *I'm feeling this one.*

마음이 가볍다 [Lit. for one's heart to be light] IDIOM 기분이 홀가분하다 = to be lighthearted (*equiv.* to feel carefree / to feel set free *ant.* 마음이 무겁다) ▌A: 사실대로 다 얘기하고 나니 한결 **마음이 가볍네요**. = *After telling the truth, I feel so liberated.* B: 그러니까 다음부터는 혼자 ⬧p.116 끙끙 앓지 말고 얘기하세요. = *Next time, talk out your problems rather than keeping it all to yourself.*

***마음이 넓다** [Lit. for one's heart to be broad] IDIOM 이해심이 많고 너그럽다 = to be understanding and magnanimous (*equiv.* to be understanding / to be magnanimous / to be bighearted *syn.* 속이 넓다 *ant.* 마음이 좁다, 속(이) 좁다) ▌A: 넌 어떤 남자가 좋아? 난 일단 키 크고 잘생긴 남자가 좋은데. = *What type of guys do you like? I like tall, handsome guys.* B: 글쎄 ……. 뭐니 뭐니 해도 **마음이 넓은** 남자가 최고 아닐까? = *Well ... Don't you think an understanding guy would be the best overall?*

마음이 놓이다 [Lit. to have one's heart set down] IDIOM 안심이 되다 = to be relieved ▌A: 119에서 곧 오겠대. = *The 911 operator says they are on the way.* B: 휴, 이제야 **마음이 놓이네**. 아까는 정말 놀라서 죽는 줄 알았어. = *Oh, what a relief. I was so shocked I thought I certainly would die.*

마음이 돌아서다 [Lit. for one's heart to turn around] IDIOM 가졌던 마음이 달라지다 = to have a change of heart (*equiv* to move on / to lose interest in someone) ▌A: 붙잡아 보지 그랬어? 헤어지자는 말에 냉큼 알았다고 했어? = *Why didn't you try to hold onto him? Did you just say "yes" when he said "let's break up"?* B: 이미 **마음이 돌아선** 사람한테 매달리면 뭐해? = *What's the use in holding onto somebody who has already moved on?*

NOTE: 주로 부정적인 맥락에서 쓰이지만 긍정적으로 쓰일 때도 있다. This expression is usually used in negative contexts, but can also be used to describe certain positive circumstances.

마음이 들뜨다 [Lit. for one's heart to be lifted] IDIOM 기대나 설렘으로 약간 흥분되다 = to be excited (*equiv.* to be walking on air / to be walking on sunshine) ▌A: 이번 연휴에 특별한 계획 있으세요? = *Do you have any plans for this holiday?* B: 네. 일본으로 여행 가려고요. 벌써부터 **마음이 들떠서** 일이 손에 안 잡혀요. = *Yeah, I'm planning a trip to Japan. I'm so excited about it I can hardly concentrate on work.*

마음이 무겁다 [Lit. for one's heart to be heavy] IDIOM 걱정거리가 있어 마음이 편하지 않다 = to feel ill at ease or concerned (*equiv.* to feel worried / to be heavy-hearted *ant.* 마음이 가볍다) ▌A: 엄마가 눈길에 넘어지

셔서 다리를 다치셨어요. 그래서 **마음이 무거워요**. = *My mother slipped on an icy road and hurt her legs. I feel so bad for her.* B: 저런. 빨리 나으셔야 할 텐데요. = Oh, that's too terrible. I hope she will get better soon.

마음이 쓰이다 [Lit. for one's heart to be used] IDIOM 자꾸 생각이 나고 걱정이 되다 = to constantly think about something and be worried by it (*equiv.* to be unnerved by something) ▌A: 왜 그렇게 불안해 보여? = *Why do you look so uneasy?* B: 집에 아이를 혼자 남겨 두고 왔거든. 계속 **마음이 쓰이네**. = *Well, I left my kid home alone. I can't stop worrying.*

마음이 약하다 [Lit. to have a weak heart] IDIOM 결심이 단단하지 못하다 = to not be firm in one's decisions (*equiv.* to be wishy-washy / to be easily swayed by others / to have a hard time turning someone down) ▌A: 거기 절대로 다시는 안 간다고 했었잖아. = *You said you would never go back there, didn't you?* B: 응, 그랬지. 그런데 꼭 와 달라고 사정하는 바람에 ……. 내가 원래 **마음이 약하잖아**. = *Yeah, that's true ... but they really wanted me to come back. You know I'm easily swayed.*

마음이 좁다 [Lit. to have a narrow heart] IDIOM 이해심이 부족하고 너그럽지 못하다 = to not be understanding or magnanimous (*syn.* 속(이) 좁다 *ant.* 마음이 넓다, 속이 넓다) ▌A: 남자가 그렇게 **마음이 좁아서** 어떡해? = *How can you call yourself a man with such a narrow mind?* B: 아니, 여기서 남자, 여자 얘기가 왜 나와? = *What does being a man or woman have to do with it?*

마음이 통하다 [Lit. for hearts to communicate] IDIOM 서로 생각이 비슷하다 = for two people to have similar thoughts (*equiv.* to be on the same wavelength / It's telepathy. / You read my mind.) ▌A: 오늘 저녁은 피자 시켜 먹을까? = *What about ordering a pizza tonight?* B: 아! 안 그래도 피자가 먹고 싶었는데. **마음이 통했나** 보다. = *Wow! I was just thinking I was in the mood for pizza. It's like you read my mind.*

마이동풍 [Lit. 馬horse + 耳ear + 東east + 風wind → wind passing over a horse's ears] CHINESE-DERIVATION 남의 말을 제대로 귀담아듣지 않음을 이르는 말＝used to describe words that do not seem to be heard (*equiv.* for words to fall on deaf hears / like water off a duck's back / in one ear and out the other *syn.* 우이독경, 소 귀에 경 읽기) █A: 재호한테 얘기 좀 해. 저렇게 놀기만 하다 나중에 후회할 텐데. ＝*You need to tell Jaeho that if he continues to just mess around like that he s going to regret it later.* B: 걔가 내 말을 듣는 애예요? 내 말은 언제나 **마이동풍**으로 흘려듣는데. ＝*Does that kid ever listen to what I say? It's like water off a duck's back.*

마침표를 찍다 [Lit. to put a period (on something)] IDIOM **1.** 끝나다＝to come to an end (*syn.* 종지부를 찍다) █A: 관용어 사전은 다 썼어요? ＝*Did you finish writing your idiom dictionary?* B: 네. 지난주로 **마침표를 찍었어요**. ＝*Yep, I put the finishing touches on it last weekend.* **2.** 끝내다＝to finish (*syn.* 종지부를 찍다) █A: 타블로 사건은 정말 무서워. 한 사람을 그렇게까지 거짓말쟁이로 몰아갈 수 있다니. ＝*The whole Tablo incident was so scary—that people could paint a person as a liar like that.* B: 그래도 스탠포드 대학에서 최종 확인을 해 줘서 논란에 **마침표를 찍어** 다행이에요. ＝*He's just lucky that it was brought to a close with final confirmation from Stanford University.*

마파람에 게눈 감추듯 [Lit. like crabs close their eyes in a southerly wind] IDIOM 음식을 아주 빨리 먹어 치우는 모습을 비유적으로 표현한 말＝used to describe very quick eating (*equiv.* to gobble up / to wolf (food) down / to inhale food) █A: 아기들이 치킨을 **마파람에 게눈 감추듯** 다 먹어 버렸어요 ＝*The kids gobbled up that chicken so fast!* B: 원래 저 나이 때는 돌도 씹어 먹을 때잖아요. ＝*At that age they'd eat rocks if they could.*

NOTE: 마파람은 뱃사람들의 은어로 남풍을 의미한다. 한국에서는 남풍이 불면 비가 올 확률이 많은데, 게가 그것을 감지하고 재빨리 눈을 감는다고 한다. 아주 재빠른 동작을 묘사할 때 쓰는 표현이다.

마파람 is seafarer slang for a wind out of the south. In Korea, a wind out of the south usually means rain is on the way. They say that crabs sense this and close their eyes early. This phrase is used to describe a very prompt action.

막다른 골목 [Lit. a dead-end alley] IDIOM 더 이상 어찌할 수 없는 절박한 상황 = a situation in which one is left with nothing more to do (*equiv.* a dead-end / an impasse / (to be backed into) a corner *cf.* 사면초가) ▌A: 오늘 새벽, A 은행장이 스스로 목숨을 끊었습니다. = *The president of the bank took his own life yesterday.* B: 은행 대출 비리 사건으로 검찰의 수사망이 좁혀 오자 **막다른 골목**에 몰려 극단적인 선택을 한 것으로 보입니다. = *After the prosecutor's net was closing in around him, his back was up against the corner and he had to take extreme measures.*

막무가내 [Lit. 莫no + 無no + 可allow + 奈what to do → not allowing any course of action] CHINESE-DERIVATION 융통성이 없고 고집이 세 다른 사람의 말을 듣지 않음 = the qualities of rigidity and stubbornness while rarely listening to the advice of others (*equiv.* as stubborn as a mule) ▌A: 아유, 나 다시는 성민 씨하고 내기 안 할래. = *I'm never going to bet on something with Seongmin again.* B: 성민 씨가 어쨌길래? = *Why? What did he do?* A: 자기가 져 놓고 다시 하자고 어찌나 **막무가내**인지. 이번에 완전히 질렸어. = *He lost and then said we should bet again. He's as stubborn as a mule. I'm really getting sick of it.*

막상막하 [Lit. 莫no + 上over + 莫no + 下under → no one over or under] CHINESE-DERIVATION 실력이 비슷하여 거의 차이가 없음 = having no discernible difference in skill (*equiv.* to be neck and neck *cf.* 도토리 키 재기) ▌A: 둘 다 세 보이는데, 누가 이길까? = *They both look strong. Who do you think will win?* B: 해 봐야 알겠지만 **막상막하**일 것 같아. = *We'll have to wait and see but I bet it'll be neck and neck.*

NOTE: '도토리 키 재기'는 정도가 고만고만한 사람끼리 서로 다툴 때 쓰는 말이고, '막상막하'는 대체로 실력이 비슷하게 뛰어난 두 사람에게 쓴다.

막상막하 is used to describe two individuals that excel in a certain field and are almost equal in skill, while 도토리 키 재기 (measuring the height of an acorn) is used to describe a situation in which two parties of underwhelming skill compete in an almost comical way.

막을 내리다 [Lit. to lower the curtain] IDIOM **1.** 무대 공연이 끝나다 = for a performance to conclude (*equiv.* to finish / for curtains to close (on a performance etc.) *syn.* 막이 내리다 *ant.* 막을 올리다) ▌A: 다음 주 토요일이면 드디어 우리 공연도 **막을 내리는군요**. = *Next Saturday, the curtains will close for the last time on our performance.* B: 그러게요. 할 때는 힘들었는데 막상 막을 내릴 때가 다가오니까 이거 서운한데요. = *Yeah. It was tough while we were doing it, but now that it's finally over, I feel a little let down.* **2.** 어떤 일이나 시기가 끝나다 = for an era or a happening to end (*equiv.* for the curtains to close (on an era etc.) *syn.* 막이 내리다 *ant.* 막을 올리다) ▌A: 요즘 아프리카 각 나라에서 민주화를 요구하는 시민들의 시위가 계속되고 있습니다. = *Recently many African nations have seen people take to the streets calling for democratization.* B: 수십 년간 지속된 독재 정권도 이제 **막을 내릴** 때가 되었나 보네요. = *It looks like the curtains are finally closing on the decades-old era of dictatorial rule.*

막을 열다 IDIOM = 막을 올리다

막을 올리다 [Lit. to raise the curtain] IDIOM **1.** 무대 공연이 시작하다 = for a performance to begin (*syn.* 막을 열다 *ant.* 막을 내리다) ▌A: 어떻게 **막을 올린** 지 사흘 만에 막을 내리냐? = *How can they already be closing the curtains just three days into their run?* B: 관객 반응이 너무 안 좋대. = *They're saying that the audience reaction was really poor.* **2.** 어떤 일이나 시기를 시작하다 = for an era or undertaking to commence (*syn.* 막을 열다 *ant.* 막을 내리다) ▌A: 소설 〈무정〉은 한국 현대소설의 **막을 올린** 작품입니다. = *The novel "Moojeong" threw open the era of modern literature in Korea.* B: 우리나라 소설사에 획을 그은 작품이군요. = *Yeah, I guess it really left its mark on the world of Korean novels.*

막이 내리다 IDIOM = 막을 내리다

막이 열리다 IDIOM = 막이 오르다

막이 오르다 [Lit. to raise the curtains] IDIOM **1.** 무대 공연이 시작되다 =

for a performance to begin (*equiv.* for the curtain to rise / for the show to get underway *syn.* 막이 열리다 *ant.* 막이 내리다) ▌A: 비보이라는 게 육체적으로 참 힘들어 보이는데, 어떠세요? =*Life as a break dancer sure looks like it would be hard physically. What's it like?* B: 힘들지만, 막상 **막이 오르고** 무대 위에 서면 다 잊어버려요. =*It is tough, but once that curtain rises, you just forget all about that.* **2.** 어떤 일이나 시기가 시작되다 =for an era or an undertaking to begin (*equiv.* to get underway / to kick off *syn.* 막이 열리다 *ant.* 막이 내리다) ▌A: 드디어 전 세계가 기다려 온 올림픽의 **막이 내일이면 오르는군요.** =*Tomorrow the day that whole world has been waiting for finally comes: the Olympics get underway.* B: 이번 올림픽은 사람들 기대가 정말 큰 것 같아요. =*This year, people do seem to be expecting a lot.*

막장까지 가다 [Lit. to go to the end of the mineshaft / to go to the final scene] IDIOM 극도로 나쁜 상황에 처하다 =to face an extremely undesirable set of circumstances (*equiv.* to arrive at the final scene / to be at the last station / to be at the end of the line *syn.* 갈 데까지 가다) ▌A: 옆집 김씨 말이야, 사람이 못쓰게 됐더군. 대낮부터 술을 얼마나 마셨는지 인사불성이 됐던데. =*You know Mr. Kim from next-door? That guy's completely out of control. He's always drinking himself into oblivion at midday.* B: 맨날 빚쟁이들한테 시달리고 마누라는 도망갔으니 그럴 만도 하죠. =*With the bill collectors hounding him and his wife running off, it's no wonder he's acting that way.* A: 이러다 **막장까지 가는** 거 아닌지 걱정이야. =*I'm just worried that the train may soon be approaching the final station if he continues on like that.*

NOTE: 이 표현의 유래에 대해서는 다음 두 가지 설이 있다. 하나는 탄광의 갱도 끝을 뜻하는 막장에서 유래했다는 설명이다. 예나 지금이나 탄광의 일이라는 게 매우 힘들고 위험하여 많은 사람들이 꺼리는 일이고, 그 중에서도 막장은 가장 위험한 작업장이었다. 막장에 갔다는 것은 탄광일을 하는 사람에게 있어 가장 위험한 상황에 있다는 것을 의미하는데, 그것이 지금과 같은 일상적인 표현이 되었다는 것이다. 다른 하나는 연극의 마지막 장(면)을 뜻하는 막장에서 왔다는 설이다. 인생을 연극에 비유해 더 이상의 무대가 없는 마지막 단계에 들어섰다는 의미로 (인생)

막장까지 갔다는 말이 생겼다는 것이다. 최근에는 내용에 개연성이 현저히 떨어지거나 불륜이나 폭력 등 자극적인 소재로 보는 이의 눈살을 찌푸리게 하는 드라마, 영화 등을 보고 '내용이 막장이다', '막장 드라마' 등의 표현을 흔히 쓴다.

There are two ways of understanding the origin of this phrase. One is that 막장 means the end of a shaft in a coal mine. In the days of old, just as today, coal mine work was extremely dangerous and most people were disinclined to take the risk. The most precarious spot to set to work would have been the very end of the mineshaft and this phrase may have made it into the lexicon after beginning as a mining term. Many also believe that this phrase originates from the word for the final scene in a play. If one's life is but a play on the stage, finding oneself in the final scene could be a very scary thing indeed. Of late, the expression has been used to describe TV dramas that are overly unrealistic, immoral, or overly violent in a way that brings a furrow to the brow.

막차를 타다 [Lit. to take the last train (or other vehicle)] IDIOM 어떤 무리에 마지막으로 합류하다 = to be the last to join a certain group (*equiv.* to get the last ticket) ▮A: 오늘 경기는 양 팀에 매우 중요한 경기입니다. = *This match is critical for both the teams.* B: 네. 오늘 이기는 팀이 플레이오프행 **막차를 타게** 되니까요. = *Yep. That's because whoever wins this game gets the last ticket to the playoffs.*

만고불변 [Lit. 萬 ten thousand + 古 old + 不 no + 變 change] CHINESE-DERIVATION 아주 오랜 옛날부터 전혀 변하지 않음 = unchanging over the millennia ▮A: 어떻게 하면 희정 씨 마음을 뺏을 수 있을까? = *What do I have to do to win Heejeong's heart?* B: 자주 만나고 잘해 주는 것밖에 더 있니? 자기한테 잘해 주는 사람한테 끌리는 건 **만고불변**의 진리야. = *Is there anything but just meeting often and being good to her? It's been true since the dawn of humankind that people are attracted to those that treat them well.*

NOTE: '만고불변의 진리'라는 말을 흔히 쓴다.
Used in the form, 만고불변의 진리 (an unchanging truism).

만리장성을 쌓다 IDIOM = 하룻밤에 만리장성을 쌓다

만사형통(하다) [Lit. 萬 ten thousand + 事 work + 亨 go well + 通 go through] CHINESE-DERIVATION 모든 일이 뜻한 대로 이루어지다 = for everything to work out according to plan ▌A: 어, 정진 씨한테서 연하장 왔네? = *Oh, here's a New Year's card from Jeongjin.* B: 뭐라고 씌어 있어? = *What does it say?* A: "올해도 건강하시고 **만사형통하시길** 바랍니다."라고 되어 있어. = *"I wish you continued health and happiness to your heart's content in the coming year."*

만수무강(하다) [Lit. 萬 ten thousand + 壽 lifespan + 無 no + 疆 border] CHINESE-DERIVATION 병 없이 오래 살다 = to live long with no diseases or ailments (*equiv.* to live a long and happy life) ▌A: 할머니 **만수무강하세요!** = *Grandma, live long and stay healthy!* B: 그래, 너도 올해 건강하거라. = *Yes, and you stay healthy too.* A: 할머니, 나 세뱃돈! = *Grandma, my New Year's money!*

만에 하나 [Lit. one in 10,000] IDIOM 가능성은 거의 없지만 혹시 = with a very slight likelihood (*equiv.* next to impossible / a sliver of a chance *cf.* 십중팔구) ▌A: 너무 일찍 출발하는 거 아냐? 왜 이렇게 서둘러? = *Don't you think we're leaving a bit too early?* B: **만에 하나** 늦으면, 지난 일 년 동안 쌓아 온 공든 탑이 무너지는 거니까. = *If by some chance we are even a little bit late, all the efforts we've made over the last year will be for naught.*

➡ p.67

만장일치 [Lit. 滿 full + 場 place + 一 one + 致 reach] CHINESE-DERIVATION 모든 사람의 의견이 같음 = the state of complete agreement among all individuals in a group (*equiv.* unanimity / to be in accord / to be of one mind) ▌A: 우리는 **만장일치가** 되지 않으면 결정을 내리지 않습니다. = *We don't make any decisions unless everyone unanimously agrees with the issue.* B: 한 사람이라도 의견이 다르면 어떡합니까? = *Then what if there are some people who don't agree.* A: 그 사람이 동의할 때까지 토론을 계속하죠. = *Then we continue the debate until that person is in agreement as well.*

말 그대로 [Lit. per one's words] IDIOM 이어서 하려는 말이 과장되지 않았음을 강조하려는 표현 = used to stress that what one is about to say is not an exaggeration (*syn.* 글자 그대로, 문자 그대로) ▌A: 아직 공무원 시험 준비 중이야? = *You're still studying for the civil service exam?* B: 네. 아시잖아요. 공무원 되기가 **말 그대로** ▶p.557 하늘의 별 따기인 거요. = *Yes. You know what it's all about. Becoming a civil servant is no less than plucking a star from the night sky.*

NOTE: See the note on 문자 그대로.

말꼬리(를) 잡다 [Lit. to catch the tail of speech] IDIOM 남이 한 말에서 사소한 부분을 집어내어 따지다 = to latch onto something insignificant someone has said and make an issue of it (*equiv* to miss the point / to nitpick *syn.* 말끝(을) 잡다) ▌A: 이 영화 오늘 밤 한 시가 넘어서 시작하네. 너무 시간이 늦는데. = *This movie doesn't start until one at night. It's too late.* B: 한 시면, 오늘 밤이 아니라, 내일 오전이라고 해야지. = *If it's one o'clock, you shouldn't say "tonight," you have to say "tomorrow morning."* A: 또 사람 **말꼬리 잡고** 늘어지는 거야? = *So you're going to nitpick everything I say now?*

말꼬리(를) 흐리다 [Lit. to slur the tail of one's speech] IDIOM 말을 정확하고 분명하게 끝맺지 않고 끝을 얼버무리다 = to speak in an unclear manner and obfuscate the ending (*equiv.* to trail off / to equivocate / to obfuscate one's words *syn.* 말끝(을) 흐리다) ▌A: 너 주말에 여행 갔다 왔다며? 누구랑 갔었어? = *I heard you went on vacation last weekend. Who did you go with?* B: 아, 그러니까 …….누구냐면 ……. = *Ah ... well ... since you're asking ...* A: 왜 **말꼬리를 흐려**? 그러니까 수상한데? = *Why is your voice trailing off like that? You're starting to look suspicious.*

말끝(을) 잡다 IDIOM = 말꼬리(를) 잡다

말끝(을) 흐리다 IDIOM = 말꼬리(를) 흐리다

말(도) 마라 [Lit. Don't even talk.] IDIOM 다음에 말하는 사실이 정도가 매우 심하다는 것을 강조하기 위해 하는 말＝used to emphasize the seriousness of what is about to be said ▌A: 군대 있을 때 얘기 좀 해 주세요. ＝*Tell me a little bit about life in the military.* B: **말도 마라.** 시간이 어찌나 안 가는지 죽는 줄 알았어. ＝*Don't bring that up. Time has never passed so slowly in my entire life.*

말도 못하다 [Lit. to not even be able to speak] IDIOM 말로 표현할 수 없을 만큼 정도가 심하다＝to be extreme to a degree that defies expression (*equiv.* to be ineffable / to defy expression / to be beyond words) ▌A: 사고로 부모를 잃고 어린 두 남매만 남았다니 정말 마음이 아프네요. ＝*They lost both their parents in an accident. My heart really aches for them.* B: 돌봐 줄 친척도 없는데 고생이 **말도 못할** 정도래요. ＝*With no relatives to look after them, it really is beyond words.*

***말도 안 되다** [Lit. to not even be words] IDIOM 이치에 맞지 않다＝to not make sense (*equiv.* to be illogical / to be ludicrous / to be ridiculous *ant.* 말(이) 되다) ▌A: 여기 사는 사람들을 강제로 쫓아내고 새로 건물을 지을 거래요. ＝*I heard that they are going to force all the residents out and put up a new building here.* B: **말도 안 돼요.** 그러면 그 사람들은 어디로 가라는 거예요? ＝*That's beyond ridiculous. Where is everyone supposed to go?*

말뚝(을) 박다 [Lit. to drive in a stake] IDIOM 의무병으로 입대한 군인이 복무 기한을 마치고도 계속 남아 직업 군인이 되다＝to stay on as a professional soldier even after one's period of mandatory military service has concluded (*equiv.* to make a career out of it / to put down one's stakes) ▌A: 철민아, 너 제대가 언제지? ＝*Hey, Cheolmin, when are you done with your military service?* B: 그게 말이야. **말뚝 박을** 생각이야. 요즘에는 사회 나와도 직장 구하기가 쉽지 않잖아. ＝*Well, that's actually something I've been thinking about. I may just settle down here and make a career out of it. It's not easy to find a job out there these days.*

말로 때우다 [Lit. to solder over with words] IDIOM 행동으로 하는 대신 말로 대충 해결하다＝to handle something in a desultory way with words (*equiv.* to pay lip service / to paper over (something with words) / to make do (with words) *cf.* 몸으로 때우다) ▌A: 이번 결혼기념일에는 뭐 하실 생각이세요?=*What are you planning for this anniversary?* B: 딱히 할 것도 없고, 그냥 **말로 때우려고요**.=*Nothing special, I think I'll just make do with some kind words.*

말만 앞세우다 [Lit. to just put words out in front] IDIOM 말만 하고 실천은 하지 않다=to just talk about something with no action (*equiv.* to talk big / to be all talk and no walk / to be a big talker *cf.* 입만 살다) ▌A: 이번 시장 선거에서 누구를 뽑아야 할까?=*Who do we have to vote for in the mayoral election?* B: 글쎄. 저번 시장처럼 **말만 앞세우는** 사람은 아니어야 할 텐데. 계획은 거창했는데 실제로 실천한 건 별로 없잖아.=*Well, it better be someone who isn't just all talk like the current mayor. He had big plans, but almost no execution.*

말문을 떼다 [Lit. to remove the door to talking] IDIOM 이야기를 시작하다=to start talking (*equiv.* to break the silence / to open the discussion / to strike up a conversation *syn.* 입(을) 떼다, 운을 떼다) ▌A: 아까 그 영업 사원 이 일 한 지 얼마 안 됐나 봐.=*I guess that salesman from early hadn't been on the job very long.* B: 왜?=*Why?* A: 땀을 뻘뻘 흘리면서 어쩔 줄 모르다가 한참 만에야 **말문을 떼는** 거야.=*He kept sweating and didn't know what to do. Then he would keep quiet for a long time before finally breaking the silence.*

NOTE: 말문은 말이 나오는 문, 즉 말을 할 때에 여는 입을 가리킨다. 말을 하거나 하지 못하는 행위들과 관련한 표현에 쓰인다.
The word 말문 means the door through which speech passes, or more precisely the lips through which words pass. It is used in expressions that relate to being able, or unable, to speak.

말문을 막다 [Lit. to block the door of speech] IDIOM 말을 꺼내지 못하게 하다=to prevent another from speaking (*equiv.* to shut someone down / to shut someone up *syn.* 입(을) 막다) ▌A: 아, 그게 어떻게 된 거냐 하면 …….=*If you're curious how that all came about ...* B: 됐어! 당신 변명

은 듣기 싫어! = *I've heard enough! I'm sick of your excuses.* A: 당신은 왜 걸핏하면 사람 **말문을 막아**? = *Why are you always trying to shut people up at the drop of a hat?*

말문이 떨어지다 IDIOM = 입이 떨어지다

말문이 막히다 [Lit. for the door of speech to be blocked] IDIOM 놀라거나 어이가 없어 말이 나오지 않다 = to be shocked or appalled to the point that one is dumbstruck (*equiv.* to be left speechless / to be dumbstruck / Words fail me. *syn.* 말을 잃다) ▌A: 낮에 윗집에서 너무 시끄럽게 음악을 틀어 놓아서 올라갔더니 내 집에서 내 마음대로 음악도 못 듣냐며 도리어 화를 내는 거야. **말문이 막히더라니까**. = *The people upstairs had the music turned up so loud today. I went up there to say something about it and the man just said, "Can't I listen to music in my own house?" I was speechless.* B: 거 참, 적반하장도 유분수지. 말이 안 통하는 사람들이네. = *Wow, he kind of turned the tables on you there, huh? You just can't get through to some people.*

*말(을) 낮추다 [Lit. to lower one's speech] IDIOM 반말을 쓰다 = to use *banmal* or other informal forms of Korean (*equiv.* to dispense with the formalities *syn.* 말(을) 놓다) ▌A: 예림 씨, 아버지도 잘 계시죠? = *Yerim, your father is doing well, right?* B: 네. 어르신 **말씀 낮추세요**. = *Yes, sir. And please feel to speak informally with me.*

*말(을) 놓다 [Lit. to put down one's speech] IDIOM 반말을 쓰다 = to use *banmal* or other informal forms of Korean (*syn.* 말(을) 낮추다) ▌A: 오늘 면접을 갔는데 사장이 초면에 **말을 놓아서** 기분이 나빴어. = *I went to a job interview today, and the boss there immediately starting speaking banmal to me. It didn't feel very good.* B: 뭐? 정말 경우 없는 사람이네. = *Huh? How rude!*

말(을) 돌리다 [Lit. to turn around one's words] IDIOM 1. 이야기하려는 내용을 직접적으로 말하지 않고 완곡하게 말하다 = to not directly state one's point but instead talk in circles (*equiv.* to beat around the bush / to talk in

circles / to not get to the point *cf.* 단도직입(적) ▌A: 경호 씨, 제발 **말 돌리지** 말고 알아듣기 쉽게 말해 주세요. = *Gyeongho, please would you just stop beating around the bush and talk in an intelligible manner?* B: 네, 지영 씨, 그러니까 ……. 저와 결혼해 주세요. = *Yes, Jiyeong. So, what I'm trying to say is ... Will you marry me?* **2.** 화제를 바꾸다 = to change the subject ▌A: 경호 씨, 그건 좀 ……. 그런데 오늘 날씨 참 덥지 않아요? = *Gyeongho, that's a little ... Isn't this hot weather we're having?* B: 지영 씨, **말 돌리지** 말고 분명히 대답해 주세요. = *Jiyeong, stop trying to change the subject and just give me a straight answer.*

말(을) 듣다 [Lit. to listen to what someone says] IDIOM **1.** 다른 사람이 시키는 대로 하다 = to do what another tells you to do (*equiv.* to listen to someone / to do as you are told) ▌A: 경민이 이제 일곱 살 됐지? 엄청 귀엽겠네. = *Gyeongmin is seven years old now, right? He must be so cute.* B: 말도 마. 미운 일곱 살이라는 말도 있잖아. **말을 안 들어.** = *Don't even bring him up. There's a reason people call that age the "detestable sevens." He never listens.* **2.** 신체나 기계 따위가 다루는 사람의 뜻대로 움직이다 = for a device or one's body to do what one wishes (*equiv.* to listen) ▌A: 나도 이제 늙었나 봐. 오랜만에 등산을 하는데 몸이 **말을 안 들어.** = *It looks like I'm getting old. I went hiking for the first time in a long time and now my body's not doing what it's told.* B: 그러니까 평소에 운동을 해야죠. = *That's why I'm telling you, you need to exercise regularly.*

말(을) 맞추다 [Lit. to match up with another's words] IDIOM 제삼자에게 같은 말을 하기 위해 다른 사람과 말의 내용을 같게 하다 = to synchronize what one is saying with another (*equiv.* to get one's story straight *syn.* 입(을) 맞추다) ▌A: 너 오늘 학교 끝나고 어디 갔었어? = *Where did you go after school today?* B: 형이랑 도서관에 있다가 저녁 사 먹고 들어왔어요. = *I was with my brother at the library for a while and then we bought something to eat and came home.* A: 네 형도 똑같이 얘기하던데, 너희 둘이 **말을 맞춘** 건 아니지? = *Yeah, that's what your brother said too. Did you guys sync up your stories?*

말(을) 붙이다 [Lit. to attach talking] IDIOM 말을 걸다 = to start talking to someone (*equiv.* to strike up a conversation / to approach someone) ▌A: 미영이한테 얘기해 봤어?=*Have you ever talked to Miyeong?* B: 아니. 어찌나 쌀쌀맞은지 **말도 못 붙여** 봤어.=*No. She seems a little cold, so I've been afraid to try to talk to her.*

말을 잃다 [Lit. to lose one's words] IDIOM 놀라거나 어이가 없어 말을 하지 못하다=to be surprised or appalled to the point of being speechless (*equiv.* to lose one's faculty of speech / to be left speechless *syn.* 말문이 막히다) ▌A: 어떻게 우리나라 양궁이 예선에서 탈락할 수 있지?=*How could Korea be disqualified in the preliminaries of the archery competition?* B: 그러게 말이야. TV로 보고 있던 사람들도 다 **말을 잃은** 거 너도 봤지?=*That's what I'm saying. Did you see how even the people watching it on TV were at a loss for words?*

말(을) 트다 [Lit. to open up speech] IDIOM 두 사람이 서로 반말로 이야기하는 사이가 되다=to get to the point in a relationship where you use informal Korean ▌A: 우리 **말 틀까요**? 나이도 같은데.=*What do you think about speaking less formally? We are the same age and all.* B: 그럴까요, 그럼?=*Sure, why not?*

말(이) 나온 김에 [Lit. on the occasion of it being mentioned] IDIOM 대화 중 의도하지 않게 나온 어떤 주제와 관련된 행위에 대해 얘기하려고 할 때 쓰는 표현=used when one wants to say more about a topic that has inadvertently come up (*equiv.* since we're talking about / while we're on the topic / now that you mention it *cf.* 말(이) 났으니 말이지) ▌A: 재미있는 영화 뭐 없을까?=*Are there any good movies out?* B: **말 나온 김에** 영화나 보러 갈까?=*Actually, since you mentioned it, want to go out and see a movie?*

말(이) 났으니 말이지 [Lit. since that has come up, I'd like to say] IDIOM 대화 중 의도하지 않게 나온 어떤 주제에 대해 자신의 생각이나 의견을 얘기할 때 쓰는 표현=used when one wants to discuss more a topic that has inadvertently been brought up (*equiv.* since you brought that up / now that you mention it *cf.* 말(이) 나온 김에) ▌A: 비서실의 안 대리

말이야, 사람이 좀 이상하지 않아? = *You know Ahn, from the secretarial division? Doesn't something seem a little off about her?* B: **말이 났으니 말이지**, 저도 평소에 좀 그런 느낌을 받았어요. 인사를 해도 잘 안 받고, 늘 딴 생각을 하는 것 같기도 하고요. = *Yeah, now that you mention it, I have kind of noticed that. She rarely responds when I say hi and always seems to be lost in her thoughts.*

말(이) 되다 [Lit. to be words] IDIOM 이치에 맞다 = to be logical or reasonable (*equiv.* to make sense *ant.* 말도 안 되다) ▌A: 너는 이게 말이 된다고 생각해? = *Does that make any sense to you?* B: **말이 안 될** 게 뭐가 있어? 다 큰 성인들끼리 여행 가는 게 어디가 어때서? = *What about it doesn't make sense? What's so strange about two fully grown adults going on vacation?*

말(이) 많다 [Lit. to have many words] IDIOM **1.** 수다스럽다 = to be talkative (*equiv.* to be wordy / to be a chatterbox) ▌A: 남자가 **말이 많으면** 못쓰는 법이야. = *A chatty man is never a good thing.* B: 엄마, 요즘에는 안 그래요. 여자들도 재미있는 남자를 좋아한다고요. = *Mom, it's not like that anymore. I'm telling you, women like men who know how to have fun.* **2.** 논란이 많다 = to be controversial (*equiv.* to be much talked about / to cause a stir) ▌A: 요즘 이 영화를 놓고 **말이 많죠**? = *There's been a lot of talk about this movie recently, huh?* B: 네. 잘 만든 오락영화라는 사람도 있고, 쓰레기 삼류 영화라고 말하는 사람도 있죠. = *Yeah, some people say it's really entertaining and others say it's third-rate trash.*

말이 많으면 쓸 말이 적다 [Lit. One who talks a lot has little useful to say.] PROVERB 말이 많으면 실속 있는 내용은 적게 마련이라는 말 = used to describe a tendency of those who say much to say little of substance (*equiv.* Those who are always talking say very little.) ▌A: **말이 많으면 쓸 말이 적은** 법이니 너도 꼭 필요한 말만 해라. = *Since we all know that those who talk a lot actually say very little, make sure that you only say what is necessary.* B: 엄마, 안 그래도 사람들이 저보고 말수 적다고 제발 말 좀 하래요. = *I don't know, Mom. People are already saying that I never talk.*

말이 씨가 된다 [Lit. for words to become a seed] IDIOM 입 밖으로 낸 말의 내용이 실제로 이루어진다는 말 = used to suggest that things people say will come true (*equiv.* Be careful what you say. It may come true. / Words can plant the seed of an idea.) ▌A: 왜 이렇게 늦지? 사고라도 난 거 아냐? = *Why is he so late? Do you think he got in an accident?* B: 그런 말 하지 마! **말이 씨가 돼**. = *Don't even talk like that! It's bad luck.*

NOTE: 이 표현은 주로 부정적인 말을 입밖에 내는 것을 경계할 때 쓰인다. 하지만 가끔 긍정적인 말을 권장하는 뜻으로도 쓰인다.
This phrase is most often used to admonish someone for speaking of some undesirable possibility, but can at times be heard encouraging a positive or wishful utterances.

말이 아니다 [Lit. to not be words] IDIOM 사정이 아주 어렵거나 외모나 형편이 몹시 안되다 = for someone's circumstances to be trying or appearance to be haggard ▌A: 그 사람 얼굴이 **말이 아니던데**. = *He looks terrible.* B: 왜 아니겠어? 식구들 먹여 살리느라 밤낮으로 일만 하니 얼굴이 좋을 리가 없지. = *Why wouldn't he? He's working all day and night to keep his family fed. How's he supposed to look good?*

말이야 바른 말이지 [Lit. These words are straight talk.] IDIOM 솔직하게 말해서 = to speak candidly (*equiv.* to be frank with you / to be honest) ▌A: 네가 나한테 어떻게 이럴 수가 있어? = *How could you do this to me?* B: **말이야 바른 말이지**, 네가 나한테 해 준 게 뭐가 있다고 생색이야? = *And just what exactly is it that you think you've ever done for me?*

말(이) 통하다 [Lit. for speech to be conveyed] IDIOM 서로 뜻이 잘 전해지고 마음이 맞다 = to communicate well and have similar interests at heart (*equiv.* to be on the same wavelength / to be on the same page) ▌A: 남자 친구 어디가 그렇게 좋아요? = *What is it that is so great about your boyfriend?* B: 관심이 비슷해서 **말이 잘 통해요**. = *We're interested in the same things and we're on the same wavelength.*

말짱 도루묵 [Lit. a complete sandfish] IDIOM 노력했던 일이 헛수고가

되었을 때 쓰는 말 = used to describe a hard-fought attempt that has come to naught (*equiv.* to cancel something out / to cause something else to be in vain *syn.* 십년공부 도로 아미타불 *cf.* 물거품이 되다) ▌A: 아, 운동하고 났더니 배고프네. 뭐 좀 먹을까? = *I'm hungry now from exercising. Do you want to get something to eat?* B: 애, 살 빼려고 운동하는 건데, 운동하고 나서 먹으면 **말짱 도루묵**이야. = *Come on now, we are exercising to lose weight. If we go out and eat something, that will just cancel everything out.*

NOTE: 옛날 조선의 14대 임금이었던 선조가 임진왜란 때 피난을 가면서 먹을 것이 궁하자 한 어부가 '묵'이라는 물고기를 바쳤다. 선조는 이 생선이 너무 맛이 좋아서 '은어'라는 이름을 붙였다. 그런데 임진왜란이 끝나고 궁궐로 돌아와 다시 그 고기를 먹어 보니 처음처럼 맛이 없었다. 이에 선조는 "도로 묵이라고 불러라."고 했다고 한다. 이때부터 이 고기의 이름은 '도로묵'이 되었는데, 나중에 '도루묵' 으로 바뀌게 되었다. '노력을 기울인 보람도 없이 헛되게 된 일'을 가리키는 말이다.
During his flight from enemy forces during the Japanese Invasion of 1592, King Seonjo was running short on food, so a fisherman offered him a 묵 fish to eat. The king was so impressed with the taste of the fish that he christened it the 은어, or "silverfish." Later, however, when he had returned to his palace after the conclusion of hostilities and ordered the fish to be served at his table again, it was not as tasty as he had remembered it. At the affront, he renamed the fish yet again. This time calling it 도로 묵, or "mook again." For a time, the fish was known that way until its name again morphed into 도루묵, as it is known today. Its idiomatic usage denotes a fruitless effort, or exertions made in vain.

말 한마디에 천 냥 빚도 갚는다 [Lit. A debt of even 1,000 *nyang* can be repaid with just a word.] PROVERB 말을 잘하면 어려운 일도 해결할 수 있다는 말 = used to suggest that careful wording can solve even serious problems ▌A: 미순 씨를 보면 참 상냥하고 고객 응대를 잘해. = *Watching Misoon at work, I found her to be amiable and good with the customers.* B: 맞아요. 불만이 가득해서 찾아온 고객들도 다 웃으며 돌아가잖아요. = *That's right. Even the customers who come in here full of* *complaints leave with a smile on their face.* A: **말 한마디에 천 냥 빚 갚을** 사람이에요. = *She's the kind of person who can accomplish anything with a few words.*

말할 수 없이 [Lit. beyond words] IDIOM 말로 표현할 수 없을 정도로 대단히 = exceedingly, beyond words (*equiv.* in a way that defies expression) ▌A: 좀 괜찮아? 많이 아팠지? = *Are you doing all right? That really hurt, huh?* B: 어. 죽는 줄 알았어. 정말 이루 **말할 수 없이** 아프더라. = *Yeah. I thought I was going to die. The pain was beyond words.*

맛(을) 들이다 [Lit. to take in a taste] IDIOM 재미와 흥미를 느끼다 = to feel amusement and interest in something (*equiv.* to get into something *cf.* 맛(이) 들다) ▌A: 이 게임에 한 번 **맛을 들이면** 밤을 새우는 경우도 흔해요. = *Once you develop a taste for this game, you often found yourself playing it all night long.* B: 아예 할 줄 모르는 게 좋겠네요. = *Then it'll be better not to know how to play it.*

맛(을)보다 [Lit. to taste] IDIOM 1. 경험하다 = to experience (*equiv.* to taste (the bitterness/sweetness etc. of an experience)) ▌A: 영수 말이야, 말투가 좀 달라진 것 같지 않아? = *Doesn't it seem like Yeongsu is speaking differently than he used to?* B: 맞아. 방학 때 서울 생활의 **맛을 본** 이후로 말투가 영 이상해졌어. = *Yeah. After getting a taste of life in Seoul over the break, he's been sounding strange.* 2. 호된 고통이나 어려움을 겪다 = to undergo intense pain or difficulty (*equiv.* to taste the bitterness of an experience *syn.* 뜨거운 맛을 보다, 매운 맛을 보다, 따끔한 맛을 보다) ▌A: 어쭈? 너 이 자식, **맛 좀 볼래**? = *Get a load of this guy. Hey, you, wanna taste some real pain?* B: 제가 뭘 어쨌다고 그러세요? = *Hey, come on. What did I do?*

NOTE: 2번 뜻으로 쓰일 때는 앞에 '뜨거운', '매운', '따끔한' 등의 관형어가 흔히 온다. 관형어가 없이 쓰일 때는 주로 '맛 좀 보다'의 꼴로 쓰인다. When used in the second meaning, the phrase is often preceded by the modifiers, 뜨거운, 매운, 따끔한. If there is no modifier present, it usually appears in the form, 맛 좀 보다.

맛(이) 가다 [Lit. for the taste to go] ɪᴅɪᴏᴍ **1.** 음식이 상하다＝for food to spoil (*equiv.* It's gone. / It's gone south. / to go bad) ▌A: 이 찌개 **맛이 간** 것 같은데?＝*I think this soup has gone bad.* B: 아, 아까 끓여 놓는 걸 깜빡했더니, 그새 상해 버렸네. 아까워라.＝*I forgot boil it earlier and it must've gone bad in that time. What a waste.* **2.** (속된 말로) 정상이 아니다＝(slang) to not be normal (*equiv.* That guy is not normal. / to be out of commission) ▌A: 컴퓨터 완전히 **맛이 간** 것 같아. 부팅이 아예 안 돼.＝*The computer is completely out of commission. It won't even boot.* B: 우리도 이번 기회에 컴퓨터 새로 살까?＝*Should we take this as an opportunity to buy a new computer?*

맛(이) 들다 [Lit. to be tinged with a taste] ɪᴅɪᴏᴍ 재미와 흥미를 느끼다＝to feel interest and amusement in something (*cf.* 맛(을) 들이다) ▌A: 어머님, 이이 혼 좀 내 주세요. 요즘 바둑에 **맛이 들어서** 밤에 잠도 안 자요.＝*Mother (in-law), please have a little talk with your son. He's gotten so into go (baduk) that he doesn't even sleep at night.* B: 정말이니? 네가 좀 봐줘라. 그게 나쁜 일은 아니잖니.＝*Really? Just let it go. It's not like he's doing anything wrong.*

망망대해 [Lit. 茫hazy + 茫hazy + 大big + 海sea] ᴄʜɪɴᴇsᴇ-ᴅᴇʀɪᴠᴀᴛɪᴏɴ 아득히 멀고 큰 바다＝a vast and boundless ocean ▌A: 기러기아빠로 생활하신 지 벌써 5년이나 되셨죠?＝*You've been keeping an empty nest for almost five years now, right?* B: 네. 가끔은 텅 빈 집에 혼자 들어가면 **망망대해**에 혼자 떠 있는 것처럼 외로운 기분이 들어요.＝*Yes. Sometimes when I come home to that empty house, it seems like I'm like a boat adrift in a vast ocean.*

망연자실하다 [Lit. 茫hazy + 然so + 自by oneself + 失lose + 하다verbal suffix] ᴄʜɪɴᴇsᴇ-ᴅᴇʀɪᴠᴀᴛɪᴏɴ 크게 놀라거나 어찌할 줄 몰라 멍한 상태로 있다＝to be stunned after a major fright (*equiv.* to be stunned / to be in shock) ▌A: 아버님은 좀 어떠세요?＝*How's your father doing?* B: 아직 **망연자실해** 계세요. 한해 농사를 하루아침에 망쳐 버렸으니 왜 안 그러시겠어요.＝*He's still in shock. Seeing a whole year's worth of farming ruined in a single morning will do that to you.*

맞불(을) 놓다 [Lit. to set a counter fire] IDIOM 상대와 같은 수단을 써서 공격하다 = to use the same methods as the enemy in a counterstrike (*equiv.* to fight fire with fire) ▌A: 저 팀이 속공 전술을 쓰네요. 감독님, 우리는 어떻게 해야 할까요? = *They're using a fast-break offense. Coach, what should we do?* B: 우리도 속공으로 **맞불을 놔야죠**. = *We have to fight fire with fire, of course.*

맞장구(를) 치다 [Lit. to beat the drum in rhythm] IDIOM 호응하거나 동의하다 = to respond in agreement (*equiv.* to chime in in agreement / to nod along / to voice one's agreement) ▌A: 그 사람은 사장님 말씀마다 **맞장구를 치던데** 잘 보이고 싶어 그러는 걸까요? = *That guy is always nodding along with everything the boss says. Do you think he's doing that to get in good with the boss?* B: 아니에요. 원래 다른 사람 말에 잘 호응을 해 주는 분이에요. = *No, he's the type of person that always agrees with what others say.*

NOTE: 장구는 전통 타악기의 일종이다. 맞장구란 여러 사람이 서로 장단을 맞추며 장구를 치는 형식을 말한다. 한 사람이 장구를 치면 다른 사람들이 장구를 쳐서 흥을 돋우는 것에서 지금의 뜻이 생겨 났다.
The 장구 is a traditional Korean drum. 맞장구 is when a group of players strike the drum in a call-and-response type rhythm. The current meaning comes from the way the excitement would build a rhythm was passed around a group in this manner.

매도 먼저 맞는 놈이 낫다 [Lit. Even when it comes to getting whipped, it's best to be first.] PROVERB 어차피 당해야 할 일이라면 먼저 겪는 것이 낫다는 말 = It's better to just get it over with. (*equiv.* Sooner begun, sooner done. / It's better to get the worst out the way first.) ▌A: 자, 그럼 누가 먼저 도전할래? = *Who wants to give it a shot?* B: 제가 먼저 할게요. **매도 먼저 맞는 놈이 낫다잖아요**. = *I'll go first. It's best just to get it over with.*

NOTE: 단순히 매를 때리는 사람의 체력만을 생각한다면 매를 먼저 맞는 것이 유리하지 않을 것이다. 하지만 자기가 매를 맞을 차례를 기다리며 다른 사람들이 맞는 것을 보는 사람의 초조한 마음을 생각한다면 이 속담이 일리가 있는 것 같다.
This expression is not simply born out of the likelihood that the whipping party would grow tired as he continued his work but more likely came from the fear that others had to endure as they watched those ahead in line writhe in pain during their punishment.

매듭(을) 짓다 [Lit. to tie a knot] IDIOM 마무리 하다 = to complete a task or project (*equiv.* to tie up loose ends / to wrap (something) up) ▌A: 다음 번 프로젝트는 뭘로 하면 좋을까요? = *What would be right for the next project?* B: 그 문제는 우선 이번 일을 **매듭 짓고** 생각합시다. = *Let's wrap this one up before we start thinking about that.*

매듭을 풀다 [Lit. to untie a knot] IDIOM 어렵거나 꼬인 문제를 해결하다 = to solve a difficult or trying problem (*equiv.* to solve the puzzle) ▌A: 아들녀석이 요즘 나하고 말을 안 하려 해요. = *My kid never wants to talk to me anymore.* B: 사춘기 때는 다들 그렇잖아요. = *That's how every child is in puberty.* A: 어릴 때는 안 그랬는데 ……. 어디서부터 **매듭을 풀어야** 할지 모르겠어요. = *He never used to be that way ... I don't even know where to start with him.*

매운 맛을 보다 [Lit. to taste something spicy] IDIOM 호된 고통이나 어려움을 겪다 = to undergo great pain or hardships (*equiv.* to learn one's lesson / to get one's fill / to learn the hard way *syn.* 따끔한 맛을 보다, 뜨거운 맛을 보다) ▌A: 이 사람 또 여성을 비하하는 얘기를 방송에서 했다나 봐. = *I guess that guy was disparaging women again on his broadcast.* B: 그 사람 얼마 전에도 같은 문제로 사람들 입에 오르내렸잖아. = *Not too long ago he caused a dustup for similar comments.* A: 응. 아직 **매운 맛을 덜 본** 모양이지. = *I guess he still hasn't had his fill.*

맥(을) 놓다 [Lit. to put down one's pulse] IDIOM 힘없이 멍하게 있다 = to zone out in a lethargic state (*equiv.* to zone out / to be listless) ▌A: 자, 이렇게 **맥 놓고** 앉아만 있지 말고 이런 때일수록 힘들 냅시다. = *Now's precisely the time we need to be working harder, not sitting around and zoning* *out.* B: 맞습니다. 정신 바짝 차려야 합니다. = *That's right. We'd better get it together right away.*

맥(을) 못 추다 [Lit. to be unable to lift one's pulse] IDIOM 제대로 힘을 쓰지 못하거나 기가 죽다 = to not be able to summon one's energy or be lethargic (*equiv.* to be unable to pull oneself together / to not have the energy) ▌A: 오늘따라 왜 그래? = *You're not yourself today.* B: 며칠 감기 때문에 고생했더니 영 **맥을 못 추겠네.** = *I've been sick with a cold for the last few days and now my energy level is at rock-bottom.*

맥(이) 풀리다 [Lit. for one's pulse to be loosened] IDIOM 기운이 빠지다 = to lose energy (*equiv.* to lose momentum / to lose steam) ▌A: 아, 결국 이번 월드컵에서도 8강 진출은 실패했네. = *In the end we didn't make it to the quarterfinals at the World Cup.* B: 나름대로 잘 싸우기는 했지만, 지고 나니 **맥이 풀리네요.** = *We did pretty well but I've been kind of down since our loss.*

맨발 벗고 나서다 IDIOM = 발 벗고 나서다

머리가 가볍다 [Lit. to have a light head] IDIOM 정신이 맑고 또렷하다 = to have a clear and bright outlook (*equiv.* to have a clear head *ant.* 머리가 무겁다) ▌A: 어때? 기분은 좀 나아졌어? = *How are you doing? Feeling a little bit better?* B: 어. 한숨 잤더니 한결 **머리가 가벼워.** = *Yep. Now that I've had a little sleep, my head has cleared.*

머리가 굳다 [Lit. to have a hard head] IDIOM 1. 생각이 유연하지 않고 완고하다 = for one's ideas to be rigid and fixed (*equiv.* to be thick-skulled / to be hard-headed) ▌A: 내가 **머리가 굳은** 탓인지 모르겠지만, 요즘 젊은 친구들이 어른들 앞에서 담배 피우는 게 내 상식으로는 이해가 안 된다. = *Maybe it's just because I'm hard-headed, but I just don't understand the way that youngsters these days just smoke in front of adults.* B: 그런 사람도 있지만 대부분은 안 그래요, 아버지. = *Some people may do that, but most people don't, Dad.* 2. 기억력이나 학습 능력이 떨어지다 = to have a bad memory or weak scholastic abilities (*ant.* 머리가

(잘) 돌아가다) █A: 이번 학기에 복학했지? 다시 대학생이 된 기분이 어때?＝*You started up college again this semester, right? How does it feel to be a student again?* B: 좋긴 한데, 군대에 있는 동안 **머리가 굳었나** 봐. 강의 시간에 집중이 잘 안 돼.＝*It's all right but during my time in the army, my skull must've gotten thicker because I'm sure having trouble concentrating during class.*

머리(가) 굵어지다 [Lit. for one's head to grow large] IDIOM 성장하여 아이 티를 벗다＝to shed all traces of childhood (*equiv.* to be full grown / to be all grown up *syn.* 머리(가) 커지다) █A: 요즘 아들 녀석이 **머리 좀 굵어졌다고** 말을 통 안 들어요.＝*I guess my son is all grown up now. We don't seem to be able to understand each other at all.* B: 원래 자식이란 게 그런 거예요.＝*That's just the way kids are.*

(머리가) 모자라다 [Lit. to lack brains] IDIOM 지능이 정상적인 수준에 이르지 못하다＝to fail to meet the average level of intellect (*equiv.* to lack the brains (for a certain activity)) █A: 너는 가끔 보면 꼭 **머리가 모자란** 사람처럼 말하더라.＝*Sometimes you really talk like someone who's lacking in the brains department.* B: 그래? 그럴 때는 꼭 지금처럼 말해 줘.＝*Really? Whenever that happens, make sure to tell me, just like you are now.*

머리가 무겁다 [Lit. to have a heavy head] IDIOM 정신이 맑지 않아 기분이 좋지 않다＝to have a dark air or be unhappy (*equiv.* to have a heavy feeling in one's head *ant.* 머리가 가볍다) █A: 어디가 안 좋으셔서 오셨습니까?＝*What's troubling you?* B: 네, 요즘 계속 잠을 잘 못 자고 **머리가 무겁습니다.**＝*Well, I've been unable to sleep now for a few days and my head is feeling a little heavy.*

머리가 복잡하다 [Lit. for one's head to be mixed up] IDIOM 고민이 많다＝to have much to worry about (*equiv.* to have many worries / to have a lot on one's mind) █A: 왜 요새 통 연락이 없었어요?＝*Why do you never call?* B: 요즘 결혼 문제 때문에 **머리가 좀 복잡해요.**＝*I've just had so much on my mind with the wedding and all.*

머리가 (잘) 돌아가다 [Lit. for one's head to spin around well] IDIOM 어떤 대상에 대해 이해가 빠르고 영리하다 = to have a quick comprehension and a fast thought process (*equiv.* to be sharp *ant.* 머리가 굳다) ➡p.232 ▌A: 젊은 친구가 왜 그렇게 **머리가 안 돌아가**? 벌써 머리가 굳은 거야? = *Why does a young guy like you have such a slow mind? Are you already set in your ways?* B: 죄송합니다. 앞으로는 이런 일 없도록 하겠습니다. = *I'm very sorry. I promise this won't happen again.*

머리(가) 커지다 [Lit. for one's head to get big] IDIOM 성장하여 아이 티를 벗다 = to grow up and shed all traces of childhood (*equiv.* to be full grown / to be headstrong *syn.* 머리(가) 굵어지다) ▌A: 경수가 이제 고3이지? = *Gyeongsu must be a senior in high school now, huh?* B: 어. 애가 **머리 좀 커졌다고** 내 말도 잘 안 듣고, 제 방에서 잘 나오지도 않아. = *Yep. He's pretty headstrong now. He never listens to what I say and rarely comes out of his room.*

머리가 (텅) 비다 [Lit. to have an empty head] IDIOM **1.** 아무 생각 없이 멍한 상태가 되다 = to be zoned out or devoid of thoughts (*equiv.* to be numb / to be stunned) ▌A: 무슨 문자길래 그래? = *Just how serious was that message?* B: 남자 친구가 이제 헤어지자네. 갑자기 **머리가 텅 비는** 느낌이야. = *Now my boyfriend is saying that we should break up. I suddenly feel numb.* **2.** 무식하다 = to be ignorant (*equiv.* to have an empty head) ▌A: 얼굴은 예쁘지만 **머리는 텅 빈** 여자가 많은 것 같아요. = *It seems like there are a lot of women out there who look pretty but are completely empty-headed.* B: 남자도 마찬가지죠. 운동만 하고 머리에 든 것은 없는 남자도 많지요. = *It's the same with men: it seems like most of them spend all their time exercising and have not a thing in their brains.*

머리(를) 굴리다 [Lit. to roll one's head] IDIOM 어떤 문제를 해결할 방법을 궁리하다 = to devise a solution to a problem (*equiv.* to come up with an idea / to find a way / to brainstorm a problem) ▌A: 무슨 좋은 방법이 없을까? = *Don't you think we can find a better way?* B: 나야 모르지. = *Me? I really have no idea.* A: 그러지 말고 네가 **머리를 좀 굴려** 봐. 너 머리 좋잖아. = *Don't say that. Just put some thought into it. You're* *smart after all.*

머리(를) 굽히다 [Lit. to bend (down) one's head] IDIOM 굴복하다 = to submit or yield (*equiv.* to bow down (before someone) / to give in *syn.* 머리(를) 숙이다) ▌A: 무슨 일 때문에 싸웠는지는 모르겠지만 그냥 네가 먼저 사과해. = *I don't know what you two have been fighting about but you need to just go and apologize first.* B: 이번에는 내가 먼저 **머리를 굽히고** 들어가고 싶지 않아. = *I don't want to be the one to give in first this time.*

머리(를) 깎다 [Lit. to shave one's head] IDIOM 승려가 되다 = to enter the (Buddhist) priesthood (*equiv.* to become a man of the cloth) ▌A: 너 이번에도 시험 떨어지면 어떻게 할 거야? = *What are you going to do if you flunk the test this time around?* B: 모르겠어요. **머리 깎고** 절에나 들어갈까 ……. = *I'm not sure ... maybe shave my head bald and head for the temple.*

머리를 들다 [Lit. to lift one's head] IDIOM 눌렸던 감정이나 일, 세력 등이 일어나다 = for an oppressed emotion, faction or group to rise up (*equiv.* to rear its head / to rise up *syn.* 고개를 들다, 고개를 내밀다) ▌A: 너 완전히 담배 끊었어? = *Have you completely quit smoking?* B: 잘 모르겠어. 한동안 안 피웠는데 요즘 들어 담배 생각이 자꾸만 **머리를 드네**. = *I'm not really sure. I hadn't been smoking for a while there, but recently the addiction seems to be rearing its ugly head again.*

머리(를) 모으다 [Lit. to gather heads] IDIOM 함께 의논하다 = to discuss (a matter) in a group (*equiv.* Let's put our heads together. / to build a brain trust) ▌A: 걱정할 것 없어. 우리 셋이 **머리를 모으면** 해결 못 할 일이 뭐 있겠니? = *We don't have anything to worry about. Is there any problem we can't solve if the three of us put our heads together?* B: 그도 그렇구나. 난 너만 믿어. = *Yeah, I suppose you're right. I'll put my faith in you then.*

머리(를) 숙이다 [Lit. to bow one's head] IDIOM **1.** 굴복하다 = to yield or surrender (*equiv.* to bow down before (a stronger power) *syn.* 머리(를) 굽히다) ▌A: 전화를 먼저 해 볼까?＝*Should I make the first call?* B: 목마른 놈이 우물 판다고 아쉬운 네가 **머리를 먼저 숙이고** 들어가야지 별 수 있니?＝*They say that it's the thirsty man who digs the well, don't they? I think there's no other way but for you to give in and take the first steps.* **2.** 존경의 뜻을 나타내다＝to demonstrate one's respect (*equiv.* to pay one's respects) ▌A: 교장 선생님의 퇴임을 맞아 학생 대표가 감사의 글을 낭독하겠습니다.＝*And now, on the occasion of the Principal's retirement, a representative from the student body will recite a statement of gratitude.* B: 학교를 위해 헌신하신 교장 선생님께 **머리 숙여** 감사드립니다.＝*We bow our heads before you in acknowledgement of your years of selfless service to this school.*

머리를 스치다 [Lit. to have one's mind grazed] IDIOM 생각이 떠오르다＝

to have a thought occur to one (*equiv.* to have a thought cross one's mind / to have a thought pop into one's mind) ▌A: 방금 좋은 생각이 **머리를 스쳤는데** 한번 들어 봐.＝*I just had a thought pop into my mind. Why don't you give it a listen?* B: 그래? 뭐야? 많은 사람들한테 우리 상품을 알릴 수 있는 방법이 있어?＝*What is it? A way to inform a lot of people about our product?*

머리(를) 식히다 [Lit. to cool one's head] IDIOM 열중하던 일을 잠시 그

만두고 휴식을 취하다＝to take a slight reprieve from something that one had passionately been engaged in (*equiv.* to cool one's head / to take a timeout) ▌A: 아, 머리 아파. 주말 내내 리포트를 쓴다고 방 안에만 있었더니 골치가 아프네.＝*Ouch, my head hurts. I spent the weekend in my room trying to finish this report and now I've got a bad headache.* B: 그럴 때는 **머리도 식힐** 겸 교외로 드라이브나 하고 와.＝*When you're feeling that way, the best thing is to take a nice drive in the countryside to cool your head.*

머리(를) 싸매다 [Lit. to wrap up one's head] IDIOM **1.** 열심히 생각하

다＝to think intensely (*equiv.* to rack one's brain / to brainstorm) ▌A: **머리를 싸매고** 궁리해도 뾰족한 방법이 생각이 안 나네.＝*I've been racking my brains, but I still can't think of a solution.* B: 일단 자고 내일

생각하는 게 어때? =*How about getting a good night's sleep and going at it again tomorrow?* **2.** 걱정거리가 있어 몸을 가누지 못하고 자리에 눕다 = for a worry to prevent one from carrying on normally ▌A: 너희들 결혼 안 하기로 했다고 엄마한테 말씀 드렸어? =*Did you tell Mom that you two decided not to get married?* B: 어. 엄마 진짜 **머리 싸매고** 누우셨어. = *Yeah, she didn't take it well and had to lie down.*

NOTE: 이 표현은 머리에 천을 두르는 실제 동작을 바탕으로 한 관용어이다. 대단한 결심을 했거나 두통이 있을 때 머리에 천을 두르는데 아마도 머리에 압박을 주어 정신을 차리기 위함이 아닌가 싶다.
This expression comes from the action of wrapping cloth around one's head. In Korea, wrapping cloth around one's head can be a way of dealing with a bad headache or when one wishes to express a resolute mindset. The pressure exerted on the skull may have been thought to help one think straight.

머리(를) 쓰다 [Lit. to use one's head] IDIOM 좋은 방법을 찾기 위해 깊이 생각하다 = to think deeply for a solution (*equiv.* to use your head / to put a lot of thought into something / to rack one's brain) ▌A: **머리를 써야지**, 힘으로 한다고 되니? = *You've got to use your head. Do you think you can handle this with brute force?* B: 머리가 안 돌아가는 걸 어떡해요? 남는 게 힘인데 ……. = *What do I do if my brain isn't working? All I've got is my strength.*

▶p.234

머리에 맴돌다 [Lit. to (have a thought) run circles in one's mind] IDIOM **1.** 잊혀지지 않고 생각나다 = for something to not be forgotten and constantly occur to someone (*equiv.* It keeps running through my mind. / I can't get it out of my mind.) ▌A: 어젯밤 영화에서 본 그 잔인한 장면이 자꾸 **머리에 맴돌아요**. = *That cruel scene from the movie last night keeps running through my mind.* B: 내가 그래서 무서운 영화를 안 본다니까. = *I told you that's why I don't watch scary movies.* **2.** 무엇이 기억이 날 듯 말 듯하다 = for something to be barely remembered (*equiv.* It's hazy in my memory.) ▌A: 그래, 생각났어! = *I just remembered!* B: 갑자기 무슨 말이야? = *What did you remember all of a sudden?* A: 이번 주

내내 그 노래 제목이 **머리에 맴돌기만** 하고 생각이 안 났는데, 지금 생각이 났어. =*I've been trying to think of the title to a song for the last week and I finally got it.*

머리에 털 나고 [Lit. ever since the first hairs sprouted on one's head] IDIOM 태어난 이후로=(ever) since one was born (*equiv.* ever since I was born / since I took one's first steps / my whole life) ▌A: 우와, 김태인 실제로 보니까 더 예쁜 것 같지 않아?=*Don't you think Kim Taein is even more beautiful in person?* B: **머리에 털 나고** 그렇게 예쁜 여자는 처음 봤어. =*She's the most beautiful woman I've ever laid eyes upon.*

머리에 피도 안 마르다 [Lit. to still have un-dried blood on one's head] IDIOM (속된 말로) 아직 어리다=(slang) to still be young (*equiv.* to be wet behind the ears / to be just a kid / a young'un *syn.* 대가리에 피도 안 마르다, 이마에 피도 안 마르다) ▌A: **머리에 피도 안 마른** 녀석이 무슨 술이야?=*What's a young'un like you doing drinking?* B: 저도 올해 열아홉 살이에요. 이제 애가 아니라고요!=*I'll be 19 this year too. I'm telling you, I'm not a kid anymore.*

머리 회전이 빠르다 [Lit. The revolutions of one's mind are fast.] IDIOM 똑똑하고 영리하다=to be smart and intelligent (*equiv.* to be a fast thinker / to be quick on one's feet) ▌A: 뛰어난 선수들은 운동도 잘하지만, **머리 회전도 빠른** 것 같아요=*Truly remarkable athletes are of course great at their chosen sport, but they also seem to be able to think on their feet.* B: 운동 선수가 머리가 나쁘다는 건 정말 잘못된 생각이지요. =*The idea that athletes aren't that smart is really a misconception.*

먹칠(을)하다 [Lit. to paint with ink] IDIOM 체면이나 명예를 더럽히다=to tarnish someone's reputation (*equiv.* to besmirch (someone's honor, reputation) / to dirty / to tarnish *syn.* 똥칠(을)하다) ▌A: 요즘 학교 폭력이 큰 사회적 문제입니다. 우리 학교도 그런 일로 학교 명예에 **먹칠을 하는** 일이 없도록 선생님들이 신경을 많이 써 주세요. =*Violence in the schools is one of society's main problems these days. I hope that our teachers will make sure that our school's reputation is never tainted* *by such incidents.* B: 네, 알겠습니다. = *Yes, we understand.*

먼 사촌보다 가까운 이웃이 낫다 [Lit A nearby neighbor is better than a distant uncle.] PROVERB 친척이라도 자주 못 보는 사이보다는 자주 만나는 이웃이 더 소중하다는 말 = used to suggest that a neighbor that one sees often can be more precious than one's distant relations ▌A: **먼 사촌보다 가까운 이웃이 낫다더니** 정말 옆집 영희 아빠 아니었으면 큰일날 뻔했어. = *I guess this is why they say that a nearby neighbor is better than a distant uncle. If it hadn't been for Yeonghee's dad next-door, we really would've had a disaster.* B: 누가 아니래. 정말 이번에 크게 신세졌어. = *That's what I'm saying. We really owe him a debt of gratitude this time.*

멍석(을) 깔다 [Lit. to lay out a straw mat] IDIOM 기회를 주거나 자리를 마련하다 = to provide someone with an opportunity or a venue (*equiv.* to set the stage for someone / to clear the path for someone) ▌A: **소영아, 할아버지 오랜만에 오셨는데 노래 한 곡 블러 봐.** = *Soyoung, your grandfather hasn't been here in a while How about singing him a song?* B: 싫어, 아빠. 부끄럽단 말야. = *No way, Dad. I'm embarrassed.* A: 원, 참. 하던 짓도 **멍석 깔아** 주면 안 한다니까. = *Jeez, once you set the stage for them, they never want to put on a show.*

NOTE: 멍석은 짚으로 만든 큰 자리로, 곡식을 너는 데 쓴다. 한편 멍석은 굿이나 광대놀이 등의 행사가 있을 때 마당에 크게 펼쳐 놓고 무대의 역할을 하기도 했다. 그 때문에 멍석을 깐다는 말이 '자리를 마련해 주다'라는 뜻을 갖게 되었다. 보통 멍석을 깔아 주면 못한다는 말을 하는데, 평소에 잘하던 것도 본격적으로 기회가 주어지면 스스로 의기소침해져서 실력 발휘를 못할 때 이런 말을 쓴다.

A 멍석 is a large mat made of straw used for sorting grains. The mat also played the role of a stage for shamanistic rituals and clown shows. As such, the phrase 멍석을 깔다 (to lay out the mat) came to signify the act of preparing a place for someone. This phrase is usually used in the form 하던 짓도 멍석을 깔아 주면 못한다 or 하던 짓도 멍석을 펴놓으면 못한다, and most commonly describes the tendency of people to fail to properly exhibit their skills when put on the spot.

멍석(을) 펴다 IDIOM = 멍석(을) 깔다

멍에를 메다 IDIOM = 멍에를 쓰다

멍에를 벗다 [Lit. to shed one's yoke] IDIOM 구속이나 통제, 인식 따위에서 벗어나다 = to break free of restraint or perception (*equiv.* to break free of the yoke / to break one's fetters *syn.* 굴레를 벗다 *ant.* 멍에를 쓰다) ▌A: 내 자식들은 한국 사회에서 이방인이라는 **멍에를 벗을** 수 있을까? = *Do you think my children will ever be able to break free of the perception that they are foreigners here?* B: 점차 한국 사회도 성숙하고 있으니 그렇게 되겠지. = *Korean society is maturing too. I'm sure that day will come.*

NOTE: See the note on 굴레를 쓰다.

멍에를 쓰다 [Lit. to wear the yoke] IDIOM 구속이나 통제, 인식 따위에 얽매이다 = to be constrained by or oppressed by a perception (of others) (*equiv.* to be labeled / to wear a certain label / to be held down *syn.* 굴레를 쓰다 *ant.* 멍에를 벗다) ▌A: 마지막으로 하실 말씀이 있습니까? = *Do you have anything that you would like to add?* B: 패배의 **멍에를 쓰고** 물러나는 마당에 무슨 할 말이 있겠습니까. = *Wearing the yoke of defeat in my resignation, what would I have to say?*

NOTE: See the note on 굴레를 쓰다.

멍에를 지다 IDIOM = 멍에를 쓰다

메가폰(을) 잡다 [Lit. to grab the megaphone] IDIOM 영화의 감독을 맡다 = to work as a director (*equiv.* to sit in the director's chair) ▌A: 이 영화는 감독이 누구예요? = *Who's directing the film?* B: 임권택 감독이 **메가폰을 잡았다고** 들었어요. = *I heard that Im Gwon-taek was sitting in the director's chair.*

NOTE: 영화 감독이 영화 촬영을 할 때 배우들에게 지시 사항을 잘 전달하기 위해 메가폰을 이용하는 데서 나온 말이다.

This expression comes from the megaphone that most directors use to bark out orders at the cast and crew.

메뚜기도 (유월이) 한철이다 [Lit. Even the grasshoppers only have one season.] PROVERB 전성기가 짧음을 빗대어 표현한 속담＝a proverb that points to the fleeting nature of success (*equiv.* All good things must come to an end. / Nothing lasts forever.) ▌A: 일 좀 쉬엄쉬엄 해. 요즘 잘나간다고 너무 무리하는 거 아냐?＝*Take it easy while you do your work. Don't you think your success has been making you overwork?* B: 잘나갈 때 많이 벌어 놔야지. **메뚜기도 한철이라는데,** 언제까지 지금처럼 잘나간다는 보장도 없잖아.＝*While I'm still successful I've got to make a lot of money. Even grasshoppers only have season. There's no guarantee that business will keep up like it is now.*

NOTE: 살아 움직이는 모든 생물은 나름대로 전성기가 있게 마련이다. 메뚜기는 여름철이 되면 논두렁과 들판에 퍼져서 제 세상을 만난 듯이 번성한다. 그러나 그 왕성한 활력과 번식도 한여름이 지나면 풀이 꺾여 자생력을 잃고 사라져 버린다. 이와 같은 현상은 메뚜기만이 아니라 모든 생명체에게 적용되는 것으로써 성장에는 한계가 있는 법이다.
Everything that lives tends to have a zenith to its life. In the summer, grasshoppers spread throughout the rice paddies and fields as if the whole world was there's for the taking. The problem looming on the horizon, however, is that after such a flurry of eating and propagating, the grass has been exhausted and they lose their ability to subsist. This law of nature applies to all living things, not just grasshoppers and shows us that there is always a limit to growth.

메스(를) 가하다 [Lit. to apply the scalpel] IDIOM 잘못을 바로잡기 위해 단호한 조치를 취하다＝to assume drastic measures to attack a problem (*equiv.* to nip (a problem) in the bud / to take the scalpel to something) ▌A: 이번에 한나라당이 내부 조직을 완전히 바꾸고 당명도 바꾼다지?＝*They're saying the Grand National Party is going to launch a complete restructuring and even change their name, right?* B: 대대적으로 **메스를**

가하나 봐. = *Yeah, it looks like they're not holding back in the measures they're willing to take.*

NOTE: 수술은 일반적인 약물 치료로는 병을 완전히 다스리는 게 가능하지 않을 때 쓰는 방법이다. 잘못을 바로잡기 위해 강한 해결책을 사용할 때 '메스를 가하다'라는 표현을 쓴다.
Surgery is usually an option of last resort, when a patient's ailments cannot be eliminated with pharmaceuticals. Accordingly, to "use the scalpel," means to resort to strong measures to catch a problem early on.

며느리 사랑은 시아버지 [Lit. Love for a daughter-in-law comes from the father-in-law.] PROVERB 며느리는 시아버지에게 더 귀염을 받는다는 말 = used to describe the tendency of father-in-laws to dote on their daughter-in-laws. (*cf.* 사위 사랑은 장모) ▌A: 시부모님이 잘해 주셔? = *Are your in-laws treating you all right?* B: 응. 특히 아버님이 예뻐해 주셔. = *Yeah, my father-in-law seems to especially think I'm cute.* A: 역시 **며느리 사랑은 시아버지**라는 말이 맞구나. = *I guess that's why they say that the most love a daughter-in-law gets is from her father-in-law.*

면목(이) 없다 [Lit. to not have the face] IDIOM 미안하거나 부끄러워 얼굴을 대하기 어렵다 = to be too sorry or ashamed of one's actions to face someone (*equiv.* I'm too ashamed to face them. / I can't even look him in the eye. *syn.* 낯이 없다) ▌A: 왜 요즘 통 연락이 없었어? = *Why don't you ever call me anymore?* B: 선생님 뵐 **면목이 없어서** 연락을 못 드렸어요. = *I couldn't face you after what happened.*

면사포(를) 쓰다 [Lit. to wear a wedding veil] IDIOM 시집을 가다 = (for a woman) to get married (*equiv.* to get hitched / to don the wedding veil) ▌A: 드디어 **면사포를 쓰게** 된 기분이 어때? = *How does it feel to be getting married?* B: 설레기도 하고 걱정도 되고 그래. = *It's thrilling and worrisome at the same time.*

NOTE: 요즈음 한국에서는 대부분 서양식 결혼을 한다. 일부 전통 혼례를 올리는 여자들은 사실 면사포를 쓰지 않지만, 관용적으로 시집을 갈 때

'면사포를 쓰다'라는 표현을 쓴다.

Many weddings in Korea are now held in the Western style. Some people, however, still get married in the traditional way. In traditional weddings, the bride does not wear a veil, but the expression can still be used as a metaphor for getting married.

면죄부를 주다 [Lit. to give someone an indulgence] IDIOM 잘못을 용서해 주다 = to forgive someone's mistakes (*equiv.* to pardon / to give someone a pardon) ▌A: 이번에 H기업 회장을 사면하 줬다지? = *I heard that the president of that firm was pardoned of all wrongdoing, right?* B: 그렇게 비리를 많이 저질러도 돈 많고 힘 있으니까 **면죄부를 주는구나**. = *I guess having plenty of money and power ensures that the government will indulge you.*

NOTE: 면죄부는 중세에 로마 가톨릭교회가 금전이나 재물을 바친 사람에게 그 죄를 면한다는 뜻으로 발행하던 증서다. 800년 경부터 대대로 교회 운영의 재원으로 상품화하였는데, 15세기 말에는 대량으로 발행하여 루터의 비판을 불러일으키고 종교개혁의 실마리가 되었다.

An indulgence was a document given to those who made offerings of gold or other valuables to the catholic church as proof that their sins had been forgiven. From the year 800, this became a commodity and source of revenue for the church. In the late 15th century, they were issued in mass which led to the objections of Martin Luther and became a flashpoint for the reformations of the church.

명맥을 유지하다 [Lit. to maintain the family name] IDIOM 사상이나 제도 등 눈에 보이지 않는 것이 계속 이어지다 = to keep alive a tradition, ideology, or system (*equiv.* to keep the name alive / to keep something alive) ▌A: 아직은 간신히 **명맥을 유지하고** 있지만, 요즘에는 이런 일에 관심을 갖는 젊은이가 거의 없어서 걱정입니다. = *We're doing our best just to keep the tradition alive, but not too many young people today are interested in what we're doing.* B: 요즘 젊은이들이 우리 전통문화에 관심을 가져야 할 텐데 말이죠. = *The youth needs to take a greater* *interest in our traditional culture.*

명실상부(하다) [Lit. 名name + 實true + 相mutual + 符be in keeping with]

CHINESE-DERIVATION 이름과 실상이 꼭 들어맞다 = for something's reputation and actuality to be in line (*equiv.* to be true to its name / to live up to its name) ▌A: 이번 월드컵 우승은 어느 나라가 하게 될까? = *Who do you think is going to win the World Cup this year?* B: 글쎄. 뚜껑은 열어 봐야 알겠지만, 브라질이 **명실상부** 최강 아닐까? = *Well, it's too early to know now, but don't you think Brazil will live up to its reputation as the strongest there is?*

➡ p.200

명암이 교차하다 IDIOM = 명암이 엇갈리다

명암이 엇갈리다 [Lit. for darkness and light to crisscross] IDIOM 기뻐하는 사람과 슬퍼하는 사람의 감정이 대조가 되다 = for a contrast to emerge between those that are happy and sad about a certain affair (*equiv.* for there to be a mixture of emotion *syn.* 명암이 교차하다, 희비가 엇갈리 다, 희비가 교차하다) ▌A: 어떻게 보면 스포츠는 참 잔인한 것 같 아. 이기는 편과 지는 편이 있고 **명암이 엇갈리잖아**. = *When you really take a look at it, sports can be really cruel: there's always a winner and a loser and joy and sadness.* B: 그게 스포츠를 하는 이유기도 하지. = *Yeah, that's also the reason people play sports.*

명함도 못 내밀다 [Lit. to not even be able to pass out one's business card]

IDIOM 도저히 상대가 되지 않아 감히 나서지도 못하다 = to be so far below a group that one cannot even show one's face among them (*equiv.* to feel utterly outclassed / to not be able to show one's face) ▌A: 오늘 참가자 들 정말 실력이 대단한 것 같지 않아요? = *Doesn't it seem like everyone who took part today was extremely talented.* B: 그러게요. 웬만 한 가수는 **명함도 못 내밀겠어요**. = *It sure does. Most of the singers out there today would be severely outclassed.*

모(가)나다 [Lit. to be rigid] IDIOM 원만하지 못하고 까다롭다 = to be temperamental and particular (*equiv.* to have a rigid personality / to have a

difficult personality) █A: 김미숙 씨는 일은 잘하는데, 사람이 좀 **모가 난** 게 흠이야. =*Kim Misook really does good work, but her rigidity is a flaw.* B: 그래도 나쁜 사람은 아니니까 차차 좋아지겠죠. =*At any rate, she's not a bad person, so I'm sure she'll get better in time.*

모가지가 잘리다 IDIOM = (목이) 잘리다

모난 돌이 정 맞는다 [Lit. The rigid stone gets the chisel.] PROVERB 성격이 너그럽지 못하거나 무리 중에서 튀는 사람은 남의 미움을 받기 쉽다는 말 = suggests that a person who lacks magnanimity or sticks out in a group is likely to be the object of scorn (*equiv.* A cornered stone meets the mason's chisel. / A tall tree catches much wind. / (You should try to) keep a low profile.) █A: 내가 군대에서 제일 많이 들은 말이 뭔지 알아? 바로 '**모난 돌이 정 맞는다**'야. 다들 중간만 하라고 하더군. =*Do you know what people told me the most when I was in the army? It was "Keep a low profile." They all just told me to do an average job of everything.* B: 우리나라 사람들은 튀는 걸 정말 싫어하니까요. =*Yep, Koreans really do hate to stick out.*

모든 일에는 다 때가 있다 [Lit. There is a time for everything.] IDIOM 어떤 일이든 적절한 시기가 있으니 그 시기를 놓치지 말라는 말 = used to encourage grasping an opportunity at the right moment or waiting for the opportune moment (*equiv.* There's a time for everything. / Strike while the iron is hot.) █A: 벌써 입사한 지도 반 년이 다 되어 가는데 아직 시시한 일만 주어지는 것 같아요. =*It's already been half a year since I started this job but it still seems like all the tasks I'm given are rudimentary.* B: **모든 일에는 다 때가 있는** 법이야. 조금만 기다려 봐. =*There is a time for everything. Just wait for your moment*

모래밭에서 바늘 찾기 [Lit. finding a needle in a field of sand] PROVERB 가능성이 매우 낮은 일 = a task that has a low likelihood of success (*equiv.* like finding a needle in a haystack) █A: 주위에 괜찮은 개발자 없어? =*Do you know any good software developers?* B: 요즘 괜찮은 프로그래머 구하기가 **모래밭에서 바늘 찾기**보다 어려운 거 몰라? =*Finding a*

good programmer these days is like finding a needle in a haystack. Hadn't you heard?

모로 가도 서울만 가면 된다 [Lit. Even if go there sideways, just get to Seoul.] PROVERB 수단과 방법을 가리지 않고 목적만 이루면 된다는 말 = used to emphasize that the methods are not important, just the outcome (*equiv.* The ends justify the means. / by any and all means) ▌A: 이 문제는 그렇게 푸는 것보다 이렇게 푸는 게 더 쉬워. = *It's easier to solve that problem like this.* B: 모로 가도 서울만 가면 된다고 답만 맞으면 되지. 나는 내 식대로 풀래. = *As long as I get the right answer, I don't think the way I do it matters. I'd rather just do it my way.*

NOTE: 서울은 한국의 수도다. 7-80년대 한국의 경제가 급격히 성장할 때 많은 사람들이 서울로 모여들었다. 당시는 교통수단이 지금처럼 발전하지 않았기 때문에 각자 다양한 수단을 이용해서 서울로 올라오곤 했다. 서울은 희망과 성공의 상징이었는데, 성공을 위해서는 수단은 아무래도 상관없다는 씁쓸한 속뜻을 지니고 있는 표현이기도 하다.
Seoul is the capital of South Korea. In the 70s and 80s, as the nation's economy grew, the population headed for Seoul. In those days, getting around the country wasn't nearly as easy as it is today, but people got to the city every which way they could. This mass exodus looks to be the origin of this phrase. Additionally, as getting to Seoul symbolized success, the phrase's true meaning is that irrespective of the means, success is all that matters.

모르긴 몰라도 [Lit. even though I don't know] IDIOM 확실하지는 않지만 십중팔구는 = most likely true (*equiv.* I'm not completely sure but ... / probably) ▌A: 우리 반에서 누가 제일 힘이 셀까? = *Who do you think is the strongest in our class?* B: 모르긴 몰라도 덩치를 보면 우근이가 제일 세지 않을까? = *I'm not 100 percent sure, but judging from size, wouldn't it be Ugeun?*

*모르는 게 약이다 [Lit. Not knowing is medicine.] PROVERB 모르면 차라리 마음이 편하다 = Being ignorant puts one's mind at ease. (*equiv.* Ignorance is

bliss. / You're better off not knowing. *ant.* 아는 것이 힘이다 *cf.* 아는 게 병이다) ▌A: 여보, 우리 집에 빚이 있어? = *Honey, do we have any debts?* B: 갑자기 그건 왜 물어? 궁금해하지 마. **모르는 게 약이야**. = *Why are you asking me that all of a sudden? Don't worry about it. Ignorance is bliss.*

모순 [Lit. 矛 spear + 盾 shield → a spear and a shield] CHINESE-DERIVATION 말이나 행동이 앞뒤가 맞지 않는 모습 = a contradiction (*equiv.* a hypocritical action / You don't practice what you preach.) ▌A: 네 행동은 네 말하고 **모순이야**. = *You never practice what you preach.* B: 왜? 건강하게 살려고 운동 열심히 한다는 얘기에 문제 있어? = *Huh? Is there something wrong with me saying that I'm exercising hard to get healthier?* A: 너는 운동 끝나고 나면 힘들다면서 기름기 있는 음식 먹잖아. 거기에 술도 꼭 몇 잔 마시고. = *You always eat greasy food as soon as you're done exercising because you say you're so worn out. And then you always have a few drinks too.*

NOTE: 한 장사꾼이 "이 창은 세상 어느 방패도 뚫을 수 있을 만큼 강합니다."라고 말한 뒤 이어서 "또 이 방패는 세상 어느 창도 뚫을 수 없을 만큼 강합니다."라고 했다. 그러자 구경꾼 한 명이 "그러면 그 창으로 그 방패를 찌르면 어떻게 됩니까?"라고 물었다. 그 장사꾼은 아무 말도 못하고 떠났다.

A slick salesman as he peddled his wares once claimed, "This spear is so sharp it can penetrate any shield." No long after he picked up a shield and said, "This shield is so strong no spear can penetrate it." One of the people who had gathered to listen to his spiel said, "What happens if you were to throw that spear at that shield?" The salesman could summon no response and left without a word.

목구멍까지 차오르다 [Lit. to be filled up to one's throat] IDIOM 분노나 하고 싶은 말 따위가 참을 수 없는 지경이 되다 = to be at that point where one can no longer contain rage or things one wants to say (*equiv.* I'm about to blow my lid. / I've had as much as I can take.) ▌A: 젠장, 팀장님 말이야, 다른 사람들 앞에서 나한테 그렇게 말할 수 있어? = *Jeez,* *how could our team leader talk to me that way in front of everybody else?* B: 과장님이 참으세요. =*Don't let it get the better of you.* A: 나도 아까는 큰소리가 **목구멍까지 차오르는** 걸 간신히 참았어. =*I was doing my best not to yell earlier myself.*

목구멍에 풀칠하다 [Lit. to paste (over) one's throat] IDIOM 겨우 먹고 살다 = to just barely get by (*equiv.* to eke out a living *syn.* 입에 풀칠하다) ▌A: 하시는 일은 어떠세요? =*How's your job?* B: 요즘 다들 어렵잖아요. 간신히 **목구멍에 풀칠하는** 정도죠 뭐. =*Everyone's having a hard time now. I just getting by, you know?*

NOTE: 옛날 시골 가난한 집에서는 먹을 것이 없을 때, 보리나 밀가루, 감자 가루 따위를 물에 풀어 끓여 먹곤 했는데 이것을 풀이라고 하였다. 목구멍에 풀칠한다는 말은 제대로 된 밥은 먹지 못하고 간신히 풀을 먹어 생계를 유지할 정도로 가난한 생활을 한다는 뜻이다.
In the old days, when there was never enough food to go around, poor households used to gather up barley, wheat, or potato flour and boil it down. This concoction was called 풀 (glue). 목구멍에 풀칠하다 is used to describe a state in which one rarely, if ever, has the money to afford a good meal but scrapes by eating whatever one can.

목구멍이 포도청 [Lit. One's throat is a police station.] PROVERB 먹고사는 문제가 다른 무엇보다 선행하는 문제라는 말 = used to emphasize that eating comes before all other problems (*equiv.* I'm working hard enough just to stay afloat. / I've got mouths to feed.) ▌A: 회사는 잘 다녀? =*How's work?* B: 만날 윗사람들 눈치 보면서 다니고 있지 뭐. **목구멍이 포도청**이잖아. =*I always have to be conscious of what my superiors are thinking. I've got mouths to feed, you know?*

NOTE: 포도청은 지금의 경찰서에 해당하는 조선 시대의 기관이었다. 포도청은 일반적으로 서민에게 막강한 권한을 행사하였는데, '목구멍이 포도청'이라는 말은 먹는 문제가 그만큼 사람들에게 가장 중요하고 다른 무엇보다는 선행하는 문제였음을 나타내는 말이다.
The 포도청 of the Joseon period was a government building akin to today's

police stations. In the Korea of old it was a place that bore the immense weight of the law and exercised a mighty influence over the masses. To say that your throat (the need to eat) is like a police station, means that one's need to get fed is more important than anything else the world can throw your way.

목마른 놈이 우물 판다 [Lit. The thirsty man digs the well.] PROVERB 급히 필요로 하는 사람이 어떤 일을 하게 되어 있다는 말 = used to suggest that the person in greatest need is the one who begins an undertaking (*equiv.* He that would eat the fruit must climb the tree. / Need makes the naked man run.) ▌A: 이 무거운 짐들을 혼자 옮기셨어요? = *You moved all these heavy bags by yourself?* B: 남편한테 해 달라니까 자꾸 나중에 하겠다고 미루잖아요. **목마른 놈이 우물 판다고** 제가 혼자 했어요. = *I asked my husband to do it but he just kept putting it off. Sometimes, if you want something done, you just have to do it yourself.*

목소리가 크다 [Lit. to have a loud voice] IDIOM 자기 주장을 강하게 말하다 = to insist on one's demands (*equiv.* to clearly voice one's demands) ▌A: 우리 회사도 여자 직원들이 옛날에 비해 많이 늘어난 것 같아요. = *It seems like we've really hired a lot of women compared to how it used to be.* B: 그렇죠. 아마 절반이 훨씬 넘을 걸요. 그래서 전반적인 회사 문제에 있어서도 여직원들의 **목소리가 커진** 것 같아요. = *That's right. I bet they're way more than half. I guess that's why the voice of the women is growing louder in overall company affairs too.*

목에 칼이 들어와도 [Lit. even with a knife at one's throat] IDIOM 어떤 어려움이 있어도 = no matter what difficulties may arise (*equiv.* no matter what / even if it kills me) ▌A: 명희 씨는 매사에 자기 생각이 뚜렷한 사람 같아요. = *Myeonghee has a clear opinion on everything.* B: 맞아요. **목에 칼이 들어와도** 틀린 걸 맞다고 하지 못할 사람이죠. = *That's right. She wouldn't say something wrong was right even if she had a knife to her throat.*

목에 핏대를 세우다 [Lit. to make one's veins bulge in the neck] IDIOM 몹시 흥분하여 말하다＝to speak in extreme anger (*equiv.* to be very upset / for one's veins to bulge in anger *syn.* 목에 핏대를 올리다) ▌A: 사고 처리는 잘 됐어?＝*Did things get handled fine with your accident?* B: 상대가 하도 **목에 핏대를 세워서** 힘들었어. 보험 회사에 연락했지 뭐.＝*That guy wouldn't let up till he was blue in the face. I just contacted the insurance company.*

목에 핏대를 올리다 IDIOM＝목에 핏대를 세우다

목에 힘(을) 주다 [Lit. to stiffen one's neck] IDIOM 거만하게 굴거나 뼈기는 태도를 취하다＝to act in an arrogant manner or assume a swagger (*equiv.* to have one's nose up high / to swagger around / to be up on one's high horse *syn.* 어깨에 힘(을) 주다 *cf.* 목에 힘(이) 들어가다) ▌A: 옆집 사람, 아들이 대기업 다닌다고 **목에 늘 힘 주고** 다녀요.＝*The people next door are up on their high horse again because their son got a job with a big company.* B: 아들 없는 사람은 서러워서 살겠나.＝*What are people who don't even have a son supposed to do?*

목에 힘(이) 들어가다 [Lit. for energy to go into one's neck] IDIOM 권위나 능력을 뽐내다＝to flaunt one's authority or abilities (*equiv.* to give off an air of confidence *syn.* 어깨에 힘(이) 들어가다 *cf.* 목에 힘(을) 주다) ▌A: 강 과장, 승진한 이후로 **목에 힘이 너무 들어간 거 아냐?**＝*You're sure holding your nose high since your promotion, Mr. Gang.* B: 에이, 왜 그러세요? 제가 언제 그랬어요?＝*Oh, why are you being like that? When did I ever do such a thing?* A: 하하, 농담이야, 농담.＝*Ha ha, it was just a joke—a joke.*

목을 길게 빼고 기다리다 [Lit. to wait with one's neck stuck out] IDIOM 애타게 기다리다＝to wait anxiously (*equiv.* to wait on pins and needles *syn.* 학수고대하다 *cf.* 목이 빠지도록 기다리다) ▌A: 김 과장, 우리 한잔만 더 하자.＝*Mr. Kim, let's get another drink.* B: 안 돼. 집에서 애들이 **목을 길게 빼고** 기다리고 있을 거야.＝*No, I can't. I'm sure my kids are waiting anxiously for me to get home.*

목(을) 놓다 [Lit. to put down one's throat] IDIOM 크게 소리를 내어 울다 = to cry loudly (*equiv.* to cry out loud / to weep bitterly / to sob) ▮A: 가족들이 모두 외국에 있고 혼자 한국에 계시다고 들었는데, 외롭지 않으세요? = *I heard that your family all lives abroad and you are alone in Korea. Aren't you lonely?* B: 왜 안 외롭겠어요? 어떤 때는 **목을 놓아** 울고 싶을 때도 있어요. = *Why wouldn't I be? Sometimes I feel like just breaking down and sobbing my heart out.*

> NOTE: '목 놓아 울다', '목 놓아 부르다'의 형태로 주로 쓰인다.
> It is normally used in the form of 목 놓아 울다 or 목 놓아 부르다 (to call out to someone).

목(을) 매다 [Lit. to tie up one's throat] IDIOM 1. 죽으려고 끈이나 줄로 목을 걸어 매다 = to hang oneself with a string or rope (*syn.* 목(을) 매달다) ▮A: 얼마나 힘이 들었으면 **목을 맸을까**? = *To get to the point of suicide ... she must've been going through so much.* B: 그러게 ……. 악플이 정말 심각한 문제야. = *That's what I'm saying ... malicious comments on the Internet are such terrible problem.* 2. 어떤 사람이나 일에 매달려 의지하다 = to depend on someone or a certain undertaking (*syn.* 목(을) 매달다) ▮A: 내가 보기에는 네가 그 남자한테 너무 **목을 매는** 것 같아. = *I think you are too closely tied to that guy.* B: 그렇게 보여? 앞으로는 안 그럴게. = *Is that what it looks like? From now on, I'll try to do things differently.*

목(을) 매달다 IDIOM = 목(을) 매다

***(목을) 자르다** [Lit. to cut (someone's throat)] IDIOM 직위나 직책에서 물러나도록 만들다 = to remove someone from the position (*equiv.* to fire someone / to cut someone loose) ▮A: 회사 게시판 봤어? 성과가 안 좋은 사람은 앞으로 **목을 자르겠다고** 쓰여 있던데? = *Did you see the company bulletin board? It says that they are going to start cutting employees that aren't performing.* B: 휴우 ……. 회사에서 버티기가 점점 힘들어지네. = *Wow ... All this time I've hung on here, but it just keeps getting harder and harder.*

목이 빠지도록 기다리다 [Lit. to wait until one's neck falls out] IDIOM 몹시 애태우며 오랫동안 기다리다 = to wait anxiously for a long time (*equiv.* to wait on pins and needles / to wait and wait *syn.* 눈이 빠지도록 기다리다 *cf.* 목을 길게 빼고 기다리다) ▌A: 어디 갔다 이제 와요? **목이 빠지도록 기다렸어요**. = *Where have you been? I've been waiting and waiting.* B: 왜 나를 그렇게 찾았어? 이거 기분 좋은데? = *Why were you so anxious to see me? That's flattering.* A: 먹을 걸 사 올 줄 알았는데, 빈손으로 왔어요? = *I thought you were going to bring something to eat. Did you come back empty-handed?*

(목이) 잘리다 [Lit. to have one's throat cut] IDIOM 직위나 직책에서 쫓겨나다 = to be removed from one's job (*equiv.* to get sacked / to be fired) ▌A: 요즘 왜 이렇게 지각이 잦아? 그러다가 **잘리면** 어떡하려고 그래? = *Why are you tardy so often these days? What do you intend to do if you get fired?* B: 에이, 될 대로 되라지 뭐. = *I guess whatever happens will happen.*

몸 둘 바를 모르다 [Lit. to not know how to hold oneself] IDIOM 부끄럽거나 민망하여 어떻게 행동해야 할지 모르다 = to be embarrassed to the point of not knowing how to act (*equiv.* I don't know how to act. / I don't know what to say. / to be at a loss) ▌A: 역시 자네는 우리 연구실의 보배야. 잘했어! = *You certainly are a treasure to our research institute. What a great job!* B: 교수님이 그렇게 칭찬해 주시니 **몸 둘 바를 모르겠습니다**. = *Hearing such kind words from you ... I'm at a loss for words.*

몸살을 앓다 [Lit. to suffer from body aches] IDIOM 어떤 일로 인해 고통을 겪다 = to be plagued by something ▌A: 본격적인 휴가 시즌을 맞아 해수욕장이 인산인해를 이루고 있습니다. = *With the peak of holiday season, beaches are extremely crowded with vacationers.* B: 그런데 피서객들이 떠난 해변은 쓰레기로 해마다 **몸살을 앓습니다**. = *But beaches are blighted with litter after vacationers leave.*

몸살(이) 나다 [Lit. to have body aches] IDIOM 어떤 일을 몹시 하고 싶어하다 = to really want to do something (*equiv.* to be dying to do something /

to be aching to do something *cf.* 몸이 근질근질하다) ▌A: 나 소개팅 좀 시켜 줘. =*Set me up with someone.* B: 너 요즘 왜 그래? 연애 못 해 **몸살 난** 사람처럼. =*Why do you keep saying that these days? You're starting to look really desperate.*

몸에 배다 [Lit. (for something) to penetrate one's body] IDIOM 익숙해지거나 습관이 되다 =to grow accustomed to something (*equiv.* to become a part of someone / to grow accustomed (to an environment) / for a practice or belief to be part of what someone is / to be in the practice of doing something) ▌A: 구두가 꽤 낡았는데, 얼마나 신으셨어요? =*Those shoes are starting to look really worn out. How long have you worn them?* B: 10년이 넘었어요. 물건을 하나 사면 오래 쓰는 습관이 **몸에 밴** 것 같아요. =*It's been more than 10 years now. Using things that I buy till the very end is part of who I am now.*

몸에 좋은 약은 입에 쓰다 [Lit. Medicine good for your body is bitter to the lips.] PROVERB 듣기 싫은 비판이나 충고가 실질적으로 도움이 된다는 말 =used to describe how criticism or advice that one hates to hear can actually be the most helpful ▌A: 아, 듣기 싫어. 잔소리 좀 그만해. =*Oh, I'm sick of hearing that. Stop nagging me.* B: 듣기 싫어도 들어. 원래 **몸에 좋은 약이 입에 쓴** 법이야. =*Listen, even though you hate it. Good medicine tastes bitter.*

몸으로 때우다 [Lit. to handle things with one's body] IDIOM 육체적인 일을 하여 다른 일을 대신하거나 대충 해결하다 =to do manual labor instead of other work or to solve things in a slipshod way (*cf.* 말로 때우다) ▌A: 이 일 하실 수 있겠어요? 육체적으로 힘들 텐데요. =*Do you think you'll be able to do this? It's going to be pretty tough physically.* B: 제가 원래 **몸으로 때우는** 일은 잘해요. =*I'm actually pretty good at manual labor.*

몸(을)담다 [Lit. to put one's body (in a place)] IDIOM 어떤 직업에 종사하거나 직장에 소속돼 있다 =to work a job or find employment ▌A: 건설업에 **몸 담으신** 지 얼마나 되셨어요? =*How long has it been now since* *you started working in construction?* B: 올해로 20년 됐습니다. =*It'll be 20 years this year.*

몸을 맡기다 [Lit. to leave one's body in someone's care] IDIOM **1.** 어떤 대상이 자기를 마음대로 하게 내버려두다=to let someone or something treat you as they please (*equiv.* to give yourself up to somebody) ▌A: 저는 정말 춤을 못 춰요. =*I can't really dance.* B: 괜찮아요. 그냥 흘러나오는 음악에 **몸을 맡기세요**. =*That's okay. Just give yourself up to the music.* **2.** 다른 사람에게 자신의 처지를 의지하다=to render oneself to somebody ▌A: 두 분은 어떤 사이십니까? =*What is the relationship between you two?* B: 제가 젊었을 때 잠시 오갈 데가 없었던 때가 있습니다. 그때 이 선생님께 **몸을 잠시 맡겼었지요**. =*I had no place to go for a time back when I was young. I then depended on this gentleman for my survival.*

몸을 버리다 [Lit. to spoil one's body] IDIOM **1.** 건강을 해치다=to ruin one's health ▌A: 공부도 좋지만 일찍일찍 자라. 그러다 **몸 버린다**. =*Studying is important but don't go to bed too late. Studying till late at night is bad for your health.* B: 네. 이것만 보고 잘게요. =*Okay. I'll just finish reading this and go right to bed.* **2.** 여자가 남자에게 정조를 빼앗기거나 신세를 망치다=for a woman to lose her chastity to a man or to ruin her life ▌A: 어제 텔레비전에 나온 그 여자 너무 불쌍해. =*I felt so bad for that woman on TV yesterday.* B: 맞아, 어렸을 때 **몸을 버린** ^{⇒p.255} 이후로 계속 몸을 팔면서 살아왔다지?=*Yeah, she said she has been selling her body like that ever since she lost her virginity at an early age.*

몸을 빼다 [Lit. to pull out one's body] IDIOM **1.** 속해 있던 단체를 나오거나 하던 일을 그만두어 책임을 회피하다=to withdraw from a group or quit employment to avoid responsibilities (*equiv.* to extract oneself (from a situation) *cf.* 손(을) 빼다, 발(을) 빼다) ▌A: 이번 일 갑자기 그만뒀다면서? 왜?=*I heard you quit your job all of sudden? Why?* B: 아무래도 나하고는 맞지 않는 일 같아서 일찌감치 **몸을 뺐지**. =*The job wasn't a good fit, so I got out of there on the early side.* **2.** 바쁜 가운데 시간을 따로 내다=to make time when one is otherwise busy (*equiv.* to make time / to get away) ▌A: 아프다면서 왜 병원을 안 가고 버텨?=*If you're so sick, why don't you just go to the hospital?* B: 일이 너무 바빠서 **몸을 뺄** 수가 있어야지.=*I'm just too busy to get away from work right now.*

몸을 사리다 [Lit. to coil up one's body] IDIOM 행동을 조심하다=to be mindful of one's behavior (*equiv.* to be careful with one's actions / to mind one's behavior) ▌A: 다들 왜 아무 말도 없어? 사장님 앞이라고 **몸을 사리는** 거야?=*Why is everyone so silent? Are you worried about how to act in front of your boss?* B: 괜찮으니까 할 말 있으면 얘기들 해 보게.=*It's all right with me. Just say what you have to say.*

몸을 섞다 [Lit. to mix bodies] IDIOM 성관계를 맺다=to have sex (*syn.* 살을 섞다, 만리장성을 쌓다, 떡(을) 치다) ▌A: 드라마를 보면 요즘 젊은 애들은 참 쉽게 **몸을 섞나** 봐.=*Judging from what I see on TV, it looks like kids today just sleep around like it's nothing.* B: 사람 나름이죠 뭐.=*Everybody's different.*

몸(을) 팔다 [Lit. to sell one's body] IDIOM 매춘하다=to prostitute oneself (*equiv.* to sell one's body) ▌A: 김 기자, 이번 인터뷰 대상자는 누구였어?=*Kim, who was the interviewee this time?* B: 가족들 모르게 **몸을 파는** 한 대학생이었어.=*A college student who sells her body without her family's knowledge.*

몸(을) 풀다 [Lit. to untie the body] IDIOM **1.** 운동을 하기 전에 스트레칭 등으로 근육의 긴장을 풀다=to relax one's tense muscles by doing stretching before exercising (*equiv.* to warm up) ▌A: 자, 바로 시작하자.=*Let's start right away.* B: 잠깐만. **몸부터 풀어야지.**=*Wait. We'd better warm up.* **2.** 아이를 낳다=to have a child (*equiv.* to give birth to) ▌A: 한국에서는 **몸을 풀고** 나면 당분간 미역국을 먹는 관습이 있어요.=*After giving birth in Korea, it's customary to eat seaweed soup for a while.* B: 그건 왜 그래요?=*Why is that?* A: 미역국이 피를 맑게 해 줘서 산모한테 특히 좋거든요.=*It's said to clear the blood, and that's especially good for new mothers.*

몸을 허락하다 [Lit. to allow one's body] IDIOM 여자가 남자에게 성관계를 가지는 것을 승낙하다 = for a woman to consent to sex with a man (*equiv.* to give it up / to go all the way) ▌A: 어쩌자고 그런 놈에게 **몸을 허락했니?** = *How could go all the way with that jerk?* B: 엄마, 그래도 사위한테 그런 놈이라니요? 그 사람 그렇게 나쁜 사람 아니에요. = *Mom, he is your son-in-law now, how could you call him a jerk? He's really not that bad.*

몸이 가볍다 [Lit. to have a light body] IDIOM 몸의 상태가 좋다 = to be in a good physical state (*equiv.* to feel good physically / to be walking on air) ▌A: 낮잠을 자고 일어났더니 한결 **몸이 가벼운걸.** = *I took a little nap and woke up walking on air.* B: 얼굴색도 아까보다 훨씬 낫네. = *You've got a little color back in your face too.*

몸이 근질근질하다 [Lit. to have an itchy body] IDIOM 어떤 일을 몹시 하고 싶어하다 = to be very eager to do something (*equiv.* to be itching to do something *cf.* 몸살(이) 나다) ▌A: 자, 오늘 컨디션 어때? = *Hey, how do you feel today?* B: 최고예요! 빨리 게임하고 싶어서 **몸이 근질근질해요.** = *Terrific! I'm very anxious to get the game started.*

***몸이 무겁다** [Lit. to have a heavy body] IDIOM 1. 피로나 병으로 몸의 상태가 좋지 않아 움직이기 힘들다 = for it to be difficult to move due to a disease or fatigue (*equiv.* to be sluggish / to feel like one's body is dragging *syn.* 몸이 천근만근이다) ▌A: 오늘은 이쯤에서 그만하죠. = *I think this is about enough for today.* B: 어? 아직 시간이 좀 남았는데, 왜요? = *Oh? We've still got some time left. Why quit now?* A: 오늘은 왠지 모르게 **몸이 무겁네요.** = *For some reason I'm feeling a little lethargic today.* 2. 임신하다 = to be pregnant ▌A: 괜찮으시면 가족이랑 같이 오세요. = *Bring your family along too, if you'd like.* B: 아, 지금 아내가 만삭이라 **몸이 무거워서** 아내는 못 올 것 같아요. = *Ah, well, my wife is pretty close to her delivery date, so I don't think she'll be able to make it.*

몸이 천근만근이다 [Lit. for one's body to weigh a thousand or ten thousand *geun*] IDIOM 피로나 병으로 몸의 상태가 좋지 않아 움직이기

힘들다 = to experience mobility difficulties due to fatigue or illness (*equiv.* I feel like my body weighs a thousand pounds. *syn.* 몸이 무겁다) ▮A: 여보세요? 명수 엄마야? 나 영희 엄만데. 나 오늘 반상회에 못 갈 것 같아요. 몸살이 났는지 **몸이 천근만근이에요**. = *Hello? Is this Myeongsu's mom? This is Younghee's mom. I think I won't be able to make it to the neighborhood meeting today. My body feels so heavy and I'm exhausted, probably because I'm coming down with a cold.* B: 아, 그래요? 그럼 집에서 몸조리하고 있어요. = *Oh, are you? Take good care of yourself, then.*

NOTE: '근'은 한국이 전통적으로 써 오던 무게의 단위이다. 지역에 따라 차이가 있지만 보통 고기 한 근은 600그램에 해당하고 과일이나 채소 따위는 375그램에 해당한다.

A 근 is a traditional measure of weight used in Korea. The exact amount varied depending on the region, but a 근 of meat is about 600 g while the same measure of vegetables would be about 375 g.

몸이 허락하다 [Lit. for the body to allow (someone to do something)] IDIOM
어떤 일을 할 수 있을 만큼 몸의 상태가 좋다 = to be in good enough shape to do a certain thing (*equiv.* (I'll continue on as long as) my body allows) ▮A: 언제까지 이 일을 계속하실 건가요? = *Until when will you do this work?* B: **몸이 허락하는** 한 계속할 생각입니다. = *I'll keep doing it as long as my body allows.*

못된 송아지 엉덩이에 뿔 난다 [Lit. A bad calf sprouts horns on its buttocks] PROVERB 됨됨이가 바르지 못한 사람이 더욱 못된 짓을 할 때 쓰는 말 = used to describe a good for nothing who has recently grown even worse ▮A: 경미가 학교에서 담배 피우다가 걸렸다고? 벌써 몇 번째야? = *Gyeongmi was caught smoking at school? How many times is it already?* B: 몰라. **못된 송아지 엉덩이에 뿔 난다더니** 점점 엇나가는 것 같아 속상해. = *I don't know. I feel so bad because she keeps going astray ... and now she's gotten even worse.*

NOTE: 모든 일에 엇나가고 부모가 시키는 일은 꼭 반대로 하는 사람을 청개구리에 비유한다. 청개구리 같은 송아지가 있어, 심지어는 머리에서 나야 할 뿔이 엉뚱하게 엉덩이에서 났다고 생각해 보라.
In Korea those who go astray and do the opposite to what their parents tell them to do are called a "tree frog." Imagine an unruly calf that has sprouted horns on its buttocks instead of its head.

못 먹는 감 찔러나 본다 [Lit. to poke a persimmon one can't eat]
PROVERB 자기가 가질 수 없다는 것을 알면서도 아쉬운 마음에 만져 보거나, 다른 사람도 그것을 갖지 못하게 하려고 할 때 쓰는 말 = used to describe a situation in which, even while knowing that one cannot possess something, one touches it once with longing or seeks to ensure others cannot have it (*equiv.* had unrealistic hope) ▌A: 어차피 돈도 안 가져와서 살 수도 없으면서 왜 이것저것 만져 보니? = *Since you didn't bring your wallet, you aren't going to be able to buy anything anyway.* B: 못 먹는 감 찔러나 보는 거야. = *What's wrong with me looking at them for a while?*

못 오를 나무는 쳐다보지도 마라 [Lit. Don't stare at a tree that you can't climb.] PROVERB 불가능한 일은 일찍 단념하라는 말 = used to encourage giving up on impossible dreams early on (*equiv.* Don't waste your time. *cf.* 열 번 찍어 안 넘어가는 나무 없다) ▌A: 애, 못 오를 나무는 쳐다보지도 마. 네가 언감생심 김동건 씨를 좋아해? = *Don't waste your time with hopeless dreams. How could you even think of having a crush on Kim Donggeon.* B: 사람 좋아하는 것도 무슨 자격이 있어야 되니? 너무 그러지 마. = *Am I not qualified to be in love with him? Don't be that way.*

못(을) 박다 [Lit. to hammer in a nail] IDIOM 어떤 사실을 꼭 집어 분명하게 하다 = to determine something for certain (*equiv.* to nail something down / to peg a date *cf.* 가슴에 못(을) 박다) ▌A: 리포트를 아직 다 못 썼는데, 교수님께 말씀드리면 기한을 연장해 주실까? = *I still haven't been able to finish writing my paper. Do you think the Professor will let me push back the deadline a little if I tell her about it?* B: 아마 안 될걸. 처음부터 오늘까지로 못을 박으셨잖아. = *I doubt it. She pegged the date for today since the very beginning.*

무게가 실리다 [Lit. for weight to be carried] IDIOM 더 중요하거나 가능성이 높은 것으로 여겨지다 = to be considered more important or to have greater possibility of success (*equiv.* (for an argument etc.) to carry weight / there's a high likelihood that ...) ▌A: 이번에 우리 사장님 연임할 수 있을까? = *Do you think our boss will get his contract extended?* B: 이사회에서 결정을 내리겠지만, 작년 한해 실적도 좋았으니, 아무래도 연임 쪽으로 **무게가 실리지** 않을까? = *The board makes the decision on that, but since his record last year was good, I think he'll most likely get the extension, don't you?*

무게를 싣다 [Lit. to carry weight] IDIOM 상대적으로 더 중요하게 여기다 = to consider something to be relatively more important (*equiv.* to give more credence to (someone's opinions or assertions etc.) *cf.* 무게가 실리다) ▌A: 너는 이번 여당과 야당의 싸움에서 누가 맞다고 생각하니? = *In the recent fights between the majority party and the opposition party, who do you think is right?* B: 나는 야당의 말에 **무게를 실어** 주고 싶어. = *I'd probably place more weight in what the opposition party is saying.*

무게를 잡다 [Lit. to hold a weight] IDIOM 점잖은 척하며 엄숙한 모습을 보이다 = to behave in an ostentatiously serious way (*equiv.* to kill the mood / to be a wet blanket) ▌A: 너한테 할 얘기가 있어. 잠깐 여기 앉아 봐. = *I have something to say to you. Sit down here for a minute.* B: 왜 갑자기 **무게를 잡고** 그래? 무섭게. = *Why are you being so serious all of a sudden? It's scary.*

무궁무진하다 [Lit. 無 no + 窮 end + 無 no + 盡 end + 하다 adjectival suffix → no end] CHINESE-DERIVATION 끝이 없을 정도로 많다 = to be limitless (*equiv.* to be endless) ▌A: 따님은 음악에 대단한 재능이 있습니다. = *Your daughter has amazing musical talent.* B: 우리 현주가요? = *My daughter, Hyunju? Really?* A: 네. 아직 나이도 어리니 잠재력이 **무궁무진합니다**. 지금부터가 중요해요. = *Yeah. She's still young, so her potential is limitless. What's important is how you raise her from now on.*

무남독녀 [Lit. 無 no + 男 son + 獨 alone + 女 daughter] CHINESE-DERIVATION 아

들이 없는 집안의 외동딸＝an only daugther in a household with no sons ▌A: 현아는 **무남독녀**로 자라서인지 남을 배려하는 게 좀 부족해. ＝*Maybe it's just because she grew up as an only daughter, but it often seems that Hyeona is inconsiderate of others.* B: 아닌 게 아니라 좀 그렇긴 하지. ＝*I can't disagree with you on that. She's always seemed that way to me.*

무대를 밟다 IDIOM ＝무대에 서다

무대를 옮기다 [Lit. to change the stage] IDIOM 활동 공간을 바꾸다＝to change the venue of one's activities ▌A: 어라? 저기 나오는 저 사람 연극배우 아냐? ＝*Hey. Is that that actor from the theater?* B: 맞아. 연극에서 영화로 활동 **무대를 옮겼대**. ＝*Yeah. I heard that he has branched out into films as well.*

무대에 서다 [Lit. to stand on the stage] IDIOM 경기나 공연에 참가하다＝to participate in a competition or performance (*equiv.* to take the stage *syn.* 무대를 밟다, 무대에 오르다) ▌A: 그 가수가 주연 배우로 뮤지컬 **무대에 설** 예정이래. ＝*They're saying that singer is planning to head up a musical.* B: 가수로서도 대성공을 거두더니 드디어 뮤지컬까지 진출했구나. ＝*After all those successes as a singer, now she's finally moving on to musicals.*

무대에 오르다 [Lit. to go up on stage] IDIOM **1.** 공연되다＝to be performed (*equiv.* to be staged *cf.* 무대에 올리다) ▌A: 올해는 창작 뮤지컬이 큰 인기를 얻었습니다. ＝*Original musicals have been really popular this year.* B: 네, 올 한해 총 50편의 창작 뮤지컬이 **무대에 오른** 것으로 조사되었습니다. ＝*That's right, more than 50 original musicals were staged this year.* **2.** 경기나 공연에 참가하다＝to participate in a competition or a performance (*syn.* 무대에 서다, 무대를 밟다) ▌A: 오랜만의 공연이시죠? 감회가 남다르실 것 같은데. ＝*This is your first performance in a while, right? I'm sure you must be overcome with emotion.* B: 네. **무대에 오르는** 게 되게 오랜만이라 지금 정말 떨립니다. ＝*It's been so long since I last took the stage. I'm quite nervous.*

무대에 올리다 [Lit. to place on top of the stage] IDIOM 공연을 하다 = to put on a performance (*equiv.* to stage a show *cf.* 무대에 오르다) ▌A: 이번 작품이 감독님 백 번째 작품인데요, 어떤 작품인가요? = *This is your one hundredth show, Mr. Director. What kind of show is it?* B: 사극입니다. 백 번째 작품으로 사극을 **무대에 올리게** 되어 기쁘게 생각합니다. = *It's an historical play. I'm happy to be staging an historical play for my hundredth.*

무릉도원 [Lit. 武military + 陵mound + 桃peach + 源source → a beautiful region where the peach trees are in bloom] CHINESE-DERIVATION 이상향 = an ideal world ▌A: 배부르고 등 따스우니 **무릉도원**이 따로 없구나! = *My belly is full and it's so nice and warm. What a wonderful world!* B: 맞아. 이제 낮잠 한숨 잘까? = *That's right. How about a little nap?*

NOTE: 시국이 혼란스러웠던 중국 진나라 때의 야기다. 무릉 지역의 한 어부가 어느 날 길을 잃고 헤매다 복사꽃이 핀 숲에 이르렀다. 끝까지 배를 저어 나아가자 굴이 하나 나왔다. 배에서 내려 굴을 따라 들어가자 갑자기 마을이 나타났다. 그런데 이 마을은, 토지는 비옥하고 경치가 매우 아름답고 모든 사람들이 행복하게 살고 있어 혼란스러운 바깥 세상과는 너무나 달랐다. 오늘날 무릉도원은 이상향의 의미로 쓰인다.
During the Qin Dynasty at the time of Taiyuan, a fisherman from Murueng was out fishing when he lost his way. He came across a meadow of beautiful peach blossoms. He took his boat to the end of the meadow when a tunnel came into view. He ventured through the tunnel and when he came out the other side, he found a exquisitely laid out town in which fields were fertile, the scenery was beautiful, and everyone looked happy. The place was entirely different from the outside world. A 무릉도원 is now used to describe a utopia.

*무릎(을) 꿇다 [Lit. to bend one's knees] IDIOM 패배하거나 굴복하다 = to be defeated or submit oneself to another (*equiv.* to surrender / to bow down before someone) ▌A: 이번에 그 팀이 질 줄은 몰랐어. = *I sure didn't think they would lose this time.* B: 나도. 그렇게 약한 팀한테 **무릎을 꿇**을 거라고는 생각도 못 했는데. = *Me neither. I never would have thought*

they would be brought to their knees by such a weak team.

무릎(을) 치다 [Lit. to hit one's knees] IDIOM 놀랍거나 기쁜 일이 있을 때나 좋은 생각이 떠올랐을 때 감탄하다 = to let out an exclamation of joy or surprise or when one suddenly thinks of something (*equiv.* for one's jaw to drop) ▌A: 동건이는 정말 머리가 좋은 것 같아. 걔가 문제 푸는 걸 보면 저절로 **무릎을 치게** 된다니까. = *Donggeon sure has a good head on his shoulders. Watching him solve problems, my jaw seems to drop all by itself.* B: 맞아. 항상 남들이 생각하지 못하는 방법으로 문제를 풀지. = *That's right. He always solves the problems in ways no one else has thought of.*

무사안일(하다) [Lit. 無no + 事work + 安comfortable + 逸leisurely] CHINESE-DERIVATION 어떤 일을 너무 쉽고 만만하게 생각하여 적당히 하려고 하다 = to consider something so easy and manageable that one does it without much thought (*equiv.* to not give much thought to something) ▌A: 이번 화재는 등산객이 버린 담배 꽁초가 원인으로 밝혀졌습니다. = *This fire was determined to have been caused by the cigarette butt a hiker tossed aside here.* B: 설마 하는 **무사안일한** 생각이 큰 재난을 불러온 것입니다. = *And that's how a single action that one hardly gives any thought to can cause a huge disaster.*

무소식이 희소식 [Lit. No news is good news.] PROVERB 소식이 없는 것이 곧 무사히 잘 있는 것이라는 말 = used to suggest that not hearing from someone likely means that they are doing fine (*equiv.* No news is good news.) ▌A: 미국으로 유학 가 있는 아들에게서 몇 주째 연락이 없어요. = *I haven't heard from my son studying in the U.S. for a few weeks now.* B: **무소식이 희소식**이라잖아요. 별일 없을 거예요. = *They say no news is good news, you know? I'm sure everything is fine.*

무슨 바람이 불어서 [Lit. what wind has blown ...] IDIOM 평소에 하지 않던 행동을 하는 사람에게 '어쩐 일로'라는 뜻으로 하는 말 = used like "what on earth could have caused ..." to a person who is engaging in behavior unlike their normal self (*equiv.* What's gotten into you? / how unlike

you to ... *cf.* 바람(이) 불다) ▌A: 철수야, 네가 **무슨 바람이 불어서** 네 방 청소를 다 하니? = *Cheolsu, has something gotten into you? Why did you clean your room?* B: 너무 지저분해서 도저히 못 견디겠어요, 아빠. = *Dad, it was too dirty and I just couldn't take it anymore.*

무아지경 [Lit. 無no + 我I + 之of + 境case] CHINESE-DERIVATION 한곳에 집중하여 자신의 존재를 잊고 있는 경지 = intense focus to the point that one forgets oneself (*equiv.* to lose oneself in (an activity) / to be in the zone) ▌A: 지영이는 춤출 때 보면 전혀 딴 사람 같아. **무아지경**에 빠져서 춤을 추잖아. = *When Jiyoung is dancing, she seems like a completely different person. She loses herself in the dance.* B: 정말 보는 사람도 **무아지경**에 빠져 든다니까. = *I'm telling you, that's how the audience feels while watching her too.*

무용지물 [Lit. 無no + 用use + 之of + 物thing] CHINESE-DERIVATION 쓸모없는 물건이나 사람 = a useless thing or person (*equiv.* a good-for-nothing) ▌A: 아, 일부러 사진 찍으려고 카메라 들고 왔는데 비가 와서 **무용지물**이 되어 버렸어. = *I made a point of bringing my camera today, but since it rained, it turned out to be useless.* B: 다음에 찍어야지 뭐. = *Guess you'll just have to get pictures of it next time.*

무자식이 상팔자다 [Lit. No children is an enviable fate.] PROVERB 자식이 없으면 걱정도 없어 마음이 편하다는 말 = used to suggest that people without children have no worries and live comfortably (*equiv.* No children, no problems.) ▌A: 그 집 애가 학교에서 또 싸움을 해서 퇴학을 당했대요. = *The kid who lives over there was fighting again at school and got expelled.* B: **무자식이 상팔자**라니까. 그 집 부모도 속을 많이 끓이겠군. = *They do say that being childless is a carefree way to live. Their parents must be having such a terrible time.*

➡p.360

무지몽매하다 [Lit. 無no + 知know + 蒙ignorant + 昧hazy + 하다 adjectival suffix] CHINESE-DERIVATION 아는 것이 없고 사리에 어둡다 = to not know anything and lack reason (*equiv.* to be unenlightened / to be benighted) ▌A: 제가 **무지몽매해서** 벌인 일이니 용서하세요. = *This* *all happened because I'm just so ignorant.* B: 무슨 말씀이세요. 희정 씨 잘못이 아니에요. = *What are you talking about? This definitely was not your fault.*

묵묵부답 [Lit. 默silent + 默silent + 不no + 答answer] CHINESE-DERIVATION 아무 대답도 하지 않음 = giving no answer (*equiv.* for one's questions to be met with silence) █ A: 왜 **묵묵부답** 말이 없어 말 좀 해 봐. ▶p.470 = *Why are you just sitting there silently? Say something.* B: 입이 열 개라도 할 말이 없다. 미안해. = *I have nothing at all to say. I'm sorry.*

묵사발(을) 만들다 [Lit. to make a bowl of *muk*] IDIOM **1.** 심하게 때리다 = to hit strongly (*equiv.* to beat someone to a pulp / to make mincemeat out of someone / to give someone a drubbing) █ A: 김형석 선수, 저번에 상대 선수를 **묵사발을 만들겠다고** ▶p.572 호언장담했는데요, 아직도 자신 있습니까? = *Kim Hyeongseok, you were spouting off about how you were going to make mincemeat of the other fighter. Are you still so confident?* B: 물론입니다. 제 이 두 주먹으로 상대 선수를 링 위에 때려 눕히겠습니다. = *Of course. I'm going to lay him flat on the ring with these here two fists.* **2.** 세력이나 기세를 완전히 누르다 = to completely oppress a group or force (*equiv.* to give someone a drubbing) █ A: 어제 청문회 봤어? = *Did you see the hearing yesterday?* B: 어. 국회의원들이 장관들을 아주 **묵사발을 만들던데.** = *Yep. The lawmakers from the National Assembly sure gave the ministers a solid drubbing.*

NOTE: 묵사발은 묵을 담는 그릇을 말한다. 그러나 이 표현에서 묵사발은 그릇 자체를 가리킨다기보다는 그 안에 든 묵의 조금만 건드려도 부서지는 성질을 차용한 것이다.

묵사발 is the word for a bowl that contains 묵 (jellied foods made of ground up nuts or other things). This expression, however, does not take its meaning from the dish but from the fragile nature of the jelly-like 묵 itself, which can be torn apart with even the lightest touch.

묵사발(이) 되다 [Lit. to become a dish of *muk*] IDIOM **1.** 심하게 맞다 = to be beaten severely (*equiv.* to get a whupping *syn.* 떡(이) 되다) █ A: 너 얼

굴이 어떻게 된 거야? = *What happened to your face?* B: 어제 불량배를 만나서 아주 **묵사발이 됐어**. = *Yesterday I mixed it up with some thugs and they really whupped me bad.* 2. 세력이나 기세가 완전히 눌리다 = for a group or force to be entirely oppressed (*equiv.* to be destroyed / to be taken apart) ▮A: 아니, 15대 0이 뭐야? 이게 야구 스코어 맞아? = *What the hell is 15 to 0? Does that sound like a baseball score to you?* B: 나도 어제 보다가 **묵사발 되는** 걸 차마 볼 수가 없어서 TV 껐어. = *Yeah, I was watching it yesterday too until I couldn't bear to watch them destroying us like that and I turned off the TV.*

NOTE: See the note on 묵사발(을) 만들다.

***문(을) 닫다** [Lit. to close the door] IDIOM 1. 폐업하다 = to shutter a business (*equiv.* to close down *syn.* 간판을 내리다 *ant.* 문(을) 열다) ▮A: 어? 이 가게 언제 **문 닫았지**? 지난주까지 했었는데. = *What? When did this place shut down? They were still open last week.* B: 요즘 작은 가게들은 살아남기 힘들잖아. = *It's hard for small stores to stay in business these days.* 2. 상점이나 기관 따위가 하루 일과를 끝내다 = to close for the day (*ant.* 문(을) 열다) ▮A: 죄송하지만, 이제 곧 **문 닫을** 시간이라서요. = *I'm sorry, but we are just about to close up for the day.* B: 아, 그렇군요. 곧 나가겠습니다. = *Ah, I see. I'll be leaving right away.*

문을 두드리다 [Lit. to knock on the door] IDIOM 어떤 단체에 들어가기 위해 신청하다 = to seek admission into an organization (*equiv.* to knock on the door) ▮A: 마흔이라는 적지 않은 나이에 연예계의 **문을 두드리기가** 쉽지 않으셨을 것 같은데요. = *At the ripe age of 40, it must not have been easy for you to knock on the door of the entertainment world.* B: 네. 하지만 젊었을 때부터 간절히 바라 왔던 일이어서 용기를 낼 수 있었어요. = *Yes, but since it was something that I had dreamed of so earnestly ever since my youth, I was able to summon the courage to do it.*

***문(을) 열다** [Lit. to open the door] IDIOM 1. 개업하다 = to open a business (*equiv.* to open the doors / to kick off / to open up *syn.* 간판을 걸다 *ant.* 문(을) 닫다) ▮A: 맞은편에 옷 가게가 또 **문을 열었네요**. = *Another* *clothing store just opened up across the street.* B: 요즘에는 자고 일어나면 새 가게가 생겨 있다니까. = *I'm telling you, new stores are popping up in the blink of an eye.* **2.** 상점이나 기관 따위가 하루 일과를 시작하다 = to commence the day's business at a store or other organization (*equiv.* to open) █ A: 병원 **문은 몇 시에 여나요?** = *What time does the hospital open?* B: 평일에는 9시에 열고, 토요일에는 9시 반에 엽니다. = *At 9 a.m. on weekdays and 9:30 on Saturdays.* **3.** 개방하다 = to be made available (*equiv.* to open the doors (for a group etc.)) █ A: 이 도서관은 이곳 주민이 아니어도 이용할 수 있나요? = *Can you use this library even if you aren't a resident here?* B: 네. 저희 도서관은 모든 분들에게 **문을 열어** 놓고 있습니다. = *Yes, we open our doors to everyone.*

문자 그대로 [Lit. as the letters (state)] IDIOM 이어서 하려는 말이 과장되지 않았음을 강조하려는 표현 = used to emphasize that the following is not an exaggeration (*equiv.* literally (when used incorrectly as an intensifier) / it wouldn't be an exaggeration to say *syn.* 글자 그대로, 말 그대로) █ A: 자, 이제 범인들은 **문자 그대로** 독 안에 든 쥐야. = *The criminals are no better than rats in a trap.* B: 석 달 동안 한 고생의 끝이 보이는군요. = *I can finally see the end to our three-month struggle.*

NOTE: '문자 그대로'는 앞서 언급한 말이나 뒤이어 하게 될 말의 사전적 의미를 강조하거나 뒤이어 하는 말이 지나치지 않음을 강조하는 표현이다. 얼핏 보면 사람을 보고 '문자 그대로' 독 안에 든 쥐라고 하는 것은 이상한 표현으로 보인다. 그러나 이때의 '문자 그대로'는 도망갈 곳이 없는 상황을 강조한 것이라고 볼 수 있다.

This expression is used to emphasize the literal meaning of the preceding statement or to assure the listener that the following statement is not an exaggeration. At first glance it may seem odd to say that criminals are "literally mice in a pot," but "literally" is similarly misused in English. In such cases, it should be understood as an intensifier.

문자(를) 쓰다 [Lit. to use flowery speech] IDIOM 어려운 단어를 섞어 말하다 = to use many difficult words in one's speech (*equiv.* to use highfalutin language / to use professorial speech *cf.* 공자 앞에서 문자 쓴다) █ A: 경

미 씨 말은 당최 알아들을 수가 없어요. =*I have absolutely no idea what Gyeongmi is saying.* B: 저도요. 어쩌나 **문자를 써** 대는지 머리가 다 아파요. =*Me neither. With all that highfalutin talk, she's really giving me a headache.*

문전성시 [Lit. 門door + 前before + 成become + 市market → It's like a market in front of the door.] CHINESE-DERIVATION 찾아오는 사람이 많음을 비유적으로 이르는 말 =used to describe a constant stream of customers or visitors (*equiv.* It's like grand central station in here.) ▌A: 우와, 저 집 앞에 왜 저렇게 사람들이 많이 모여 있어요? =*Why are there so many people in front of that house?* B: 얼마 전에 저 집 사연이 TV에 소개된 이후 연일 **문전성시**를 이루고 있어요. =*Those people had their story broadcast on TV and ever since, it's been a constant stream of visitors.*

문턱에 들어서다 [Lit. to cross the threshold] IDIOM 어떤 상태나 단계가 시작되려 하다 =to enter a phase or take on a state (*equiv.* to cross the threshold / to cross the line into (a new state)) ▌A: 이제 아침 저녁으로 쌀쌀하지 않아요? =*Recently the evenings and early mornings have been pretty chilly, huh?* B: 네. 가을의 **문턱에 들어선** 것 같아요. =*Yeah, it seems like we've crossed the threshold into fall.*

문턱을 낮추다 [Lit. to lower the threshold] IDIOM 쉽고 편하게 접근할 수 있도록 조건이나 자격을 완화하다 =to relax the qualifications or requirements to make something more accessible (*equiv.* to lower the bar *ant.* 문턱을 높이다) ▌A: 우리 호텔 식당은 이제 **문턱을 낮추어** 호텔 외부 손님들에게도 개방할 예정입니다. =*The hotel restaurant here is going to be relaxing its requirements and allowing non-guests to dine there as well.* B: 아, 그것 참 반가운 소식이군요. =*Ah, I'm really glad to hear that.*

문턱을 넘어서다 [Lit. to stand on the other side of the threshold] IDIOM 어떤 환경이나 상태에서 벗어나다 =to leave an environment or state (*equiv.* to break free of (a state) / to shed (a state)) ▌A: 우리나라는 짧은 시간에 참 많이 발전했어요. =*Korea sure has advanced a lot in a short amount of time.* B: 맞아요. 사실 가난의 **문턱을 넘어선** 것도 그리

오래되지 않았죠. = *It sure has. It really hasn't been long since we broke free of our poverty as a nation.*

문턱을 높이다 [Lit. to raise the threshold] IDIOM 조건이나 자격을 강화하여 접근을 까다롭게 만들다 = to raise the qualifications or requirements to limit accessibility (*equiv.* to raise the bar / to raise the threshold *syn.* 문턱을 낮추다 *cf.* 문턱이 높다) ▌A: 요즘 불법 이민 문제가 심각해지고 있다는 기사 봤어? = *Did you see that article about how serious illegal immigration is becoming?* B: 어. 정부에서 이민의 **문턱을 높이겠다고** 하던데. = *Yeah, and the government is saying its going to raise the bar for immigrants.*

문턱이 높다 [Lit. for the threshold to be high] IDIOM 조건이나 자격이 까다로워 접근이 어렵다 = to be difficult of access due to hard requirements or demand for high qualifications (*equiv.* to have high standards / a high bar to cross / to have a high threshold *cf.* 문턱을 높이다) ▌A: 오늘 첫 무대는 어땠어? = *How was it giving your first performance today?* B: 너무 긴장을 많이 해서 실수를 많이 했어요. = *I was so nervous, I made a lot of mistakes.* A: 역시 프로 무대의 **문턱이 높구나**. = *The threshold really is high to make it on the pro stage.*

문턱이 닳도록 드나들다 [Lit. to wear out the threshold by being in and out] IDIOM 자주 드나들다 = to be constantly in and out of a place (*equiv.* to always be in and out / to stop by all the time) ▌A: 왜 요즘 당신 후배 우리 집에 놀러 안 와요? 한동안 우리 집 **문턱이 닳도록 드나들더니**. = *Why isn't your younger friend coming by anymore? He used to stop by all the time.* B: 그 후배 얼마 전에 딴 데로 이사 갔거든. = *That's because he just moved to a different part of town.*

물거품이 되다 [Lit. to become a water bubble] IDIOM 그동안의 꿈이나 노력이 모두 헛되게 되다 = for a long-fought effort or dream to come to naught (*equiv.* to go up in smoke / to pop like a bubble *cf.* 십년공부 도로 아미타불, 말짱 도루묵, 수포로 돌아가다) ▌A: 내년에는 집을 살 수 있을 줄 알았는데, 집값이 너무 많이 뛰어서 **물거품이 되어** 버렸

어. = *I thought I would be able to buy a house next year but those plans went up in smoke when the prices of houses shot up.* B: 눈을 좀 낮춰 보는 게 ▶p.146 어때? = *What about lowering your standards a little bit?*

물 건너가다 [Lit. to cross the water] IDIOM 일이 이미 이루어지기 힘들게 되다 = The time to achieve one's aims has passed. (*equiv.* It's water under the bridge. *syn.* 버스(를) 놓치다) ▮A: 아, 내가 그때 조금만 잘했으면 우리 팀이 이겼을 텐데. = *If I had only done a little better back then, our team could've won.* B: 이미 **물 건너간** 일이야. = *It's all water under the bridge now.*

물고기는 물을 떠나 살 수 없다 [Lit. A fish cannot live outside of the water.] PROVERB 누구나 자신에게 어울리는 곳이 있으며 그곳에서 지내는 것이 가장 낫다는 말 = used to emphasize that everyone does best in a certain environment ▮A: 이태현 선수가 격투기를 그만두고 씨름계로 돌아왔다며? = *I heard that Lee Taehyeon has given up mixed matial arts and returned to ssireum.* B: 그러니까 물고기는 **물을 떠나 살 수 없는** 거야. 씨름판이 본인에게 가장 어울리는 자리인 거지. = *Yep, fish can't live outside the water. The ssireum mat is where he belongs.*

*****물과 기름** [Lit. water and oil] IDIOM 서로 어울리지 못하여 겉도는 사이 = a relationship in which the two parties do not get along (*equiv.* to be like oil and water / to not mesh well *syn.* 물 위의 기름, 물과 불) ▮A: 과장님하고 차장님은 원래부터 저렇게 **물과 기름**이었어요? = *Have the bureau chief and the deputy chief always been like water and oil?* B: 원래는 안 그랬는데 언젠가 한번 크게 싸운 이후로 저렇게 서먹서먹하게 지내. = *No, they weren't always that way, but after they had one major fight they've been awkward around each other.*

물과 불 [Lit. water and fire] IDIOM 서로 어울리지 못하여 적대적인 상태나 그런 상태에 있는 두 대상 = the antagonistic state of two parties who do not get along or those two parties themselves (*equiv.* to be like fire and ice *syn.* 물과 기름) ▮A: 동생이랑 친하세요? = *Are you close with your little brother?* B: 사실 별로 안 친해요. 저랑 동생이 성격이 완전히

반대라서 **물과 불**이에요. = *Honestly, not really. Our personalities are exact opposites, so we're like fire and ice when we're together.*

물꼬를 트다 [Lit. to clear the sluice gates] IDIOM 막혀 있는 상태를 해소하다 = to alleviate a blockage or impasse (*equiv.* to open the doors (to a new era) / to open the sluice gates) █ A: 이번 남북 단일 축구 팀이 남북 교류의 **물꼬를 트는** 계기가 될 것이라 확신합니다. = *I'm sure that the establishment of a combined North and South Korean soccer team will open the sluice gates to exchange between our two countries.* B: 네, 그런 점에서 오늘 경기는 그 의미가 아주 큰 시합이죠. = *Yes, today's match certainly does have a deeper meaning in that regard.*

물 만난 고기 [Lit. a fish that has met water] IDIOM 자신이 매우 잘하거나 익숙한 환경에 놓인 사람이나 상황 = used to describe a person who is in their ideal environment or such a situation itself (*equiv.* to be like a fish in water / to be in one's element) █ A: 한솔 씨가 그렇게 노래를 잘하는지 몰랐어요. = *I had no idea Hansol was that good at singing.* B: 그러게 말이에요. 노래방 가니까 완전히 **물 만난 고기**던데요. = *That's what I'm saying. You take her out for karaoke, and she's like a fish in water.*

물먹은 솜 [Lit. cotton that has drunk water] IDIOM 몸이 몹시 무겁고 처지는 상태를 비유하는 말 = a metaphor for feeling droopy and lethargic (*equiv.* to be dragging around / to feel droopy) █ A: 오늘 왜 이렇게 빨리 왔어? = *Why did you get here so early today?* B: 오늘 몸이 **물먹은 솜**처럼 무거워서 조퇴하고 일찍 왔어. = *I've been dragging around all day today, so I left early and came home.*

물불(을) 가리지 않다 [Lit. to not distinguish between water or flame] IDIOM 위험이나 어려움을 신경쓰지 않고 일을 강행하다 = to not concern oneself with danger or difficulty and resolutely carry out a task (*equiv.* to go to hell and back (to get something done) / to go through hell and high water (for one's kids etc.)) █ A: 한국의 부모들은 자기 자식 일이라면 **물불을 가리지 않는** 것 같아요. = *Korean parents would go to hell for their kids.* B: 맞아요. 그런데 그게 문제가 될 때도 많죠. = *That's* *true, but that's also the root of many problems.*

물샐틈없다 [Lit. to have no leaks] IDIOM 철저하고 빈틈이 없다 = to be thorough and without blind spots (*equiv.* to have no leaks / to have no holes) ▌A: 이러다 전쟁 터지는 거 아닐까? 북한이 어제 또 방송에서 위협하는 말을 했잖아. = *If things continue on like this, will war break out? North Korea made threatening statements again in their broadcasts last night.* B: 우리 군이 **물샐틈없이** 경계를 하고 있는데, 별일이야 있겠어? = *Our border defenses have no blind spots. Do you really think something could happen?*

물에 물 탄 듯 술에 술 탄 듯 [Lit. as if water was been mixed with water and liquor mixed with liquor] PROVERB 말이나 행동이 주관이 없고 흐리멍덩한 사람에게 쓰는 말 = used to describe someone who seems to possess no definite opinions or is dull (*equiv.* to be bland *syn.* 술에 술 탄 듯 물에 물 탄 듯) ▌A: 사람 참 답답하네. 사람이 **물에 물 탄 듯 술에 술 탄 듯** 왜 그래? = *You're kind of annoying to be around. Why are you so bland?* B: 죄송합니다. 이번 건은 제가 책임 지고 제대로 처리하겠습니다. = *I'm sorry. I take full responsibility for this and I'll handle it.*

NOTE: 물 위에 물을 더 붓거나 술 위에 술을 더 부어 봤자 본질적으로 달라지는 것은 없다.
Pouring more water into a glass of water or more liquor into a bottle of liquor causes no fundamental change. That's where this idiom derives its meaning.

물에 빠지면 지푸라기라도 잡는다 [Lit. If one falls in the water, one will even grab at straw.] PROVERB 아주 다급한 상황이 되면 아무것도 아닌 것에도 의지하게 된다는 말 = *In a very tense situation, there's nothing you won't rely on.* (*equiv.* A drowning man will clutch at straw.) ▌A: 이 사람 정말 나쁜 사람이네. 말기 암 환자들을 대상으로 사기를 쳤대. = *This guy is a really bad fellow. He defrauded late-stage cancer patients.* B: **물에 빠지면 지푸라기라도 잡는** 사람들의 심리를 악용한 거네. = *When people are going through hard times, they tend to latch onto* *anything they can. It looks like he exploited that tendency.*

물에 빠진 놈 건져 놓으니까 내 봇짐 내라 한다 [Lit. I rescued a man who was drowning and he responded by asking for his backpack.] PROVERB 남의 은혜를 입고서도 그 고마움을 모르고 오히려 트집을 잡을 때 쓰는 말 = used when people who are the beneficiaries of a good deed are far from thankful and instead find fault with those who aid them (*equiv.* No good deed goes unpunished. / Give them an inch and they'll take a mile. / Save a thief from the gallows and he'll cut your throat.) ▌A: 저기요, 아까 지갑 놓고 가셨죠? = *Excuse me, you left your wallet here earlier, right?* B: 아, 네. 감사합니다. 잃어버린 줄 알고 한참을 찾았는데. 그런데 안에 돈이 삼만 원 있었는데 없어졌네요. = *Ah, yes. Thank you. I looked all over for it. But what happened to the 30,000 won that was in it.* A: 지금 저를 의심하는 건가요? **물에 빠진 놈 건져 놓으니까 내 봇짐 내라 한다더니** 좋은 일 하려다가 도둑으로 몰리는군요. = *Are you accusing me of taking it? No good deed goes unpunished, huh? Now you're trying to make me out to be a thief.*

물에 빠진 생쥐 [Lit. a rat that has fallen in the water] IDIOM 물에 흠뻑 젖어 몰골이 초췌해진 모양 = the haggard appearance of someone who is completely drenched (*equiv.* (to look like) a drowned rat) ▌A: 밖에 비 와? 왜 **물에 빠진 생쥐**가 됐어? = *Is it raining outside? You look like a drowned rat!* B: 집에 거의 다 와 가는데 갑자기 소나기가 내려서. = *I was almost home and then I got caught in a downpour.*

물 위의 기름 IDIOM = 물과 기름

물(을)들이다 [Lit. to dye] IDIOM 어떤 환경이나 사상 따위를 전파하다 = to spread an environment or ideology (*equiv.* for people to be infected (with an ideology) *cf.* 물(이)들다) ▶p.276 ▌A: 미꾸라지 한 마리가 온 웅덩이를 흐린다더니 승철이가 학원에 들어온 다음부터 다른 애들도 나쁜 **물을 들이는** 것 같아요. = *I guess this is why they say one bad apple spoils the bunch. Ever since Seungcheol started here, he's been a bad influence on the other children.* B: 아무래도 승철이 부모님께 말씀드

려야겠죠?=*I think we have no choice but to talk to his parents about this.*

물(을)먹다 [Lit. to drink water] IDIOM **1.** 곤란을 겪다=to be put in an awkward or embarrassing situation (*equiv.* to be short-changed) ▌A: 요즘 당신 왜 맨날 야근이야?=*Why have you been working so much overtime recently?* B: 회사 감사 기간인데 만만한 우리 부서가 **물먹고** 있어서 그래.=*Well, it's audit time at work now and our division always gets pushed around. So that's why.* **2.** 시험에 떨어지다=to fail on a test (*equiv.* to flunk a test / to blow it *syn.* 미역국(을) 먹다) ▌A: 이번에 대위 승진 시험 있었지? 남편은 승진했어?=*There was a promotion examination recently, right? Did your husband make captain?* B: 이번에도 **물먹었어.** 그것 때문에 요즘 집안 분위기가 말이 아니야.=*No, he flunked again. That's why the mood at our house has been bad for a long time.* **3.** 어떤 직종에 종사하거나 자신이 지내 오던 곳이 아닌 다른 곳에서의 생활을 경험하다=to experience life in another country or work in an environment other than what one is used to ▌A: 웁스! 이걸 빠뜨렸네.=*Oops! We left this out.* B: 뭐? 웁스? 애가 석 달 동안 외국 **물을 먹더니** 이상한 것만 배워 왔네.=*What do you mean, "oops"? You've lived abroad for three months and all you managed to learn were words like that.*

NOTE: 요즘도 가끔씩 고기의 무게를 늘리기 위해 소나 돼지에게 물을 먹이는 사람들의 얘기가 신문에 오르내리곤 한다. '물먹다'나 '물을 먹이다'는 이와 같은 행동에서 온 표현이다. '물을 먹다'가 1,2번의 뜻으로 쓰일 때는 주로 조사 '을'이 생략된 형태로 쓰이는 반면 3번의 의미로 쓰일 때는 조사가 잘 생략되지 않는다. 또한 그때는 앞에 직종이나 지역명이 오는 경우가 많다.

Even now, it is not uncommon to see people in the paper who were caught trying to fatten up pigs or cows by feeding them water and thereby make more money when selling them. This expression comes from the unethical practice of trying to deceive the buyer of an animal as to the animals true weight by such means. When this expression is used in either of the first two meanings, the particle 을 is usually omitted but in the case of the third definition, is rarely left off. Also, when used in this third meaning, the name of an occupation or region appears before the idiom.

물(을) 먹이다 [Lit. to feed (someone) water] IDIOM 곤경에 빠뜨리다 = to place someone in a difficult situation (*equiv.* to drive someone into a corner *syn.* 엿 먹이다) ▌A: 감히 이 자식이 나를 **물 먹여**? = *How dare he back me into a corner like this!* B: 참아요. 일부러 그러기야 했겠어요? = *Keep it together. Do you think he did it on purpose?*

NOTE: See the note on 물(을)먹다.

물(을) 흐리다 [Lit. to spoil water] IDIOM 속해 있는 무리에 나쁜 영향을 끼치거나 분위기를 망치다 = to have a bad influence on or ruin the mood in the group one is a part of (*equiv.* to spoil the vibe / to bring down the mood / to be a buzzkill *cf.* 미꾸라지 한 마리가 온 웅덩이를 흐린다) ▌A: 어제 회식 때 김 대리님 때문에 분위기가 너무 이상하지 않았어요? = *Wasn't the vibe a little weird yesterday at the staff party because of Mr. Kim?* B: 누가 아니래요. 어디를 가나 **물을 흐리는** 사람이 꼭 있다니까요. = *I can't disagree with you on that. No matter where you go, there's always someone who kills the buzz.*

물이 너무 맑으면 고기가 없다 [Lit. If the water is too clear, there won't be any fish.] PROVERB 사람이 지나치게 올곧으면 사람들이 가까이하기를 꺼린다는 말 = used to describe how people who are too upstanding may end up being shunned (*equiv.* upright to a fault) ▌A: 박 과장은 참 성실하고 바른 사람인데 융통성이 너무 없는 게 흠이야. = *Department chief Park is sincere and hardworking, but his lack of flexibility is a problem.* B: **물이 너무 맑으면 고기가 없다는데**, 조금만 더 유들유들해지시면 좋을 텐데 말이죠. = *I guess that's why they say that some people can be upright to a fault. He'd be better off if he loosened up a bit, you know?*

물(이)들다 [Lit. to be dyed] IDIOM 어떤 환경이나 사상 따위가 다른 사람과 닮아 가다 = to begin to resemble others or think like the others in a given environment (*equiv.* to mix in / to assimilate / to drink the Kool-Aid *cf.* 물(을)들이다) ▌A: 착한 정권이가 어쩌다 패싸움에 휘말린 거야? = *How did our sweet little Jeongguon get wrapped up in a group scuffle?*

B: 중학교 가더니 나쁜 친구를 사귀었나 봐. 걔들한테 **물든** 것 같아. =*Once he started middle school, he started hanging out with the wrong crowd and it looks like they had a bad influence on him.*

물(이)오르다 [Lit. for the water to rise] IDIOM 능력이나 형편, 외모 등이 아주 좋은 상태에 있다 = for one's capabilities, state of affairs or appearance to reach a high point ⬛A: 지현 씨는 요즘 보면 연기에 눈을 완전히 뜬 것 같아. =*It looks like Jihyun has finally achieved enlightenment in her acting.* B: 제가 보도 그래요. 정말 연기에 **물이 올랐어요.** =*That's what I was thinking too. She's really reaching new heights.* ➡p.147

물(이)좋다 [Lit. The water is good.] IDIOM (속된 말로) 술집이나 나이트클럽 등 유흥업소의 분위기가 좋다 = (slang) for the atmosphere to be good at a bar, night club or other such establishment (*equiv.* to have a good vibe) ⬛A: 이 주변 나이트 중에서 제일 **물좋은** 곳이 어디야? =*Out of all the nearby night clubs, which one would you say has the best vibe?* B: 요 주변에는 다 별로야. 차를 타고 좀 나가야 돼. =*Around here, there's nothing special. You've got to drive out of this area a bit.*

> **NOTE:** '물이 좋다'는 '생선 따위가 싱싱하다'는 뜻이다. 그러나 비유적으로 위와 같이 쓰이기도 한다.
> This expression was originally used to describe the waters in a certain area as containing fresh fish, but is now used metaphorically as above.

물 찬 제비 [Lit. a swallow that kicked the water] IDIOM **1.** 몸매나 옷 맵시가 매우 깔끔한 남자나 물건 = a man who dresses in a chic way or has a clean-cut look or a sleek item ⬛A: 저기 저 차 좀 봐. **물 찬 제비**처럼 잘 빠졌는데! =*Take a look at that car. Those are some clean lines!* B: 아마 새로 나온 외제차일 거야. =*I bet that's the new import.* **2.** 동작이 민첩한 사람 = someone who makes quick, agile movements ⬛A: 와, 저 녀석 달리기할 때는 거북이 같더니, 수영하는 걸 보니 **물 찬 제비**가 따로 없구먼. =*Wow, when that guy runs, he looks like a turtle, but seeing him swim is like seeing swim is like watching a dolphin.* B: 어릴 때 바닷가 근처에 살았거든요. =*That's probably because he lived near the water as a boy.*

NOTE: 제비는 동작이 매우 빠르고 민첩하다. 제비가 물 위의 먹이를 잡아 먹기 위해 물을 깃으로 차면서 수면 위를 나는 모습을 보면 아주 날렵해 보인다. '물 찬 제비'라는 표현은 제비의 그러한 동작에서 온 것이다. The movements of a swallow are very agile and rapid. When catching prey, the swallow hits the water (물을 차다) with its wings as it swoops in to snag the bugs that live on the water. This slick action is why 물 찬 제비 is where the phrase comes from.

*뭐니 뭐니 해도 [Lit. even if you say this or that] IDIOM 다른 무엇보다 = more than anything else ▌A: 논문 쓴다고 또 밤을 새운 거예요? 그러다가 몸 상하겠어요. 뭐니 뭐니 해도 건강이 최고인데. = *Did you stay up all night writing your thesis? If you keep on like that, you're going to lose your health. Don't forget that your health comes before all else.* B: 걱정해 줘서 고마워요. = *Thanks so much for your concern.*

뭐 잘못 먹었냐? [Lit. Did you eat wrong?] IDIOM 엉뚱한 말이나 행동을 할 때 하는 소리 = used when someone speaks or acts in an unexpected way (*equiv.* What was in that burger (or other food)? / What's gotten into you? *syn.* 어디 아프냐?) ▌A: 당신 오늘따라 유난히 예쁜데? = *You look especially beautiful today.* B: 당신 오늘 뭐 잘못 먹었어? = *Was something in that burrito you ate?*

(미꾸라지) 용 됐다 [Lit. (for a loach) to have become a dragon] PROVERB 별 볼 일 없던 사람이 크게 되었을 때 쓰는 말 = used to describe someone rather unremarkable who becomes very successful (*cf.* 개천에서 용 (이) 나다 ➡p.273) ▌A: 철민이 녀석 서울 물을 먹더니 용 됐던데? = *There must be something in the water in Seoul. Cheolmin has made quite the man of himself.* B: 서울 가기 전에는 그냥 철부지 아이였는데, 이제 신사가 다 됐어. = *Before going to Seoul he was just a whippersnapper and now he really is a refined gentleman.*

미꾸라지 한 마리가 온 웅덩이를 흐린다 [Lit. One mudfish makes the whole pond murky.] IDIOM 못된 사람 하나가 전체 무리에 해를 끼칠 때 쓰는 말 = used to describe how one individual can negatively affect an entire group (*equiv.* One bad apple spoils the bunch.) ▌A: 요즘에 우리 동아리 분위기가 좀 이상해진 것 같지 않아? = *Doesn't it seem like the mood at our club meetings has been strange recently?* B: 그러게. 얼마 전에 새로 들어온 사람이 뒤에서 안 좋은 얘기를 하고 다닌다던데. = *Yeah, that guy who joined not too long ago is talking about people behind their backs.* A: 미꾸라지 한 마리가 온 웅덩이를 흐리는구먼. = *One bad apple really does spoil the bunch.*

***미역국(을) 먹다** [Lit. to eat seaweed soup] IDIOM 시험에 떨어지다 = to fail a test (*equiv.* to flunk an exam *syn.* 물(을)먹다) ▌A: 이번에는 붙었어? = *Did you make it this time?* B: 아니, 또 미역국 먹었어. = *No, I blew it again.* A: 휴, 벌써 몇 번째냐. = *Ah, how many times has it been?*

> NOTE: 한국 사람들은 시험을 보기 전 관습적으로 미역국을 먹지 않는다. 이는 미역의 미끄러운 성질과 관련이 깊어 보인다. '미역국을 먹었다'라는 말은 '시험에서 떨어지다'라는 말이다.
>
> The normally popular dish, 미역국 or seaweed soup, is avoided like the plague by Koreans on test days. The slippery texture of seaweed has long been associated with slipping up. The phrase 미역국을 먹다 is now a euphemism for failing a test.

미운 놈 떡 하나 더 준다 PROVERB = 미운 아이 떡 하나 더 준다

미운 아이 떡 하나 더 준다 [Lit. to give the child one despises an extra piece of *tteok*] PROVERB 미울수록 다정하게 대해야 미워하는 마음이 없어진다는 말 = used to describe how one can overcome dislike for another by treating them kindly (*syn.* 미운 놈 떡 하나 더 준다) ▌A: 지난 번에는 경희랑 그렇게 싸우더니 왜 요즘에는 그렇게 잘해 주니? = *You got in a fight with Gyeonghee not too long ago, why are you being so nice to her lately?* B: 미운 아이 떡 하나 더 준다는 말도 몰라? = *Haven't you ever heard that you're supposed to be extra kind to those you dislike.*

> NOTE: 이 표현은 '친구를 가까이하되 적은 더 가까이하라.'는 말과 일맥상통한다.

This phrase is related to "Keep your friends close and your enemies closer."

미운 오리 새끼 [Lit. a despised duckling] IDIOM 남에게 천대를 받는 사람 = someone who is scorned by others (*equiv.* the ugly duckling) ▎A: 너 폴 포츠 알아? = *Have you heard of Paul Potts?* B: 알지. 오디션 프로그램에서 유명해진 사람이잖아. = *Of course. He's that guy who got famous from being on a talent show, right?* A: 어. 원래는 **미운 오리 새끼** 같은 존재였다는데, 이번에 백조로 거듭났잖아. = *Yep, he really was an ugly duckling reborn as a beautiful swan.*

NOTE: 안데르센의 유명한 동화 '미운 오리 새끼'에서 온 표현이다. '미운 오리 새끼에서 백조로 거듭나다'라는 말을 흔히 쓴다.
This expression comes from the Hans Christian Andersen story, *The Ugly Duckling*. The phrase 미운 오리 새끼에서 백조로 거듭나다 is also used to describe a positive transformation of an originally underwhelming individual.

미운 정 고운 정 [Lit. despised compassion, beautiful compassion] IDIOM 오래도록 가까이 지내면서 때로는 다투기도 하면서 쌓인 깊은 정 = a deep relationship in which two individuals sometimes fight and sometimes get along ▎A: 두 분은 어쩌면 아직도 그렇게 금실이 좋으세요? = *After all these years, how do you two manage such marital harmony?* B: 부부로 오래 살면서 **미운 정 고운 정** 다 든 것 뿐이에요. 특별히 사이가 좋거나 하지는 않아요. = *It's no more than going through so many ups and downs together. Our relationship isn't really all that great.*

미운털이 박히다 [Lit. to have a despised hair implanted] IDIOM 미움을 받다 = to be despised (*equiv.* to be on someone's blacklist / to get on someone's bad side) ▎A: 팀장님이 한턱 낸대요. 얘기 들었죠? = *Our boss says he's paying. Didn't you hear?* B: 아니요. 제가 팀장님한테 **미운털이 박혔잖아요**. 저한테는 말씀을 잘 안 하세요. = *No. I'm on his bad side, you know? He doesn't say much to me at all.*

미주알고주알 [Lit. anus-banus] IDIOM 사소한 것까지 모두 = even the

trivial things ▌A: 어제 회사 결근하고 어디 갔었어요? 통화할 때 들리는 소리로 봐서 집은 아닌 거 같던데. = *Where did you go after work yesterday? It didn't sound like you were at home when we talked.* B: 뭘 그리 **미주알고주알** 캐물어요? 텔레비전 소리였어요. = *Why are you being so nosy? That was just the sound of the TV.*

> NOTE: 미주알은 항문을 가리키는 말이다. '미주알 고주알'은 그와 같이 남의 은밀한 부분까지 시시콜콜 간섭하고 캐묻는 사람에게 쓰는 말이다. 고주알은 특별한 뜻이 없고 미주알과 운율을 맞추기 위해 만들어 낸 말이다.
>
> 미주알 is a word for the anus and this phrase is used to describe someone who is pestering you with way too many questions as if prodding and probing your private parts. The second part of the phrase, 고주알, has no special meaning—it just makes a nice rhyming conclusion to the couplet.

믿는 도끼에 발등 찍힌다 [Lit. You are hit in the toe by an axe that you believed in.]

PROVERB 잘될 거라고 믿고 있던 일이 틀어지거나 믿고 있던 사람이 배신하여 해를 입게 될 때 쓰는 말 = used when something one had believed would work out comes to naught or when betrayed by someone one had trusted ▌A: 어, 휴가 나왔어? 요즘 미진이랑은 잘 지내지? = *Are you on break? How are things going with Mijin?* B: 걔 얘기는 하지도 마. 고무신 거꾸로 신었어. = *Don't even bring her up. She left me.* A: 우와, 너 입대할 때 울고불고하던 애가 ……. **믿는 도끼에 발등 찍힌** 셈이구나. = *Really? The same girl who cried and carried on like that when you left for the army? What a betrayal.*

→ p.57

밑도 끝도 없다 [Lit. to have no bottom or end]

IDIOM 앞뒤의 연관 관계가 없이 불쑥 말을 꺼내다 = to bring up something that is unrelated to the conversation ▌A: 야, 네가 나한테 어떻게 이럴 수가 있어? = *How could you do this to me?* B: **밑도 끝도 없이** 무슨 말이야? 여기 앉아서 차근차근 얘기해 봐. = *Well that was right out of left field. Sit here, calm down, and tell me what's going on.*

밑 빠진 독에 물 붓기 [Lit. pouring water into a pot with no bottom]

IDIOM 아무리 노력해도 소용없는 일 = a task in which no amount of effort will make a difference (*equiv.* an exercise in futility) ▌A: 내가 아무리 한 푼이라도 아끼려고 노력해도 당신이 이렇게 흥청망청 돈을 물쓰듯 하면 **밑 빠진 독에 물 붓기**야. 여보, 제발 정신 좀 차려. = *No matter how hard I try to save a penny, with you out there painting the town red, it's an exercise in futility. Please, honey, pull yourself together.* B: 미안해, 다시는 안 그럴게. = *I'm sorry. I won't let it happen again.*

밑져야 본전 [Lit. Even if one loses money one still breaks even.] IDIOM 일이 잘못되어도 손해는 아닐 때 쓰는 말 = Even if an attempt ends in failure, one risks nothing. (*equiv.* You've got nothing to lose. / might as well) ▌A: 이 일을 내가 할 수 있을까? = *Do you think I'll be able to do this?* B: 뭐 **밑져야 본전**이잖아. 한번 해 봐. = *Well, you've got nothing to lose. Give it a shot.*

밑지는 장사 [Lit. a (money) losing business] IDIOM 이득 없이 손해 보는 행위 = an activity that only brings loses with no benefits (*equiv.* a losing proposition) ▌A: 아무리 생각해도 정민이 그만 만나야 할까 봐. 내가 **밑지는 장사** 같아. = *No matter how I look at it, I've got to stop seeing Jeongmin. I think I'm on the losing team.* B: 너는 연애가 산수인 줄 아니? 이것저것 재지 말고 사람을 봐. = *Is love just math to you? Don't think about this and that, just consider what kind of a person she is.*

밑천도 못 찾다 [Lit. to not even be able to find the seed money] IDIOM 일한 보람이 없이 오히려 손해만 입다 = to be left with no compensation for one's work and instead sustain losses (*equiv.* to have nothing to show for (all one's hard work) *syn.* 본전도 못 찾다) ▌A: 도저히 못 참겠다. 이번 신입생들 해도 해도 너무해. 한마디해야겠어. = *I just can't stand it anymore. These new hires are just too much. I'm going to have to speak my mind.* B: 참아. 애들이 맹랑해서 얘기해 봤자 **밑천도 못 찾을 거야**. = *Hold on there. Those newcomers are really something else. Nothing good could come of it.*

밑천이 드러나다 [Lit. for the source to be exposed] IDIOM 숨겨져 있던 본

성이나 역량이 나타나다 = for a hidden true character or ability to appear (*equiv.* for one's true (character, abilities) to shine through *syn.* 바닥이 드러나다) █ A: 아까 그 녀석 내 앞에서 하는 말 들었지? **밑천이 드러나서 못 배운 티가 나는 거지.** = *You heard what that guy said to me, right? He's low-class background is starting to show through.* B: 엄마, 하지만 엄마가 먼저 너무 심하게 말씀하셨어요. = *But, Mom, you were the one who went too far first.*

밑천(이) 떨어지다 [Lit. to run out of sources] IDIOM 이야깃거리가 궁해지다 = for topics of conversation to become scarce (*equiv.* to be fresh out of things to talk about) █ A: 할아버지, 옛날이야기 하나 더 해 주세요. = *Grandpa, tell me more about the old days.* B: 아, 이제 할아비도 **밑천이 떨어졌는걸.** = *I think even Grandpa is fresh out of stories.*

ㅂ

***바가지(를) 긁다** [Lit. to scratch on the pans] IDIOM 아내가 남편에게 잔소리를 하다 = for a wife to nag her husband (*equiv.* to henpeck one's husband / to nag) ▌A: 왜 밖에 나와 계세요? = *Why are you outside?* B: 아내가 어찌나 **바가지를 긁던지** 잠깐 바람 쐬러 나왔어요. = *My wife's been nagging me again, so I had to step out for some fresh air.*

NOTE: 옛날 사람들은 전염병이 돌 때 바가지를 긁으면 그 소리가 전염병을 옮기는 귀신을 쫓아낸다고 믿었다. 그러다 시간이 지나면서 '아내가 남편에게 잔소리를 하다'라는 뜻으로 바뀌었다. 바가지를 긁는 그 소리가 듣는 사람에게 몹시 거슬리기 때문일 것이다.
Long ago, people would scratch gourds at the first signs of a disease outbreak as the sound was traditionally thought to ward off the spirit bearers of disease. Its meaning may have changed over the years to mean a wife nagging her husband, but one thing is still true: scraping on a gourd makes a terrible racket.

***바가지(를) 쓰다** [Lit. to wear a gourd] IDIOM 요금이나 물건값을 제값보다 비싸게 지불하다 = to be overcharged for a fare or price of goods (*equiv.* to get ripped off / to be swindled *cf.* 덤터기(를) 쓰다, 바가지(를) 씌우다) ▌A: 아무래도 이 시계 너무 비싸게 주고 샀나 봐. = *Anyhow, I think I paid too much for this watch.* B: 얼마 줬는데? = *How much did you pay?* A: 50만 원. = *500,000 won.* B: **바가지 쓴 거** 맞네. = *Then you did get ripped off.*

NOTE: 바가지는 여러 가지 물건을 담기도 하지만 주로 물을 담는 데 쓴다. 따라서 바가지를 (뒤집어)쓴다는 것은 물을 (뒤집어)쓴다는 뜻으로 이해할 수 있다. 뜻하지 않게 머리에 물을 뒤집어써서 온통 몸이 물에 젖었으니 재수 없는 일을 당한 것이다.
Gourds are useful for carrying all kinds of things but were primarily used to carry water. That's why turning over a gourd and wearing it on one's head meant pouring out all the water. Being suddenly drenched is an unfortunate turn of events indeed. So is getting ripped off, as this idiom denotes.

***바가지(를) 씌우다** [Lit. to make someone else wear a gourd] IDIOM 요금이나 물건값을 제값보다 비싸게 받다 = to take more for a product than the actual price (*equiv.* to rip somebody off *cf.* 덤터기(를) 씌우다, 바가지(를) 쓰다) ▌A: 일부 택시 기사들이 외국인들한테 **바가지를 씌워서** 문제가 되고 있대요. = *They say that some taxi drivers intentionally ripping off foreigners has become a major problem.* B: 정말 나라 망신을 시키는 사람들이군요. = *Those people are truly an embarrassment to our nation.*

NOTE: See the note on 바가지(를) 쓰다.

바가지(를) 차다 [Lit. to wear a gourd] IDIOM 거지가 되다 = to become a beggar (*equiv.* to be out on the streets *syn.* 깡통(을) 차다, 쪽박(을) 차다 *cf.* 거리로 나앉다) ▌A: 너처럼 그렇게 경제 관념이 없으면 **바가지 차기** 딱 좋아. = *For a person like you with absolutely no financial sense, being a beggar would be the perfect occupation.* B: 걱정하지 마. 알뜰한 마누라 만나면 돼. = *Don't worry. All I've got to do is meet a frugal wife and I'll be fine.*

NOTE: See the note on 깡통(을) 차다.

바늘 가는 데 실 간다 [Lit. Where the needle goes, the thread goes.] PROVERB 늘 같이 있는 두 사람이나 사물의 긴밀한 관계를 가리키는 말 = used to refer to a very close relationship between two people or objects (*equiv.* They're like two peas in a pod. / They're like peanut butter and jelly. *cf.* 바늘과 실) ▌A: 너희 부부는 어쩌면 그렇게 늘 붙어다니니? = *How can you two always be together like that?* B: **바늘 가는 데 실 가는** 건 당연한 거 아니니? = *Where the needle goes, so goes the thread. I think it's only natural.*

바늘과 실 [Lit. a needle and thread] IDIOM 아주 밀접한 사이 = a very close relationship (*equiv.* to be inseparable *cf.* 바늘 가는 데 실 간다) ▌A: 언니랑 참 친하신가 봐요. = *You sure seem close to your older sister.* B: 네. 어릴 때부터 늘 같이 다녀서 사람들이 **바늘과 실**이라고 했어요. = *Yeah, everyone has always called us inseparable since childhood.*

바늘 도둑이 소도둑 된다 [Lit. A needle thief becomes a cow thief.] PROVERB 사소한 나쁜 짓도 자주 하면 버릇이 되어 나중에는 큰 죄를 저지르게 된다는 말 = used to describe the tendency of criminal behavior to start out small and grow into more serious crimes (*equiv.* It's a slippery slope (to full-blown criminality). / Petty theft is a gateway crime.) ▌A: 동현이가 반 아이 펜이 갖고 싶어서 훔쳤대요. = *Donghyeon said that he wanted a classmate's pen so he took it.* B: 펜을? 이 녀석, **바늘 도둑이 소도둑 된다는데**, 따끔하게 혼을 내요. = *A pen? It's a slippery slope to full-blown thievery. Give him a serious scolding.*

(바늘로) 찔러도 피 한 방울 안 나오겠다 [Lit. Even if you prick (someone) they wouldn't shed a drop of blood.] IDIOM **1.** 사람이 매우 야무져서 빈틈이 없다 = for someone to be so shrewd that they have almost no weaknesses (*equiv.* a smooth operator / a cool customer) ▌A: 참 저 친구 **바늘로 찔러도 피 한 방울 안 나오게** 생겼네. = *Hey, that guy sure seems like a cool customer.* B: 보기에는 저렇게 야무져 보여도 알고 보면 허술해요. = *Yeah, that may be what he looks like, but once you get to know him, he's pretty down to earth.* **2.** 아주 독하고 냉정하다 = to be very intense and cold ➡ p.532 ▌A: 인호 말이야, 경진이가 이번에 그렇게 큰일을 당했는데 코빼기도 안 보일 수가 있어? **찔러도 피 한 방울 안 나올** 녀석 같으니라고. = *What's the deal with Inho? How could he not show up once when Gyeongjin was going through so much stuff? He's starting to look really coldhearted.* B: 못 들었어? 인호가 경진이 입원비 다 냈다던데. = *Didn't you hear? Inho paid for her entire hospital stay.*

바늘방석에 앉다 [Lit. to sit on a cushion of needles] IDIOM 마음이 불편한 상황에 처하다 = to be in a very uncomfortable situation (*equiv.* to be in hot water / to be in the hot seat *syn.* 가시방석에 앉다) ▌A: 요즘 회사에서

팀장님 눈치가 보여서 **바늘방석에 앉아** 있는 기분이에요. = *Recently I think my boss is on to me, so I may be in hot water.* B: 뭐 잘못한 거라도 있어요? = *Did you do something wrong?*

바닥(을) 기다 [Lit. to crawl on the floor] IDIOM 정도나 수준이 아주 낮다 = for one's level or results to be very low

▌A: 너 이번에 성적이 왜 이래? 특히 수학 성적은 **바닥을 기는데**. = *What's going on with your grades this semester? Your math scores especially seem to have hit rock-bottom.* B: 아빠, 저는 아무래도 수학 쪽에는 재능이 없는 것 같아요. = *Dad, I just don't think I have any talent for math.*

바닥을 치다 [Lit. to hit the floor] IDIOM 지표 따위가 심하게 하락하다 = for an index etc. to drop drastically (*equiv.* to bottom out)

▌A: 이번에 미국 대통령이 재선에 성공할 수 있을까? = *Do you think the US president will get reelected?* B: 글쎄. 듣기로는 지지율이 **바닥을 치고** 있다는데, 아무래도 어렵지 않을까? = *Well, I've heard that his support levels are scraping the floor. Don't you think that's unlikely?*

바닥(이)나다 [Lit. for the floor to show up] IDIOM 돈이나 물건 따위가 다 사용되어 없어지다 = for money or other products to be used up (*equiv.* to be exhausted / to be used up *syn.* 바닥이 드러나다)

▌A: 조금만 더 참아 봐. = *Just hold on a little longer.* B: 알았어. 그런데 서둘러. 내 인내심도 **바닥나고** 있으니까. = *OK. But hurry up. My patience is wearing thin.*

바닥이 드러나다 [Lit. for the floor to show through] IDIOM 1. 다 소비되어 없어지다 = to be all used up (*equiv.* to run dry / to be exhausted *syn.* 바닥(이)나다)

▌A: 여보 왜 밥 안 하? = *Honey, why didn't you make any rice?* B: 우리 집 쌀통이 **바닥이 드러난** 지가 언제인 줄 알아? = *Do you have any idea how long it's been since our rice ran dry.* 2. 숨겨져 있던 정체가 드러나다 = for someone's hitherto hidden identity to show through (*syn.* 밑천이 드러나다)

▌A: 돈 얘기가 나오니까 그 사람 얼굴 표정이 확 바뀌는 거 봤어? = *As soon as we brought up money, did you see how his face changed?* B: **바닥이 드러나는** 거지 뭐. = *It's just his true character showing through.*

바람 앞의 등불 [Lit. a flame in front of the wind] PROVERB 매우 위태로운 상황 = a perilous situation (*equiv.* a candle in the wind) ▌A: 이순신 장군은 어떤 인물인가요? = *What kind of person was Admiral Lee Sunshin?* B: 아, 이순신 장군은 임진왜란 때 **바람 앞의 등불**이었던 나라를 구한 영웅이에요. = *He's the admiral that saved our nation when it didn't seem that Korea had a prayer against the onslaught of the Japanese.*

바람(을) 넣다 [Lit. to put wind into (someone or something)] IDIOM **1.** 남을 부추겨서 무슨 행동을 하려는 마음이 생기게 하다 = to push someone into doing something or make them want to do something (*equiv.* to egg someone on / to inflate someone *syn.* 바람(을) 잡다 *cf.* 바람(이) 들다) ▌A: 정민아, 이번 주말 삼촌이랑 스키 타러 갈까? = *Hey, Jeongmin. How'd you like to go skiing with me this weekend?* B: 너는 왜 마음잡고 ➡ p.208 공부하려는 애한테 **바람을 넣고** 그러니? = *Why are you distracting a child that's already made up her mind to study.* **2.** 기분 전환을 위해 탁 트인 곳으로 나가다 = to go to an open area to change one's mood (*syn.* 바람(을) 쐬다) ▌A: 좋아요, 삼촌. = *All right, Uncle.* B: 너는 수험생이 공부해야지 스키장이 웬 말이야? = *What is all this skiing talk? You should be studying for your exams.* A: 엄마, 저도 콧구멍에 **바람 좀 넣어야** 살 것 같아요. = *Mom, I've got to get out of the house for a little bit or I'm going to die.*

NOTE: 1번 뜻에서 바람은 마음이 들뜬 상태나 행동을 비유한 말이다. '바람을 잡다'나 '바람이 들다'의 '바람'도 같은 의미이다. 2번 뜻의 바람은 신선한 공기, 기분 전환을 뜻한다. '바람을 쐬다'도 같은 맥락에서 이해할 수 있다. '콧구멍에 바람을 넣다', '콧바람을 쐬다'와 같이 직접적으로 공기를 마시는 행위를 표현할 수도 있다.

In the case of the first meaning, 바람 (wind) is a metaphor for a buoyed state of mind or such behavior. The meaning is similar in the expressions 바람을 잡다 or 바람이 들다. The second meaning uses 바람 as a stand-in for fresh air or a change in one's state of mind. The expression 바람을 쐬다 can be understood in this manner. The expressions 콧구멍에 바람을 넣다 and 콧바람을 쐬다 signify the more concrete action of actually breathing in fresh air.

***바람(을)맞다** [Lit. to be hit with a wind] IDIOM 약속한 사람이 나타나지 않아 허탕을 치다 = for the other party not to show up for an appointment (*equiv.* to get stood up / to get blown off *cf.* 바람(을)맞히다) ▌A: 왜 그렇게 저기압이야? = *Why do you look so down?* B: 오늘 데이트 약속이 있었는데 **바람맞았어**. = *I had plans for a date today, but I got stood up.*

NOTE: 약속 장소에 나갔지만 상대는 나타나지 않고 쓸쓸히 바람만 불고 있는 상황을 상상해 보라.
Imagine you went to meet someone at the appointed time and place but all that was there to greet you was the lonely wind. This is the expression to use in such a case.

***바람(을)맞히다** [Lit. to hit someone else with a wind] IDIOM 상대와 만날 약속을 지키지 않아 허탕을 치게 하다 = to not keep a scheduled appointment and thereby cause someone to travel pointlessly to the prescribed location (*equiv.* to stand someone up *cf.* 바람(을)맞다) ▌A: 감히 우리 딸을 **바람맞혀**? 괘씸한 놈이네. = *He dares to stand up my daughter? What an impertinent fool.* B: 당신이 그 녀석 만나서 혼 좀 내 줘요. = *You'd better give him a piece of your mind.*

NOTE: See the note on 바람(을) 맞다.

바람(을) 쐬다 [Lit. to expose oneself to the wind] IDIOM 기분 전환을 위해 탁 트인 곳으로 나가다 = to head outdoors to improve one's state of mind (*equiv.* to get some (fresh) air / to cool one's head *syn.* 바람(을) 넣다) ▌A: 어디 가니? = *Where are you heading?* B: 집 안에만 있으니까 갑갑해서 **바람 쐬러** 잠깐 나가요. = *I couldn't handle being cooped up in the house anymore, so I'm heading out for some fresh air.*

NOTE: See the note on 바람(을) 넣다.

바람(을) 잡다 [Lit. to catch the wind] IDIOM 남을 부추겨서 무슨 행동을 하려는 마음이 생기게 하다 = to egg someone on until they become inclined to take a certain course of action (*equiv.* to egg someone on / to pressure someone (into doing something) *syn.* 바람(을) 넣다) ▌A: 여행 갔다 오면서 뭘 이렇게 많이 사 왔어요?=*Why did you buy so much stuff on your vacation?* B: 현지 가이드가 기념품을 사라고 어찌나 **바람을 잡던지** 안 살 수가 있어야지. =*The guide there kept pressuring us to buy souvenirs to the point where we almost had no choice but to buy them.*

NOTE: See the note on 바람(을) 넣다.

***바람(을)피우다** [Lit. to kick up a breeze] IDIOM 배우자나 사귀는 사람이 아닌 이성과 관계를 갖다=to carry on a romantic relationship with someone other than one's spouse or significant other (*equiv.* to cheat on / to have an affair *syn.* 한눈(을)팔다 *cf.* 바람(이)나다) ▌A: 당신이 만약 **바람피우면** 그날로 나랑 끝이에요. 명심해요.=*If you ever cheat on me, that's the end of us. Bear that in mind.* B: 알았어요. 당신도 마찬가지 예요. =*OK, I got it. The same goes for you.*

NOTE: '바람피우다', '바람나다'에서의 '바람'은 몰래 다른 이성과 관계를 가지는 것을 뜻한다.
바람 in the expressions 바람피우다 and 바람나다 means having a secret affair with a member of the opposite sex.

바람(이)나다 [Lit. for a wind to occur] IDIOM 배우자나 사귀는 사람이 아닌 이성에게 마음을 빼앗기다=to have romantic feelings for someone other than one's spouse or significant other (*equiv.* to cheat on someone / to be messing around on someone *cf.* 바람(을)피우다) ▌A: 요즘 드라마를 보면 온통 **바람이 난** 사람들 얘기네.=*TV dramas these days are all just stories of people cheating on each other.* B: 그만큼 바람피우는 사람 이 많다는 얘기 아니겠어?=*Don't you think that's because that many people are out there cheating?*

바람(이) 들다 IDIOM = 허파에 바람(이) 들다

바람(이) 불다 [Lit. for the wind to blow] IDIOM 유행이 되거나 분위기가 형성되다=for a trend to be kicked off or a certain mood to arise (*equiv.* to be in full force / for the winds (of a certain movement) to blow *cf.* 무슨 바람이 불어서) ▌A: 지금 아프리카에는 민주화 **바람이 거세게 불고** 있습니다. = *The winds of democracy are blowing across the African continent.* B: 튀니지에 이어 이집트에서도 독재 정권에 저항하는 시위가 벌어지고 있습니다. = *First in Tunisia and now in Egypt too, people are gathering to oppose the autocratic regimes that rule their countries.*

바통을 넘기다

[Lit. to pass on the baton] IDIOM 해 오던 일을 인계하다 = to pass off the work one had been engaged in to a successor (*equiv.* to pass on the baton / to hand the reins to) ▌A: 오늘이 제가 9시 뉴스를 진행하는 마지막 날입니다. 내일부터는 이지혜 아나운서가 **바통을 넘겨** 받아 9시 뉴스를 책임지겠습니다. = *Today is the last day I will be anchoring the Nine O'Clock News. I will be passing the baton to Lee Jihye, and she will be assuming my post tomorrow.* B: 그동안 고생 많으셨습니다. = *Thanks for your years of distinguished service.*

박리다매(하다)

[Lit. 薄little + 利benefit + 多much + 賣sell] CHINESE-DERIVATION 이익을 적게 보면서 많이 팔다 = to sell a lot but only earn a small amount ▌A: 이거 너무 싸게 파시는 거 아니에요? = *Don't you think you're selling this for too little?* B: **박리다매**가 저희 집 전략입니다. = *Our sales strategy has always been to make up for our narrow profit margin with extra high volume.*

박(이) 터지다

[Lit. for the gourd to burst] IDIOM (속된 말로) 치열하게 노력하다 = (slang) to make strenuous exertions (*equiv.* to bust one's brain / to bust one's gourd) ▌A: 졸업 후에는 뭐할 생각이니? = *What are you planning on doing after graduation?* B: 사법시험을 준비할 생각이에요. = *I'm thinking about studying for the Judicial Examination.* A: 그렇게 어려운 시험을? 정말 **박이 터지게** 공부해야 할 텐데. = *That's such a hard test. You're really going to have to bust your brains for that one.*

NOTE: '박'은 머리를 속되게 이르는 말이다. 주로 '박(이) 터지게'의 형태로 쓰인다.
The word 박 is slang for the head. This expression is most commonly used in the form: 박(이) 터지게.

박장대소(하다) [Lit. 拍hit + 掌palm + 大big + 笑laugh] CHINESE-DERIVATION

손뼉을 치며 크게 웃다 = to clap and let out a large laugh (*equiv.* to erupt with laughter / to explode with laughter) ▌A: 코미디언으로서 가장 행복할 때가 언제인가요? = *As a comedian, when are you the happiest?* B: 관객들이 제 코미디를 보고 **박장대소하는** 것을 보는 순간입니다. = *The moment that the audience erupts with laughter during my routine.*

박학다식(하다) [Lit. 博extensive + 學learn + 多much + 識know] CHINESE-DERIVATION

많이 배워 아는 것이 많다 = to have learned much and possess great knowledge (*equiv.* to be learned) ▌A: 선생님처럼 **박학다식한** 사람이 되려면 어떻게 해야 하나요? = *What do I have to do if I want to be as wise as you, sir?* B: 아무래도 독서만 한 것이 없겠지요. = *I suppose there's nothing more important than reading.*

반신반의(하다) [Lit. 半half + 信believe + 半half + 疑doubt → half-believing and half-doubting] CHINESE-DERIVATION

한편으로는 믿지만 다른 한편으로는 의심하다 = to partially believe something while partially doubting it (*equiv.* to half-believe) ▌A: 수영이가 이번 시험에서 등수가 50등이나 올랐다고요? = *I heard Suyeong moved up 50 spots in her test rank this time.* B: 글쎄, 그렇게 됐지 뭐예요. 저도 처음에는 **반신반의했다니까요**. = *Well, yes, I suppose she did. I only half-believed it myself at first.*

반죽이 좋다 [Lit. to have good dough] IDIOM

웬만해서는 화를 내거나 부끄러워하는 일이 없다 = to rarely get angry or embarrassed (*equiv.* to have good stuffing / I like the stuff you're made of. / Nothing much gets to you.) ▌A: 아까 보니까 어떤 사람이 지나가면서 너를 심하게 밀치던데, 괜찮아? = *I noticed somebody bumped into you pretty hard earlier. Are you all right?* B: 응, 괜찮아. 그럴 수도 있지 뭐. = *Yeah, I'm fine. It's unavoidable sometimes.* A: 하여튼 **반죽도 좋아**. = *Anyhow, nothing seems to get to you.*

NOTE: 반죽은 가루에 물을 붓고 이겨 갠 것이다. 잘 개진 반죽은 부드럽고 차지다. 반죽이 좋은 사람이란 성격이 부드럽고 유들유들해서 노여움이나 부끄러움을 타지 않고 조금은 뻔뻔한 사람을 가리킨다.

Dough is made by mixing water with flour and kneading it. If the mixture has been kneaded properly, it is soft and sticky. This expressions relates dough to someone who has a soft but unabashed personality or is plucky but not easily angered or embarrassed.

발걸음이 떨어지지 않다 IDIOM = 발이 떨어지지 않다

발길에 차이다 IDIOM = 발에 차이다

발길(을) 끊다 IDIOM = 발(을) 끊다

발길이 떨어지지 않다 IDIOM = 발이 떨어지지 않다

발동을 걸다 [Lit. to start moving] IDIOM 어떤 일을 시작하다 = to begin an undertaking (*equiv.* to kick something off / to get going with (an undertaking) *ant.* 제동을 걸다 *cf.* 발동이 걸리다) ▌A: 시험 준비는 언제부터 시작할 거니? = *When are you going to start studying for the test?* B: 이제 슬슬 발동을 걸어야지. = *Well, I'd better get going on it pretty soon.*

발동이 걸리다 [Lit. to be started up] IDIOM 어떤 일이 시작되다 = for something to begin (*equiv.* for something to be underway *ant.* 제동이 걸리다 *cf.* 발동을 걸다) ▌A: 민수가 이제 마음을 완전히 잡았나 보네. 방에서 나오지도 않고 공부만 하는 거 보면. = *It looks like Minsu's really made up his mind to work hard this time. Judging from the way he's been studying in his room like that.* B: 뒤늦게 **발동이 걸렸나** 봐요. = *It took him a while to get going, but now he's on a roll.*

발뒤꿈치도 따를 수 없다 IDIOM = 발뒤꿈치도 못 따라가다

발뒤꿈치도 못 따라가다 [Lit. to not even be able to follow the heels of someone] IDIOM 능력 따위의 차이가 매우 커 비교가 되지 않는다 = to be so far behind in terms of capability etc. that it is beyond compare (*equiv.* He can't hold a candle to you. / to be a distant second *syn.* 발뒤꿈치도 못 따라가다) ▌A: 야, 맛있다! 너 한 요리하는데? = *Hey, this is pretty good!*

You're somewhat of a cook. B: 그래? 엄마 요리하는 거 어깨 너머로 ^{▶p.410}
보고 배운 건데. 사실 나는 우리 엄마 **발뒤꿈치도 못 따라가**. =
*Really? I just learned by looking over my mother's shoulder. Honestly, though,
my cooking couldn't hold a candle to hers.*

NOTE: 발뒤꿈치는 신체의 가장 낮은 부분에 해당한다. 어깨는커녕, 가장 낮
은 부분에도 미치지 못한다는 것은 많이 뒤처졌음을 의미한다.
In this case, the heel represents the lowest part of the body. Not even being
able to reach that, let alone the shoulders, shows just how far behind
someone is.

발등에 불이 떨어지다 [Lit. to have fire fall on one's feet] IDIOM 일이 몹
시 절박하게 닥치다 = to be very close to a deadline (*equiv.* to have one's
feet to the flame / to be up against the wall) ▌A: 민호야, 엄마 좀 도와줄
래? = *Minho, mind helping your mother out a bit?* B: 죄송해요. 지금 바
빠요. 내일이 개학인데 아직 숙제를 다 못 했어요. = *I'm sorry, but
I'm really busy right now. School starts again tomorrow, and I still haven't
done all of my homework.* A: 너는 꼭 **발등에 불이 떨어져야** 하니? 미
리미리 해 두면 좋잖아. = *Do you always have to wait until your back's up
against the wall? Getting things done ahead of time is a much better way to go.*

발등의 불을 끄다 [Lit. to put out the fire on one's feet] IDIOM 눈앞에 닥
친 어려움을 해결하다 = to solve the difficulty immediately before one
(*equiv.* to put out the most urgent fire) ▌A: 휴우, 일단 이 돈으로 **발등
의 불은 끄겠군요**. = *Phew, well at least we can put out the most urgent fire
with this money.* B: 네. 그런데 내일 돌아올 어음이 또 걱정이에
요. = *Yes, but I'm worried about what we're going to do when that debt is due
tomorrow.*

발로 뛰다 [Lit. to run with one's feet] IDIOM 직접 현장을 찾아다니다 = to
visit the site (of construction, of a crime etc.) in person (*equiv.* to put one's feet
on the ground (at the scene) / to pound the pavement) ▌A: 김선영 씨는 어
떤 기자가 되고 싶나요? = *What kind of reporter do you seek to become,
Kim Seonyeong?* B: 언제까지나 **발로 뛰는** 기자로 남고 싶습니다. =

I always wanted to be the kind of reporter that is out there pounding the pavement.

발로 쓰다 [Lit. to write with one's feet] IDIOM 글씨가 몹시 엉망이다 = for one's handwriting to be atrocious (*equiv.* chicken scratch / chicken scrawl) ▎A: 이거 **발로 썼어**? 왜 이렇게 알아보기 힘들어? = *Did you write this with your feet? Why's it so hard to decipher?* B: 제가 아까 졸면서 받아 적었더니 …… . 죄송합니다. = *I copied it down while I was dozing off earlier and ... I'm really sorry.*

발목(을) 잡다 [Lit. to grab someone's ankle] IDIOM 약점이나 고난이 되어 속박에서 벗어나지 못하게 하다 = for something to be a weakness or hardship that restricts someone (*equiv.* for something to hold someone back *cf.* 발목(을) 잡히다) ▎A: 김 교수도 참 운이 없어. = *Professor Kim really seems to have no luck.* B: 그러게. 자기가 옛날에 한 말이 자기 **발목을 잡게** 될 줄은 몰랐을 거야. = *That's what I'm saying. I bet he never would've guessed that something he said so long ago would end up holding him back.*

발목(을) 잡히다 [Lit. to have one's ankle caught] IDIOM 약점이나 고난으로 인해 속박에서 벗어나지 못하다 = to be unable to break free of a weakness or hardship (*cf.* 발목(을) 잡다) ▎A: 아빠, 엄마랑 어떻게 만나셨어요? = *Dad, how did you and Mom first meet?* B: 옛날에 술 마시고 네 엄마한테 뽀뽀했다가 그 길로 **발목 잡혀서** 결혼했다. = *I got drunk and kissed her once a long time ago, and then could never break free of her, so we got married.*

발바닥에 불이 나다 [Lit. for a fire to burn on the soles of one's feet] IDIOM 여기저기 돌아다니다 = to travel here and there (*equiv.* to be all over the place / to really get around *syn.* 발에 불이 나다) ▎A: 요즘 많이 바빠? = *Have you been busy recently?* B: 어. 딸아이 혼수 준비 때문에 돌아다니느라 **발바닥에 불이 날** 지경이야. = *Yep, I've been running all around town like my feet were on fire trying to get this house ready for my daughter and her husband.*

발 벗고 나서다 [Lit. to take off one's feet and step forward] IDIOM 적극적으로 나서다 = to take a proactive approach (*equiv.* to roll up one's sleeves / to get one's hands dirty *syn.* 소매를 걷고 나서다, 팔을 걷어붙이다, 맨발 벗고 나서다) ▌A: 내 친구 동원이는 친구 일이라면 늘 **발 벗고 나서는** 성격이야. = *My friend Dongwon is always ready to roll up his sleeves when it comes to helping out a friend.* B: 그런 친구가 있으면 참 든든하겠어요. = *Having a friend like that must be reassuring.*

NOTE: '발 벗다'는 꽤 이상한 말처럼 들릴 수 있다. 그러나 실제로는 신발을 벗는 것을 의미한다.

At first blush, 발 벗다 (literally, to take off one's feet) sounds like a frightful expression. The actual meaning of this expression, however, is to remove one's shoes.

발 없는 말이 천 리 간다 [Lit. Words with no legs travel 1,000 *li* (a unit of distance).] PROVERB 소문은 매우 빨리 퍼진다 = Rumors travel fast. (*equiv.* That rumor really has legs.) ▌A: 요즘 보면 **발 없는 말이 천 리 간다는** 속담을 바꿔야 할 것 같아. = *I think it's about time someone changed the expression "legless words travel 1,000 li."* B: 맞아. 어디 말이 천 리만 가겠어? 유명인이 한 말은 전 세계로 퍼지는 데 얼마 걸리지도 않잖아. = *That's right. Nowadays, what is 1,000 li? It takes but a moment for something someone famous said to make its way all around the world.*

NOTE: '리'는 거리의 단위이다. 1리는 약 0.4km에 해당하므로 천 리는 400km쯤 된다. 한반도의 최남단에서 수도 서울까지의 거리가 약 천 리 정도이기 때문에 한국의 관용어 속에서 천 리가 아주 먼 거리를 상징하는 표현으로 자주 등장한다.

A 리 is a measurement unit of distance. One 리 is equal to 0.4 km, so 1,000 리 works out to be about 400 km. Since the distance from the southernmost area to the captial, Seoul, measures about 1,000 리, 1,000 리 is a metaphorical stand-in for "a vast distance."

발에 불이 나다 IDIOM = 발바닥에 불이 나다

발에 차이다 [Lit. to be hit by a foot] IDIOM 아주 흔하다 = to be extremely common (*equiv.* to be everywhere one looks / to be everywhere one puts one's feet / to be so common you have to step over them *syn.* 발길에 차이다) ■ A: 우와, 서울에 오니까 예쁜 여자들이 진짜 많다! = *Wow, in Seoul there really are beautiful women everywhere.* B: 야, 저 정도 예쁜 여자는 **발에 차일** 정도로 많아. = *Girls like that are everywhere you look.*

발을 구르다 [Lit. to stomp one's feet] IDIOM 몹시 안타까워하다 = to be filled with regret (*equiv.* to stomp in anger) ■ A: 이 영화 진짜 감동적이었어. = *That movie was very touching.* B: 응. 특히 엄마가 아이를 찾아 **발을 동동 구르는** 장면에서는 눈물이 나더라. = *Yeah, especially the scene where the mother was breaking down when she couldn't find her daughter. It made me cry.*

NOTE: 흔히 '동동'이라는 부사와 같이 쓰인다.
This expression is commonly used with the adverb 동동.

발(을) 끊다 [Lit. to cut off one's steps] IDIOM 더 이상 왕래를 하지 않다 = to no longer visit a place (*equiv.* to keep away from *syn.* 발길(을) 끊다) ■ A: 요즘 정 사장 여기 자주 와요? = *Does Mr. Jeong come by here often?* B: 어유, 정 사장님 여기 **발 끊으신** 지 오래됐어요. = *Mr. Jeong stopped showing his face here long ago.*

발(을) 들여놓다 [Lit. to bring in one's feet] IDIOM 처음으로 접하다 = to encounter something for the first time (*equiv.* to set foot on) ■ A: 너 정말 여기가 어떤 곳인지 알고 **발을 들여놓겠다는** 거야? = *Did you really come here knowing what kind of a place this was?* B: 알아. 나도 각오는 돼 있어. = *Yes, I'm ready.*

발(을) 디딜 틈이 없다 [Lit. to have no place to put one's feet] IDIOM 매우 혼잡스럽다 = to be very crowded (*equiv.* to have no breathing room *syn.* 입추의 여지가 없다) ■ A: 정말 아침 출근길에 지하철 타는 일은 고역이야. = *Taking the subway to work in the morning really is the pits.* B: 누가 아니래. **발 디딜 틈도 없는** 경우가 대부분이야. = *I can't say no* *to that. There's hardly even a place to stand.*

발(을)맞추다 [Lit. to match up one's feet (with those of another)] IDIOM 흐름을 따르다＝to follow the overarching trends (*equiv.* to go with the flow / to get in line) ▌A: 이 가방은 신제품인가요?＝*Is this bag new?* B: 네. 이 모델은 요즘 유행에 **발맞추어** 심플한 디자인을 강조한 제품입니다.＝*Yes. This model was designed to reflect the latest trends and emphasizes simplicity in design.*

발을 묶다 [Lit. to bind someone's feet] IDIOM 활동을 제한하다＝to restrict the activities of someone (*equiv.* to bind someone's feet *cf.* 발(이) 묶이다) ▌A: 정민이 또 접촉 사고 냈다며? 차 키 뺏어야겠군.＝*I heard Jeongmin got into another fender-bender? I'm going to take away his car keys.* B: 그렇다고 애 **발을 묶는** 건 너무하지 않아요?＝*But don't you think taking away his freedom of movement is going a little too far?*

발(을)붙이다 [Lit. to attach one's feet (to the ground etc.)] IDIOM 정착하다＝to settle down somewhere (*equiv.* to put down roots) ▌A: 세상은 넓은데 내가 **발을 붙일** 곳이 하나 없다니.＝*In the whole, wide world, how could there be no place for me to settle down?* B: 왜 그렇게 약한 소리를 하고 그래?＝*Why are you talking like a defeated man?*

발(을) 빼다 [Lit. to remove one's feet (from a place)] IDIOM 관계를 끊고 물러나다＝to end a relationship and stand down (*equiv.* to step back / to extricate oneself from a situation *cf.* 손(을) 빼다, 몸을 빼다) ▌A: 조직 폭력의 세계에 발을 일단 들여놓으면 **발을 빼기가** 어렵다고 알고 있는데 어떻게 새 삶을 찾으셨나요?＝*Once you've set foot in the world of organized crime, I've heard that it's very hard to extricate oneself. How did you manage to begin a new life?* B: 죽을 각오로 그곳을 나왔습니다.＝*I was willing to die just to get out of there.*

발(을) 뻗고 자다 [Lit. to stretch out one's feet and sleep] IDIOM 걱정거리가 해결되어 마음 편히 자다＝to resolve one's worries and sleep soundly (*equiv.* to get a good night's rest / to sleep soundly) ▌A: 그동안 고생 많았

다. 어때? 속이 시원하지? = *You had a lot to worry about there for a while. How are you feeling now? Relieved?* B: 네. 이제 **발 뻗고 잘 수 있을 것 같아요, 아버지**. = *Yes, Dad, I think I'll finally be able to get a good night's rest now.*

***발(이) 넓다** [Lit. to have broad feet] IDIOM 아는 사람이 많다 = to know many people (*equiv.* to have a broad social network / to be a social butterfly / to be well connected) ▌A: 정말 손님이 많이 오셨네요! = *Wow, so many people showed up!* B: 네. 저희 시아버지가 **발이 넓으시거든요**. = *Yes, my father-in-law is quite the social butterfly.*

발이 닳다 [Lit. for one's feet to be worn out] IDIOM 이곳저곳을 많이 다니다 = to travel around often (*equiv.* to wear through the soles of one's shoes (looking around etc.)) ▌A: 목격자는 찾았어? = *Did you find a witness?* B: 아니요. **발이 닳도록** 뛰어다녔지만 어젯밤 그 사고를 본 사람은 못 찾았어요. = *No. We almost wore through the soles of our shoes we've been out there so much, but no one seems to have seen the accident last night.*

> **NOTE:** 주로 '발이 닳도록'의 형태로 쓰인다.
> This expression is usually used in the form of 발이 닳도록.

발이 떨어지지 않다 [Lit. for one's feet not to detach] IDIOM 미련이나 걱정으로 인해 선뜻 떠나지 못하다 = to be prevented from leaving by lingering attachment (*equiv.* I just can't bring myself to leave (this job, my wife etc.) *syn.* 발길이 떨어지지 않다, 발걸음이 떨어지지 않다) ▌A: 아이가 많이 아프다면서요? = *I heard your son is really sick.* B: 네. 요즘 병원에 있는데 오늘도 녀석을 두고 **발이 떨어지지 않는** 걸 간신히 출근했어요. = *That's right. He's in the hospital right now. I could barely bring myself to leave his side this morning when I left for work.*

발(이) 묶이다 [Lit. for one's feet to be tied] IDIOM 교통수단이 없거나 기타 이유로 이동에 제한을 받다 = to be restricted in movement due to transportation problems or other reasons (*equiv.* to be immobilized / to be stranded / to be tied down *cf.* 발을 묶다) ▌A: 김 대리한테서 연락이 왔

어요. 주말에 섬에 놀러 갔는데, 태풍 때문에 **발이 묶였대요**. = *We just got a call from Kim. He says he was out vacationing on an island and the typhoon stranded him there.* B: 그래? 어쩔 수 없지. 그럼 오늘 회의는 김 대리 없이 우리끼리 합시다. = *Really? Well, I guess there was nothing he could do then. Then let's do today's meeting by ourselves.*

발이 손이 되도록 빌다 IDIOM = 손이 발이 되도록 빌다

발톱을 숨기다 [Lit. to hide one's toenails] IDIOM 본모습이나 실력을 감추다 = to hide one's true self or abilities (*equiv.* to keep something under wraps) ▌A: 원선 씨 보면 있는 듯 없는 듯 했는데 그렇게 야심이 큰 줄 몰랐네. = *Wonseon has always seemed to be neither here nor there. I had no idea he had such ambition.* B: 여태까지 **발톱을 숨겨** 왔나 봐요. = *I guess he's kept it under wraps until now.*

발판으로 삼다 [Lit. to consider something a step] IDIOM 목적을 달성하기 위한 계기나 수단으로 하다 = to use something as a means for achieving one's aims (*equiv.* to use something as a stepping stone) ▌A: 이번 수출을 **발판으로 삼아** 올해를 본격적인 해외 진출의 해로 만듭시다. = *Let's use this export operation as a stepping stone to making this the year of the export for us.* B: 네. 저희는 사장님만 믿겠습니다. = *Yes, sir. We'll put our faith in you.*

발판을 마련하다 [Lit. to prepare a step] IDIOM 목적을 달성하기 위한 계기나 수단을 마련하다 = to create a path or opportunity towards one's goals (*equiv.* to take the first steps towards one's goals) ▌A: 올해 회사의 목표는 무엇인가요? = *What is the company's goal for the year?* B: 모바일 시장에 안정적으로 진입하는 **발판을 마련하는** 것입니다. = *Laying the groundwork for our steady advancement into the mobile industry.*

밤낮을 가리지 않다 [Lit. to not care whether it is night or day] IDIOM 쉬지 않고 계속하다 = to continue incessantly (*equiv.* to work (or carry on any activity) day and night) ▌A: 박 서방은 어쩌다 쓰러진 거냐? = *What caused your husband to collapse?* B: 요즘 회사에 일이 많아서 **밤낮을**

가리지 않고 일하다가 그렇게 됐더요. = *He's been working night and day recently and that's what brought him to this.*

***밤이나 낮이나** [Lit. night or day] IDIOM 언제나 = anytime (*equiv.* all night and day *syn.* 낮이나 밤이나, 자나 깨나, 눈이 오나 비가 오나, 앉으나 서나) ▌A: 제발 당신도 정신 좀 차려. **밤이나 낮이나** 게임만 하지 말고. = *Please would you wake up! You can't just play video games all night and day.* B: 잔소리 좀 그만해. 귀에 못이 박히겠어. = *Stop nagging me. You're hurting my ears.*

밥 먹듯(이) 하다 [Lit. to do something (as much) as one eats rice] IDIOM 예사로 자주 하다 = to do something very often (*equiv.* to do something very often / (for a certain action) to be part of one's daily life) ▌A: 결혼 생활은 어때요? 재미있어요? = *How's married life? Is it fun?* B: 남편 얼굴 보기도 힘들어요. 야근을 **밥 먹듯이 하거든요**. = *I barely even see my husband. Overtime is such a part of our daily lives.*

밥상을 차리다 [Lit. to prepare a table] IDIOM 다른 사람이 일하기 좋게 여러 가지 준비를 하다 = to make it comfortable for someone to work by preparing everything necessary (*equiv.* to lay the table for someone / to clear the way for something) ▌A: 아이고, 어떻게 그걸 못 넣냐? **밥상을 차려** 놓아도 걷어 차 버리는구먼. = *How could you not make that goal? They cleared the way for him and everything, and that's the best he could do?* B: 선수라고 늘 잘할 수 있냐? = *Even pros can't always get it right.*

밥알(을) 세다 [Lit. to count grains of rice] IDIOM 밥을 마지못해 굼뜨게 먹다 = to eat slowly (*equiv.* to pick at one's food) ▌A: 입맛이 없니? 왜 **밥알을 세고** 있어? = *Don't you have an appetite? Are you counting the grains of rice?* B: 아까 배가 고파서 군것질을 했더니 영 밥 생각이 없네요. = *I was hungry earlier so I had a snack and now I lost my appetite.*

NOTE: 밥을 아주 조금씩, 주로 젓가락으로 맛없게 먹는 사람에게 밥알을 세고 있냐며 핀잔을 준다. 나이 많은 사람들은 그래서 밥을 젓가락으로 먹는 것을 좋아하지 않는다.

People who eat rice bit by bit, usually with chopsticks, are often sarcastically asked, "Are you counting each grain of rice?" Because eating rice in this manner has long been considered unsightly, the older generation of Koreans prefers eating rice with a spoon.

방귀 뀐 놈이 성낸다 [Lit. for the person who farted to get angry] PROVERB 잘못을 한 사람이 오히려 남에게 화를 낸다는 말 = The person who made a mistake audaciously blame others. (*equiv.* to try to turn the tables on someone / to try to pin the blame on someone else *cf.* 적반하장) ▌A: 나 참 ➡P.97 기가 막혀서. = *I'm really fed up.* B: 왜? 무슨 일 있어? = *Why? What's wrong?* A: 길을 가다가 달려오는 어떤 사람하고 부딪혔는데, **방귀 뀐 놈이 성낸다더니** 자기가 막 화를 내는 거야. = *I was walking down the street and this guy was running in the opposite direction and hit into me. Then he had the gall to get mad at me.*

***방바닥(을) 긁다** [Lit. to scratch the floor of one's room] IDIOM 특별히 하는 일 없이 집에 있다 = to be at home with nothing much to do (*equiv.* to hang out at home / to lounge around at home) ▌A: 주말에는 뭐했어요? = *What did you do over the weekend?* B: 그냥 **방바닥 긁었어요.** = *I just hung out at home.*

NOTE: 고양이나 개가 어떤 물건을 긁는 것을 어렵지 않게 볼 수 있다. 사람이 특별히 할 일이 없어 집에 있으면 누워서 잠을 자거나 텔레비전을 보며 시간을 보내기 쉽다. 그것도 지쳐 마치 저 동물들처럼 바닥을 긁을 정도니 얼마나 심심하고 무료하게 집에서 시간을 보냈다는 뜻이겠는가. It's easy to see cats and dogs scratching at things. When people have nothing special to do, they often lie down for a nap or watch television. When one has even tired of such things and resorts to scratching the floor for kicks, one is truly bored beyond compare.

방방곡곡 [Lit. 坊village + 坊village + 曲bent + 曲bent → every corner of every village] CHINESE-DERIVATION 한 곳도 빠짐이 없는 모든 지역 = everywhere, with no exclusions (*equiv.* here, there and everywhere / in every nook and cranny) ▌A: 우리 민수를 잃어버린 지 벌써 3년이 되었어 요. = *It's been three years now since we lost our dear Minsu.* B: 그동안 얼 마나 마음 고생이 심하셨어요? = *You must have had such a terrible time.* A: 사실 전국 **방방곡곡** 안 가 본 데가 없습니다. = *There's nowhere in this whole country we haven't looked for him.*

방방곡곡 '방방곡곡'의 잘못된 말 = a mistaken form of 방방곡곡

배(가)부르다 [Lit. to have a full stomach] IDIOM 생활이 넉넉하여 아쉬 울 것이 없다 = to have an abundant lifestyle and want for nothing ▌A: 야, 좋은 알바 자리 나왔는데, 너 할래? = *Hey, a great part time job just opened up. Want to give it a try?* B: 난 됐어. 이번 방학에는 스키 배울 거야. = *I'm OK. I'm going to learn how to ski this vacation.* A: 네가 **배가 불렀구나.** 싫으면 관둬라. = *What a charmed life you live. Fine, don't do it then.*

> NOTE: 실제로 밥을 많이 먹어 배부른 사람이나 배가 나온 임신부에게도 당 연히 쓸 수 있다.
> This expression is of course also used to describe the state of actually being full and also for pregnant women with bulging stomachs.

배(가) 아프다 [Lit. to be sick to one's stomach] IDIOM 남이 잘되어 질투 가 나다 = to be jealous of another's success (*equiv.* to be jealous / to be green with envy *syn.* 속(이) 쓰리다 *cf.* 사촌이 땅을 사면 배가 아프다) ▌A: 내 친구 명수 알지? 걔가 이번에 부장으로 승진했대. = *You know my friend Myeongsu? He just got promoted to department manager.* B: 아 잘 됐네. 당신은 승진 얘기 없어? = *Wow, that's great. Was there any talk of a promotion for you?* A: 나는 아직 멀었지. 친구지만 솔직히 약간 **배 가 아픈걸.** = *I've still got a long way to go. He's my friend and all, but I do feel a little green.*

배꼽(을) 빼다 [Lit. to pluck someone's belly button] IDIOM 몹시 우습다 = to be very amused (*equiv.* to crack people up *cf.* 배꼽(이) 빠지다) ▌A: 철 민이는 참 재미있어. 코미디언이 따로 없다니까. = *Cheolmin really is*

a funny guy. Pro comedians have got nothing on him. B: 아까 녀석 웃긴 표정 봤어? 다들 **배꼽을 뺐잖아**. = *Did you see him making funny faces earlier? He completely cracked everyone up.*

배꼽(을) 잡다 IDIOM = 배꼽(을) 쥐다

배꼽(을) 쥐다 [Lit. to grasp one's belly button] IDIOM 웃음을 참지 못해 크게 웃다 = to not be able to hold back one's laughter (*equiv.* to burst out laughing *syn.* 배꼽(을) 잡다) ▌A: 아, 오랜만에 정말 재미있는 영화 봤네. = *It had been a while since I had seen such a funny movie.* B: 나도. 특히 아까 그 장면에서는 **배꼽을 쥐고** 한참 웃었어. = *Yeah, especially during that one scene, I couldn't help but burst out laughing.*

배꼽(이) 빠지다 [Lit. for one's navel to fall off] IDIOM 몹시 우습다 = to be very amused (*equiv.* to laugh till one bursts / to laugh one's head off *cf.* 배꼽(을) 빼다) ▌A: 어제 개그콘서트 봤어? 웃겨 죽는 줄 알았어. = *Did you see that standup comedy show on TV yesterday? It was hilarious.* B: 그러게 말야. 나도 **배꼽이 빠지는** 줄 알았다니까. = *That's what I'm saying. I was laughing my head off.*

배(를) 불리다 [Lit. to fill someone up] IDIOM 물질적 욕심을 채우다 = to satisfy one's appetite for material gain (*equiv.* to satisfy one's appetite / to take one's fill *syn.* 배(를) 채우다) ▌A: 정말 일할 맛이 안 나. 아무리 열심히 일을 해도 월급은 안 오르고 사장님 **배를 불려** 주는 꼴이니. = *I'm really not feeling like working today. No matter how hard I work my paycheck never gets any bigger and I'm just feeding my boss.* B: 우리 사장님은 돈은 조금 주고 일은 너무 시키는 것 같아. = *Yeah, compared to the amount we get paid, I think our boss asks for way too much.*

배(를) 채우다 IDIOM = 배(를) 불리다

*배보다 배꼽이 (더) 크다 [Lit. for one's navel to be larger than one's belly] PROVERB 주가 되는 것보다 부가 되는 것이 더 많거나 크다 = for a secondary matter to outweigh the matter or primary import (*equiv.* the tail

wagging the dog) ▌A: 이번에 중고 컴퓨터를 30만 원 주고 한 대 샀는데, 고장 나서 수리하려니까 40만 원 달래요. 이게 말이 돼요?＝ *I bought a used computer for 300,000 won and when it broke down, they asked me for 400,000 won to fix it. Isn't that ridiculous?* B: 배보다 배꼽이 더 크네요. ＝ *That's all out of whack.*

배부른 소리(를) 하다 [Lit. to make the noises of someone who is full] IDIOM 상대적으로 사정이 나은 사람이 푸념을 늘어놓다＝for someone who is relatively better off to be complaining (*equiv.* You're one to talk. / At least you (have a job, have a girlfriend etc.) / You should be counting your blessings. *cf.* 배(가)부르다) ▌A: 아, 내일이면 또 출근해야 하는구나. 정말 가기 싫다. ＝ *I've already got to head back to work tomorrow. I really hate my job.* B: 배부른 소리 하고 앉았네. 지금 우리나라 실업률이 얼마인지 알아?＝ *At least you have a job. Do you have any idea how many unemployed people there are in Korea right now?*

NOTE: '배부른 소리 하고 앉았네.'라는 형태로 많이 쓰인다.
  This expression is most often used in the form 배부른 소리 하고 앉았네.

배은망덕(하다) [Lit. 背betray + 恩favor + 忘forget + 德thanks] CHINESE-DERIVATION 남에게 입은 은혜를 잊고 배신하다＝to forget the favor one has received and betray the benefactor (*equiv.* to be ungrateful) ▌A: 엄마가 저한테 해 준 게 뭐가 있다고 그러세요?＝ *What have you ever done for me, Mom?* B: 참 나. 기껏 키워 놓으니까 뭐가 어째? 이런 배은망덕한 놈아!＝ *What nerve! Well, I raised you, didn't I? What an ungrateful jerk you turned out to be!*

백기(를) 들다 [Lit. to lift the white flag] IDIOM 항복하다＝to surrender (*equiv.* to wave the white flag / to throw in the towel *syn.* 두 손(을) 들다, 수건(을) 던지다) ▌A: 우와, 정말 모르겠어. 이 문제는.＝ *Wow, I really have no idea what to do with this problem.* B: 벌써, 백기 드는 거야? 실망인데 ……. ＝ *You're already throwing in the towel? How disappointing!*

NOTE: 백기(白旗)는 흰 깃발을 뜻한다. 예전에 전쟁을 할 때는 그 군대를 상징하는 깃발을 항상 세우고 다녔는데, 항복의 뜻을 내비칠 때 흰 깃발을 들었다.
A 백기 is a white flag. In the olden days when flags were still the primary means of communication on the battlefield, hoisting the white flag, indicated surrender.

백년가약 [Lit. 百hundred + 年year + 佳beautiful + 約contract] CHINESE-DERIVATION 젊은 남녀가 부부가 되어 평생을 같이할 것을 다짐하는 약속 = an engagement in which a young couple vow to spend their lives together ▮ A: 우리가 검은 머리 파뿌리가 될 때까지 같이하자며 **백년가약**을 맺은 지 벌써 50년이 되었네. = *It's already been 50 years since we vowed to stay together until we were old and gray.* B: 참 세월이 정말 빠르네. = *My, how time flies.*

NOTE: 주로 '백년가약을 맺다'라는 형태로 쓰인다.
This expression is usually used in the form, 백년가약을 맺다.

백년해로(하다) [Lit. 百hundred + 年year + 偕together + 老old] CHINESE-DERIVATION 부부가 되어 평생을 같이하다 = for a couple to spend their lives together ▮ A: 재은 씨, 나와 **백년해로합시다**. = *Jaeun, let's spend our lives together.* B: 지금 나한테 청혼하는 거예요? = *Are you proposing to me?*

백발백중 [Lit. 百hundred + 發shoot + 百hundred + 中center] CHINESE-DERIVATION **1.** 총이나 활을 쏠 때마다 늘 정확히 맞힘 = hitting the target every time one shoots a bow or gun (*equiv.* to be a perfect shot) ▮ A: 우와, 아무리 장난감 총이지만 너 되게 잘 쏜다! = *It may just be a toy gun, but you really are a good shot!* B: 당연하지! 이래 보여도 군대 있을 때 **백발백중**의 명사수였다고. = *Of course I am! I may not look like much now, but when I was in the army, I was a famous marksman.* **2.** 무슨 일이든지 틀리지 않고 다 맞힘 = being perfect at whatever one is doing ▮ A: 새해도 됐는데 점 보러 갈까? **백발백중**으로 맞힌다는 집 얘기를 들

있었어. = *Do you want to start of the new year by going to see a fortuneteller? I heard of a place that is always right on the mark.* B: 너는 젊은 애가 뭐 그런 걸 믿니? = *How can someone as young as you believe in that kind of thing?*

백전백승 [Lit. 百 hundred + 戰 fight + 百 hundred + 勝 win] CHINESE-DERIVATION 싸울 때마다 이김 = winning every fight (*equiv.* to be unbeatable) ▌A: 어때? 이번 시합 이길 자신 있어? = *What do you think? Are you going to be able to win this match?* B: 당연하지. 우리 팀이 홈 경기는 **백전백승**인 거 몰라? = *Of course I am. Don't you know our team is unbeatable at home?*

백지장도 맞들면 낫다 [Lit. Even sheets of paper are better when carried together.] PROVERB 쉬운 일도 힘을 합치면 더 쉽게 할 수 있다는 말 = Even easy work is made easier when many people help out. (*equiv.* Many hands make light work.) ▌A: 오늘 이사하느라 다들 고생 많았다. **백지장도 맞들면 낫다는** 말처럼, 막내부터 엄마, 아빠까지 다 같이 짐을 옮긴 덕분에 생각보다 빨리 끝났어. = *We had a tough day moving today, didn't we? It's just like the saying goes: Many hands make light work. With everyone from our youngest to Mother helping out, we finished sooner than I'd anticipated we would.* B: 아빠, 우리 이사 온 기념으로 자장면 시켜 먹어요. = *Dad, how about we order some jajangmyeon for the special occasion?*

백팔십도 달라지다 [Lit. to change 180 degrees] IDIOM 완전히 달라지다 = to change completely (*equiv.* to do a 180) ▌A: 민수가 군대 갔다 와서 많이 달라진 것 같네요. 예전보다 훨씬 어른스러워졌어요. = *Minsu sure has changed since he got back from the army. He seems a lot more mature than he ever used to be.* B: 네. **백팔십도 달라졌어요.** = *Yep, he really did a 180.*

백해무익(하다) [Lit. 百 hundred + 害 harm + 無 no + 益 benefit] CHINESE-DERIVATION 해롭기만 하고 이로운 바가 없다 = to be very harmful and not at all beneficial ▌A: 제발 담배 좀 끊어. 그 **백해무익한** 걸 뭐하러

시작했어? = *Could you please stop smoking? Why did you ever start doing something that only harms you?* B: 나도 끊고 싶어. 하지만 그게 마음처럼 되는 건 줄 알아? = *Trust me, I'd like to quit. You think it's enough to just want it?*

밴댕이 소갈머리 IDIOM = 밴댕이 속

밴댕이 속 [Lit. the inside of a large-eyed herring] IDIOM 아주 마음이 좁은 사람을 두고 하는 말 = used to describe someone who is very petty (*syn.* 밴댕이 소갈머리 *cf.* 속(이) 좁다) ▌A: 민수 자식 어떻게 나한테 그런 말을 할 수가 있지? 다시는 민수하고 말도 안 할 거야. = *How could Minsu speak to me that way? I'm never going to talk to him again.* B: 너는 남자가 돼 가지고 어떻게 된 게 속이 **밴댕이 속**이니? = *How could a grown man be so petty?*

NOTE: 밴댕이는 청어과에 속하는 물고기로 몸 길이가 15–20cm 정도 되니 그렇게 작은 물고기는 아니다. 하지만, 밴댕이를 갈라 보면 내장기관이 몸집에 비해 매우 작다. 외모나 인상에 비해 마음이 좁은 사람을 가리켜 밴댕이 속이라 표현한다.

The 밴댕이 is a kind of herring that measures between 15 and 20 cm when fully grown. Its external size is not that small, but when sliced open anglers of old were surprised to find that the size of its internal organs is very small. This is the reason why 밴댕이 속 is a phrase now used to describe someone who, relative to the impression they give or their image, is surprisingly shortsighted or lacks compassion.

뱁새가 황새 쫓아가면 가랑이가 찢어진다 [Lit. The Korean crow is split in two trying to keep up with the stork.] PROVERB 자신보다 나은 사람을 무턱대고 따라 하다가 낭패를 본다는 말 = to undergo great hardships while trying to mimic someone of greater abilities (*cf.* 숭어가 뛰니까 망둥이도 뛴다) ▌A: 우와, TV에 나오는 남자들은 어쩌면 저렇게 몸이 좋을까. 이제부터 나도 하루에 운동 다섯 시간씩 할 거야. = *How do you think those guys on TV get a physique like that? From now on, I'm going to work out for at least five hours a day.* B: 그만둬. **뱁새가**

황새 쫓아가려고 하면 가랑이가 찢어지는 법이야. = *You'll never be able to match the people you see on TV. Just give it up.*

NOTE: 뱁새는 아주 작은 새이고 황새는 다리가 아주 긴 큰 새이다. 키가 작은 사람이 키가 큰 사람을 흉내내어 브폭을 크게 하여 걸으려고 무리하면 다리에 무리가 올 것이다. 자기보다 잘난 사람을 따라 하려고 자기 역량보다 과하게 무리를 하면 탈이 날 수도 있다는 뜻이다.
The Korean crow (뱁새) is a rather small bird, while the stork (황새), is a very large, long bird. If a person of short stature attempts to walk with the long strides of a taller person, their legs won't be able to take the stress for long. In much the same way, when one mimics the actions of someone of much greater abilities, one may soon run into trouble.

뱃가죽이 등에 붙다 [Lit. to have one's stomach skin attached to one's back] IDIOM 배가 몹시 고프다 = to be very hungry (*equiv.* to be famished) ▌A: 여보 나 밥 좀 줘. **뱃가죽이 등에 붙었어.** = *Honey, please feed me. I'm starving over here.* B: 어디서 뭐하길래 아직 밥도 못 얻어먹었어? = *What we're you up to that kept you from eating until now?*

뱃속이 검다 [Lit. for the inside of one's stomach to be dark] IDIOM 마음속에 나쁜 생각을 갖고 있다 = to have dark thoughts (*equiv.* to have a black heart) ▌A: 우리 과 김 조교는 일을 참 잘해요. = *The TA for our department does a really good job.* B: 그건 그렇지만 너무 믿지는 마세요, 교수님. 그 친구 **뱃속이 검은** 친구예요. = *That may be true, but don't trust him too much. He's got a black heart.*

버스(가) 지나가다 [Lit. for the bus to pass] IDIOM 기회나 차례가 지나가다 = for an opportunity of turn to come and go (*equiv.* The train has left the station.) ▌A: 날이면 날마다 오는 기회가 아닙니다. **버스 지나간** 다음에 손 흔들지 마시고 이번 기회에 싸게 겨울 코트 준비하세요. = *Good opportunities don't come around every day. Don't make a fuss after it's already too late. Buy a winter coat now.* B: 아저씨, 이거 얼마예요? = *Excuse me, how much is this?*

버스(를) 놓치다 [Lit. to miss the bus] IDIOM 기회를 놓치다＝to miss an opportunity (*equiv.* The train has left the station. / You've lost your chance. *syn.* 물 건너가다) ▌A: 너 아직까지 수정이한테 좋아한다고 고백 못 했지? **버스 놓치고 후회하지 말고, 얼른 고백해.**＝*You still haven't told Sujeong that you're interested in her, have you? Don't wait till it's too late. Just hurry up and do it!* B: 나도 이렇게 우유부단한 내 자신이 ◆p.438 싫다.＝*I also hate myself for being so wishy-washy about it.*

번갯불에 콩 볶아 먹다 [Lit. to roast beans in the fire of a lightning bolt and eat them] PROVERB 행동이나 일 처리가 매우 빠르다＝for one's actions or work flow to be very quick ▌A: 벌써 다 했어? **번갯불에 콩 볶아 먹겠다!**＝*You're already done? You're like greased lightning!* B: 딴 건 몰라도 내가 일 하나는 빨리 하잖아.＝*When it comes to work, I'm pretty fast.*

번데기 앞에서 주름 잡다 [Lit. to make wrinkles in front of silkworm larva] PROVERB 지식이나 실력이 부족한 사람이 자신보다 나은 사람 앞에서 가소롭게 잘난 체할 때 쓰는 말＝for a person who lacks capability or knowledge to act proud in front of someone far superior (*equiv.* to show off in front of the wrong person *syn.* 공자 앞에서 문자 쓴다) ▌A: 제가 한 일본어 하니까 모르는 게 있으면 물어보세요.＝*I'm pretty ◆p.561 OK when it comes to Japanese, so let me know if there's something you don't understand.* B: 애, 여기 있는 민수 씨는 일본에서 10년 동안 살다 오셨어.＝*Hey, man. Minsu's lived ten years in Japan.* A: 아, 그래요? 제 가 **번데기 앞에서 주름 잡았군요.**＝*Oh, really? I guess I chose the wrong person to show off in front of.*

NOTE: 번데기 몸에 얼마나 많은 주름이 있는지 생각해 보라.

Consider the number of wrinkles on the skin of silk larvae and you will understand why it wouldn't make sense to try to outdo the creature in terms of wrinkly skin.

번지수가 틀리다 [Lit. to have the wrong address] IDIOM 엉뚱한 대상을 찾았거나 잘못된 방향으로 나가다＝to locate the wrong party or head off in the wrong direction (*syn.* 번지수를 잘못 짚다) ▌A: 김세현 씨, **번지수가 틀린 거 아니에요? 컴퓨터에 문제가 있으면 해당 부서로 가야지 왜 엉뚱한 곳에 와서 따지고 그래요?** = *Kim Sehyeon, don't you think you've come to the wrong place? When you've got a computer problem, you need to see the proper department about it, not go and complain to the wrong people.* B: 아, 죄송합니다. 제가 잘못 알았군요. = *Oh, I'm so sorry. I guess I misunderstood.*

번지수를 잘못 짚다 IDIOM = 번지수가 틀리다

벌린 입을 다물지 못하다 [Lit. to not be able to close one's wide-open mouth] IDIOM 몹시 감탄하거나 어이가 없다 = to be overwhelmed or dumbfounded (*equiv.* to be jaw-dropping) ▌A: 우리 보라카이 놀러 갔을 때 생각나? 참 좋았잖아. = *Do you remember our vacation to Borocay? It really was great.* B: 응. 특히 바닷물이 너무 맑고 예뻐서 우리 둘 다 **벌린 입을 다물지 못했잖아.** = *Yeah, the water was so clear we almost couldn't believe it.*

벌집(을) 건드리다 IDIOM = 벌집(을) 쑤시다

벌집(을) 쑤시다 [Lit. to stir up a wasps' nest] IDIOM 건드려서는 안 될 것을 공연히 건드려 문제를 일으키다 = to needlessly cause trouble (*equiv.* to stir up a hornet's nest *syn.* 벌집(을) 건드리다) ▌A: 요즘에 엄마가 너무 반찬에 신경을 안 쓰는 것 같지 않아, 누나? = *Mom doesn't seem to be putting much effort into the side dishes recently, huh?* B: 엄마가 바쁘셔서 그래. 괜히 엄마한테 그런 얘기 할 생각 마. **벌집을 쑤시는** 꼴이 될 테니까. = *That's because she's busy. Don't even think about telling her that and stirring up a hornet's nest.*

법 없이도 살 사람 [Lit. someone who could live without even laws] IDIOM 착하게 사는 사람 = someone who lives in a kind and just way ▌A: 태민 씨가 그렇게 화내는 건 처음 봤어요. = *That's the first time I've ever seen Taemin get so upset.* B: 저도요. 그 사람 **법 없이도 살 사람**인데 이번에는 단단히 화가 났나 봐요. = *Me too. He's normally such a kind*

man. I guess he was just really upset this time.

법은 멀고 주먹은 가깝다 [Lit. to be far from the law and close with the fists] PROVERB 화가 나거나 억울한 일이 있을 때 차분하게 이성적으로 일을 처리하기보다는 감정적으로 폭력을 쓰는 사람에게 쓰는 말 = used to refer to people who, when angered, choose to handle things with violence instead of through more reasonable means (*equiv.* to live by the rules of the street) ▌A: 아무리 화가 나도 그렇지 함부로 주먹을 쓰면 되냐? = *No matter how upset you were, do you think it's OK to just start throwing punches like that?* B: 법은 멀고 주먹은 가깝더라고. = *I guess I just live by the rules of the street.*

벙어리 냉가슴 앓다 [Lit. for a mute to suffer in silence] IDIOM 겉으로 표현을 못 하고 속으로 괴로워하다 = to be unable to express one's hardships and suffer in silence (*equiv.* to suffer in silence) ▌A: 벙어리 냉가슴 앓지 말고 속 시원하게 털어놔 봐. = *Don't just suffer in silence, tell me all that's on your mind.* B: 실은 나, 누나 몰래 누나 일기 훔쳐봤어. = *I took your diary and read it.* A: 뭐? 너 죽고 싶어? = *What? You wanna die?*

베일에 가리다 IDIOM = 베일에 싸이다

베일에 싸이다 [Lit. to be surrounded by a veil] IDIOM 비밀스럽게 가려져 있다 = to be covered in secrecy (*equiv.* to be veiled) ▌A: 도대체 그 회사는 어떤 회사야? = *Just what kind of company is that place anyway?* B: 글쎄, 소문만 무성하지 실제로 뭐하는 회사인지는 **베일에 싸여** 있잖아. = *Well, there are definitely a lot of rumors going around, but as to what it really does, it's wrapped in a veil of secrecy.*

베일을 벗기다 [Lit. to lift someone's veil] IDIOM 비밀스럽게 가려져 있는 것의 정체를 밝히다 = to expose the true nature of something that had been kept secret (*equiv.* to lift the veil (of secrecy) *cf.* 베일을 벗다) ▌A: 내가 기자의 명예를 걸고 이 사건의 **베일을 벗겨** 내겠어. = *I'll stake my reputation as a reporter to lift the veil of secrecy surrounding this incident.*

B: 조심하라고. 그러다 다치는 수가 있어. = *I'm just saying you should be careful. You may end up getting hurt.*

베일을 벗다 [Lit. to take off a veil] IDIOM 비밀스럽게 가려져 있는 것의 정체가 드러나다 = for something that had been secret to be exposed (*equiv.* to shed the veil of secrecy *cf.* 베일을 벗기다) ▌A: 너도 이 책 읽는구나? 어디까지 읽었어? = *Oh, so you've been reading this book too! How far have you gotten?* B: 범인이 **베일을 벗기** 직전이야. = *I'm at the part right before the criminal is unveiled.*

벼는 익을수록 고개를 숙인다 [Lit. Rice bows its head as it matures.] PROVERB 잘난 사람일수록 더 겸손해져야 한다는 말 = The more you mature, the more modest you should become. ▌A: 너 이번 시험에서 또 백 점 받았다며? 대단하네! = *I heard that you got a perfect score on this test again? You're amazing.* B: 뭐 별 거 아니에요. 만날 백 점 받는걸요 뭐. 저한테는 시험이 너무 쉬워요. = *That's nothing. I've got perfect scores all the time. To me, tests are too easy.* A: **벼는 익을수록 고개를 숙이는** 법이다. 사람이 겸손해야지. = *People should gain modesty with maturity. That's something you should work on.*

벼락(을) 맞다 [Lit. to be struck by lightening] IDIOM 1. 심하게 꾸중을 듣다 = to be severely rebuked (*equiv.* to catch a lot of flak / to catch hell) ▌A: 아, 큰일났다. 내가 학원 안 간 거 엄마가 알면 **벼락 맞을** 텐데. = *I'm in big trouble. I'll catch hell from my mom if she finds out I didn't go to academy today.* B: ▶p.230 매도 먼저 맞는 게 낫다는데, 얼른 집에 가 봐. = *It's better to just get it over with. Hurry home and tell her.* 2. 못된 짓을 하여 천벌을 받다 = to be punished by the heavens for one's bad deeds (*equiv.* to be struck by a bolt of lightening from the heavens) ▌A: 언니가 너무 미워, 엄마. 그냥 언니가 없어졌으면 좋겠어! = *Mom, I really hate my sister. I wish she would just go away and never come back!* B: 그런 **벼락 맞을** 소리가 어디 있니? = *Don't even say such a thing.*

벼랑(끝)에 몰리다 [Lit. to be driven to the brink] IDIOM 위험한 상황에 처하다 = to face a very dangerous situation (*equiv.* to be driven to the edge /

to be backed up against a wall *syn.* 벼랑(끝)에 서다) ▌A: 오늘 경기는 우리가 쉽게 이기겠지? = *I think we'll be able to easily win today's game.* B: 장담할 수는 없지. 상대도 오늘 지면 끝이잖아. **벼랑 끝에 몰린** 만큼 죽기 살기로 할 게 뻔하니까. = *I wouldn't be so sure. If they lose today, it's over for them. With their backs up against the wall, it's life or death for them today.*

벼랑(끝)에 서다 IDIOM = 벼랑(끝)에 몰리다

벼룩도 낯짝이 있다 [Lit. Even a flea has a face.] PROVERB 사람은 염치와 체면이 있어야 한다는 말 = used to suggest that people must always have honor and dignity (*syn.* 빈대도 낯짝이 있다) ▌A: 누나한테 돈을 좀 빌려 볼까? = *Should we borrow some money from my sister?* B: **벼룩도 낯짝이 있지,** 누나한테 또 어떻게 돈을 빌려? = *Have you no shame? How could we go to her again for money?*

NOTE: 벼룩을 실제로 본 적이 있나? 벼룩의 몸길이는 몇 밀리미터에 불과하다. 이렇게 작은 벼룩에게도 얼굴이 있다는 말은 그만큼 얼굴이 중요하다는 뜻이다. 여기서 얼굴은 체면이나 염치를 상징하는 것이다.
Have you ever seen a flea? Its body is no more than a few millimeters long. To say that even a creature of this size has a face, emphasizes the importance of the face. In this idiom, "face," means honor and dignity.

*벼룩의 간을 빼 먹다 [Lit. to remove and eat a flea's liver] IDIOM 어려운 처지에 있는 사람에게서 물품을 뜯어내다 = to take valuables from someone who has very little (*equiv.* You're skinning a flea for its hide.) ▌A: 오늘 아르바이트비 받았다며? 오늘 한턱 내. = *I heard you got paid today? You pay for this.* B: 어이구, 차라리 **벼룩의 간을 빼 먹어.** 그게 얼마나 된다고. = *Come on now, you'd be better off stealing money from a bum. How much do you think I make?*

NOTE: 벼룩은 실제로 간이 없다. 다만 여기서 벼룩은 매우 작고 보잘것없는 것을 의미하고 간은 그런 대상에게 있어 없어서는 안될 중요한 것을 의미한다.

Fleas don't actually have a liver. In this idiom, the "flea" represents someone who has very little and the "liver" means something that person cannot do without.

벽에도 귀가 있다 [Lit. Even the walls have ears.] PROVERB 아무도 안 듣는 데서라도 말조심해야 한다는 말 = used to suggest care in one's words even when no one seems to be around (*syn.* 낮말은 새가 듣고 밤말은 쥐가 듣는다) ▌A: 우리 팀장님은 너무 짠돌이야. = *Our team leader is so stingy.* B: 쉿! **벽에도 귀가 있다**는 말 몰라? 요즘 같은 때에 입조심해야지. = *Quiet! Don't you know, even the walls have ears around here. You've got to be careful in times like these.*

벽에 부딪치다 [Lit. to hit up against a wall] IDIOM 장애나 한계에 가로막히다 = to be blocked by an obstacle or limit (*equiv.* to hit a brick wall / to be banging one's head against the wall) ▌A: 새 소설 구상은 잘돼 가? = *Are you making good progress on the new novel?* B: 아니. 또 **벽에 부딪치고** 말았어. = *Nope. It's like I'm banging my head against the wall.*

벽(을) 쌓다 [Lit. to build a wall] IDIOM 전혀 관계하지 않다 = to have absolutely no relationship with someone or something (*equiv.* to cut oneself off from something *syn.* 담(을)쌓다) ▌A: 지금 가장 고마운 분은 누구인가요? = *Who are you most thankful for?* B: 아내한테 고맙다는 말을 하고 싶습니다. 제가 집안일에는 **벽을 쌓고** 살아와서 늘 미안했거든요. = *I want to say how thankful I am towards my wife. I've never cared one iota about household affairs, and I've always been sorry to her for that.*

변덕이 죽 끓듯 하다 [Lit. for one's whims to be like boiling porridge] IDIOM 변덕이 심하다 = to be very whimsical (*equiv.* to run hot and cold / to be wishy-washy / to be capricious) ▌A 참 나, 팀장님 말이야, 오전에는 기분 좋아서 일찍 퇴근하라고 하더니, 이제 와서 야근하라니 너무하지 않아? = *Our team leader this morning tells us that we can leave early because he's in a good mood, but then tells us now that we have to work overtime today. He's really outdone himself this time.* B: 내 말이. **변덕이**

죽 끓듯 한다니까. = *That's what I'm talking about. He is a capricious character.*

NOTE: 죽은 끓을 때 이쪽저쪽에서 작은 거품들이 풍선처럼 부풀었다가 터진다. 마음이 쉽게 변해 이쪽저쪽으로 옮겨다니는 사람을 가리켜 변덕이 죽 끓듯 한다고 한다.
When boiling Korean porridge, 죽, many tiny bubbles gurgle up to the surface and pop. The fleeting and scattered nature of these bubbles, is why this expression is used to describe someone who is darting here and there in a flippant and whimsical nature.

변죽(을) 울리다 [Lit. to make the rims ring] 1. 바로 집어 말을 하지 않고 둘러서 말을 하다 = to not get to the point and carry on with superfluous talk (*equiv.* to beat around the bush) ▌A: 야, 갑갑하게 왜 이리 말을 빙빙 돌려? **변죽 울리지** 말고 얼른 시원하게 말해. = *The way you're beating around the bush like that is really frustrating. Stop talking in circles and just say what you want to say.* B: 아, 미안. 내가 너무 뜸을 들였지? = *Oh, I'm sorry. I was really taking my time, wasn't I?* 2. 사물이나 사건의 본질이 아닌 부분만 건드리고 정작 중요한 것은 하지 않다 = to only address the insignificant parts of an issue and leave the essence untouched (*equiv.* to miss the point) ▌A: 학교 폭력을 뿌리 뽑겠다고 하더니 요즘 또 잠잠하네. = *There was so much talk about attacking school violence at the root but things sure quieted down fast.* B: 또 **변죽만 울리**다 말겠지. = *I'm sure they just lashed out in the wrong direction again.*

NOTE: 변죽은 그릇이나 과녁의 가장자리를 말한다.
A 변죽 is the rim of a bowl or target.

변죽이 좋다 IDIOM '반죽이 좋다'의 잘못된 말 = a mistaken form of 반죽이 좋다

변화무상하다 [Lit. 變change + 化become + 無no + 雙compare + 하다 adjective suffix] CHINESE-DERIVATION 변화가 아주 심하다 = for there to be vast changes (*equiv.* to undergo a sea change / to be all of the place) ▌A: 아

침에는 그렇게 비바람이 몰아치더니 낮이 되니 해가 쨍쨍 나네요. 참 날씨가 **변화무쌍하군요**. = *This morning it was windy and rainy and now the sun is out. The weather sure is all over the place here.* B: 여기가 섬이라서 그래요. = *Yeah, that's because it's an island.*

별(을) 달다 [Lit. to attach a star (to something)] IDIOM (속된 말로) 죄를 지어 감옥에 갔다 오다 = (slang) to serve time in a penitentiary for crimes one has committed and be released (*equiv.* to do one's time / to pay for one's crimes *syn.* 콩밥(을) 먹다, 호적에 빨간 줄(이) 그이다) ▌A: 너 이제 어떻게 살래? = *How are you going to live now?* B: 뭐 이제 **별까지 달았는데** 뭐가 두렵겠어요? = *I've done my time. What have I got to be afraid of?*

NOTE: 별은 전과자가 감옥살이를 한 횟수를 가리키는 속어다.
 One's 별 (stars) are the amount of times one has been incarcerated.

별이 보이다 [Lit. for stars to be visible] IDIOM 물리적으로 큰 충격을 받아 정신이 없다 = to be shocked, usually physically, in such a way that is nearly rendered unconscious (*equiv.* to see stars) ▌A: 괜찮아? 크게 넘어진 것 같은데. = *Are you OK? That was quite a fall.* B: 그게 괜찮지 않네. 아직도 **별이 보여**. = *No, not really. I'm still seeing stars.*

병아리 눈물만큼 [Lit. as much as a chick's tear] IDIOM 아주 조금 = only a very little ▌A: 비가 너무 안 와서 큰일이야. = *This lack of rain is a major problem.* B: 그저께 조금 왔잖아요. = *It rained a little just the other day.* A: **병아리 눈물만큼** 온 거? 그걸로는 ➡p.413 어림도 없어. = *You mean those three drops that fell? That barely even counts.*

병 주고 약 준다 [Lit. to give someone a disease and give them the medicine too] PROVERB 해를 입힌 뒤에 달래는 것을 가리키는 말 = describes the action of impairing or injuring someone and then trying to comfort them ▌A: 이거라도 마시고 해. = *At least have something to drink first.* B: 지금 **병 주고 약 주는** 거야? 내가 누구 때문에 이 고생을 하는지 알긴 아나 보지? = *Are you giving me a disease and then* *offering me a cure? It looks like you know who's causing me to have a hard time right now, huh?*

보기 좋은 떡이 먹기도 좋다 [Lit. *Tteok* that looks good is also good to eat.] PROVERB 겉모양이 좋은 것이 내용도 좋다는 말 = used when the appearance of something and its content are both good (*equiv.* good in name and nature *ant.* 뚝배기보다 장맛이다) ▌A: 영희야, 저기 저 새 접시 좀 꺼내 와. = *Yeonghee, would you get out that new plate over there?* B: 엄마, 그냥 쓰던 접시 쓰면 안 돼? = *Mom, can't we just use the dishes we always use?* A: 애는. 보기 **좋은 떡이 먹기도 좋다**는 말 몰라? = *Oh, honey, don't you know that the presentation makes the dish?*

***보는 눈이 있다** [Lit. to have a seeing eye] IDIOM 안목이 있다 = to have discerning taste (*equiv.* to have an eye for (fashion etc.) *syn.* 눈이 높다) ▌A: 애, 아까부터 저 남자가 너를 자꾸 쳐다보는 것 같아. = *That guy's been staring at you for the last few minutes.* B: 참, 나, **보는 눈은 있어** 가지고. 이놈의 인기는 식을 줄을 모르네. = *Jeez, it looks like he has a an for beauty. My popularity never cools off.*

보따리(를) 싸다 [Lit. to wrap up in a bundle] IDIOM 하던 일을 그만두다 = to quit the work one had been doing (*equiv.* to wrap up / to call it quits) ▌A: 휴우, 또 떨어졌구나. 벌써 세 번째네. = *Gosh, I flunked again. That makes three times now.* B: 이제 어떡할 거야? = *What are you going to do now?* A: **보따리 싸서** 집에 내려가야지. = *It's time to call it quits and head home.*

보따리(를) 풀다 [Lit. to open up a bundle] IDIOM 이야기하다 = to talk (*equiv.* Out with it! / to spill the beans) ▌A: 자, 아까 하려던 얘기가 뭐야? 어서 **보따리 풀어** 봐. = *OK, so what was it you were going to say earlier? Out with it.* B: 별것 아니에요. 혹시 내일 시간 되면 같이 영화 보러 가실래요? = *Ah, it's nothing much. If you're not too busy tomorrow, what about catching a movie?*

보란 듯이 [Lit. as if telling others to watch] IDIOM 남들 앞에서 자랑스럽

고 당당하게 = proudly or haughtily in front of others (*equiv.* for everyone to see / to put on a show) ▌A: 나는 네가 **보란 듯이** 해낼 줄 알았어. = *I knew you would show us all by getting it done.* B: 다 선생님 덕분입니다. = *It was all thanks to you, sir.*

NOTE: '여봐란듯이'라는 말도 쓰는데 같은 표현이다.
여봐란듯이 is also commonly used to express the same meaning.

보자 보자 하다 [Lit. to say, "Let's watch. Let's watch."] IDIOM 참고 넘어가다 = to bear something and move on (*equiv.* to grin and bear it) ▌A: **보자 보자 했더니** 네가 눈에 보이는 것이 없나 보구나. = *I tried to just let it go, but it's starting to seem like you're blind.* B: 제가 뭘 어쨌다고 그렇게 심한 말을 하십니까? = *What exactly did I do to make you so upset?*

➡ p.142

NOTE: 못마땅한 상황을 참다 못해 마음속에 있는 말을 하려고 할 때 쓰는 표현이다. '보자 보자 하니까', '보자 보자 했더니'의 형태로 주로 쓰인다. 때로는 "보자 보자 하니까 누구를 보자기로 알아?"와 같이 말하기도 하는데, 여기서 보자기는 특별한 의미로 쓰인 것이 아니라 '보자 보자'와 쌍을 이룬 언어유희로서 쓰인 것이다.
This is used when one has taken all one can of a certain situation and intends to speak one's mind. It is most often used in the forms 보자 보자 하니까 and 보자 보자 했더니. Sometimes it occurs in the form "보자 보자 하니까 누구를 보자기로 알아?" In this sentence 보자기 has no special meaning, but is a play on the 보자 part from the beginning of the phrase.

복병을 만나다 [Lit. to meet an ambush] IDIOM 예상하지 못한 어려움을 겪다 = to meet with an unexpected difficulty (*syn.* 암초에 부딪치다) ▌A: 잘나가던 유럽이 경제 위기라는 **복병을 만날** 줄 누가 알았겠어? = *Who could've guessed that mighty Europe would fall prey to economic woes?* B: 어떤 사람들은 충분히 예상 가능한 일이었다던데? = *Some people are saying that it was predictable outcome.*

본전도 못 건지다 IDIOM = 본전도 못 찾다

본전도 못 찾다 [Lit. to not even be able to find the principal] IDIOM 일한 보람이 없이 오히려 손해만 입다 = for one's efforts to be met with no benefit and instead lead to losses (*syn.* 본전도 못 건지다, 밑천도 못 찾다) ▌A: 팀장님한테 우리 회식 언제 하냐고 물어볼까? = *How about asking the boss when we're going to have our staff party?* B: 그만둬. 요즘 회사 분위기도 안 좋은데. **본전도 못 찾지 말고.** = *Just leave it alone. The vibe isn't very good around here right now. Don't make things worse.*

~ 부 능선을 넘다 IDIOM '~ 분 능선을 넘다'의 잘못된 말 = a mistaken form of ~ 분 능선을 넘다

부모 말을 들으면 자다가도 떡이 생긴다 [Lit. If you listen to your parents, there'll be *tteok* waiting for you when you wake up.] PROVERB 부모 말을 잘 들어야 한다는 말 = emphasizes the importance of listening to one's parents ▌A: 민철아, 자기 전에 이 닦아라. = *Mincheol, brush your teeth before you go to bad.* B: 아빠, 제가 한두 살 먹은 애예요? = *Am I still a two-year-old, Dad?* A: **부모 말을 들으면 자다가도 떡이 생긴다는 말 모르니?** = *Don't you know that listening to your parents has its rewards?*

부부 싸움은 칼로 물 베기 [Lit. A couple fighting is like cutting water with a knife.] PROVERB 부부는 싸웠다가 화해하는 일이 흔히 있는 일이라는 말 = emphasizes how commonplace it is for married couples to fight and make up ▌A: 이제 **부부 싸움은 칼로 물 베기라는** 말도 못 하겠어. 세 쌍 중 한 쌍이 이혼한다니 말이야. = *It doesn't seem like married couples really stick it out like they used to. I mean, I've heard that one in three marriages end in divorce.* B: 맞아. 아무리 부부 사이라도 싸워서 좋을 건 없지. = *Yeah, now being married is no guarantee that a couple will stay together after a fight.*

부전자전 [Lit. 父father + 傳convey + 子son + 傳convey] CHINESE-DERIVATION 아들이 여러 면에서 아버지를 닮았을 때 쓰는 말 = used to describe a son that resembles his father in many ways (*equiv.* like father, like son / a chip off the old block / The apple doesn't fall far from the tree. *syn.* 그 아버지에

그 아들) █A: 정민이가 제 아빠 운동 신경을 물려받았나 봐. =*It seems like Jeongmin inherited his father's athletic abilities.* B: **부전자전**이지 뭐. 운동 하나는 잘해. =*Like father, like son, I guess. He's good at sports—I'll give him that.*

부정부패 [Lit. 不no + 淨clean + 腐rotten + 敗rotten] CHINESE-DERIVATION 바르지 않고 썩음 = depravity and moral coruption (*equiv.* corruption) █A: 새로 뽑은 대통령은 **부정부패**를 척결할 수 있을까? =*Do you think the new president will be able to root out corruption?* B: 대통령 스스로가 깨끗해야 가능하겠지. =*The president has to be clean himself for that to happen.*

북 치고 장구 치고 [Lit. to hit the *buk* (a large Korean drum) and the *janggu* (an hourglass-shaped Korean drum)] IDIOM 혼자서 이 일 저 일 모두 할 때 쓰는 말 = used to describe someone who, by themselves, does a little bit of this and a little bit of that (*equiv.* to dabble) █A: 새로 가게 열었다며? 주방에 사람은 구했어? =*So, you opened up your own store? Did you find someone for the kitchen?* B: 아니, 지금은 내가 음식 만들고 서빙하고 다 해. =*Nope, I'm making the food and serving it at this point.* A: 혼자서 **북 치고 장구 치고** 하는구나. 힘들겠다. =*Wow, you're like a one-man band, huh? Must be tough.*

NOTE: 북과 장구를 치려면 두 사람이 필요하다. 혼자서 북도 치고 장구도 치듯, 여러 사람이 필요한 일을 혼자서 해 나가는 모양을 일컫는 표현이다.
If you want to play the 북 and the 장구 at the same time, it takes two people. This expression is used to describe someone doing some work, which normally takes several people to do, by oneself like someone darting back and forth between these two drums to hit every beat on time.

~ 분 능선을 넘다 [Lit. to cross ... tenths over the ridge] IDIOM 어떤 일의 진행이 고비를 넘기다 = for a certain job to be beyond the hardest point (*equiv.* to get through the worst of it / It's all downhill from here.) █A: 오늘 이겼으니 이제 남은 세 경기에서 한 경기만 더 이기면 우승이

야. = *Since we won today, all we have to do is win one of the next three matches and we'll make it to the finals.* B: 우승까지 **9분 능선을 넘은** 셈이네. = *We're as good as there at this point.*

NOTE: 여기서 '분'은 10분의 1을 가리키는 말이다. 9분 능선을 넘었다는 말은 전체 고갯길의 90%를 왔다는 말이니 힘든 고비를 넘겼다는 뜻이 된다. 흔히 '분'이 아닌 '부'를 써서 '9부 능선'이라는 말을 많이 쓰는데 '9분 능선'이 맞는 표현이다.

분 means one tenth. Crossing the ridge of nine 분 means one has come 90 percent of the ridge, which means overcoming a difficult point. Usually people use 부 instead of 분, as in 9부 능선, but the correct form is 9분 능선.

분초를 다투다 [Lit. to fight over minutes and seconds] IDIOM 아주 급하다 = to be very urgent (*equiv.* to come down to the seconds / to be extremely time-sensitive) ▌A: 이 일은 **분초를 다투는** 일입니다. 조금만 시간이 지나도 국물이 식어 맛이 없어지거든요. = *This is all very time-sensitive. If you miss the target time by even a few seconds, the broth will cool down and it will lose its taste.* B: 아, 그래서 주방이 이렇게 바쁜 거군요. = *Ah, so that's why the kitchen is always this hectic.*

불가사의(하다) [Lit. 不 no + 可 allow + 思 think + 議 discuss] CHINESE-DERIVATION 일반적인 생각으로는 이해할 수 없을 만큼 기이하다 = to be so esoteric as to defy common understanding (*equiv.* to defy understanding) ▌A: 어떻게 한여름에 산에 얼음이 얼 수 있을까요? = *How could ice form like this on a mountain in the middle of summer?* B: 정말 **불가사의한** 일이네요. = *It really does defy understanding.*

불꽃(이) 튀다 [Lit. to bounce sparks] IDIOM 1. 겨루는 모양이 매우 치열하다 = to be engaged in a intense dispute (*equiv.* for sparks to fly) ▌A: 오늘 경기 정말 재미있었지? = *That game today sure was fun, huh?* B: 어. **불꽃 튀는** 접전이었어. = *Yep, the sparks were really flying.* 2. 분노가 나타나다 = for rage to be expressed ▌A: 아까 예림이랑 예슬이랑 싸울 때 봤어? = *Did you see Yerim and Yeseul fighting earlier?* B: 둘이 노려보는

데 눈에서 **불꽃이 튀던데**. = *They had some serious fire burning in their eyes when they looked at each other.*

불난 집에 부채질한다 [Lit. to fan the flames of a burning house] PROVERB 화난 사람이나 어려운 상황에 있는 사람을 자극해 화나 어려움을 더 크게 만들 때 쓰는 말 = to further excite a person or situation in a way that makes matters worse (*equiv.* to fan the flames / to add insult to injury) ▶p.188 ▌A: 또 딱지 뗐어? 이번 달만 벌써 몇 번째야? 당신은 운전하면 안 되겠네. = *You got another ticket? How many times has it been this month? I don't think you should be driving.* B: 지금 **불난 집에 부채질하는 거야?** = *Are you trying to fan the flames?*

불똥(이) 튀다 [Lit. to bounce sparks] IDIOM 어떤 사건이 다른 것에 영향을 미쳐 화를 입히다 = to have wrath directed at one as an unconcerned party (*equiv.* to get embroiled in another's quarrel) ▌A: 네 아빠는 왜 맨날 술 마시고 이 시간까지 안 들어오니? 너도 앞으로 집에 늦게 들어오면 혼날 줄 알아. = *Why does your father have to drink every day and still out late? You'd better not come home late either or else.* B: 엄마는. 왜 **불똥이 나한테 튀어?** = *Mom, why are you taking it out on me?*

불면 꺼질까 쥐면 터질까 [Lit. (to worry if) for something to burn down when being blowed, and for something to burst if being clutched] PROVERB 어린 자녀를 귀하게 기르는 것을 가리키는 말 = used to describe rearing children in a precious, overprotective way (*cf.* 금지옥엽) ▌A: **불면 꺼질까 쥐면 터질까** 기른 자식이 벌써 커서 결혼을 한다니 실감이 안 나네요. = *It was just yesterday that I was changing his diapers, and now here he is, getting married. I can't believe it.* B: 이제 김 선생님도 마음 편하게 자신의 인생을 즐기세요. = *Now it's time for you to relax and start enjoying your own life, sir.*

불씨가 꺼지지 않다 IDIOM = 불씨가 남아 있다

불씨가 남아 있다 [Lit. for there to still be some burning embers] IDIOM **1.** 희망이나 가능성이 남아 있다 = for there to be some remaining hope (*equiv.* for there to still be a flicker of hope) ▌A: 우리나라는 아직 16강의 **불씨가 남아 있습니다**. = *There is still a flicker of hope for Korea to reach the Round of 16.* B: 그러나 16강 진출을 위해서는 남은 한 경기를 반드시 이겨야 합니다. = *But if that's going to happen, we absolutely have to win the one match that is left.* **2.** 문제를 일으킬 수 있는 불안 요소가 남아 있다 = for there to still exist some chance of creating a problem (*equiv.* The first isn't completely out.) ▌A: 독도 문제는 한일 외교에서 뜨거운 감자인 것 같아요. **◆p.202** = *It seems like the Dokdo issue is a hot potato for diplomatic relations between Japan and Korea.* B: 네. 양국 관계에서 늘 **불씨로 남아 있죠**. = *The fire never seems to be all the way out between the two countries.*

불씨가 되다 [Lit. to become an ember] IDIOM 원인이나 계기가 되다 = to become the cause or opportunity ▌A: 내가 무심코 한 말이 **불씨가 되어** 이렇게 일이 커질 줄은 몰랐어. = *I never thought that just a few words of mine would be enough to cause so much trouble.* B: 결자해지라고 네가 **◆p.51** 나서서 일을 수습해. = *Since you caused it, you should be the one to step forward and fix it.*

불(을) 보듯 뻔하다 [Lit. to be as clear as watching a fire] IDIOM 아주 명백하다 = to be very obvious (*equiv.* to be clear to see *syn.* 불(을) 보듯 훤하다) ▌A: 너 오늘 학교에서 선생님한테 혼났지? = *You got in trouble at school today, didn't you?* B: 어? 엄마 어떻게 알았어? = *What? How did you know?* A: 숙제 안 해 갔잖아. **불을 보듯 뻔한** 일이지. = *You didn't do your homework. Of course you were going to get yelled at.*

불(을) 보듯 훤하다 IDIOM = 불(을) 보듯 뻔하다

불철주야 [Lit. 不no + 撤distinguish + 晝day + 夜night] CHINESE-DERIVATION 밤낮을 가리지 않음 = not distinguishing night and day ▌A: 수고하십니다. 경비에는 아무 문제 없죠? = *Keep up the good work, everyone. You aren't having any problems with the guarding, correct?* B: 네, 저희가 **불철주야**로 감시를 하고 있으니 걱정하지 마십시오. = *No, sir. We are* *on guard night and day. You have nothing to worry about.*

NOTE: 주로 '불철주야(로)'의 꼴로 쓰인다.
This expression is most often used in the 불철주야(로) form.

붓을 꺾다 [Lit. to break the brush] IDIOM 글 쓰는 활동을 그만두다 = to give up on writing (*equiv.* to put down the quill / to put away the typewriter *syn.* 붓을 놓다) ▋A: 선생님, 이번 작품을 끝으로 **붓을 꺾겠다고** 선언하셨는데 그 이유가 무엇입니까? = *Sir, you've stated that after this work, you'll be putting down the quill for good. May I ask the reason?* B: 제 스스로에게 한계를 느꼈습니다. = *I've come to realize my own limitations.*

NOTE: 요즘 젊은 작가들은 컴퓨터로 글을 쓰기 대문에 이런 표현을 잘 쓰지 않는다.
As most of today's young authors use computers to write their works, this expression has fallen out of common use.

붓을 놓다 IDIOM = 붓을 꺾다

비가 오나 눈이 오나 [Lit. if rain or snow comes] IDIOM 항상 = always (*equiv.* all night and day / rain or shine *syn.* 눈이 오나 비가 오나, 앉으나 서나, 자나 깨나, 밤이나 낮이나) ▋A: 돌아가신 모친께서는 어떤 분이셨습니까? = *What was your mother like?* B: **비가 오나 눈이 오나** 자식 걱정뿐인 분이셨습니다. = *She was the kind of person who always was concerned about the welfare of her children.*

비몽사몽 [Lit. 非no + 夢dream + 似be like + 夢dream] CHINESE-DERIVATION 반쯤 잠들고 반쯤 깨어 있는 상태 = the state of being half-asleep (and half-awake) (*equiv.* to be half-asleep / to be half-awake) ▋A: 어쩌다 무릎에 멍이 든 거야? = *How'd you get that bruise on your knee?* B: 오늘 새벽 **비몽사몽** 중에 화장실 가다가 탁자에 부딪쳤어. = *Early this morning I got up and bumped into the table on my way to the bathroom.*

비싼 수업료를 내다 [Lit. to pay expensive tuition] IDIOM 큰 낭패를 보거나 아픔을 겪고 난 뒤 교훈이나 깨달음을 얻다 = to learn a lesson after suffering an ignominious defeat (*equiv.* to learn one's lesson / to learn the hard way) ▌A: 건강보다 소중한 게 없다는 걸 이번에 크게 아프고 난 뒤 알게 됐어요. = *After getting really sick this time, I realized that there is nothing more important than one's health.* B: **비싼 수업료를 낸** 셈이 군요. = *I guess you learned the hard way.*

비 온 뒤에 땅이 굳어진다 [Lit. The earth hardens after rain falls.] PROVERB 시련을 겪은 뒤에 더 강해진다는 말 = describes how people grow stronger after going through trials (*equiv.* That which doesn't kill me, can only make me stronger.) ▌A: 명은 씨 부부는 재결합한 뒤에 더 사이가 좋아 보이네. = *Since Myeongeun and her husband got back together, they look better than ever.* B: **비 온 뒤에 땅이 굳어진다는** 말도 있잖아. = *I guess that's why they say that a good fight can actually bring a couple closer together.*

비일비재(하다) [Lit. 非no + 一one + 非no + 再again → not once nor twice] CHINESE-DERIVATION 자주 여러 번 일어나다 = to commonly occur (*equiv.* an everyday occurrence / It's not the first time (something has happened). / an everyday thing) ▌A: 어디 다친 데는 없으세요? = *Are you hurt anywhere?* B: 네, 괜찮아요. 술 취한 손님이 시비 거는 일은 **비일비재한데요** 뭘. = *No, I'm fine. It's not the first time drunken patrons have picked a fight with me.*

비행기(를) 태우다 [Lit. to put someone on a plane] IDIOM 남을 정도 이상으로 칭찬하다 = to praise someone excessively (*equiv.* to praise someone to the skies / to sing someone's praises) ▌A: 우와, 오늘 정말 근사하신데요. 스무 살이라고 해도 믿겠어요. = *Wow, you're really looking good today. You don't look a day over 20.* B: 왜 갑자기 **비행기를 태우고** 그러세요? 부끄럽게. = *Why are you buttering me up like that? You're embarrassing me.*

NOTE: 한국어나 영어나 하늘을 나는 것은 기분이 좋은 상태를 비유할 때가 많다.

In both Korean and English, metaphors dealing with soaring or flying denote positive states of mind and elation. This expression literally means to take someone for a plane ride and metaphorically is similar to the English expression, "to butter someone up."

빈 깡통이 요란하다 IDIOM = 빈 수레가 요란하다

빈대도 낯짝이 있다 IDIOM = 벼룩도 낯짝이 있다

빈대 붙다 [Lit. to attach (oneself like) a bedbug] IDIOM (속된 말로) 노력하지 않고 다른 사람에게 붙어 이득을 보다 = (slang) to not make efforts for oneself and instead seek benefit by becoming close to someone successful (*equiv.* to mooch off / to be like a parasite / to suckle off someone's breast)

▌A: 요즘 어디에서 지내? = *Where are you living these days?* B: 사촌 형네에서 **빈대 붙어** 지내요. = *I'm living like a parasite at my cousin's house.*

NOTE: 빈대는 밤에만 활동하는 야행성 해충으로 사람이나 동물의 몸에 달라붙어 피를 빨아먹고 산다. 이러한 빈대의 습성에 빗대어 '남에게 빌붙어서 무엇이든지 공짜로 해결하고 득을 보려는 사람의 행동'을 '빈대 붙다'라고 한다.

Bedbugs are nocturnal creatures that affix themselves to warm bodies and subsist by sucking the blood of animals and people. Someone who latches onto someone else and mooches off of them can be well described with this expression.

빈대 잡으려다 초가삼간 다 태운다 [Lit. to burn down a three-room thatch house while trying to catch a bedbug] PROVERB 작은 문제를 해결하려고 하다 큰 손해를 입게 될 때 쓰는 말 = describes a situation where, in the course of trying to resolve a small problem, one causes a much larger problem (*equiv.* to throw the baby out with the bathwater / to burn down the

house to kill a rat) ▌A: 우리 이번 기회에 도배를 다 다시 할까? 벽지에 얼룩도 많이 묻었고. = *Should we take this as an opportunity to re-wallpaper the walls? The walls are covered with spots and marks.* B: **빈대 잡으려다 초가삼간 태울** 일 있어? 얼룩 몇 개 때문에 도배를 다시 하면 돈이 얼마인지나 알아? = *Don't you think that would be going a little bit overboard? Do you have any idea how expensive it would be to replace all the wall over a few spots?*

빈 수레가 요란하다 [Lit. An empty cart makes a lot of noise.] PROVERB 실속 없는 사람이 더 떠들어 댄다는 말 = suggests a tendency of those with little in terms a real ability to have the loudest voices (*equiv.* Empty vessels make the most sound. *syn.* 빈 깡통이 요란하다) ▌A: 저 선배, 말로는 자기가 엄청 잘하는 것처럼 떠들어 대더니 막상 시합에서 보니 별로던데. = *That guy was always carrying on about how great he was, but when it came time for the test he sure wasn't anything special.* B: 그러니까 **빈 수레가 요란하다는** 거야. = *I guess that's why they say an empty vessel makes the most noise.*

빙산의 일각 [Lit. the tip of an iceberg] IDIOM 극히 일부분 = one extremity of a whole (*equiv.* to be (just) the tip of the iceberg) ▌A: 그 정치인 지난 설날에 아랫사람들한테 뇌물 받아 먹었다는 기사 봤어? = *Did you read that article about the politician who accepted bribes from his underlings last New Year's Day?* B: 응, 봤어. 그게 전부겠어? **빙산의 일각**이겠지. = *Yep, I saw that. Do you think that's all? I'm sure it was just the tip of the iceberg.*

NOTE: 빙산은 수면 위로 나와 있는 부분이 전체의 7분의 1밖에 되지 않는다고 한다. 바람직하지 못한 일의 대부분이 숨겨져 있고 겉으로 드러나 있는 것은 일부분에 지나지 않음을 비유하는 말이다.
They say that the portion of an iceberg visual from the surface is sometimes as little as one seventh of its overall size. When something, usually unsightly, is still mostly concealed, this phrase is often employed. Its usage is almost identical to that of the analogous English phrase, "the tip of the iceberg."

빛을 발하다 [Lit. to emit light] IDIOM 제 값어치를 발휘하다 = to exhibit one's value (*equiv.* to demonstrate one's true worth) ▌A: 내일이면 드디어 지난 1년 동안 만든 제품이 시장에 출시되네. = *Tomorrow's the day the product we've been working on for more than a year will finally be hitting the market.* B: 그동안 우리 고생한 게 **빛을 발해야** 할 텐데. = *I hope it was worth all we put into it.*

빛을 보다 [Lit. to see light] IDIOM 그동안 잘 알려져 있지 않던 것이 세상에 알려지거나 인정을 받다 = for something that had been largely unknown to the world to become known or receive recognition (*equiv.* to be brought (out of the shadows and) into the light *syn.* 햇빛을 보다 *ant.* 그늘에 가리다) ▌A: 그동안 세상에 알려져 있지 않던 김 화백의 작품 세 점이 **빛을 보게** 되었습니다. = *Three of Kim's paintings, which were previously unknown to the world, have now seen the light of day.* B: 한 개인 소장가가 김 화백의 작품 세 점을 미술관에 기증했기 때문입니다. = *That's because a private collector donated the three pieces to a museum.*

빛을 잃다 [Lit. to lose its light] IDIOM 가치나 의미가 줄어들다 = for something to lose value or meaning (*equiv.* to lose some of its shine *syn.* 빛(이)바래다) ▌A: 오늘 김 감독의 천 번째 경기인데 경기를 져서 안타깝네요. = *Today was Coach Kim's 1,000th game. It's a real shame that it ended in a loss.* B: 그러게요. 의미 있는 기록인데 좀 **빛을 잃은** 느낌이에요. = *That's what I'm saying. It kind of takes some of the shine off of such a meaningful record.*

빛(이)바래다 [Lit. for the shine of a thing to fade] IDIOM 가치나 의미가 줄어들다 = for something to lose value or meaning (*equiv.* to lose some of its shine *syn.* 빛을 잃다) ▌A: **빛이 바랜** 건 사실이지만 기록은 영원한 법이죠. = *It may have lost some of its shine but a record is forever.* B: 네, 시간이 지날수록 빛을 발하는 기록이 될 거예요. = *Yes, as time passes his record will remain as a shining example.*

빛 좋은 개살구 [Lit. a good-looking wild apricot] PROVERB 겉으로 보기에는 좋으나 실제로는 좋지 못한 것 = something that looks outwardly desirable but is not all that great in actuality (*equiv.* a deceptive appearance *cf.* 뚝배기보다 장맛이다) ▌A: 우와, 너희 집 정말 좋다. 넓고 구조도 정말 좋아. = *Wow, your house is awesome. The layout is nice and it's so big.* B: 어휴, 그게 다 **빛 좋은 개살구**야. 은행에 매달 갚아야 하는 대출금이 얼마인지 아니? = *Appearances can be deceiving. Do you have any idea what my mortgage payments are like?*

NOTE: 개살구는 겉만 보면 맛있어 보이지만 실제로는 아무 맛이 없다. 이처럼 겉은 그럴듯하지만 실속은 없는 상황을 가리켜 '빛 좋은 개살구'라고 한다.

Wild apricots look very delicious, but if you've ever been unfortunate enough to bite into one, you know that they are far less tasty than their store-bought cousins. This little deception is why the fruit is now inextricably associated with things that have a sparkly exterior but are, upon further inspection, quite underwhelming.

ㅃ

빨간불이 켜지다 [Lit. for a red light to turn on] IDIOM 위험을 알리는 조짐이 나타나다 = for a sign of danger to present itself (*equiv.* for a red light to go off in one's mind / for warning flags to pop up *syn.* 적신호가 켜지다 *ant.* 파란불이 켜지다, 청신호가 켜지다) ▌A: 주식 시장이 이렇게 불안정해서 큰일이에요. = *The stock market being so unstable is a major problem.* B: 우리 경제에 **빨간불이 켜진** 셈이죠. = *It's as if all the economic indicators are flashing red.*

빼다(가) 박다 [Lit. to take away and then hammer in] IDIOM 매우 비슷하다 = to be very similar (*equiv.* to be the spitting image of (someone)) ▌A: 얘는 제 엄마를 **빼다 박았네.** = *That girl is the spitting image of her mom.* B: 정말이야. 얼굴도 그렇지만 목소리도 똑같아. = *No fooling. Her looks just like her mom but her voice sounding exactly the same is even more amazing.*

빼도 박도 못하다 [Lit. to be unable to take away or hammer in (something)] IDIOM 이러지도 저러지도 못하는 난처한 입장이 되다 = to be left with no suitable course of action (*equiv.* to be left with nothing to do / to be at an impasse / to be in a pickle / to be in a bind) ▌A: 엄마, 내일 남편 회사 사람들 집들이 초대했는데, 어떻게 해야 할지 모르겠어요. 큰소리쳐 놓아서 **빼도 박도 못하겠고.** = *Mom, I got carried away and invited a bunch of my husband's work friends over for a housewarming tomorrow. I'm really in a bind.* B: 저런. 몇 명쯤 오는데? = *Oh my! How many people did you invite?*

NOTE: 이 표현은 그 기원을 생각하면 사용을 주의해야 하는 표현이다. 남녀가 섹스를 하려고 하는데 다른 사람이 들이닥쳐 남자가 어찌할 바를 모르는 데서 나온 원색적인 표현이기 때문이다.
Considering the origin of this phrase, it would be prudent to exercise caution in its use. The origin was the image of a man and woman about to engage in sexual intercourse when another person suddenly busts into the room. The man would of course be left in an awkward situation, not knowing what to do.

~ 빼면 시체 [Lit. Without ... you're corpse.] IDIOM 무엇이 대단하다는 뜻 = used to describe something as great (*equiv.* He's nothing without his (money).) ▍A: 네 동생 정말 귀엽다. 나를 처음 보는데도 오빠, 오빠 하면서 잘 따르네. = *Your little sister is so cute. Right from the start she called me "big brother," and listens to what I say.* B: 걔가 원래 애교 **빼면 시체야**. = *Her charm is what makes her who she is.*

뻔할 뻔 자 [Lit. the character *ppeon* for obvious] IDIOM 아주 뻔하고 명백한 것 = something exceedingly clear and obvious (*equiv.* as clear as day / as plain as the nose on your face / obvious with a capital o *cf.* 놀랄 노 자) ▍A: 그럼 네 말은 범인이 남편이라는 거지? = *So what you're saying is that the culprit was her husband?* B: **뻔할 뻔 자** 아냐? = *Yeah, wasn't that obvious?*

NOTE: See the note on 놀랄 노 자.

뼈(가) 빠지게 일하다 [Lit. to work until one's bones fall out] IDIOM 몹시 고되게 일하다 = to work extremely hard (*equiv.* to work like a dog) ▍A: 1년 365일 하루도 안 쉬고 **뼈 빠지게 일했지만** 아무도 알아 주는 사람이 없어요. = *I worked 365 days a year all year long and not a single person even acknowledged that.* B: 언젠가 좋은 날이 올 거예요. 기운 내세요. = *Someday things will get better. Cheer up.*

뼈(가) 있다 [Lit. to have bones] IDIOM 말에 비판적인 의도가 숨겨져 있다 = for words to have a hidden negative message (*equiv.* for there to be some truth in what someone is saying *cf.* 가시가 있다) ▌A: 아까 네가 한 말 말이야, 농담처럼 하기는 했지만 **뼈가 있는** 말이지?=*You know what you said earlier? You were only half-joking, huh?* B: 아니야. 그냥 별 뜻 없이 한 말이야.=*No. There was no deeper meaning to it.*

뼈도 못 추리다 [Lit. to be unable to pull together one's bones] IDIOM 강한 상대에게 호되게 당하다=to be attacked severely by a strong opponent

▌A: 야, 상대는 대기업이야. 우리 같은 작은 회사가 아무리 덤벼 봤자 **뼈도 못 추려**.=*Hey, we're going up against a major corporation. No matter what we do, we'll be the ones who get hurt.* B: 길고 짧은 건 대 봐야 알지.=*We'll never know until we try.* ➡ p.102

뼈를 깎다 [Lit. to grind one's bones] IDIOM 매우 고통스럽다=to be very painful (*syn.* 살을 깎다)

▌A: 성공하려면 **뼈를 깎는** 노력을 해야 합니다.=*If you want to succeed, you have to work yourself to the bone.* B: 저는 외모를 가꾸기 위해 **뼈를 깎는** 노력을 했어요. 성형수술을 통해 턱을 깎았죠.=*For my looks, I worked myself to the bone: I had my jawbones ground down when I got plastic surgery.*

> **NOTE:** '뼈를 깎는 고통', '뼈를 깎는 노력'이라는 표현이 자주 쓰인다.
> This expression is most commonly used as 뼈를 깎는 고통 or 뼈를 깎는 노력.

뼈를 묻다 [Lit. to bury one's bones] IDIOM 단체나 분야에 평생토록 헌신하다=to be self-sacrificing and completely immersed in a certain field or organization

▌A: 요즘 젊은이들은 우리 때보다 애사심이 부족한 거 같아요.=*Youngsters today don't seem to have any company pride like we used to.* B: 맞아요. 우리 때는 회사에 **뼈를 묻을** 각오로 일했었는데 말이에요.=*That's right. Back in our time we were ready to go to our graves if the company so much as asked.*

뼈만 남다 [Lit. to only have bones left] IDIOM 심하게 야위다=to be emaciated (*equiv.* to be a bag of bones *syn.* 뼈와 가죽뿐이다)

▌A: 경자 씨 보기 애처로워 혼났어요.=*It was hard to look at Gyeongja, she's so pitiful nowadays.* B: 그동안 마음 고생이 얼마나 심했는지 **뼈만 남았더라니까요**. = *Imagine just how terrible things must have been for her to turn into a bag of bones like that.*

뼈에 사무치다 [Lit. to permeate one's bones] IDIOM 어떠한 감정이 매우 깊고 강하다 = to feel a deep and strong emotion (*equiv.* to feel (an emotion) in one's bones / ... to the core / with every bone in one's body) ▌A: 하이옌 씨는 한국 생활에서 제일 힘든 점이 뭐예요? = *What's hardest for you about living in Korean, Hayen?* B: 아무래도 고국에 있는 가족들에 대한 그리움이죠. 베트남에 있는 부모님이 **뼈에 사무치도록** 보고 싶을 때가 많아요. = *Well, I'd have to say it's the longing I feel in my heart for those I left behind in Vietnam. Every bone in my body aches to see my parents again.*

뼈와 가죽뿐이다 [Lit. to be only skin and bones] IDIOM 심하게 야위다 = to be emaciated (*equiv.* to be just skin and bones *syn.* 뼈만 남다) ▌A: 애, 다이어트도 좋지만 적당히 해라. **뼈하고 가죽뿐이야**. = *Dieting is good, but you shouldn't overdo it like that. You're just skin and bones.* B: 아직 더 빼야 해요, 엄마. = *I've still got to be prettier, Mom.*

뼈와 살이 되다 [Lit. to become flesh and bones] IDIOM 정신적으로 도움이 되다 = to help mentally (*equiv.* to nourish the soul) ▌A: 오늘 오후에 세미나 있는데 같이 갈래? = *We have a seminar later this afternoon. Do you want to go together?* B: 귀찮아. 너 혼자 갔다 와. = *What a bother. You just go by yourself.* A: 그래도 그런 게 다 **뼈가 되고 살이 되는 거야**. = *Yeah, it's a hassle but this kind of thing is nourishment for the soul.*

뿌리(가) 깊다 [Lit. to have deep roots] IDIOM 역사나 기원이 오래되다 = to have long history (*equiv.* to have deep roots) ▌A: 한국에는 아직도 남아 선호 사상이 남아 있나요? = *Do Korean parents still prefer male children?* B: 젊은 세대들 사이에서는 거의 없어졌지만, 나이 많은 사람들 사이에서는 아직도 있죠. 유교 문화가 **뿌리 깊으니까요**. = *Amongst the younger generation, that type of thinking has almost disappeared, but older Koreans still often think that way. Confucian thought has deep roots*

in Korean.

뿌리(를) 내리다 [Lit. to put down roots] IDIOM 정착하다 = to live in a place long-term (*equiv.* to put down roots (in a new land etc.) / to settle down) ▌A: 너도 이제 나이가 있는데 결혼해서 한 곳에 **뿌리를 내려야** 하지 않겠니? = *You're getting on in the years now. Don't you think it's about time to get married and settle down someplace?* 3: 네. 저도 그럴 생각이에요, 아버지. = *Yes, Father, I've also been thinking that.*

뿌리(를) 뽑다 [Lit. to pluck the root] IDIOM 근원을 없애다 = to eliminate the cause (*equiv.* to nip it in the bud / to get at the root cause) ▌A: 이어서 교장 선생님께서 말씀하시겠습니다. = *Next, the Principal has some remarks he'd like to share with us.* B: 학생 여러분, 최근 심각한 사회 현상이 되고 있는 학교 폭력을 **뿌리 뽑아야** 합니다. = *Students, violence in the schools has become a major societal problem and it is imperative that we tear it out by the root.*

뿌린 대로 거둔다 [Lit. to gather what (the seeds) one has scattered] PROVERB 잘했으면 잘한 만큼, 못했으면 못한 만큼 결과가 나타난다는 말 = emphasizes that people are rewarding for their labors and punished for their indolence (*equiv.* You reap what you sow. / You made your bed, now lie in it. *syn.* 콩 심은 데 콩 나고 팥 심은 데 팥 난다) ▌A: 너도 후회할 날 있을 거야. **뿌린 대로 거두는** 법이야. = *A day will come when you will regret this. You reap what you sow.* B: 듣기 싫으니까 어서 나가! = *I'm sick of hearing you talk. Get out!*

入

사공이 많으면 배가 산으로 간다 [Lit. Too many sailors steer the ship up a mountain.] PROVERB 일을 주도하려는 사람이 많으면 일이 제대로 되기 힘들다는 말 = points out the tendency of endeavors to fail when too many people attempt to take the lead (*equiv.* Too many cooks (in the kitchen) spoil the broth.) ▌A: 으악, 이거 맛이 왜 이래? = *Yuck, what's wrong with this food?* B: 요리하는데, 언니랑 엄마가 자꾸 이래라 저래라 하잖아. 시키는 대로 했더니 이래. = *When I was cooking, my mother and sister kept telling me to do this and that and this is how it turned out.* A: **사공이 많으면 배가 산으로 가는** 법이지. 네 소신껏 해. = *Too many cooks in the kitchen spoil the broth. Just do it your way.*

사돈 남 말 한다 [Lit. for one's child's in-laws to talk about someone else] PROVERB 자신에게도 같은 잘못이 있는데 남을 탓할 때 쓰는 말 = describes someone who criticizes someone for a fault that they themselves possess (*equiv.* You're such a hypocrite! / Look who's talking! / Worry about yourself first.) ▌A: 야, 약속 시간 좀 잘 지켜. = *Hey, you need to be on time.* B: **사돈 남 말 하는** 거 아냐? 너야말로 지난번에 약속 시간에 한 시간이 늦었잖아. = *Oh, look who's talking! You were an hour late last time we met.*

NOTE: 여기서의 남은 결국 말하는 사람('나')을 가리킨다. 사돈 입장에서 보면 내가 곧 남이기 때문이다. 다시 말하면, 사돈이 내가 할 말을 한다는 뜻이 된다. 사돈이라는 관계는 다른 쪽 부모가 내 자식의 흉을 볼 때, 나는 그쪽 자식을 욕할 수 있는 어려운 사이이다. 상대편 자식에 대한 불만이 있지만 말을 하지 않고 있는데, 오히려 그쪽이 내 자식 욕을 하면 내 입장에서는 기가 막힐 것이다. 자기 자신의 허물을 보지 못하는 사람에게 핀잔을 줄 때 쓰는 표현이다.

남 usually refers to "others," but in this case is in fact oneself. 사돈 is the word for a son or daughter-in-law's parents, and from their perspective, oneself is the "other" in this case. If the child of one set of in-laws is rebuked by the other set of parents, the first set of in-laws may seek revenge by criticizing their son or daughter's spouse. If I am not fond of my son's choice in women, but have been holding my tongue only to have my daughter-in-law's parents say something nasty about my son, of course I wouldn't be able to contain myself. When someone's critique of another's flaws precisely pertain to themselves, this is the perfect expression to call them on their hypocrisy.

사돈의 팔촌 [Lit. one's child's in-law's third cousin] IDIOM 아주 먼 관계에 있는 사람 = a very distant relation (*equiv.* a far-off cousin) ▌A: 청첩장을 돌려야 하는데 누구 누구에게 줘야 할지 고민이야. **사돈의 팔촌**까지 알리는 게 예의인지, 아니면 가까운 사람들한테만 드려야 할지 말이야. = *I have to send out wedding invitations, but I'm not sure who I should send them to. I mean, do I have to invite even my most distant relatives, or just those I'm close to?* B: 가까운 지인들한테만 청첩장 드리고, 다른 분들한테는 전화 드리는 거 어때? = *What about just sending invitations to the people you are close to and calling the rest?*

사람들 눈이 있다 [Lit. There are people's eyes.] IDIOM 다른 사람의 이목이 있다 = Other people are watching. (*equiv.* People are watching. / There are eyes everywhere.) ▌A: 큰일났네. 애가 으줌 쌌어. 기저귀 갈아야겠네. = *What a mess. He just peed himself. I'll guess we'll have to change his diaper.* B: 여기 지하철에서? **사람들 눈이 있잖아.** 일단 내리자. = *Right here, on the subway? People are watching. Let's get off first.*

사람(을) 잡다 [Lit. to catch a person] IDIOM 상대를 심한 곤경으로 몰아넣다 = to put someone in a difficult position (*equiv.* to drive someone into a corner / to hold something over someone's head *cf.* 생사람(을) 잡다, 선무당이 사람 잡는다) ▌A: 아, 저런 여자들은 좋겠다. 결혼할 때 프

러포즈도 받고. = *It must be nice to be a girl like that. To be proposed to and all.* B: 결혼한 지 10년이 넘었는데, 아직도 나 프러포즈 안 한 걸로 **사람을 잡는 거야?** = *We've been married now for ten years and you're still holding the fact that I didn't propose to you over my head?*

사람(이)되다 [Lit. to become a person] IDIOM 기본적인 인격을 갖추다 = to attain the foundation of character ▌A: 학생들에게 제일 강조하시는 부분이 뭡니까? = *What do you emphasize most to your students?* B: 공부도 중요하지만 우선 **사람이 되라고** 늘 애기합니다. = *I'm always telling them that of course studying is important, but it's important to be a good person as well.*

사면초가 [Lit. 四four + 面face + 楚Chu + 歌song → The song of Chu is heard on all sides.] CHINESE-DERIVATION 주위에 도움을 청할 사람이 없는 외롭고 곤란한 상황 = the state of being in a precarious spot with no one to ask for aid (*equiv.* to be caught between a rock and a hard place *cf.* 막다른 골목) ▌A: 여당도 김 총리에게 퇴진을 권유했다는데, 정말 물러날까? = *Now, even the ruling party is asking for Prime Minister Kim's resignation. Do you think he'll really step down?* B: 야당에 여당까지 그러는데 별 수 있겠어? **사면초가**에 몰린 격이네. = *With both parties pressuring him now, does he have any choice? He's pretty much backed into a corner now.*

NOTE: 초나라의 항우가 적인 한나라와 전투를 벌이고 있었다. 그런데 한밤중에 사방에서 초나라 노래가 들려왔다. 한나라에서 항복한 초나라 군사들을 시켜 고향 노래를 부르게 한 것이었다. 초나라 병사들은 그 노래 때문에 감상적이 되어 사기가 떨어졌고, 그 때문에 초나라는 패하고 말았다.

Hsiang Yu of Chu was engaged in a fierce battle with Han soldiers in a dispute known as the Chu-Han Contention. As they camped for the night, suddenly the song of the Chu rang out on all sides. The Han generals had forced surrendered Chu soldiers to sing their songs from back home. The Chu soldiers, being suddenly overwhelmed with emotion from hearing the songs of their countrymen lost their spirit and were defeated by the Han.

사사건건 [Lit. 事work + 事work + 件case + 件case] CHINESE-DERIVATION 매사에 = in all matters (*equiv.* every single thing) ▌A: 내가 하는 말마다 **사사건건** 반대하는 이유가 뭐니? = *Why do you oppose everything that I tell you?* B: 내가? 나는 단지 내 의견을 말했을 뿐이야. = *Do I? I was just sharing my opinion.*

NOTE: 이 표현은 주로 부사로 쓰인다.
This expression is mostly used as an adverb.

사생결단 [Lit. 死die + 生life + 決decide + 斷determine] CHINESE-DERIVATION 죽을 각오로 끝장을 내려고 함 = being ready for a fight to the death (*equiv.* to fight to the death / to fight tooth and nail *cf.* 너 죽고 나 죽자, 이판사판) ▌A: 뭐라고? 이게 또 내 잘못이라고? 너랑 나랑 오늘 **사생결단**을 내 보자. = *What? You're saying this is my fault too? Today is the day we finish this once and for all!* B: 미안해. 나는 그런 뜻이 아니었어. = *Sorry. That's not what I meant by it.*

NOTE: 주로 '사생결단을 내다'의 꼴로 쓰인다.
Most often used in the form, 사생결단을 내다.

사서 고생(을)하다 IDIOM = 고생을 사서 하다

사실무근 [Lit. 事work + 實true + 無no + 根root → an incident not grounded in fact] CHINESE-DERIVATION 근거가 없거나 사실이 아님 = having no basis in fact (*equiv.* groundless / baseless) ▌A: 그 교수님 정말 실망이야. 여기저기서 뇌물을 받았다던데? = *I'm so disappointed in that professor. I heard he's been taking all kinds of bribes.* B: 본인은 **사실무근**이라고 말하지만, 아니 땐 굴뚝에 연기 나겠어? = *He has said that it's a groundless rumor but would there be smoke without fire?*
▶p.396

사위는 백년손님이다 [Lit. A son-in-law is a guest of 100 years.] PROVERB 사위는 대하기 어렵다는 말 = describes the difficulty in how to treat one's son-in-law ▌A: 장인 어른하고 장모님은 잘해 주셔? = *How are your in-laws? Are they good to you?* B: 어. 갈 때마다 어찌나 잘해 주시는

지 어떨 때는 죄송하기까지 해. = *They take such good care of me I'm almost sorry to impose on them.* A: 사위는 백년손님이라잖아. = *I guess that's why they say people never get comfortable with their sons-in-law.*

사위 사랑은 장모

[Lit. Love for a son-in-law comes from the mother-in-law.] PROVERB 사위는 장모에게 더 예쁨을 받는다는 말 = describes the tendency for mothers-in-law to be fond of their sons-in-law (*cf.* 며느리 사랑은 시아버지) ▌A: 엄마, 엄마는 왜 박 서방한테 그렇게 차갑게 대해? 사위 사랑은 장모라는데. = *Mom, why are you being so cold to your son-in-law like that? I thought that mothers-in-law are supposed to be close to their sons-in-law.* B: 내가 뭘 어쨌다고 그러니? 이 정도 했으면 됐지. = *What did I do? I think I've done more than enough.*

사자 없는 산에 토끼가 왕 노릇 한다

[Lit. On a mountain with no lion, the rabbit plays the role of king.] PROVERB 뛰어난 사람이 없는 곳에서 보잘것없는 사람이 잘난 체하는 것을 비꼬는 말 = a sardonic description of the tendency for a lesser individual to rise up to a powerful position when a stronger individual is not present (*equiv.* When the cat's away, the mice will play.) ▌A: 요즘 팀장님 해외 출장 가신 이후로 김 대리님 너무 어깨에 힘 주고 다니는 거 같지 않아? = *Ever since the boss has been abroad on business, Mr. Kim is walking around like he owns the place.* B: 그러게, 사자 없는 산에 토끼가 왕 노릇 한다잖아. = *When the cat's away, the mice will play.*

➧ p.411

사족

[Lit. 蛇 snake + 足 foot → (as unnecessary as) feet on a snake] CHINESE-DERIVATION 쓸데없는 군더더기 = an unnecessary addition (*equiv.* a third wheel / superfluity) ▌A: 자, 여기 네가 부탁한 물건 있어. 사족이지만 깨끗하게 쓰고 돌려줘야 하는 거 알지? = *Hey, here's that stuff you asked to borrow. It goes without saying, but keep it clean.* B: 당연하지. 고마워. 잘 쓸게. = *Of course. Thanks.*

NOTE: 옛날 고대 중국에서 여러 사람들이 모여 술을 마시려 했다. 그런데 술의 양이 부족하자 다들 뱀의 그림을 그려 제일 먼저 그리는 사람이 술을 마시기로 했다. 그리하여 한 남자가 가장 먼저 그림 그리기를 마치고 술을 마시려 했다. 그런데 다른 남자가 술잔을 빼앗으며 "당신 그림에는 뱀에 발이 있군요. 어떻게 발이 있는 게 뱀이라고 할 수 있겠습니까?"라고 말하며 자신이 술을 마셔 버렸다. 쓸데없는 것을 추가하여 오히려 일을 그르칠 때 쓰는 표현이다.

Long ago in China, a group of people gathered to drink together. There wasn't enough to go around, however, so they decided to all draw a picture of a snake and the person who finished first would get to drink. One especially speedy drawer finished his work and was heading for the bottle. But right at that instant, another man snatched the bottle, saying, "There are feet on your snake! How can you call that creature a snake?" He then downed the bottle. Just like the flashy addition of feet to the snake worked against this man's liquor ambitions, unnecessary filigree is never a good thing. This phrase is used to describe such instances.

사족을 못 쓰다 [Lit. to be unable to use one's limbs] IDIOM 무엇을 매우 좋아하거나 절대적으로 신뢰하다 = to really like something or absolutely trust (someone or something) (*syn.* 오금을 못 쓰다, 껌뻑 죽다, 자다가도 벌떡 일어난다) ▌A: 나 먼저 들어갈게. 일이 좀 있어서. = *I'll go ahead and head home first. I have some things to take care of.* B: 자네가 어쩐 일이야? 술이라면 **사족을 못 쓰는** 사람이. = *You? What do you have to do? A man who never turned down a drink in his life ...*

사죽을 못 쓰다 IDIOM '사족을 못 쓰다'의 잘못된 말 = a mistaken form of 사족을 못 쓰다

사촌이 땅을 사면 배가 아프다 [Lit. to feel sick to your stomach if your cousin buys land] PROVERB 남이 잘되는 것을 질투할 때 쓰는 말 = describes feeling envious of another's success (*cf.* 배(가) 아프다) ▌A: 참, 옆집의 종원이가 명문대에 합격했다지? 정말 대단하네. = *They're saying Jongwon from next-door got into a famous university. He really is amazing.* B: 알고 보면 지방 캠퍼스야. 대단할 것 없어. = *He just got into a regional campus. There's nothing amazing about it.* A: **사촌이 땅을 사면 배가 아프다더니**, 왜 말을 그렇게 해? = *You're just saying that* *because you're jealous. Why are you being that way?*

사후 약방문 [Lit. a prescription after someone has died] PROVERB 때가 지난 뒤에 어리석게 애를 씀 = to show concern after it is already too late (*equiv.* to have missed the boat / after death comes a doctor / to be a day late and a dollar short *syn.* 소 잃고 외양간 고치기) ▌A: 어떻게 비가 좀 왔다고 도시 전체가 마비가 될 수 있지? = *How could a little rain paralyze the whole city like this?* B: 또 정부는 뒤늦게 홍수 대비한다고 **사후 약방 문**을 하겠군. = *And now the city is going to, in their usual way, stress the importance of flood preparedness.*

사흘이 멀다 하고 IDIOM = 하루가 멀다 하고

***산 넘어 산이다** [Lit. another mountain beyond this mountain] IDIOM 갈수록 더욱 어려운 상황에 처함 = for one's lot to grow even more difficult with the passage of time (*equiv.* It's one thing bad after another. *syn.* 갈수록 태산) ▌A: 부모님께 결혼 허락은 받았어요? = *Did your parents approve of your marriage?* B: 어. 그런데 **산 넘어 산이야**. 집 구하는 일이 만만치가 않아. = *Yeah, but it's just one hurdle after another. Finding a house has been no walk in the park.*

산 입에 거미줄 치랴 [Would a spider put up its web on a mouth that's alive?] PROVERB 아무리 살림이 어려워도 그럭저럭 살아가기 마련이 라는 말 = describes the tendency of people to get by some way or another no matter how hard their lives may be (*cf.* 입에 거미줄 치다) ▌A: 이제 곧 애도 나오는데, 주인이 전세금도 올려 달라네. 이거 참 걱정이 야. = *Pretty soon we're going to be parents and now, all of a sudden, our landlord is raising the rent. This is going to be a serious problem.* B: **산 입 에 거미줄 치겠어?** 너무 걱정 마. = *We always find a way to get by. Don't worry too much.*

NOTE: 사람들이 자주 드나들지 않는 곳에는 거미가 거미줄을 치기 마련이 다. 입에 거미줄이 생길 정도로 먹을 것이 오랫동안 입에 들어가지 않 은 상황, 즉 오랫동안 굶은 상황을 가리켜 '입에 거미줄 친다'라고 한

다. '산 입에 거미줄 치랴'는 그래도 사람이 살아있는데 설마 굶어 죽기야 하겠냐는 의미이다.
Spiders usually go with low-traffic spots when choosing where to erect their houses. When someone hasn't eaten for a long time, the phrase '입에 거미줄 친다' is often used. The phrase 산 입에 거미줄 치랴 means that if people are around, there's no way one will starve to death.

산전수전 [Lit. 山mountain + 戰fight + 水water + 戰fight → battles with mountains and water] CHINESE-DERIVATION 세상의 온갖 고생 = all sorts of hardships (*equiv.* every difficulty the world can throw at you) ▌A: 어제 방송 봤어? 방송 중에 마이크가 꺼졌는데도 그 진행자는 당황하지 않고 잘 넘기더라. = *Did you see the show yesterday? The mic cut off right in the middle of the show, but the announcer didn't panic and just kept on going.* B: 워낙 **산전수전** 다 겪은 베테랑이잖아. = *Yeah, he's a battle-tested veteran, that's why.*

NOTE: '산전수전을 겪다'라는 형태로 주로 쓰인다.
This phrase is almost always used in the form 산전수전을 겪다.

산통(을) 깨다 [Lit. to break the counting stick box] IDIOM 잘되어 가던 일을 망치다 = to suddenly bring failure to something had been going well (*syn.* 쪽박(을) 깨다 *cf.* 산통(이) 깨지다) ▌A: 야, 이제 그만하고 놀자. = *Hey, let's quit this and just hang out.* B: 조금만 더 하면 끝나. 산통 깨지 말고 가만 있어 봐. = *We're almost done. Don't ruin everything when we're so close. Just hold on a little longer.*

NOTE: 길이 10cm 가량의 나뭇가지에 숫자 따위를 적은 것을 산가지 혹은 산대라고 한다. 산통은 이 산대를 넣는 통을 말한다. 산통을 대여섯번 흔든 다음 산통 속의 산대를 무작위로 꺼내 거기에 새겨진 숫자에 따라서 치는 점을 산통점이라 한다. 산통이 깨지면 점쟁이가 점을 볼 수가 없다.
A twig of about 10 cm in length with numbers written on it is called a 산가지 or 산대. A 산통 is a receptacle for these kind of sticks. After shaking the

container around five or six times, pulling out the sticks randomly and writing down the numbers was one way of telling someone's fortune. If this container broke in the process, the fortuneteller wouldn't be able to provide his client with the valuable insights they had paid for.

산통(이) 깨지다 [Lit. for the counting stick box to break] IDIOM 잘되어 가던 일이 뒤틀리다 = for something that had been going well to suddenly end in failure (*cf.* 산통(을) 깨다) ▌A: 부장님은 왜 젊은 사람들 노는 데 눈치 없이 끼시는지 모르겠어. = *I don't know why our VP doesn't has the sense to stay away when us younger employees are trying to have a good time.* B: 분위기 좋았는데 부장님 오셔서 **산통 다 깨졌지** 뭐야. = *Things were going great until he showed up.*

NOTE: See the note on 산통(을) 깨다.

산해진미 [Lit. 山 mountain + 海 sea + 珍 treasure + 味 taste] CHINESE-DERIVATION 산과 바다에서 나는 귀하고 좋은 음식 = all the delicacies of the land and sea ▌A: 역시 호텔 뷔페라 다르구나. **산해진미**가 다 있네. = *Hotel buffets really are something else. They have everything a person could want.* B: 그러게요. 우리 저녁까지 이걸로 때우게 많이 먹고 갑시다. = *That's what I'm saying. Let's eat enough to last us till dinner.*

살얼음판을 걷다 [Lit. to walk on a sheet of ice] IDIOM 위태롭고 아슬아슬하다 = to be precarious or risky (*equiv.* to walk on thin ice) ▌A: 건강 검진 결과 나왔어? = *Did you get the results of your physical?* B: 아니. 하루하루가 **살얼음판을 걷는** 기분이야. = *Nope. I'm waiting on pins and needles.* A: 뭐 큰 병이야 있겠어? 너무 걱정 마. = *It's not like you've got any major problems. Don't worry too much.*

살을 깎다 IDIOM = 뼈를 깎다

살을 붙이다 [Lit. to attach flesh] IDIOM 어떤 이야기에 다른 내용을 더하다 = to add or enhance a dialogue to flesh out ▌A: 어때? 읽어 본 소

감이? = *How was it? What are your thoughts after reading it?* B: 재미는 있는데, 몇몇 장면은 **살을 더 붙이는** 게 좋을 것 같아. = *Well, it was entertaining but I think some of the scenes need to be fleshed out a little more.*

살을 섞다 IDIOM = 몸을 섞다

삼삼오오 [Lit. 三three + 三three + 五five + 五five → in threes and fives]
CHINESE-DERIVATION 몇몇 사람이 무리를 지어 다니는 모양 = the appearance of others moving about in small groups (*equiv.* in twos and threes) ▌A: 여고생들은 왜 늘 **삼삼오오** 떼를 지어 다니는 걸까? = *Why do high school girls always walk around in groups of twos and threes.* B: 원래 저맘때면 다들 그래. = *That's just how kids are at that age.*

삼십육계 [Lit. 三three + 十ten + 六six + 計scheme → the 36th scheme]
CHINESE-DERIVATION 형편이 불리하여 달아나는 게 최선인 상황에서 쓰는 말 = used to describe a situation so dire that one's best option is to run away (*equiv.* to cut and run / to hightail it out of somewhere *cf.* 걸음아 날 살려라) ▌A: 오늘은 전문가를 모시고 산에서 야생 짐승을 만났을 때의 대처법을 알아보겠습니다. 선생님. 산에서 멧돼지를 만나면 어떻게 해야 하나요? = *Today we've arranged for some experts to tell us what to do when we come across a wild animal on the mountain side. Please tell us, what's the best course of action if we come across a wild pig?* B: **삼십육계** 줄행랑이 최고입니다. = *The best thing to do is hightail it out of there.*

NOTE: 옛날 중국 고서 손자병법에 보면 36가지 전투 전략이 소개된다. 그 중 마지막 36번째 계략이 도망치는 것이라 했다. '삼십육계' 혹은 '삼십육계 줄행랑'이라는 말은 도망친다는 뜻이다.
In ancient Chinese texts, 36 battle strategies are outlined. The 36th method was to cut and run. That's why '삼십육계' and '삼십육계 줄행랑' means to save one's hide by hightailing it out of there.

삼척동자 [Lit. 三three + 尺unit of length + 童child + 子child → a child of

no more than three *cheok*] CHINESE-DERIVATION 철없는 어린아이 = a mere schoolboy (would know) (*equiv.* Every school child knows that!) ▌A: 어떻게 이런 문제를 틀릴 수가 있니? **삼척동자도** 이 문제는 풀 수 있겠다. = *How could you get this question wrong? An elementary-schooler could do this.* B: 실수야, 실수. 설마 내가 이걸 몰라서 틀렸겠니? = *It was a mistake—a mistake. Do you really think I wouldn't know how to do this?*

NOTE: 1척은 30cm 정도에 해당한다. 삼척동자는 키가 1m도 되지 않는 어린아이를 일컫는 말이다.

A 척 is a traditional measure that equals around 30 cm. A 삼척동자 is a child that is still less than a meter in height.

삼천포로 빠지다 [Lit. to head off towards Samcheonpo] IDIOM 일이나 이야기가 엉뚱한 방향으로 진행되다 = for work or a conversation to move in a strange or surprising direction (*equiv.* to get off track / to go off on tangents) ▌A: 교장 선생님이 훈화 말씀 중에 갑자기 나라 경제에 관한 말씀을 왜 하시죠? = *Why did the principle suddenly start talking about the economy during the middle of his directions?* B: 그러게요. 교장 선생님은 다 좋은데, 가끔 **삼천포로 빠지시는** 게 탈이에요. = *Yeah. I like almost everything about the man, but he does have a tendency to go off on tangents.*

NOTE: 삼천포는 경상남도의 한 지명이다. 지리적으로 다른 지역에 비해 고립되어 있어 다른 곳으로 가려다가 실수로 이곳 삼천포로 오는 경우가 많았다고 한다.

삼천포 is a place in South Gyeongsang Province. The place is rather isolated, and it is said that many a traveler of yore ended up there by accident.

삽질(을)하다 [Lit. to shovel] IDIOM 쓸데없는 짓으로 시간 낭비를 하다 = to waste time with meaningless labor (*equiv.* to do busywork) ▌A: 알고 보면 이렇게 간단한데, 이걸 몰라 여태까지 **삽질을 했네**. = *I can see now just how simple this is. I've wasted so much time doing this the wrong way.* B: 그래도 결국 알아냈구나. 대단한데! = *Well, you finally figured*

it out. I'm impressed!

NOTE: 삽으로 무엇인가를 푸는 것은 가장 원초적인 노동력으로 일을 하는 것이다. 포클레인과 같이 일을 더 빨리 더 쉽게 할 수 있는 수단이 있는 데도 미련하게 가장 힘든 방법을 택하여 비효율적으로 일을 할 때 이 표현을 쓴다.

Shoveling is one of the most basic, raw kinds of labor there is. When the same job can be carried out much more quickly and easily with a backhoe, it doesn't make sense to waste a whole day shoveling by hand. Choosing an inefficient means to achieve a certain aim is often described with this phrase.

상다리가 부러지다
[Lit. for the table legs to break] IDIOM 상에 음식을 매우 많이 차려 놓다 = to put a great amount of food on the table (*equiv.* The table legs bent under the weight of the food. / What a spread! *syn.* 상다리가 휘어지다, 떡 벌어지게 차리다) ▌A: 차린 건 없지만 많이 드세요. = *It's not much of a spread, but have your fill.* B: 차린 게 없다니요? 상다리가 부러지겠는걸요. = *Not much of a spread? The table is bending under the weight of it all.*

상다리가 휘어지다
IDIOM = 상다리가 부러지다

상부상조(하다)
[Lit. 相mutual + 扶help + 相mutual + 助help] CHINESE-DERIVATION 서로 돕다 = for two parties to help each other (*equiv.* I'll scratch your back, you scratch mine.) ▌A: 도와줘서 정말 고맙다. = *Thanks so much for helping out.* B: 뭘. 저번에는 네가 나 도와줬잖아. 친구끼리 상부상조하는 거지. = *Well, you helped me a lot that time too. Being friends means being there for each other.*

*새 발의 피
[Lit. blood in a bird's foot] PROVERB 아주 적은 분량 = a very small amount ▌A: 너도 어제 축구 경기에 내기 걸었어? 나는 2만 원이나 잃었어. = *Did you bet on the soccer match yesterday too? I lost 20,000 won on it.* B: 겨우 그거 가지고? 그 정도는 내가 잃은 돈에 비하면 새 발의 피야. = *That's all? That's but a fraction of what I lost on that game.*

NOTE: 이 표현에서의 새는 참새와 같이 작은 새를 가리킨다. 참새의 작은 발에서 피가 나 봤자 그 양이 많지 않다는 데서 나온 말이다.
The bird referred to in this expression is likely a small one. The amount of blood found the feet of a small finch would likely be a minuscule amount.

새옹지마 [Lit. 塞 frontier + 翁 old man + 之 of + 馬 horse → the horse of an old man in the frontier] CHINESE-DERIVATION 인생의 행복이나 불행은 예측할 수 없다는 말 = describes how one can never tell what is a blessing or a curse (*equiv.* a blessing in disguise / God works in mysterious ways.) ▌A: 정말 인생사 **새옹지마**라는 말이 맞나 봐. = *You sure never know what is going to be a blessing or a curse.* B: 무슨 일이 있었는데? = *Why? What happened?* A: 어제 뉴스 보니까 복권에 당첨된 사람이 돈을 흥청망청 쓰다가 거리로 나앉았대요. = *There was a guy on the news yesterday who won the lottery but then frittered all his money away till he was out on the streets.*

NOTE: 어느 경계 지역에 노인이 살고 있었다. 어느 날 그가 기르는 말이 도망쳐 적군이 있는 지역으로 가 버렸다. 사람들이 위로했지만 노인은 조금도 슬퍼하지 않았다. 몇 달 후 도망 갔던 말이 적군의 좋은 말과 함께 돌아왔다. 사람들은 축하했지만 노인은 기뻐하지 않았다. 좋은 말이 생기자 노인의 아들이 그 말을 타고 달리다 말에서 떨어져 다리가 부러졌다. 마을 사람들이 위로하자 노인은 다시 "이것이 오히려 복이 될 수도 있다"며 태연했다. 얼마 안 있어 적군이 쳐들어왔고, 마을의 젊은이들은 모두 징집되어 거의가 전쟁터에서 죽었다. 그러나 노인의 아들은 다리 부상 때문에 끌려가지 않아 무사할 수 있었다.
Once upon a time, there was an old man living in the border regions of his country. A horse that he had been raising escaped and fled to where the enemy troops were stationed. People offered the old man words of solace concerning his plight, but he appeared not to be sad at all. A few months later, the escaped horse returned, and it brought a friend with it: a prized horse that belonged to the enemy troops. The whole town was in a tizzy about his felicitous turn of fate, but the man was stoic. One day the man's son was riding the new horse when he fell to the ground and broke his leg. Again, the townspeople gather ed to offer him solace and again the man was

placid, saying "This may too turn out to be a good thing." Not long after, the enemy forces attacked and all of the town's able-bodied men were conscripted to repel the onslaught. Almost all of the town's young men died on the battlefield, save for the man's son, who was safe at home.

색안경(을) 끼다 IDIOM = 색안경(을) 쓰다

색안경(을) 쓰다 [Lit. to wear tinted glasses] IDIOM 선입관을 가지고 좋지 않은 감정으로 보다 = to have a bias against something or someone (*equiv.* look on something or someone from a biased viewpoint / to see the world through the lens of bias / to have a skewed vision (of things) *syn.* 색안경(을) 끼다) ▌A: 나는 정치인들이 싫어. 다 거짓말쟁이 같아. = *I hate politicians. They all seem like liars.* B: 왜 그 사람들을 **색안경을 쓰고 보니?** = *Why are you so prejudiced against them?*

> NOTE: 선글래스를 끼고 사물을 보면 밝은 색의 물건도 어둡게 보인다. 다른 사람이나 현상에 편견을 갖고 있다는 뜻이다.
> English also has metaphors about tinted glasses, but the meaning here is a little different. This phrase is similar to "a skewed look." And has a negative connotation. After all, even a bright, shinny object is dim when viewed through sunglasses.

생각이 짧다 [Lit. to have short thoughts] IDIOM 생각의 깊이가 얕다 = to have no depth to one's thoughts (*equiv.* to be shortsighted / to not think something through) ▌A: 아무리 철이 없어도 그렇지 어떻게 그런 말을 할 수가 있니? = *You may still not be all grown up, even so, how could you say those things?* B: 죄송합니다. 제가 **생각이 짧았어요**. = *I'm so sorry. I didn't think it through.*

생사람(을) 잡다 [Lit. to catch an innocent] IDIOM 아무 관계 없는 사람에게 죄를 씌우다 = to blame an innocent person (*cf.* 사람(을) 잡다) ▌A: 악! 이것 봐요, 왜 이러세요? = *Ah! Hey, what do you think you're doing?* B: 뭘 말이에요? = *What are you talking about?* A: 방금 제 다리 몰래

만졌잖아요. = *You just tried to touch my leg.* B: 아니, 이 아가씨가 **생 사람 잡네. 나는 그런 적 없어요.** = *You've got the wrong guy. I've done no such thing.*

NOTE: 접두사 '생(生)-'은 억지스럽다는 뜻을 가지고 있다. 생사람, 생트 집, 생고생, 생이별 등이 그렇다.
The prefix 생(生) often means abstinence or coercion. 생사람, 생트집, 생 고생, 생이별 are examples of this.

샴페인을 너무 일찍 터뜨리다 [Lit. to break open the champagne too soon] IDIOM 성급하게 성공을 확신하고 긴장을 풀다 = to let celebrate victory and let down one's guard too soon (*equiv.* to count one's chickens before they've hatched / to break open the champagne too soon) ▎A: 지금 경제 위기를 슬기롭게 이겨야 하는데. = *We have to seek a smart way of beating this economic crisis.* B: 10년 전 외환 위기 때는 **샴페인을 너 무 일찍 터뜨렸다는** 지적을 받았는데 이번에는 그런 실수를 하지 말아야죠. = *Ten years ago we were criticized for celebrating victory too soon after the financial crisis and that's something we must avoid this time around.*

서당개 삼 년이면 풍월을 읊는다 [Lit. The schoolhouse dog recites the primer after three years.] PROVERB 어떤 분야에 대해 아는 것이 없어 도 그 부문에 오래 있으면 약간의 지식은 생기게 마련이라는 말 = Even if one lacks special intelligence in a field, working in that area for a long time will ensure the acquisition of at least some knowledge (*equiv.* A saint's maid quotes Latin. / to learn by osmosis) ▎A: 아버지, 이 차 엔진 소리 가 이상한데요. = *Dad, the engine is sounding a little weird.* B: 그렇구나. 우리 아들, 대단한데? 어떻게 알았니? = *You're right. Not too shabby. How did you know?* A: 제가 아버지 일을 도운 지가 벌써 몇 년인데 요. **서당개 삼 년이면 풍월을 읊는다잖아요.** = *It's been a long time since I started helping you out in the shop. I guess I picked up a few things by osmosis.*

서슬이 시퍼렇다 [Lit. for a blade to be deep blue (sharp)] IDIOM 기세가 날

카롭고 대단하다 = for someone's spirit to be keen and great ▌A: 야, 빨리 도망가. 엄마가 **서슬이 시퍼레서** 널 찾고 있어. = *Hey, you'd better run. Mom's got fire in her eyes to catch you.* B: 정말? 성적표 나왔나 보네. 난 죽었다. = *Really? It looks like my report card came. I'm a dead man.*

NOTE: See the note on 두 눈(을) 시퍼렇게 뜨고 있다.

서울 가서 김 서방 찾는다 [Lit. to head for Seoul and look for Mr. Kim]

PROVERB 구체적인 정보 없이 사람을 찾는 경우에 쓰는 말 = to look for a person without enough specific information(*equiv.* to look for a needle in a haystack) ▌A: 야, 이름도 모르고 주소도 모르는데 사진 한 장만으로 어떻게 사람을 찾니? 이거야말로 **서울 가서 김 서방 찾기지.** = *Hey, how are we supposed to find someone with no name or address and just one picture to go on? It's like trying to find a certain Mr. Kim who lives in Seoul.* B: 인터넷에 올리면 어떨까? = *How about we post it on the Internet?*

NOTE: 서울은 한국의 수도로 한국에서 가장 큰 도시이며, 김 씨는 한국에서 가장 흔한 성이다.
As the capital of South Korea, Seoul is the largest and most populous region, and the last name Kim, is the most common surname.

서투른 목수가 연장 탓한다 [Lit. The novice carpenter blames the tools.]

PROVERB 실력이 없는 사람이 제 실력이 부족한 것을 인정하지 않고 도구 탓만 할 때 쓰는 말 = used to describe a novice who blames the equipment for their failures and fails to acknowledge their own lack of skills. (*syn.* 선무당이 장구 탓한다) ▌A: 오늘따라 왜 이렇게 못 쳐? = *Why are you playing so badly today?* B: 큐가 내가 늘 쓰던 게 아니라서 그런가 봐. = *I guess it's because this isn't the cue I normally use.* A: **서투른 목수가 연장 탓하는** 법이야. 왜 큐 탓을 하냐? = *It's the novice carpenter who blames his tools. Why is it the cue's fault?*

선견지명 [Lit. 先first + 見see + 之of + 明bright] CHINESE-DERIVATION 앞으로

일어날 일을 내다보는 지혜 = knowledge or insight into what will occur in the future (*equiv.* foresight) ▌A: 어떻게 주가가 폭락하기 직전에 주식을 팔았어? **선견지명**이 있었던 거야?=*How did you manage to sell your stock right before the price crashed? Do you have foresight or something?* B: 그냥 소 뒷걸음질치다 쥐 잡은 거지 뭐.=*No, I just saw what everyone else was doing and stumbled upon a windfall.*

선남선녀 [Lit. 善good + 男man + 善good + 女woman → good men and women] CHINESE-DERIVATION 외모가 준수한 젊은 남자와 여자=a good-looking younger man and woman ▌A: 이 **선남선녀**들은 누구야? 자네 아들딸인가?=*And who is this attractive young duo? Is that your son and daughter?* B: 아니, 아들하고 며느리야. 애들아, 아빠 친구다. 인사 드려라.=*No, that would be my son and my daughter-in-law. Kids, this here is one of my friends. Say hi.*

선무당이 사람 잡는다 [Lit. A novice shaman catches people.] PROVERB 능력이 부족한 사람이 나서다가 오히려 일을 그르친다는 말=describes how the efforts of an incompetent person may make matters worse (*cf.* 사람(을) 잡다) ▌A: 왜 그래? 체했어?=*What's with you? Are you sick to your stomach?* B: 응. 아까 저녁 먹은 게 소화가 안 되네.=*Yeah, I've been having a little indigestion since dinner.* A: 이리 와. 내가 따 줄게.=*Come over here, I'll prick your finger (a folk remedy).* B: 됐어. **선무당이 사람 잡을라**. 그냥 소화제 먹을래.=*That's all right. Care from a quack doctor like you might actually make it worse. I'll just take something for my indigestion.*

선무당이 장구 탓한다 PROVERB=서투른 목수가 연장 탓한다

선(을) 긋다 [Lit. to draw a line] IDIOM 한계를 정하거나 구분을 명확히 하다=to set a clear boundary or distinction (*equiv.* to draw the line *syn.* 금(을) 긋다) ▌A: 너는 정호랑 사귀는 거야, 안 사귀는 거야?=*Are you going out with Jeongho or aren't you?* B: 말했잖아. 정호하고 나는 그냥 친구 사이라고.=*I already told you. We're just friends.* A: 애, 그럼 네가 **선을 분명히 그어야지**. 어정쩡하게 그게 뭐니?=*Oh really? Then you need to be a little more clear about drawing the line. You can't just* *keep on being noncommittal like that.*

선을 넘다 [Lit. to cross a line] IDIOM 한도나 경계를 넘다 = to exceed a limit or boundary (*equiv.* to cross the line *ant.* 선을 지키다) ▎A: 누나, 제발 시집 좀 가. 누나 때문에 밤에 잠이 안 와. = *You've really got to get married, Sis. I'm losing sleep over this.* B: 동생아, 걱정해 주는 건 고맙지만 **선을 넘지는** 마라. 넌 내 동생이야. = *I appreciate the concern, but don't cross the line. You are my little brother after all.*

선을 지키다 [Lit. to keep the line] IDIOM 정도를 지나치지 않게 하다 = to not exceed proper limits (*ant.* 선을 넘다) ▎A: 직장 생활을 하다 보면 **선을 지키는** 게 참 쉽지 않은 것 같아요. = *Sometimes it's hard not to cross the line at work.* B: 맞아요. 적당한 거리를 유지하는 게 참 어렵죠. = *That's right. It's hard to always keep the proper amount of distance.*

설마가 사람 잡는다 [Lit. "There's no way" can come back to get you.] PROVERB 그럴 리가 없을 것이라는 안일한 생각이 큰 문제를 일으킨다는 말 = Believing that something will never happen can cause major problems. ▎A: 뒷문도 잠갔어? = *Did you lock the back door too?* B: 아니. 뭐 고작 하루 집을 비울 건데 별일 있겠어? = *No. We're just leaving the house empty for one day. What could go wrong?* A: **설마가 사람 잡는다는** 말 몰라? = *It's that lax attitude that's going to come back and get you.*

***설상가상** [Lit. 雪snow + 上over + 加add + 霜frost → adding frost to the snow] CHINESE-DERIVATION 어렵거나 불행한 일이 겹쳐 일어남 = a confluence of two undesirable events (*equiv.* to make matters worse *syn.* 엎친 데 덮친 격) ▎A: 어머님이 교통사고로 병원에 입원하셨다면서요? 걱정이 많으시겠어요. = *I heard your mom has been in the hospital since her car accident.* B: 네. **설상가상**으로 아내도 몸이 많이 안 좋아서 큰일이에요. = *Yes. And on top of that, my wife has been really weak lately too. It's a real mess.*

섬섬옥수 [Lit. 纖fine + 纖fine + 玉jade + 手hand → slender hands that are as beautiful as jade] CHINESE-DERIVATION 여성의 아름다운 손＝beautiful hands of a woman ▌A: 왜 이래요? 갑자기 사람 손은 잡고 그래요?＝*Why are you suddenly grabbing my hand like that?* B: 당신 손이 언제 이렇게 됐죠? 젊었을 때의 그 **섬섬옥수**가 나랑 살면서 이렇게 거칠어져 버렸네.＝*When did your hands get this way? Your dainty, smooth hands have grown rough during our life together.*

성을 갈다 [Lit. to change one's last name] IDIOM 맹세하거나 장담할 때 쓰는 말＝used when taking an oath or vow (*syn.* 손가락에 장(을) 지지다, 손에 장(을) 지지다) ▌A: 네가 이번 시험에서 반에서 10등 안에 들겠다고? 정말 그러면 내가 **성을 갈겠다**.＝*You're saying you're going to make it into the top ten on this test? If you do that, I'll change my last name.* B: 내가 너 **성 가는** 걸 보기 위해서라도 꼭 10등 안에 들 거야.＝*I'll do it just so I can see you change your last name.*

NOTE: 이름은 개명 신청을 통해 바꿀 수도 있지만, 성은 부모에게 물려 받는 것으로 개인이 마음대로 바꿀 수 없다. 상대의 어림없는 말이나 행동을 보고 성을 갈겠다고 큰소리치는 것은 그만큼 그것이 이루어지지 않을 것임을 확신한다는 말이다.

Such feelings have diminished recently, but Koreans traditionally took great pride in their lineage. As one's surname was an example of this lineage, it was synonymous with one's identity. To vow to change such an important aspect of one's was a serious promise indeed. First names can be changed through a report with related offices, but last names cannot be changed as one likes. If one vows to change their last name when someone else makes an absurd assurance that they will do something or something will happen, that suggests they are confident that such a thing will never happen.

세 살 (적) 버릇 여든 간다 [Lit. The habits (one has) at three go till eighty.] PROVERB 어릴 때 들인 버릇은 고치지가 어렵다는 말＝used to point out how difficult it is to fix bad habits ▌A: 저 녀석 자기 마음에 안 들면 물건 집어던지는 버릇을 이번 기회에 꼭 고쳐야겠어.＝*I hope this can be an opportunity for him to fix his habit of knocking things down whenever he gets upset.* B: 아직 어리니까 그렇겠죠.＝*That's just*

because he's still so young. A: 세 살 버릇 여든 간다는 말 몰라? = *Don't you know, the habits he forms now will stick with him for life.*

세상만사 [Lit. 世 world + 上 over + 萬 ten thousand + 事 work] CHINESE-DERIVATION 세상에서 일어나는 온갖 일 = all the things going on in the world(*equiv.* everything under the sun) ▌A: 야, 왜 하루 종일 방에 처박혀 ▶p.287 있어? 바람 쐬러 나가자. = *Hey, why did you stay cooped up in your room all day long? Let's go out and get some fresh air.* B: 됐어. 난 그냥 집에 있을래. 지금은 **세상만사**가 다 귀찮아. = *That's all right. I'd rather just hang out here at home. Everything's getting on my nerves right now.*

세상없어도 [Lit. even if there is no (longer a) world] IDIOM 무슨 일이 있어도 = no matter what happens (*equiv.* even if the world ends tomorrow *syn.* 하늘이 두 쪽(이) 나도, 죽었다 깨어나도) ▌A: 민정이 시집 언제 보낼 거야? = *When are you going to marry off Minjeong?* B: 올해 안으로는 **세상없어도** 보낼 생각이야. = *I plan to get her married this year even if it kills me.*

세상(을) 등지다 [Lit. to turn one's back on the world] IDIOM **1.** 사람이 없는 깊은 산속 같은 곳에 들어가 사회와 교류하지 않고 살다 = to go deep into the mountains or some other unpopulated place and cease interaction with society. (*equiv.* to live as a hermit *syn.* 세상(을) 버리다) ▌A: 텔레비전을 보면 의외로 산속에서 혼자 사는 사람이 많은 것 같아요. = *Judging from what I've seen on TV, there are a lot of people who live in the mountains by themselves.* B: 사는 게 각박하니까 **세상을 등진** 사람이 많은 거겠지. = *I'm sure there are a lot of people who have turned their backs on this heartless world.* **2.** 사람이 죽다 = to die (*syn.* 세상(을) 버리다) ▌A: 실은 몇 해 전에 **세상을 등지려고** 한 적이 있었습니다. = *Honestly, a few years ago, there was a time when I just wanted to end it all.* B: 저런, 무슨 일이 있었나요? = *That's terrible. What happened?* A: 회사에서 잘리고 우울증이 왔었거든요. = *I had just gotten fired at work,* ▶p.252 *and I had fallen into a deep depression.*

NOTE: See the note on 세상(을) 뜨다.

*세상(을) 떠나다 IDIOM = 세상(을) 뜨다

세상(을) 뜨다 [Lit. to depart this world] IDIOM '죽다'를 완곡하게 이르는 말 = a euphemism for "to die" (*syn.* 세상(을) 떠나다) ▎A: 할아버지는 살아 계세요? = *Is your grandfather still alive?* B: 작년 봄에 **세상을 뜨셨어요**. = *He passed on in the spring of last year.*

NOTE: 다른 대부분의 사회와 마찬가지로 한국에서도 죽음을 직접적으로 언급하는 것은 금기시된다. 그래서 한국어에는 죽음을 에둘러 표현하는 다양한 말들이 있다. • 죽다: 가장 기본적인 말. 사람과 동식물에 두루 쓸 수 있다. 이하는 사람에게만 쓰는 표현들이다. • 눈(을)감다, 세상(을) 뜨다, 숨을 거두다, 유명을 달리하다, 요단 강(을) 건너다, 한줌(의) 흙이 되다: 완곡한 표현. • 사망하다: 공식적, 법률적인 말. • 돌아가(시)다, 운명하다, 작고하다, 별세하다, 타계하다: 높여서 이르는 말. • 서거하다: 왕, 대통령, 애국지사 등 사회적, 정치적으로 지위가 매우 높은 사람이 죽었을 때 쓴다. • 골로 가다: 비속하게 이르는 말. • 세상(을) 등지다: 한을 품은 채 세상을 떠났다는 뉘앙스가 있다.

In almost every culture, the discussion of death is a taboo. In Korean as well, there are many euphemisms for death. • 죽다 is of course the most basic expression and is used for people, plants and animals. The following expressions are only used for people. • 눈(을)감다, 세상(을) 뜨다, 숨을 거두다, 유명을 달리하다, 요단 강(을) 건너다, and 한줌(의) 흙이 되다 are euphemisms. • 사망하다 is a formal, legal term for dying. • 돌아가(시)다, 운명하다, 작고하다, 별세하다, and 타계하다 are all examples of honorific ways of expressing death. • 서거하다 is the term used for the death of a king, president, patriot or someone else whose status in society was very exalted. • 골로 가다 is a slang, vulgar expression for death. • 세상(을) 등지다 has the nuance of "departing this world with a grudge."

세상(을) 버리다 IDIOM = 세상(을) 등지다

세월아 네월아 [Lit. Years schmears.] IDIOM 태평스럽게 시간을 흘려보

내는 모습을 익살스럽게 표현한 말 = used to describe someone's lackadaisical approach to life in a humorous way (*equiv.* to watch the years go by) ▌A: 정수야, 벌써 방학도 열흘이나 지났는데 뭐라도 해야 되지 않니? 언제까지 그렇게 **세월아 네월아** 있을 거야? = *Jeongsu, it's already been ten days since school got out. Don't you think it's about time you did something? How much longer are you going to just laze through life.* B: 알았어요, 엄마. 내일부터 알바 자리 있나 알아볼게요. = *All right, mom. I'll look into getting a job tomorrow.*

NOTE: '세월'의 '세'는 '해'를 뜻하는 한자 '歲'를 의미한다. 하지만 이 표현에서는 '세'를 숫자 3을 뜻하는 관형사 '세'처럼 받아들여 4를 뜻하는 '네'를 덧붙인 '네월아'라는 말을 만들어 낸 것이다. 언어유희에 해당한다.

Expressions like 세월아 네월아 fall into the category of wordplay. Taking the first syllable of 세월 to mean "three," adding the prefix 네, which also means "four," makes for a humorous sequence used to describe a less than proactive approach to life.

세월 앞에 장사 없다 [Lit. There is no man whose strength is greater than that of time.] IDIOM 누구나 나이를 많이 먹으면 쇠약해지게 마련이라는 말 = describes how even those of great physical strength weaken and grow feeble with time ▌A: 아까 선생님 뵈니까 마음이 많이 아팠어. 그렇게 당당하던 분이 많이 쇠약해지셨더라그. = *It was sad to see the way our old teacher is looking nowadays. How could someone who was once so full of vitality grow so feeble?* B: **세월 앞에 장사 없는** 법이잖아. = *Truly even the mightiest of men grow weak with the passage of time.*

세월이 약이다 [Lit. Time is medicine.] PROVERB 가슴 아프고 슬픈 일도 시간이 흐르면 괴로움이 줄어든다는 말 = describes how even the deep pain and sadness is lessened with the passage of time (*equiv.* Time heals all. *syn.* 시간이 약이다) ▌A: 그렇게 아픈 상처가 있으셨군요. 어떻게 그 고통을 견뎌 내셨어요? = *You must've been so scarred emotionally. How did you get over it?* B: **세월이 약이더군요.** 시간이 지나면서 조금씩 고통이 줄어들더라고요. = *Time really does heal all. As time has* *passed, the pain has lessened, bit by bit.*

*소 귀에 경 읽기 [Lit. reading texts into a cow's ear] PROVERB 아무리 말

해 주어도 이해하지 못하거나 귀담아듣지 않을 때 하는 말 = used when no matter what one says, it has no effect on the listener (*equiv.* to sing psalms to a dead horse / for one's words to fall on deaf ears / an exercise in futility *syn.* 우이독경, 마이동풍) ▌A: 보라야, 일찍 일찍 들어오라고 엄마가 몇 번이나 말하니? 이건 **소 귀에 경 읽기**니 원. = *Bora, how many times have I told you? You need to come home earlier. It's an exercise in futility.* B: 알았어요, 엄마. 내일부터 일찍 들어올게요. = *OK, Mom. I'll come home earlier starting tomorrow.*

소금(을) 뿌리다 [Lit. to sprinkle salt] IDIOM 잘되어 가는 일을 망치

다 = to ruin an endeavor that had been going smoothly (*syn.* 고춧가루(를) 뿌리다, 재(를) 뿌리다, 초(를) 치다, 찬물(을) 끼얹다) ▌A: 애들 아, 오늘 자율학습 땡땡이치고 영화 보러 갈까? = *Hey. Wanna ditch study hall today and go see a movie?* B: 야, 내일 쪽지 시험 있는 거 몰라? = *Did you forget we have a quiz tomorrow?* A: 애는 꼭 분위기 좋을 때 **소금을 뿌린다니까**. = *This guy always spoils the fun just when things are going great.*

소 닭 보듯 하다 [Lit. like a cow looks at a chicken] PROVERB 상대방을

무관심하게 대하다 = to have absolutely no interest in one's counterpart ▌A: 신혼 생활이 깨가 쏟아지지? = *The honeymoon stage is really great, huh?* B: 그 정도는 아니어도 행복하게 잘살고 있습니다. = *Well, it's not really all that, but we are getting along just fine.* A: 나도 자네 때는 그랬어. 그런데 결혼한 지 20년이 넘어가니 이제 서로를 **소 닭 보듯 한다네**. = *That's how I was when I was your age too. But now, after 20 years of marriage, we don't really concern ourselves much with each other.*

NOTE: 닭은 소의 주변을 어슬렁거리면서 땅에 있는 벌레나 소의 몸에 붙어 있는 벌레를 잡아 먹는다. 소로서는 닭이 자기 몸에 붙은 성가신 벌레를 먹어 주기 때문에 쫓아 버리거나 위협하지 않는다. 그렇다고 서로 친할 것도 없으니 그야말로 소와 닭은 무심한 관계다.
Chickens that live nearby cattle often feed on insects on the ground or insects that live on the cows themselves. Cows must be thankful for the assistance provided in getting rid of the insects in all the hard-to-reach places. That's why cows never attempt to shoo away the chickens. Despite their close proximity, these two animals both seem to go about their lives without paying much attention to each other. Thus, this expression is used to describe a relationship that doesn't involve meddling in each other's affairs.

소도 언덕이 있어야 비빈다 [Lit. Even cows need a hill to rub (themselves against)] PROVERB 누구나 의지할 곳이 있어야 어떤 일을 시작할 수 있다 = Everyone needs someone to depend on when they embark on a new endeavor. ▌A: 이번에 통장으로 새로 뽑힌 김영민이라고 합니다. = *Hello, my name is Kim Yeongmin and I was chosen as neighborhood chief.* B: 아, 네, 축하드립니다. 잘 부탁합니다. = *Ah, yes. Congratulations. Take good care of us.* A: 많이들 도와주십시오. **소도 언덕이 있어야 비비는** 거 아니겠습니까? = *Please help me out. Everyone needs a helping hand sometimes.*

NOTE: 소가 자라면서 뿔이 나기 시작하면 뿔이 나는 부분이 간지럽게 된다. 이러한 증세는 뿔이 다 자라고 난 후에도 계속되어 습관적으로 언덕의 경사를 이용해 뿔이나 몸의 가려운 부분을 비비고는 한다.
When cattle first start sprouting horns, the spot on their heads where the horns will come in begins to itch. This continues even after the horns have grown in, so cattle often seek inclines or other outcroppings they can use to scratch themselves with.

소 뒷걸음질치다 쥐 잡기 [Lit. a cow walking backwards and catching a rat] PROVERB 우연히 성공을 거둠 = being met with a fortunate success ▌A: 어떻게 핸드폰이 화장대 밑에 있는 줄 알았어? = *How did you know my phone was under the vanity?* B: 내가 뭐 알고 그랬겠니? 그냥 **소 뒷걸음질치다 쥐 잡기**였어. = *What did I know? I just found it while I was looking for something else.*

소리 소문(도) 없이 [Lit. without either sound or rumor] IDIOM 슬그머니 = stealthily ▌A: 너는 **소리 소문 없이** 어디 갔다가 지금 오는 거니? = *Where did you slip off to?* B: 화장실 갔었어요. 그런 것도 보고해야 하나요? = *I went to the bathroom. Do I have to report that to you too?*

소매를 걷고 나서다 [Lit. to roll up one's sleeves and step forward] IDIOM 적극적인 태도를 취하다 = to assume an proactive stance (*equiv.* to roll up one's sleeves *syn.* 발 벗고 나서다, 팔을 걷어붙이다, 소매를 걷고 나서다) ▌A: 영자 너도 얼른 **소매 걷고 나서**. = *Yeongja, roll up your sleeves and get to work.* B: 나는 싫어, 애. 나는 얼굴 타는 거 질색이란 말이야. = *No way. I hate getting a tan on my face.*

소문난 잔치에 먹을 것 없다 [Lit. There is nothing to eat at the party we've heard so much about.] PROVERB 소문은 떠들썩한데 실제는 그에 못 미칠 때 쓰는 말 = used to describe a situation where the rumors were big but in actuality the event was small (*equiv.* all hype and no substance / much ado about nothing / big boast, small roast) ▌A: 에이, 일주일 전부터 잔뜩 기대했는데, 너무 게임이 싱거운데? = *Man, I was full of anticipation about this since last week. Why's this game such a letdown?* B: 그러니까 **소문난 잔치에 먹을 것 없다**잖아. = *Guess that's why you have to be wary of too much hype.*

소설(을) 쓰다 [Lit. to write a novel] IDIOM 지어내어 말하다 = to make something up (*equiv.* to tell stories / to spin a tale) ▌A: 이 기사 좀 봐 봐. 사실을 완전히 왜곡해 놓았어. = *Take a look at this article. It's a complete fabrication.* B: 그 신문 원래 **소설 잘 쓰기로** 유명하잖아. = *That newspaper is famous for telling tall tales.*

소 잃고 외양간 고치기 [Lit. fixing one's barn after losing the cattle] PROVERB 일이 틀어진 후에 뒤늦게 대책을 세움 = taking action when it's too late (*syn.* 사후 약방문) ▌A: 이 사이트 진짜 웃기네. 해킹 당해서 고객 정보가 다 유출되고 나니까, 보안을 강화하겠대. = *The people who run this site really make me laugh. Now that they've been hacked and their customer information has been leaked, they are talking abut beefing up* *security.* B: 소 잃고 외양간 고치는 격이네. = *That's what they call shutting the stable door after the horse has bolted.*

속(도) 모르다 [Lit. to not know the insides cf others] IDIOM 다른 사람의 마음을 알지 못하다 = to not know the thoughts of others (*equiv.* to not know what someone else is going through) █ A: 우리 맛있는 거 먹으러 갈까? = *Let's go find something good to eat, shall we?* B: 주인이 전셋값 올려 달라 그래서 나는 걱정이 태산인데, 당신은 내 **속도 모르고** 그런 말이 나와? = *With my landlord demanding more money, I'm up to my neck with worries right now. Judging from the fact that you would say that, I can tell you have no idea what I'm dealing with right now.*

속 빈 강정 [Lit. a hollow rice cracker] PROVERB 겉은 그럴듯하지만 내용물은 보잘것없음 = something that appears passable but lacks substance in actuality (*equiv.* It's all looks and no substance. / It's a lemon.) █ A: 저 사람 말은 얼핏 들으면 그럴싸한데, 내용이 없어. = *When you hear him talk, it's so easy to believe what he says but there's really no substance to it.* B: 맞아. **속 빈 강정**이라니까. = *Yeah, that's right. He's got no depth.*

NOTE: 강정은 찹쌀가루 반죽을 말려 기름에 튀긴 전통 과자의 일종이다. 강정을 기름에 튀기면 부풀면서 겉이 그럴듯하게 풍성해 보이지만 실상 속은 텅 비어 있다.
A 강정 is a kind of traditional cracker that is made by drying dough and frying it in oil. When the treat is fried, it swells up, making it appear to be quite substantial. It is in fact, hollow inside.

속수무책 [Lit. 束bind + 手hand + 無no + 策plan → for one's hands to be bound and be left with no options] CHINESE-DERIVATION 어찌할 도리가 없음 = having no path forward (*equiv.* to have one's hands tied) █ A: 어제 집에 오다가 소매치기를 당했어. 오토바이 탄 놈들이 내 가방을 순간적으로 낚아채 달아났어. = *I was the victim of a pick pocket yesterday on my way home. Some kids on a motorcycle suddenly grabbed my bag and made off with it.* B: 그래서 그걸 보고만 있었어? = *So you just stood by and watched that happen?* A: 뭐 어떡하겠어? **속수무책**으로 당하기만 했지. =

What was I supposed to do? There was nothing I could do except be victimized.

속(을) 긁다 [Lit. to scratch someone's insides] IDIOM 기분을 상하게 만들다＝to hurt someone's feelings (*syn.* 속(을) 뒤집다) ▌A: 영희 엄마, 오늘따라 왜 이렇게 얼굴이 푸석해 보여?＝*Why does your face look so puffed up today?* B: 남의 **속 긁는** 소리 그만하고 관리비나 빨리 내. ＝*Why don't you just give me the management fee and stop saying hurtful things?*

속(을) 끓이다 [Lit. to boil one's insides] IDIOM 걱정이나 답답함으로 인해 마음을 졸이다＝to be in consternation because of worry or vexation (*equiv.* to be about to explode *syn.* 속(을)썩이다, 속(을) 태우다, 애(를)태우다, 가슴(을) 태우다 *cf.* 속(이) 끓다) ▌A: 정말 더러워서 회사 때려치우든가 해야지. ＝*My job is such a mess, I think I'm going to have to quit.* B: 야, 직장인이란 게 원래 그런 거야. 괜한 일로 **속 끓이지** 말고 기분 풀어. ＝*Hey, that's what working life is all about. Don't get yourself worked up over nothing. Just let it go.*

속(을) 뒤집다 [Lit. to turn over one's insides] IDIOM **1.** 남이 자신의 말을 믿지 못할 때 답답해하며 하는 말＝used when one is frustrated because others do not believe what one is trying to say ▌A: 그 말을 지금 나보고 믿으라는 거야?＝*You're telling me to believe that?* B: 우와, 정말이라니까! 내 **속을 뒤집어** 보여 줄 수도 없고!＝*What? I'm telling you, it's the truth! I can't just turn my insides out and show you.* **2.** 기분을 상하게 만들다＝to hurt someone else's feelings (*syn.* 속(을) 긁다 *cf.* 속(이) 뒤집히다) ➡p.220 ▌A: 은혜는 말 잘 듣지?＝*Eunhye listens to you, right?* B: 말도 마. 맨날 내 **속을 뒤집어**. ＝*Don't even bring that up. She is always hurting my feelings.*

속(을)썩이다 [Lit. to let someone's insides rot] IDIOM **1.** 마음을 몹시 상하게 만들다＝to deeply hurt the feelings of another ▌A: 도대체 우리 마누라 **속을 썩이는** 놈이 누구야?＝*Who on earth would make you feel this way?* B: 누구기는 누구야? 바로 당신이지. ＝*Who? You, of course.* **2.** 괴로워하다＝to be upset or bothered (*syn.* 속(을) 끓이다, 속(을) 태우다, 애(를)태우다, 가슴(을) 태우다) ➡p.310 ▌A: 벙어리 냉가슴 앓듯

혼자 **속썩이지** 말고 속 시원하게 털어놔 봐. ➡p.363 = *Don't just suffer in silence like that, let me know what's going on.* B: 사실 나 직장에서 잘렸 ➡p.252 어. = *Well, honestly I was fired from my job.*

속(을) 차리다 [Lit. to pull one's insides together] IDIOM 자기의 실속을 챙기다 = to gather up one's insides (*equiv.* to pull oneself together *cf.* 냉수 먹고 속 차려라) ▌A: 야, 거 되지도 않을 독권은 그만 사고 이제 **속 차려**. = *Hey, stop wasting money on lottery tickets that never pay off and pull yourself together.* B: 이게 제 유일한 낙이어요, 아빠. = *Dad, this is the only enjoyment I have in life.*

속(을) 태우다 [Lit. to burn one's insides] IDIOM 1. 걱정이 되어 마음을 졸이다 = to consternate in worry (*syn.* 속(을) 끓이다, 애(를)태우다, 가슴(을) 태우다 *cf.* 속(이) 타다) ▌A: 내가 어제 너 때문에 **속 태운** 거 생각하면 …… . 한 번만 더 그러면 정말 혼날 줄 알아. = *When I think about how upset I was yesterday because of you, I'm sure that I won't let you get away with this again.* B: 네, 알았어요. 잘못했어요. = *Yes, I understand. I made a mistake.* 2. 다른 사람을 걱정하게 만들다 = to worry another (*syn.* 속(을) 끓이다, 애(를)태우다 *cf.* 속(이) 타다) ▌A: 병헌 씨는 참 효자인 것 같아요. = *Byeongheon, you really seem like a good son.* B: 제가요? 제가 부모님 **속을 얼마나 태웠는데요**. = *Me? You have no idea how much consternation I've caused my parents.*

속(을) 풀다 [Lit. to relax one's insides] IDIOM 1. 불편한 속을 다스리다 = to alleviate one's abdominal symptoms ▌A: 어제 술이 과했나 봐. 우리 점심은 해장국으로 하는 게 어때요? = *I think I overdid it yesterday with the drinking. Do you want to have haejangguk for lunch?* B: 네, 좋아요. **속 푸는** 데는 해장국이 최고죠. = *For fixing up your insides, it is the best.* 2. 분하거나 답답한 마음을 해소하다 = to alleviate one's feeling of uneasiness or vexation ▌A: 마음속에 걱정을 쌓아 두지 마시고, 그때그때 **속을 푸세요**. = *Don't just store up your worries in your heart, let it out bit by bit.* B: 저도 그러고 싶은데 그게 잘 안 돼 요. = *That's what I'd like to do too, it's just not that easy.*

속(이) 깊다 [Lit. to have deep insides] IDIOM **1.** 생각이 깊고 이해심이 많다=to have deep thoughts and a broad scope of understanding ▌A: 효신이는 어쩌면 애가 이렇게 **속이 깊어요**?=*How could Hyoshin be so deep?* B: 사실 저도 가끔 쟤가 내 배 아파 낳은 내 자식이 맞나 싶어요.=*Sometimes I too wonder how I could give birth to such a child.* **2.** 마음속 깊은 곳에 있다=to reside deeply in one's mind or heart (*equiv.* deep (thoughts, conversation etc.)) ▌A: 경진 씨는 친구가 많아요?=*Gyeongjin, do you have a lot of friends?* B: 네. 하지만 **속 깊은** 얘기를 나눌 친구는 몇 명 안 돼요.=*Yes, but there's only a few that I can have deep talks with.*

NOTE: 2번 뜻으로 쓰일 때는 주로 '속 깊은 얘기', '속 깊은 대화'라는 말을 많이 쓴다.
When used in the second sense, this expression most commonly appears as 속 깊은 얘기 or 속 깊은 대화.

속(이) 끓다 [Lit. for one's heart to be boiling] IDIOM 마음속에서부터 화가 치밀어 오르다=for anger to suddenly rise up inside of one (*equiv.* for anger to swell up inside (of one's heart) *cf.* 속(을) 끓이다) ▌A: 남편도 잘 있지?=*Your husband is doing well too, isn't he?* B: 남편이 아니라 원수야, 원수. 그 인간 생각만 하면 지금도 **속이 끓어**.=*He's not my husband. He's my enemy, I tell you. Whenever I think of him the anger just swells up inside of me.*

속이 넓다 [Lit. to have a broad inside] IDIOM 이해심이 많고 너그럽다=to be understanding and magnanimous (*syn.* 마음이 넓다 *ant.* 속(이) 좁다, 마음이 좁다) ▌A: 어떤 남자를 원하세요?=*What kind of guy are you interested in?* B: 제가 좀 제멋대로인 성격이라서, **속이 넓은** 남자였으면 좋겠어요.=*I kind of live by my own rules, so it would be nice if he was very understanding.*

속(이) 뒤집히다 [Lit. to turn one's insides out] IDIOM **1.** 토가 나올 듯이 속이 메스껍다=to be nauseous to the point of vomiting ▌A: 밥 먹는데 꼭 화장실 얘기해야겠어요? **속이 뒤집히려고** 그러잖아요.=*Do you* *really have to carry on with that bathroom talk while we're eating? I feel like I'm going to throw up.* B: 무슨 남자가 그렇게 비위가 약해요? = *What kind of man has such a weak stomach?* **2.** 화가 나다 = to be angry ▌A: 명수야, 제발 장가 좀 가라. 내가 너만 보면 **속이 뒤집힌다**. = *Myeongsu, please hurry up and get married. Just looking at you makes me upset.* B: 이제 삼촌까지 그러세요? = *Now even you're saying that, uncle?*

속(이) 보이다 [Lit. for one's insides to be shown] IDIOM 엉큼한 마음이 들여다보이다 = for one's insidious heart to be exposed (*equiv.* to show what one is truly made of) ▌A: 예진 씨, 집까지 제 차로 모셔다 드릴게요. = *Yejin, allow me to drive you home.* B: 우와, 명호 씨, 예진 씨한테만 잘해 주기야? **속이 빤히 보인다고**. = *Wow, Myeongho, you're just going to be that nice to Yaejin? You are making your intentions too clear.*

***속(이)상하다** [Lit. for ones insides to go bad] IDIOM 괴롭거나 우울하다 = to be tormented or depressed ▌A: **속상해** 죽겠어. = *I'm having such a hard time, I feel like I could die.* B: 무슨 일 있어? = *What's wrong?* A: 수학에서 한 문제 틀렸어. = *I got one question wrong in mathematics.* B: 너 지금 자랑하는 거지? = *You're actually trying to brag right now, aren't you?*

***속(이)시원하다** [Lit. for one's insides to cool] IDIOM 좋은 일이 생기거나 걱정거리가 사라져 마음이 상쾌하다 = for one's heart to be refreshed because a worry has vanished or something positive has happened ▌A: 거 봐. 청소를 싹 하니 깨끗하고 얼마나 좋니? **속이 다 시원하다**. = *Look at that. Now that we've got everything sparkling clean, it's great, isn't it? I feel so refreshed inside.* B: 이제부터 자주 치울게요. = *From now on, I'll clean up more often.*

속(이) 쓰리다 [Lit. for one's insides to be sore] IDIOM 남이 잘되어 질투가 나다 = to be jealous of the successes of others (*syn.* 배(가) 아프다) ▌A: 소연이 엄마는 무슨 복이 많아서 의사 사위를 얻었대? 솔직히 **속이 좀 쓰린데**? = *A doctor for a son-in-law? What makes you so lucky? I'm*

honestly quite jealous. B: 복은 무슨. 의사 사위가 무슨 대수라고. =
Luck? What luck? What's the big deal about a doctor?

속(이)없다 [Lit. to have no insides] IDIOM **1.** 자존심이나 줏대가 없다 =
to have no pride or definite opinions (*equiv.* to have no spine) ▌A: 너는 **속**
도 없니? 그렇게 딱지를 맞고도 계속 쫓아다니게? = *Don't you have*
any spine? You get rejected like that and still keep chasing her around? B:
좋아하는데 자존심 세워서 뭐해? = *I like her. What's pride going to get*
me? **2.** 악의가 없다 = to have no bad intentions (*equiv.* to have no ill will)
▌A: 세호 씨가 말투는 좀 거칠어도 **속없이** 하는 소리니까 기분 나
빠하지 마세요. = *Seho's way of talking can be a little rough sometimes but*
he doesn't mean anything by it, so don't let it hurt you. B: 네. 저도 잘 알
아요. 괜찮아요. = *Yes, I know. It's okay*

속(이) 좁다 [Lit. to have small insides] IDIOM 이해심이 부족하고 너그럽
지 못하다 = to lack understanding or magnanimity (*syn.* 마음이 좁다 *ant.*
속이 넓다, 마음이 넓다 *cf.* 밴댕이 속) ▌A: **속 좁은** 아이처럼 유치
하게 왜 그래? = *Why are you acting as immature as a small-minded child?*
B: 유치하다고? 그럼 너는 이게 별일 아니라는 거니? = *I'm*
immature? You're saying you don't think this is a big deal?

속(이) 좋다 [Lit. to have good insides] IDIOM 성품이 너그럽거나 마음이
편안하다 = to have a magnanimous character or a calm heart ▌A: 내가 지
금 **속이 좋아서** 이러고 있는 줄 알아? = *Do you think I'm doing this*
because I have a good heart? B: 속 끓이면 뭐가 달라져? 그러지 말고
우리 나가자. = *Is being upset about it going to change anything? Come on,*
let's just go out.

속(이) 타다 [Lit. for one's insides to burn] IDIOM 걱정이나 답답함으로
인해 마음이 괴롭다 = to be anguished by worry or uneasiness (*syn.* 가슴
이 타다, 애(가)타다 *cf.* 속(을)태우다) ▌A: 왜 안 자고 깨어 있
어? = *Why are you still up?* B: 벌써 열두 시가 다 돼 가는데, 은주한
테서 전화가 없어서 **속이 타.** = *It's after 12 and we still haven't heard*
from Eunju. I'm on pins and needles over here.

속(이) 터지다 [Lit. for one's insides to explode] IDIOM 화가 나거나 답답하다 = to be upset or ill at ease (*syn.* 애(가) 터지다) ▌A: 이리 비켜. 내가 너 설거지 한번 시키려다가 **속이 터져** 죽겠다. = *Step aside. I wanted you to wash the dishes once but I don't think I can bear to watch it any longer.* B: 엄마, 처음부터 잘하는 사람이 어디 있어? = *Mom, nobody does it well right from the start.*

속전속결 [Lit. 速fast + 戰fight + 速fast + 決decide] CHINESE-DERIVATION 어떤 일을 빨리 진행하여 빨리 끝냄 = executing and finishing a project promptly (*equiv.* a blitz / a flurry of activity) ▌A: 나 날 잡았어. 다음 달 20일이야. = *I set the date. It's the 20th of next month.* B: 뭐? 엊그제 상견례하고 다음 달에 결혼한다고? 완전히 **속전속결**이구나! = *What? You just introduced the in-laws the other day and now you're already getting married next month? You really aren't fooling around.*

손가락(안)에 들다 IDIOM = 손가락에 꼽히다

손가락에 꼽히다 [Lit. to be counted on one's fingers] IDIOM 무리 중에서 몇 안 될 정도로 특별하다 = to be one of the most prominent in a certain group (*syn.* 손가락(안)에 들다, 손에 꼽히다 *cf.* 손가락(을) 꼽다) ▌A: 친구들 중에 결혼한 사람 많아요? = *Have many of your friends gotten married?* B: 아니요. 아직 대부분 결혼 안 했어요. 결혼한 친구는 다섯 **손가락에 꼽힐** 정도여요. = *No. The majority still haven't gotten married. Actually, I could count the number that are married on one hand.*

NOTE: 구체적으로 '첫 손가락에 꼽히다', '세 손가락에 꼽히다', '다섯 손가락에 꼽히다'와 같이 말하기도 한다.
This phrase is also used to more concretely to express numbers. For example, 첫 손가락에 꼽히다, 세 손가락에 꼽히다, 다섯 손가락에 꼽히다.

손가락에 장(을) 지지다 [Lit. to sear one's palm with a hot iron] IDIOM 맹세하거나 장담할 때 쓰는 말 = used when one takes a vow (*equiv.* (If you do that) I'll eat my hat. *syn.* 손에 장(을) 지지다, 성을 갈다) ▌A: 나 앞

으로 일주일 내에 5kg 뺄 거야. = *I'm going to lose 5 kg in one week.* B: 네가? 네가 정말로 일주일 안에 5kg을 빼면 내 **손가락에 장을 지진다**. = *You? If you really lose 5 kg in one week I'll sear my hand with a hot iron.*

손가락(을) 꼽다 [Lit. to count one's fingers] IDIOM **1.** 셀 수 있을 정도로 많지 않다 = to be so few as to easily be countable (*syn.* 손(을)꼽다 *cf.* 손가락에 꼽히다) ▌A: 제가 어릴 적만 해도 집에 컴퓨터가 있는 사람이 **손가락을 꼽을** 정도였어요. = *Even when I was a child the number of people who had a computer was so few you could count them on a single hand.* B: 요즘이야 컴퓨터 없는 집이 없잖아요. = *And now, there isn't a single household that doesn't have a computer.* **2.** 간절히 기다리는 모양을 표현한 말 = used to express the image of someone waiting earnestly (*syn.* 손(을)꼽다) ▌A: 도대체 무슨 일이야? = *What in the world is wrong with you?* B: 형우가 지금 다쳐서 병원에 있대요. = *I just heard that Hyeongoo is in the hospital injured.* A: 아니, 제대 날짜만 **손가락 꼽으며** 기다리고 있었는데 이게 웬 마른 하늘에 날벼락이야! = *But he was just days away from being discharged from the military. What a bolt from the blue!*

손가락(을) 빨다 [Lit. to lick one's fingers] IDIOM 굶다 = to starve ▌A: 요즘 일거리가 없어 큰일이야. **손가락 빨게** 생겼어. = *Still not being able to find work is going to be a major problem. It looks like I'm going to be starving.* B: 좀만 참아. 겨울만 지나면 일거리가 들어오겠지. = *Just hold on for a little longer. Once the winter passes, I'm sure you'll be able to find work.*

NOTE: 갓난아기들의 경우 손가락을 빠는 모습을 쉽게 볼 수 있다. 엄마의 젖이 먹고 싶은데 그럴 수 없을 때 본능적으로 그런 행동을 한다고 한다. 다 큰 어른이 손가락을 빤다는 말은 정말로 그런 행동을 한다는 것이 아니라 먹을 것이 없다는 뜻이다.
It is commonplace for babies to suck their fingers. They do instinctively when they hunger for their mother's milk but mother is not around. When we say an adult sucks their fingers, that means metaphorically that they don't have anything to eat.

손가락질(을)하다 [Lit. to point fingers] IDIOM 비난하고 흉을 보다＝to criticize or find fault (*equiv.* to point fingers *syn.* 돌(을) 던지다, 침(을) 뱉다) ▌A: 제발 술 좀 그만 먹어. 동네 사람들이 **손가락질할까** 겁이 나. ＝*Please stop drinking so much. I'm worried that people in the neighborhood will start to point.* B: 내 돈 내고 내가 술 먹는데 누가 뭐라 그래? ＝*I paid for this drink and now I'm going to drink it. What could they possibly say?*

손가락 하나 까딱 않다 [Lit. to not move a finger] IDIOM 조금도 일을 하려 하지 않다＝to be absolutely disinclined towards work (*equiv.* to not lift a finger / to not raise a finger *syn.* 손 하나 까딱 안 하다, 손끝 하나 까딱 안 하다) ▌A: 명절이 되면 남자들은 **손가락 하나 까딱 않고** 여자들만 일하는 게 너무 불공평해요. ＝*On all of the holidays the men don't lift a finger to help and the women work terribly hard. It's so unfair.* B: 맞아. 여자들은 명절이 오히려 스트레스야. ＝*That's right. Holidays are actually a stressful time for women.*

손끝에 물 한 방울 안 묻히다 IDIOM＝손에 물 한 방울 안 묻히다

손끝이 맵다 IDIOM＝손이 맵다

손끝 하나 까딱 안 하다 IDIOM＝손가락 하나 까딱 않다

손(도) 안 대고 코 풀다 [Lit. to blow your nose without touching it] IDIOM 별 노력 없이 의도한 바를 이루다＝for one's wishes to come true with little or no effort (*equiv.* It fell into one's lap.) ▌A: 오늘 경기는 아주 쉽게 이긴 것 같아요. ＝*I think we won this game pretty easily today.* B: 상대팀이 실책을 너무 많이 해서 **손도 안 대고 코 푼** 셈이죠 뭐. ＝*Yeah, the other team made so many errors it just kind of fell into our lap.*

손바닥 뒤집기보다 쉽다 [Lit. to be easier than flipping over one's hand] IDIOM 매우 손쉽다＝to be very easy (*equiv.* as easy as pie) ▌A: 너 앞으로 조심해! 너 하나 쥐도 새도 모르게 사라지게 만드는 것쯤 **손바닥 뒤집기보다 쉬워**. ＝*You'd better be careful from now on! Making you*

▶p.502

vanish without a trace would be nothing for me. B: 지금 저를 협박하시는 겁니까? = *Are you threatening me?*

손바닥 뒤집듯이 [Lit. as if one were flipping over one's hand] IDIOM 태도를 바꾸거나 결정을 번복하기를 아주 쉽게 = used when someone easily changes their demeanor or reverses their decisions (*equiv.* He has an (opinion) for every day of the week.) ▌A: 정치인들은 말 바꾸기를 **손바닥 뒤집듯이** 하니 믿을 수가 있어야지. = *Politicians seem to have a new opinion for every day of the week. It's hard to believe them anymore.* B: 그래서 공약(公約)의 공 자가 빌 공(空) 자라고 하잖아요. = *That's why they say gong* (公: *public*) *in gongyak* (公約: *a pledge to the public*) *actually means empty* (空).

손바닥 (들여다)보듯 훤하다 [Lit. to be as clear as looking into one's palm] IDIOM 속속들이 잘 알고 있다 = to know the ins and outs of a thing (*equiv.* to see right through something *cf.* 뛰어 봤자 부처님 손바닥) ▌A: 과장님, 오늘 날씨가 너무 좋지 않습니까? = *Boss, isn't the weather just great today?* B: 자네 일하기 싫어서 그러지? 자네 마음이 **손바닥 들여다보듯이 훤해**. = *You're just saying that because you don't want to work, huh? I can see right through you.*

손바닥으로 하늘을 가리다 [Lit. to block out the sky with the palm of one's hand] PROVERB 아무리 숨기려고 해도 소용이 없다 = to be unable to hide something no matter how hard one tries ▌A: 네가 이번에도 시험 떨어지면 포기하겠다고 선언한 걸 식구들이 다 알고 있는데, 그런 적이 없다니? **손바닥으로 하늘을 가릴** 셈이니? = *The whole family remembers how you swore you would give up if you failed the test again this time. And now you're saying that never happened? You're not fooling anyone.* B: 제 속뜻은 그게 아니었어요. = *That's not how I meant it.*

손발을 맞추다 [Lit. to match up feet and hands] IDIOM 생각이나 행동을 서로 맞게 하다 = to match up thoughts and actions with another (*equiv.* to bring oneself into line *cf.* 손발이 맞다) ▌A: 이번에 새로 옮긴 팀에서 적응은 잘하고 있나요? = *Are you getting used to your new team?* B: 네.

대부분의 선수들과 예전에 대표팀에서 **손발을 맞춰** 본 경험이 있어서 별 어려움 없습니다. = *Yes. I had already worked with most of the other athletes during our time on the national team. So it wasn't that big of a deal.*

NOTE: 군인들이 줄을 지어 팔과 다리의 동작을 하나처럼 맞추어 걷는 모습을 생각해 보라.
Imagine soldiers marching in a line with arms and legs in perfect sync.

손발이 따로 놀다 [Lit. for feet and hands to play separately] IDIOM **1.** 생각이나 행동이 서로 맞지 않다 = for one's thoughts and actions to not match those of another (*equiv.* to not mesh *ant.* 손발이 맞다) ▌A: 우리 이번 공연 걱정이야. = *I'm really worried about this performance.* B: 저도요. 연출이랑 주연 배우랑 저렇게 **손발이 따로 놀아서** 큰일이에요. = *Me too. For the producer and the main actor cannot mesh like that is a major problem.* **2.** 몸이 생각한 대로 움직이지 않다 = for one's body to not move as they wish ▌A: 춤 잘 추세요? = *Are you good at dancing?* B: 아니요. 저 몸치예요. **손발이 따로 놀아요.** = *No, I'm so clumsy at dancing. My body doesn't move as I want.*

***손발이 맞다** [Lit. for hands and feet to match] IDIOM 생각이나 행동이 서로 맞다 = for someone's way of thinking and behavior to match another's well (*ant.* 손발이 따로 놀다 *cf.* 손발을 맞추다, 도둑질을 해도 손발이 맞아야 한다) ▸p.132 ▌A: 이 두 사람은 누가 부부 아니랄까 봐 **손발이 척척 맞는구먼.** = *The two are in perfect harmony.* ▸p.518 B: 천생연분인가 봐요. = *They are made for each other.*

손발이 오그라들다 [Lit. for one's hands and feet to shrink] IDIOM 몹시 민망하고 창피한 마음이 들다 = to feel so embarrassed and ashamed ▌A: 연기할 때 국어 책을 읽는 연기자도 심심찮게 있어요. = *There are many actors whose acting seems more like they are reading out of a book.* B: 그럴 때는 제가 다 **손발이 오그라드는** 느낌이라니까요. = *Watching that kind of performance makes me so uncomfortable.*

NOTE: 원래 한 인터넷 사이트에서 은어처럼 쓰던 말이지만 요즘은 특히 방송에서 아주 흔하게 쓰는 표현이다. 몹시 낯뜨거운 말이나 행동 때문에 이를 지켜보거나 듣고 있는 사람이 도리어 민망해질 때 쓰는 말이다. This expression originated on the Internet and came to be widely used in daily life and especially on TV entertainment programs. It is used to desribe a situation when listeners or the audience cringe at the sight of some embarrassing behavior or laughable statements.

손뼉도 마주 쳐야 소리가 나는 법이다 [Lit. Two hands need to be clapped to make sound.] PROVERB 말다툼이나 싸움은 양쪽 모두 잘못이 있기 때문에 일어난다는 말 = suggests that arguments or fights occur only when both sides have problems. (*equiv.* It takes two to tango.) ▌A: 엄마, 지형이 좀 보세요. 제 옷을 자기 마음대로 입고 나갔어요. = *Mom, look what Jihyeong did. He went out with my clothes on without even asking me.* B: **손뼉도 마주 쳐야 소리가 나는 법이지.** 너는 지형이 옷 입은 적 없니? = *It takes two to tango. Are you saying you've never worn Jihyeong's clothes?*

손에 꼽히다 IDIOM = 손가락에 꼽히다

손에 넘어가다 [Lit. for something to pass to one's hands] IDIOM 누군가의 소유가 되다 = for something to fall into someone's possession ▌A: 사장님이 힘들게 키우신 회사가 이렇게 남의 **손에 넘어가다니.** = *The company that the president worked so hard to grow fell into someone else's hands.* B: 그러게 말이야. 사장님이 괜찮으셔야 할 텐데. = *That's what I'm saying. I hope the boss will be okay.*

손에 넣다 [Lit. to put something into your hands] IDIOM 자기 소유로 만들다 = to make something your possession ▌A: 이 노트북 요즘 물량이 달려서 구하기 힘들다던데 어떻게 **손에 넣었어?** = *How did you buy the laptop? I heard that it's hard to get due to the short supply.* B: 나오기도 전에 주문했었거든. = *I ordered it before it is released.*

손에 달리다 [Lit. for something to depend on one's hands] IDIOM 어떤 일이 누구의 힘에 의해 좌우되다 = for something to be controlled by somebody ▍A: 김 팀장만 믿겠어요. 이 일의 성패가 김 팀장의 **손에 달렸습니다**. = *I'll believe in you, Kim. The outcome of this work depends on you.* B: 네, 열심히 하겠습니다, 사장님. = *Okay, I'll do my best, Mr. President.*

손에 들어가다 [Lit. for something to go into hands] IDIOM 어떤 힘이나 세력이 미치는 범위 내에 들어가다 = to enter within range on which a certain power and influence affect ▍A: 중요한 서류니까 잘 보관해야 한다. 다른 사람 **손에 들어가면** 큰일나. = *Since it is an important document so you have to keep it safe. It would be a big trouble if it falls into someone else's hands.* B: 알았어요, 걱정 마세요. = *I understand. Don't worry.*

손에 땀을 쥐다 [Lit. to hold sweat in one's palms] IDIOM 아슬아슬하여 마음이 몹시 조마조마하다 = to be very agitated because of one's precarious position (*equiv.* (to keep one) on the edge of one's seat) ▍A: 오늘 게임 정말 **손에 땀을 쥐게** 하는군요. = *The game is really keeping me on the edge of my seat today.* B: 네. 정말로 양팀 대단한 시합을 하고 있습니다. = *Yeah, both teams are really putting up a good fight.*

손에 물 한 방울 안 묻히다 [Lit. for one to not even wet one's hands with a drop of water] IDIOM 여자가 힘든 일을 하지 않고 편하게 살다 = for a woman to live a comfortable life with little toil (*syn.* 손끝에 물 한 방울 안 묻히다) ▍A: 선화는 복이 터졌어. = *Sunhwa is so lucky.* B: 왜? = *Why?* A: 부잣집 시집가서 **손에 물 한 방울 안 묻히고** 살잖아. = *She married a guy from a wealthy family and lives such a comfortable life.*

손에 익다 [Lit. to become used to] IDIOM 일이 손에 익숙해지다 = to grow accustomed ▍A: 좀 익숙해지셨나요? = *Are you getting used to things?* B: 네. 덕분에 이제 일이 좀 **손에 익었어요**. = *Yes, thanks to you I've gotten acclimated very quickly.*

손에 잡히지 않다 [Lit. for something to not be grasped by one's hands]

IDIOM 마음이 불안하거나 들떠 일에 집중이 안 되다 = *for it to be impossible to concentrate on work due to anxiety or excitement* ▌A: 아, 오늘 일이 **손에 안 잡혀**. = *Oh, I can't concentrate on work today.* B: 왜요? 무슨 일 있어요? = *How come? Did something happen?* A: 우리 큰아이가 아픈데 집에 혼자 두고 왔거든요. = *My eldest kid is sick, but I had to leave him home alone.*

손에 잡힐 듯하다 [Lit. for something to seem within one's grasp] IDIOM 매우 가깝게 보이다 = *for something to appear as though it is very close* ▌A: 우와, 산에 올라오니까 정말 구름이 **손에 잡힐 듯해**. = *Wow, here at the summit, it really feels like we could just reach out and touch the clouds.* B: 그러게. 정말 구름이 옆에 있는 것 같지? = *That's what I'm saying. It feels like the clouds are right next to you, doesn't it?*

손에 장(을) 지지다 IDIOM = 손가락에 장(을) 지지다

손(을)꼽다 IDIOM = 손가락(을) 꼽다

손(을) 내밀다 [Lit. to extend one's hands] IDIOM 1. 금전적으로 도움을 요청하다 = *to ask for financial help* (*syn.* 손(을) 벌리다) ▌A: 너한테까지 손 **내밀게 되어** 민망하다. = *I'm so embarrassed to come to you for money.* B: 무슨 소리야. 어려운 때는 도와야지. = *What are you talking about? We have to help out each other when we are in need.* 2. 도움을 주겠다는 의사를 보이다 = *to show one's intention to help* ▌A: 윤 선생님은 저한테 은인 같은 분이십니다. 제가 힘들 때 **손을 내밀어 주신** 유일한 분이셨어요. = *I owe a great deal to Mr. Yoon. He was the only person who lent me a helping hand when I was going through terrible times in my life.* B: 그런 분이 돌아가셨으니 얼마나 마음이 아프세요. = *It must be such a terrible loss for you.*

손(을)놓다 [Lit. to let go one's hands] IDIOM 하던 일을 그만두다 = *to stop what one was doing* ▌A: 그렇게 **손놓고** 있을 거야? = *Are you going to just stand idle?* B: 일해야지. 그런데 어디서부터 손을 대야 할지 엄두가 안 나네. = *Yeah, I know I have to get to work. But I don't even*

▶p.373

know where to start.

손(을)대다 [Lit. to touch something with hands] IDIOM **1.** 관여하기 시작하다 = to start or get involved in (*ant.* 손(을)떼다) ▌A: 아니, 이 사건에 **손댄** 지가 벌써 두 달이 넘었는데 아직 단서도 못 찾았다는 게 말이 돼? = *Do you think it makes sense that you have yet to find a single clue even though you've been on the case for two months?* B: 조금만 더 기다려 주십시오. = *Please give me just a little bit more time.* **2.** 남의 물건을 몰래 쓰다 = to use someone else's stuff without permission ▌A: 어쩌다가 그 사람은 회사 공금에까지 **손을 댔대**? = *What brought him to embezzle company funds?* B: 아이가 아픈데 병원비가 없어서 순간적으로 그랬나 봐. = *He lost control and did it because his kid is sick and he didn't have money for his medical care.* **3.** 고치거나 매만지다 = to fix or mend ▌A: 원고가 워낙에 훌륭해서 **손댈** 부분이 없습니다. = *Your manuscript is so perfect that there's nothing to fix.* B: 아, 그럼 다행이군요. 감사합니다. = *That's good to hear. Thank you.* **4.** 때리다 = to hit ▌A: 아버지는 술만 마시면 저희들에게 **손을 대고는** 했어요. = *My father used to hit us whenever he was drunk.* B: 어렸을 때 참 힘들었겠군요. = *You must have had such a hard time when you were kid.*

손(을)들다 IDIOM = 두 손(을) 들다

손(을)들어 주다 [Lit. to raise hands] IDIOM 찬성하거나 편을 들다 = to approve or to take sides ▌A: 이번만큼은 나도 네 **손을 들어 줄 수가** 없겠다. = *I can't side with you this time.* B: 맞아, 이번 일은 내가 입이 열 개라도 할 말이 없어. = *Yeah. I can't make any excuse for what I did this time.* ➡p.470

손(을)떼다 [Lit. to take off hands] IDIOM 하던 일을 그만두다 = to quit what one was doing (*ant.* 손(을)대다) ▌A: 너는 이 일에서 **손떼라**. = *Quit this work.* B: 아버지, 제가 벌인 일이니 제가 마무리하게 해 주세요. = *Father, this is what I started, so let me finish it.*

손(을) 벌리다 [Lit. to spread hands] IDIOM 금전적으로 도움을 요청하

다＝to ask for financial help (*syn.* 손(을) 내밀다) ▌A: 번번이 미안해. 내가 손 **벌릴** 사람이 너밖에 더 있냐?＝*Sorry for doing this again. I don't have anybody else to ask for money.* B: 괜찮아. 뭐 큰 돈도 아닌데 뭘.＝*That's okay. It's not even that much money.*

손(을)보다 [Lit. to look at hands] IDIOM **1.** 어떤 물건을 손질하다＝to repair or touch up (*equiv.* to repair / to touch up) ▌A: 다 고쳤어?＝*Is it all fixed?* B: 아니, 아직 **손볼** 데가 좀 남았어.＝*No, I still have some work left to do.* **2.** 자기 뜻에 따르게 하기 위해 다른 사람을 때리거나 겁 주다＝to hit others or threaten them to make them obey ▌A: 새로 들어온 신입 녀석, 버릇이 너무 없지 않아?＝*Isn't that new guy rude?* B: 맞 아, 그 녀석 내가 **손 좀 봐야겠어**.＝*Yeah, you're right. I'd better teach him a lesson.*

손(을) 빼다 [Lit. to pull out hands] IDIOM 하고 있던 일에서 빠져나오 다＝to extract oneself from a job or endeavor (*syn.* 발(을) 빼다, 몸을 빼 다) ▌A: 이제 와서 너 혼자 **손을 빼겠다고**? 그렇게는 안 되지.＝ *You mean you're going to extract yourself from this? You can't.* B: 내가 어 떻게 하면 되겠어요?＝*What do I have to do?*

손(을) 뻗치다 [Lit. to stretch out hands] IDIOM 이제까지 하지 않던 일까 지 활동 범위를 넓히다＝to extend one's realm of work and activity ▌A: 우와 대기업이 이제 야식 사업에까지 **손을 뻗치다니**, 해도 해도 너무하네.＝*Don't you think it's crossing the line for big corporations to now be extending their reach into the late-night snacking industry?* B: 맞아. 이 런 건 정부가 규제를 좀 해야 되지 않을까?＝*You're right. I guess the government should regulate such things.*

손(을)쓰다 [Lit. to use hands] IDIOM 조치를 취하다＝to take a step ▌A: 죄송합니다. 최선을 다했지만 제가 **손쓸** 수 있는 상황이 아니 었어요.＝*I'm sorry. I did my best, but the situation was beyond my capacity.* B: 네, 이해합니다. 감사합니다.＝*Yeah, I understand that. Thank you.*

손(을) 씻다 [Lit. to wash hands] IDIOM 부정적인 일을 그만두다 = to quit something bad (*syn.* 손(을) 털다) ▌A: 가만 보면 감옥에서 나와 **손 씻고** 종교를 갖는 사람이 참 많은 것 같아. = *If you take a closer look, there are many who quit their bad behavior and became religious after serving their time in prison.* B: 감옥 안에서 마음의 변화를 겪게 되나 보지. = *They might experience a deep change of heart in prison.*

***손(을)잡다** [Lit. to hold hands] IDIOM 힘을 합하여 함께 일하다 = to cooperate and work together (*equiv.* to join hands) ▌A: 우리 두 사람이 **손 잡으면** 두려울 게 뭐가 있겠어? = *If we join hands, what do we have to fear?* B: 맞아. 앞으로 잘해 보자. = *You're right. Let's do better from now on.*

손(을) 털다 [Lit. to shake off hands] IDIOM 1. 부정적인 일을 그만두다 = to quit something bad (*syn.* 손(을) 씻다) ▌A: 자네, 요즘도 나쁜 짓 하고 다니는 거 아니지? = *You're not still engaging in bad behavior, are you?* B: 아, 아닙니다. 저 이제 **손 털었습니다**. = *No. I'm done with it.* 2. 노름판에서 가진 돈을 모두 잃다 = to lose all you have at a gambling house ▌A: 노름이라는 게 얼마나 무서운 건 줄 알아? **손 털기** 전에는 절대로 일어나지 못하는 곳이 바로 노름판이야. = *Do you know how horrible gambling is? You won't be able to leave the casino until you've lost every penny.* B: 그걸 알면서도 사람들이 노름에 빠지는 거 보면 참 한심해. = *It's pitiful that people fall into gambling even though they know that simple fact.*

손(이) 가다 [Lit. for hands to go] IDIOM 번거롭고 노력이 많이 필요하다 = to be a hassle or require much effort ▌A: 김밥은 먹을 때는 참 편한데, 만들기는 참 번거로워요. = *Gimbap is easy to eat but hard to make.* B: 맞아요, 재료도 많이 들고 싸기도 해야 하고, **손이 많이 가는** 음식이에요. = *That's right. You need so many ingredients and have to roll it up just right. It's a lot of work.*

손(이) 달리다 [Lit. for hands to be lacking] IDIOM 일손이 모자라다 = for hands to be in short supply ▌A: 애들아, 이번 방학 때 농활은 우리 삼

촌네로 가자. 지금 농번기라 **손이 많이 달린대**. = *Hey, guys. Why don't we go to my uncle's house over vacation and do some volunteer work? They said they're short on labor because it's such a busy farming season.* B: 좋아. 언제 출발할까? = *That's a good idea. When should we go?*

손이 맵다 [Lit. for hands to be spicy] IDIOM 손으로 슬쩍 때려도 몹시 아프다 = used when someone's light slapping with hands is very painful (*equiv.* to have a sharp hand *syn.* 손끝이 맵다) ▌A: 야, 아파! 왜 이렇게 세게 때리는 거야? = *Hey, it hurts. Why did you hit me that hard?* B: 그냥 살살 친 건데, 미안. 내가 원래 **손이 좀 매워**. = *I just slapped you lightly. I guess I'm just naturally a heavy hitter.*

손이 발이 되도록 빌다 [Lit. to pray until one's hands become feet] IDIOM 간절하게 빌다 = to desperately beg for forgiveness (*syn.* 발이 손이 되도록 빌다) ▌A: 아버지는 뭐라셔? = *What did your father say?* B: **손이 발이 되도록 빌어도** 눈썹도 까딱하지 않으세요. = *No matter how much I pleaded for forgiveness, he wouldn't budge an inch.*

NOTE: 대체로 발은 손에 비해 거칠다. 다른 사람에게 용서를 구하느라 손이 발처럼 거칠어질 때까지 빈다는 뜻이다. 혹은, 손바닥을 발처럼 지면에 대고 바닥에 엎드려 용서를 비는 모습에서 유래했다고도 이해할 수 있다.
Usually feet are rougher than hands. To beg for forgiveness, one rubs their hands so eagerly that their hands become rough like feet. Or it is possible to assume that the expression came from a person's image facing down with their hands on the ground like feet.

손(이)부끄럽다 [Lit. for hands to be embarrassing] IDIOM 무엇을 주거나 받으려고 손을 내밀었는데 상대가 물건을 받거나 주지 않아 무안해지다 = to feel embarassed after extending one's hand because an act of giving or receiving did not take place as it was intended to ▌A: 얼른 받아. **손이 부끄럽잖아**. = *Hurry up and take this. Don't just leave me hanging.* B: 아, 이걸 받아도 되는 건지 모르겠어요. 아무튼, 감사합니다. = *I really don't know if I should be accepting this. Anyway, thank you very much.*

손이 열 개라도 모자라다 [Lit. Even ten hands would be insufficient.]

IDIOM 몹시 바쁘다 = to be very busy ▌A: 아, 너 마침 잘 왔다. 가게 일 좀 도와줘. = *Good, you're here. Help me out in the store.* B: 많이 바쁜가 봐? = *You must be very busy.* A: 말도 마. **손이 열 개라도 모자랄** 지경이야. = *Don't even bring that up. I'm so busy that even ten hands would not be enough.*

손(이) 작다 [Lit. for hands to be small] IDIOM 씀씀이가 작다 = to buy little

and not be generous when serving others (*ant.* 손(이) 크다) ▌A: 사람이 열 명이나 온다는데 겨우 음식을 이거밖에 안 했니? **손이 그렇게 작아서** 어떡하니? = *This is all you made for ten people? How could you be so stingy?* B: 이렇게 많은 손님이 오는 게 처음이라 양을 잘 못 맞추겠더라고요, 어머님. = *Mother, this is the first time I've ever made food for so many guests, so I didn't know how much food to prepare.*

손(이) 크다 [Lit. for hands to be big] IDIOM 씀씀이가 크고 넉넉하다 =

buy a lot of something or be generous when serving others (*equiv.* buy a lot of something or be generous when serving others *ant.* 손(이) 작다) ▌A: 이걸 다 어머니 혼자 하신 거예요? = *Did your mother make all this food by herself?* B: 저희 어머니가 원래 **손이 크셔요**. = *My mother is generous by nature.*

손톱도 안 들어가다 [Lit. for not even a fingernail to fit] IDIOM 사람이 아

주 냉정하고 인색하다 = used to describe a person who is very cold-hearted and stingy ▌A: 집이 너무 추워. 집주인한테 보일러 좀 바꿔 달라고 부탁해 볼까? = *The house is so cold. Should we ask for the landowner to change the furnace?* B: 주인 아저씨 못 봤어? **손톱도 안 들어가게** 생겼던데. = *Didn't you meet him? He looked so stingy.*

NOTE: 손톱처럼 얇은 것이 들어갈 틈도 없으니 조그마한 틈도 없다는 뜻이다. 그처럼 빈틈이 전혀 없는 사람에게 쓰는 표현이다.

If a fingernail cannot fit into it, that means there is no crack at all. This expression is used to describe someone who is very tight and strict.

손 하나 까딱 안 하다 IDIOM = 손가락 하나 까딱 않다

솔선수범(하다) [Lit. 率obey + 先first + 垂hang down + 範rule] CHINESE-DERIVATION 남보다 앞장서서 행동하여 다른 사람에게 모범을 보이다 = to set an example by taking initiative ▌A: 우리 반 애들이 너무 말을 안 들어서 고민이에요. = *I'm worried because my students just won't listen.* B: 네가 먼저 **솔선수범해야지** 시키기만 하면 안 된다. = *You have to set an example first, don't just order them around.*

송구영신 [Lit. 送send + 舊old + 迎welcome + 新new] CHINESE-DERIVATION 묵은해를 보내고 새해를 맞음 = seeing the old year out and the new year in (*cf.* 근하신년) ▌A: 요즘에는 보기 드물지만 옛날에는 음력 설이 되면 연을 날리는 풍습이 있었어요. = *It's hard to see these days, but people used to fly kites on Lunar New Year's.* B: 특별한 의미가 있나요? = *Was there a special meaning in doing that?* A: **송구영신**의 의미가 들어 있는 거죠. = *It was a metaphor for seeing out the old year and bringing in the new year.*

송충이는 솔잎을 먹어야 한다 [Lit. A pine caterpillar should eat pine tree leaves.] PROVERB 자기 분수에 맞게 살아야 한다는 말 = One should live according to their place. (*equiv.* Don't bite off more than you can chew. / Know your station.) ▌A: 또 하루 종일 잠만 자는 거야? 당신도 주말이면 등산 다닐 거라며? = *Are you sleeping all day again? I thought you said you were going to go hiking on the weekends.* B: 아, 힘들어. **송충이는 솔잎을 먹어야** 하는 건가 봐. 역시 난 잠이 좋아. = *I'm tired. I think I have to know my place and live accordingly. I like sleeping—that's just who I am.*

쇠뿔도 단김에 빼라 [Lit. to remove cow horns in one sitting] PROVERB 하려고 마음먹었을 때 행동으로 옮기라는 말 = Put into action when you make up your mind to do it. (*equiv.* Strike while the iron is hot.) ▌A: 자, 그럼 언제부터 시작할까요? = *Then, when should we start?* B: **쇠뿔도 단김에 빼랬다고**, 지금 당장 시작합시다. = *Like the saying says, strike while the iron is hot. Let's get going right now.*

NOTE: 소의 뿔은 사람에게나 소 자신에게나 위험할 수 있다. 때문에 소의 뿔이 나기 시작할 무렵 제거하거나 살을 찌르지 못하도록 안으로 묶어 준다. 소의 뿔을 뽑을 때는 쇠막대를 불에 지져 열을 가한 후 뿔이 나오는 살 주변에 대어 뿔이 나는 자리를 흐물흐물하게 만들었다. '단김에'는 바로 그 쇠막대가 '뜨겁게 달구어져 있는 동안에'라는 뜻이다.

Cattle's horns can be a threat to themselves and their masters. That's why people cut off the horns or tie them inward when they start to grow. When removing the horns, one must heat up an iron stick and put it on the area of horns to make it soft. 단김에 means, "while the iron is hot."

수건(을) 던지다 [Lit. to throw in the towel] IDIOM 포기하다 = to give up

(*equiv.* to throw in the towel *syn.* 두 손(을) 들다, 백기(를) 들다 *cf.* 돌(을) 던지다) ▌A: 이제 그만 **수건 던지지** 그래? = *Why don't you throw in the towel now?* B: 아냐. 아직 역전의 기회가 있어. = *No way. There is still chance of turning this game around.*

NOTE: 권투에서 시합을 포기할 때 링 안으로 수건을 던진다. 이 관습에서 비롯된 표현이다.

When a boxer gives up a match, they throw a towel inside the ring. This expression originates with this custom.

수면 아래로 가라앉다 [Lit. to sink below the surface of water] IDIOM 문제나 사건 등에 대한 논의가 잠잠해지다 = for talks on problems and incidents to subdue (*ant.* 수면 위로 떠오르다) ▌A: 월드컵이 시작되면서 정치 얘기가 쏙 들어갔네. = *Talks on political issues disappear as the World Cup starts.* B: 덕분에 뇌물 수수 사건이 **수면 아래로 가라앉아** 버렸지 뭐야. = *The allegation on bribery subdued thanks to it.*

수면 위로 떠오르다 [Lit. to emerge above the surface of water] IDIOM 문제나 사건 등이 공개적으로 드러나다 = for an issue or incident to be revealed to the public (*ant.* 수면 아래로 가라앉다) ▌A: 정말 이번 사건은 너무 충격적이야. = *This incident is so shocking.* B: 소문으로만 떠돌던 승부 조작이 **수면 위로 떠오른** 거지 뭐. = *The rumors surrounding*

the fabrication of results have finally made it out into the light.

***수박 겉 핥기** [Lit. licking the surface of a watermelon] PROVERB 어떤 일을 제대로 하지 않고 형식적으로 대강 하는 것을 가리키는 말＝doing something in a sloppy way and meeting the minimum requirements █A: 얼마 전에 안전 검사도 통과했다는 다리가 어떻게 무너지지?＝*How could the bridge collapse after passing the safety inspections not so long ago?* B: 검사를 **수박 겉 핥기**로 했다는 뜻이겠지.＝*I guess that means they did a sloppy job with the inspections.*

수수방관(하다) [Lit. 袖sleeve + 手hand + 傍side + 觀see → watching with arms folded] CHINESE-DERIVATION 간섭하지 않고 그대로 내버려 두다＝to not meddle with and leave untouched (*equiv.* to stand by idly / to stand at the sidelines) █A: 야, 좀 어떻게 해 봐. 왜 남의 일 보듯 **수수방관**만 하고 있어?＝*Do something. Why are you just standing by idly?* B: 이럴 때는 그냥 가만히 있는 게 상책이야.＝*In this situation, standing back is the best policy.*

수염이 석 자라도 먹어야 양반이다 [Lit. Even a *yangban* with a beard three *ja*-long must eat to be a *yangban*.] PROVERB 체면보다 먹는 것이 더 중요하다는 말＝used to describe how eating is more important than saving face █A: 공부도 좋지만 밥부터 먹자. **수염이 석 자라도 먹어야 양반이라는** 말도 있잖아.＝*Studying is important, but let's eat first. There is a saying that eating is more important than saving face.* B: 그럴까, 그럼? 짜장면 어때?＝*Wanna eat then? Okay, what about jajangmyeon?*

수포로 돌아가다 [Lit. to go back to bubbles] IDIOM 허사가 되다＝for something to come to naught (*equiv.* to go down the drain / to burst like a bubble *cf.* 물거품이 되다) █A: 김지민 선수가 시즌 마지막 경기에서 우승에 도전했지만, 아깝게 실패했습니다.＝*Kim Ji-min went for a win at the last game of this season, but unfortunately he failed.* B: 그러면, 명예의 전당 입성도 **수포로 돌아가겠군요**.＝*This means his attempt to enter the Hall of Fame has come to naught.*

수혈을 받다 [Lit. to receive a blood transfusion] IDIOM 외부의 도움을 받다 = to receive help from an external source ▌A: 부실한 은행들에 또 정부에서 공적 자금을 투입한다는군 = *The government decided to inject public funds again into ailing banks.* B: **수혈을 받아** 회복이 된다는 보장도 없는데, 매번 그런 식이네. = *There is no guarantee the banks will survive even with injection, but the goverament always addresses the issue the same way.*

순진무구하다 [Lit. 純pure + 眞true + 無no + 垢dirt + 하다adjectival suffix] CHINESE-DERIVATION 착하고 순진하다 = to be nice and innocent ▌A: 저 녀석, 용돈 달라고 할 때만 꼭 저렇게 **순진무구한** 표정을 짓는다니까. = *That boy always gives me the puppy dog eyes when he asks for his allowance.* B: 그게 재 전략인 걸 몰라요? = *Don't you know that's his strategy?*

술에 술 탄 듯 물에 물 탄 듯 IDIOM = 물에 물 탄 듯 술에 술 탄 듯

술잔을 기울이다 IDIOM = 잔을 기울이다

숨도 크게 못 쉬다 [Lit. to not even be able to breathe loudly] IDIOM 위축되다 = to be intimidated (*equiv.* I can't even make a peep (in front of someone).) ▌A: 재민 씨, 오늘 우리 아버지 앞이라 힘들었지? 아까 보니 **숨도 크게 못 쉬던데.** = *Jaemin, you must have had a hard time with my father today. You looked intimidated.* B: 응. 아버님이 좀 무서워서. = *Yeah, your father is scary.*

숨을 거두다 [Lit. to gather breath] IDIOM '죽다'를 완곡하게 이르는 말 = a euphemism for "to die" ▌A: 화재 현장에서 사람을 구하다 중태에 빠졌던 소방관이 끝내 **숨을 거두고** 말았습니다. = *The fireman who was in critical condition after rescuing others in a fire has passed on.* B: 자신의 몸을 돌보지 않고 여러 생명을 구한 소방관의 죽음에 많은 사람들이 안타까워하고 있습니다. 김영신 기자가 보도합니다. = *Many were touched by the death of the man who sacrificed his life to save others. Reporter Kim Youngshin will cover the story.*

NOTE: See the note on 세상(을) 뜨다.

숨이 턱에 닿다 [Lit. for breath to reach the jaw] IDIOM 몹시 숨이 차다 = to be out of breath ▮ A: 왜 그렇게 헉헉거려? = *Why are you gasping like that?* B: 지각 안 하려고 **숨이 턱에 닿도록** 뛰었거든요. = *I ran, huffing and puffing not to be late for the class.*

숭어가 뛰니까 망둥이도 뛴다 [Lit. A gray mulet leaps, and a goby leaps too.] PROVERB 자신의 입장이나 처지는 생각하지 않고 남이 한다고 하니까 덮어놓고 따라 할 때 쓰는 말 = to blindly copy others without considering one's own situation and circumstances (*cf.* 뱁새가 황새 쫓아가면 가랑이가 찢어진다) ▮ A: 저도 이대오 선수만큼 연봉을 올려 주십시오. = *Please raise my salary to what Lee Daeoh gets.* B: **숭어가 뛰니까 망둥이도 뛴다더니,** 네가 대오만큼 팀에 공헌했다고 생각하니? = *Just because he gets that, you think you deserve it too? Do you think you've contributed as much to our team as he has?*

NOTE: 숭어는 뛰는 힘이 강해서 수면 위로 매우 높이 뛰어오를 수 있다. 망둥이는 숭어에 비해 크기도 작고 생긴 것도 못난 물고기다. 망둥이 역시 뛰어오르기를 잘하지만 숭어만은 못하다. 그래서 자신의 능력이나 분수를 생각하지 않고 자기보다 잘난 사람을 무턱대고 따라하는 사람을 가리켜 이 표현을 쓴다.
The gray mulet fish is a good jumper. It often leaps high out of the water. The goby is smaller than the gray mulet and looks ugly. The goby is not too shabby when it comes to the jumping game either, but can not top the gray mulet. This expression is used to refer to one who blindly follows and tries to copy someone who is better than them without considering their ability or circumstances.

승승장구하다 [Lit. 乘ride + 勝win + 長long + 驅drive + 하다verbal suffix] CHINESE-DERIVATION 계속해서 승리하거나 성공하여 기세가 대단하다 = to accomplish a string of victories ▮ A: 내일 결승전은 어떻게 예상하십니까? = *How do you predict tomorrow's final match will turn out?* B: 결승까지는 **승승장구하며** 올라왔지만 결승전은 쉽지 않은 시

합이 될 것 같습니다. = *We've been on a roll until now, but the finals are a different story.*

시간이 약이다 IDIOM = 세월이 약이다

시기상조 [Lit. 時time + 機momentum + 尙still + 早early] CHINESE-DERIVATION 때가 이름 = a premature time (*equiv.* The time is not yet ripe.) █ A: 이번 FTA 협상에 대해 어떻게 생각하세요? = *What do you think about the negotiations over the free trade agreement?* B: 농산물 시장의 전면적인 개방은 **시기상조** 아닐까요? = *Wouldn't it be too premature to completely open to the agricultural market?*

시도 때도 없이 [Lit. without time and season] IDIOM 늘 아무 때나 = all the time █ A: 너는 무슨 이를 **시도 때도 없이** 닦니? = *How come you brush your teeth all the time?* B: 입속이 찝찝해서 못 견디겠어요. = *I can't stand bad taste in my mouth.*

NOTE: '시(時)'와 '때'는 같은 말이다. 단순히 운율을 맞추기 위해 반복한 것이다. '시시때때로'라는 말도 있다.
시 and 때 mean the same thing. They are repeated for rhythm. In a similar vein is the expression, 시시때때로.

***시작이 반이다** [Lit. Starting is half.] PROVERB 무슨 일이든 시작하기가 어려운 법이니 일단 시작했으면 꽤 많이 진행한 것과 마찬가지라는 말 = suggests that just getting started can be the hardest part of an endeavor and if one has accomplished that, one has already made much progress (*equiv.* Well begun is half done.) █ A: 어휴, 이제 시작해서 언제 이걸 다 끝내지? = *Phew, now we've started, but when are we ever going to finish?* B: **시작이 반이라잖아.** 힘내. = *Well begun is half done, you know? Keep up the good work.*

시장이 반찬이다 [Lit. Hunger is an appetizer.] PROVERB 배가 고프면 특별한 반찬이 없어도 밥이 맛있다는 말 = suggests that if one is hungry, a meal tastes good without special side dishes (*equiv.* Hunger is the best sauce.)

▌A: 밥하고 김치밖에 없는데 이걸로 되겠어?=*All we've got is kimchi and rice. Is that going to do it?* B: 괜찮아. **시장이 반찬이잖아.** =*That's fine. Hunger is the best sauce.*

시종일관 [Lit. 始beginning + 終end + 一one + 貫penetrate] CHINESE-DERIVATION 처음부터 끝까지 한결같음=unchangingly, from beginning to end ▌A: 어쩌면 그렇게 비행기에 앉아 있는 내내 자세가 똑같을 수가 있어요? **시종일관** 허리를 꼿꼿하게 세우고 계신 것 같아요.=*How were able to sit exactly the same way during the whole plane ride? From beginning to end you were sitting straight.* B: 어릴 때부터 그렇게 앉는 게 습관이 됐거든요.=*I developed that habit in childhood and it stuck with me.*

NOTE: 주로 부사로 쓰인다. This expression is mainly used as an adverb.

시치미(를) 떼다 [Lit. to take a label off a falcon's foot] IDIOM 알면서도 모르는 척하거나 하고도 하지 않은 척하다=to pretend to not know or pretend that one hasn't done something (*equiv.* to play dumb / to feign ignorance *syn.* 딱 잡아떼다, 오리발(을) 내밀다) ▌A: 너 유미가 여기 왔을 때 유미 봤지?=*You saw Yumi when she came here, didn't you?* B: 유미요? 그게 누구예요?=*Yumi? Who's that?* A: **시치미 떼지** 마.=*Don't play dumb.*

NOTE: 옛날 사람들은 매를 이용해 사냥을 하고는 했다. 이때 매에 표식을 달아 자신의 것임을 나타냈는데 이 표식을 '시치미'라고 불렀다. 그런데 간혹 남의 매를 잡아 시치미를 떼 버리고는 자신의 매라고 우기는 사람들이 있었다. '시치미를 떼다'라는 표현은 이렇게 해서 생겨났다. Long ago, people used to hunt using hawks. To keep track of whose bird was whose, they would attach a bracelet to the hawk's talon. This mark of ownership was called 시치미. It wasn't long though before dishonest folks started ripping off these name tags in order to rip off the hawks. Owing to this custom, the phrase, "removing the name tag," came to mean playing dumb.

시퍼렇게 살아 있다 [Lit. to be alive blue] IDIOM 죽지 않고 멀쩡하게

살아 있다＝to be alive in perfect shape (*syn.* 두 눈(을) 시퍼렇게 뜨고 있다) ▌A: 회장님, 몇몇 이사들이 회장님을 몰아내려고 계획을 꾸미고 있다고 합니다. ＝*Mr. President, rumor has it that some directors are making a plot to remove you from your position.* B: 내가 아직 **시퍼렇게 살아 있는데** 나를 쫓아내겠다고? 어림도 없지! ＝*I'm standing here in perfect shape, and they are trying to kick me out of here? Absurd!*

NOTE: See the note on 두 눈(을) 시퍼렇게 뜨고 있다.

시행착오 [Lit. 試try + 行do + 錯incorrect + 誤mistake] CHINESE-DERIVATION 시험과 실패를 거듭하며 학습이 이루어지는 일＝learning through a process of many attempts and failures (*equiv.* trial and error) ▌A: 이런 책을 쓰시게 된 동기가 있습니까? ＝*What was your motivation to write this book?* B: 제가 겪은 **시행착오**를 다른 사람들은 경험하지 않게 도와주고 싶었습니다. ＝*I wanted to help others to avoid the trials and errors that I went through.*

***식은 죽 먹기** [Lit. (it's like) eating porridge that's already cooled down] PROVERB 아주 쉬운 일＝a very easy task (*equiv.* as easy as pie / a piece of cake *syn.* 땅 짚고 헤엄치기, 누워서 떡 먹기 *ant.* 하늘의 별 따기) ▌A: 이 문제 좀 가르쳐 줄래? 아무리 봐도 모르겠어. ＝*Would you mind teaching me how to do this problem? I just can't figure it out.* B: 이 문제는 공식만 알면 **식은 죽 먹기**야. ＝*Once you know the formula, it's a piece of cake.*

신물(이)나다 [Lit. to have acid reflux] IDIOM 지긋지긋하다＝to be sick of something (*syn.* 진저리(가) 나다, 진절머리(가) 나다) ▌A: 우리 짜장면 먹을까? ＝*What about having jajangmyeon?* B: 짜장면? 이번 방학 때 집에서 혼자 얼마나 먹었던지 짜장면이라면 이제 **신물이 나**. ＝*Jajangmyeon? I had way too much jajangmyeon over vacation and now I'm sick of it.*

신출귀몰하다 [Lit. 神ghost + 出come out + 鬼ghost + 沒hide + 하다 verbal suffix] CHINESE-DERIVATION 1. 남들 모르게 나타났다 사라지다＝to appear without others' knowing and then disappear again (*cf.* 동에 번쩍 서

에 번쩍) ▋A: 뭐? 영식이가 지금 거기 일본에 있다고? 어제 나랑 만났었는데. **신출귀몰하네.** = *What? Is Youngsik in Japan now? I just saw him yesterday. That was fast.* B: 그래서 영식이 별명이 홍길동이잖아요. = *That's why his nickname is Hong Gildong (a teleporter of Korean lore).* **2.** 솜씨나 재주가 아주 뛰어나다 = for abilities or skills to be very excellent ▋A: 옛날에는 명절이면 텔레비전에서 서커스 공연을 많이 했었는데 요즘은 통 보기가 힘들어. = *There used to be so many circus shows on TV long ago, but they're hard to find anymore.* B: 맞아. 그 사람들 보면 재주가 **신출귀몰한** 게 참 신기한데. = *You're right. Whenever I watch that kind of show, I'm just astounded by the skills.*

신토불이 [Lit. 身body + 土soil + 不no + 二two → One's body and the soil where one was born is the one.] CHINESE-DERIVATION 자기가 사는 땅에서 나온 농산물이 체질에 맞음 = used to emphasize that products grown from the soil where one lives are the best for one's body. ▋A: 요즘 아이들은 빈대떡이나 한과 같은 우리 전통 음식을 잘 모를 거예요. = *I bet kids today don't even know about traditional Korean foods like bindaetteok or hangwa.* B: **신토불이**라고 우리 전통 음식이 몸에 더 맞는데 말이에요. = *Yeah, they say Local food is good for local people.*

NOTE: 이 말은 1980년대 말, 우루과이 라운드(Uruguay Round)로 인하여 농산물 시장 개방에 대한 불안이 심할 때 농협이 우리 농산물을 애용하자는 운동을 벌이면서 만들어 낸 조어다.
This expression came into being in the late 1980s as concern spread over the possible effects on Korean farmers by opening agricultural market to the world with the Uruguay Round Agreements of Multilateral trade negotiations (MTN). The National Agricultural Cooperative Federation coined the expression to boost the use of domestic agricultural products.

실패는 성공의 어머니 [Lit. Failure is the mother of success.] PROVERB 성공을 거두기 위해서는 실패도 있게 마련이라는 말 = suggests that failures are always a part of attaining success (*equiv.* Failure is a stepping stone to success.) ▋A: 기죽지 마. **실패는 성공의 어머니**잖아. = *Don't be let down. Failure is the mother of success.* B: 고마워. 정신 차리고 다음번

을 준비해야겠어. = *Thanks. I've got to pull myself together and get ready for my next shot.*

심사숙고(하다) [Lit. 深 deep + 思 think + 熟 ripe + 考 think] CHINESE-DERIVATION 오랫동안 깊이 생각하다 = to ponder for a long time ▌A: 선생님, 저는 대학에 가지 않겠습니다. 심사숙고 끝에 내린 결정입니다. = *I'm not going to college. I made up my mind after mulling it over for a long time.* B: 그래? 그럼 다른 계획이라도 있니? = *Did you? So, do you have another plan?*

십년공부 도로 아미타불 [Lit. Ten years of study goes back to Amitabha.] PROVERB 오랫동안 해 온 일이 헛수고가 되어 버린 경우에 쓰는 말 = used when long efforts and hardships end in failure (*syn.* 말짱 도루묵, 도로 아미타불 *cf.* 물거품이 되다) ▌A: 그 육상 금메달리스트 말이야, 약물 복용이 발각돼서 금메달도 박탈당했잖아. = *You know that gold medallist track star? They found out he was doping and stripped his medal away.* B: 어. 십년공부 도로 아미타불 된 거지 뭐. = *Yeah. All that effort was for nothing.*

NOTE: 아미타불은 서방 극락 세계를 세웠다고 전해지는 부처의 이름이다. 옛날에 한 남자가 이 부처의 이름을 매일 새기며 10년간 수련을 했다. 그런데 10년째 되는 날, 예쁜 여자를 보고는 손을 잡아 버렸다. 그 순간 10년의 노력이 모두 물거품이 되고 말았다. 아미타불이 되지 못하고 도로 원래대로 돌아가고 만 것이다.
Amitabha is the name of a celestial Buddha that created the heavens. There once lived a man who spent ten years training himself by meditating while writing the buddha's name every day. But on the very day that ten years had passed since he began this regimen, a beautiful woman walked by, and being unable to control himself, he reached out for the woman's hand. In that one moment, his ten years of training came to naught. This expression comes from the man's failure to attain enlightenment and return to the street in his original state.

십 년 묵은 체증이 내려가다 [Lit. for something that has been

undigested in the stomach for ten years to pass] IDIOM 속이 후련하다 = to feel relief (*equiv.* to take a load off of one's mind / to feel relieved *syn.* 앓던 이(가) 빠지다) ▌A: 창고에 쌓여 있던 잡동사니들을 다 버리니까 **십 년 묵은 체증이 내려가는** 것 같아. = *I feel like a weight as been lifted off my shoulders after clearing all my junk out of storage.* B: 그러니까 안 쓰는 물건들은 그때그때 버려야 하는 거예요. = *That's why you have to clean out the stuff that you don't use whenever you can.*

십 년이면 강산도 변한다 [Lit. In ten years, even the rivers and mountains change.] PROVERB 십 년이면 대부분의 것이 바뀐다는 말 = implies that after ten years, most things will have changed (*equiv.* Time changes everything.) ▌A: 부산은 처음이세요? = *Is this your first time in Busan?* B: 20년 만에 와 보는 거예요. 정말 많이 바뀌었네요. = *It's been twenty years since I was here last. So much has changed.* A: **십 년이면 강산도 변하는데**, 이십 년이면 말할 필요도 없겠죠. = *Even in ten years a lot changes, but after 20, it must be a world of difference.*

십자가를 지다 [Lit. to carry a cross on one's back] IDIOM 어려운 일을 맡거나 희생을 감수하다 = to take up difficult work or endure sacrifice (*equiv.* to bear a cross) ▌A: 아버지, 얼마 전에 돌아가신 김근태 씨는 어떤 분이세요? = *Father, who was the Kim Geuntae that passed away a while ago?* B: 독재 정권 시절에 민주화를 위해 **십자가를 지셨던** 분이란다. = *He was the man who bore the cross for democratization during the times of dictatorships in Korea.*

십중팔구 [Lit. 十ten + 中among + 八eight + 九nine → eight or nine out of ten] CHINESE-DERIVATION 거의 대부분이거나 거의 틀림없음 = almost for sure (*equiv.* nine times out of ten *cf.* 만에 하나) ▌A: 영희가 오늘 여기 올까? = *Do you think Yeonghee will show up today?* B: **십중팔구** 안 올 거야. 걔는 원래 일요일 오후에는 집 밖으로 잘 안 나와. = *There's maybe a one-in-ten chance of it. She rarely leaves the house on Sunday afternoons.*

NOTE: 조사 없이 부사처럼 쓰이기도 한다.
　　Also used without a particle as an adverb.

从

싹수가 노랗다 [Lit. for the sprouts to be yellow] IDIOM 가능성이나 희망이 애초부터 보이지 않다 = There is little possibility and hope from the outset. (*ant.* 될성부른 나무는 떡잎부터 알아본다) █ A: 저 녀석은 어린 놈이 벌써부터 담배나 피우고 **싹수가 노랗군**. = *That little kid is already smoking. Talk abut a failure right out of the gate.* B: 그러게 말이야. 초등학생인 것 같은데. = *That's what I'm saying. He looks like an elementary-schooler.*

싹을 꺾다 IDIOM = 싹을 자르다

싹을 밟다 IDIOM = 싹을 자르다

싹을 자르다 [Lit. to cut the bud] IDIOM 새로 시작하는 것이 더 성장하기 전에 막거나 없애다 = to stave off or eliminate something before it gets bigger or out of hand (*equiv.* to nip it in the bud *syn.* 싹을 꺾다, 싹을 밟다) █ A: 어린 아이까지 죽이는 건 너무하지 않아? = *Don't you think killing a kid is going too far?* B: 무슨 소리야? 지금 **싹을 잘라** 놓지 않으면 나중에 후회하게 될 거야. = *What are you talking about? We will regret it later if we don't nip it in the bud.*

싼 게 비지떡 [Lit. Cheap things are (like) *tteok* made from tofu residue.] IDIOM 값이 싼 물건은 품질이 나쁘기 마련이라는 말 = used to suggest that cheap products naturally have bad quality █ A: 엊그제 시장에서 산 청바지 말이야, 싸다고 좋아했는데 빨았더니 물이 다 빠져서 못 입겠어. = *You know the jeans that I bought a few days ago at the market. I was happy because I bought them cheap but they faded after one wash. I can't* *wear them anymore.* B: 그러니까 **싼 게 비지떡**인 거야. = *That's why people say you get what you pay for.*

NOTE: 비지는 두부가 될 성분을 빼내고 남은 찌꺼기를 말한다. 비지는 딱딱하고 맛도 없어 보통 버리거나 사료로 쓴다. 먹을 게 부족하던 시절, 비지에 쌀가루나 밀가루를 넣고 반죽하여 부친 것이 비지떡이다. 값이 싸기는 하지만 그만큼 맛이나 영양가가 없는 음식이다.
비지 refers to dregs left when one makes tofu. Normally, this residue is hard and tasteless , so it is thrown away or used for animal feed. 비지떡 is a sort of pancake made by mixing the residue with rice or wheat powder. When there was not enough food to go around, people often made 비지떡. The food is cheap, but not tasty or nutritious.

쌀독에서 인심 난다 PROVERB = 광에서 인심 난다

쌍지팡이(를) 들고 나서다 [Lit. to set out holding a pair of crutches]
IDIOM 완강하게 반대하다 = to strongly oppose (*syn.* 쌍지팡이(를) 짚고 나서다) ▌A: 너 아까 그 사람하고 결혼은 절대 안 돼. = *You can't marry him.* B: 왜 언니는 내 일에 그렇게 **쌍지팡이를 들고 나서는** 거야? = *Why are you always putting your nose in my business and opposing everything I do?*

쌍지팡이(를) 짚고 나서다 IDIOM = 쌍지팡이(를) 들고 나서다

NOTE: 쌍지팡이는 다리를 못 쓰는 사람이 짚고 다니는 한 쌍의 지팡이를 말한다. 다리가 불편한 사람이 쌍지팡이를 짚고 일어서며 어떤 사람을 말릴 정도로 다급하고 강한 어조로 반대할 쓰는 표현이다.
쌍지팡이 is a set of two crutches used by those who, for one reason or another, cannot use their legs. This expression depicts a feeling of disapproval so great that even a person who can't walk would rise up in opposition.

썩어도 준치 [Lit. Even though it's rotten, it's still herring.] IDIOM 본래 훌륭한 것은 약간의 손상을 입는다 해도 어느 정도 값어치를 한다는

말＝suggests that something of great value is still valuable even when it has sustained some damage ▌A: 저 선수는 이제 한물간 줄 알았는데 아직 그래도 성적이 괜찮네. ＝*I thought that athlete was past his prime, but he still seems to be getting the job done.* B: 썩어도 준치라는 말도 있잖아. ◆p.561 한가락 하던 그 실력이 어디 가겠어? ＝*A winner past his prime is still a winner. His talent isn't likely going anywhere.*

NOTE: 준치는 청어목에 속하는 바닷물고기로 맛이 아주 좋다고 한다. 썩은 준치라고 해도 다른 맛없는 생선보다는 맛있다는 뜻에서 나온 표현으로 보인다. 실제로 썩은 고기를 먹을 수야 없을 테니 과장된 표현으로 생각할 수 있다.

준치 is a fish of the herring variety that is thought to be very delectable. This expression likely suggests that this fish, even when rotten, is still tastier than other fish that were tasteless to begin with. As eating any kind of rotten meat or fish is likely unadvisable, this expression is a bit of an exaggeration.

썩은 동아줄을 잡다 [Lit. to clutch at a rusty chain] IDIOM 도움이 되지 않는 사람이나 대상에 의지하다＝to rely on someone or something that are not be of a help ▌A: 이번에 상무님이 명예퇴직하시면서 그 밑에 있던 김 차장도 사직서 냈다며? ＝*I heard that as the managing director quit, assistant director Kim also quit.* B: 썩은 동아줄을 잡은 셈이지 뭐. ＝*Yeah, it is like Kim had clutched at a bad rope.*

NOTE: 이 표현은 아래 설화와 관련이 있다. 옛날에 세 남매를 둔 어머니가 하루는 산 너머로 품팔이를 갔다가 돌아오는 길에 그만 호랑이에게 속아서 잡아먹히고 말았다. 호랑이는 어머니의 옷을 입고 집에 나타나서 아이들을 속여 잡아먹으려 했다. 이에 집에 있던 남매는 우물가로 도망간 뒤 하느님께 빌어 하늘에서 내려온 동아줄을 타고 하늘로 올라갔다. 호랑이도 두 아이들과 같이 하늘에 빌자 동아줄이 내려왔다. 그러나 이 동아줄은 썩은 동아줄이어서 매달려 하늘로 올라가다가 떨어져 죽었다. 하늘에 올라간 두 남매는 각각 해와 달이 되었다고 한다.

This expression originates from the following old tale. Once upon a time, the mother of three went to peddle her wares in the neighborhood beyond the mountain. On the way back home, she was tricked by a tiger and eaten by the animal. The tiger wore the woman's clothes, went to the woman's house and tried to prey on her children as well. The kids ran away to the well and prayed to God to save them. A rope came down to them and they were able to escape from the tiger by climbing up and grasping the rope. Then, the tiger also prayed for a rope. A rope came down and the tiger held to it, but it was a rotten rope, so the animal fell from the air and died. The two kids who ascended to the sky became the sun and moon.

쐐기(를) 박다 [Lit. to drive a wedge] IDIOM 다짐을 두거나 확실히 결정 짓다 = to make something clear or firm decision on something ▌A: 아, 이 번 골은 결정적이다. 승부에 **쐐기를 박는** 골이네. = *That was a decisive goal. It has cemented the results.* B: 더 볼 것도 없어. 승부는 결정이 났어. = *We don't even need to keep watching. The outcome is clear.*

쑥대밭을 만들다 [Lit. to make a field of mugwort] IDIOM 매우 어지럽히 거나 완전히 망치다 = to make a mess or turn something into ruins ▌A: 조 카 녀석이 왔다 가면서 집을 **쑥대밭을 만들어** 놓았네. = *My nephew came to visit and left the house a terrible mess.* B: 나는 좀 쉬어야겠으니 당신이 다 치워. = *I have to take it easy, so you clean it up.*

NOTE: 쑥은 번식력이 강해 매우 잘 자란다. 쑥이 자라기 시작한 곳은 금세 쑥이 우거진 밭, 쑥대밭이 된다. 무성한 쑥대밭은 볼품이 없다.
Mugwort grows so fast that it thickly covers any field in a short amount of time. The rank mugwort field is unpleasant to look at.

쑥대밭이 되다 [Lit. to become a field of mugwort] IDIOM 매우 어지러워 지거나 완전히 망해 버리다 = to become very cluttered or end in complete failure (*equiv.* to be a mess) ▌A: 집이 어쩌다가 이렇게 **쑥대밭이 되었 어?** = *Why is the house such a mess?* B: 창문 열어 놓고 외출했었는데 아까 소나기 왔었잖아. 빗물이 다 들어왔어. = *I left the window open when I went out earlier and there was a sudden downpour, you know? A lot of rain came in the window.*

NOTE: See the note on 쑥대밭을 만들다.

쓴맛 단맛 다 보다 [Lit. to experience sweet and bitter tastes] IDIOM 괴로움과 즐거움을 다 겪다=to undergo hardships and enjoyment (*equiv.* to experience the good and the bad *syn.* 단맛 쓴맛 다 보다 *cf.* 쓴맛(을) 보다) ▌A: 회사 생활은 어떠니?=*How is company life treating you?* B: 아직은 재미있어요.=*It's been fun so far.* A: 그래. 좀 지나면 **쓴맛 단맛 다 보게** 될 거야.=*Yeah, that's right. After a while, you'll have gone through both good times and bad.*

쓴맛(을) 보다 [Lit. to taste a bitter taste] IDIOM 실패하거나 좌절하여 괴로움을 겪다=to experience torment following a failure or major frustration (*cf.* 쓴맛 단맛 다 보다) ▌A: 정민이는 늘 자신감이 가득한 게 참 보기 좋아.=*Jeongmin is so full of confidence it's nice to be around him.* B: 애가 아직 어려서 인생의 **쓴맛을 못 봐서** 그런 거죠 뭐.=*That's because he is young and still hasn't experienced the hardships of life.*

쓴입을 다시다 [Lit. to smack one's bitter lips] IDIOM 못마땅하여 말을 하지 않다=to be displeased and unable to speak ▌A: 우리 회사 사람들이 나만 빼고 자기들끼리 회식하러 간 거 있지?=*My friends from work all left me behind and had a staff party. Can you believe that?* B: 저런. 그래서 어떻게 했어?=*That's terrible. So what did you do?* A: **쓴입만 다셨지.** 어떡하겠어?=*I had to grin and bear it. What else could I do?*

쓴잔을 들다 IDIOM=고배를 들다

쓴잔을 마시다 IDIOM=고배를 들다

쓸개(가) 빠지다 [Lit. for one's gallbladder to fall out] IDIOM 위엄이나 품위, 자존심이 없다=to lack dignity, class or confidence ▌A: 이 **쓸개 빠진** 녀석아, 사내 녀석이 앞치마 두르고 부엌에서 뭐하는 거냐?=*What a spineless little twit! What do you think you're doing in the kitchen with an apron on?* B: 할아버지, 요즘어는 남자도 다 부엌일 해야 해요.=*Grandpa, men have to take part in the kitchen work nowadays too.*

씨가 마르다 [Lit. for the seed to dry up] IDIOM 완전히 없어져 찾아볼 수

없다 = to completely disappear (*cf.* 씨를 말리다) ▌A: 요즘 농촌에는 노인들밖에 없어요. 처녀 총각들 **씨가 마를** 지경이에요. = *There's nothing left but old people now in the farming villages. I'm worried that our unmarried young men and women will totally disappear.* B: 큰 문제네요. = *That's a major problem.*

씨를 말리다 [Lit. to try a seed] IDIOM 모조리 없애고 다시는 생겨나지 못하게 만들다 = to completely eliminate and make sure that something will never appear again (*equiv.* to wipe something off the face of the earth *cf.* 씨가 마르다) ▌A: 옛날에는 산에 야생 동물들이 많았는데 요즘에는 통 볼 수가 없네요. = *Long ago there used to be many wild animals on the mountain but now it's impossible to find one.* B: 밀렵꾼들이 불법으로 야생 동물들을 잡아서 **씨를 말리고** 있으니까요. = *That's because the poachers are busy wiping them off the face of the Earth with all of their illegal hunting.*

아는 것이 힘이다 [Lit. Knowing is power.] QUOTE 지식의 중요성을 강조한 말 = used to emphasize the importance of knowledge (*equiv.* Knowledge is power. *ant.* 아는 게 병이다) ▌A: 너는 그렇게 공부를 안 해서 나중에 어떻게 하려고 그러니? "**아는 것이 힘이다**"라는 말도 모르니? = *If you continue to not study like that, what do you intend to become later on in life? Haven't you heard that knowledge is power?* B: 엄마, "아는 게 병이다"라는 말도 있어요. = *Mom, there is also a saying that knowing too much is torture.*

◆p.395

NOTE: 프랜시스 베이컨이 한 말이다.
 This saying is originally attributed to Francis Bacon.

***아는 게 병이다** [Lit. Knowing is a disease.] PROVERB 차라리 모르면 마음이 편한데 알고 있어서 괴로울 때 쓰는 말 = describes how one can be blissfully ignorant but is tormented upon finding something out (*ant.* 아는 것이 힘이다 *cf.* 모르는 게 약이다) ▌A: 컴퓨터에서 전자파가 나온다는 기사를 어제 봤더니 괜히 눈이 더 침침한 느낌이야. = *Yesterday I read an article that said computers give off electromagnetic waves and now my eyes are more blurry when I look at the screen than ever.* B: 그러게 **아는 게 병이라고** 하는 거야. = *I guess that's why they say it's better not to know some things.*

아는 길도 물어 가라 [Lit. Ask the way even when it's a road you know well.] PROVERB 잘 아는 것을 할 때도 주의를 하라는 말 = used to encourage caution even when carrying out an activity one knows well (*syn.* 돌다리도 두드려 보고 건너라) ▌A: 잘할 수 있겠어? = *Do you think* *you'll be able to handle this?* B: 내가 이거 한두 번 해 본 줄 알아? 누워서 떡 먹기야. = *You think this is the first time I'm doing this? It's easy as pie.* A: 그래도 조심해. 아는 길도 물어 가라는 말이 있잖아. = *Even so, be careful.*

아니나 다를까 [Lit. Is it any different from knowing?] IDIOM 예상한 바와 같을 때 쓰는 말 = used to describe a situation in which the outcome is exactly what one had anticipated ▌A: 왜 그래? 감기 걸렸어? = *What's up with you? Are you sick?* B: 응. 어제부터 몸이 으슬으슬 춥더니 **아니나 다를까** 열도 나고 기침까지, 아주 죽겠네. = *Yeah, I've been getting the chills constantly since yesterday and it's just as I thought: now I have a fever and a cough too. I'm a goner for sure.*

아니 땐 굴뚝에 연기 나겠어? [Lit. Would smoke come from a chimney if there were no fire?] PROVERB 실제로 어떤 일이 있기 때문에 소문이 난다는 말 = suggests that a rumor wouldn't arise if there weren't basis for it in fact (*equiv.* Where there's smoke, there's fire.) ▌A: 우리 팀 영민 씨하고 총무 팀 경숙 씨하고 사귄다는 소문이 있던데 진짜일까? = *Do you think it's true that Youngmin from our team and Gyeongsuk from the General Affairs Team are a couple?* B: **아니 땐 굴뚝에 연기 나겠어?** = *Where there's smoke, there's fire.*

아닌 게 아니라 [Lit. It's not not that,] IDIOM 생각이나 앞서 한 말이 실제와 같음을 강조하는 말 = used to emphasize that the preceding statement is factual ▌A: 그런데, 너는 몸 괜찮아? 나는 어제 운동을 무리하게 했나 봐. 여기저기 몸이 쑤셔. = *By the way, how are you feeling? I think I overdid it yesterday with the exercise. I'm aching all over.* B: **아닌 게 아니라**, 나도 죽겠어. = *I can't say that's not the case for me. I feel like I'm going to die.*

아닌 밤중에 홍두깨 [Lit. a wooden paddle on an unlikely night] PROVERB 1. 상대가 예상하지 못한 말이나 행동을 하는 경우에 쓰는 말 = used to describe an unexpected statement or action ▌A: 참, 너 옛날에 사귀었던 현식이 소식 알아? = *Hey, have you heard anything recently about* *that guy Hyeonshik that you used to date?* B: **아닌 밤중에 홍두깨**라고 그 애 얘기는 갑자기 왜 꺼내? = *Why would you just bring him up suddenly out of the clear blue like that?* **2.** 뜻밖의 일을 당한 경우에 쓰는 말 = used when one suffers an unfortunate turn of events ▌A: 오늘 범칙금을 20만 원이나 내라는 통지서가 날아왔는데 이게 무슨 **아닌 밤중에 홍두깨**야? = *I just got a bill in the mail here for a 200,000 won fine. What's this out of the clear blue?* B: 내가 그저께 딱지 뗐거든. 미안해. = *I got a ticket a few days ago. I'm sorry.*

➡p.188

NOTE: 홍두깨는 다듬이질할 때 쓰는 나무 방망이다. 남편이 죽어 혼자 된 여자가 밤중에 홍두깨로 다듬이질을 하며 외로움을 달래는 모습에서 유래한 표현이다. 여기서 '아닌 밤중'은 밤이 아니라는 의미가 아니라 '때아닌 밤중' 즉 '밤중에 느닷없이'라는 의미이다.

홍두깨 is a wooden paddle used for ironing out clothing. Often widows, out of loneliness, would iron late into the evening. The 아닌 밤 part of this expression does not mean "not night," rather it means "unexpectedly, in the middle of the night." This phrase is used to describe an activity that seems ridiculous or out of place.

아 다르고 어 다르다 [Lit. Ah and uh are different.] PROVERB

같은 내용이라도 표현에 따라 다르게 들릴 수 있다는 말 = describes how words can be heard differently depending on their expression despite having the same content ▌A: 꼬마야, 이리 좀 와 봐. = *Come here, child.* B: 아저씨, 같은 말이라도 **아 다르고 어 다른** 건데, "아이야, 이리 좀 와 볼래?"라고 하면 듣기 좋잖아요. = *Mr., how about instead of calling me "child," you just say "excuse me, young man"?*

NOTE: '아'와 '어'는 각각 대표적인 양성모음과 음성모음이다. '아'는 밝고 작은 느낌을, '어'는 어둡고 큰 느낌을 준다. 예를 들어 "아기 볼이 '발갛다'."라고 하면 연하고 고운 아기 피부를 연상시키지만, "아기 볼이 '벌겋다'."라고 하면 열이 있거나 아프다는 느낌을 준다. 이처럼 말이라는 것이 표현에 따라 다른 느낌을 전달하기 때문에 말을 정확하고 조심해서 해야 한다는 말이다.

아 and 어 are the most representative positive- and negative-sounding vowels. 아 is thought of as bright and small, while 어 gives off a darker and larger feeling. For example, to say, 아기 볼이 발갛다 brings to mind a beautiful, pure-looking child, whereas to say 아기 볼이 벌겋다 implies that the child is red with a fever or sick in someway. In this way a slight change of vowel can have a major effect on the meaning conveyed. That's why this expression is used to suggest prudence in one's word choice.

아비규환 [Lit. 阿hill + 鼻nose + 叫shout + 喚shout] CHINESE-DERIVATION 많은 사람이 참혹한 지경에 빠져 울부짖는 상황 = a situation in which many people are crying at the sight of something terrible ▌A: 어제 뉴스 봤어? 일본에 쓰나미 온 거. = *Did you watch the news yesterday? About the tsunami in Japan.* B: 그럼. 정말 **아비규환**이 따로 없더라고. 그래도 그 와중에도 일본 사람들 침착한 게 정말 대단하더라. = *Of course. What a terrible disaster! But it was amazing how calm the Japanese people remained even in the midst of such a calamity*

NOTE: '아비(阿鼻)'는 불교에서 말하는 8대 지옥 중 가장 아래에 있는 지옥을 가리킨다. 이곳에 떨어진 죄인들은 하루에 수천번씩 죽고 되살아나는 고통을 받으며 잠시도 쉬지 못한다고 한다. '규환(叫喚)'은 8대 지옥 중 네 번째 지옥으로 살아 있을 때 다른 사람을 죽이거나 절도, 음주를 일삼은 자들이 떨어지게 된다. 이들은 물이 펄펄 끓는 가마솥에 빠지거나 몹시 뜨거운 방에 들어가는 고통을 받는다고 한다.
아비(阿鼻) is the word for the lowest of the eight hells described in Buddhism. In this place, the condemned are forced to endure a thousand deaths and rebirths every day and never enjoy a moment of respite. 규환(叫喚) is the fourth hell and the final destination of those who make debauchery, thievery, murder, and drinking the way of their lives. They burn in a gigantic cauldron of boiling water or in a room of scorching flames.

아쉬운 소리 [Lit. the sound of want] IDIOM 남에게 무엇인가를 부탁하는 말 = words used to ask a favor of another p.262 ▌A: 무슨 바람이 불어서 네가 날 찾아왔냐? **아쉬운 소리**를 할 게 있나 보지? = *What wind blew you* *here to see me today? Looks like you have a favor of some sort to ask of me, right?* B: 왜 그러세요, 형님. 그냥 형님 생각이 나서 와 봤어요. = *Why would you say that? I've just been wondering about you. That's why I came.*

아연실색하다 [Lit. 啞speechless + 然so + 失lose + 色color + 하다verbal suffix] CHINESE-DERIVATION 뜻밖의 일에 몹시 놀라 말을 하지 못하고 얼굴빛이 변하다 = to be so shocked that one loses one's faculties of speech and one's face changes color (*equiv.* to turn white as a sheet) ▌A: 소영이가 많이 놀랐겠구나. = *Soyoung must've been so shocked.* B: **아연실색했죠** 뭐. 집이 난장판이 되어 있으니 처음에는 도둑이 든 줄 알았어요. = *She was as white as a sheet. The whole house was turned upside down and at first I thought that we had been robbed.*

아이 보는 데는 찬물도 못 먹는다 [Lit. One cannot even drink cold water where a child is watching.] PROVERB 아이들은 보는 대로 따라 하기 때문에 아이들 앞에서 말이나 행동을 조심해야 한다는 말 = used to suggest prudence in one's speech and actions in front of children as they have a tendency to mimic everything they see ▌A: 영수야, 너 왜 신발을 구겨 신니? 똑바로 신어야지. = *Yeongsu, why do you have your shoes only half on? You better put them on right.* B: 전에 아빠도 신발을 구겨 신었잖아. = *I saw you wear them like this.* A: **아이 보는 데는 찬물도 못 먹겠구나.** 아빠도 안 그럴 테니, 너도 똑바로 신어라. = *This is exactly why they say you can't make a single misstep in front of kids. Listen, I promise I won't do that anymore, so you too need to wear your shoes properly.*

NOTE: 아이들은 어른들이 하는 말이나 행동을 그대로 따라한다. 가령 물을 마실 때 벌컥벌컥 마시거나 물을 흘리면서 마시는 등의 행동을 하면 아이들이 그것을 보고 배울 수 있는데. 이 표현은 이처럼 아이들 앞에서는 사소한 행동도 조심해야 한다는 의미를 담고 있다.

Children have a tendency to mimic the actions and speech of adults. If one were to gulp down a glass of water, spilling it in the process, it's likely that any child nearby would ape these actions. This phrase is used to emphasize how careful adults have to be about how they act in front of children.

아픈 데를 건드리다 [Lit. to poke at a sore spot] IDIOM 상대의 약점을 건드리다 = to go after the weaknesses of one's counterpart (*syn.* 아픈 데를 찌르다) ▌A: 너도 이제 그만 포기하고 취직 자리 알아봐야 하지 않겠니? 벌써 다섯 번이나 떨어졌잖아. = *Don't you think it's about time you gave up and started looking for a job? You've already failed five times.* B: 너는 꼭 그렇게 남의 **아픈 데를 건드려야겠니**? = *You sure have a knack for prodding people's sore spots.*

아픈 데를 찌르다 IDIOM = 아픈 데를 건드리다

안개 속 [Lit. in the midst of fog] IDIOM 상황이 드러나 있지 않아 알 수 없는 상태 = when one cannot discern the actual state of affairs because the situation is unclear or obscured ▌A: 오늘 일본 팀이 중국 팀을 이기면서 세 팀의 순위 경쟁이 **안개 속**에 싸이게 됐네요. = *With the Japanese team beating the Chinese today, the rank of all three teams has been shrouded in fog.* B: 결국 우리나라와 일본의 최종 경기 결과에 따라 순위가 결정되겠네요. = *I guess the final rank of Korea will be determined after the last match with Japan.*

안되는 사람은 뒤로 넘어져도 코가 깨진다 PROVERB = 재수 없는 놈은 뒤로 자빠져도 코가 깨진다

안에서 새는 바가지 밖에서도 샌다 [Lit. A gourd that leaks indoors will leak outdoors as well.] PROVERB 품성이 나쁜 사람은 어디에서도 드러난다는 말 = Someone of vile character will be that way regardless of the surroundings. (*equiv.* Once a villain always a villain. / You can take the man out of the ghetto, but you can never take the ghetto out of the man. / It's like putting lipstick on a pig.) ▌A: 너 얼굴이 왜 이래? 싸웠니? = *What happened to your face? Did you get in a fight?* B: 어떤 녀석이 자꾸 까불잖아요. = *Some guy kept taunting me.* A: 아이고, **안에서 새는 바가지 밖에서도 샌다**더니 학교 가서까지 싸움질이냐? = *Jeez, it's always the same story with you, isn't it? Now you're even fighting at school?*

안하무인 [Lit. 眼eye + 下under + 無no + 人people] CHINESE-DERIVATION 다른

사람을 무시하는 태도를 가리키는 말 = describes condescending behavior towards others ▌A: 옆집 남자 말이야, 사람이 왜 그래? 사람이 인사를 해도 아는 체를 안 하고. 완전히 **안하무인**이던데? = *Hey, you know the guy next door? Why does he have to be that way? When I try to say hi to him, he just ignores me. It's like he's too good for everyone else.* B: 당신 몰랐어? 옆집 아저씨 시각장애인이잖아. = *Didn't you know? The guy next door is blind.*

앉아서 보고만 있다 [Lit. to sit down and just watch] IDIOM 참견하지 않고 방관하다 = to not interfere in an affair and let it run its course (*equiv.* to stand idly by *syn.* 뒷짐만 지고 있다, 팔짱(을) 끼고 구경만 하다, 가만히 앉아 있다) ▌A: 여보 들었어? 맞은편에 또 새 빵집이 들어온대. = *Honey, did you hear? Yet another bakery is set to open across the street.* B: 큰일이야. 정말 이대로 **앉아서 보고만 있어서** 될 일인지 모르겠네. = *What a disaster! I don't know if we can just stand idly by this time.*

앉으나 서나 [Lit. whether one stands or sits] IDIOM 항상 = always (*syn.* 밤이나 낮이나, 비가 오나 눈이 오나, 자나 깨나) ▌A: 당신은 어떻게 된 게 **앉으나 서나** 돈 벌 생각밖에 안 해? = *Why is it that all you think about is making money all day and all night?* B: 우리가 그나마 이 정도 살게 된 게 그런 나 덕분인 건 왜 몰라? = *Don't you know it's all thanks to that behavior that we live as well as we do today?*

앉은 자리에 풀도 안 난다 [Lit. for grass not to even grow where one has sat] IDIOM 몹시 냉정하고 독한 사람을 두고 하는 말 = used to describe a person who is extremely cold or intense (*equiv.* to be cold) ▌A: 용준아, 돈 있으면 좀 빌려 줘. = *Yongjun, could you lend me some money if you have any?* B: 미안, 나도 지금 가진 돈이 없는데. 영민이한테 빌려 봐. = *Sorry, I don't have any. Borrow some from Yeongmin.* A: 그 녀석 몰라서 그래? **앉은 자리에 풀도 안 날** 애잖아. = *Apparently you don't know what he's like. That guy is as cold as ice.*

NOTE: 잠깐 앉았다 일어났는데도 그 사람의 독기 때문에 풀이 자라지 않을 정도라면 얼마나 독한 사람이겠는가.

If someone is so noxious that even sitting in a place briefly kills the grass where one has sat, one is obviously as cold as ice.

알게 모르게 [Lit. being aware or unaware] IDIOM 자기도 잘 모르는 사이에 = without one's knowing it (*equiv.* when one wasn't paying attention) ▌A: 왜 온몸에 멍이야? = *Why are you covered in bruises?* B: 아, 이사하다가 **알게 모르게** 그렇게 됐나 봐. = *Oh, I guess I must have bumped myself while moving.*

알다가도 모를 일 [Lit. something that one has known and then not known] IDIOM 이해가 가지 않는 일 = something that one cannot understand (*equiv.* I just don't get it. / It's beyond me.) ▌A: 나라 경제는 어렵다는데 백화점 명품 매장에는 물건이 없어 못 팔 지경이라니, 참 **알다가도 모를 일**이야. = *Everyone keeps saying the country is going through hard economic times right now, but department stores sell luxury goods so fast they can't even keep them in stock. I just don't get it.* B: 정말 우리나라 사람들 명품이라면 사족을 못 쓰는데, 큰 문제야. = *Koreans really do go crazy for luxury brands. It's a major problem.*

➡ p.339

앓느니 죽지 [Lit. It's better to die than be sick.] PROVERB 다른 사람에게 일을 맡겼으나 영 마음에 들지 않을 때 차라리 자신이 직접 하는 게 낫겠다는 뜻으로 하는 말 = used when one has entrusted another with a certain task but the results are so unsatisfactory that one must do it oneself (*equiv.* You want something done right, you do it yourself. / I'd rather do it myself.) ▌A: 내가 부탁한 거 다 했어? = *Did you do what I asked you to?* B: 텔레비전에서 갑자기 재미있는 게 하네. 이것만 보고 할게. = *There's a show I really want to watch on TV right now. I'll do it right after this.* A: **앓느니 죽지.** 됐어, 그냥 내가 할게. = *If you want something to get done, you really have to just do it yourself, don't you? Don't worry about it. I'll just do it.*

NOTE: 잔병치레를 자주 하는 것보다 그냥 죽는 게 낫다는 말로, 성가시게 늘 시달리기보다는 크게 한 번 당하고 마는 것이 낫다는 말이다.

Meaning that it's better to die than get sick frequently, this expression is used to suggest that instead of undergoing frequent annoyances, it is better to suffer once and get it over with quickly.

앓는 소리(를) 하다 [Lit. to make sickly noises] IDIOM 자신의 아픔이나 괴로움을 엄살스럽게 호소하다 = to carry on about one's hurt or hardships (*equiv.* to whine / to carry on (about one's hardships) *syn.* 죽는소리 (를) 하다) ▌A: 이번에도 1등 자신 있지? = *Are you confident you'll be first again this time?* B: 아니야. 이번에는 공부를 많이 못 해서 정말 힘들 것 같아. = *No. I wasn't able to study that much this time around, so I think it'll be tough.* A: 너는 또 앓는 소리를 하니? = *Are you whining again?*

앓던 이(가) 빠지다 [Lit. for one's teeth that had been sick to fall out] IDIOM 걱정거리가 없어져 마음이 후련해지다 = for one's heart to clear because a certain worry has vanished (*syn.* 십 년 묵은 체증이 내려가다) ▌A: 참, 집 나갔다면서? 몇 달 동안 집이 안 나가서 애태웠지? = *Hey, I heard you finally got your house sold. You must've been waiting on pins and needles until your house finally sold huh?* B: 응. 앓던 이 빠진 기분 이야. = *Yeah. I feel like a weight has finally been lifted off my shoulders.*

암초를 만나다 [Lit. to meet a hidden reef] IDIOM 예상하지 못한 문제를 맞닥뜨리다 = to come across an unforeseen difficulty (*equiv.* to run aground / to hit a sandbar) ▌A: 저 선수는 진짜 아까워. 월드컵을 앞두고 부상 이라는 암초를 만나다니. = *What a waste! I can't believe that with the World Cup right around the corner he would get injured like that.* B: 저번 월드컵 때도 부상 때문에 못 나갔었잖아. = *He wasn't able to compete in the last World Cup either because of an injury.*

암초에 걸리다 IDIOM = 암초에 부딪치다

암초에 부딪치다 [Lit. to bump into hidden reef] IDIOM 예상하지 못한 문 제를 맞닥뜨리다 = to come up against an unforeseen problem (*equiv.* to run aground / to hit a sandbar) ▌A: 대통령의 개혁 의지에 검찰에서 반발

한다는 뉴스 봤어?=*Did you see the news about the prosecutors opposing the president's plan for reform?* B: 어, 봤어. 시작부터 **암초에 부딪친** 셈이네.=*Yeah, I saw that. It's like the ship has already run aground before even getting out of the harbor.*

앙금이 남다 [Lit. for sediment to remain] IDIOM 마음속에 개운치 않은 감정이 남다=to be left unfulfilled or dissatisfied (*equiv.* to be left with a bad taste in one's mouth / to have lingering resentment) ▌A: 내일 애들 다 모일 건데 너도 나와.=*Everyone's getting together tomorrow, you should come too.* B: 경자도 나와? 걔 오면 난 안 갈래.=*Is Gyeongja coming too? If she's coming, I don't want to go.* A: 너는 아직도 저번 일로 경자랑 **앙금이 남았니?** 이번 기회에 훌훌 털어 버려.=*You two still haven't gotten over what happened last time? Take this as an opportunity to finally clear the air.*

앞길이 구만리 같다 [Lit. for the road ahead to seem like 90,000 *li*] PROVERB 아직 나이가 젊어 살아갈 세월이 많이 남아 있다=to still have a long life to live because of one's youthful age (*equiv.* You still have your whole life ahead of you.) ▌A: 소희 없으면 제 인생은 의미가 없어요. 살아도 사는 게 아니라고요.=*Without Sohee, my life is pointless. I can live, but I'll never truly be alive again.* B: **앞길이 구만리 같은** 애가 못 하는 소리가 없네.=*You've got your whole life ahead of you. You sure say some wacky things!*

앞뒤가 다르다 [Lit. for the front and back to be different] IDIOM 과거에 했던 말이나 행동과 다르다=to not be in line with what one said or did in the past ▌A: 수고비는 일이 끝난 다음에 드리겠습니다.=*I'll be compensating you once we're finished.* B: 네? 말이 **앞뒤가 다르지** 않습니까? 저는 분명 일을 시작할 때 받는 걸로 들었는데요.=*What? That's not what you said before, right? I clearly heard you say that you would be paying me as soon as we got started.*

앞뒤가 막히다 [Lit. for the front and back to be blocked] IDIOM 융통성이 없고 답답하다=to lack flexibility and be hard to deal with ▌A: 당신도

부장님한테 잘 좀 보여. 높은 분이랑 친하게 지내면 떡고물이라도 [→ p.193] 떨어질지 누가 알아? = *You should also try to do your best in front of the VP. Cozy up to someone in a high position and they may throw you some table scraps, right? You never know.* B: 회사에서 일만 열심히 하면 됐지, 뭐하러 아부를 해? = *I think I'll be fine just working hard and keeping to myself. What's flattery going to get me?* A: 참, 당신도 **앞뒤가 이렇게 막혀서야** ……. = *Geez, you're such a square.*

앞뒤가 맞다 [Lit. for the front and back to match] IDIOM 말이 이치에 맞다 = for one's words to be logical (*equiv.* to make sense) ▌A: 김 대리. 이 보고서 **앞뒤가 전혀 안 맞잖아**. = *Mr. Kim, this report makes absolutely no sense.* B: 아, 어느 부분 말씀이세요? = *Ah, exactly which part are you referring to?*

앞뒤(를) 가리지 않다 [Lit. to not distinguish between front and back] IDIOM 어느 하나에 열중하여 다른 것을 생각하지 않다 = to be so enthralled in one activity that one does not think of anything else (*equiv.* to lose oneself in a certain pursuit) ▌A: 왜 그래? 배 아파? = *What's wrong with you? Are you sick?* B: 아까 너무 많이 먹었나 봐요. = *I guess I overate earlier.* A: **앞뒤 안 가리고** 정신없이 먹어 댈 때 내가 알아 봤다. = *When you were really going at it earlier, I knew this was going to happen.*

***애(가)타다** [Lit. for one's innards to burn] IDIOM 몹시 답답하거나 걱정스럽다 = to be frustrated or worried (*equiv.* to burn with the worry or anticipation / to be on tenterhooks *syn* 가슴이 타다, 속(이) 타다 *cf.* 애(를)태우다) ▌A: 남들은 애들 영어다 뭐다 일찌감치 가르치는데, 우리 민수는 저렇게 아무것도 안 시켜도 될까? = *Other parents start early, teaching the kids English and this and that. Do you think it's really okay that we aren't teaching Minsu anything?* B: 애들은 노는 게 최고야. = *Playing is what's best for kids.* A: 남은 이렇게 **애가 타는데** 태평한 소리는! = *I'm hemming and hawing over this and that's all you've got to say? Why are you so relaxed?*

NOTE: '애가 타다', '애가 터지다', '애 떨어질 뻔하다', '애태우다' 등의 '애'는 창자를 의미한다.
The 애 in the expressions, 애가 타다, 애가 터지다, 애 떨어질 뻔하다, 애태우다 etc. means "intestines" or "viscera."

***애(가) 터지다** [Lit. for one's innards to explode] IDIOM 화가 나거나 답답하다＝to be very angry or frustrated (*equiv.* to blow up / to explode *syn.* 속(이) 터지다) ▌A: 안나푸르나에서 실종된 박영석 대장 시신을 꼭 찾아야 할 텐데. ＝*It's imperative that they recover the body of Park Yeongseok, the expedition leader who went missing in Annapurna.* B: 그러게. 우리 국민들도 마음이 이런데 가족들은 얼마나 **애가 터질까**. ＝*That's what I'm saying. If the public feels this bad about it, imagine how terrible his family must feel.*

애 떨어질 뻔하다 [Lit. to almost have one's innards fall out] IDIOM 순간적으로 몹시 놀라다＝to suddenly be extremely surprised (*equiv.* to have the living daylights scared out of you / to have the bejesus scared out of you *syn.* 간(이) 떨어질 뻔하다) ▌A: 미숙아! ＝*Misuk!* B: 아이고, 깜짝이야! **애 떨어질 뻔했네**. ＝*What the ...! You scared the bejesus out of me!*

***애(를)태우다** [Lit. to burn one's innards] IDIOM **1.** 걱정이 되어 마음을 졸이다＝to fret over something or be worried (*syn.* 가슴(을) 태우다, 속(을) 태우다, 속(을) 끓이다 *cf.* 애(가)타다) ▌A: 민수야, 밤이 늦었는데 집에 그만 가야지? 부모님 **애태우시겠다**. ＝*Minsu, it's late. Don't you think you'd better finish up here and get home? Your parents must be worried.* B: 지금 하는 게임만 끝내고요. ＝*Let me just finish this game and go.* **2.** 다른 사람을 걱정하게 만들다＝to make someone worry (*syn.* 속(을) 태우다, 속(을) 끓이다, 애(를)태우다) ▌A: 그러지 말고, 어서 일어나라. 부모님 **애 좀 그만 태워라**. ＝*Come on, hurry and get up. Stop worrying your parents.* B: 아, 조금밖에 안 남았는데 ……. 내일 다시 해야지. ＝*Ah, I was almost done ... I guess I'll have to come back and finish tomorrow.*

***애매모호하다** [Lit. 曖obscure ＋ 昧hazy ＋ 模vague ＋ 糊vague ＋ 하다

adjectival suffix] CHINESE-DERIVATION 말이나 터도가 분명하지 않다 = for someone's actions or words to be ambiguous and uncertain (*equiv.* to vacillate) ▌A: 네 태도를 분명히 해. 그 **애매모호한** 태도는 뭐야? = *Show me exactly where you stand on the issue. What's with all the ambiguity?* B: 나한테 시간을 좀 줘. = *Give me some more time.*

애 이름 [Lit. a child's name] IDIOM 대단치 않은 돈이나 일 = a rather small amount of money or an insignificant task (*equiv.* child's play / chump change) ▌A: 돈 있으면 삼백만 원만 빌려 줘. = *If you have the money, would you mind lending me 3 million won?* B: 돈 삼백만 원이 **애 이름**인 줄 알아? 나한테 그렇게 큰돈이 어겄어? = *Do you think 3 million is just chump change? Where am I going to find that kind of money?*

애지중지(하다) [Lit. 愛love + 之this + 重cherish + 之this] CHINESE-DERIVATION 매우 사랑하고 소중하게 여기다 = to love something deeply or cherish it ▌A: 이거 네가 **애지중지하던** 옷 아니야? = *Aren't these the outfits that you cherished the most?* B: 아, 그 코트요? 이제 안 입어요. 버릴 거예요. = *Ah, that coat? I don't wear it anymore. I'm going to throw it out.*

야단법석 [Lit. 野field + 壇platform + 法Buddhism preach + 席seat → a place for preaching Buddhism outdoors] CHINESE-DERIVATION 여러 사람이 모여 떠들고 소란을 떠는 것 = many people gathering and causing a commotion (*equiv.* hoopla / a fuss / commotion) ▌A: 무슨 일이라도 났어요? 왜 이리 다들 **야단법석**이에요? = *Did something happen? Why is everyone making such a fuss?* B: 그게 아니라 유명 가수가 와서 다들 모여서 구경하고 있어요. = *It's not that. A famous singer showed up, so everyone started crowding around.*

NOTE: '야단법석이다', '야단법석을 떨다'의 꼴로 주로 쓰인다.
This expression is most often used in the following forms: 야단법석이다, 야단법석을 떨다.

약방에 감초 [Lit. licorice at the pharmacy] PROVERB 꼭 있어야 하는 사람

이나 물건＝an indispensable person or thing (*equiv.* a must-have) ▌A: 저 개그맨은 오락 프로그램 안 나오는 곳이 없는 것 같아.＝*I think that comedian is in every single comedy show there is.* B: **약방에 감초** 같은 역할을 잘하니까 그런 거 아닐까?＝*Yeah, that's because he plays an indispensable role, don't you think?*

NOTE: 한약을 지을 때 빠지지 않는 약재 중의 하나가 바로 감초다. 감초는 성질이 순해 다른 약재와 잘 어울리며 약초의 쓴맛 등을 없애 주기 때문에 웬만한 한약의 처방전에는 꼭 끼어 있다. '약방의 감초'라고도 한다.

In the creation of Oriental pharmaceuticals, one product is absolutely indispensable: licorice. That is because its mild properties allow it to mix well with other medicinals and its flavor helps mask the more bitter flavors of other ingredients. This expression is also sometimes iterated as, 약방의 감초.

약방의 감초 PROVERB＝약방에 감초

약육강식 [Lit. 弱weak + 肉flesh + 强strong + 食eat → The weak are to be eaten by the strong.] CHINESE-DERIVATION 강자가 약자를 지배하는 세상 이치＝the principle of those strong ruling over the week (*equiv.* survival of the fittest / Might makes right. / It's a dog-eat-dog world. *cf.* 적자생존) ▌A: 동물이나 사람이나 힘없고 약한 것들은 무리에서 처지고 잡아먹히는구나.＝*It's the same in the animal kingdom as it is amongst humans: those who are weak are ostracized from the group and end up becoming someone's pray.* B: **약육강식**의 세계에서는 어쩔 수 없지.＝*It's a dog-eat-dog world out there. What are you gonna do?*

얌전한 고양이 부뚜막에 먼저 올라간다 [Lit. It's the mild-mannered cat that jumps up on the stove first.] PROVERB 얌전해 보이는 사람이 딴짓을 하거나 약삭빠르게 자기 실속을 차릴 때 쓰는 말＝used when someone who looks meek or mild acts in a surprising manner or seeks their own benefit first (*equiv.* I never would've expected this from him. / I didn't think he was the type to do such a thing.) ▌A: 미선이 걔는 순진한

줄 알았는데 벌써 남자를 알았다고? = *Mison looked so innocent, but now she's saying she's already been with a man?* B: 원래 **얌전한 고양이 부뚜막에 먼저 올라가는** 법이잖아. = *It's always the ones that look the most innocent that you have to watch out for.*

NOTE: 부뚜막은 옛날 부엌에 솥을 걸어두고 음식을 놓아 두던 장소를 말한다. 오늘날의 선반 역할을 하는 곳이다. 먹을 것에 관심이 없는 척하던 고양이가 사람이 사라지자 냉큼 음식이 있는 곳으로 올라가는 모습을 그러한 사람의 행동에 빗댄 표현이다
In the kitchens of yesteryear, the 부뚜막 was where the kettles of food were hung. This place performed a role similar to what shelves do for us today. This expression portrays the kind of people that often surprise us just as a cat that ordinarily looked to have no interest in food suddenly jumping up to grab a bite as soon as its master had left the room.

***양다리(를) 걸치다** [Lit. to lay a leg on each side] IDIOM 동시에 두 명의 이성을 사귀다 = to be involved in a romantic relationship with two members of the opposite sex at the same time (*equiv.* to two-time / to have an affair) ▍A: 소미랑 왜 헤어진 거야? = *Why did you break up with Somi?* B: 글쎄, 걔 나 모르게 **양다리를 걸치고** 있었던 거 있지. = *Well, I found out she was cheating on me.*

양반은 못 된다 [Lit. to not be able to become a *yangban*] IDIOM 다른 사람에 관한 이야기를 하고 있는 도중에 그 사람이 나타났을 때 쓰는 말 = used when people are discussing a certain person and suddenly that person shows up (*equiv.* speak of the devil *syn.* 호랑이도 제 말 하면 온다) ▍A: 너희들 여기 있었어? = *Oh, here you guys are.* B: 어? 참 너도 **양반은 못 되는구나.** = *Huh? Speak of the devil.* A: 왜? 내 얘기 하고 있었어? = *What? Were you guys talking about me?*

NOTE: 조선 시대 양반은 체면을 소중히 여겼다. 양반은 남의 흉을 보지 않고 설사 누가 자신의 흉을 보아도 못 들은 치해야 했다. 그러니 의도하지 않았더라도 자신을 흉보고 있는 자리에 나타난다는 것은 양반으로서 할 행동이 아니라고 여겼던 것이다.

During the Joseon period, the yangban considered honor to be of utmost importance. They spoke no ill of others and weren't even supposed to acknowledge it when they heard others speak ill of them. Showing up suddenly where others were speaking ill of you, even if it was unintentional, was something that the *yangban* were never supposed to allow to happen.

얘기가 다르다 [Lit. The talk is different.] IDIOM 처음에 약속한 내용과 다르다 = for someone to say something that contradicts what they said before (*equiv.* That's not what you said before. / Why do you keep changing your story? *syn.* 이야기가 다르다) ▮A: 도배는 저희가 해야 한다니 **얘기가 다르잖아요**. 저번에 분명히 주인집에서 도배를 해 주시겠다고 했잖아요. = *What do you mean we have to do the wallpapering? That's not what was said before. Last time, you clearly said that you would wallpaper the house for us.* B: 저희는 그런 약속을 한 적이 없습니다. = *We never made such a promise.*

어깨가 가볍다 [Lit. for one's shoulders to be light] IDIOM 무거운 책임에서 벗어나 마음이 홀가분하다 = to unload an important or weighty responsibility and feel relieved (*equiv.* to feel like a weight has been lifted *ant.* 어깨가 무겁다) ▮A: 이제 자식들이 시집 장가 다 갔으니 **어깨가 가볍겠어?** = *With all of your kids finally married off, it must be a major weight off your shoulders, huh?* B: 아닌 게 아니라 무거운 짐을 내려 놓은 기분이야. = *I can't disagree. It's a major load off my chest.*

어깨가 무겁다 [Lit. to have heavy shoulders] IDIOM 무거운 책임을 져서 마음이 부담스럽다 = to feel burdened by a heavy responsibility (*equiv.* to bear a weight on one's shoulders *ant.* 어깨가 가볍다) ▮A: 아버지가 외국에 계셔서 집에 남자는 저 혼자예요. = *With my dad away overseas, I'm the man of the house.* B: **어깨가 무겁겠군요**. = *What a responsibility!*

어깨너머로 배우다 [Lit. to learn over someone else's shoulders] IDIOM 남이 하는 것을 옆에서 보거나 들어 익히다 = to learn by watching another or by listening to what they say ▮A: 어떻게 네가 이런 음식을

할 줄 아니?=*How did you learn to make this?* B: 어릴 때 엄마가 하시는 걸 **어깨너머로 배웠어요**.=*I learned by watching my mom when I was young.*

어깨를 겨루다 [Lit. to pit one's shoulders against those of another] IDIOM 대등한 위치에서 경쟁하다=to compete from similar standing (*syn.* 어깨를 견주다) ▌A: 우리나라가 육상 단거리에서 세계적인 선수들과 **어깨를 겨루게** 될 날이 올까요?=*Do you think that the day will ever come when South Korean athletes will compete with the strongest runners of the world?* B: 글쎄요. 아무래도 신체 조건이 불리하니 쉽지는 않겠지만, 불가능하지는 않다고 봅니다.=*Well, their lesser stature will be an obstacle, but I don't see it as impossible.*

어깨를 견주다 IDIOM = 어깨를 겨루다

어깨를 나란히 하다 [Lit. to put one's shoulders in a row with others] IDIOM 서로 실력이나 지위가 비슷한 상태가 되다=for one's abilities or status to be similar to that of others (*equiv.* to stand shoulder to shoulder with (the best etc.)) ▌A: 우리나라는 짧은 시간에 놀라울 만큼 빠른 성장을 했습니다.=*Korea has really grown at an alarming rate in such a short time.* B: 어느새 선진국들과 **어깨를 나란히 할** 정도가 되었잖아요.=*Before we even realized it Korea has come to stand in line with other advanced nations.*

어깨(를) 펴다 [Lit. to spread one's shoulders] IDIOM 당당하게 행동하다=to act imposing or dignified (*equiv.* to raise one's head high / to keep one's chin up *syn.* 가슴(을) 펴다) ▌A: 죄송해요, 아버지. 이 나이 먹도록 취직도 못 하고 아버지한테 ►p.373 손이나 벌리네요.=*I'm so sorry, Father. At this age, to have to come to you with my hand out ...* B: 괜찮아. 기죽지 마라, 아들. 이런 때일수록 **어깨 펴고** 다녀.=*It's all right. Don't let yourself lose hope, my son. This is precisely when you must keep your head held high.*

어깨에 힘(을) 주다 [Lit. to prop up one's shoulders] IDIOM 거만하게 굴

거나 뻐기는 태도를 취하다 = to act arrogantly or ostentatiously (*equiv.* to act (all) high and mighty / to prance around arrogantly *syn.* 목에 힘(을) 주다 *cf.* 어깨에 힘(이) 들어가다) ▌A: 명자가 요즘 **어깨에 잔뜩 힘을 주고** 다니는 거 알아? = *Myeongja sure has been prancing around with her head held high recently, huh?* B: 그래? 왜? = *Really? Why?* A: 이번에 큰딸이 서울대에 합격했대. = *Because her eldest daughter got into Seoul National University.*

어깨에 힘(이) 들어가다 [Lit. for energy to go into one's shoulders] IDIOM

권위나 능력을 뽐내다 = to be boastful of one's authority or capabilities (*syn.* 목에 힘(이) 들어가다 *cf.* 어깨에 힘(이) 들어가다) ▌A: 자네 요즘 살맛 나겠어. 직장에서는 승승장구하지, 자식들은 다 잘나가지. = *You must be so happy with the way your life has been going recently. You're on a roll at work, and your kids are doing so well.* B: 사실 나도 모르게 **어깨에 힘이 들어가기는** 해. = *Yeah, honestly I find myself walking around with my head held high without even realizing I'm doing it.*

어느 세월에 [Lit. In what year?] IDIOM

매우 긴 시간이 지나야 함을 강조할 때 쓰는 말 = used to emphasize that a great amount of time will need to pass (before something comes true etc.) (*equiv.* In what century? *syn.* 어느 천년에) ▌A: 집 좋다! = *Your house is amazing!* B: 빛 좋은 개살구지 뭐. 은행에서 빌린 돈을 **어느 세월에** 다 갚을지 모르겠어. = *It's all just a façade. I'll never be able to pay back the bank all the money I owe them.*

어느 장단에 춤을 춰야 할지 모르겠다 [Lit. not to know which rhythm one should dance to] IDIOM

일을 시키는 사람의 지시가 자주 변해 일을 수행하기가 어려울 때 쓰는 말 = describes a situation where constantly changing orders leave a person confused about what to do (*equiv.* Whose drumbeat do I need to follow?) ▌A: 우리 팀장님 때문에 피곤해 죽겠어요. = *I'm sick and tired of our team leader.* B: 왜요? 무슨 일 있어요? = *Why? What's going on?* A: 어제는 이렇게 하라고 하고 오늘은 또 저렇게 하라고 하니, **어느 장단에 춤을 춰야 할지 모르겠어요.** = *He told me to do things one way yesterday, and then another way today. I don't know what to do.*

어느 천년에 IDIOM = 어느 세월에

어디 아프냐? [Lit. Are you sick somewhere?] IDIOM 엉뚱한 말이나 행동을 할 때 하는 소리 = used when someone says something unexpected or acts in a surprising way (*equiv.* Are you feeling all right? *syn.* 뭐 잘못 먹었냐?) ▌A: 너 **어디 아프냐**? 아까부터 왜 혼자 그렇게 웃어? = *Are you feeling all right? Why have you been laughing to yourself like that?* B: 그냥 무슨 생각 좀 하고 있었어요. = *I've just been thinking about something.*

어림(도)없다 [Lit. to not even have an estimate] IDIOM **1.** 말이나 행동이 터무니없다 = for someone's words or actions to be preposterous (*equiv.* That's preposterous! / Not a chance! / Stop your blathering! *syn.* 어림 반 푼 어치도 없다) ▌A: 지금 돈으로 이 회사를 사겠다는 거요? **어림없는** 소리 마시오! = *You're telling me you intend to buy this company? That's preposterous!* B: 그러지 마시고 천천히 생각해 보십시오. = *Come on, just think it over.* **2.** 도저히 감당해 낼 수 없다 = to be far beyond one's powers (*equiv.* The likelihood of that is next to nil. *syn.* 어림 반 푼어치도 없다) ▌A: 미선이가 서울대를? **어림도 없어**. = *Miseon? To Seoul National University? Not a chance.* B: 사람 일을 어떻게 알아? 미선이라고 서울대 가지 말라는 법은 없잖아. = *How can you be so sure? Who says she can't go?*

NOTE: '어림'은 대강 짐작으로 헤아리는 것을 말한다. '어림도 없다'는 '어림 반 푼어치도 없다'가 줄어든 말로 이해할 수 있다. '말의 이치나 가능성을 대충 헤아려 봐도 얼마 되지 않는다'라는 뜻이다.
An 어림 is an estimate based on guesswork. The expression 어림도 없다 can be understood as a shortened form of 어림 반 푼어치도 없다 (The estimate is less than half a penny). This phrase means that the value of what someone has said or the likelihood of it coming to pass is extremely low.

어림 반 푼어치도 없다 IDIOM = 어림(도)없다

어부지리 [Lit. 漁fish + 夫man + 之of + 利benefit → the benefit of a

fisherman] CHINESE-DERIVATION 두 사람이 다투는 사이에 엉뚱한 사람이 이익을 보게 될 때 쓰는 말 = used to describe a situation where a third party is the beneficiary of a fight between two others (*equiv.* to play one's enemies against each other) ▌A: 이거 제가 가져도 되나요? **어부지리** 같은데. = *Is it really okay for me to be taking this? It just doesn't seem right.* B: 재석이랑 용운이랑 둘 다 안 갖겠다고 하니까 어차피 주인 없는 물건인데 뭐. = *Jaeseok and Yongoon both said that they won't take it, so it's up for grabs at this point anyway.*

NOTE: 중국 전국시대의 한 이야기에서 유래한 표현이다. 냇가에서 황새 한 마리가 조갯살을 먹으려고 부리를 넣었는데, 그 순간 조개가 입을 오므려 부리가 껍질에 끼었다. 그 상태로 둘이 낑낑대는 걸 어부가 발견하고 그 둘을 한번에 잡아 집으로 돌아갔다.
This idiom is derived from a story of China during the Warring States period. Along the banks of a river, a stork stuck its bill into a clam's shell to find himself some clam meat. Just at that moment, however, the clam snapped shut, catching the stork's bill in its mouth. A passing fishermen discovered the pair in this state and took them both home for his supper.

어불성설 [Lit. 語word + 不no + 成become + 說say] CHINESE-DERIVATION 말이 이치에 맞지 않음 = illogical statements (*equiv.* to be illogical / to be ludicrous) ▌A: 나는 큰 집에서 살고 싶은데, 돈을 많이 벌고 싶은 생각은 없어. = *I want to live in a big house, but I'm not interested in making a lot of money.* B: 그게 말이 되냐? **어불성설**이지. = *Do you think that makes sense? That's ridiculous.*

어안이 벙벙하다 [Lit. for one's tongue to be dumbfounded] IDIOM 놀랍거나 기막힌 일을 당하여 얼떨떨하다 = to be bewildered because of a surprising or perplexing happening (*equiv.* to be wide-eyed in astonishment / to be dumbstruck) ▌A: 수상 소감 부탁드립니다. = *How do you feel about winning this award?* B: 제가 대상을 받게 될 줄은 꿈에도 몰랐어요. 그래서 지금 좀 **어안이 벙벙합니다**. = *I never in my wildest dreams imagined I would be holding this prize in my hands. That's why my jaw is still hanging wide open.*

어제오늘 일이 아니다 [Lit. It's not a issue from today or tomorrow.] IDIOM 늘 있어 왔던 일이다＝Something has consistently occurred since long ago. (*equiv.* It happens all the time. / It's nothing new.) ▌A: 아기를 낳아도 걱정이에요. 누구 봐 줄 사람도 없고, 그렇다고 직장을 그만둘 수도 없고. ＝*I'm worried about what's going to happen if I have a child. There'll be no one to look after it, but even so, I can't just quit my job.* B: 어제오늘 일이 아니죠. 뾰족한 해결책도 없고요. ＝*Such problems are nothing new for parents. Unfortunately, there is no easy solution.*

어처구니(가)없다 [Lit. The pestle handle is gone. (Or possibly, the animal statuette is gone.)] IDIOM 너무 황당하거나 한심해서 언짢다＝to be in bad humor because one is perplexed or displeased (*syn.* 기(가)막히다, 기(가)차다) ▌A: 어제 걔 말하는 거 들었어? 자기가 잘못해 놓고 오히려 큰소리치는 걸 보니 참 **어처구니가 없더라고**. ＝*Did you hear what he said to me yesterday? It was all his fault but he tried to blame me. It was unbelievable.* B: 네가 이해해. 뭔가 오해가 있었겠지. ＝*Try to understand. I'm sure it was all just a big misunderstanding.*

> **NOTE:** 이 표현에는 다음 두 가지 설이 있다. 하나는 어처구니가 맷돌의 손잡이를 가리킨다는 설명이다. 맷돌을 돌려야 하는데 그 손잡이가 없는 난처한 상황에서 어이없다는 뜻이 파생되었다는 것이다. 다른 하나는 어처구니가 집의 안녕을 위해 전통 한옥의 지붕에 세워 놓은 동물 모양의 구조물이라는 설이다. 어처구니가 없으면 집에 화가 닥칠 수 있기 때문에 그만큼 당혹스러운 상황이 되는 것이다.
>
> There are two stories about the origin of this phrase. 어처구니 is the word for the handle of a pestle. Yes, the pestle of mortar and pestle fame. Not being able to find the pestle when you need to grind something up can truly put you in a bad mood. Some say that this is the root of the phrase. On the other hand, the animal-shaped charm that adorned traditional hanoks was also called by this name. These statuettes were believed to ensure the welfare of the inhabitants, and naturally, if one went missing, it would send the household into a panic.

억장이 무너지다 [Lit. for a 100 million-story (wall) to collapse] IDIOM 극

심한 슬픔이나 절망감을 느끼다 = to feel profound sadness or disappointment (*equiv.* to feel as if one's entire life has shattered / to feel as if the sky has fallen *syn.* 하늘이 무너지다) ▌A: 처음 암이라는 얘기를 들으셨을 때 심정이 어떠셨어요? = *When you first heard that it was cancer, how did you feel?* B: **억장이 무너지는** 것 같았죠 뭐. = *I felt like my whole life was collapsing around me.*

NOTE: '억장'은 '억장지성(億丈之城)'의 줄임말로 성의 높이가 억 장(한 장은 사람 키에 해당)에 이를 정도로 높은 성을 말한다. 그처럼 높은 성이 무너지는 듯한 느낌을 받을 때 이 표현을 쓴다.
억장 is a shortened form of 억장지성(億丈之城), and therefore means a fortress 100 million *jang* (one *jang* is approximately the height of an average person) high. Imagine such a colossal fortress collapsing to the ground and you will understand what this expression is all about.

억지 춘향 [Lit. a forced *Chunhyang*] IDIOM 원치 않은 일을 어쩔 수 없이 함 = doing something one does not want to do (*equiv.* to do something against one's will) ▌A: 어제 선 봤다며? 어땠어? = *I heard your parents set up a meeting with an eligible bachelor for you yesterday? How was it?* B: 별로 결혼 생각도 없는데, 엄마가 하도 성화여서, **억지 춘향**으로 끌려 나간 거지 뭐. = *I really have no interest in marriage whatsoever, but my mom just won't let up. So I was kind of dragged there against my will.*

NOTE: 이 표현과 관련해서는 두 가지 설이 있다. 첫째는, 한국의 전통 소설인 〈춘향전〉의 주인공 춘향에서 유래했다는 설이다. 춘향이는 억지로 수청을 들게 하려는 변 사또를 끝내 거부했는데, 여기서 억지 춘향이라는 말이 생겨 났다는 것이다. 두 번째는 '억지 춘양'이라는 말에서 왔다는 설이다. 춘양은 경북의 한 지명으로, 원래는 이 인근까지 철도가 놓여질 계획이었는데 어떤 이유에선지 춘양에 철도를 억지로 놓아 철도 노선이 뒤죽박죽이 되어 버렸다고 한다. 이 때문에 억지 춘양이라는 말이 생겨 났는데, 이것이 나중에 억지 춘향으로 바뀌게 되었다고 한다.
There are two schools of thought on the origin of this phrase. The first theory is that the phrase originates with the main character of the Korean

classic, *The Story of Chunhyang*. The local magistrate, Mr. Byun, was constantly trying to convince her to be his concubine but she refused. 억지 means "compulsion" and 춘향 is the name of the character, so many believe that the phrase originates here. As for the other theory, there is a place named 춘양 in North Gyeongsang Province. There were plans to put a railway in the area, but not to bring the railroad to town. After wrangling over the issue, the town was included in the line but extending the line to the town meant that the railroad had become a zigzagging mess. From this debacle, the phrase was coined as 억지 춘양 and later changed to 억지 춘향.

언감생심 [Lit. 焉how + 敢dare + 生grow + 心heart] CHINESE-DERIVATION 감히 바랄 수도 없음 = inability to even dream (of such things) (*equiv*. to not even dare to dream) ▌A: 지금은 세상 참 많이 좋아진 거예요. 적어도 밥 굶을 걱정은 안 하니까요. = *The world is a much better place than it used to be. At the very least we don't have to worry about starving anymore.* B: 우리 어릴 때만 해도 삼시 세 끼 하얀 쌀밥을 먹는다는 건 **언감생심** 꿈도 못 꿀 일이었지요. = *Even as recently as when we were young, we wouldn't even dare to dream of having three meals of white rice per day.*

언 발에 오줌 누기 [Lit. to pee on a frozen foot] PROVERB 잠시의 효력은 있으나 근본적인 해결책은 되지 못할 때 쓰는 말 = used to describe a course of action that generates a short-lived positive effect but is not fundamentally effective (*equiv*. a temporary fix *syn*. 임시방편) ▌A: 아이고, 허리야. 청용아, 이리 와서 엄마 허리 좀 밟아라. = *Ouch, my back! Cheongyong, come over here and walk on my back for a bit.* B: 엄마, 그래 봤자 **언 발에 오줌 누기**죠. 병원을 가세요. = *Even if I do, it'll only be a temporary fix, Mom. You need to see a doctor about that.*

NOTE: 발이 얼었을때 오줌을 누면 물론 잠깐 녹긴 하겠지만, 물은 열을 잘 흡수하기 때문에 다시 차가워져 사태가 더욱 악화된다.

Peeing on a frozen foot does, of course, cause it to thaw momentarily, but as liquids absorb heat well, the foot would immediately become cold again and the overall situation would quickly grow worse.

언행일치 [Lit. 言word + 行do + 一one + 致reach] CHINESE-DERIVATION 말과 행동이 일치함 = for one's words and actions to be in accord (*equiv.* keeping one's word / practicing what you preach) ▌A: 정치인에게 있어 가장 중요한 것이 뭐라고 생각하세요? = *What do you think is the most important principle for a politician?* B: **언행일치** 아닐까요? = *Well, that would most likely be keeping their word, don't you think?*

얼굴에 똥칠(을)하다 [Lit. to paint one's face with poop] IDIOM 체면을 깎거나 명예를 더럽히다 = to destroy someone's reputation (*syn.* 얼굴에 먹칠(을)하다) ▌A: 아니 왜 술을 마셨으면 곱게 잠이나 잘 일이지, 이웃집 대문에 토는 하고 그러니? 어미 **얼굴에 똥칠을 하는구나**, 네가. = *I don't understand, if you were drunk why wouldn't you just come in the house to sleep? Why did you go throw up in front of our neighbor's door like that? You're trashing our reputation.* B: 저는 우리 집 대문인 줄 알았어요. = *I thought it was our front door.*

얼굴에 먹칠(을)하다 IDIOM = 얼굴에 똥칠(을)하다

얼굴에 씌어 있다 [Lit. It's written on one's face.] IDIOM 기분이나 감정이 표정에 그대로 나타나다 = for one's feelings or emotions to be apparent (*equiv.* to be written all over one's face) ▌A: 오늘 학교에서 무슨 일 있었니? 표정이 왜 그렇게 안 좋아? = *Did something happen today at school? You don't look very happy.* B: 아무 일 없었어요. = *No, nothing happened.* A: 안 좋은 일이 있었다고 **얼굴에 씌어 있는데** 뭘. 엄마한테 얘기해 봐. = *Come on now, it's written all over your face. Now come here and tell me what happened.*

얼굴에 철판(을) 깔다 [Lit. to lay a steel plate across one's face] IDIOM 염치나 체면도 없이 몹시 뻔뻔스럽다 = to act in a brazen or shameless manner (*equiv.* to have no shame *cf.* 얼굴(이) 두껍다) ▌A: 갑자기 돈이 필요한데 누구한테 부탁하지? = *All of a sudden I'm in need of a lot of money, but who should I ask?* B: **얼굴에 철판을 깔고** 사장님한테 얘기해 보는 게 어때? = *If you can take the shame of it, you could always ask the boss.*

얼굴(을) 내밀다 [Lit. to push out one's face] IDIOM 모임 따위에 모습을 나타내다 = to show up at a meeting or event (*equiv.* to show one's face) ▌A: 얘, 너 요즘 얼굴 보기가 왜 이렇게 힘들어? 모임에 **얼굴 좀 내밀어**. = *Why haven't I seen you around much recently? Why don't you show your face at the meeting?* B: 미안. 요즘에 너무 바빠서 정신이 좀 없네. = *I'm sorry. I've been really busy lately. Things are so chaotic right now.*

얼굴을 들지 못하다 IDIOM = 낯을 들지 못하다

얼굴(을) 보다 [Lit. to see someone's face] IDIOM 체면을 고려하다 = to consider someone's reputation ▌A: 내 **얼굴 봐서** 네가 참아. = *Just let it go, because I'm asking you too.* B: 내가 네 형 때문에 참는다. 다음부터는 국물도 없을 줄 알아. = *I'm just letting it slide because of your brother. It won't happen again.*

> NOTE: '누구누구의 얼굴을 봐서', '누구누구의 얼굴을 봐서라도'의 꼴로 쓰인다.
> Most often used in the following forms: 누구누구의 얼굴을 봐서, 누구누구의 얼굴을 봐서라도.

얼굴(을) 붉히다 [Lit. to make one's face red] IDIOM 1. 화를 내다 = to be angry (*equiv.* to be red in the face) ▌A: 아파트 층간 소음 때문에 이웃끼리 **얼굴 붉히는** 경우가 많대요. = *They say that noisy upstairs neighbors are the cause of many angry tenants.* B: 그것 때문에 살인도 일어날 정도니 심각한 문제죠. = *Sometimes it's enough to drive people as far as murder. It's a serious problem.* 2. 수줍어하다 = to be shy (*equiv.* for one's face to turn red (with embarrassment)) ▌A: 예림이는 어릴 때나 지금이나 참 수줍음이 많아. = *Yerim, ever since she was a little child, has always been so shy.* B: 그래도 지금은 많이 나아진 거예요. 예전에는 누가 쳐다만 봐도 **얼굴 붉히고는** 했잖아요. = *Well, she's a lot better than she used to be. Back in the old days her face used to turn crimson whenever anyone would as much as stare at her.*

얼굴(이) 간지럽다 IDIOM = 낯(이)간지럽다

얼굴(이) 두껍다 IDIOM = 낯(이) 두껍다

얼굴이 반쪽이 되다 [Lit. Your face is half (of what it used to be).] IDIOM 살이 많이 빠져 얼굴이 안돼 보이다 = to lose so much weight that one is pitiful to look at ▌A: 엄마, 저 왔어요. = *Mom, I'm here.* B: 아이고, 내 새끼 어디 얼굴 좀 보자. 객지 생활 석 달 만에 **얼굴이 반쪽이 됐네**. = *Oh my, look at your face. After only three months of living in a new place, your face has shrunk by half.*

얼굴이 팔리다 [Lit. to have one's face sold] IDIOM 주로 좋지 않은 일로 여러 사람에게 알려지다 = for one's face to become well-known, most commonly for an untoward reason ▌A: 이 동네에서는 내 **얼굴이 팔려** 있으니까 딴 데로 가자. = *I'm too well known around these parts. Let's go somewhere else.* B: 그래. 여기는 눈이 너무 많다. = *All right. There're too many eyes on us right now.*

업어 가도 모르다 [Lit. to not even know that one is being carried somewhere] IDIOM 잠이 아주 깊이 들다 = to sleep very deeply (*equiv.* to be a heavy sleeper / to sleep through anything) ▌A: 쉿! 조용히 해. 영수 자. = *Shhh! Be quiet. Youngsu is sleeping.* B: 괜찮아. 애는 한번 잠들면 **업어 가도 몰라**. = *It's fine. A marching band couldn't wake him up.*

없는 말 [Lit. words that don't exist] IDIOM 사실이 아닌 말 = a statement that is not true ▌A: 뭐? 내가 민수 씨한테 추파를 던졌다고? = *What? You're saying that I was making eyes at Minsu?* B: 사실 내가 **없는 말** 지어낸 건 아니잖아. 네가 민수 씨한테 꼬리 친 건 사실 아냐? = *You think I just made it up out of thin air? So you're saying it's not true that you made moves on him first?*

엉덩이가 근질근질하다 [Lit. to have an itchy rear end] IDIOM 가만히 앉아 있지 못하고 자꾸 일어나 몸을 움직이고 싶어하다 = to not be able to sit still for long and want to get up and move around (*equiv.* to have ants in your pants / to be antsy) ▌A: 하루 종일 책상 앞에만 앉아 있었더니 **엉덩이가 근질근질하네**. = *Sitting at my desk all day long is starting to*

make me feel really antsy. B: 그럼 잠깐 바람이라도 쐬러 나갈까?= ➡p.287
Well then how about getting some fresh air?

엉덩이가 무겁다 [Lit. to have a heavy rear end] IDIOM 한번 자리에 앉으면 일어나지 않고 오래 앉아 있다 = to stay seated for a long time whenever one has sat down ▌A: 공부 벌써 다 한 거야?= *You're already finished studying?* B: 게임 한 판 하면서 머리 좀 식히고 다시 하려고 ➡p.236 요. = *I'm just going to cool my head while I play one game and get right back to it.* A: 공부를 잘하려면 **엉덩이가 무거워야** 되는데 ……. 쯧쯧. = *If you want to get good grades, you should strap yourself down to the chair.*

엎드려 절 받기 PROVERB = 옆구리 찔러 절 받기

엎어지면 코 닿을 데 [Lit. the place one's nose would touch if one fell down] PROVERB 매우 가까운 거리 = a very close spot (*equiv.* a stone's throw away) ▌A: 또 지각이야? 넌 집이 **엎어지면 코 닿을 데**에 있으면서 왜 만날 늦니?= *You're tardy again? Your house is a stone's throw away and yet you still manage to be late every day?* B: 죄송해요. 집이 가까우니까 자꾸 게으름을 피우게 되네요. = *I'm so sorry. I guess because my house is so close by I always take my time getting ready.*

엎질러진 물 [Lit. spilt water] PROVERB 바로잡거나 돌이킬 수 없는 일 = something that cannot be stopped or reversed (*equiv.* spilt milk / water under the bridge) ▌A: 아까 그런 약속은 하는 게 아닌데. 야단 났어. = *I shouldn't have made that promise. I'm going to get in big trouble.* B: 이미 **엎질러진 물**이야. 잊어버려. = *It's water under the bridge now. Forget about it.*

엎친 데 덮친 격 [Lit. to be thrown over and then knocked over] IDIOM 어려운 일이나 불행한 일이 겹쳐 일어나다 = for difficult or unfortunate events to occur almost simultaneously (*equiv.* (to be like) kicking someone when they're down / and to make matters worse ... *syn.* 설상가상) ▌A: 요즘 왜 그렇게 피곤해 보여요?= *Why are you looking so tired recently?* B: 회사에서 일도 많은데, **엎친 데 덮친 격**으로 남편이 교통사고가

나서 입원하는 바람에 병 간호까지 해야 하거든요. = *Well, there's always a heavy workload at the office, and on top of that my husband got into a car accident and had to be hospitalized. So I have to nurse him as well.*

여자가 한을 품으면 오뉴월에도 서리가 내린다 [Lit. When a woman holds a grudge, it will frost even in May or June.] PROVERB 여자가 앙심을 품지 않도록 하라는 말 = a warning to avoid incurring the rancor of a woman (*equiv.* Hell hath no fury like a woman scorned.) ▌A: 저게 말이 돼? 이혼한 전 남편한테 복수하려고 10년 동안 칼을 간다는 게? = *Does that make any sense to you? For a woman to be out for revenge like that for over 10 years after divorcing her husband?* B: **여자가 한을 품으면 오뉴월에도 서리가 내린다는** 말도 있잖아. = *That's why they say hell hath no fury like a woman scorned.*

역지사지(하다) [Lit. 易exchange + 地place + 思think + 之this] CHINESE-DERIVATION 처지를 바꾸어서 생각해 보다 = to consider an issue from a new standpoint (*equiv.* to walk a mile in another's shoes / to see (the world, a situation etc.) through another's eyes) ▌A: 지하철에서 자리를 잡고 앉아서 술 마시는 등산객 기사 봤어? = *Did you see that article about the hikers who sat down in the middle of the subway train and started drinking?* B: 어. 어떻게 사람들이 그렇게 이기적일 수 있지? **역지사지한다면** 도저히 있을 수 없는 일일 텐데. = *Yeah. How can people act so selfishly? If people would just look upon their own actions through the eyes of others, things like that would never happen.*

연극(을)하다 [Lit. to perform to play] IDIOM 남을 속이기 위해 거짓으로 말이나 행동을 꾸미다 = to act or speak in an affected manner to deceive others (*equiv.* to put on a show) ▌A: 엄마, 미정이 학교 갈 시간 아냐? = *Mom, isn't it time for Mijeong to go to school?* B: 미정이 오늘 아파서 못 가겠단다. = *She's saying she's too sick to go to school today.* A: 엄마, 그 말을 믿어? 학교 가기 싫어서 **연극하는** 거잖아. = *Mom, you believe that? She's putting on a show for you because she doesn't want to go to school.*

연막(을) 치다 [Lit. to create a smokescreen] IDIOM 수단을 써서 사실을

숨기다＝to use means at one's disposal to hide the truth (*equiv.* to put up a smokescreen) ▌A: 이번에 그 팀 핵심 선수가 부상으로 출전 못 한다는 게 사실일까? ＝*Do you think the rumors that that team's most powerful player won't be able to compete in the next match because of an injury are true?* B: 모르지. 연막을 치는 것일 수도 있어. ＝*I have no idea. It could be a smokescreen.*

열 길 물속은 알아도 한 길 사람 속은 모른다 [Lit. Even if one knows the water to a depth of ten *gils* (unit of depth), one can never know even one *gil* into the heart of another.] PROVERB 사람의 속마음을 알기가 매우 어렵다는 말＝describes the difficulty of truly knowing the inner thoughts of another (*equiv.* You can't judge a book by its cover.) ▌A: 김 과장한테 뒤통수를 맞을 줄은 정말 꿈에도 몰랐어요. ＝*I never in my wildest dreams thought that department chief Kim would betray me like this.* B: **열 길 물속은 알아도 한 길 사람 속은 모르는** 거라잖아요. ＝*That's why they say you can never know what intentions reside in the hearts of men.*

> NOTE: '길'은 사람 키 정도에 해당하는 길이를 말한다.
> A *gil* is approximately the height of an average man.

열매(를) 맺다 [Lit. to bear fruit] IDIOM 노력의 성과가 나타나다＝for one's efforts to be met with accomplishment or reward ▌A: 주례 선생님의 주례사가 있겠습니다. ＝*And next will be the officiant's message.* B: 오늘은 두 사람의 사랑이 마침내 **열매를 맺는** 날입니다. ＝*Today is the day that the love of these two has finally borne fruit.*

열 번 찍어 안 넘어가는 나무 없다 [Lit. There's no tree that cannot be felled in ten strokes.] PROVERB 아무리 의지가 굳어도 여러 번 권유하면 마음이 변하게 마련이라는 말＝suggests that no matter how resolute one's heart may be, persistent persuasion is bound to change it (*equiv.* Little strokes fell great oaks. / If at first you don't succeed, try, try again. / There's nothing you can't do if you keep at it long enough. *cf.* 못 오를 나무는 쳐다보지도 마라) ▌A: 두 분은 첫눈에 반하셨어요? ＝*Did you two fall for each other at first sight?* B: 아니요. 제가 혼자 쫓아다녔어요. **열 번**

찍어 안 넘어가는 나무 없다고, 계속 따라다니다 사귀게 됐죠. = *No. I one-sidedly kept after her. This must be why they say if at first you don't succeed, try try again. After pursuing her for a long time, she finally gave in.*

열 손가락 깨물어 안 아픈 손가락이 없다 [Lit. If you bite anyone of your ten fingers, there isn't a single one that won't hurt.] PROVERB 부모에게 자식들은 하나같이 다 소중하다는 말 = Parental love that is spread equally among all children. (*equiv.* Every child is (equally) dear to their parents.) ▌A: 아빠는 왜 나보다 언니를 더 좋아해? = *Why is she Dad's favorite?* B: **열 손가락 깨물어 안 아픈 손가락이 어디 있니?** 아빠가 왜 언니를 편애해? = *Every child is equally dear to their parents. Why do you think your father would ever play favorites?*

열쇠를 쥐다 [Lit. to grasp the key] IDIOM 어떤 일을 해결하는 결정적인 실마리를 갖고 있다 = to possess the critical elements to a solution (*equiv.* to hold the key(s) *syn.* 키를 쥐다) ▌A: 내일 경기는 어떻게 전망하십니까? = *What's your outlook for the match tomorrow?* B: 역시 부상에서 회복한 지 얼마 되지 않는 김승현 선수가 경기의 **열쇠를 쥐고** 있다고 생각합니다. = *Well, obviously I think that Kim Seunghyeon, who's only recently recovered from an injury, is holding the keys to victory tomorrow.*

열 일 제치다 [Lit. to push aside ten tasks] IDIOM 어떤 중요한 일 때문에 다른 모든 일을 미루거나 그만두다 = to quit or delay all one's other work to focus on an urgent task ▌A: 뭐야? 고작 발가락 다친 거였어? 많이 다쳤다고 해서 **열 일 제치고** 달려왔더니. = *What's the deal? All you did was hurt your toe? I heard you were severely injured, so I cleared my schedule and ran all the way over here.* B: 언니가 몰라서 그래. 피가 엄청나게 나왔단 말이야. = *You just weren't here to see it, but I really did bleed a lot.*

NOTE: '열 일 제치고'나 '열 일 제쳐 두고'의 꼴로 쓰인다.
This phrase is most often used as, 열 일 제치고 or 열 일 제쳐 두고.

열풍이 불다 [Lit. for a hot wind to blow] IDIOM 크게 유행하거나 사회적 분위기가 형성되다 = for a major trend to be underway or a societal change to take place (*equiv.* for a movement to sweep the land / for the winds of change to blow) ▌A: 유럽에서 케이 팝의 **열풍이 불고** 있대요. = *I hear that K-pop is sweeping across Europe.* B: 반가운 소식이기는 한데, 앞으로가 중요하겠군요. = *I'm glad to hear it, but how things go from here on out will make the difference.*

엿 먹이다 [Lit. to feed someone *yeot*] IDIOM (속된 말로) 남을 속이거나 골탕을 먹이다 = (slang) to deceive someone or give them a hard time (*syn.* 물(을) 먹이다) ▌A: 박 형사, 왜 그렇게 화를 내? = *Detective Park, why are you so upset?* B: 지금 저 녀석이 저 **엿 먹이려고** 하잖아요. = *That bastard just tried to trick me, that's why.*

NOTE: 1964년 중학 입시 문제 중에 "엿기름 대신 넣어서 엿을 만들 수 있는것은 무엇인가?"라는 것이 있었다. 당시 무즙이 보기에 있었는데 정답은 다른 것이었다. 그런데 실제로는 무즙으로도 엿을 만들 수 있다고 한다. 이에 학부모들의 항의가 이어졌고 급기야는 무즙으로 엿을 만들어 입시 기관에 찾아가 들이밀기에 이르렀다. 결국은 무즙을 답으로 써서 떨어진 학생들을 추가 합격시켰다. 이 사건 이후로 '엿 먹이다'가 지금의 관용 표현으로 자리잡게 되었다.

In the 1964 national middle school entry examinations, one of the questions read, "What can be used instead of barley germ to make *yeot*?" Among the possible answers, radish pulp was listed, but the correct answer was a different ingredient. It is, however, possible to make the traditional treat with radish pulp. This seemingly misleading question touched off a firestorm among parents who went as far as to make the candy with radish pulp and shove it in the faces of those working at the agency that administered the test. The upshot was that those students who had missed this particular questions were admitted to middle school. Ever since, the expression 엿 먹이다 has had a special place in the colloquial lexicon.

엿장수 마음대로 [Lit. It's up to the *yeot* salesman.] IDIOM 자기 마음대로 = as one wishes (*equiv.* at someone's discretion) ▌A: 왜 갑자기 출근

시간이 아홉 시에서 여덟 시 반으로 당겨진 거죠?=*Why was the start of our workday suddenly rolled back from 9:00 to 8:30?* B: 사장님 지시래요.=*It was the boss's orders.* A: 완전 **엿장수 마음대로**군요.=*Wow, I guess everything really is up to him.*

NOTE: 군것질거리가 귀하던 시절, 엿은 아이들에게 최고의 군것질거리였다. 이때는 다들 가난해서 돈을 주고 엿을 사기보다는 고철이나 빈병 등과 엿을 바꾸어 먹었다. 이때 얼마만큼의 엿을 줄 것인지는 순전히 엿장수의 판단에 달려 있었다. 그로 인해 이 표현이 생겨 났다.
Back in the old days, there weren't too many treats for kids. The traditional Korean candy 엿 (*yeot*) was the best there was. The impecunious masses, instead of paying for the treat in cash would more often barter scrap metal or empty bottles. As to how much the *yeot* seller was going to fork over, the decision was entirely his to make. The whimsical nature of his rulings on such business matters gave root to this phrase.

옆구리가 시리다 IDIOM = 옆구리가 허전하다

옆구리가 허전하다 [Lit. for one's flank to feel empty] IDIOM 사랑하는 사람이 없어 쓸쓸하다=to feel deserted or lonely due to the absence of a lover (*syn.* 옆구리가 시리다) ▌A: 아, 좀 있으면 크리스마스인데 **옆구리가 허전해**.=*With Christmas just around the corner, I'm starting to feel really lonely.* B: 나도. 이번 크리스마스는 누구랑 보내지?=*Me too. Who should we spend this Christmas with?*

***옆구리 찔러 절 받기** [Lit. poking someone's side and receiving their bow] PROVERB 상대를 강요하여 억지로 대접받는 경우를 가리키는 말=compelling someone to treat you in a certain manner (*syn.* 엎드려 절 받기) ▌A: 이번 생일에 남편한테 비싼 가방 받았다며? 좋겠다.=*I heard that you received an expensive bag as your birthday gift. I'm so jealous.* B: 일주일 전부터 사 달라고 졸랐거든. **옆구리 찔러 절 받기야.**=*I've been begging him for a whole week. I forced him to buy it for me.*

NOTE: 절은 무릎을 바닥에 꿇고 몸을 엎드린 채 올리는 인사를 말한다. 만

약 어떤 사람에게 절을 받고 싶은데 그 사람이 절을 하지 않는 상황에서 옆구리를 찔러 강제로 허리를 숙이게 만든다고 생각해 보자. '옆구리 찔러 절 받기'란 이처럼 억지로 다른 사람에게 대접을 받는 상황을 말한다. 같은 표현으로 '엎드려 절 받기'라는 표현도 있다. 이 표현은 상대에게서 절을 받고 싶어 내가 먼저 엎드리는 익살스러운 상황에서 비롯했다. 내가 먼저 엎드리면 상대도 당황하여 나에게 엎드릴 수밖에 없을 것이다. 그런 식으로라도 상대에게서 대접을 받으려는 것이다.

A 절 is the kind of deep bow performed by bending one's knees and lowering one's torso to the ground. Imagine a situation where you feel that you are deserving of a bow but your counterpart just keeps standing there awkwardly, so you jab him in the ribs to get him to bend over. This is a situation where one compels a certain level of treatment from another. In a similar vein is the expression, 엎드려 절 받기, which illustrates the farcical situation of one bowing down first in order to get one's counterpart to bow down as well. If one commences a deep bow, the other person will be perplexed into bowing as well. This phrase denotes the act of forcing special treatment or acknowledgement at any cost.

오금을 못 쓰다 [Lit. to not be able to use one's joints] IDIOM 무엇을 매우 좋아하다 = to like something very much (*syn.* 사족을 못 쓰다, 껌뻑 죽다, 자다가도 벌떡 일어난다) ▮ A: 저 친구 많이 늙었군. = *Wow, he's really aged.* B: 술이라면 오금을 못 쓰던 친구가 술을 마다하다니. = *For a guy who used to go gaga at the sight of alcohol to turn down a drink like that ...*

오금을 못 펴다 [Lit. to not be able to extend one's arms or legs] IDIOM 기세에 눌려 기를 펴지 못하다 = to be oppressed in a way that prevents one from acting in an uninhibited way ▮ A: 아직도 우리 아빠가 그렇게 어려워? = *Is my dad still that hard to be around?* B: 응. 장인어른 앞에서는 오금을 못 펴겠어. = *Yeah. I can never let down my guard in front of him.*

오금이 쑤시다 [Lit. for one's joints to ache] IDIOM 무엇인가 하고 싶은

생각에 가만히 있지 못하다＝to not be able to sit still due to excitement about a certain activity (*equiv.* to be itching to do something *cf.* 좀이 쑤시다) ▌A: 병원에만 있으려니 **오금이 쑤셔서** 괴로워요.＝*Having to stay all day in the hospital like this is really making me itch to get outside.* B: 그래도 가만 누워 있으라고 의사 선생님이 그랬잖니.＝*Even so, the doctor told you to stay in bed.*

오금이 저리다 [Lit. for one's joints to be numb] IDIOM 초조하여 마음을 졸이다＝to be fretful or nervous (*equiv.* to be a bundle of nerves *cf.* 도둑이 제 발 저리다) ▌A: 면접은 많이 보셨어요? 힘드시죠?＝*Have you been to a lot of job interviews? It's tough, isn't it?* B: 네. 면접 대기하고 있으려니 **오금이 저리네요.**＝*Yes. Waiting for the interview, I'm always a bundle of nerves.*

오냐오냐하다 [Lit. to say "yes" (to everything)] IDIOM 어린아이의 응석을 다 받아 주다＝to indulge one's children (*equiv.* to spoil one's children) ▌A: 엄마, 저거 사 줘, 사 줘.＝*Mom, buy me that one. Please, please.* B: 너, 엄마가 안 된다고 했지? 애가 **오냐오냐했더니** 요즘 버릇이 통 없네.＝*Didn't I say no already? I've been spoiling you recently and now you have no manners.*

오뉴월 감기는 개도 안 걸린다 [Lit. Even dogs don't catch a cold in May and June.] PROVERB 여름에 감기에 걸린 사람을 놀릴 때 하는 말＝used to make fun of someone who has caught a cold in summer ▌A: 감기 걸렸어? 한여름에 웬 감기야?＝*Are you sick? How does someone catch a cold in the middle of summer?* B: 그러게. **오뉴월 감기는 개도 안 걸린다는데.**＝*That's what I'm saying. Dogs don't even catch colds in summer.*

NOTE: 음력 5,6월은 양력으로 6,7월에 해당한다. 즉 오뉴월 감기는 여름 감기를 의미한다.
The fifth and sixth month of the lunar calendar correspond to the sixth and seventh month of the solar calendar. A 오뉴월 감기 is a summer cold.

오뉴월 개 팔자 [Lit. A dog's fate for the months of May and June] PROVERB

아무 걱정이 없는 매우 편한 신세 = a very carefree and relaxed state of affairs (*cf.* 개 팔자가 상팔자) ▮A: 다니 저 녀석은 왜 방학 내내 집에서 잠만 자? **오뉴월 개 팔자가** 따로 없구먼. = *But why does he just stay home and sleep all through vacation like a lazy dog?* B: 그러게 말이에요. 아버님이 혼 좀 내 주세요. = *That's what I'm saying. Why don't you get on him about it a little bit?*

NOTE: 음력 5, 6월은 양력으로 6,7월에 해당하는데, 이때는 농사일이 매우 바쁜 시기다. 더운 날씨에 사람들은 일하느라고 힘들고 바쁜데, 개들은 시원한 나뭇그늘에서 낮잠을 자기만 한다. 이 모습을 사람들이 부러워하여 생긴 속담이다.
The fifth and six months of the lunar calendar correspond to the sixth and seventh months of the solar calendar, and are an extremely busy time for farmers. As the farmer and his family toil in the fields under the hot sun, the family dog would often coil up in the shade of the tree for a rest. People envied the dog's lot during this time, giving rise to this expression.

오늘내일하다 [Lit. It's today or tomorrow.] IDIOM 1. 죽을 때가 가까이 다가오다 = for one's dying day to draw near ▮A: 아버님은 병세는 좀 어떠셔? = *How's your father getting along with his condition?* B: **오늘내일하셔**. = *He's only got a few days left.* 2. 해산할 때가 가까이 다가오다 = for the expected delivery date of a child to draw near (*equiv.* (to be expecting) any day now) ▮A: 배가 많이 불렀군요. 출산일이 언제예요? = *Wow, your stomach is getting pretty big. When's the big day?* B: **오늘내일해요**. = *Any day now.*

오도 가도 못하다 [Lit. to be unable to come or go] IDIOM 자리를 옮길 수 없는 상태가 되다 = to be in a situation where one cannot relocate (*equiv.* to be immobilized) ▮A: 오늘 폭설 때문에 차 안에서 **오도 가도 못하고** 두 시간이나 있었어요. = *The sudden snowfall today left us immobilized for two hours.* B: 저런. 고생스러웠겠어요. = *Jeez. That must've been rough.*

오르막이 있으면 내리막이 있다 [Lit. Wherever there is an upturn, there is also a downturn.] PROVERB 사람이나 일이나 잘될 때가 있으면

못될 때가 있게 마련이라는 말 = *If there is ever a time when things go well, there will also be a time when things go poorly. (equiv. What goes up must come down. / All good things must come to an end. / Everything has its ebbs and flows. syn. 달도 차면 기운다)* ▌A: 지금 한창 절정의 인기를 얻고 계신데요, 인기를 실감하시나요? = *Your popularity seems to be greater than ever right now. Does it feel like you're dreaming?* B: **오르막이 있으면 내리막이 있잖아요**. 순간적인 인기에 연연하지 않으려 합니다. = *You know what they say, all good things must come to an end. I don't intend to get too attached to fleeting fame.*

오르지 못할 나무는 쳐다보지도 마라 [Lit. Don't even look at a tree that you can't climb.] PROVERB 자신의 능력 밖이거나 분수에 넘치는 대상에 대해서는 처음부터 욕심을 내지 않는 게 좋다는 말 = suggests that it is better from the outset to not develop a will to do something if it is beyond one's abilities (*equiv.* Don't bother trying the impossible. / You are out of your league. / Dream on.) ▌A: 야, 선미 씨 진짜 예쁘지 않아? 사귀자고 해 볼까? = *Hey, don't you think Sunmi is pretty? Should I ask her out?* B: 선미 씨 좋아하는 직원이 얼마나 많은데. **오르지 못할 나무는 쳐다보지도 마**. = *A lot of guys at the office have a thing for her. Don't waste your time even trying.*

오리무중 [Lit. 五 five + 里 unit of length + 霧 mist + 中 middle → in the midst of a five-*li* fog] CHINESE-DERIVATION 사람의 행방이나 사건의 실체 따위를 전혀 알 수가 없음 = being utterly unable to determine someone's whereabouts or the real state of a situation (*equiv.* to be groping (for answers etc.) in a sea of fog / to be lost in a haze) ▌A: 범인은 잡았대요? = *Have they apprehended the criminal?* B: 아직 행방이 **오리무중**이래요. = *His whereabouts are still veiled in a shroud of fog.*

NOTE: 1리는 약 0.4km에 해당한다. 따라서 5리는 2km쯤 된다. 안개가 2km나 끼어 있으니 앞이 잘 보이지 않을 것이다. 어떤 일의 상황을 잘 알 수 없을 때 이 표현을 쓴다.
One *li* is approximately 0.4 kilometers. Accordingly 5 *li* is about 2 kilometers. In a fog that deep, one wouldn't be able to make out anything. This expression is used when one cannot delineate what lies ahead.

***오리발(을) 내밀다** [Lit. to extend the duck leg] IDIOM 엉뚱하게 딴전을 부리다 = to attempt a ridiculous diversion (*equiv* to play innocent *syn.* 딱 잡아떼다, 시치미(를) 떼다 *cf.* 닭 잡아먹고 으리발 내민다) ▌A: 네가 안 했다고 자꾸 **오리발 내밀** 거야? = *Are you going to keep pretending that you didn't do it?* B: 정말이에요. 믿어 주세요. = *I'm telling the truth. Please believe me.*

NOTE: See the note on 닭 잡아먹고 오리발 내민다.

오만방자(하다) [Lit. 傲arrogant + 慢arrogant + 放release + 恣act freely] CHINESE-DERIVATION 태도나 행동이 건방지고 거만하다 = for one's comportment or actions to be impudent or arrogant (*syn.* 오만불손(하다)) ▌A: 모르는 게 있으면 선생님한테 물어보아라. = *If there's something you don't understand, just ask me.* B: 제가 선생님보다 나은데 누구한테 물어보라는 거예요? = *But I'm better at this than you are. Why should I ask you?* A: 이런 **오만방자한** 놈 같으니라고! = *Why you arrogant little …!*

오만불손(하다) [Lit. 傲arrogant + 慢arrogant + 不no + 遜modest → being arrogant and not modest] CHINESE-DERIVATION 태도나 행동이 건방지고 거만하다 = for one's behavior or actions to be impudent and arrogant (*syn.* 오만방자(하다)) ▌A: 이봐 젊은이, 그 **오만불손한** 태도는 뭔가? 나이 많은 어른한테. = *Look here, youngster. How could you speak that way in front of a senior citizen?* B: 당신은 또 뭐야? 내가 뭘 잘못했다고 이래? = *Who are you? And what are you saying I did wrong?*

오매불망(하다) [Lit. 寤awaken + 寐asleep + 不no + 忘forget → being awake and unable to forget] CHINESE-DERIVATION 늘 잊지 않다 = to never forget someone ▌A: 3년간 **오매불망** 기다려 온 사람이 다음 주면 오네요. 기분이 어때요? = *That unforgettable person that you've been losing sleep over for the last three years is finally coming back next week.* B: 벌써부터 설레서 잠이 잘 안 와요. = *I'm so excited I can barely sleep.*

NOTE: '오매불망'은 보통 부사처럼 쓰인다.
오매불망 is most often used as an adverb.

오십보백보 [Lit. 五 five + 十 ten + 步 step + 百 hundred + 步 step → the difference between 50 steps and 100 steps] CHINESE-DERIVATION 약간의 차이는 있지만 본질적으로 차이가 없음 = having a small difference while being essentially the same (*equiv.* six of one and half-dozen of the other *syn.* 거기서 거기, 그 나물에 그 밥, 그놈이 그놈이다, 대동소이하다) ▌A: 너 몇 등 했니? = *How did you do?* B: 35등. 넌? = *I ranked 35th. You?* A: 난 34등. 너나 나나 **오십보백보**구나. = *I got 34th. I guess we're almost one and the same.*

NOTE: 전쟁터에서 패해 오십 보 물러난 사람이나 백 보를 물러난 사람이나 본질적으로 차이가 없다.
To cut and run on the battlefield is equally cowardly, whether it is 50 steps you fled or 100. For the man who fled 50 paces to scoff at the man who fled 100 would be quite ridiculous, wouldn't it?

오지랖(이) 넓다 [Lit. for a coat's front hem to be wide] IDIOM 주제넘게 남의 일에 참견을 잘하다 = to meddle in the affairs of others in an intrusive manner (*equiv.* to be meddlesome / to stick one's nose where it doesn't belong) ▌A: 제 남편은 **오지랖이 어찌나 넓은지** 동네 일 중에 참견 안 하는 일이 없어요. = *My husband is so meddlesome that he interferes in everything that's happening in my neighborhood.* B: 그만큼 관심이 많으신 거겠죠. = *That's just because he takes an interest in the neighbors.*

NOTE: 오지랖이란 윗옷의 앞자락을 말한다. 오지랖이 넓으면 그 안에 입은 다른 옷을 가릴 수 있다. 원래는 남의 일을 적극적으로 도와준다는 긍정적 의미로 쓰였지만 지금은 남의 일에 쓸데없이 잘 끼어드는 사람을 부정적으로 묘사할 때 보통 쓰인다.
오지랖 is the name for the outer hem of a top layer of clothing. If this part is broad, it can conceal the clothing underneath. The original meaning of this

phrase was positive and denoted a person who was helpful and participatory. Now the phrase is largely used to describe people who stick their nose where it doesn't belong.

오합지졸 [Lit. 烏crow + 合join + 之of + 卒soldier → solidiers like a flock of crows] CHINESE-DERIVATION 규율이 없고 훈련이 안 된 병사＝troops with no discipline or training (*equiv.* a ragtag bunch / a motley crew) ▌A: 상대편의 수가 우리보다 두 배는 더 많은 것 같은데, 우리가 이길 수 있을까?＝*The opposing side has at least two times greater numbers. Can we really win?* B: 걱정 마. 수만 많았지 **오합지졸**에 불과해.＝*Don't worry. They are many, but they are a motley assortment of men indeed.*

옥에 티 [Lit. a flaw in jade] IDIOM 아주 좋은 것에 있는 작은 흠＝a small flaw in something otherwise great (*equiv.* a fly in the ointment) ▌A: 어제 콘서트 갔었다며? 어땠어?＝*I heard that you went to that concert yesterday. How was it?* B: 좋았어. 그런데 좌석이 좀 불편했어. 그게 **옥에 티**였어.＝*It was good except my seat was uncomfortable. That was the only fly in the ointment.*

온실 속의 화초 [Lit. a flower in a greenhouse] IDIOM 어려움을 모르고 곱게만 자란 사람＝someone who has lived a trouble-free life, not knowing strife or hardship (*equiv.* a boy in a bubble / a sheltered child) ▌A: 우리 범균이는 애는 착한데 좀 야무지지 못해.＝*My Beomgyun is kind, but I sometimes feel he's not tough enough.* B: 언니가 범균이를 **온실 속의 화초**처럼 키워서 그렇잖아.＝*That's because you raised him like a rose in a greenhouse.*

올가미(를) 씌우다 [Lit. to ensnare someone in your trap] IDIOM 계략을 써서 곤경에 빠뜨리다＝to use a ruse or other trickery to ensnare someone (*equiv.* to set someone up) ▌A: 사실대로 얘기하세요. 당신이 한 짓 맞죠?＝*Speak the truth. This is your handiwork, isn't it?* B: 아니라니까요. 누군가 저를 **올가미를 씌운** 거라고요.＝*I've already said no. It was all a setup.*

올 것이 오다 [Lit. for what will come to come] IDIOM 예상하고 있던 좋지 않은 일이 일어나다 = for the unfortunate events one has anticipated to come to pass (*equiv.* to get what's coming to you / for it to only be a matter of time) ▌A: 참, 너 영장 나왔다며? 기분이 어떠냐? = *I heard they finally called you in to report for duty. How do you feel?* B: 뭐, **올 것이 왔구나** 싶지 뭐. = *Well, it was only a matter of time.*

옷걸이(가) 좋다 [Lit. for the clothes hanger to be good] IDIOM 몸매가 좋아 옷이 잘 어울린다 = for a person who has a well-proportioned body to look good in anything they wear (*equiv.* to look good in anything) ▌A: 내일 중요한 모임 있는데 뭘 입고 가야 할지 모르겠어. = *I have an important meeting tomorrow. I don't know what to wear.* B: 너는 **옷걸이가 좋아서** 뭘 입어도 잘 어울려. = *You look great in everything, so I'm sure you can't go wrong.*

옷(을) 벗다 [Lit. to take off clothes] IDIOM 어떤 지위나 자리에서 물러나다 = to step down from a position or post (*equiv.* to step down *syn.* 짐(을) 싸다) ▌A: 경호 씨, 자신 있어요? 이번 일이 회사에 얼마나 중요한지 잘 알죠? = *Kyeongho, are you confident? I trust you know how important this is to our company.* B: 네. 이번 일이 성공하지 못하면 **옷을 벗을** 각오가 돼 있습니다. = *Yes, I know. I'm ready to step down if this doesn't turn out well.*

***옷이 날개** [Lit. Clothes are wings.] PROVERB 좋은 옷을 입으면 사람이 근사해 보인다는 말 = suggests that wearing fine clothing makes a person look more appealing (*equiv.* The clothes make the man. / The tailor makes the man. / Fine feathers make fine birds.) ▌A: 이게 누구야? 옷을 이렇게 입으니까 몰라보겠다. = *Who is this? Dressed like that, it's hard to recognize you.* B: 왜 그러세요, 부끄럽게. = *Oh stop it. You're making me blush.* A: 정말 **옷이 날개**라더니 그 말이 딱 맞네. = *I guess it's true: fine feathers make fine birds.*

왈가왈부(하다) [Lit. 曰 say + 可 correct + 曰 say + 否 no → to say yes and to say no] CHINESE-DERIVATION 서로 자신이 옳다고 말다툼을 하다 = to argue back and forth with each side maintaining that they are in the right (*equiv.* to argue back and forth / to discuss the pros and cons) ▌A: 우리끼리 여기서 **왈가왈부할** 게 아니라 다른 사람 얘기를 들어 보자. =*Let's just ask somebody else for their opinion instead of arguing back and forth all day.* B: 좋아. 과연 누구 말이 옳은지 다른 사람한테 물어보자고. =*Okay. Let's ask them who they think is in the right.*

요단 강(을) 건너다 [Lit. to cross the River Jordon] IDIOM 죽다 = to die (*syn.* 눈(을)감다) ▌A: 간밤에 탤런트 고은경 씨가 죽었대. =*TV personality Koh Eungyeong died last night, they're saying.* B: 며칠 전에 중환자실에 있다는 기사 봤는데, 결국 **요단 강을 건넜구나.** =*I read in the news that she was in critical care just a few days ago. I guess she didn't make it after all.*

NOTE: See the note on 세상(을) 뜨다.

요람에서 무덤까지 [Lit. from the cradle to the grave] QUOTE 태어나서 죽을 때까지 = from one's birth until one's death (*equiv.* from the cradle to grave) ▌A: 나도 스웨덴 같은 나라 가서 살고 싶어. 스웨덴은 **요람에서 무덤까지** 국가에서 복지를 책임진대. =*I'd like to live in a country like Sweden. I heard that the state provides welfare from the cradle to the grave.* B: 다 일장일단이 있지. 대신 그 나라는 세금을 많이 낼걸? =*There are pluses and minuses to that I'm sure. I bet they have to pay a lot of taxes.*

➡ p.455

요 모양 요 꼴이다 [Lit. this shape, this form] IDIOM 좋지 않은 처지 = an undesirable situation ▌A: 아침에 좀 일찍 일어나. =*Why don't you get up earlier in the morning?* B: 일찍 일어난다고 딱히 할 일도 없는데 뭘. =*Even if I get up early. I won't have anything to do.* A: 네가 그러니까 **요 모양 요 꼴이지.** =*That's why you're stuck in a rut.*

요조숙녀 [Lit. 窈 elegant + 窕 quiet + 淑 ladylike + 女 woman] CHINESE-DERIVATION 말과 행동이 고상하고 품위가 있는 여성 = a woman whose mannerisms and behavior are of the utmost refinement (*equiv.* a lady of

refinement) ▌A: 이게 누구야? 정민이 아니냐? 어릴 때 보고 한동안 못 봤더니 어느 새 **요조숙녀**가 되었구나! = *And who's this? Jeongmin, is that you? Last time I saw you you were still a child but now you've blossomed into an elegant woman.* B: 네, 아저씨. 오랜만에 봬요. = *Yes. It has been a long time.*

요지부동 [Lit. 搖shake + 之but + 不no + 動move] CHINESE-DERIVATION 어떠한 자극에도 움직이지 않거나 태도의 변화가 없음 = being on unshakable even under the greatest of stimuli or being unchanging in one's behavior (*equiv.* to be unflappable / to be unshakeable) ▌A: 영호한테 같이 가자고 다시 말해 봤어? = *Did you try again to persuade Yeongho to go with us?* B: 응. 소용없어. **요지부동**이야. = *Yep. It was worthless. He's unshakeable.*

용용 죽겠지 [Lit. *Yong, yong* you're gonna die.] IDIOM 남을 약 올리면서 하는 말 = used when one is taunting another ▌A: 우리 막내는 엄마 따라 백화점 가는 거야? = *Is our baby going to follow mom to the department store?* B: 응. 장난감도 사고 맛난 것도 많이 먹을 거다. 언니, **용용 죽겠지**. = *Yep. And I'm going to get some toys and eat some good food. I'll rub it in my big sister's face.*

NOTE: 여기서 '용용'은 별다른 뜻이 있는 말이 아니라 어린 아이들이 상대를 놀릴 때 쓰는 감탄사이다. 보통 양 엄지손가락 끝을 양쪽 볼에 대고 나머지 네 손가락을 흔드는 동작을 하면서 '용용 죽겠지'라고 말한 후 혓바닥을 죽 내민다.

The *yong, yong* part of this phrase has no special meaning but is simply used by children when they tease others (akin to "nanny boo-boo"). As in the US, this taunt is usually accompanied by waving one's hands with the thumbs extended into one's cheeks and the finale, of course, is sticking out one's tongue at the intended target.

용의 꼬리보다 뱀의 머리가 낫다 [Lit. A snake's head is better than dragon's tail.] PROVERB 큰 조직에서 남의 밑에 있는 것보다 작은 조직에서 우두머리 노릇을 하는 것이 더 낫다는 말 = suggests that it is better to be at the head of a small organization than to be working below others

in a large firm (*equiv.* Better to be the head of an ass than the tail of a horse. / It's better to walk before a hen than behind an ox.) ▌A: 네 성적이면 서울에 있는 명문대학도 갈 수 있을 텐데, 왜 지방 대학에 갔어? = *With your test scores, you probably would've been able to get into some good universities in Seoul. Why did you choose a school out in the provinces?* B: 용의 꼬리보다 뱀의 머리가 낫겠다 싶어서. = *I've always thought that it's better to be the head of an ass than the tail of a lion.*

용의주도하다 [Lit. 用use + 意intention + 周widespread + 到reach + 하다 verbal suffix] CHINESE-DERIVATION 사람이나 계획 따위가 철저하여 빈틈이 없다 = for a person or set of plans to have no blind spots or weak points ▌A: 지문은커녕 흔적조차 전혀 없군. = *He didn't even leave behind a trace, let alone fingerprints.* B: **용의주도한** 놈인 것 같은데요. = *Yeah, he doesn't seem to make mistakes.*

우는 아이 젖 준다 [Lit. The crying baby is given milk.] PROVERB 무슨 일이나 요구해야 얻을 수 있다는 말 = suggests that one must make demands in order to receive what is due (*equiv.* The squeaky wheel gets the grease.) ▌A: 보고서 다 썼어? = *Did you finish that report?* B: 아직. 어떤 책을 참고로 해야 할지 감을 못 잡겠어. = *Not yet. I don't know what books I should be using as a reference.* A: 그러지 말고 선생님께 조언을 구해 봐. **우는 아이 젖 준다**는 말도 있잖아. = *Just ask the teacher for some advice. The squeaky wheel gets the grease.*

***우물 안 개구리** [Lit. a frog in a well] PROVERB 보고 들은 것이 적어 넓은 세상의 형편을 알지 못하는 사람 = someone who has not seen or heard much and therefore has a limited worldview (*equiv.* a man of limited scope / a small- or narrow-minded person) ▌A: 이번 방학 때 미국 갔다 왔다며? 부럽다! = *I heard that you went to the States during the vacation. I'm jealous of you.* B: 우리나라에만 있다가 외국에 가 보니까 내가 그동안 얼마나 **우물 안 개구리**였는지 알겠더라고. = *Now that I've been abroad, I realized how narrow my outlook used to be.*

NOTE: 우물 안에만 있는 개구리는 그곳이 세상의 전부인 줄 안다.
    A frog in a well thinks his realm is the entire world.

우물에 가 숭늉 찾는다 [Lit. to seek scorched-rice water in front of a well] PROVERB 일의 순서를 무시하고 재촉하거나 서두른다는 말 = to ignore the order of things and impatiently press for results (*equiv.* to jump the gun / to put the cart before the horse) ▌A: 내가 아까 부탁한 거 다 됐어? = *Are you done with all the things that I asked you to do before?* B: **우물에 가 숭늉 찾지** 말고 좀 기다려. 아직 30분밖에 안 지났잖아. = *Give me a few minutes would you? It's been only 30 minutes since you asked.*

NOTE: 밥을 지은 후 솥에 남은 밥에 물을 붓고 데운 것이 숭늉이다. 우물에는 밥을 할 물을 푸러 가는 것인데 그곳에 숭늉이 있을 리가 없다. When a pot of rice has been almost entirely cleaned out and all that remains is hardened burnt rice stuck to the sides, water is added and 숭늉 is made. Seeking this refreshing treat in front of a well would truly be putting the cart before the horse.

우여곡절 [Lit. 迂circuitous + 餘extra + 曲circuitous + 折break → the winding path] CHINESE-DERIVATION 복잡한 사정 = a complicated set of circumstances (*equiv.* the vicissitudes of life / a rough patch / hard times) ▌A: 어? 왜 영선이 대신 네가 왔니? = *Why are you here instead of Yeongseon?* B: **우여곡절**이 좀 있었어요. = *It's a long story.*

우왕좌왕(하다) [Lit. 右right + 往go + 左left + 往go] CHINESE-DERIVATION 당황하여 허둥대다 = to be flustered and in disarray (*equiv.* a muddle of motion / to be all helter-skelter) ▌A: 여러분, 이럴 때일수록 침착해야 합니다. **우왕좌왕하시면** 큰 사고가 날 수도 있습니다. = *Ladies and gentlemen, it's precisely in times such as these that you must remain calm. Causing a commotion could be very dangerous.* B: 맞습니다. 다들 진정하시고 자리에 좀 앉아서 얘기를 하시죠. = *That's right. Please calm down and take a seat so we can have a discussion.*

우유부단하다 [Lit. 優excellent + 柔soft + 不no + 斷cut + 하다adjectival suffix→ to be too soft to cut] CHINESE-DERIVATION 결정을 쉽게 내리지 못하고 자꾸만 망설이다 = to not easily make decisions and often delay (*equiv.* to be wishy-washy / to be indecisive) ▌A: 자장면 먹을까, 아니 짬뽕도

먹고 싶은데. 아, 뭘 시켜야 할지 결정을 못 내리겠어! = *How about having jajangmyeon? No, wait, I really want jjambbong too.* B: 하여튼 너 **우유부단한** 건 알아줘야 해. = *At any rate, you've got to admit that you're really wishy-washy.*

우이독경 [Lit. 牛cow + 耳ear + 讀read + 經writing → reading into a cow's ears] CHINESE-DERIVATION 아무리 말해 주어도 이해하지 못하거나 귀담아듣지 않는 것 = used when no matter how many times you say something, your counterpart never seems to grasp it or take heed (*equiv.* like water off duck's back / for one's words to fall on deaf ears *syn.* 소 귀에 경 읽기, 마이동풍) ▮ A: 큰딸 아직 결혼 안 했지? = *Your eldest daughter still hasn't gotten married, has she?* B: 응. 이제 결혼하라는 말도 안 해. **우이독경**이거든. = *Yeah. I don't even try anymore. My words are like water off a duck's back.*

우후죽순 [Lit. 雨rain + 後after + 竹bamboo + 筍bamboo shoot → bamboo shoots that grow after rain] CHINESE-DERIVATION 짧은 시간 안에 어떤 일이 많이 생겨남 = something occurring or coming into existence many times in a short period (*equiv.* to be springing up everywhere) ▮ A: 요즘에는 TV만 틀면 온통 토크쇼뿐이야. = *The only thing on TV these days is talk shows.* B: 맞아. 프로그램 하나가 인기를 끄니까 여기저기서 **우후죽순**처럼 생겨나는 것 같아. = *Yeah. One show gets a little popularity and the next thing you know, similar shows are springing up all over the place.*

운을 떼다 [Lit. to take off a letter] IDIOM **1.** 이야기를 시작하다 = to begin talking about something (*syn.* 입(을) 떼다, 말문을 떼다) ▮ A: 무슨 얘기길래 그렇게 **운을 떼기가** 힘들어? 괜찮으니까 어서 말해 봐. = *What is it that you're having so much trouble talking to me about it? I promise I'll be fine. Just spit it out.* B: 정식아, 돈 있으면 좀 빌려 줄래? = *Jeongshik, do you have any money you can spare?* **2.** 삼행시 따위의 머리글자를 부르다 = to call out the first letter of a three-line poem ▮ A: 우리 삼행시 짓기 할까? = *How about playing the acronym game?* B: 그래. 설악산 어때? 네가 **운을 떼** 줘 봐. = *Sounds good. How about starting with Seoraksan? You kick it off.* A: 오케이. 설! = *All right. Seol!*

NOTE: '운'이란 시에서 각 행의 동일한 위치에 규칙적으로 쓰인 글자를 말한다. 원래는 한시를 지을 때 쓰지만 요즘에는 일상에서 삼행시를 지을 때 많이 쓰인다. 삼행시란 세 글자로 된 단어의 각 글자를 머리글자로 하는 세 개의 행으로 된 시를 말하는데, 고전적 의미의 시라기보다는 언어유희에 해당한다. 삼행시를 지을 때는 보통 다른 한 사람이 운에 해당하는 세 개의 글자를 불러주는데, 이를 두고 '운을 뗀다'고 한다.

An 운 is a letter that is used in the same position in every line of a poem. It was originally used in Chinese-style poetry but nowadays is also used often in three-line poetry. This 삼행 poetry takes each letter of a three letter word and uses those letters to form the first letter in three lines. More than being a historical form of poetry, this is a type of wordplay. When carrying out this kind of word game, it is common for another person to provide the three words. This is also called 운을 뗀다.

운을 띄우다 IDIOM '운을 떼다'의 잘못된 표현 = an incorrect form of 운을 떼다

***울며 겨자 먹기** [Lit. crying while eating mustard] PROVERB 싫은 일을 억지로 함 = being forced into doing something that one dislikes (*equiv.* to bite the bullet / to grin and bear it / to resign oneself to a certain course of action) ▌A: 보험을 또 들었어? = *You signed up for more insurance?* B: 어. 남편 친구가 부탁해서 **울며 겨자 먹기**로 들었어. = *Yes. My husband's friend asked me to do it as a favor, so I had to bite the bullet.*

NOTE: 겨자는 아주 조금만 넣어도 특유의 향이 코를 쏜다. 겨자를 처음 먹어 보는 사람이 멋도 모르고 겨자를 많이 넣는다면 아마 눈물이 쏙 빠질 것이다. 그렇다고 음식을 버릴 수도 없는 노릇이니 눈물을 흘리면서 억지로 먹을 수밖에 없다.

Just a drop of mustard can bring that peculiar mustard tingle to the nose. People trying mustard for the first time, not knowing its intensity, will likely put so much in their meal that they find themselves tearing up while eating it. Even so, one cannot just throw away an entire meal, so one must eat right through the tears. Imagining this scenario will make this expression clear to anyone.

웃는 낯에 침 뱉으랴 [Lit. Would anyone spit on a laughing face?] PROVERB 웃고 있는 사람에게는 모질게 하지 못한다는 말 = describes how it is difficult to be harsh on someone who is laughing ▌A: 아, 이거 내가 실수했네. 팀장님한테 문서 다시 보내야겠네. = *I made a mistake here. I'll have to send the file to the boss again.* B: 아까 보니 팀장님 기분이 별로 안 좋아 보이던데. = *He didn't look to be in a very good mood today.* A: 그래? 뭐 커피 한 잔 들고 가면 **웃는 낯에 침이야 뱉으시겠어**? = *Really? Well, maybe I can soften him up with a cup of coffee in hand.*

웃음을 팔다 [Lit. to sell one's laughter] IDIOM 화류계 생활을 하다 = to engage in prostitution or a similar line of work (*equiv.* to engage in the world's oldest profession / to be a woman of the night) ▌A: 요즘 여대생들 중에는 알바로 술집에서 **웃음을 파는** 사람도 있다죠? = *They are saying that many female college students these days moonlight at clubs and the like, huh?* B: 네. 각자 사정이야 있겠지만 참 딱하네요. = *Yes. I'm sure they all have their reasons, but it's truly a sad state of affairs.*

원님 덕에 나팔 분다 [Lit. to blow one's trumpet thanks to the magistrate] PROVERB 세력이 있는 사람과의 친분으로 인해 좋은 대접을 받거나 우쭐대다 = to enjoy a special treatment due to one's acquaintance with an individual of prestige within a certain organization (*equiv.* to have friends in high places) ▌A: 저 사람 누구야? = *Who is that?* B: 사장님 조카래. **원님 덕에 나팔 분다더니** 자기가 이 회사 사장처럼 행세하네. = *That's the nephew of our boss. Having friends in high places sure makes people walk around like they own the place.*

NOTE: 옛날에 마을의 원님이 길을 지나갈 때면 맨 앞에서 나팔을 불어 사람들에게 원님의 행차를 알렸다. 그러면 거리에 있는 사람들이 길 가장자리로 물러나며 원님 쪽을 향해 고개를 숙였다. 나팔을 부는 사람은 원님 덕분에 사람들에게 인사를 받게 되니 의기양양해져 더욱 신나게 나팔을 불었을 것이다. 힘이 있는 사람의 옆에 있어 덩달아 이익을 볼 때 쓰는 표현이다.
In the days of yore, a trumpeter headed off the procession of the village magistrate and signaled his coming with a blast of the horn. At that, the

people in the street would move off to the edge of the road and bow their head as the retinue passed by. Thanks to the magistrate, the horn blower too became the beneficiary of these reverential bows. Riding high on this wonderful treatment, he probably blew his horn even harder. This expression is used to describe a situation in which being near someone of power leads to secondary benefits for those in the vicinity.

원수는 외나무다리에서 만난다 [Lit. You meet your enemy at a single log bridge.] PROVERB 몹시 사이가 나쁜 사람과 피할 수 없는 곳에서 만나게 될 때 쓰는 말 = Used to describe a situation in which two individuals of terribly ill rapport come together unavoidably and by fate. (*equiv.* to encounter one's enemy at the worst place and at the worst time) ▌A: 원수는 외나무다리에서 만난다더니, 어쩌다 네가 원미랑 같은 팀이 됐니? = *You know how they say you always run into your enemy at the worst time and place? Well, I just found out that I'm on the same team as Wonmi.* B: 그러게 말이야. 서로 엄청 어색할 텐데, 걱정이야. = *Yeah, that's what I'm saying. You guys are going to be so awkward around each other. I'm worried about you.*

원숭이도 나무에서 떨어질 때가 있다 [Lit. Sometimes even monkeys fall out of trees.] PROVERB 아무리 익숙하고 잘하는 일이라도 실수할 때가 있다는 말 = describes how despite being extremely adroit and practiced at a certain task, it is inevitable that one will at times make mistakes ▌A: 이십 년 동안 이 일을 하셨으면 눈 감고도 하시겠어요? = *Now that you've been doing this for 20 years, I bet you could do it with your eyes closed, huh?* B: 그렇죠. 하지만 그래도 워낙 위험한 일이라 조심해야 합니다. 원숭이도 나무에서 떨어질 때가 있으니까요. = *That's right. But since it's a pretty dangerous job, I always have to be careful. Even monkeys sometimes fall from trees.*

월척을 건지다 IDIOM = 대어를 낚다

월척을 낚다 IDIOM = 대어를 낚다

웬 떡이냐 [Lit. What's with the *tteok*?] IDIOM 기대하지 않던 행운을 만났을 때 하는 말 = used when one is the beneficiary of an unexpected boon (*equiv.* a windfall / a boon *cf.* 굴러 온 호박) ▌A: 이 모자 네가 쓸래? 나한테는 맞지를 않네. = *Do you want to wear this hat? It doesn't really fit me.* B: 우와, 이게 **웬 떡이냐**! 고마워! = *Wow, what an unexpected surprise! Thanks!*

위기일발 [Lit. 危 danger + 機 momentum + 一 one + 髮 hair → the moment a strand of hair bears a heavy weight] CHINESE-DERIVATION 절박한 순간 = the critical moment (*equiv.* the nick of time) ▌A: 휴우, 하마터면 차에 부딪힐 뻔했어. = *Phew, we almost got into a car accident.* B: 정말 **위기일발** 이었어. = *Yeah, we got out just in the nick of time.*

위풍당당하다 [Lit. 威 power + 風 appearance + 堂 dignified + 堂 dignified + 하다 adjectival suffix] CHINESE-DERIVATION 겉모습이나 기세가 위엄이 있고 당당하다 = for one's appearance or aura to be dignified and imposing ▌A: 이게 자네 개야? 고 녀석 참 잘생겼네. 덩치도 커서 아주 **위 풍당당하구먼**. = *Is that your dog? That's a good-looking animal. He's built well and has a dignified air about him.* B: 그렇지? 이 놈이랑 같이 다니면 마음이 든든하다니까. = *Yeah, huh? Walking around with him, I have nothing to worry about.*

윗물이 맑아야 아랫물이 맑다 [Lit. The water above must be clear for the water below to be clear.] PROVERB 윗사람이 잘해야 아랫사람도 보고 배워 잘한다는 말 = suggests that people in high positions must comport themselves well for those in lower positions to mimic them and also do right (*equiv.* As is the king, so are the people.) ▌A: 민수가 공부는 안 하고 텔레비전만 봐서 걱정이에요. = *Minsu's never studying and always just watching TV is becoming a major worry for me.* B: **윗물이 맑아야 아랫물 이 맑지**. 너도 회사 갔다 오면 텔레비전만 보잖아. = *You have to set a good example for him. When you get back from work all you do is watch TV.*

유명무실(하다) [Lit. 有 exist + 名 name + 無 no + 實 content] CHINESE-DERIVATION 이름만 있고 실속은 없다 = to have only a title and no content (*equiv.* in name only / titular) ▌A: 옛날에는 이 집 참 장사 잘됐었는데, 이제 썰렁하네. = *This place used to do really good business, but now it's like a ghost town.* B: 지금은 **유명무실해졌지** 뭐. = *Now all that's left is the name, I guess.*

유명을 달리하다 [Lit. to switch between the living world and the dead]

IDIOM '죽다'를 완곡하게 이르는 말 = a euphemism for "to die" (*equiv.* to cross the great divide) ▌A: 오늘은 며칠 전 불의의 사고로 **유명을 달리한** 한 팝 가수의 노래를 들어 보겠습니다. = *Today we'll be listening to a song from a pop singer who was taken from us unexpectedly just a few days ago.* B: 팝 역사에 한 획을 그은 가수죠. = *He definitely left his mark on the pop music world, that's for sure.*

NOTE: See the note on 세상(을) 뜨다.

유비무환 [Lit. 有exist + 備prepare + 無no + 患worry] CHINESE-DERIVATION

준비가 되어 있으면 걱정할 것이 없음 = Being prepared means having nothing to worry about. (*equiv.* Better safe than sorry. / An ounce of prevention is worth a pound of cure.) ▌A: 돈이 좀 남는데 먹을 것 좀 더 살까? = *We still have a little bit of money left. Want to get some more food?* B: 만사가 **유비무환**인데 돈을 좀 남겨 두자. 무슨 일이 생길지 모르잖아. = *Don't you think you'd better save that for a rainy day? You never know what the future holds.*

유야무야(되다) [Lit. 有exist + 耶particle + 無no + 耶particle → Something may or may not exist.] CHINESE-DERIVATION

흐지부지되다 = for things to come to naught (*equiv.* for things to be left unresolved / to fade away) ▌A: 얼마 전까지 공무원 뇌물 사건 때문에 전국이 떠들썩했는데, 요즘 잠잠하네. = *Not too long ago, a bribery incident involving a civil servant caused a stir, but it has largely subsided now.* B: 일본 지진 때문에 그 일이 **유야무야되는** 느낌이야. = *I think the earthquake in Japan made that issue fade away in the public consciousness.*

유언비어 [Lit. 流flow + 言word + 蜚fly + 語talk → flowing words with no

talk] CHINESE-DERIVATION 근거 없이 널리 퍼진 소문=a groundless rumor that has spread broadly (*equiv.* a groundless rumor / a canard) ▌A: 너 영희 씨랑 사귄다며? 손 잡고 걸어가는 것도 본 사람이 있다던데?=*I heard you're dating Yeonghee. Someone is saying they saw you two holding hands.* B: 다 **유언비어**야. 나 좋아하는 사람 따로 있어.=*People are just flapping their lips. I am interested in someone else.*

유유상종 [Lit. 類group + 類group + 相mutual + 從follow] CHINESE-DERIVATION 비슷한 사람들끼리 무리를 이루어 어울림=illustrates the tendency of similar people to form social groups (*equiv.* Birds of a feather flock together.) ▌A: 어쩌면 네 친구들도 하나 같이 너처럼 노는 걸 좋아하니?=*How is it that all your friends like to party just as much as you do?* B: **유유상종**이란 말도 있잖아요, 아빠.=*They do say birds of a feather flock together.*

유유자적(하다) [Lit. 悠leisurely + 悠leisurely + 自by oneself + 適enjoy] CHINESE-DERIVATION 걱정 없이 한가롭고 여유 있게 지내다=to spend time in a leisurely carefree manner ▌A: 시골 생활은 어때?=*How's country life?* B: 조용하고 좋아. 이렇게 **유유자적** 사는 것도 나쁘지 않은 것 같아.=*It's quiet and very nice. I don't see anything wrong with just idling my days away like this.*

유일무이하다 [Lit. 唯only + 一one + 無no + 二two + 하다adjectival suffix] CHINESE-DERIVATION 오직 하나뿐이다=for there only to exist one of something (*equiv.* the one and only) ▌A: 홈쇼핑 광고를 보면 맨날 하는 말이 똑같아.=*The things they say on the home shopping channels are always the same.* B: 응. **유일무이한** 기회라는 둥, 주문이 폭주하고 있다는 둥 시청자를 현혹하잖아.=*Yeah. "This is a once-in-a-lifetime opportunity," "The orders are flooding in," etc.—they're always just trying to dazzle the viewing audience.*

음으로 양으로 돕다 [Lit. to help in both darkness and light] IDIOM 남이 모르게 도와주다=to help in ways unknown to others (*equiv.* to help in ways seen and unseen) ▌A: 그동안 저희 가족을 **음으로 양으로 도와**

주신 모든 분들께 감사드립니다. =*I want to extend my thanks to all of you who helped us in ways seen and unseen throughout the years.* B: 그동안 정이 많이 들었는데 떠나신다니 아쉽네요. =*We've grown so close during our time together. It's a shame that you have to leave.*

응어리(가)지다 [Lit. to become a clump] IDIOM 한이나 불만이 가슴에 남아 있다 = for one to be left with a grudge or unsatisfied feeling (*equiv.* to leave a bad taste in one's mouth *ant.* 응어리(를) 풀다) ▌A: 민수야, 그동안 선생님한테 섭섭한 거 많았지? **응어리진** 게 있으면 다 풀어라. =*Minsu, I am sure I disappointed you as a teacher in so many ways, right? If you have any grudges against me, let's get it all out right now.* B: 선생님, 무슨 말씀이세요? 그런 거 없어요. =*Oh what ever do you mean? I feel nothing of the sort.*

응어리(를) 풀다 [Lit. to break a clump] IDIOM 가슴에 남아 있는 한이나 불만을 해소하다 = to ameliorate a grudge or dissatisfaction held in one's heart (*equiv.* to take a load off one's mind / to get something off one's chest *ant.* 응어리(가)지다) ▌A: 늦은 나이에 다시 공부를 시작하신 계기가 있었나요? =*What was it in particular that motivated you to begin studying again at such a late age?* B: 어릴 때 가난해서 공부를 못 한 게 한이 되어서요. **응어리를 풀고** 싶었어요. =*I could never get over the fact that as a child our poverty didn't allow me to study. I wanted to finally get that off my chest.*

의기소침하다 [Lit. 意intention + 氣spirit + 銷scattered + 沈submerge + 하다adjectival suffix] CHINESE-DERIVATION 기운이 없고 풀이 죽다 = to be out of energy or crestfallen (*equiv.* to be dispirited / lethargic) ▌A: 왜 그리 **의기소침해** 있어? =*Why do you look so down in the dumps today?* B: 전 아무래도 음악에 재능이 없나 봐요. 아무리 연습해도 좀처럼 실력이 늘지를 않아요. =*I guess I just don't have any talent when it comes to music. No matter how much I practice, I never seem to get any better.*

의기양양(하다) [Lit. 意intention + 氣spirit + 揚rise + 揚rise] CHINESE-DERIVATION 마음이 만족스러워 뽐내는 모양이 가득하다 = to look proud or in high spirits because one is deeply satisfied (*equiv.* to have a triumphant air about one) ▌A: 진영이 녀석, 왜 저렇게 **의기양양해서** 돌아다녀? = *Why do you think Jinyeong is walking around with his head held so high?* B: 오늘 학교에서 선생님한테 칭찬 받았대. = *Today in class, the teacher paid him a compliment.*

이(가) 없으면 잇몸으로 산다 [Lit. If one doesn't have teeth, one survives with just gums.] PROVERB

꼭 필요한 것이 없으면 그보다 좀 못한 것으로 대신해서 그럭저럭 살아간다는 말 = describes the act of getting by under less than perfect conditions when a better situation cannot be attained (*equiv.* to get by (with what we've got) / to make do (with what one has)) ▌A: 정희 씨가 이제 안 나온다면서요? 도와주는 사람 없이 힘들지 않으시겠어요? = *I heard that Jeonghee no longer works here. Won't it be tough for you to get this all done by yourself?* B: **이 없으면 잇몸으로 사는 거죠 뭐.** = *Well, I'll just have to make do, won't I?*

이구동성 [Lit. 異different + 口mouth + 同same + 聲sound → The lips are different but the voice is the same.] CHINESE-DERIVATION

여러 사람의 말이 같음 = used when the statements of many are in accord (*equiv.* to be of one mind) ▌A: 이 영화 재미있을까? = *Do you think this movie will be any good?* B: 신문 보니까 평론가들이 **이구동성**으로 칭찬하던데? = *From what I saw in the papers, all of the critics are of one mind in singing its praises.* A: 그럼 재미없겠네. = *Then I'm sure it's going to be bad.*

이를 갈다 [Lit. to grind one's teeth] IDIOM

몹시 분하여 앙갚음을 하려고 벼르다 = to be motivated by rage and be making designs on vengeance (*equiv.* to have it out for someone / to have one's mind set on revenge) ▌A: 너 조심해야겠어. 민수가 너 잡히면 가만 안 두겠다고 **이를 갈고** 있던데? = *You'd better watch out. Minsoo is out to get you.* B: 난 잘못한 거 없으니까 무서울 것도 없어. = *I haven't done anything wrong, so I don't see what I should be afraid of.*

이를 악물다 [Lit. to bite down on one's teeth] IDIOM

힘든 상황을 참고 견디다 = to endure a difficult set of circumstances (*equiv.* to bite the bullet / to grin and bear it) ▌A: 우와, 그 어려운 시험에 한 번 만에 합격한 비결이 뭐야? = *Wow! What's your secret to passing such a difficult test on your first try?* B: 어머니가 몸이 안 좋으셔서 병원에 계시거든요. 어머니 생각하면서 **이를 악물고** 공부했어요. = *My mother's sick in the hospital right now. I did it for her.*

이(를) 잡듯 [Lit. as if (one is) catching lice] IDIOM 샅샅이 뒤져 찾는 모양을 비유적으로 표현한 말 = a metaphor for looking closely for something (*equiv.* to comb (a place for something)) ▌A: 소식 들어온 거 있어? = *Any news yet?* B: 아직이요. 하지만 이 근방을 **이 잡듯이** 찾고 있으니 곧 좋은 소식이 있을 겁니다. = *Not yet. But we're going over the area with a fine-toothed comb, so I'm sure we will have good news shortly.*

NOTE: 과거에는 사람들의 위생 상태가 지금처럼 좋지 않아 머리에 이가 기생하고 있는 경우가 흔했다. 때문에 머리를 촘촘한 빗으로 빗으며 이를 잡고는 했다. 눈에 잘 보이지도 않는 이를 꼼꼼히 찾듯 무엇인가를 꼼꼼하게 찾는 모양을 가리키는 표현이다.

In the old days, the state of hygiene wasn't what it is today and lice was a major problem. Using a fine-toothed comb, it was not uncommon to find lice. This expression depicts the action of looking intently at something as if one is trying to pick out lice.

이름(이)높다 [Lit. to have a high name] IDIOM 유명하다 = to be famous (*equiv.* to be a big name) ▌A: 오만 원권 지폐 속의 이 분은 누구인가요? = *Who is this person on the 50,000 won bill?* B: 신사임당이에요. 조선 시대 현모양처로 **이름높았던** 분이죠. = *That's Shinsaimdang. She was famous during the Joseon era for being a paragon of feminine virtue.*

NOTE: 주로 '…(으)로 이름이 높다'의 꼴로 쓰인다.
Most often used in the form, ...(으)로 이름이 높다.

이름(이) 없다 [Lit. to have no name] IDIOM 세상에 널리 알려져 있지 않다 = to not be widely known in the world (*equiv.* to be unknown to the world / to be nameless *ant.* 이름(이) 있다) ▌A: 이 그림 정말 멋지네

요. 누가 그린 거예요? = *This painting is really good. Who did it?* B: 이름 없는 화가가 그린 거예요. 우연히 보고 마음에 들어서 샀어요. = *An unknown artist. I came across it by chance and was fond of it, so I bought it.*

NOTE: 주로 '이름 없는 …'의 꼴로 쓰인다.
Most often used in the form, 이름 없는 …

이름(이) 있다 [Lit. to have a name] IDIOM 세상에 널리 알려져 있다 = to be broadly known to the world (*equiv.* to be well known / to have made a name for oneself *ant.* 이름(이) 없다) ▌A: 이번 축제에 연예인들도 온다며? = *I heard some celebrities are coming to the festival this time.* B: 응. 이름 있는 가수며 개그맨이 많이 온다던데? = *Yeah, there're going to be a few big-name singers and comedians.*

이마에 피도 안 마르다 IDIOM = 머리에 피도 안 마르다

이맛살을 찌푸리다 [Lit. to wrinkle up the skin on one's forehead] IDIOM 못마땅해하다 = to be displeased (by something) (*equiv.* to furrow one's brow *syn.* 눈살(을) 찌푸리다) ▌A: 주말에도 출근한다고 남편이 뭐라고 안 해요? = *Your husband didn't say anything about you having to go to work on the weekends?* B: 이맛살을 찌푸리던데요. = *Well, he furrowed his brow a bit.*

이빨 빠진 호랑이 [Lit. a tiger whose teeth have fallen out] IDIOM 예전에는 세력이 있었으나 지금은 그 세력을 잃어 힘이 없는 사람 = someone who used to be powerful but has lost all their influence (*cf.* 종이호랑이) ▌A: 아빠가 정년 퇴임하신 이후로는 집에서 엄마가 아빠보다 목소리가 더 큰 것 같아. = *Since Dad retired it seems like Mom runs the show at home.* B: 내가 느끼기어도 그래. 아빠도 **이빨 빠진 호랑이**가 되어 버린 건가. = *Yeah, that's what I've noticed too. I guess he was just a paper tiger all along.*

이실직고(하다) [Lit. 以 by + 實 true + 直 straight + 告 tell] CHINESE-

DERIVATION 바른대로 말하다 = to tell the absolute truth (*equiv.* telling it like it is / straight talk) ▌A: 좋게 말할 때 **이실직고해라**. = *You'd better tell me the real story while I'm still asking nicely.* B: 왜 제 말을 안 믿어 주세요? = *Why won't you believe me?*

이심전심 [Lit. 以by + 心heart + 傳convey + 心heart → conveyance from heart to heart] CHINESE-DERIVATION 마음이 서로 통함 = unspoken communication between two individuals (*equiv.* telepathy / reading each other's minds) ▌A: 우리 아이스크림 먹을까? = *Do you want to grab some ice cream?* B: 좋아. 안 그래도 나도 아이스크림 먹자고 얘기할 참이었는데, **이심전심**이라고 마음이 통했구나. = *Sure. I was actually just about to suggest that we get some ice cream. I guess you read my mind.*

이야기가 다르다 IDIOM = 얘기가 다르다

이야기꽃을 피우다 [Lit. for the flower of conversation to bloom] IDIOM 여러 사람이 한 자리에 모여 즐겁게 이야기를 나누다 = for a group of people to gather and enjoy conversing with each other ▌A: 엄마는 이모들만 오면 되게 신나나 봐. 시간 가는 줄 모르고 **이야기꽃을 피우는** 거 보면 말이야. = *Whenever her sisters come around, Mom sure gets excited. She loses track of time and gets lost in conversation.* B: 그렇지? 역시 핏줄이 좋은 건가 봐. = *That's true, huh? I guess there's nothing better than being with one's kin.*

이열치열 [Lit. 以by + 熱heat + 治control + 熱heat → controlling heat using heat] CHINESE-DERIVATION 더울 때 오히려 뜨거운 음식을 먹거나 땀을 내어 더위를 이김 = the idea that it's better to beat the heat by eating hot food or purposely making oneself sweat (*equiv.* fighting fire with fire) ▌A: 더워 죽겠는데 시원한 냉면 먹을까? = *This heat is killing me. Want to grab a bowl of cold noodles?* B: 그보다는 뜨끈한 설렁탕 어때? **이열치열**이랬잖아. = *Wouldn't some hot food like seolleongtang be better? They say you've got to fight fire with fire, you know?*

이왕이면 다홍치마 PROVERB = 같은 값이면 다홍치마

이판사판 [Lit. *ipan* and *sapan*] CHINESE-DERIVATION 막다른 데 이르러 어찌할 수 없게 된 지경 = the state of being blocked in on all sides and left with nothing to do (*equiv.* to be caught between a rock and a hard place *cf.* 너 죽고 나 죽자, 사생결단) █A: 너 수업 끝나고 철민이랑 싸우기로 했다며? 걔 싸움 잘하는 거 몰라? = *I heard that you decided to fight Cheolmin after school. Don't you know he's a great fighter?* B: 뭐 **이판사판**으로 덤비면 어떻게 되겠지. = *I'll just go for broke and see what happens then, won't I?*

NOTE: 이판사판은 불교의 이판승과 사판승에서 유래했다고 한다. 조선 시대 승려들 중 공부에만 몰두하는 쪽을 이판승, 공부보다는 절의 살림살이를 담당했던 부류를 사판승이라고 했다. 이들은 상호보완적인 관계였지만 서로에 대한 이해가 부족해 갈등의 골이 깊었다고 한다. 이판사판은 이판과 사판의 사이처럼 막다른 데 이르러 어찌할 수 없게 된 상황에서 쓰는 말이다.

The 이판사판 in this phrase apparently originates in Buddhist ideas of 이판승 and 사판승. Monks during the Joseon period who only focused on studies were part of the 이판승, while the group who devoted their time to temple life were called 사판승. These two groups actually complemented each other in a mutually beneficial way, but there was a fundamental lack of understanding between them that led to much discord. This phrase is used to describe and unwinnable situation, as if one were caught on the fence between these two factions.

인과응보 [Lit. 因cause + 果result + 應answer + 報respond] CHINESE-DERIVATION 착한 일을 하면 복을, 나쁜 짓을 하면 벌을 받는다는 말 = suggests that if one carries out good deeds, one will be rewarded and if one acts in an immoral way, one will be punished (*equiv.* What goes around comes around. / It's karma.) █A: 엄마, 동민이가 너무 말을 안 들어요. = *Mom, Dongmin never listens.* B: 네가 클 때 엄마 속을 좀 썩였니? 다 **인과응보**다. = *Well you put me through hell too, didn't you? It's all just karma.*

인사불성 [Lit. 人man + 事work + 不no + 省aware] CHINESE-DERIVATION 자신에게 일어나는 일을 알 수 없을 만큼 정신을 잃은 모습 = losing awareness to the point that one doesn't even know what is taking place (*equiv.* unconsciousness / oblivion) ▌A: 어쩌자고 술을 **인사불성**이 될 때까지 마셨어요? = *What happened to you that made you think it was necessary to drink yourself into oblivion?* B: 오늘 기분 좋은 일이 있어서 마시다 보니 그렇게 됐어요. = *I started drinking because something good happened today and that's just the way it turned out.*

인산인해 [Lit. 人people + 山mountain + 人people + 海sea → a sea and mountain of people] CHINESE-DERIVATION 사람이 수없이 많이 모인 상태 = an uncountable number of people gathered together (*equiv.* a mass of humanity) ▌A: 여기는 농구 결승전이 열리는 서울 체육관입니다. = *This is the Seoul Gymnasium that is currently hosting the basketball finals.* B: 이곳은 현재 관중들로 **인산인해**를 이루고 있습니다. = *The spectators are quite the mass of humanity.*

NOTE: 주로 '인산인해를 이루다'라는 형태로 쓰인다.
Usually used in the form, 인산인해를 이루다.

인생무상 [Lit. 人human + 生life + 無no + 常always] CHINESE-DERIVATION 인생이 덧없다는 말 = emphasizes the fleeting nature of human existence (*equiv.* No one lives forever. / the transience of life) ▌A: 당신 흰머리가 왜 이렇게 많아? = *Why do you have so much gray hair?* B: 벌써 내 나이가 이렇게 됐나. **인생무상**이란 말이 참 실감이 나네. = *Am I already that old? Now I know what they mean when they say your life passes by in the blink of an eye.*

인지상정 [Lit. 人human + 之of + 常always + 情feeling] CHINESE-DERIVATION 사람이면 누구나 가지는 보통의 마음 = the normal feelings that all humans feel (*equiv.* normal human sentiment) ▌A: 기부를 많이 하시기로 유명한데 참 대단하시네요. = *It's really amazing how much you have donated to help others over the years.* B: 어려운 사람들을 보면 돕고 싶은 게 **인지상정**이잖아요. 특별히 대단할 것 없습니다. = *The desire* *to help others in need is nothing more than a basic human instinct. It's really not that big of a deal.*

일거양득 [Lit. 一one + 擧raise + 兩both + 得get] CHINESE-DERIVATION 한 가지 일을 하여 두 가지 이익을 얻음 = carrying out one task that brings two rewards (*equiv.* killing two birds with one stone *syn.* 일석이조, 꿩 먹고 알 먹기, 도랑 치고 가재 잡기, 임도 보고 뽕도 딴다) ▌A: 시간이 날 때는 주로 뭐하세요? = *What do you normally do when you have free time?* B: 미국 드라마를 봅니다. 시간도 때우고 영어 공부도 하고 **일거양득**이죠. = *I usually watch shows from America. It fills up the time and helps me study English—it's killing two birds with one stone.*

일맥상통하다 [Lit. 一one + 脈stem + 相mutual + 通go through + 하다 verbal suffix] CHINESE-DERIVATION 생각이나 현상 따위가 서로 비슷하거나 통하는 데가 있다 = for thoughts or phenomena etc. to be similar or to be in accord (*equiv.* to have a thread of connection / to be analogous with each other) ▌A: 마이클 씨, 미국 속담에는 어떤 것이 있나요? = *Michael, what are some American proverbs?* B: Scratch my back and I will scratch yours.라는 말이 있습니다. "내 등을 긁어 주면 네 등을 긁어 주겠다"라는 뜻이죠. = *Well, there is "Scratch my back and I'll scratch yours." I guess that means,* "내 등을 긁어 주면 네 등을 긁어 주겠다." A: 우리나라 속담 "가는 정이 있어야 오는 정이 있다"와 **일맥상통하는** 말이군요. = *The Korean analog to that would probably be "There's got to be warm feelings on the way out for there to be warm feelings headed in."*

일목요연하다 [Lit. 一one + 目eye + 瞭clear + 然so + 하다adjectival suffix] CHINESE-DERIVATION 한눈에 알아볼 수 있을 만큼 분명하다 = to be so clear that one can grasp it immediately (*equiv.* to be clear as day) ▌A: 역시 넌 참 말을 잘 해. 네가 설명을 해 주니까 **일목요연하게** 정리가 되는 것 같아. = *You really are a good speaker. After hearing your explanation, I really feel like I have a good grasp of things.* B: 그래? 도움이 되었다니 다행이네. = *Really? I'm glad to hear it was helpful.*

일사불란하다 [Lit. 一one + 絲thread + 不no + 亂messy + 하다adjectival suffix → an unfrayed thread] CHINESE-DERIVATION 질서나 체계가 잘 잡혀 있다 = for things to be in order or organized according to a system (*equiv.* to be in lockstep / to have one's ducks in a row) ▌A: 자, **일사불란하게** 움직입시다. 시간이 별로 없어요. = *Let's move as one. We don't have much time.* B: 네, 몇 시에 출발하나요? = *What time should we leave?*

일사천리 [Lit. 一one + 瀉pour + 千thousand + 里unit of length → One branch of a river goes a thousand *li* (unit of distance).] CHINESE-DERIVATION 거침없이 빨리 진행됨 = describes a situation in which things are proceeding with great rapidity ▌A: 새로 오신 팀장님은 추진력이 강하신 것 같아. = *The new chief has a strong drive.* B: 응. 그분이 온 이후로 그동안 밀려 있던 일이 **일사천리**로 진행되네. = *Yeah. Things that were left undone for a long time are finally getting dealt with.*

***일석이조** [Lit. 一one + 石stone + 二two + 鳥bird → throwing one stone and catching two birds] CHINESE-DERIVATION 한 가지 일을 하여 두 가지 이익을 얻음 = refers to an action in which one action is met with two rewards (*equiv.* to kill two birds with one stone *syn.* 일거양득, 꿩 먹고 알 먹기, 도랑 치고 가재 잡기, 임도 보고 뽕도 딴다) ▌A: 점심은 주로 어디서 드세요? = *Where do you usually eat lunch?* B: 구내 식당에서 먹어요. 값도 싸고 시간도 아낄 수 있어서 **일석이조**거든요. = *At the company cafeteria. It's cheap and I can get in and get out fast. It's like killing two birds with one stone.*

일심동체 [Lit. 一one + 心heart + 同same + 體body] CHINESE-DERIVATION 여러 사람이 마음을 모으는 일이나 그런 상태 = a consensus of opinion or being of the same mind (*equiv.* to be of one mind) ▌A: 부부는 **일심동체**라는데 당신은 왜 이렇게 내 마음을 몰라? = *They say that married couples are of one mind, but why can't you seem to understand where I'm coming from?* B: 내가 내 마음도 잘 모르겠는데 당신 마음을 어떻게 알아? = *I don't even know what it is that I want, how am I supposed to know anything about you?*

일자무식 [Lit. 一one + 字letter + 無no + 識know → not knowing how to

read even a letter] CHINESE-DERIVATION 전혀 아는 것이 없음 = knowing absolutely nothing (*equiv.* to be dumb as a door nail) ▮ A: 어떻게 이렇게
➡ p.474
자식 농사를 잘 지으셨어요? = *How did you raise your children so well?*
B: 저는 **일자무식**이지만 제 자식만은 잘 키우고 싶었어요. = *I'm dumb as a door nail about most things, but I just really wanted to do a good job with my own kids.*

일장일단 [Lit. 一one + 長merit + 一one + 短demerit] CHINESE-DERIVATION 한 가지 사건이나 현상에 공존하는 장점과 단점 = the positive and negative aspects of a single affair or phenomenon (*equiv.* strength and weakness) ▮ A: 이 집은 어떤 것 같아? = *What do you think about this house?* B: **일장일단**이 있겠지. 회사에서 가까워지는 대신 예전 집보다 좁아서 불편할 것 같은데. = *Well, it has its pluses and minuses. It is closer to my workplace than my old house, but it's smaller than the old house so it may be a little cramped.*

일 절만 해라 [Lit. Just do one verse.] IDIOM 잘 알고 있는 얘기이니 길게 말할 필요가 없다는 말 = suggests that the two parties already know the point of what is being said so there's no reason to be long about it (*equiv.* Don't go on and on. / Enough is enough.) ▮ A: 제발 네 방 청소는 네가 알아서 좀 해라. = *Please, would you just clean up your room yourself?* B: 알았어요, 엄마. 제발 **일 절만 하세요**. = *All right, Mom. Please don't go on and on.*

일찍 일어나는 새가 벌레를 잡는다 [Lit. The bird that wakes up early catches the bug.] PROVERB 성공하려면 아침에 일찍 일어나는 부지런함이 있어야 한다는 말 = suggests that the diligence to wake up early in the morning is the key to success (*equiv.* The early bird gets the worm.) ▮ A: 동민아, 좀 일찍 일어나라. **일찍 일어나는 새가 벌레를 잡는다**는 속담도 있잖니. = *Dongmin, try and get up a little earlier. There's a reason people always say that the early bird gets the worm.* B: 엄마, 저는 새도 아니고 벌레 잡을 일도 없어요. = *Mom, I'm not a bird and I have no intention of catching any worms.*

일침을 가하다 IDIOM = 일침을 놓다

일침을 놓다 [Lit. to put in a needle] IDIOM 따끔한 충고를 하다 = to give someone advice that may be hard to hear (*equiv.* to give some stinging advice *syn.* 일침을 가하다, 침을 놓다) ▌A: 저희 남편은 예의 없는 사람을 보면 그냥 지나치지 못해요. 어제도 엘리베이터에서 내리기 전에 타는 사람이 있었는데 **일침을 놓더라고요**. = *When my husband sees someone who is rude, he can never just walk on by. Just yesterday he offered a harsh rebuke to someone who was getting on the elevator before we had gotten off.* B: 훌륭한 분이네요. 그런 분이 꼭 있어야 해요. = *What an amazing man! The world needs more people like that.*

일파만파 [Lit. 一one + 波wave + 萬ten thousand + 波wave → One wave causes ten thousand waves.] CHINESE-DERIVATION 한 사건이 잇따라 많은 사건으로 번짐 = one incident immediately spawning many more (*equiv.* to kick up a firestorm / the ripple effect / to rock the boat) ▌A: 그 국회의원 많은 사람들 앞에서 성희롱 발언을 했대요. = *That assemblyman has made lewd remarks in front of many people.* B: 지금 그 사건이 **일파만파**로 번져서 국회의원 자리도 위태로워졌어요. = *That situation has metastasized into a full-blown case, and now he's in a lot of trouble.*

일편단심 [Lit. 一one + 片piece + 丹red + 心heart → a piece of red heart] CHINESE-DERIVATION 변치 않는 진실된 마음 = single-hearted devotion (to a lover) ▌A: 영희는 참 대단해. 남자 친구가 군대 가 있는 동안 어쩌면 하루도 안 빼고 편지를 쓰네. = *Yeonghee is really something special. How was she able to write a letter to her boyfriend like that every day he was in the army?* B: **일편단심** 민들레가 따로 없어. = *Her love is like an ever-blooming rose.*

NOTE: '일편단심 민들레'라는 말을 자주 한다. 민들레는 생명력이 매우 강한 식물이다. 열악한 환경에서도 잘 자라고 밟혀도 다시 살아난다. 사랑하는 사람을 향한 마음이 단단하여 변치 않는 사람을 민들레에 비유하는 것도 바로 그런 이유에서다.

This expressions often used in the form, 일편단심 민들레. The dandelion is known to possess an extremely strong life force. Even under the most adverse conditions, when often stepped on, it always springs back to life. That's the reason why a lover who is cf one mind and unwavering in their adoration, is often compared to a dandelion.

일확천금 [Lit. 一one + 攫catch + 千thousand + 金money] CHINESE-DERIVATION 단번에 많은 재물을 얻음 = earning a fortune in one fell swoop (*equiv.* to strike it rich / to strike gold / to get rich overnight) ▌A: 나는 왜 사람들이 땀 흘려 일할 생각을 안 하고 **일확천금**을 노리는지 이해가 안 돼. = *I really don't understand why people always shy away from hard work and instead just look for ways to strike it rich overnight.* B: 나는 사실 그 마음을 알 것 같아. 뉴스를 보면 대달 월급날만 기다리는 내 자신이 초라하게 느껴질 때가 있거든. = *Well, I for one understand that. Watching the news, I start to think less of myself if I just sit around waiting for my paycheck every month.*

임기응변 [Lit. 臨face + 機momentum + 應respond + 變change] CHINESE-DERIVATION 그때그때 형편에 따라 달맞게 일을 처리함 = dealing with matters in a method well tailored to the current circumstances (*equiv.* rolling with the punches / to take matters as they come) ▌A: 어제 노래를 하다가 가사를 잊어버려서 당황했었어요. = *I forgot the lyrics yesterday and was so embarrassed.* B: 그래서 어떻게 했어요? = *So what did you do?* A: **임기응변**으로 마이크를 관객들에게 돌렸죠. = *Well, I had to roll with the punches. I just turned the mike towards the audience.*

임도 보고 뽕도 딴다 [Lit. to see one's lover and pluck mulberry leaves too] PROVERB 한 가지 일을 하여 두 가지 이익을 얻음 = to engage in a single effort and be met with two rewards (*syn.* 꿩 먹고 알 먹기, 도랑 치고 가재 잡기, 일거양득, 일석이조) ▌A: 여자 친구랑 주로 어디서 데이트하세요? = *When you go on a date with your girlfriend, where do you two usually go?* B: 저희는 둘 다 학생이라 주로 도서관에서 같이 공부해요. = *Because we're both students, we usually just study at the library.* ▶p.219 A: 말 그대로 **임도 보고 뽕도 따는** 거네요. = *I guess that's what they* *mean by killing two birds with one stone.*

NOTE: 과거 60년대에는 누에를 기르느라 뽕나무가 많았다. 여인네들에게 뽕잎을 따는 것은 중요한 생계 수단이었다. 뽕나무 밭은 우거진 뽕잎 때문에 다른 사람의 눈에 잘 띄지 않아 남녀가 몰래 데이트를 즐기는 장소로도 이용되었다. 그 때문에 사랑하는 사람도 만나고 일도 한다는 의미의 '임도 보고 뽕도 딴다'는 표현이 생겨 났다.
In the 1960s, there were many mulberry trees around as a byproduct of people raising silkworms. Plucking the leaves of these trees was an important means of survival for many women of the time. The thick leaves of the trees also made patches of mulberry trees a popular date spot because of the privacy they afforded. That gave rise to the expression, "meeting one's lover and plucking mulberry leaves," as a metaphor for getting two things done at once.

임시방편 [Lit. 臨face + 時time + 方way + 便comfortable] CHINESE-DERIVATION 어떤 문제에 대한 일시적인 해결책=a temporary solution to a problem (*equiv.* a temporary fix / a stopgap / a workaround *syn.* 언 발에 오줌 누기) ▌A: 여기 이 종이는 뭐야?=*What's this paper for?* B: 아까 보니까 벽지에 구멍이 나 있더라고. **임시방편**으로 막아 놓은 거야.=*I noticed there was a hole in the wallpaper earlier. I'm going to use it as a temporary fix.*

임자(를) 만나다 [Lit. to meet one's owner] IDIOM 실력이 뛰어나 자신을 제압할 만한 상대를 만나다=to meet someone whose skills far outshine one's own abilities (*equiv.* I've been bested. / to meet one's match) ▌A: 기영이가 어쩐 일로 요즘에 숙제를 꼬박꼬박 하네요.=*For some reason Giyoung has been getting her homework done on time recently.* B: 새 담임 선생님이 되게 엄하신가 봐요. **임자 제대로 만난** 거죠.=*Her new homeroom teacher is really strict. I think she finally met her match.*

입김을 넣다 [Lit. to put in steam from one's lips] IDIOM 영향력을 행사하다=to exercise influence ▌A: 이제 아이돌이 안 나오는 드라마가 없군요.=*It seems like idol stars are in every TV drama out there right now.* B:

소속사에서 방송국에 **입김을 넣는다고** 하더라고요. = *They say that the stars' PR firms hold sway over the broadcasting companies.*

입김이 세다 [Lit. to have strong steam from one's lips] IDIOM 영향력이 강하다 = to have strong influence (*syn.* 콧김이 세다) ▋A: 선생님이시라고요? 교사 생활은 좀 어떠세요? = *You said you're a teacher right? How is life in the teaching profession?* B: 힘들어요. 특히 요즘에는 학부모들의 **입김이 세서** 이래저래 눈치 봐야 해요. = *It's tough. Especially since the parents have so much sway over things now. I have to be careful about my every move.*

입만 뻥긋하다 [Lit. to spread just one lips] IDIOM 말을 하다 = to speak (*equiv.* Every time he opens his mouth (he always ...).) ▋A: 김 과장, 왜 싱글벙글이야? 좋은 일 있어? = *Kim, why are you all smiles today? Did something good happen?* B: 우리 딸한테 넥타이 선물 받았어. = *I got a necktie from my daughter.* A: 저 친구, **입만 뻥긋했다** 하면 자식 자랑이구먼. = *Every time this guy opens his mouth, all he does is brag about his kids.*

> NOTE: 주로 '입만 뻥긋하면', '입만 뻥긋했다 하던'의 꼴로 쓰인다.
> This phrase is usually used in the following forms: 입만 뻥긋하면, 입만 뻥긋했다 하면.

입만 살다 [Lit. for one's lips only to be alive] IDIOM 행동은 하지 않으면서 말만 그럴듯하게 잘하다 = to never carry out anything in actuality but often speak of doing great things (*equiv.* He's just a big talker. / to talk big *cf.* 말만 앞세우다) ▋A: 내가 마음만 먹으면 너보다 훨씬 잘할 수 있어. = *If I just set my mind to it, I can do a much better job than you ever could.* B: 자식, **입만 살아** 가지고. 말만 하지 말고 한번 해 봐. = *You're talking big. Let's see what you can really do.*

입만 아프다 [Lit. Only one's lips are sore.] IDIOM 말한 보람이 없다 = for one's words to be in vain (*equiv.* to waste one's breath / to not be worth saying) ▋A: 너희 남편 아직 안 들어왔어? 요즘도 만날 그렇게 늦

게 들어와? = *Your husband still isn't home? He's still coming home that late every day?* B: 말해 뭐 해. **입만 아프지**. = *What's the use in saying anything about it? It's just a waste of my breath.*

입바른 소리 [Lit. words from straight lips] ɪᴅɪᴏᴍ 내용은 옳지만 듣는 사람이 다소 불편하게 느낄 만한 이야기 = a statement that, although proper, is likely to make the listener feel uncomfortable (*equiv.* to tell it like it is *cf.* 입에 발린 소리) ▌A: 참 경수 씨는 높은 분들 앞에서도 기죽지 않고 할 말은 다 하네요. = *That Gyeongsoo sure is good at staying strong even in front of the bigwigs.* B: 그 친구 **입바른 소리** 잘하는 건 알아 줘야 해. = *Yep, there's no denying that he tells it like it is.*

입 밖에 내다 [Lit. to send (words) outside one's lips] ɪᴅɪᴏᴍ 말하다 = to speak (*equiv.* to let something slip) ▌A: 오늘 내가 여기 왔었다는 얘기 **입 밖에 내면** 죽을 줄 알아! = *If you let it slip that I was here today, you're dead!* B: 알았어요. 아무한테도 얘기 안 할게요. = *Got it. I won't tell anyone.*

입방아(를) 찧다 [Lit. to pound the lip pestle] ɪᴅɪᴏᴍ 남에 관한 얘기를 이러쿵저러쿵하다 = to talk haphazardly about someone else (*equiv.* to chatter / to gossip / to flap one's lips) ▌A: 옆집 여자랑 무슨 할 말이 그렇게 많아? = *What were you talking about with the woman next-door for so long?* B: 801호 사는 새댁에 대해 **입방아를 찧더라고**. 나는 잠자코 듣고만 있었어. = *She was talking up a storm about the newly married woman in 801, but I was just dozing off.*

ɴᴏᴛᴇ: 방아를 찧을 때 보면 절굿공이가 절구에 닿았다 떨어졌다를 반복한다. 이 모양이 사람이 말을 할 때 윗입술과 아랫입술이 닿았다 떨어졌다 하는 것과 닮은 데서 유래한 표현이다. 입방아는 단순히 말을 하는 행위를 가리키는 것이 아니라 다른 사람의 험담을 가리킨다.

When people grind things with a mortar and pestle, the pestle is constantly rising and falling into the mortar. This is similar to the way people's lips flap together when talking. This expression, however, means not simply talking, but talking about another person in a negative way.

입방아에 오르내리다 IDIOM = 입방아에 오르다

입방아에 오르다 [Lit. to be on the tip of the lip pestle] IDIOM 좋지 않은 일로 남의 대화의 화제가 되다 = to become the subject of the conversations of others for a regrettable reason (*syn.* 입에 오르다, 입방아에 오르다, 입방아에 오르내리다) ▎A: 너는 다 큰 계집애가 맨날 술 마시고 늦게 들어오면 되니? 그러다 동네 사람들 **입방아에 오를까** 두렵다. = *Do you think it's all right for a full-grown woman to go out drinking every night and come home late? I'm just worried you're going to be the talk of the neighborhood for it.* B: 엄마, 그게 뭐가 그리 중요해요? = *Mom, why is that so important?*

NOTE: See the note on 입방아(를) 찧다.

입술에 침이나 바르고 (거짓)말해라 [Lit. Apply spit to one's lips and tell a lie.] IDIOM 속이 빤히 보이는 거짓말은 그만두라는 말 = used to tell one's counterpart to stop telling transparent lies (*equiv.* Who do you think you're fooling? / Give it up already.) ▎A: 당신 지금 어디 갔다 오는 거야? = *Where have you been?* B: 응? 말했잖아. 야근했다고. = *Huh? I told you I put in some overtime.* A: **입술에 침이나 바르고 거짓말해.** 술 냄새가 여기까지 나는데, 야근을 했다고? = *Who do you think you're fooling? I can smell the alcohol from here, but you're telling me it was "overtime"?*

NOTE: 사람이 거짓말을 하면 들킬까 긴장하여 입에서 침이 잘 나오지 않아 마르게 된다. 입술에 침이나 바르라는 말은 입술이 바짝 마른 것이 거짓말하는 티가 다 난다는 뜻이다.
When one tells a lie, their mouth often becomes dry because of nerves. 입술에 침이나 발라라 means one can tell their counterpart is telling a lie because they notice the person's mouth is dry.

입술을 깨물다 [Lit. to bite one's lips] IDIOM 고통이나 분을 참다 = to endure pain or a grudge ▎A: 어제는 선생님이 반 아이들 앞에서 나한

테 어찌나 무안을 주시던지 눈물이 나오려는 걸 **입술을 깨물고** 참 았어요. = *Yesterday, my teacher insulted me so harshly in front of other students I had to bite my lips to hold back tears.* B: 네가 가만히 있는데 그러시든? = *I doubt she did it for no reason.*

입에 거미줄 치다 [Lit. to have spider web across one's lips] IDIOM 가난하 여 먹지 못하고 굶다 = to be starving because of poverty (*cf.* 산 입에 거 미줄 치랴) ➡ p.544 ▌A: 장사는 잘돼? = *Is your business going well?* B: 잘되 긴. 파리만 날려. 이러다 **입에 거미줄 치게 생겼어.** = *No, it's a downright ghost town over there. If things keep on like this, we're going to be starving soon.*

입에 (게)거품을 물다 [Lit. to have foam at the mouth] IDIOM 몹시 흥분 하여 떠들어 대다 = to make a great fuss in a frenzied state ▌A: 정치인들 은 참 이상해. 왜 다른 정당이 무슨 말만 하면 **입에 게거품을 물고** 반대하는 걸까? = *I don't understand politicians. Why are they always foaming at the mouth in opposition to anything the other party says?* B: 그러 게 말이야. 나도 참 이해가 안 돼. = *That's what I'm saying. I can't understand why they act that way either.*

NOTE: 게거품은 말 그대로 게가 토하는 거품같은 침을 말한다. 여기서는 어떤 사람이 흥분해서 입 주변에 거품처럼 침이 고인 모습을 비유하는 말이다.
The phrase 게거품 refers to the bubbles, or foam, that gathers around a crab's mouth. This expression is akin to the English phrase "to foam at the mouth." It is used metaphorically about someone who is extremely agitated or in a frenzied state.

입에 곰팡이가 슬다 [Lit. to have mold growing on one's lips] IDIOM 말을 오랫동안 하지 않다 = to not speak for a long time (*equiv.* to be a man of few words / to be taciturn) ▌A: 너는 어쩌면 그렇게 말이 없니? **입에 곰팡이 슬겠다,** 말 좀 해. = *What is it that makes you so quiet? Your lips are going to rust from lack of use.* B: 그래서 나 양치질 자주 하잖아. = *Yeah, that's why I'm always brushing my teeth.*

입에 담다 [Lit. to put something in one's mouth] IDIOM 무엇에 대해 말하다 = to talk about a certain topic ▌A: 인터넷 댓글들을 보면 참 한심해요. 어쩌면 **입에 담지도** 못할 얘기들을 아무렇지 않게들 하는지……. = *Some comments on the Internet are so absurd. How could people say something so terrible without a blink or qualm?* B: 얼굴이 안 보인다고 함부로 글을 쓰는 거죠. = *They make reckless remarks because they don't have to show their face.*

NOTE: 주로 '입에 담지 못할'의 형태로 쓰인다. '차마 입 밖으로 꺼내기도 민망한'이라는 뜻이다.
This expression is most often used in the form 입에 담지 못할, which means, "too shameful or embarassing to even speak."

입에 대다 [Lit. to put (something) to one's lips] IDIOM 음식을 먹거나 담배를 피우다 = to eat, drink or smoke ▌A: 음식을 **입에도 안 댔네.** 좀 먹어 보지 그래? = *You haven't even had a bite. Why don't you at least give it a try?* B: 나도 먹고 싶은데, 지금 이가 아파서 아무것도 못 먹겠어. = *I want to eat too, but my teeth are too sore right now.*

입에 발린 소리 [Lit. sound applied on one's lips] IDIOM 마음에 없이 듣기 좋으라고 그냥 하는 말 = remarks made to please someone that lack true meaning (*equiv.* lip service / sweet talk *cf.* 입바른 소리) ▌A: 부장님, 오늘따라 어쩌면 이렇게 화사하세요? 누가 보면 20대인 줄 알겠어요. = *Chief, you look so vibrant today. If you're not careful, people might mistake you for a twenty-something.* B: 호호. **입에 발린 소리**인 줄 알면서도 기분은 좋네. 고마워. = *Ho ho, I know that's just lip service, but I'm still happy to hear it. Thanks.*

NOTE: '입에 발린 말', '입에 붙은 말'이라고도 한다. 말은 머릿속으로 한 생각이나 가슴속으로 느낀 것을 입을 통해 표현하는 것이다. 그런데 말이 머리나 가슴을 통하지 않고 늘 입에 붙어 있다면, 진짜 속마음을 담지 않고 습관처럼 그냥 내뱉는 것이다.
This phrase is also seen in the forms, 입에 발린 말 and 입에 붙은 말. Words are, of course, an expression through the lips of thoughts and

feelings. If these words, however, do not pass through the mind or heart and are constantly stuck to the lips, they do not express one's true feelings and are simply spoken out of habit or necessity.

입에 오르내리다 IDIOM = 입방아에 오르다

입에 오르다 IDIOM = 입방아에 오르다

입에 자물쇠를 채우다 [Lit. to put a lock into one's mouth] IDIOM 아무 말도 하지 않다 = to not say anything (*equiv.* to zip it / to keep a lid on it *syn.* 입(을)다물다, 입(을) 닫다) ▌A: 이거 비밀인 거 알지? = *You know this is a secret, right?* B: 그럼. **입에 자물쇠 채울** 테니까 염려 마. = *Sure, don't worry. I won't tell a soul.*

입에 재갈(을) 물리다 [Lit. to put a gag into someone's mouth] IDIOM 강제로 말을 하지 못하게 하다 = to prohibit someone from talking by force (*equiv.* to gag someone) ▌A: 이번 선거와 관련해서 트위터에 글을 잘못 올렸다가 선거법 위반이라고 고발 당한 사람이 한둘이 아니지? = *There were not just a few people who were accused of violating election law for posting remarks on Twitter in regards to this election.* B: 응. 국민의 입에 **재갈을 물리려나** 봐. = *Yeah, they might be trying to gag the public.*

입에 침도 마르기 전에 [Lit. even before the spit dries] IDIOM 말한 지 얼마 되지 않아 = right after one has said something ▌A: 연예인 A씨 결혼한다는 기사 봤어? = *Did you read the news that a certain celebrity will get married?* B: 아니. 며칠 전에 결혼 안 한다고 하지 않았어? = *No, didn't she say she wouldn't be getting married just a few days ago?* A: 그랬지. **입에 침도 마르기 전에** 말을 뒤집네. = *She did. She reversed that pretty quickly.*

입에 침이 마르다 [Lit. for spit to dry in the mouth] IDIOM 다른 사람이나 물건을 거듭해서 칭찬하다 = to praise someone or something repeatedly ▌A: 이 책 읽어 봤어? = *Have you read this book?* B: 네. 읽어 본 사

람들마다 하도 **입에 침이 마르게** 칭찬하길래 궁금해서 저도 읽어 봤어요. = *Yeah, everybody who read the book said it was so great that I just had to read it.*

입에 풀칠하다 IDIOM = 목구멍에 풀칠하다

입은 비뚤어져도 말은 바로 해라 [Lit. Even if your lips are crooked, you should speak straight.] PROVERB 상황이 어떻든지 진실을 말하라는 말 = One should speak the truth no matter what the circumstances may be. ▌A: 엄마, 형이 저 때렸어요. = *Mom, my brother hit me.* B: **입은 비뚤 어져도 말은 바로 해야지**, 내가 너를 언제 때렸니? 그냥 살짝 건 드렸지. = *You should speak the truth. When did I hit you? I just slightly tapped you.*

입(을) 놀리다 [Lit. to move one's mouth] IDIOM (속된 말로) 말을 건방 지게 함부로 하다 = (slang) to speak rudely and recklessly (*equiv.* to run one's mouth *syn.* 주둥이(를) 놀리다. 혀(를) 놀리다) ▌A: 말조심해! 누구 앞이라고 **입을 함부로 놀리는** 거야? = *Be careful with your words! You'd better be careful before you start running your mouth off like that, huh?* B: 제가 무슨 없는 말 했나요? = *What? Is it not the truth?*

p.420

***입(을)다물다** [Lit. to shut one's mouth] IDIOM 말을 하지 않거나 하던 말을 중단하다 = to not talk or stop talking (*equiv.* to bite one's tongue *syn.* 입(을) 닫다, 입에 자물쇠를 채우다 *ant.* 입(을) 벌리다) ▌A: 뭐래? = *What did he say?* B: **입을 꾹 다물고** 아무 말도 안 하네요. = *He kept his mouth shut the whole time.*

입(을) 닦다 IDIOM = 입(을) 씻다

입(을) 닫다 [Lit. to close one's lips] IDIOM 말을 하지 않거나 하던 말을 중단하다 = to not talk or stop talking (*equiv.* to clam up / to bite one's tongue *syn.* 입(을)다물다, 입에 자물쇠를 채우다 *ant.* 입(을) 벌리다) ▌A: 어때? 뭐 좀 알아냈어? = *What's going on? Did you find something?* B: 아니요. 아예 **입을 닫아** 버렸어요. = *No, he just clammed up.*

입(을) 떼다 [Lit. to detach one's lips] IDIOM 말을 꺼내다 = to begin to talk (*equiv.* to open up *syn.* 말문을 떼다, 운을 떼다 *cf.* 입이 떨어지다) ▌A: 회의실 분위기는 좀 어때? = *How's the atmosphere in the meeting room?* B: 싸늘하지 뭐. 아무도 **입을 떼는** 사람이 없어. = *It's a little chilly in there. Nobody even opened their mouths.*

입(을) 막다 [Lit. to cover one's mouth] IDIOM 사실을 있는 대로 말하지 못하게 하다 = to stop someone from speaking the truth (*syn.* 말문을 막다) ▌A: 이 돈 받으십시오. = *Here, take this money.* B: 지금 돈으로 제 **입을 막을** 생각이십니까? = *Are you trying to buy my silence?*

입(을) 맞추다 [Lit. to match lips] IDIOM 제삼자에게 같은 말을 하기 위해 다른 사람과 말의 내용을 같게 하다 = to sync up the statements a group will later tell a third party (*equiv.* Let's get our story straight. *syn.* 말(을) 맞추다) ▌A: 두 사람 진술이 완전히 같은데요. = *They made identical statements.* B: 사전에 **입을 맞춘** 모양이군. = *They might have gotten their stories straight in advance.*

입(을) 모으다 [Lit. to gather lips] IDIOM 여러 사람이 같은 의견을 말하다 = for many people to voice the same opinion ◀ p.425 ▌A: 요즘 여성, 남성 할 것 없이 다이어트 열풍이 불고 있습니다. = *Regardless of gender, everybody is going for slender bodies these days.* B: 하지만 무리한 다이어트는 건강을 해칠 수 있다고 의사들은 **입을 모아** 강조합니다. = *But doctors stress in chorus that excessive dieting will ruin your health.*

입(을) 벌리다 [Lit. to open one's lips] IDIOM 말을 시작하다 = to begin speaking (*ant.* 입(을) 닫다, 입(을) 다물다, 입에 자물쇠를 채우다) ▌A: 경미 걔는 **입만 벌렸다** 하면 다른 사람 험담이니? = *Why does Kyungmi always talk trash about others whenever she speaks?* B: 그러는 너는 지금 경미 험담하는 거 아냐? = *Aren't you talking trash about Kyungmi right now?*

입(을) 씻다 [Lit. to clean one's lips] IDIOM 이익을 혼자 차지하고서 모른 체하다 = to abscond with all the profits or benefits of an enterprise and play dumb about it (*syn.* 입(을) 닦다) ▌A: 정희 걔는 어쩌면 애가 그러니? 이번에 반장으로 뽑힌 게 누구 덕분인데 고맙다는 말 한마디 없네. = *What makes Jeonghee be that way? Who does she think is responsible for getting her chosen as class president? And to not even thank us.* B: 그러게 말야. 반장 되고 난 뒤에 **입을 싹 씻어** 버리더라. = *That's what I'm saying. After she become class president, she completely turned her back on us.*

입(을) 열다 [Lit. to open one's lips] IDIOM 꺼내기 힘든 말을 시작하다 = to open up to someone about a secret etc. ▌A: 나한테만 살짝 말해 줘. = *Just go ahead and tell me.* B: 안 돼. 내가 **입을 열면** 여러 사람이 다쳐. = *No way. If I open my mouth, a lot of people will get hurt.*

입(이) 가볍다 [Lit. to have light lips] IDIOM 비밀이나 해서는 안 될 남의 얘기를 경솔하게 잘하다 = to thoughtlessly divulge another's secrets or other sensitive information (*equiv.* to have a big mouth *syn.* 입(이) 싸다 *ant.* 입(이) 무겁다) ▌A: 다음 달에 회사 그만두신다면서요? = *So, you're quitting next month?* B: 어? 어떻게 아셨어요? = *What? Who told you that?* A: 김 대리가 그러던데요. = *That's what Mr. Kim was saying.* B: 하여튼 김 대리는 **입이 가벼워요**. 아무한테도 말하지 말랬는데. = *Mr. Kim sure has a big mouth. I told him not to tell anyone.*

입이 간지럽다 IDIOM = 입이 근질근질하다

입이 거칠다 [Lit. to have rough lips] IDIOM 거친 말을 쉽게 하다 = to make rude remarks easily (*equiv.* to be course *syn.* 입이 걸다, 입이 험하다, 입이 더럽다) ▌A: 저는 사회 생활하면서 저렇게 **입이 거친** 사람은 처음 봤어요. = *I've never seen a person who talks that way.* B: 저도 처음에는 적응이 안 됐는데, 지내다 보면 속마음은 따뜻한 분이에요. = *At first, I couldn't get used to it either, but I've actually found that he has a warm heart.*

입이 걸다 IDIOM = 입이 거칠다

입이 궁금하다 [Lit. for one's lips to be curious] IDIOM 군것질을 하고 싶

다 = to be hungry for a snack (*syn.* 입이 심심하다) ▌A: **입이 궁금한데, 뭐 좀 먹을 것 없어?** = *I'm in the mood for a snack. Do you have anything to eat?* B: 고구마 있는데 먹을래? = *I have some sweet potatoes. Do you want some?*

입이 귀밑까지 찢어지다 IDIOM = 입(이) 찢어지다

입이 귀에 걸리다 [Lit. to have one's lips caught on one's ears] IDIOM 기분이 매우 좋아 얼굴에 웃음이 가득하다 = to have a broad smile on one's face because one is in especially good humor (*equiv.* to grin from ear to ear) ▌A: **좋은 일 있어요? 입이 귀에 걸렸네.** = *What happened? You're grinning from ear to ear.* B: 보너스가 생각보다 많이 나왔네. = *My bonus was bigger than I expected.*

입이 근질근질하다 [Lit. to have itchy lips] IDIOM 자기가 알고 있는 것을 말하고 싶어하다 = to want to tell others what one knows (*equiv.* I can't hold it in anymore. / I'm itching to tell someone. *syn.* 입이 간지럽다) ▌A: **사실은 말이야. 아까 그거 내가 한 거야.** = *Honestly, it was me. I did it.* B: 그래? **입이 근질근질해서** 어떻게 참았어? = *Really? How did you keep yourself from blurting it out earlier?*

입이 더럽다 [Lit. to have dirty lips] IDIOM 말을 거칠고 사납게 하다 = to speak in a very rude and violent way (*equiv.* to have a dirty mouth *syn.* 입이 거칠다, 입이 걸다, 입이 험하다) ▌A: 이런 제기랄, 사람 좀 지나가게 비켜요. = *Damn it, let me pass by.* B: 아니 이 양반이 왜 이렇게 **입이 더러워?** 아침부터 싸우자는 거요? = *Why are you talking that way? Are you picking a fight this early in the morning?*

입이 딱 벌어지다 [Lit. for one's lips to break open] IDIOM 좋은 일로 매우 놀라다 = to be very surprised at a fortunate occurrence (*equiv.* to be jaw-dropping) ▌A: 어제 이 대리 집들이 갔었다며? 어땠어? = *You went to Mr. Lee's home-warming party yesterday, right?* B: **입이 딱 벌어지게** 음식을 차렸더라고. = *They prepared such a feast, my jaw nearly hit the floor.*

입이 떨어지다 [Lit. for one's lips to fall off] IDIOM 말이 나오다＝for a topic to be brought up (*cf.* 입(을) 떼다) ▮A: 다음 주에 휴가 쓴다고 말했어?＝*Did you tell them you're going to go on a vacation next week?* B: 아니. 다들 바쁜 거 아는데 나 혼자 휴가 내겠다고 말하려니까 **입이 떨어져야** 말이지.＝*No, I couldn't bring it up because I know everybody at work is so busy these days.*

입이 많다 [Lit. for there to be many mouths] IDIOM 식구가 많다＝to have many family members (*equiv.* to have many mouths to feed) ▮A: 안녕하세요? 빵 사 가시려고요? 무슨 빵을 이렇게 많이 사세요?＝*How are you? Are you going to buy bread? That's a lot of bread you're buying!* B: 저희 집에 **입이 좀 많잖아요**.＝*You know we've got plenty of mouths to feed.*

***입(이) 무겁다** [Lit. to have heavy lips] IDIOM 신중하여 말을 함부로 하지 않다＝to refrain from thoughtless words due to one's discretion (*ant.* 입(이) 가볍다, 입(이) 싸다) ▮A: 이 얘기는 아무한테도 하지 마.＝*Don't tell anybody about what I said.* B: 걱정 마. 나 **입 무거운** 편이야.＝*Don't worry. I'm not a big talker.*

입이 심심하다 [Lit. to have bored lips] IDIOM 군것질을 하고 싶다＝to feel like having a snack (*syn.* 입이 궁금하다) ▮A: 왜 요즘 들어 그렇게 과자를 먹어?＝*Why have you been snacking so much lately?* B: 담배를 끊어서 그런지 자꾸 **입이 심심하네**.＝*Probably because I quit smoking, I feel like I always need to have something in my mouth.*

입(이) 싸다 [Lit. to have cheap lips] IDIOM 비밀이나 해서는 안 될 남의 얘기를 경솔하게 잘하다＝to thoughtlessly divulge another's secrets or other sensitive information (*equiv.* to have a big mouth / to have loose lips *syn.* 입(이) 가볍다 *ant.* 입(이) 무겁다) ▮A: 야, 너 사람들한테 내가 규리랑 사귄다고 다 얘기했다며? 너는 왜 그리 **입이 싸냐**?＝*Hey, I heard you've been telling people I'm dating Gyuri. Why do you have such a big mouth?* B: 미안해. 어쩌다 보니 나도 모르게 그렇게 됐어.＝*I'm sorry. It just happened without me even thinking about it.*

입이 열 개라도 할 말이 없다 [Lit. One has nothing to say, even with ten mouths.] PROVERB 잘못이 명백하여 변명의 여지가 없다 = One's wrongdoing is so clear that there is no room for excuses. (*equiv.* There's no way I can talk my way out of this one, is there?) ▌A: 네가 나한테 어떻게 이럴 수가 있어? = *How could you do this to me?* B: 내가 정말 **입이 열 개라도 할 말이 없다**. = *There's nothing I can say to fix this.*

***입이 짧다** [Lit. to have short lips] IDIOM 식성이 까다롭거나 음식을 조금만 먹다 = to be a picky eater or only eat small quantities (*equiv.* to be a picky eater / to eat like a bird) ▌A: 왜 그렇게 조금만 드세요? 맛이 없어요? = *Why aren't you eating more? Doesn't it taste good?* B: 아니에요. 맛있어요. 제가 원래 **입이 좀 짧아요**. = *It tastes great. I'm just not a big eater.*

입(이) 찢어지다 [Lit. for one's mouth to be torn] IDIOM 기뻐서 어쩔 줄을 모르다 = to be beside oneself with joy (*equiv.* to be overjoyed / to be beside oneself (with joy) *syn.* 입이 귀밑까지 찢어지다) ▌A: 이번에 새로 온 교생 선생님 진짜 예쁘지 않아? = *Isn't the new TA drop-dead gorgeous?* B: 맞아. 다른 애들도 전부 **입이 찢어지던데**? = *Right. All the guys were just beside themselves.*

입이 험하다 IDIOM = 입이 거칠다

입추의 여지가 없다 [Lit. There is no room for (even) a gimlet.] PROVERB 많은 사람들이 꽉 들어찼다 = to be filled with many people (*equiv.* to be jam-packed / to be filled to capacity *syn.* 발(을) 디딜 틈이 없다) ▌A: 시청자 여러분 안녕하십니까? 드디어 고대하던 2012 프로야구 개막전이 펼쳐지겠습니다. = *Hello, everyone. The much-awaited opening ceremony of the 2012 professional baseball season is at last underway.* B: 네. 관중석은 이미 만원 관중으로 **입추의 여지가 없습니다**. = *Right. The stands are already filled to capacity.*

자격지심 [Lit. 自 by oneself + 激 violent + 之 of + 心 heart] CHINESE-DERIVATION 자신이 처한 상황이나 자신이 한 일에 대해 스스로 부끄럽거나 못 마땅하게 여기는 마음 = feeling embarrassed or displeased with one's situation or about what one has done ▮A: 너는 왜 잘사는 사람들만 보면 그렇게 안 좋은 시선으로 보니? = *Why do you see the rich in such a bad light?* B: 내가 못사니까 **자격지심**이 있어서 그래. = *It's because I have some dissatisfaction with myself about my poverty.*

자급자족(하다) [Lit. 自 by oneself + 給 provide + 自 by oneself + 足 adequate] CHINESE-DERIVATION 자기에게 필요한 것을 스스로의 힘으로 생산하다 = to produce what one needs on one's own (*equiv.* to be self-sufficient) ▮A: 이렇게 깊은 산골에 살면 시장이 없어 불편하지 않으세요? = *Isn't it inconvenient to live in this little mountain town with no market?* B: 웬만한 건 **자급자족하고**, 한 달에 한 번 시내에 나갑니다. = *We're self-sufficient and go down to the town once a month.*

자나 깨나 [Lit. waking or sleeping] IDIOM 언제나 = all the time (*syn.* 밤이나 낮이나, 눈이 오나 비가 오나, 앉으나 서나) ▮A: 태희야, 나랑 사귀자. 나 요즘 **자나 깨나** 네 생각뿐이야. = *Taehee, why don't we start going out? I've been thinking about you all the time.* B: 미안해. 나 다음 달에 결혼해. = *I'm sorry. I'm going to get married next month.*

자다가도 벌떡 일어난다 [Lit. to abruptly wake up in the middle of sleeping] IDIOM 1. 몹시 좋아하다 = to be very fond of (*syn.* 사족을 못 쓰다, 오금을 못 쓰다, 껌뻑 죽다) ▮A: 왜 벌써 숟가락을 놓니? = *Why did you put down your spoon already?* B: 입맛이 없어요. = *I don't* *have an appetite.* A: 밥이라면 **자다가도 벌떡 일어나는** 애가, 무슨 고민 있어?＝*Even when you're asleep you normally spring right out of bed at the mention of food. Do you have something on your mind?* 2. 억울함이나 분노가 가슴에 깊이 남아 있다＝for a grudge or anger to remain deep in one's heart ▌A: 인터넷의 악플 때문에 마음 고생이 심하셨죠?＝*You must have had such a hard time because of the malicious things people have said on the Internet.* B: 지금도 악성 댓글을 생각하면 **자다가도 벌떡 벌떡 일어나요**.＝*I definitely lose sleep over it.*

자다가 봉창 두드린다 [Lit. to tap a sealed window while sleeping]

PROVERB 상황과 전혀 관계없는 말을 불쑥 꺼내다＝to abruptly bring up an irrelevant issue ▌A: 우리 점심은 뭐 먹을까?＝*What should we eat for lunch?* B: 너는 이 상황에서 먹는 얘기가 나오니? **자다가 봉창 두드리지** 말고 가만히 있어.＝*Why are you talking about food in this situation? Don't talk off topic and just be quiet, would you?*

NOTE: 봉창은 채광과 통풍을 위해 벽을 뚫어 구멍을 내고 창틀 없이 종이를 발라 봉한 창을 말한다. 이 표현은 얼핏 생각하면, 잠을 자다가 잠결에 자기 집 봉창을 두드린다는 의미로 이해하기 쉽다. 그러나 그보다는, 곤하게 잠을 자고 있는데 누군가가 밖에서 집의 봉창을 두드린다는 뜻으로 이해하는 게 맞을 것 같다. 사람이 곤하게 자고 있을 새벽 시간에 엉뚱하게 남의 집 문도 아닌 봉창을 두드리는 돌출행동을 표현한 말이다.
봉창 is a window bored in the wall and sealed with paper for light and ventilation. This expression might sound as if one taps his own house's sealed window but it is more appropriate to think of it as somebody tapping the another's window while he is sleeping. This expression describes an unexpected action, like knocking on the window—not the door—of somebody's house late at night.

자라 보고 놀란 가슴 솥뚜껑 보고 놀란다 [Lit. Once you are surprised at the sight of a snapping turtle you'll startle at a pot lid.] PROVERB 어떤 것에 몹시 놀란 사람은 그와 비슷한 것만 보아도 놀란다는 말＝A person who was very surprised at something feels startled to see

something similar. (*equiv.* once bitten, twice shy) █A: 어, 엘리베이터에서 왜 소리가 나지? 또 멈추는 거 아냐?＝*Huh? Why is the elevator making so much noise? Won't it stop?* B: 비상 버튼을 실수로 눌렀어요.＝*I accidently pressed the emergency button.* A: 아, 그랬구나. **자라 보고 놀란 가슴 솥뚜껑 보고 놀란다더니**. 저번에 엘리베이터가 고장 나서 갇혀 있었잖아. 그때부터 이래.＝*Ah, you did? Like they say, "once bitten twice shy," I have been this way ever since I got stuck in a broken elevator.*

자리(를) 걷다 [Lit. to roll up a mat] IDIOM **1.** 병이 낫다＝to recover from sickness (*syn.* 자리를 털다 *ant.* 자리에 눕다) █A: 여기까지 와 주시고 감사합니다.＝*Thank you for coming to see me.* B: 어서 **자리 걷고** 일어나셔야죠.＝*I hope you will be better soon.* **2.** 다른 곳으로 옮기려고 준비하다＝to get ready to move to another place (*syn.* 자리를 털다) █A: 도대체 공연은 언제 시작하는 거야?＝*When is this performance going to start?* B: 날 샌 것 같은데, **자리 걷고** 가자.＝*It looks like it'll never start. Let's forget about it and leave.*

자리(를) 털다 IDIOM ＝자리(를) 걷다

자리에 눕다 [Lit. to lie down on the bed] IDIOM 병으로 앓아눕다＝to lie down with illness (*ant.* 자리(를) 걷다) █A: 너 대학 안 가겠다고 하니 부모님이 뭐라셔?＝*What did your parents tell you when you said you would not go to college?* B: 엄마는 **자리에 누우셨고** 아버지는 집 나가래.＝*My mom fell ill and went to lie down and my father told me to leave home.*

자수성가(하다) [Lit. 自 by oneself + 手 hand + 成 accomplish + 家 family] CHINESE-DERIVATION 물려받은 재산 없이 혼자 힘으로 집안을 일으키거나 재산을 모으다＝to make one's own fortune or support a family without the help of inheritance (*equiv.* to be a self-made man (or woman) / to pull oneself up by one's own boot straps) █A: 아버지는 **자수성가하신** 분이에요. 그래서 저한테도 독립심을 기르라고 자주 말씀하셨어요.＝*My father is self-made man. So he often told me to be independent.* B: 아, 훌륭한 아버지를 두셨군요.＝*Oh, you have a great father.*

자식 농사 [Lit. farming of children] IDIOM 자녀를 낳아 기르는 일 = giving birth to offspring and taking care of them ▌A: 자제분들은 뭐하나요? = *What are your children doing for a living?* B: 큰아이는 외교관이고 작은아이는 의사예요. = *The older one is a diplomat and the younger one is a doctor.* A: **자식 농사**를 정말 잘 지으셨군요. = *You raised your children well.*

자업자득 [Lit. 自by oneself + 業work + 自by oneself + 得get] CHINESE-DERIVATION 자신이 한 행동으로 인해 스스로에게 좋지 않은 결과가 돌아옴 = describes a situation in which one's actions bring about a self-injurious result ▌A: 진수 말이야, 학사경고 받았다며? = *Was Jinsu put under academic probation?* B: 다 **자업자득**이지 뭐. 수업 안 들어가고 연애만 할 때 알아봤어. = *That's all of his own making. I knew it when he started dating instead of attending classes.*

자초지종 [Lit. 自from + 初beginning + 至to + 終end] CHINESE-DERIVATION 처음부터 끝까지의 과정 = a process from start to finish ▌A: 김정연 씨, 도대체 무슨 일을 이 따위로 하는 거예요? = *Mr. Kim Jyeongyeon, how could you handle it like this?* B: 제가 **자초지종**을 설명드리겠습니다, 팀장님. = *I'll explain everything, chief.*

자충수를 두다 [Lit. to make a move that reduces one's own score during a game of go] IDIOM 스스로에게 해가 되는 행동을 하다 = to act in a self-injurious way (*equiv.* to shot oneself in the foot *syn.* 제 무덤을 파다, 제 꾀에 제가 넘어간다, 제 발등을 제가 찍는다) ▌A: 일 많아? 야근해야 돼? = *Do you still have a lot to do? Do you have to work overtime?* B: 네. 원래 내일까지 해야 되는 일인데, 제가 오늘까지 끝낼 수 있다고 큰소리쳤거든요. = *Yes, I was supposed to be done by tomorrow, but I bragged that I could do all today.* A: 저런. **자충수를 둔** 셈이구먼. = *Gee. You really shot yourself in the foot there.*

NOTE: 자충은 바둑에서 자기 집에 자기가 돌을 놓아 자신의 점수를 줄이는 것을 말한다. 스스로에게 해가 되는 짓을 할 때 쓰는 표현이다.
자충 is a move in the game of go that reduces one's own score by putting

stone in one's own area. This phrase is used to describe an action that is self-injurious.

자포자기(하다) [Lit. 自by oneself + 暴torture + 自by oneself + 棄abandon] CHINESE-DERIVATION 절망에 빠져 자기 자신을 돌보지 않다 = not to take care of oneself in despair ▌A: 너답지 않게 그깟 일로 **자포자기한 거야**? 왜 만날 술이야? = *Did you give up yourself over that? It's not like you. Why do you keep drinking every day?* B: 나다운 게 뭔데? 네가 내 마음 알아? = *What do you know about me? Do you know how I feel right now?*

자화자찬(하다) [Lit. 自by oneself + 畵picture + 自by oneself + 讚praise → to paint oneself and flatter oneself] CHINESE-DERIVATION 자기가 한 일을 스스로 칭찬하다 = to self-aggrandize (*equiv.* to toot one's own horn) ▌A: 역시 난 천재야! 나는 못하는 게 없어! = *Naturally. I'm a genius. There's nothing I can't do!* B: **자화자찬**도 심하면 병이야. 그만해. = *That kind of self-aggrandizement can be a disease That's enough.*

작살(을)내다 [Lit. to smash (something) to pieces] IDIOM (속된 말로) 심리적, 물리적으로 심한 타격을 입히다 = (slang) to deal a blow to something or someone physically and psychologically (*equiv.* to break someone to pieces / to destroy someone *cf.* 작살(이)나다) ▌A: 감히 내 딸을 차? 내 이놈 **작살을 내야겠군**. = *How could he dump my daughter? I'll smash him to pieces.* B: 아빠, 참으세요. 그 사람 잘못이 아니에요. = *Please don't do that. It's not his fault.*

작살(이)나다 [Lit. to be smashed to pieces] IDIOM (속된 말로) 심리적, 물리적으로 심한 타격을 입다 = (slang) to be harmed physically and psychologically (*cf.* 작살(을)내다) ▌A: 이렇게 비가 안 오니 올해 농사는 아주 **작살이 나겠군**. = *This year's harvest is going to be decimated by this draught.* B: 기우제라도 지내야 되는 거 아니야? = *Do we need to do a rain dance?*

작심삼일 [Lit. 作make + 心heart + 三three + 日day → the tendency of only adhering to a new plan for three days] CHINESE-DERIVATION 결심이 굳지 못해

쉽게 포기함＝used when someone is not resolute and gives up easily (*equiv.* to not stick to anything / to lack follow-through) ▌A: 올해에는 담배를 꼭 끊을 거야. ＝*I definitely will quit smoking this year.* B: 너 작년에도 그렇게 말했잖아. 올해는 제발 **작심삼일** 안 되도록 해 봐. ＝*You said the same thing last year. Why don't you stick to your plan this time?*

작은 고추가 맵다 [Lit. Small peppers are spicy.] PROVERB 몸집이 작은 사람이 뛰어난 능력을 가지고 있을 때 쓰는 말＝used to describe someone of small stature with great abilities (*equiv.* Big things come in small packages.) ▌A: 저 선수는 다른 선수들보다 키가 훨씬 작은데도 어쩌면 저렇게 잘할까요? ＝*He's smaller than all the other athletes. I wonder what makes him so good on the field.* B: **작은 고추가 맵다**는 속담도 있잖아요. ＝*They say big things come in small packages.*

잔뼈가 굵다 [Lit. for small bones to become thick] IDIOM 오랫동안 어떤 일이나 업종에 종사하다＝to become involved in a certain field of work for long time ▌A: 팔씨름은 김 씨를 따라갈 사람이 없어. ＝*No one can beat Mr. Kim when it comes to arm-wrestling.* B: 공사판에서 **잔뼈가 굵은** 사람이라 아주 다부진 사람이지. ＝*His strength is due to the many years he spent as a construction worker.*

잔을 기울이다 [Lit. to tilt a glass] IDIOM 술잔에 부어 놓은 술을 마시다＝to have a glass of liquor (*equiv.* to tilt the glass / to throw one back *syn.* 술잔을 기울이다) ▌A: 남편은 어디 갔어요? ＝*Where has your husband gone?* B: 아마 지금쯤 동네 어느 술집에서 **잔을 기울이고** 있을 거예요. ＝*He's probably throwing a few back at the neighborhood bar.*

잘되면 제 탓 못되면 조상 탓 [Lit. If things work out, it's my doing. If not, it's the fault of my ancestors.] PROVERB 일이 안될 때 그 책임을 다른 사람에게 돌리는 태도를 가리키는 말＝describes the action of blaming others when things don't work out (*equiv.* to take credit for the good, and blame others for the bad) ▌A: 이게 다 엄마 때문이야. 엄마가 아침에 나를 늦게 깨워 줘서 늦은 거잖아. ＝*This is all your fault, Mom! You woke me up late, and that made me late for class.* B: 참 나. **잘되면 제 탓**

못되면 조상 탓이라더니, 네가 늦잠 잔 거 가지고 왜 엄마 핑계를 대니? = *That's ridiculous. You're always blaming others for your mistakes.*

장군 멍군 [Lit. check and checkmate] IDIOM 두 사람이 한 차례씩 승리를 주고받음 = a situation in which two contenders each win once ▌A: 자, 내가 이겼지? = *Well, I guess I won, didn't I?* B: 그래. 네가 이겼어. **장군 멍군**이네. = *Sure, you won. It's kind of hard to tell.* A: 그래 이제 1:1이니까 3세트를 이기는 사람이 이기는 거야. = *Well, it's 1 to 1 now, so whoever wins the next match wins it all.*

NOTE: 장기에서는 상대편의 왕을 잡으려고 놓는 수를 장군이라고 말하고, 장군을 받아 막는 일을 멍군이라고 한다.
In Korean chess, 장기, a move meant to ensnare the opponent's king is called a 장군 and foiling this attempt is called 멍군.

장님 코끼리 만지기 [Lit. a blind person touching an elephant] PROVERB 일부분만 알면서 전체를 안다고 착각하는 것 = describes the illusion that one knows everything even though they know just a part of it ▌A: 몸을 따뜻하게 하시고 찬 음식을 드시면 안 됩니다. = *You have to keep yourself warm, and stay away from cold food.* B: 예전에 신문에서 보니 인후염에 아이스크림이 좋다고 하던데요. = *I read that ice cream is good for a sore throat on newspapers on the other day.* A: **장님 코끼리 만지기** 식의 상식입니다. = *That's just a misleading information.*

NOTE: 코끼리가 어떻게 생겼는지 모르는 장님 몇 사람이 코끼리를 만져 보았다. 코끼리의 다리를 만져 본 사람은 코끼리를 기둥처럼 생겼다고 말했고, 몸통을 만져 본 사람은 벽처럼, 코 부분을 만져 본 사람은 긴 대롱처럼 생겼다고 묘사했다. 이처럼, 어느 한 부분만을 가지고 전체를 판단하는 오류를 범할 때 '장님 코끼리 만지기'라고 말한다.
A group of blind people unaware of an elephant's appearance tried to touch the animal. The one who touched its legs said the elephant looked like a column, the one who touched the body said a wall, while the last one touched its nose and said a long tube. As such, this expression is used when one makes a mistake from judging the whole after only seeing a small part.

장단(을) 맞추다 [Lit. to keep time to the music] IDIOM **1.** 남의 기분을 맞춰 주는 말이나 행동을 하다＝to make oneself agreeable to another in words or behavior ▌A: 야, 네 이야기 중에 그 부분은 좀 이상한데?＝*Hey, that part sounds weird in your story.* B: 너는 그러지 말고 동생 얘기에 **장단 좀 맞춰** 줘라.＝*Why don't you just nod along with what your brother is saying?* **2.** 서로 조화를 이루어 일을 처리하다＝to handle things in sync (*cf.* 장단이 맞다) ▌A: 이 가게는 저희 가족이 다 같이 꾸려 나가고 있습니다.＝*All of my family members are working for this store.* B: 모든 가족이 **장단을 맞춰** 일하는 모습이 참 부럽네요.＝*It's enviable for all family members to work in harmony.*

장단이 맞다 [Lit. for the rhythm to be in sync] IDIOM 같이 일하는 데 있어서 생각과 행동이 잘 맞다＝for people's minds and actions to be in sync in their work (*cf.* 장단(을) 맞추다) ▌A: 아주 두 부부가 **장단이 잘 맞는구먼**.＝*That couple makes such beautiful harmony.* B: 부부는 일심동체라잖아요.＝*That's why there's a saying that husband and wife are one.*

▶p.454

재(를) 뿌리다 [Lit. to sprinkle ashes] IDIOM 잘되어 가는 일을 망치다＝to ruin something that has been going well (*syn.* 고춧가루(를) 뿌리다, 소금(을) 뿌리다, 초(를) 치다, 찬물(을) 끼얹다) ▌A: 뭐하러 벌써부터 그렇게 열심히 공부하냐? 시험도 아직 멀었는데.＝*Why are you studying that hard even when the test is still a long way off?* B: 너는 왜 삼촌이 되어 가지고 조카 공부하는데 **재를 뿌리고** 그러니?＝*Why are you trying to disturb your nephew when he is studying?*

재수 없는 놈은 뒤로 자빠져도 코가 깨진다 [Lit. When an unlucky man falls on his back, he still manages to break his nose.] PROVERB 운이 몹시 없는 상황을 가리키는 말＝describes a very unlucky situation (*equiv.* The bread always falls buttered side down. / If anything can go wrong, it will. / Murphy's Law *syn.* 안되는 사람은 뒤로 넘어져도 코가 깨진다) ▌A: 아, 큰일났어. 어제 접촉사고가 났는데, 하필이면 제일 비싼 외제차야. 수리비가 5백만 원이나 나왔대.＝*Yesterday I got into an accident, and of course it had to be with someone driving an expensive* *import. They're telling me it's going to be 5 million won to fix.* B: 참, **재수 없는 놈은 뒤로 자빠져도 코가 깨진다더니**, 어쩌면 좋니. = *I guess the bread does always fall on the buttered side.*

~ 저리 가라다 [Lit. to say something/someone should go away] IDIOM ⋯과 견줄 수 있을 만큼 아주 대단하다 = for something or someone to be just as great as ... ▮A: 우와 김 선생 노래 정말 잘하네요. = *Wow, Mr. Kim is a really excellent singer.* B: 그러게요. 완전히 가수 **저리 가라네요**. = *That's what I'm saying. The pros have got nothing on him.*

적나라하다 [Lit. 赤red + 裸naked + 裸naked + 하다adjectival suffix] CHINESE-DERIVATION 있는 그대로 다 드러내다 = to expose everything as it is ▮A: 그 책 어때? 재미있어? = *How's that book? Is it interesting?* B: 응. 이 작가 소설을 보면 인간의 잔인함이 **적나라하게** 드러나 있어. = *Yeah. This writer's novels graphically reveal the cruelty of human beings.*

적반하장 [Lit. 賊thief + 反reverse + 荷load − 杖stick → for the thief to shake the stick at the the owner] CHINESE-DERIVATION 잘못한 사람이 잘못이 없는 사람을 나무람 = blaming another for something you caused (*cf.* 방귀 뀐 놈이 성낸다) ▮A: 이것 봐요. 사람하고 부딪혔으면 미안하다고 사과를 해야죠! = *Hey now! When you bump into someone, you're supposed to say sorry.* B: **적반하장**도 유분수지. 그쪽이 딴 데 보다가 부딪힌 거잖아요. = *You're really going to say that to me? You were the one who was looking the other way and hit into me.*

적신호가 켜지다 IDIOM = 빨간불이 켜지다

적을 알고 나를 알면 백전백승 [Lit. If you know the enemy and yourself, you will never be defeated.] PROVERB 적과 자기 자신을 알면 싸움에서 늘 이긴다는 말 = used to suggest that knowing oneself and knowing one's enemy is always a formula for success (*cf.* 지피지기) ▮A: 연습 안 하고 왜 비디오만 봐? = *Why are you watching video clips and not practicing?* B: 상대팀 분석 중이야. **적을 알고 나를 알면 백전백승**이라잖아. = *I'm analyzing the other team. If one knows one's enemy and* *oneself, one cannot be defeated.*

적자생존 [Lit. 適suitable + 者person + 生live + 存exist → The fittest survives.] CHINESE-DERIVATION 환경에 적응하는 것만 살아남고 그렇지 못한 것은 도태되는 현상 = the phenomenon of individuals most suited to an environment surviving while others cease to exist (*equiv.* survival of the fittest *cf.* 약육강식) ▎A: 동물의 세계는 **적자생존**의 법칙이 지배하잖아. = *In the wild, the rule of survival of the fittest dominates.* B: 뭐 사람 사는 세상도 크게 다르지 않지. = *The world of human beings is hardly any different.*

NOTE: 다윈이 '종의 기원'에서 사용한 말이다.
From Darwin's "The Origin of Species."

적재적소 [Lit. 適suitable + 材material + 適suitable + 所place → to put the right material in the right place] CHINESE-DERIVATION 어떠한 사람에게 알맞은 자리 = the right position for the right person (*equiv.* (to be) the right man or woman for the job) ▎A: 강진수 씨는 리더의 요건이 뭐라고 생각하십니까? = *Gang Jinsu, what do you think are some of the necessities to be a leader?* B: 여러 가지가 있겠지만 사람을 **적재적소**에 쓰는 것이라고 생각합니다. = *Well, there are a lot of things, but I think putting the right people in the right positions is critical.*

전광석화 [Lit. 電lightning + 光light + 石stone + 火fire → a flash from lightning or flint] CHINESE-DERIVATION 대단히 짧은 시간이나 매우 빠른 동작 = a very short amount of time or an extremely quick movement (*equiv.* in a flash / lightning fast) ▎A: 아, 왕기춘 선수 멋진 업어치기로 한판승을 거둡니다! = *Ah, Wang Gichun's adroit take-down skills win another victory for him!* B: 정말 **전광석화** 같은 공격이었습니다. = *It really was a lightning-quick attack.*

전기가 통하다 [Lit. to convey electricity] IDIOM 남녀가 서로 좋아하게 되다 = for a man and woman to begin to like each other (*equiv.* for there to be sparks (of passion) between two people *cf.* 눈(이) 맞다) ▎A: 두 사람 언

제 **전기가 통한 거야**? = *When did you start to feel there was chemistry between you two?* B: 처음 만난 순간 아, 이 사람이다 싶었어요. = *The very first moment we met, I thought to myself "This may be the one."*

전도유망하다 [Lit. 前before + 途road + 有exist + 望hope + 하다adjectival suffix] CHINESE-DERIVATION 앞날이 밝고 성공할 가능성이 많다 = for the days ahead to be bright and for there to be a high likelihood of success ▌A: 이번 신입사원 김명철 씨 말이에요. 카이스트 나왔다죠? = *Do you know that new guy, Kim Myeongcheol? He went to KAIST, right?* B: 네. 박사 마치고 연구원으로 입사했대요. 듣기로는 5개 국어를 한다더군요. = *Yeah I heard he finished his doctorate there and is working here now as a researcher. They also say he speaks five languages.* A: **전도유망**한 분이군요. = *That guy's got a bright future ahead of him.*

전무후무(하다) [Lit. 前before + 無no + 後after + 無no] CHINESE-DERIVATION 이전에도 없었고 이후에도 없을 것이다 = for something to happen that has never happened before and will likely never happen again (*equiv.* to be unprecedented / a once-in-a-lifetime event) ▌A: 정말 엄청난 기록이군요. 한 경기에 삼진을 25개나 잡았습니다. = *What an amazing record: 25 strikeouts in one game!* B: 네. 아마도 **전무후무한** 대기록이 되지 않을까 싶습니다. = *That's right. It's the first and last time that we will ever see that happen.*

전쟁을 치르다 [Lit. to wage war] IDIOM 소동을 겪다 = to suffer through a commotion (*equiv.* to wage war) ▌A: 아이 다섯을 키우시려면 힘드시겠어요. = *Raising five kids like that must be hard.* B: 아침마다 아이들 학교 보내느라 **전쟁을 치르고** 나면 기운이 하나도 없어요. = *Every morning I have to wage war just to get the kids out the door. It leaves me feeling completely depleted.*

전전긍긍하다 [Lit. 戰shiver + 戰shiver + 兢afraid + 兢afraid + 하다verbal suffix] CHINESE-DERIVATION 두려워하며 걱정하다 = to worry in fear (*equiv.* to quake with fear) ▌A: 내가 유리창 깬 걸 엄마가 알면 나는 죽을 텐데 어떡하지? = *If Mom finds out that I am the one who broke the window,* *she's going to kill me. What should I do?* B: 여기서 **전전긍긍할** 게 아니라 그냥 솔직하게 얘기해. = *You don't need to quiver in fear about it. Just tell her the truth.*

전철을 밟다 [Lit. to walk the tracks of a cart] IDIOM 이전 시대나 사람의 잘못을 되풀이하다 = to repeat the mistakes of a preceding person or era ▌A: 메이저리그에 도전했던 김대성 선수가 한국 무대로 복귀하기로 결정했습니다. = *Kim Daeseong, the athlete who tried his hand at the Major Leagues, has decided to return to Korean baseball.* B: 작년에 한국 프로 야구로 돌아온 이민기 선수의 **전철을 밟게** 된 셈이네요. = *It looks like he'll be following in the footsteps of Lee Mingi, who returned to the Korean leagues last year.*

NOTE: 전철은 수레가 지나가고 난 뒤 남은 바퀴 자국을 가리킨다. 다른 사람이 남긴 전철을 밟으며 따라간다는 말은 앞서 먼저 간 누군가의 잘못된 행동을 되풀이한다는 것을 의미한다.
전철 is the word for the tracks left behind by a cart. To step on those tracks means to follow on the heels of an unsuccessful predecessor.

전파를 타다 [Lit. to ride the airwaves] IDIOM 방송 매체에 나오다 = to be on TV (*equiv.* to take (to the) airwaves / to be on air) ▌A: 참, 들었어? 혼자 네 쌍둥이를 키우는 남자 말이야, 이번에 재혼했대. = *Hey, did you hear? I mean about the guy who's raising quadruplets by himself. I heard he just got remarried.* B: 저번에 사연이 **전파를 탄** 후에 방송을 보고 찾아온 어떤 여자랑 결혼했다고 하데. = *They're saying he's marrying a woman who saw his story on TV and went looking for him.*

전화위복 [Lit. 轉change + 禍disaster + 爲do + 福good fortune] CHINESE-DERIVATION 좋지 않은 일이 계기가 되어 오히려 좋은 일이 생김 = a disaster that turns out in one's favor (*equiv.* When life gives you lemons, make lemonade. / It was a blessing in disguise.) ▌A: 저번 경기에서 패한 게 오히려 **전화위복**이 됐어요. 선수들이 그전보다 훈련을 더 열심히 해요. = *Losing that last game could've been a blessing in disguise. The players are training harder than ever.* B: 때로는 지는 게 약이 될 때도 있죠. =

Sometimes losing can be a good thing.

절이 싫으면 중이 떠나야 한다 [Lit. If he hates the temple, the priest has to leave.] PROVERB 어떤 장소나 대상이 마음에 들지 않으면 그 장소나 대상이 아니라 마음에 들어하지 않는 그 사람이 떠나야 한다는 말 = suggests that if a person hates a certain environment or person, they'd be better off moving on than trying to change the way things are (*equiv.* If you can't stand the heat, get out of the kitchen.) ▌A: 대리님, 회사 그만두신다면서요? = *I heard you're leaving the company?* B: 네. 이 회사는 비전이 없는 것 같아요. 절이 싫으면 중이 떠나야죠. = *Yes, this place just seems to lack vision. They just seemed like it was time for me to move on.*

젊어서 고생은 사서도 한다 [Lit. Even if you have to pay for your problems, you'll do it when you're young.] PROVERB 젊을 때 한 고생은 인생을 살아가는 데 큰 도움이 되기 때문에 두려워할 필요가 없다는 말 = suggests that the hardships of youth are invaluable and therefore nothing to be afraid of (*cf.* 고생을 사서 하다) ▌A: 요즘에 서빙 알바한다며? 힘들지? = *I heard you've been waiting tables recently. Isn't that a tough job?* B: 아니에요. 젊어서 고생은 사서도 하는데요 뭘. = *No, it's not like that. At this age, it's not like I'm going to be living on easy street.*

*__점수(를) 따다__ [Lit. to pluck points] IDIOM 좋게 평가를 받다 = to be appraised well (*equiv.* to earn brownie points) ▌A: 아버님이 뭘 좋아하셔? = *What is your dad into?* B: 바둑이 취미셔. = *His hobby is go.* A: 그래? 잘됐네. 나도 바둑 좋아하는데. 이번 기회에 **점수 좀 따야겠다**. = *Really? That's great. I really like go too. I'd better earn some brownie points with him this time.*

점(을)찍다 [Lit. to draw a point] IDIOM 마음속으로 정해 두다 = to decide something in one's mind ▌A: 나 차 바꾸려고 하는데 조언 좀 해 줘. = *I'm planning on getting a new car, why don't you give me some advice?* B: **점찍어** 둔 건 있고? = *Do you have your eye on anything?* A: 아니. 이제부터 알아볼 생각이야. = *Nope. I'm just kicking off the search right now.*

NOTE: 조선 시대에는 높은 관직을 선임할 때 세 명의 후보를 우선 뽑고 그 중 한 명의 이름 위에 임금이 직접 점을 찍어 최종 선택했다. '점을 찍다'라는 표현은 여기에서 유래했다.
During the Joseon Period, when a person was under review for a high-ranking position, it was customary to select three candidates and give their names to the king who would then place a dot above his choice. The expression of "to draw a point" comes from this.

접시 물에 코 박고 죽다 [Lit. to submerge one's nose in a bowl of water and die] IDIOM 처지가 몹시 궁하여 답답할 때 자조적으로 쓰는 말 = used to express scorn and contempt at oneself over one's continued plight (*equiv.* I just want to kill myself and get it over with. / I just want to end it all.) ▌A: 아직 취직 못 했어? = *You still haven't been able to find a job?* B: 응. 벌써 백수 생활 2년째인데, 정말 **접시 물에 코 박고 죽고** 싶은 심정이야. = *Yeah. It's been two years now that I've been unemployed. I'm at the point right now where I just wish I could die.*

정곡을 찌르다 [Lit. to hit the bullseye] IDIOM 핵심을 찌르다 = to get at the gist ▌A: 결국 이 문제는 누가 더 빨리 사람들을 모으느냐에 달려 있는 거군요. = *At the end of the day, this is just a matter of who can bring in the people faster.* B: 네, 맞아요. 바로 **정곡을 찌르셨어요.** = *Yes, that's correct. You hit the nail on the head.*

NOTE: 정곡은 과녁의 한가운데에 해당하는 점을 가리킨다.
정곡 is the word for the bullseye of a target.

정정당당하다 [Lit. 正straight + 正straight + 堂dignified + 堂dignified + 하다adjectival suffix] CHINESE-DERIVATION 태도가 떳떳하고 방법이나 수단이 공정하다 = for the behavior of all involved parties to be upright and the methods and means used to be fair (*equiv.* fair and square / on the straight and narrow) ▌A: 우리 이번에야말로 누가 더 달리기를 잘하는지 겨뤄보자. = *Let's finally see who's the better runner.* B: 좋아. 대신 **정정당당하게** 하기야, 알았지? = *Good. But let's keep it fair and square, okay?*

젖내(가) 나다 [Lit. to smell of (mother's) milk] IDIOM 정신적, 육체적으로 아직 성숙하지 못한 면이 보이다 = to give off the impression that one has not fully matured physically or mentally (*equiv.* He still smells of his mother's milk. / He's still green. *syn.* 젖비린내(가) 나다) ▌A: 내가 그런 **젖내 나는** 열 살짜리 애랑 대결을 해야 하다니. = *I just can't believe that I have to compete with that little baby 10-year-old.* B: 어리다고 얕보면 안 돼. 들리는 소문으로 탁구 신동이래. = *Don't look down on him just because he's young. I heard he's a prodigy at table tennis.*

젖비린내(가) 나다 IDIOM = 젖 내(가) 나다

제 꾀에 제가 넘어간다 [Lit. to fall for one's own deceit] PROVERB 잘하려고 한 일이 오히려 자신에게 허가 되다 = for a project that one had expected a lot from to inadvertently become injurious (*equiv.* for a scheme or plan to backfire / to get caught in one's web of deceit *syn.* 제 무덤을 파다, 제 발등을 제가 찍는다, 자충수를 두다) ▌A: 참, 있는 사람들이 더 하는 것 같아. 세금 덜 내겠다고 꼼수 쓰다가 걸린 것 좀 봐. = *People who already have so much just don't know when to call it quits. They scheme and scheme to try to evade taxes, and now look what happened to them.* B: **제 꾀에 제가 넘어간** 꼴이네. = *Yeah, their plan kind of backfired on 'em.*

***제 눈에 안경** [Lit. glasses for the wearer's eye] IDIOM 보잘것없는 물건도 자기 마음에 들면 좋게 보인다는 말 = describes how something even of little beauty can be perceived as beautiful if one has affection for it (*equiv.* Beauty is in the eye of the beholder.) ▌A: 어때? 우리 신랑 잘생겼지? = *What do you think? Isn't my husband handsome?* B: 그래, 뭐, **제 눈에 안경**이니까. = *Sure, if you say so. I guess beauty is in the eye of the beholder.*

NOTE: 눈이 나쁜 사람이 처음으로 안경을 쓰면 세상이 달라 보이는 느낌을 받는다. 어떤 사물이나 현상에 대한 평가는 개개인의 관점에 따라 달라질 수 있는데, '제 눈에 안경'이라는 표현에서 안경이 바로 그러한 개인의 주관적인 관점을 상징한다.
Once someone with poor vision puts on glasses for the first time, it is as if

they were reborn into a new and beautiful world. This phrase reminds us that is not what is beheld that is important, but the vision or perspective of the beholder.

제동을 걸다 [Lit. to apply the brakes] IDIOM 행동을 제한하거나 방해하다 = to restrict or impede someone's actions (*equiv.* to put the brakes on (the actions of another) / to put a stop to *ant.* 발동을 걸다 *cf.* 제동이 걸리다) ▌A: 우리나라 정치는 왜 항상 그 모양인지 모르겠어. = *I just don't understand why Korean politics is always like that.* B: 맞아. 이번에 정부가 하는 일에 또 야당이 **제동을 걸고** 있잖아. = *That's right. The minority party is again just trying to put the brakes on everything the administration is doing.*

제동이 걸리다 [Lit. to have the brakes applied] IDIOM 행동에 제한을 받다 = to be restricted in one's actions (*ant.* 발동이 걸리다 *cf.* 제동을 걸다) ▌A: 이번 사건으로 인해 정부의 도덕성이 큰 타격을 입었습니다. = *The perceived ethics of this administration have taken a major hit with this scandal.* B: 또, 정부의 개혁 정책에도 **제동이 걸릴** 전망입니다. = *Again, it looks as if the brakes will be applied to the government's policy of reform.*

제 무덤을 파다 [Lit. to dig one's own grave] IDIOM 잘하려고 한 일이 오히려 자신에게 해가 되다 = for one's project to become self-injurious (*equiv.* That really came back to bite you in the rear. / for an attempt etc. to backfire *syn.* 제 발등을 제가 찍는다, 제 꾀에 제가 넘어간다, 자충수를 두다) ▌A: 이번에 K사에 특허 침해 소송을 낸 P사 말이야, 오히려 자기네가 K사의 특허를 침해했다고 판결을 받았다지? = *You know how a certain company sued another for breach of patent? In the end, they are the ones who got in trouble for a patent violation.* B: 제 무덤을 제가 판 거죠. = *Yep, they kind of dug their own grave.*

제 발등을 제가 찍는다 [Lit. to step on one's own foot] PROVERB 자기가 한 일이 오히려 자신에게 해가 될 때 쓰는 말 = describes a situation in which one's own actions have been injurious to oneself (*equiv.* to shoot oneself in the foot *syn.* 제 무덤을 파다, 제 꾀에 제가 넘어간다, 자충수를 두다) ▌A: 강 의원 말이야, 맨날 다른 사람 비난하고 고발하다가 결국 의원직 사퇴하네. = *You know Representative Gang? He's always criticizing and persecuting others and now, after all that, he's resigning his position.* B: 참 이상한 사람이야. 제 발등을 제가 찍은 셈이지 뭐. = *What a strange fellow. I guess he shot himself in the foot.*

제 버릇 개 못 준다 [Lit. You can't give your habits to a dog.] PROVERB 한 번 들인 나쁜 버릇은 고치기가 어렵다는 말 = describes how difficult it is to fix a habit once it is acquired (*equiv.* Once a thief, always a thief. / A leopard cannot change his spots.) ▌A: 우리 조카 영수 말이에요. 개가 또 싸움질하다가 경찰서 잡혀갔대요. = *You know my nephew Youngsoo? He was carted down to the police station again for fighting.* B: 제 버릇 개 못 준다더니, 또? = *I guess a leopard can't change his spots, huh?*

***제사(를) 지내다** IDIOM = 고사(를) 지내다

제 살 깎아 먹기 [Lit. scraping off one's own flesh] IDIOM 스스로에게 손해가 되는 짓 = an action that injures oneself (*equiv.* to cannibalize (the industry, one's own product etc.)) ▌A: 아니 여기 또 편의점이 들어섰어? 이 편의점은 바로 저기에도 있잖아. = *What? Now they're opening up another store here? There's another one right over there.* B: 제 살 깎아 먹기인 거지 뭐. = *Yep, they're kind of cannibalizing each other, aren't they?*

제자리걸음(을) 하다 [Lit. to walk in place] IDIOM 진척이 없다 = to make no progress (*equiv.* to walk in place / to tread water) ▌A: 프로젝트가 시작된 지 벌써 석 달이 지났는데 아직도 **제자리걸음을 하고** 있으니 참 답답하네요. = *It's already been three months since this project started and it feels like we're just walking in place. I'm starting to get a little frustrated.* B: 이러다 유야무야되는 거 아닌지 모르겠어요. = *If we continue on like this, it may just all go up in a puff of smoke.*

조강지처 [Lit. 糟dregs + 糠chaff + 之of + 妻wife → the wife from when one ate meals of dregs and chaff] CHINESE-DERIVATION 힘든 시기를 함께 겪은 아내 = a wife who stayed by one through the hard times (*equiv.* She's been with me for the good times and the bad, the ups and the downs.) ▌A: 이놈아, 네가 **조강지처**를 두고 바람을 피우다니. 왜 그랬니? = *How could you cheat on a wife who's been by your side like that through all the ups and downs? Why would you do a thing like that?* B: 제가 미쳤었나 봐요. 이혼 당해도 싸죠. = *I guess I just wasn't thinking straight. A divorce would be getting off easily.*

조삼모사 [Lit. 朝morning + 三three + 暮dusk + 四four → three in the morning, four in the evening] CHINESE-DERIVATION 교활한 꾀를 써서 남을 속이는 일 = deceiving another with transparent trickery (*equiv.* a cheap trick) ▌A: 우와, 이번 달에는 월급이 많이 들어왔네! = *Wow, I got paid a lot this month!* B: 그거 연말 보너스를 월급으로 미리 준 거야. = *They just gave out the end-of-the-year bonus this month.* A: 거 참, **조삼모사**가 따로 없군. = *Geez, what a cheap trick!*

NOTE: 오랜 옛날 중국의 한 남자가 원숭이를 여러 마리 길렀다. 그런데 살림이 어려워져 먹이로 주는 도토리 수를 줄일 수밖에 없었다. 처음에는 원숭이들에게 도토리를 아침에 세 개, 저녁에 네 개 주었다. 그러자 원숭이들이 몹시 화를 내었다. 그래서 다음날부터 아침에 네 개, 저녁에 세 개를 주었다. 그러자 원숭이들이 모두 만족하며 기뻐했다.
Long ago in China there lived a man who raised monkeys. The monkey business, however, wasn't booming and he was forced to cut down on the number of acorns he fed them each day. He started giving the monkeys three acorns in the morning and four in the evening. The monkeys were not pleased. He decided to switch it up the next day and gave the monkeys four acorns in the morning and three in the evening. The monkeys were happy with the new arrangement. Such weak trickery is referred to with this phrase.

졸로 보다 [Lit. to look at someone as a *jol*] IDIOM 우습게 보다 = to think little of someone (*equiv.* to treat someone like a pawn / to treat someone like a pushover *syn.* 졸로 알다) ▌A: 우리 팀장은 나를 **졸로 보나** 봐. 걸핏하면 나보고 당직을 서라 하니 말이야. = *Our team leader treats me like a pushover. At the drop of a hat, he puts me on call.* B: 네가 팀 막내니까 그런 거겠지. = *I'm sure that's just because you're the newest member of the team.*

NOTE: 졸은 장기에서 맨 앞에 위치하는 다섯 개의 작은 말이다. 앞과 옆으로 한 칸씩만 이동할 수 있어서 일반적으로 힘이 가장 약한 기마이다. 누군가를 졸로 본다는 것은 그 사람을 얕본다는 말이다.
졸 is name of five small pieces used in Korean chess. They can only be moved one space to the front or side and are generally the weakest piece on the board. That is why considering someone to be a 졸 means taking them lightly.

졸로 알다 IDIOM = 졸로 보다

좀이 쑤시다 [Lit. for the moths to poke] IDIOM 마음이 들뜨거나 초조해 가만히 있지 못하다 = to be unable to sit still because of one's jubilant attitude or nerves (*equiv.* to have cabin fever / I'm just so excited, I can't sit still. / to be antsy *cf.* 오금이 쑤시다) ▌A: 주말 내내 집에만 있었더니 **좀이 쑤시네.** = *I spent the whole weekend cooped up at home and now I'm feeling a little antsy.* B: 영화 보러 갈까? = *How about seeing a movie?*

NOTE: 좀벌레가 몸을 쑤셔대면 가려워서 참을 수가 없게 된다. 그래서 가만히 참고 기다리지 못하고 몸을 들썩이는 것을 '좀이 쑤시다'라고 말한다.
When small moths bounce against one's skin at night, it tickles and becomes impossible to bear. That's why when one is feeling antsy and can barely sit still, it is referred to in Korean as "moths poking."

종로에서 뺨 맞고 한강(에) 가서 눈 흘긴다 [Lit. to get slapped in the face in Jongno and look daggers (at someone) over by the Han River] PROVERB 화를 엉뚱한 사람에게 풀 때 쓰는 말 = describes a situation in which one takes one's anger out on the wrong person (*equiv.* Don't take your

anger out on me!) ▌A: 왜 어머님은 맨날 나만 갖고 그러시는지 모르 겠어. 그러니까 당신이 평소에 중간에서 잘해야 할 거 아냐. =*I don't know why your mother always treats me this way. This is why you should try to keep the peace between us as much as you can.* B: **종로에서 뺨 맞고 한강 가서 눈 흘긴다더니, 왜 갑자기 불똥이 나한테 튀어?** ◆p.321 =*I don't know why you're taking this out on me. Why are you picking a fight with me?*

종(이) 치다 [Lit. for the bell to be struck] IDIOM 일이 성사될 가망이 없 다 = for a project or task to have no likelihood of success (*equiv.* It's all over. / The fat lady has sung. *syn.* 날(이) 새다) ▌A: 야, **종 쳤다.** 집에 가자. = *Hey, the fat lady has sung. Go home.* B: 기다려 봐. 대상 발표가 남았잖 아. = *Just hold on a minute. The grand prize still hasn't been announced.*

종이 한 장 차이 [Lit. the difference of one sheet of paper] IDIOM 매우 작 은 차이 = a very small difference (*equiv.* by a hair) ▌A: 결승전에서는 누 가 이길까? = *Who do you think will win the finals?* B: 글쎄. 실력은 **종 이 한 장 차이**니까 당일 컨디션이 좋은 선수가 이기겠지. = *Well, since the difference in ability is about the width of a single hair, I think it'll come down to how the athletes are feeling on that particular day.*

종이호랑이 [Lit. a paper tiger] IDIOM 겉보기에는 아주 센 것 같지만 사 실은 약한 것 = something that initially appears to be very strong but in fact is quite weak (*equiv.* a paper tiger / all bark and no bite *cf.* 이빨 빠진 호랑 이) ▌A: 저 선수 스캔들 이후로 좀처럼 예전 실력이 안 나오네 요. = *Ever since the scandal erupted, he just hasn't been the same on the greens.* B: **종이호랑이**가 된 것 같아요. = *I guess he really was just a paper tiger.*

NOTE: 원래 이 표현은 중국의 紙老虎(지노호)라는 표현에서 비롯한 것이 다. 한편, 영어에도 paper tiger라는 표현이 있다. 1956년 마오쩌둥은 미 국을 겉으로 보기에는 아주 강력하지만 실제로는 두려워할 필요가 없 는, 종이호랑이에 불과하다고 평가했다. 이때부터 서양 언론에서 paper tiger라는 표현을 본격적으로 사용하게 되었다.
This expression originally comes from the Chinese expression, 紙老虎. The

same Chinese expression led to the phrase, "paper tiger," in English. In 1956 Mao Zedong appraised the US as a power that looked imposing from a distance, but was truly no more than a paper tiger. This was when the western press adopted the phrase and commenced its regular usage.

종지부를 찍다 IDIOM = 마침표를 찍다

좋은 게 좋다 [Lit. Good things are good.] IDIOM 약간의 문제가 있더라도 적당히 타협을 하는 것이 서로에게 좋다는 말 = suggests that even when there are slight problems, a little compromise can be beneficial to both parties ▌A: 이 문구는 좀 고쳐야 할 것 같은데요. = *We're going to have to fix the wording here a bit.* B: 우리 **좋은 게 좋은 거**라고 자주 얼굴 보는 사이에 너무 까다롭게 그러지 맙시다. = *Since we're going to have to continue to see each other on a regular basis, I think we should gloss over the little things if possible.*

좌불안석(하다) [Lit. 坐sit + 不no + 安comfortable + 席seat] CHINESE-DERIVATION 마음이 불안하고 초조하여 자리에 편안히 앉아 있지 못하다 = to be unable to sit comfortably because one is ill at ease or nervous (*equiv.* I'm so nervous I just can't sit still.) ▌A: 왜 그렇게 **좌불안석**이야? = *Why are you so fidgety?* B: 아내 출산일이 오늘내일하거든요. = *Because my wife's delivery is going to happen either today or tomorrow.*

좌지우지(하다) [Lit. 左left + 之do + 右right + 之do → (to tell someone to go) left or right] CHINESE-DERIVATION 이리저리 자기 마음대로 다루다 = to treat someone according to one's whim (*equiv.* to boss someone around / to run the show / to hold the reins) ▌A: 감독님도 계신데 선수들 모두 주장 말만 듣네. = *Even with the coach here, the players are just listening to the team captain.* B: 응. 실질적으로 주장이 모두 **좌지우지하지**. = *Yeah, honestly, it's the captain that runs the show.*

좌충우돌(하다) [Lit. 左left + 衝clash + 右right + 突dash forward] CHINESE-DERIVATION 이쪽 저쪽으로 사물이나 사람과 마구 부딪히다 = to bump up against people and things on each side (*equiv.* It's a bumpy road. / It's still pretty haphazard.) ▌A: 영수 씨, 새 업무에 적응은 잘하고 있어요?＝*Youngsu, are you getting used to your new job?* B: 아직 일을 배우는 단계라서 매일 **좌충우돌하고** 있죠 뭐.＝*I'm still in the learning stages, so it's pretty chaotic.*

주가를 올리다 [Lit. to raise the stock value] IDIOM 인기나 명성, 평판 등이 높다＝to raise the popularity, fame, or reputation (of someone, or oneself)
▶ p.407
▌A: 오늘은 약방에 감초 역할로 요즘 한창 **주가를 올리고** 있는 김영호 씨를 만나 보겠습니다.＝*Today we're going to meet the actor, Kim Yeongho, who has recently raised his stock by becoming an indispensable character on many TV shows.* B: 박수로 맞아 주세요.＝*Let's give him a warm welcome.*

주객전도(하다) [Lit. 主host + 客customer + 顚turn over + 倒fall → for the customer and owner to switch roles] CHINESE-DERIVATION 중요한 것과 부차적인 것 따위가 서로 뒤바뀌다＝for something important and something ancillary to switch roles (*equiv.* for the tables to turn / a role reversal / to put the cart before the horse) ▌A: 우리 기숙사 식당에는 기숙사 사는 학생보다 외부 시민들이 더 많은 것 같아요.＝*It seems like there are more customers from outside the school at our dormitory cafeteria than actual students.* B: 그래서 학생들이 밥을 못 먹는 경우도 있잖아요. **주객이 전도된** 거죠.＝*Yeah, that's why sometimes the students can't even eat there. We've been kicked out of our own house.*

주는 것 없이 밉다 [Lit. to dislike (someone) without giving them anything] IDIOM 특별한 이유 없이 밉다＝to be annoyed by someone for no particular reason (*equiv.* I don't know why, he just bugs me.) ▌A: 너는 왜 그렇게 미영이를 싫어해?＝*Why do you hate Miyoung so much?* B: 그냥 **주는 것 없이 미워.**＝*I don't know; she just bugs me.*

주도면밀하다 [Lit. 周widespread + 到reach + 綿continuous + 密meticulous + 하다adjectival suffix] CHINESE-DERIVATION 꼼꼼하고 세심하여 빈틈이 없다＝to be careful, meticulous and leave no blind spots (*equiv.* to

leave no stone unturned / to always be on the one's toes) ▌A: 갑자기 컴퓨터가 꺼졌는데 데이터에는 이상 없어요?=*The computer suddenly shut off. Are there any irregularities with the data?* B: 네, 괜찮아요. 미리 백업을 해 뒀거든요.=*No, everything's fine. I already backed it all up ahead of time.* A: **주도면밀하시네요**.=*You really are cautious about your work, aren't you?*

주둥이(를) 놀리다 IDIOM=입(을) 놀리다

주머니가 가볍다 [Lit. for one's pockets to be light] IDIOM 가지고 있는 돈이 적다=to not have very much money (*ant.* 주머니가 두둑하다) ▌A: 또 라면이에요? 뭐 좀 제대로 된 걸 먹지 않고서요?=*It's ramen again? Why don't you just eat a real meal?* B: 요즘 **주머니가 가벼워서** 아껴야 해요.=*I'm running on empty these days. I've got to be careful with my money.*

주머니가 두둑하다 [Lit. for one's pockets to be thick] IDIOM 가지고 있는 돈이 많다=to have a lot of money (*equiv.* to have deep pockets *ant.* 주머니가 가볍다) ▌A: 오늘 내가 한턱낼게.=*Today is my treat.* B: 어쩐 일이야?=*Oh, what's the occasion?* A: 오늘 월급 받아서 **주머니가 두둑해**. 가자.=*I just got paid today, so the money's burning a hole in my pocket. Let's go.*

주머니가 비다 [Lit. for one's pockets to be empty] IDIOM 가진 돈이 없다=to have no money (*equiv.* to have empty pockets) ▌A: 여보 나 용돈 좀 줘. **주머니가 완전히 비었어**.=*Honey, could you give me some spending cash? My pockets are empty.* B: 용돈 벌써 다 쓴 거야?=*You've already used up all the cash I gave you?* A: 한 달에 5만 원으로 어떻게 버텨?=*How am I supposed to get by on 50,000 won per month?*

주머니(를) 털다 [Lit. to shake one's pockets] IDIOM 1. 가지고 있는 돈을 다 내놓다=to put out all the money one has (*equiv.* to turn one's pockets inside out / to empty one's pockets *syn.* 호주머니(를) 털다) ▌A: 왜 지갑에 돈이 하나도 없어?=*Why don't you have a penny in your wallet?* B:

오다가 보니 불우 이웃 돕기를 하길래 **주머니를 털었지**. =*On the way home, I made a donation to help the poor and I emptied out my pockets.* 2. 강도짓이나 도둑질을 하다=to steal or commit robbery (*equiv.* to shakedown (a victim) / to turn someone's pockets inside out (looking for money) *syn.* 호주머니(를) 털다) ▌A: 요즘 은행에서 돈 찾아서 나오는 사람들 **주머니를 터는** 놈들이 많대요. =*I heard there are lots of criminals who shake down customers after they leave the bank with money.* B: 그래? 당신도 조심해야겠네. =*Really? You better be careful too.*

주머닛돈이 쌈짓돈 [Lit. pocket money or pouch money] PROVERB 한 가족의 재산은 결국 공동의 것이므로 네 것 내 것을 굳이 따질 필요가 없다는 말=used to express that the property of a family is shared and therefore there is no reason to squabble over it. ▌A: 오늘 밥값은 당신이 내요. =*You pay for the food today.* B: 아무나 내면 어때? 어차피 **주머닛돈이 쌈짓돈**이지. =*What difference does it make who pays? It all comes from the same place anyway.*

NOTE: 쌈지는 담배나 돈 따위를 넣어 가지고 다니는 작은 주머니를 말한다. 돈이 다른 주머니에 있으나 쌈지에 있으나 결국 그 사람 돈이기는 마찬가지다.
A 쌈지 is the word for a small pouch used to carry cigarettes or money. Whether the money is in one's pouch or pocket, it still belongs to the owner.

주먹이 운다 [Lit. My fists are crying.] IDIOM 때리고 싶은 것을 참으면서 하는 말=said when one is resisting the urge to hit someone (*equiv.* I really want to punch you right now. / One's fists are itching to hit someone.) ▌A: 너 하는 것 보니 사람 치겠다. 어디 한번 때려 봐. =*You look like you're getting ready for a fight. Let's do this.* B: 우와, **주먹이 운다**, 주먹이 울어. =*Wow, my fists are just itching to punch you right now.*

주사위가 던져지다 [Lit. for the dice to be thrown] QUOTE 어떤 일이 이미 결정되다=for a certain matter to have been decided (*equiv.* The dice has been cast. / to be passed the point of no return) ▌A: 정말 이번 결정은 너무 어이없어. =*I was really taken aback by this decision.* B: 이제 왈가왈

부해 봤자 소용없어. **주사위는 이미 던져졌잖아**. = *There's no use and going back and forth over it now. The dice has been cast.*

NOTE: 역사가 수에토니우스에 의하면, 이 표현은 줄리어스 시저가 그의 군대를 이끌고 로마를 향해 진군하면서 루비콘 강을 건넜을 때 썼다고 한다.
From the quote attributed by Suetonius to Julius Caesar as he led his army across the Rubicon towards Rome.

주인(을) 만나다

[Lit. to meet one's owner] IDIOM 어떤 물건이 그것을 잘 사용할 수 있는 사람의 손에 들어가다 = for a certain item to end up in the hands of someone who knows how to put it to good use ▌A: 이 목걸이는 직접 만드신 거예요? = *Did you make this necklace all by yourself?* B: 네. 참 힘들게 만든 물건인데 아직 **주인을 못 만났네요**. = *Yes. It was really tough to make, but I still haven't found the right person to wear it.*

주체(를) 못하다

[Lit. to be unable to take the burden] IDIOM 감당할 수 없다 = to be beyond one's abilities ▌A: 민수야, 나 좀 도와줘. 짐이 너무 많아 **주체를 못하겠어**. = *Hey, Minsu, could you help me out a bit? I have too much to carry and I don't think I can handle it.* B: 어, 잠깐만. = *Yeah, just a second.*

주판알(을) 튀기다

[Lit. to flick the counter bead] IDIOM 이익과 손해를 따져보다 = to calculate the benefits and losses (*equiv.* to run the numbers / to go over the pros and cons *syn.* 계산기(를) 두드리다) ▌A: 어떤 요금제를 하는 게 제일 나을까? = *What billing plan do you think would be the* ➡ p.455 *best for me?* B: 아무리 **주판알을 튀겨도** 마찬가지야. 다 일장일단이 있는 건데 뭐. = *There's no need to keep running the numbers, it looks like they're both about the same. They both have their strengths and weaknesses.*

죽기보다 싫다

[Lit. to hate (something) more than death] IDIOM 몹시 싫다 = to hate immensely (*equiv.* I'd rather die than (do that).) ▌A: 너 이 문제 알아? = *Do you get this problem?* B: 수학은 경호가 제일 잘하잖

아. = *Gyeongho is the one who's best at math.* A: 됐어. 걔한테 물어보는 건 죽기보다 싫어. = *Never mind. I'd rather die than ask that guy.*

죽기 살기로 [Lit. (to consider something) life and death] IDIOM 굳은 각오로 매우 열심히 = with stalwart resolution and absolute motivation (*equiv.* It's a matter of life and death. *syn.* 죽기 아니면 까무러치기로) █ A: 이번에는 정말 **죽기 살기로** 열심히 해 볼게요. = *This time I'm going to approach it as if it were life or death.* B: 그래, 그렇다고 너무 무리하지는 말고. = *Fine, just don't go overboard.*

죽기 아니면 까무러치기로 IDIOM = 죽기 살기로

죽는소리(를) 하다 [Lit. to make a dying sound] IDIOM 자신의 아픔이나 괴로움을 엄살스럽게 호소하다 = to bemoan one's pain or suffering in an overblown manner (*equiv.* to act like you're about to die *syn.* 앓는 소리(를) 하다) █ A: 휴우, 요즘같이 장사가 안되면 가게 문을 닫게 될지도 모르겠어요. = *With business as bad as it is these days, I may have to close down the store.* B: **죽는소리 좀 하지** 마. 다들 힘들잖아. = *Don't carry on like that. Everyone is having a hard time.*

죽도 밥도 안 되다 [Lit. to be neither porridge nor rice] IDIOM 일이 제대로 되지 않다 = for a project to not proceed smoothly (*equiv.* It's neither here nor there. / It's all come to naught. *cf.* 죽이 되든 밥이 되든) █ A: 이러다가는 **죽도 밥도 안 되겠어**. = *If we continue on like this, it will all come to naught.* B: 맞아요. 이제 빨리 결정을 내립시다. = *You're right. Let's hurry up and make a decision.*

죽마고우 [Lit. 竹bamboo + 馬horse + 故old + 友friend → a friend that one has known since the days one played around on a bamboo horse] CHINESE-DERIVATION 어릴 때부터 가까이 지내며 자란 친구 = a friend that one grew up with (*equiv.* a bosom buddy / I've known him since we were (both) in diapers.) █ A: 이쪽은 제 회사 동료인 고미영 씨, 이쪽은 제 **죽마고우**인 조태수입니다. = *This is my colleague from work Go Miyeong, and this is my childhood friend, Jo Taesu.* B: 안녕하세요, 말씀 많이 들었습

니다. = *Hi, nice to meet you. I've heard so much about you.*

죽 쒀서 개 준다 [Lit. to boil porridge and give it to a dog] PROVERB 애써서 한 일이 엉뚱한 사람을 이롭게 하는 결과가 되었을 때 하는 말 = used when a project that one put a lot of effort into ends up benefiting an uninvolved third party (*equiv.* for one's efforts to come to naught / for all one's efforts to go up in flames / What a waste!) ▌A: 어? 여기 있던 과자 어디 있지? 미영 씨 주려고 사 온 건데. = *Hey, what happened to the food that was right here? I bought that for Miyeong.* B: 앗! 그런 줄 모르고 팀원들이 하나씩 먹어 버렸는데 ……. = *Oops! I didn't know what it was for and I handed it out to the team. We ate it all ...* A: 그래요? **죽 쒀서 개 준** 꼴이네. = *Really? Well, that plan sure went up in flames.*

죽어라 (하고) [Lit. to oneself to die] IDIOM **1.** 있는 힘을 다해 = with all one's strength (*equiv.* to resign oneself to death / to work oneself to the death) ▌A: 참 나. 도와 달라고 사정을 하길래 **죽어라 하고** 도와줬는데 고맙다는 인사도 없네. = *That guy asks for my help, I gave it everything I've got, and he doesn't even say thanks.* B: 그러게 사람 마음이라는 게 화장실 갈 때랑 나올 때가 다른 법이잖아요. = *People do have fickle hearts.* **2.** 기가 막힐 정도로 = to an extremely annoying degree ▌A: 아이가 지금 몇 살이죠? = *How old is your son now?* B: 일곱 살이에요. **죽어라** 말도 안 들어요. = *He is seven. The way he never listens is killing us.*

죽었다 깨어나도 [Lit. even if one dies and wakes back up] IDIOM **1.** 무슨 일이 있어도 = no matter what happens (*syn.* 하늘이 두 쪽(이) 나도, 세상없어도) ▌A: 저 분 믿어도 되는 분인가요? = *Is it all right for me to trust him?* B: 걱정 마세요. 비밀은 **죽었다 깨어나도** 지키는 사람입니다. = *Don't worry about it. He'll take your secrets to the grave.* **2.** 아무리 해도 = no matter what one does ▌A: 이 문제는 **죽었다 깨어나도** 모르겠어. = *No matter how hard I try, I just can't solve this problem.* B: 그러지 말고 그냥 해답지를 읽어 봐. = *Come on, just check the answer sheet.*

죽으나 사나 [Lit. whether one lives or dies] IDIOM **1.** 다른 일은 생각하지

않고 항상＝without thinking of anything else ▮A: 우리 애는 가수가 꿈이에요. **죽으나 사나** 노래 생각뿐이에요.＝*Our daughter dreams of one day being a singer. All she ever thinks about is singing.* B: 한 가지를 그렇게 열심히 하면 성공하는 거죠.＝*When someone has that kind of single-minded devotion, they're bound to succeed.* **2.** 어쩔 수 없이＝unavoidably ▮A: 어쩌다 내가 민영 씨랑 짝이 되었나 몰라요.＝*I don't know how I ended up being paired with you.* B: 너무 그러지 마세요. **죽으나 사나** 우리는 끝까지 함께 가야 해요.＝*Oh, come on. Don't be that way. No matter what may come, we're in this together to the end.*

죽으라는 법은 없다 [Lit. There is no law that says we must die.] IDIOM 아주 어려운 상황에서도 살아 나갈 방법이 있다는 말＝suggests that even in a terribly difficult situation, there is always a means of survival (*equiv.* Things always work out for the best. / There's always a way out. *syn.* 하늘이 무너져도 솟아날 구멍이 있다) ▮A: 참 사람 **죽으라는 법은 없나** 봐. 생활비가 떨어져서 오늘 저녁은 굶어야 하나 생각하고 있었는데, 마침 돈이 들어왔어.＝*I guess things really do work out in the end. I was all out of spending cash and set to starve today but then my money showed up just in the nick of time.* B: 그것 참 다행이네.＝*We really lucked out.*

죽을 둥 살 둥 [Lit. whether one lives or dies] IDIOM 다른 일을 돌보지 않고 한 가지 일에 마음을 빼앗긴 모양을 비유하는 말＝used to metaphorically depict ones single-minded concentration on a given project ▮A: 명진 씨 소식 들었어? 큰애가 결국 하늘 나라로 갔대.＝*Have you heard anything about Myeongjin? In the end, he lost his eldest child.* B: 아이 살려 보겠다고 **죽을 둥 살 둥** 매달리더니 그것도 소용없었나 보네.＝*He was so focused on taking care of his daughter, but it was all of no use.*

죽(을) 쑤다 [Lit. to make rice porridge] IDIOM 어떤 일을 망치다＝to ruin a project or attempt ▮A: 시험은 어땠어?＝*How was the test?* B: 완전히 **죽을 쑤었어.** 너무 어려워서 문제를 다 풀지도 못했어.＝*I really messed up. It was so hard I didn't even try to do some of the problems.*

NOTE: 밥을 하는 시간을 넘겨서 끓이면 죽이 된다. 일부러 죽을 끓일 수도 있지만, 밥을 하다가 깜빡하고 시간을 넘겨 죽이 되는 경우도 있다. '죽을 쑤다'는 밥을 하려다 실수로 죽을 쑨 것처럼 어떤 일을 망쳤을 때 쓰는 말이다.
When rice is boiled too long, it becomes *juk*. Sometimes one starts out with the intention of making *juk*, but sometimes, it is an accident that results from overcooking the rice. The expression, 죽을 쑤다, is used when the results of one's actions lead to unintended results, as if one had inadvertently boiled *juk* when attempting to make rice.

죽이 되든 밥이 되든 [Lit. whether it makes porridge or rice] IDIOM 일이 제대로 되든 안 되든＝whether things turn out well or not (*cf.* 죽도 밥도 안 되다) ▌A: 에라, 모르겠다. **죽이 되든 밥이 되든** 일단 시작해 보자. ＝*Ah, just forget it. No matter what may happen, let's at least give it a shot.* B: 그래. 벌써부터 너무 걱정할 필요 없으니까. ＝*Yeah. It's too early to worry that much.*

죽이 맞다 [Lit. to make a perfect set of ten] IDIOM 서로 뜻이 맞다＝for the aims of two parties to be in accord (*syn.* 꿍짝이 맞다) ▌A: 너희 둘은 어떻게 그렇게 **죽이 잘 맞니**? ＝*How come you two always seem to be of one mind?* B: 어릴 때부터 늘 같이 있었으니까 그렇겠지 뭐. ＝*I guess that's just because we've spent so much time together ever since we were young.*

NOTE: 여기에서 '죽'은 옷이나 그릇 따위의 열 개를 묶어 이르는 말이다. 어떤 물건의 개수가 10의 배수로 딱 떨어질 때 죽이 맞다고 하는데, 여기에서 지금의 뜻이 파생되었다.
The word 죽 in this expression means a group of 10 bowls or pieces of clothing etc. When a bundle of items turns out to be a multiple of 10, people say 죽이 맞다. The phrase originates from this usage.

줄(을) 서다 [Lit. to stand in line] IDIOM 1. 차례나 기회를 기다리다＝to wait one's turn or for an opportunity (*equiv.* to wait in line) ▌A: 이거 왜 이래? 밖에 나가면 지금도 나 좋다는 남자가 **줄을 섰어!** ＝*What's* *wrong with you? Even now there are plenty of men who would stand in line just to have a moment of my time!* B: 그래, 알았어. 어련하시겠어. = *All right, I got it. I bet that's true.* **2.** 도움이 될 만한 사람을 따르다 = to follow or obey someone who may be of benefit to you (*equiv.* to cozy up to powerful people) ▌A: 사회 생활은 결국 **줄을 잘 서는** 사람이 성공하는 거야. = *Society is all about cozying up to the right people.* B: 맞아. 내가 **줄을 잘못 서서** 지금 요 ▶p.435 모양 요 꼴이잖아. = *That's right. My inability to kiss up to the right people is why I'm still where I am.*

중구난방 [Lit. 衆multitude + 口mouth + 難difficult + 防protect → It's difficult to cover the mouths of many people.] CHINESE-DERIVATION **1.** 여러 사람이 저마다 떠들어 댐 = the spectacle of many people chattering boisterously ▌A: 다들 좀 조용히 하세요. **중구난방**으로 저마다 자기 얘기만 하니까 회의 진행이 안 되잖아요. = *Please quiet down, everyone. If you all keep on speaking out of turn, we won't be able to carry on with this meeting.* B: 그럼 제가 먼저 말씀드리겠습니다. = *Then I guess I will go ahead and speak first.* **2.** 매우 어지럽고 정리가 안 됨 = a mass of confusion that's impossible to tidy up ▌A: 이게 뭐야? 가나다순으로 정렬을 해야지 이렇게 **중구난방**으로 책을 꽂아 넣으면 어떻게 찾아? = *What's all this? You need to put the books back in alphabetical order, not in a jumble like this. How do you expect anyone to be able to find anything?* B: 네, 죄송합니다. 다시 할게요. = *I understand. I'm very sorry. I'll redo it.*

중언부언(하다) [Lit. 重repeat + 言speak + 復again + 言speak] CHINESE-DERIVATION 같은 말을 계속 되풀이하다 = to repeat the same statements (*equiv.* a (superfluous) reiteration / to repeat (a statement) / to keep saying the same things over and over) ▌A: 그러니까, 어제 그 사람을 만난 건 아니지만, 만날 약속을 하기는 했었는데 ……. = *It's not that I met that person yesterday ... just that we had talked about meeting and ...* B: 왜 자꾸 **중언부언**이야? 똑바로 말하지 못해? = *Why do you keep repeating yourself? Can't you talk straight?*

중이 제 머리 못 깎는다 [Lit. A monk can't shave his own head.]

PROVERB 아무리 솜씨가 좋은 사람도 그것이 자기 자신과 관련되면 잘하기 힘들다는 말＝describes how, despite someone's great abilities, when it comes to themselves, they might not be up to carrying out a certain task ▌A: 주식 강의하는 사람들은 주식으로 돈 많이 벌까?＝*Do you think those people who lecture on the stock market actually make very much money on stocks themselves?* B: **중이 제 머리 못 깎는** 법이지. 이론과 실전은 다른 거 아니겠어?＝*Those who can't do, teach. I think theory and practice are not the same thing, you know?*

쥐고 흔들다 [Lit. to grab and shake] IDIOM 자기 마음대로 하다＝to have one's way (with a person, object) (*equiv.* to have someone at your beck and call / to have someone under your thumb *syn.* 꽉 잡고 있다, 쥐었다 폈다 하다) ▌A: 너는 남편을 **쥐고 흔들면서** 사는 비결이 뭐니?＝*What's your secret to having your husband at your beck and call like that?* B: 내가 무슨 남편을 **쥐고 흔들어**? 나 잡혀 살아, 애.＝*What do you mean "beck and call"? He's got me under his thumb, don't you know?*

쥐구멍에도 볕 들 날 있다 [Lit. The sun even shines in the rat hole some days.] PROVERB 고생만 하는 사람에게도 좋은 때가 온다는 말＝suggests that fortune will even shine on those who struggle constantly (*equiv.* Every cloud has a silver lining. / Every dog has his day. / Fortune knocks at every door. / There's a light at the end of every tunnel.) ▌A: 야호! **쥐구멍에도 볕 들 날 있다더니**, 나한테도 이런 날이 오는구나!＝*I guess every dog does have its day. How could such a wonderful thing happen to me?* B: 왜, 좋은 일 있어?＝*What? Do you have good news?* A: 복권 당첨 됐어!＝*I bought a winning lottery ticket.*

쥐구멍에라도 들어가고 싶다 [Lit. Even if it's a rat hole, I'd like to go inside.] IDIOM 몹시 부끄러워 얼른 그 자리를 피하고 싶다＝to be so embarrassed that one wants to leave immediately (*equiv.* (I'm so embarrassed,) I want to just crawl into a hole somewhere.) ▌A: 오늘 아침 조회 시간에 전교생 보는 데서 넘어졌어요.＝*I fell down this morning at roll call and everyone saw me.* B: 저런. 많이 안 다쳤니?＝*That sucks. Did you hurt yourself?* A: 다치지는 않았는데, 너무 창피해서 **쥐구멍에라도 들**

어가고 싶은 심정이었어요. = *No, I didn't get hurt, but I was so embarrassed I wanted to crawl into a hole somewhere and hide.*

***쥐꼬리** [Lit. a rat's tale] IDIOM 매우 적은 분량 = a very small amount (*equiv. a thimble full*) ▌A: 내년에는 연봉이 좀 올라야 할 텐데. = *They'd better raise your salary next year.* B: 오른다고 해 봤자 **쥐꼬리**만큼일 게 뻔해. = *Even so, it'll be by just some inconsequential amount.*

NOTE: 20세기 중반 한국에서는 쥐를 잡는 운동이 있었다. 학생들은 쥐를 잡았다는 증거로 쥐의 꼬리를 교사에게 제출해야 했다. 그러면 교사는 학생들에게 연필이나 공책 등을 상으로 주고는 했다. 어떤 학생들은 상을 더 받고 싶어 쥐꼬리를 두세 토막으로 자르기도 했다. 가뜩이나 작은 쥐꼬리가 그럴 경우에는 더욱 더 작아졌을 것이다. 이때부터 매우 적은 분량을 쥐꼬리라고 부르기 시작했다.

In the 1950s, a major campaign was underway to deal with the country's burgeoning rat population. If students brought a rat tail to their teachers at school, they were awarded a pencil or notebook. Always quick to deceive the teacher, students soon found that they could cut a single rat tail into many pieces and submit them all, thereby doubling or even tripling their reward. After they had their way with the rat's tail, the remaining pieces were extremely small, and ever since, an extremely tiny quantity as been referred to with this phrase.

쥐도 궁지에 몰리면 고양이를 문다 [Lit. Even a rat will bite a cat when it's cornered.] PROVERB 약한 자도 막다른 지경이 되면 있는 힘을 다해 저항한다는 말 = describes how even a weak entity will lash out with all its might when backed into a corner ▌A: 저도 저 혼자 이렇게 당하고 있지는 않을 겁니다. **쥐도 궁지에 몰리면 고양이를 무는 법입니다.** = *I won't stand here and take the blame for this all on my own. A cornered man fights like there's nothing to lose.* B: 지금 나를 협박하는 건가? = *Are you threatening me?*

쥐도 새도 모르게 [Lit. so even the birds and rats don't know] IDIOM 아무도 모르게 감쪽같이 = stealthily, so that no one knows ▌A: 요즘 같으면 어디 무서워서 인터넷에 글이라도 남기겠어요? = *With things as scary*

as they are now, I sure wouldn't write anything up on the Internet. B: 맞아
요. 정부 정책에 반대하는 글을 남겼다가 **쥐도 새도 모르게** 끌려
간 사람들도 많대요. = *Me neither. I heard that a lot of people who spoke
out against government policy were just taken away without a peep.*

NOTE: 한국 사람들은 새와 쥐를 각각 낮과 밤을 대표하는 동물로 여겼다.
'낮말은 새가 듣고 밤말은 쥐가 듣는다'라는 속담도 있다.
Rats were thought to be the representative creatures of the night, while birds
stood for the daytime. There's a saying that goes 낮말은 새가 듣고 밤말은
쥐가 듣는다 (Lit. Birds may hear you during the day and rats at night. This
phrase is roughly analogous to "The walls have ears.")

쥐뿔도 모르다 [Lit. to not even know a rat's horns] IDIOM 아무것도 모르
다 = to know nothing (*syn.* 개뿔도 모르다) ▌A: 아무튼 성현이 녀석
쥐뿔도 모르면서 아는 척하기는. = *Anyway, that Seonghyeon doesn't
know anything but he's always pretending to be so smart.* B: 성현이가 원
래 약간 허세가 있잖아. = *Yeah, he's always been a big talker.*

NOTE: '쥐꼬리'라는 표현에서 알 수 있듯 쥐는 아주 작고 보잘것없는 것과
관계가 있다. 물론 쥐에게 뿔이 있을 리 없지만 만약 쥐뿔이 있다면 얼
마나 작을 것인가. '쥐뿔도 모르다', '쥐뿔도 없다', '쥐뿔도 아니다'의
쥐뿔은 결국 하고자 하는 말을 강조하기 위한 장치이다.
As is seen in the expression 쥐꼬리, rats are often equated metaphorically
with things of little value. Rats don't have horns, but if they did, they'd be
awfully small. In the expressions, 쥐뿔도 모르다, 쥐뿔도 없다 and 쥐뿔도
아니다, the word 쥐뿔 simply plays the role of an intensifier.

쥐뿔도 아니다 [Lit. to not even be a rat's horn] IDIOM 보잘것없다 = to be
worthless (*equiv.* to be less than nothing *syn.* 가뿔도 아니다) ▌A: 저 사람
은 **쥐뿔도 아니면서** 사람을 얼마나 무시하는지 몰라. = *He's nothing
much at all himself but he's always looking down on others.* B: 맞아. 정말
사람 참 별로야. = *Yep, that guy really is a zero.*

NOTE: See the note on 쥐뿔도 모르다.

쥐뿔도 없다 [Lit. to not even have a rat's horn] IDIOM 아무것도 없다=to have nothing (*syn.* 개뿔도 없다) ▌A: 형은 왜 **쥐뿔도 없으면서** 좋은 것만 사려고 해?=*Why are you always wanting to buy expensive stuff when you don't have a penny to your name?* B: 야, 모르는 소리 마. 없는 사람일수록 좋은 옷을 입어야 무시를 안 당하는 거야.=*Hey, you don't know what's up. Us have-nots have to dress nicely to avoid being looked down upon.*

NOTE: See the note on 쥐뿔도 모르다.

쥐었다 폈다 하다 [Lit. to do a contract-and-release] IDIOM 자기 마음대로 하다=to do as one pleases (*syn.* 꽉 잡고 있다, 쥐고 흔들다) ▌A: 이 동네에서 장사하려면 김 씨한테 잘 보여야 해.=*If you want to run a business in this neighborhood, you've got to do well by Mr. Kim.* B: 왜요?=*Oh? Why?* A: 이 동네 상권을 **쥐었다 폈다 하는** 사람이거든.=*He controls all the business in the area.*

쥐 죽은 듯이 [Lit. like a mouse dies] IDIOM 매우 조용하게=very quietly ▌A: 분위기가 왜 이렇게 가라앉아 있어요?=*Why is the mood here so down?* B: 감원한다는 소문이 있잖아요. 이런 때일수록 **쥐 죽은 듯이** 있는 게 최고예요.=*There are rumors of layoffs. This is precisely the time when we have to keep quiet.*

NOTE: 옛날에는 집집마다 쥐가 많았다. 특히나 밤이 되면 천장에서 쥐들이 뛰어다니는 소리가 무척 시끄러웠다. 그래서 매우 조용한 상태를 쥐가 다 사라져 버린 상황과 연결하여 생각했을 것이다.
In the old days, all houses had mice. At night, the sound of the vermin crawling around in the rafters was especially loud. This is probably why the disappearance of all mice is associated with an extremely quiet environment.

***지갑(을) 열다** [Lit. to open up one's wallet] IDIOM 돈을 쓰다=to spend money ▌A: 시장에 가도 **지갑을 열기가** 망설여져요.=*I'm even afraid to open up my wallet at the market.* B: 저도 그래요. 하루가 다르게 물가가 오르는 것 같아요.=*Me too. The prices of everything just keep rising every day.*

지고지순하다 [Lit. 至reach + 高high + 至reach + 順pure + 하다adjectival suffix] CHINESE-DERIVATION 매우 고결하고 순수하다 = to be of high purity and refinement ▌A: 이 영화는 왜 인기가 있는 것 같아? 사실 불치병으로 죽어 가는 남편과 그 아내 얘기는 별로 새롭지 않잖아. = *Why do you think this movie is so popular? Honestly, that plot of a woman and her husband dying of an incurable disease is nothing new.* B: 그야 그렇지만, 요즘 세상에 그런 **지고지순한** 사랑이 흔치는 않으니까 감동적인 거 아닐까. = *That's true, but that kind of pure, absolute love is a rare thing in today's world. I think it struck a chord.*

지나가는 말 [Lit. words that pass by] IDIOM 별다른 의미 없이 한 말 = words with no special meaning (*equiv.* words said in passing / offhand remarks) ▌A: 지나가는 말로 한 건데 뭘 그걸 갖고 화를 내? = *I didn't mean anything by it. Why are you getting so upset?* B: **지나가는 말**이라고? 속을 들킨 게 아니고? = *"Didn't mean anything"? Don't you mean that you've spoken your true mind?*

지나가던 개가 웃다 IDIOM = 지나가던 소가 웃다

지나가던 소가 웃다 [Lit. for a passing cow to laugh] IDIOM 말도 안 되는 얘기를 듣고 어이가 없을 때 쓰는 말 = used when one is taken back by a ridiculous statement (*equiv.* That's ridiculous / Yeah, right. / That's laughable. *syn.* 지나가던 개가 웃다) ▌A: 나 결심했어. 나 이제 공부 열심히 할 거야. = *I've made up my mind. I'm going to study hard from now on.* B: 네가 공부를? 얘, **지나가던 소가 웃겠다**! = *You? Study hard? Yeah, right.*

지도(를) 그리다 [Lit. to draw a map] IDIOM 이불에 오줌을 싸다 = to pee on the bedclothes ▌A: 이불 빨래해? = *Are you washing the comforter?* B: 응. 작은애가 간밤에 또 **지도를 그렸어**. = *Yep, the little one wet the bed again last night.*

지렁이도 밟으면 꿈틀한다 [Lit. If you step on a worm, it will squirm.] PROVERB 아무리 순하고 보잘것없는 사람도 너무 함부로 대하면 가

만 있지 않는다는 말＝warns that even those who look meek or lackluster will fight back when treated roughly ▌A: 너무하시는 거 아닙니까? **지렁이도 밟으면 꿈틀하는 법입니다**.＝*Aren't you going just a little bit overboard here? Even though I am just a nobody, I won't stand for this!* B: 내가 뭘 어쨌길래 화를 내고 그래요?＝*What did I do to get you so upset?*

지성이면 감천 [Lit. If (there's) sincerity, the heavens will be moved.] PROVERB 무슨 일이든 정성을 다하면 어려운 일도 잘 풀린다는 말＝suggests that in every pursuit, working with devotion will help one overcome all obstacles (*equiv.* Faith moves mountains.) ▌A: 들었어? 옆 동에 사는 암에 걸린 아저씨 있잖아, 기적적으로 나았대.＝*Did you hear? You know the man next door who has cancer? They're saying he's had a miraculous recovery.* B: 그 집 딸이 지극정성으로 간호한다고 하더니만, **지성이면 감천**이라는 말이 맞구먼.＝*His daughter took such good care of him. I guess this is why they say that faith can move mountains.*

지지고 볶다 [Lit. to fry and roast] IDIOM **1.** 머리카락을 곱슬곱슬하게 만들다＝to make one's hair curly ▌A: 파마했어? **지지고 볶으니까** 좀 낫네.＝*Did you get a perm? It looks a lot better with some curl to it.* B: 지난주에 파마했는데 무슨 소리야? 제발 나한테 관심 좀 가져.＝*What do you mean? I got my hair permed last week. Could you please show a little more interest in me?* **2.** 희로애락을 함께하며 살아가다＝to experience sadness and pleasure in one's life (*equiv.* to go through the ups and downs of life) ▌A: 딴 건 다 필요 없고, 너희끼리 재미있게 **지지고 볶고** 살아라.＝*Nothing matters as much as you two living all life has to offer by each other's side.* B: 네, 행복하게 잘 살겠습니다, 아버님.＝*Thanks. We are going to spend the rest of our years happily together.* **3.** 다른 사람을 못살게 굴다＝to pester someone ▌A: 어미야, 너는 네 남편 좀 그만 **지지고 볶아라**.＝*(Daughter-in-law), you need to stop nagging your husband.* B: 죄송해요, 어머님.＝*I'm sorry, Mother.*

지지부진(하다) [Lit. 遲late ＋ 遲late ＋ 不no ＋ 進advance] CHINESE-DERIVATION 일이 매우 더디어 잘 진척되지 않다＝for an undertaking to progress extremely slowly █A: 공사 완공 예정이 원래 지난 달이었는데 아직도 멀었네요. 왜 이렇게 공사가 **지지부진해요**? = *Completion of construction was originally scheduled for last month, but we've still got a long way to go. Why are things moving at a snail's pace?* B: 시공사가 부도 났대요. = *They're saying the builder defaulted on a debt.*

지푸라기라도 잡고 싶다 IDIOM = 물에 빠지면 지푸라기라도 잡는다

지피지기 [Lit. 知 know + 彼 that + 知 know + 己 oneself] CHINESE-DERIVATION

적의 사정과 나의 사정을 두루 잘 앎 = knowing the state of one's enemy and oneself (*cf.* 적을 알고 나를 알면 백전백승) █A: **지피지기**면 백전백승이라는 말이 있잖아. 그런데 만약에 나도 상대를 잘 알고 상대도 나를 잘 알면 누가 이기지? = *They say that knowing one's enemy guarantees victory 100 percent of the time. But what if I know my enemy well, but he knows me well too—then what happens?* B: 그 말은 원래 지피지기면 백전불태라는 말에서 온 거야. 적을 알고 나를 알면 결코 위태롭지 않다는 거지. = *That saying originally came from the saying "If one knows the enemy and knows oneself, even a hundred battles will not be a true threat." So the point is to know thyself and the enemy.*

직성이 풀리다 [Lit. for one's stars (fate) to get better] IDIOM 바라던 것이

이루어져 만족스럽다 = for something that one had wished for to come true █A: 아, 집안 청소를 했더니 마음이 한결 후련한걸! = *I cleaned house today and now I feel like a weight has been lifted.* B: 당신 성미도 참. 항상 모든 게 그렇게 정리가 되어 있어야 **직성이 풀리니** 원. = *You've really got some character. You need everything to be tidied up before you're satisfied.*

NOTE: 직성은 나이에 따라 사람의 한해 운명을 관장한다는 아홉 개의 별을 가리킨다. 사람은 9년마다 한 번씩 동일한 직성과 그에 따른 동일한 운을 갖게 된다고 한다. 개중에는 특별히 운이 없다고 믿어지는 별도 있어 이때에는 그 불운을 막기 위해 특별한 의식을 치르기도 했다. 그를 통해 좋지 않은 직성을 잘 넘기고 다음 직성을 맞이하게 되면 '(좋지 않은) 직성이 풀린다'고 했다.

직성 is the word for nine stars that were said to determine a person's fate for the year based on their age. Once every nine years, a person would end up with the same horoscope. Of course some of these stars were thought to be more unlucky than others and to block the misfortune they brought, special diligence was in order. If one got through the year unscathed, people would say (좋지 않은) 직성이 풀린다 and so the phrase is now used when someone gets their wish and is satisfied with the result.

진도(가) 느리다 [Lit. for progress to be slow] IDIOM (속된 말로) 사귀는 두 남녀가 신체적으로 친밀해지는 속도가 느리다 = (slang) for the pace of physical closeness in a relationship to be slow (*equiv.* We're taking it slowly. / We're making slow progress.) ▌A: 저희는 사귄 지 1년이 될 때까지 손도 못 잡았어요. = *We had dated for a whole year before we even held hands for the first time.* B: 진도가 엄청 느렸네요. = *Wow, you guys really made slow progress.*

진도(가) 빠르다 [Lit. for progress to be fast] IDIOM (속된 말로) 사귀는 두 남녀가 신체적으로 친밀해지는 속도가 빠르다 = (slang) for the physical closeness in a relationship to proceed rapidly (*equiv.* We're moving right along. / We've been moving pretty fast.) ▌A: 사귀기로 한 날에 손을 잡았다고? = *They held hands the first day they started going out?* B: 확실히 요즘 아이들은 진도가 빠르네요. = *Kids today really do move fast!*

진도(를) 나가다 [Lit. to make (go out) progress] IDIOM (속된 말로) 사귀는 두 남녀의 신체적인 친밀도가 높아지다 = (slang) for a couple to become more intimate physically (*equiv.* to make progress) ▌A: 뭐? 사귄 지 6개월이나 됐는데 아직 뽀뽀도 못 했다고? = *What? You guys have been going out for six months now and you still haven't kissed?* B: 네. 진도 나가기가 너무 힘들어요. = *Yeah. It's kind of hard to make progress with her.*

진땀(을) 빼다 [Lit. to give off a sweat] IDIOM 어려운 일이나 난처한 일을 당해 몹시 애를 쓰다 = to suffer much consternation because of a difficult assignment or task that is beyond one's abilities (*syn.* 진땀(을) 흘리

다) █A: 영호 녀석 자꾸 아이는 어떻게 해야 생기냐고 물어보는 통에 **진땀 뺐어요**. = *Yeongho's constantly asking me how kids are made and it's keeping me up at nights.* B: 저런. 그래서 뭐라고 했어? = *What a mess. So what did you say?* A: 몰라도 된다고 쥐어박았죠. = *I shut it down by saying that it's not something he needs to know right now.*

진땀(을) 흘리다 IDIOM = 진땀(을) 빼다

진수성찬 [Lit. 珍treasure + 羞food + 盛grand + 饌meal → a treasure trove of food] CHINESE-DERIVATION 푸짐하게 잘 차린 음식 = a plentiful meal (*equiv.* a sumptuous meal / a feast fit for a king) █A: 차린 건 없지만 많이 드세요. = *It's nothing special, but please have your fill.* B: 차린 게 없으시다니요. 완전히 **진수성찬**인데요. = *What do you mean, "nothing special"? It's a veritable feast!*

진(을) 빼다 [Lit. to remove the sap from someone] IDIOM 1. 몹시 힘들게 하다 = to be very hard on someone (*equiv.* to put someone through hell / to give someone hell) █A: 왜 그리 기운이 없어 보여요? = *Why do you look so worn out?* B: 아기가 밤새 울어서 **진을 빼더라고요**. = *My son was crying all night long. He's really not making this easy on us.* 2. 기운이 하나도 없을 정도로 힘을 쓰다 = to use up every bit of one's energy (*equiv.* to deplete one's energy) █A: 아이들 장난이 심하죠? = *The kids are always messing around, aren't' they?* B: 네. 수업 시간에 하도 떠들어서 조용히 시키느라 **진 뺐어요**. = *That's right. They're so noisy during class and it's next to impossible to get them to quiet down.*

NOTE: 진은 식물의 줄기나 나무 껍질에서 분비되는 끈끈한 물질을 말한다. 진이 다 빠지면 식물은 말라서 죽게 된다. 사람에게도 쓸 수 있는 에너지가 한정되어 있는데 진을 다 뺐다는 말은 에너지를 모두 소진했다는 말이다.

The word *jin* is analogous to "resin" or "sap" in English. If the sap in a plant disappears, the plant will dry up and die. The amount of energy people have is also finite, and to say 진을 다 뺐다 means that one's energy has been exhausted.

진(을) 치다 [Lit. to set up camp] ɪᴅɪᴏᴍ 여러 사람이 자리를 차지하고 있다 = for many people to be occupying a location (*equiv.* to set up camp (in a place) / to move in) ▌A: 저기 건물 앞에서 매일 **진을 치고** 있는 애들은 뭐예요? = *What's the deal with all those young people gathered in front of that building every day?* B: 저 건물에 유명한 가수가 산다는 것 같던데요. = *I think some famous singer lives there.*

진(이) 빠지다 [Lit. for one's sap to be depleted] ɪᴅɪᴏᴍ 힘이나 의욕이 없다 = for one's energy or volition to be depleted ▌A: 이틀 연속으로 밤을 새웠더니 **진이 빠진** 느낌이야. = *After staying up for two nights straight, I feel like I'm going to collapse.* B: 어쩐지 너 무리한다 싶더라. = *Yeah, I thought you might be overdoing it.*

진저리(가) 나다 [Lit. to shiver] ɪᴅɪᴏᴍ 몹시 지긋지긋하고 싫다 = to be disgusted by something and quiver at the sight of it (*equiv.* to quiver (at the sound or sight of something) *syn.* 신물(이)나다, 진절머리(가) 나다 *cf.* 진저리(를) 내다) ▌A: 요 며칠 계속 회의만 했더니, 이제 회의라면 **진저리가 나**. = *After having to go to meetings for the last four days straight, now I tremble at the word, "meeting."* B: 정말 결론 안 나는 회의만큼 지겨운 것도 없어요. = *There's truly nothing more annoying than a meeting that reaches no conclusion.*

ɴᴏᴛᴇ: 진저리는 원래 차가운 것이 살갗에 닿거나 오줌을 눈 뒤에 무의식적으로 떨쳐지는 몸짓을 말한다.
진저리 is the word for a shiver when one's flesh touches something cold or an unconscious shake that comes after urination.

진저리(를) 내다 [Lit. to shiver] ɪᴅɪᴏᴍ 몹시 지긋지긋하고 싫다 = to be disgusted by something and quiver at the sight of it (*equiv.* to quiver (at the sound or sight of something) *syn.* 진저리(를) 치다 *cf.* 진저리(가) 나다) ▌A: 언니, 우리 경민이 피아노 시킬까? = *Sis, do you think I should have Gyeongmin take piano lessons?* B: 아이가 원하면 그렇게 해도 억지로 시키지는 마. 민경이도 어릴 때 억지로 피아노 시켰더니 지금은 피아노 소리만 들어도 **진저리를 내**. = *If he shows interest in it,* *that's fine, but don't force it. I forced Mingyeong to take piano when she was young and now she quivers at the sound of a piano.*

진저리(를) 치다 IDIOM = 진저리(를) 내다

진절머리(가) 나다 IDIOM = 진저리(가) 나다

짐(을) 싸다 [Lit. to pack one's bags] IDIOM **1.** 관계하고 있던 일을 그만두다 = to quit the work one had been doing (*equiv.* to pack one's bags (and leave) *syn.* 옷(을) 벗다) ▌A: 강 부장, 이번 일 성공하지 못하면 **짐 쌀** 생각하는 게 좋을 거요. = *Mr. Gang, if this project doesn't pan out, you should think about packing your bags.* B: 네, 저도 잘 알고 있습니다. = *Yes, I'm well aware of that myself.* **2.** 다른 곳으로 옮기려고 준비하다 = to prepare for a relocation ▌A: 옛날에는 이 마을이 참 살기 좋았는데요. = *Life in the village used to be really nice.* B: 그랬죠. 그런데 이제 다 떠나고 몇 가구 안 남았네요. 남은 사람도 언제 **짐 쌀지** 모를 일이고요. = *Yes, it did. But now, almost everyone has left and there are just a few households that remeain. And for all we know, they may be fixing to leave too.*

짐(을) 풀다 [Lit. to unpack one's bags] IDIOM 거처를 정해 생활을 시작하다 = to find a place to live and commence life in a new place (*equiv.* to unpack one's bags / to find a place to rest one's head) ▌A: 잘 곳은 정했어? = *Have you found a place to live?* B: 일단 고시원에 **짐을 풀었어.** 차차 알아봐야지. = *For now, I've set myself up in a boarding house. I'm taking things one step at a time.*

집도 절도 없다 [Lit. to have neither house nor temple] IDIOM 머물 곳이나 가진 것이 없다 = to have no place to sleep and no worldly possessions (*equiv.* to be without house and home) ▌A: 돌아가신 코치님은 제게 아버지와도 같은 분입니다. **집도 절도 없는** 저를 먹여 주고 재워 주시면서 야구를 가르쳐 주셨습니다. = *Coach, God rest his soul, was just like a father to me. When I had nowhere to turn, he took me in and kept me fed.* B: 그런 분이 돌아가셨으니 슬픔이 크시겠어요. = *It must be so hard for you to lose someone like that.*

NOTE: 옛날에는 사람이 생활하는 공간이 크게 집과 절 두 군데였다. 집은 보통의 사람들이 사는 곳이고 절은 승려들이 사는 곳이다. 집도 절도 없다는 말은 기거할 곳이 전혀 없다는 말이다.
In the Korea of yore, the two main spheres of activity were the house and the temple. People of the world live in houses, while religious men reside in the temple. That's why when one has no place to lay one's head, people say, 집도 절도 없다.

짖는 개는 물지 않는다 [Lit. The dog that barks doesn't bite.] PROVERB 겉으로 떠들어 대는 사람은 실속이 없다는 말 = suggests that those who talk big rarely can back it up (*equiv.* to be all bark and no bite / to be all talk) ▌A: 내일 드디어 결승전이네. 상대는 네 코를 납작하게 만들어 주겠다고 큰소리치던데 걱정 안 돼? = *The finals are tomorrow. The competition has said they're going to flatten you. Aren't you worried?* B: 원래 **짖는 개는 물지 않는** 법이야. 걱정할 거 없어. = *They're all bark and no bite. I've got nothing to worry about.*

짚고 넘어가다 [Lit. to touch and pass over] IDIOM 따지거나 밝혀서 분명히 하다 = to nitpick or to make something clear (*equiv.* to go over (a topic, issue etc.)) ▌A: 이정민 씨, 또 지각이야? 이번만큼은 **짚고 넘어가야겠어.** 도대체 왜 늦은 거야? = *Lee Jeongmin, you're late again? I think we're going to have to go over this again. Why on earth were you late?* B: 아침에 늦잠을 자서요 ……. 죄송합니다. = *I overslept this morning. I'm really sorry.*

짚신도 제짝이 있다 [Lit. Even a straw shoe has its match.] PROVERB 아무리 못난 사람도 결혼을 할 짝이 있다 = Even the most undesirable people can find someone to marry. (*equiv.* Every Jack has his Jill.) ▌A: **짚신도 제짝이 있다더니** 네가 장가를 갈 줄은 정말 꿈에도 몰랐다. = *They say every Jack has his Jill, but I never dreamed I'd live to see you getting married.* B: 나도 내가 장가 한번 못 가고 늙어 죽는 줄 알았어. = *Me too. I thought I'd grow old all alone.*

双

짜고 치는 고스톱 [Lit. a prearranged game of go-stop] IDIOM 누군가를 속이기 위해 사전에 한 약속에 따라 벌이는 행동이나 일 = actions taken per an earlier agreement to deceive another (*equiv.* a setup) ▌A: 가상 결혼 프로그램 말이야, 저러다 정 들면 진짜 사귀는 거 아냐? = *You know the TV programs where people pretend to be man and wife? I wonder if people actually end up falling for each other.* B: 멍청하긴. 저거 다 **짜고 치는 고스톱**인 거 몰라? = *That's pretty stupid. Don't you know that's all just a setup?*

쪽박(을) 깨다 [Lit. to break open a small gourd] IDIOM 일을 망치다 = to ruin a project (*equiv.* to throw a monkey wrench in the plans *syn.* 산통(을) 깨다) ▌A: 연말인데 우리도 불우 이웃 돕기 성금 낼까? = *What with it being the end of the year and all, how about we make a little contribution to charity?* B: 정말로 전달이 되는지 안 되는지도 모르는데 내면 뭐 해? = *We don't even know if it will get to the people who need it.* A: 왜 당신은 없는 사람들 도와주지는 듯할망정 **쪽박을 깨**? = *What won't you just let me help people in need?*

쪽박(을) 차다 IDIOM = 바가지(를) 차다

차(떼고)포 떼고 [Lit. after getting rid of the *cha* and the *po*] IDIOM 중요한 것을 다 빼고 = after getting rid of all the important parts (*equiv.* to play with a handicap / to be hamstrung) ▌A: 오늘 경기는 이길 것 같아요? = *Do you think you guys will win today?* B: 잘 모르겠어요. 주전 선수들이 대부분 부상이니. = *I don't really know ... since all our best players are out with injuries and all.* A: 참, **차 떼고 포 떼고** 경기하려니 힘드시겠어요. = *Yes, it must be difficult to put up a good fight with the team handicapped like that.*

NOTE: 차와 포는 한국의 장기에서 가장 힘이 센 기물이다. 장기를 둘 때 한쪽의 실력이 달리면 핸디캡으로 상수가 차나 포를 없애고 게임을 시작하는데, 이것을 두고 '뗀다'고 말한다. 차나 포를 뗀다는 것은 전력의 손실을 안고 싸운다는 의미이다.

차 and 포 are the names of the two knights in Korean chess. They are both very powerful pieces and play an important role in the game. If one player is leaps and bounds ahead of the other player, they may handicap themselves by playing without these pieces. In that case, the verb used to describe their removal from the board is 떼다. This expression accordingly means to be competing without one's best players on the field, or to have lost one's previous power.

차일피일(하다) [Lit. 此this + 日day + 彼that + 日day] CHINESE-DERIVATION 약속이나 해야 할 일을 자꾸 미루다 = to constantly put off one's work or appointments (*equiv.* to put off / to procrastinate) ▌A: 너 도서관에 책 반납해야 되지 않아? = *Don't you have to take those books back to the library?* B: 모레까지만 반납하면 돼요. = *I have until the day after* *tomorrow.* A: 그렇게 **차일피일하다** 늦으면 연체료 내야 한다. =*If you keep on procrastinating like that, you'll have to pay late fines.*

찬물도 위아래가 있다 [Lit. Even cold water has an up and down.]

PROVERB 윗사람을 공경해야 한다는 말 =used to encourage respect for one's superiors ▌A: 팀장님, 어서 오세요. 기다리고 있었어요. =*Boss, please come on in. We've been waiting for you.* B: 아니, 먼저들 먹지 그랬어요? =*You should've just eaten without me.* A: **찬물도 위아래가 있는데**, 저희가 먼저 먹을 수가 있나요. =*There's a right and wrong way of doing everything; how could we just go on without you?*

NOTE: 이 말은 찬물 한 잔을 마시는 것과 같이 일상적인 일에도 누가 먼저 마실 것인지 순서가 정해져 있다는 뜻이다. 한국의 전통적인 위계 문화가 드러나 있는 표현이다.
This phrase tells us that even in the most quotidian of daily tasks, such as drinking water, there is an order the way things are done: namely, top to bottom. This phrase illustrates Korea's rigid class system.

*찬물(을) 끼얹다 [Lit. to douse with cold water] IDIOM 훼방을 놓거나 분위기를 망치다 =to disturb or ruin the atmosphere (*equiv.* to be a downer / to be a wet blanket *syn.* 소금(을) 뿌리다, 재(를) 뿌리다, 초(를) 치다, 고춧가루(를) 뿌리다) ▌A: 들었어요? 우리 회사 곧 인수된대요. =*Did you hear? Our company is going to be taken over soon.* B: 이제 열심히 일 좀 해 보려고 했더니, 의욕에 **찬물을 끼얹는군요**. =*I was just about to get serious about my work, but that news definitely puts a damper on things.*

찬밥 더운밥 가리다 [Lit. to choose between warm rice or cold rice] IDIOM 자신의 어려운 처지는 생각하지 않고 까다롭게 굴다 =to not consider one's lot and act in a picky manner (*equiv.* Now's not the time for us to be picking and choosing. / Don't look a gift horse in the mouth.) ▌A: 여기 원래 창고로 쓰던 데인데, 지금 남는 방이 여기밖에 없어. 그래도 괜찮겠어? =*We originally used this room for storage but now it's all we've got left. Is that going to be OK with you?* B: 괜찮아. 내가 지금 **찬밥 더운밥 가릴** 때가 아니거든. =*Yes, it'll be fine. I can't afford to be picky*

right now.

찬밥 신세 [Lit. a cold-rice lot] IDIOM 남들로부터 환영 받지 못하는 처지 = a circumstance in which one is not welcomed by others (*equiv.* to be unwelcome / to be left out in the cold) ▌A: 공부 잘하는 형이 있어서 좋았겠다. = *It must've been nice to have an older brother who was so good in school.* B: 모르는 소리 마. 형은 공부 잘한다고 부모님한테 칭찬 받는데 나는 늘 **찬밥 신세였어.** = *You have no idea. My parents were always complimenting him for being such a good student and I was left out in the cold.*

참는 자에게 복이 있다 [Lit. Luck comes to he who endures.] PROVERB 억울하고 화가 나도 참는 게 낫다는 말 = suggests that keeping anger and exasperation at unfair treatment to oneself is best (*equiv.* Good things come to those who wait. / Patience is a virtue.) ▌A: 왜 나만 맨날 밥하고 설거지 하고 다 해야 돼? 너무 불공평하잖아. = *Why do I always have to make the food and do the dishes? It's so unfair.* B: 네가 참아라. **참는 자에게 복이 있는** 거야. = *Just keep quiet. Sometimes it's best to just bear down and take it.* A: 참을 게 따로 있지. 이건 못 참아. = *There's a time for just "taking it," and now's not that time.*

참새가 방앗간을 그냥 지나랴 [Lit. Would a sparrow just pass by the mill?] PROVERB 사람이 자기가 좋아하는 것을 보고 그냥 지나치지 못할 때 쓰는 말 = describes how people can't just walk past something they like ▌A: 우와, 이거 고기 냄새 아냐? 출출한데 우리 고기 먹을까? = *Wow, isn't that meat I smell cooking? I'm hungry. Why don't we get something to eat?* B: 과연. **참새가 방앗간을 그저 지나가나** 싶었어. = *Yeah, I didn't figure a bear could just pass by the honey pots.*

척하면 삼천리 [Lit. 3,000 *li* in an instant] IDIOM 상대의 의도나 돌아가는 상황을 눈치 빠르게 알아차리는 것을 가리키는 말 = describes a quick ability to sense the intentions of others or the state of affairs (*syn.* 척하면 착이다) ▌A: 왜? 밖에 나가게? = *Why? You're heading out?* B: 응. 올 때 과자 사다 줘? = *Yeah, do you want me to buy you something to eat* *while I'm out?* A: 역시. **척하면 삼천리**구먼. = *Wow, you really are sharp.*

> NOTE: 한국은 예로부터 국토의 세로 길이가 삼천 리(1200km)라고 했다. 전국을 훤히 꿰뚫어 보듯 어떤 일을 잘 알고 있을 때 쓰는 표현이다.
> The length of Korea has traditionally been calculated as 3,000 *li* (1,200 km). This expression means that someone seems to see in a glance all that is taking place across the entire peninsula.

척하면 착이다 [Lit. In an instant it's *chak*.] IDIOM 약간의 암시만으로 상대가 하고자 하는 말이나 의도를 금세 알아차리다 = to be able to tell, with only the slightest hint, the intentions of another (*equiv.* Nothing gets by you. *syn.* 척하면 삼천리) ▌A: 담배 사 왔니? 불은? = *Did you bring cigarettes? A lighter?* B: 라이터 가져오라는 얘기는 안 하셨잖아요. = *You didn't tell me to bring a lighter.* A: **척하면 착이지**, 아들아. = *You should have picked up on that yourself, son.*

> NOTE: '착'은 여기서 별다른 뜻이 있는 것이 아니라 '척'과 운율을 맞추기 위해 쓰인 글자이다.
> The 착 in this phrase has no special meaning but just rhymes nicely with 척.

천 리 길도 한 걸음부터 [Lit. Even a road of 1,000 *li* begins with a single step.] PROVERB 무슨 일이든 차근차근 해 나가는 것이 중요하다는 말 = suggests that no matter what the endeavor, taking it one step at a time is the best way (*equiv.* A journey of a thousand miles starts with a single step. / Slow and steady wins the race. / Step by step one goes a long way. / He who would climb the ladder must begin at the bottom.) ▌A: 우와 무슨 짐이 이렇게 많아? 이거 다 정리하려면 오늘밤까지 해야겠다. = *Why do you have so many bags? It's going to be nighttime before we get this all cleared away.* B: **천 리 길도 한 걸음부터**잖아. 슬슬 시작하자고. = *Even a journey of a thousand miles begins with a single step. Let's get going.*

천방지축 [Lit. 天heaven + 方direction + 地earth + 軸axis → not knowing which direction is heaven and which direction is earth] CHINESE-DERIVATION 몹시

덤벙대고 함부로 날뛰는 모양이나 사람 = describes a person or undertaking that is proceeding in an entirely slipshod, helter-skelter manner ▌A: 큰아이는 얌전한데 둘째는 완전히 **천방지축**이야. = *Our oldest is a good kid but his younger brother is all over the place.* B: 둘째가 너 닮았나 보네. = *I guess the younger one takes after you.*

천생연분 [Lit. 天heaven + 生born + 緣connect + 分connection → a connection born in heaven] CHINESE-DERIVATION 아주 잘 맞는 부부나 연인 = a couple that seems to be perfectly suited for each other (*equiv.* a match made in heaven) ▌A: 어쩌면 너희 둘은 그렇게 죽이 잘 맞니? = *How can you two get along so well?* B: 사람들이 모두 저희더러 **천생연분**이래요. = *People call us a match made in a heaven.*

천의 얼굴을 가지다 [Lit. to have a thousand faces] IDIOM 여러 가지 성격을 동시에 가지다 = to have many different personalities (*equiv.* to wear many hats / a man of a thousand faces) ▌A: 저 배우는 저번 영화에서는 그렇게 선해 보이더니 지금은 또 완전히 악당 그 자체네. = *That actor gave off such a wholesome vibe in his last film and this time, he's like evil itself.* B: 그래서 **천의 얼굴을 가졌다고** 하잖아. = *That's why they call him the man of a thousand faces.*

천재지변 [Lit. 天heaven + 災disaster + 地earth + 變change → a shift in the heavens and earth] CHINESE-DERIVATION 지진, 홍수 등 자연현상에서 비롯된 재앙 = an earthquake, flood or other natural disaster (*equiv.* a natural disaster / a cataclysm) ▌A: 이게 웬 **천재지변**이야? 이렇게 눈이 많이 오는 건 내 평생 본 적이 없어. = *Is this the end of the world? I've never seen so much snow fall in my life.* B: 큰일이네. 밖에 나가지도 못하고 집 안에만 갇혀 있게 생겼잖아. = *What a disaster. It looks like we'll be trapped indoors for a while.*

천진난만하다 [Lit. 天heaven + 眞true + 爛in full bloom + 漫all over + 하다adjectival suffix] CHINESE-DERIVATION 말이나 행동에 아무런 거짓이나 꾸밈이 없다 = to not lie or practice any sort of affectation ▌A: 집이 왜 이렇게 엉망이야? 민수 혼 좀 내. = *Why's your house such a mess? I think* *you need to give Minsu a talking to.* B: 그 **천진난만한** 미소를 보고 있으면 차마 화를 낼 수가 없어요. =*I just can't yell at him when he looks at me with those innocent eyes of his.*

천차만별 [Lit. 千thousand + 差different + 萬ten thousand + 別distinguish] CHINESE-DERIVATION 여러 가지 대상이 모두 달라 차이가 있음 = an assortment of kinds and varieties that all differ from each other (*equiv.* to be multifarious / a wide array) ▌A: 보통 결혼 비용은 얼마나 드나요? = *How much do weddings usually cost?* B: 사람에 따라 **천차만별**이죠. 천만 원도 안 드는 사람도 있는가 하면 몇십 억을 쓰는 사람도 있죠. = *It really runs the gamut. Some people do it for less than 10 million won, while others end up spending 100s of millions.*

천편일률 [Lit. 千thousand + 篇poem − 一one + 律rhythm → the monotony of a thousand poems of the same meter] CHINESE-DERIVATION 여럿이 별 차이가 없이 비슷비슷함 = a multitude (*equiv.* monotony / humdrumness) ▌A: 요즘 드라마는 어쩌면 저렇게 다 똑같은지 모르겠어. 너무 **천편일률**적이야. = *Why do all the dramas have to be exactly the same these days? It's always just the same old, same old.* B: 맞아. 내용도 다 너무 자극적이고 현실성도 떨어지고. = *Yep. The content just tries to get a reaction from the viewers and the stories are always so unrealistic.*

철두철미하다 [Lit. 徹penetrate + 頭head + 徹penetrate + 尾tail + 하다 adjectival suffix → to penetrate from head to tail] CHINESE-DERIVATION 처음부터 끝까지 빈틈이 없고 철저하다 = to not have one blind spot and be very thorough (*equiv.* through and through / from head to toe) ▌A: 이 사건에 대해 국민들의 관심이 높은 만큼 다들 **철두철미하게** 조사해 주기 바랍니다. = *As public interest in this affair is exceedingly high, please remember to leave no stone unturned in your investigation.* B: 네, 최선을 다하겠습니다. = *Yes, we will give it everything we've got.*

철면피 [Lit. 鐵iron + 面face + 皮skin → a face made of iron] CHINESE-DERIVATION 부끄러움이나 염치가 없는 사람 = someone who does not seem to feel shame or have a sense of honor (*equiv.* to be brazen / to be shameless / to have no shame) ▌A: 어제 뉴스 봤어? 사람을 죽여 놓고도 어쩌면 그렇게 태연할 수가 있지?=*Did you see the news yesterday? How could someone be that calm after killing someone?* B: **철면피**라는 말이 딱 맞지 뭐야.=*I guess that's what they mean by a calloused killer.*

철퇴를 가하다 [Lit. to swing the mace] IDIOM 엄한 처벌을 내리다=to hand out a severe punishment (*equiv.* to bring the ax down on someone / to throw the book at them) ➡p.434 ▌A: 이번에 뇌물 받은 공무원들 전부 옷을 벗었다지?=*All the government workers caught up in this bribery scandal quit, right?* B: 응. 당연히 **철퇴를 가해야지**.=*Yeah, of course they were going to throw the book at them.*

철퇴를 맞다 [Lit. to be struck with the mace] IDIOM 엄한 처벌을 받다=to receive a severe punishment (*equiv.* to get the book thrown at you *syn.* 된서리를 맞다) ▌A: 어라? 방송 말미에 웬 사과 방송이지?=*Oh? What's this apology announcement at the end of the broadcast?* B: 이 드라마 간접 광고 때문에 말이 많더니, **철퇴를 맞았나** 보네.=*There was a lot of chatter about how much product placement they had been doing on this show. I guess they got busted for it.*

첩첩산중 [Lit. 疊fold + 疊fold + 山mountain + 中middle] CHINESE-DERIVATION **1.** 매우 깊은 산속=very deep in the mountains ▌A: 도대체 이런 **첩첩산중**에 사람이 살기는 하는 거야?=*People really live this deep in the mountains?* B: 조금만 더 가면 돼. 봐, 저기 불빛이 보이잖아.=*We're almost there. There, don't you see the lights?* **2.** 여러 가지 어려움이 겹친 상황=many difficult events coming together (*equiv.* a confluence of unfortunate events) ▌A: 길을 잃은 것 같은데. 핸드폰 꺼내 봐. 전화가 되나 보자.=*I think we're lost. Get out the cell phone. Let's see if it works.* B: 핸드폰 배터리가 다됐어.=*I ran out of batteries.* A: 이거 갈수록 **첩첩산중**이네.=*Things are just getting worse and worse.*

첫걸음마를 떼다 IDIOM=걸음마를 떼다

첫 단추를 끼우다 [Lit. to button the first button] IDIOM 새로운 일이나

과정을 시작하다＝to begin a new undertaking or commence a proceeding (*equiv.* to kick off / to get underway / to take the first steps) ▌A: 내일 첫 출근이지? 오늘 일찍 자고 내일 일찍 가거라.＝*Tomorrow's your first day, huh? Get to bed early and be there early tomorrow.* B: 뭐하러요? 시간 맞춰서 가면 되죠.＝*Why should I get there early? I think it'll be fine if I just get there on time.* A: 뭐든지 **첫 단추를 잘 끼우는** 게 중요한 거야. 아빠 말 들어라.＝*It's important to start off on the right foot. Just trust me on this.*

첫발을 내딛다 [Lit. to take the first step] IDIOM 어떤 일이나 과정에 들어서다＝to begin a new job or undertaking (*equiv.* to take the first step *syn.* 첫발을 떼다) ▌A: 사회에 **첫발을 내디딘** 소감이 어때?＝*How do you feel now, having just taken your first steps in the real world?* B: 아직 어리둥절해요. 열심히 해야죠.＝*I'm still a little bewildered by it all. I'll just have to keep doing my best.*

첫발을 떼다 IDIOM＝첫발을 내딛다

첫 삽을 뜨다 [Lit. to lift the first shovel] IDIOM 건설 사업이나 그와 관련된 일을 처음으로 시작하다＝to begin a construction-related undertaking (*equiv.* to break ground) ▌A: 오늘은 지난 2005년 **첫 삽을** 뜬 이후 7년 만에 드디어 새로운 철도가 모습을 선보이는 날입니다.＝*After first breaking ground in 2005, today, seven years later, our new railroad is finally unveiled.* B: 김대기 기자가 나가 있습니다. 나와 주시죠.＝*And now we turn to Reporter Kim Daegi, who is on the scene with the story.*

첫술에 배부르랴 [Lit. Is one's first spoonful enough to fill one up?] PROVERB 무슨 일이든 처음부터 단번에 만족할 수는 없다는 말＝used to suggest that one should not expect immediate satisfaction from a new endeavor (*equiv.* Rome wasn't built in a day.) ▌A: 애개, 고작 월급이 이거밖에 안 돼?＝*This is all I get per month?* B: **첫술에 배부를** 수야 있니? 실망할 것 없다.＝*Don't expect everything to happen in a day. It's nothing to be disappointed about.*

청렴결백(하다) [Lit. 淸clear + 廉simple + 潔clean + 白white] CHINESE-DERIVATION 마음이 맑고 재물에 대한 욕심이 없다＝to have purity of heart and be free of avarice ▌A: 아버지는 평생을 **청렴결백하게** 살다 가신 분입니다. ＝*My father lived his entire life with a pure heart and never coveted the possessions of others.* B: 훌륭한 분을 아버지로 두셨군요. ＝*How lucky you were to have such a great man as a father.*

청산유수 [Lit. 靑blue + 山mountain + 流flow + 水water → water flowing from a blue mountain] CHINESE-DERIVATION 거침없이 말을 잘하는 모습＝the image of an elaborate speaker (*equiv.* to be very smooth / a glib talker / silver-tongued) ▌A: 말은 **청산유수**군. ＝*Wow, that guy has a way with words.* B: 저 사람 아나운서 출신이잖아. ＝*That's because he used to be a TV anchor.*

청신호가 켜지다 IDIOM ＝파란불이 켜지다

청천벽력 [Lit. 靑blue + 天heaven + 霹lightning + 靂lightning → a lightening bolt in a blue sky] CHINESE-DERIVATION 뜻밖의 사건이나 사고＝an unexpected incident or accident (*equiv.* a bolt out of the blue *syn.* 마른하늘에 날벼락) ▌A: 암이라는 얘기를 처음 들었을 때 많이 놀라셨죠?＝*You must've been shocked when you first heard it was cancer.* B: **청천벽력** 같았죠 뭐. ＝*It was like a lightening bolt in a clear blue sky.* A: 그래도 수술이 잘 끝나서 다행이에요. ＝*Even still, we're so lucky that the surgery went well.*

청출어람 [Lit. 靑blue + 出come out + 於than + 藍grass → The blue made from the grass is even bluer than the grass iteself.] CHINESE-DERIVATION 제자가 스승보다 나을 때 쓰는 말＝used when a pupil's skill surpasses that of his teacher (*equiv.* to outshine one's teacher) ▌A: 이게 자네가 그린 그림인가? 오히려 나보다 낫구먼. **청출어람**이야. ＝*Did you draw this picture? This is even better than my work. And thus the pupil outshines the teacher.* B: 아닙니다. 선생님께서 그렇게 말씀하시니 몸 둘 바를 모르겠습니다. ＝*Oh, I don't know about that. Hearing you say that, though, leaves me speechless.*

NOTE: 중국의 사상서인 〈순자〉의 한 대목인 '청출어람 청어람(靑出於藍 靑於藍: 쪽에서 뽑아낸 푸른 물감이 오히려 쪽보다 더 푸르다)'에서 나온 표현이다.
This is phrase is taken from the verse, '청출어람 청어람(靑出於藍 靑於藍) (the blue dye extracted from indigo is bluer than the indigo itself)' found in the book of philosophy, "순자," or "Xunzi," as it is known in English.

초록은 동색 [Lit. *Cho* and *rok* are the same color.] PROVERB 입장이나 처지가 같은 사람들끼리 편을 짓게 되어 있다는 말 = describes how people of the same opinion or circumstances join together (*equiv.* Takes one to know one. / Birds of a feather flock together. / to look out for one's own *syn.* 가재는 게 편, 팔이 안으로 굽는다) ▮ A: 이번에 성희롱한 국회의원 말이야, 결국 제명 안 당했잖아. 어떻게 그럴 수가 있지? = *You know that assemblyman who got in trouble for sexual harassment? In the end, he wasn't even expelled from the assembly. How does that happen?* B: **초록은 동색**이잖아. 국회의원들이 다 감싸고 도니까 그런 거지. = *Those politicians always look out for their own. It's because the others shielded him.*

NOTE: 초색(草色)과 녹색(綠色)은 이름은 다르지만 같은 계열의 비슷한 색이다. 사람도 자신과 비슷한 사람의 편을 들게 마련이라는 말이다.
초색 (草色: the color of the grass, vegetation etc.) and 녹색(綠色: green) may have different names, but they are essentially the same color. This phrase is used to describe how similar individuals always seem to group together.

초(를) 치다 [Lit. to splash vinegar] IDIOM 훼방을 하거나 좋은 분위기를 망치다 = to obstruct or ruin the mood (*equiv.* to be a wet blanket / to rain on someone's parade *syn.* 고춧가루(를) 뿌리다, 소금(을) 뿌리다, 재(를) 뿌리다, 찬물(을) 끼얹다) ▮ A: 이 복권이 당첨되면 얼마나 좋을까. 일단 차부터 한 대 사야지. = *Wouldn't it be great if this was a winning lottery ticket? First, I'd go out and buy a car.* B: 야, 꿈 깨. 확률이 얼마인 줄 알아? = *Hey, snap out of it. Do you have any idea what the odds of that are?* A: 왜 **초를 치고** 그래? 꿈도 못 꾸냐? = *Do you have to rain*

◆ p.112

on my parade? What's wrong with dreaming?

NOTE: 음식의 간을 맞추기 위해 조금만 넣어야 하는 초를 지나치게 많이 넣으면 신맛이 강해져 음식 맛을 버리게 된다. 남이 먹으려는 음식에 초를 확 뿌려 음식을 못 먹게 만드는 행위에서 비롯된 표현이다.
The right amount of vinegar can make a dish go down smoothly, but too much can sour the food. This phrase comes from the idea of someone pouring too much vinegar on another's dish to the point that it becomes inedible.

초읽기에 들어가다 [Lit. to go into the countdown] IDIOM 어떤 일이 시작 되기까지 얼마 남지 않다 = for an event to be about to begin (*equiv.* to be in the final countdown (for an event to start) / The countdown has begun.) ▎A: 오늘이 29호 홈런이지? = *Today's homerun was his 29th, right?* B: 그렇지. 이제 30호 홈런이 **초읽기에 들어갔네**. = *That's right. Now the countdown has begun for his 30th.*

초지일관(하다) [Lit. 初beginning + 志will + 一one + 貫penetrate] CHINESE-DERIVATION 처음 세운 뜻을 끝까지 밀고 나가다 = to push ahead with one's original intention ▎A: 너는 어쩌면 10년 전이나 지금이나 머리 모양이 그대로냐? = *How can you have the same hairstyle for 10 years?* B: 사람이 **초지일관해야지**. = *People have to choose something and stick with it, don't they?*

촉각(을) 곤두세우다 [Lit. to make one's feelers stand up] IDIOM 상황의 변화를 놓치지 않으려고 정신을 집중하다 = to be intently watching a situation to ensure one misses nothing (*equiv.* to have one's feelers out) ▎A: ➡p.424 이번 선거의 열쇠는 권 교수가 쥐고 있는 것 같아요. = *I think Prof. Kwon holds the key to this election.* B: 언론도 권 교수의 행보에 **촉각을 곤두세우고** 있잖아요. = *Yeah, and the press has their feelers out for any indication of movement on his part.*

총대(를) 메다 [Lit. to hold up a gun stock to one's shoulder] IDIOM 1. 아무 도 나서지 않는 일을 맡다 = to assume the hard task no one wants to take

on (*equiv.* to take one for the team / to rise to the occasion / to step up to the plate) ▌A: 이번에 대표팀 감독은 누가 맡는대? 아무도 안 하려 한다며? = *Who's going to coach the national team this time? I heard nobody is interested in doing it.* B: 결국 박 감독이 **총대를 메기로** 했대. = *Coach Park finally rose to the occasion.* 2. 어떤 일의 결과에 책임을 지다 = to take responsibility for the outcome (*equiv.* to take the fall (for a failed project etc.)) ▌A: 들었어? 이번 프로젝트 실패에 책임을 지고 조 부장님이 퇴사하신대. = *Did you hear? Department Chief Jo took responsibility for the failure of the project and is stepping down.* B: 정작 물러나야 할 사람은 가만히 있는데, 조 부장님이 **총대를 메셨네**. = *The people who should've taken responsibility stood by silently and watched Jo take the fall.*

NOTE: 과거에는 총이 모든 병사들에게 지급되지 않았다. 총을 받은 병사들은 총을 관리해야 하는 책임을 져야 하는 동시에 상대편 공격의 첫 번째 표적이 되었다. 게다가 당시의 총은 지금보다 훨씬 무거워 총을 들고 다니는 자체가 힘든 일이었다. 그러므로 총을 지급받는 것이 달갑지 않았을 것이다.
Long ago, guns were extremely heavy and were not given out to every soldier. Soldiers who were entrusted with a firearm were in charge of its maintenance and also became the primary target of enemy attacks. On top of that, the guns of the time were much heavier and a burden just to carry. As such 총대(를) 메다 soon came to be a metaphor for taking on a task that others are trying to shirk.

추파를 던지다 [Lit. to cast amorous glances] IDIOM 이성을 유혹하다 = to attempt to seduce a member of the opposite sex (*equiv.* to make eyes at / to give someone that come-hither look) ▌A: 야, 아까부터 저 여자가 너한테 추파를 던지는데? = *Hey, that woman over there has been checking you out for a while now.* B: 나도 알아. 그냥 모른 체해. = *Yeah, I noticed it too. Just ignore it.*

출사표를 내다 IDIOM = 출사표를 던지다

출사표를 던지다 [Lit. to throw certificate of enlistment] IDIOM 경기나 경

쟁 따위에 참가 의사를 밝히다 = to indicate one's intentions to participate in a contest or election etc. (*equiv.* to throw one' hat in the ring *syn.* 출사표를 내다) █A: 이번 대통령 선거에 김대선 씨가 출마 의사를 밝혔습니다. = *Kim Daeseon announced his intentions to run for president in this year's election.* B: 이로서 이번 대선에 **출사표를 던진** 후보는 모두 일곱 명이 되었습니다. = *That makes it seven candidates in the race now.*

취사선택(하다) [Lit. 取take + 捨abandon + 選select + 擇select] CHINESE-DERIVATION 여럿 가운데서 쓸 것과 버릴 것을 결정하다 = to decide what to keep and what to throw away (*equiv.* to pick and choose) █ A: 저는 되고 싶은 게 너무 많아요. 의사도 되고 싶고 과학자도 되고 싶고. = *I want to do so many things with my life. I want to be a scientist, and a doctor ...* B: 다 잘할 수는 없으니까 **취사선택**이 중요하지. = *Well, you can't do it all, so you'd better pick and choose.*

치가 떨리다 [Lit. for one's teeth to chatter] IDIOM 몹시 분하거나 지긋지긋하다 = to be extremely agitated or disgusted (*cf.* 치를 떨다) █A: 가해자를 용서할 마음이 있으신가요? = *Do you have any intention to forgive the perpetrator?* B: 아니요, 그럴 마음 없습니다. 지금도 제가 당한 일을 생각하면 **치가 떨립니다**. = *None whatsoever. Even now, when I think of what was done to me, I shake with rage.*

치를 떨다 [Lit. to chatter one's teeth] IDIOM **1.** 몹시 분해하거나 지긋지긋해하다 = to be filled with rage or disgust (*cf.* 치가 떨리다) █A: 여기는 경치는 참 좋은데 동네 사람들이 좀 불친절한 것 같아요. = *The landscape is beautiful here but the townspeople seem a little rude.* B: 관광객들이 놀러 와서 시끄럽게 떠들고 쓰레기를 마구 버려서 마을 사람들이 관광객이라면 **치를 떨어요**. = *They are disgusted by the way tourists come here and cause a commotion while trashing the place.* **2.** 매우 인색하여 내놓으려 하지 않다 = to be very stingy and unwilling to share anything █A: 내 참, 내가 머리에 털 나고 나서 저렇게 지독한 구두쇠는 처음 봤어. = *I've never seen such a stingy person in my whole life.* B: 나도. 돈 백 원에도 **치를 떠네**. = *Me neither. He balks at even sharing 100 won.*

친구 따라 강남 간다 [Lit. to follow a friend to Gangnam] PROVERB 자신의 뚜렷한 주관 없이 남이 하자고 하는 대로 하는 사람을 보고 하는 말 = used to describe someone who blindly follows the actions of another (*equiv.* If all your friends jumped off a cliff, would you do it too?) ▌A: 어제 학원 안 가고 어디 갔니? 사실대로 말해 봐. = *I know you didn't go to your institute classes yesterday. Where did you go? Tell me the truth.* B: 민수 따라 놀러 갔었어요. = *I went to hang out with Minsu.* A: **친구 따라 강남 간다더니,** 너는 왜 맨날 민수 하자는 대로만 하니? = *If your friend jumped off a cliff, would you do that too? Why do you always just do what Minsu wants to do?*

NOTE: 여기서 강남은 중국 양쯔강의 남쪽을 뜻한다. 친구 말만 믿고 먼 곳까지 무턱대고 따라갔다가 낭패를 볼 수 있다는 뜻으로, 주관 없는 태도를 경계하는 표현이다.
The 강남 of this expression denotes the area of China south of the Yangtze River. This expression refers to a fiasco of a trip that has befallen one after tagging along with a friend. The idea is that one should never blindly follow the actions of another.

칠전팔기 [Lit. 七 seven + 顚 fall + 八 eight + 起 rise → fall seven times and rise up eight times] CHINESE-DERIVATION 여러 번 실패해도 포기하지 않고 계속해서 도전하는 정신 = the idea continuing to challenge oneself even after successive failures (*equiv.* dogged perseverance / to not know when to stay down) ▌A: 엄마, 죄송해요. 이제는 그만 시험 준비 그만하고, 취직 준비할게요. = *Mom, I'm really sorry, but I think I'm going to give up on preparing to take more tests and start thinking about getting a job.* B: 아니야. **칠전팔기** 정신으로 한 번 더 도전해 보자, 응? = *No. Now's the time to show your dogged perseverance and give it one more shot. All right?*

NOTE: 엄밀히 따지면 이 표현은 말이 안 된다. 일곱 번 넘어지면 일곱 번 일어나게 되지, 여덟 번 일어날 수는 없다. 넘어지는 것에 굴하지 않고 씩씩하게 일어나는 행동이나 정신을 강조하기 위해 일부러 7보다 하나 더 큰 숫자를 쓰게 된 것 같다.
Looking closely at this expression, it would seem to not make sense. If one

falls down seven times, getting up seven times is possible, but eight times? It seems like the extra time was added to emphasize the importance of rising up again whenever one has been knocked to the ground.

침묵은 금이다 [Lit. Silence is gold.] PROVERB 말을 하지 않는 것이 좋을 때가 있다는 말＝suggests that sometimes it is better to remain silent (*equiv.* Silence is golden.) ▌A: 아, 그 말은 정말 안 했으면 좋았을 텐데 ……. ＝*Arghh, I really wish I hadn't said that ...* B: 그러니까 **침묵은 금이라고** 했잖아. ＝*That's why they say silence is golden.*

침을 놓다 IDIOM＝일침을 놓다

침(을) 뱉다 [Lit. to spit (out spit)] IDIOM 멸시하고 비난하다＝to disdain and criticize (*syn.* 돌(을) 던지다, 손가락질(을)하다 *cf.* 누워서 침 뱉기, 웃는 낮에 침 뱉으랴) ▌A: 저 사람은 참 불쌍한 사람이야. ＝*I really feel bad for that guy.* B: 왜? 엄청난 부자잖아. ＝*Why? He's super rich.* A: 부자면 뭐해? 동네에서 인심을 완전히 잃었어. 다들 저 사람 하는 일이라면 **침을 뱉잖아**. ＝*What difference does that make? He's completely lost the goodwill of the neighborhood. Everyone just curses everything that he does.*

침(을) 삼키다 IDIOM＝침(을) 흘리다

침(을) 흘리다 [Lit. to drip saliva] IDIOM 몹시 탐내다＝to lust after something (*equiv.* to salivate over something *syn.* 침(을) 삼키다) ▌A: 이 가방 정말 예쁘다!＝*What a beautiful bag!* B: 내가 찍어 둔 거니까 괜히 **침 흘리지** 마. ＝*I've already claimed it, so don't waste your time dreaming.*

ㅋ

칼을 갈다 [Lit. to sharpen the knives] IDIOM 독한 마음을 먹고 실력을 쌓다 = to better one's skills with an intensity of purpose (*equiv.* to be sharpening up the knives for battle / to be out for revenge *syn.* 독을 품다) ▌A: 오늘 한국 대 일본 축구 경기는 정말 흥미진진할 거 같아. = *The Korea-Japan game tonight is shaping up to be an enthralling match.* B: 맞아. 저번에 한국이 승부차기 끝에 진 후로 **칼을 갈아** 왔잖아. = *Ever since Korea lost the last match on a penalty shoot-out, the team has been just waiting for revenge.*

칼(을) 대다 [Lit. to touch the knife (to one's skin)] IDIOM 수술을 하다 = to have a surgical procedure (*equiv.* to go under the knife / to have some work done) ▌A: 저 탤런트는 한동안 안 보이더니 또 얼굴에 **칼 댔나봐**. = *She was nowhere to be seen for a while and now here she is again. Looks like she went under the knife again.* B: 왜? 얼굴이 달라졌어? = *Really? Is there something different about her face?*

칼자루(를) 잡다 IDIOM = 칼자루(를) 쥐다

칼자루(를) 쥐다 [Lit. to grasp the hilt of a sword] IDIOM 유리한 입장에 있거나 결정권을 갖고 있다 = to be in an advantageous position or hold the decision-making authority (*equiv.* to have the final say / to hold all the cards *syn.* 칼자루(를) 잡다) ▌A: 이 차는 어떠세요? = *What about this car?* B: 제 마음에는 드는데 집에 가서 아내하고 상의해 볼게요. 저희 집의 **칼자루는 아내가 쥐고** 있거든요. = *Well, I do like it, but I'll have to consult with my wife about it first. She's the one who wears the pants in our relationship, you know?*

코가 꿰이다 [Lit. to have one's nose threaded] IDIOM 약점이 잡히다 = for one's weakness to be found out ▌A: 자네는 왜 그렇게 마누라한테 꼼짝을 못 하나? = *Why does your wife keep you on such a short leash?* B: 제가 젊었을 때 사고를 한번 쳤었거든요. 그때 **코가 꿰인** 이후 줄곧 이래요. = *I caused some trouble back in my younger days and that's the way it's been ever since.*

코가 납작해지다 [Lit. to have one's nose flattened] IDIOM 기세가 꺾여 풀이 죽다 = to be disheartened or dispirited (*equiv.* to be shown up / to be dispirited (by another's excellence) *cf.* 기(가)죽다) ▌A: 어제 영업팀의 김은하 씨랑 테니스 쳐서 졌다면서? = *I heard you lost at tennis to Kim Eunha from the sales team.* B: 네. 여자라고 얕보다 **코가 납작해졌어요**. = *Yeah, I didn't take her seriously because she's a woman, and I ended up getting schooled.*

코가 높다 IDIOM = 콧대(가) 높다

코가 비뚤어지게 [Lit. so that one's nose becomes crooked] IDIOM 몹시 취할 정도로 = till one is severely intoxicated (*equiv.* to be wasted / to be very drunk / to be trashed) ▌A: 오늘은 우리 **코가 비뚤어지게** 마셔 보자. = *Let's drink till our eyes go crooked.* B: 좋지. 오늘은 내가 살게. = *Sounds good. Tonight's on me.*

코가 빠지다 [Lit. for one's nose (mucus) to fall out] IDIOM 기가 죽고 맥이 빠지다 = to be dispirited and lose heart ▌A: 민수 녀석 오늘 시험 아니야? = *Did Minsu have a test today?* B: 안 그래도 그것 때문에 지금 **코가 빠져서** 제 방에 있어. 시험 망쳤나 봐. = *Yeah, I was just about to tell you. He's in his room with a crestfallen look on his face. It looks like he flunked the test.*

NOTE: See the note on 코(를) 빠뜨리다.

코끝도 안 보인다 IDIOM = 코빼기도 안 보인다

코끝이 찡하다 [Lit. to have tingling in one's nose] IDIOM 몹시 감동하거나 슬퍼하다 = to be deeply moved or very sad (*equiv.* to get all chocked up *syn.* 콧등이 시큰하다) ▌A: 엄마, 뭘 보고 계시길래 눈에 눈물이 그렁그렁하세요? = *What on earth are you watching that would cause your eyes to fill up with tears like that, Mom?* B: 부모 없이 동생들 돌보는 아이 이야기인데, 보다 보니 **코끝이 찡하네**. = *It's the story of a kid raising his younger brothers without parents. It's got me all choked up.*

코너에 몰리다 IDIOM = 구석에 몰리다

코(를) 박다 [Lit. to hammer in one's nose] IDIOM 무엇인가를 열중해서 들여다보다 = to peer very intently into something ▌A: 뭘 그렇게 **코를 박고** 보고 있어? = *What are you looking at so intently?* B: 아, 신문에 재미있는 기사가 있어서요. = *Ah, there was just a really interesting article in the paper.*

코(를) 빠뜨리다 [Lit. to drip out snot] IDIOM 다 되어 가는 일을 망치다 = to ruin a project that had been close to completion (*equiv.* to ruin something at the last minute) ▌A: 그런데, 엄마한테 거짓말하고 우리끼리 놀러 가도 될까? = *Hey, but do you think it's really all right for us to tell Mom a lie and go off by ourselves like this?* B: 얘가 다 된 밥에 **코 빠뜨릴** 일 있어? 엄마한테 얘기하면 우리끼리 놀러 가라고 허락할 것 같아? = *Why are you trying to ruin everything at the last minute? Do you think she would let us go if we told her?*

NOTE: 여기서의 코는 콧물을 의미한다. '다 된 밥에 코 빠뜨렸다'라고도 한다.

In this idiom, 코 does not just mean "nose" but "runny nose." As seen in the example, this expression is often iterated as 다 된 밥에 코 빠뜨렸다.

코 묻은 돈 [Lit. snot-covered money] IDIOM 어린아이들이 가지고 있는 적은 돈 = small quantities of money that little kids carry around ▌A: 요즘에 동네에 불량 학생들이 나타나서 아이들 **코 묻은 돈**을 빼앗는대. = *Some hooligans in the neighborhood are popping up and stealing the* *kids' lunch money.* B: 그래? 방법을 찾아야겠네. 경찰에 연락하는 게 낫겠지? =*Really? We'd better do something about that. Don't you think we should contact the police?*

NOTE: 추운 겨울, 아이들은 흐르는 콧물을 손으로 대충 훔치며 뛰어논다. '코 묻은 돈'은 아이들이 콧물을 훔친 그 손을 벌려 부모님에게서 타 낸 용돈을 의미한다.
In wintertime, kids often clean up their runny noses in a halfhearted way with their hands. 코 묻은 돈 means the small amounts of pocket money that parents put in their young children's snotty hands.

코빼기도 안 보인다 [Lit. to not even see someone's nose] IDIOM

(속된 말로) 도무지 나타나지 않아 볼 수가 없다 =(slang) Someone who seems to never be around and is rarely seen. (*equiv.* to not need hide nor hair of someone *syn.* 코끝도 안 보인다) ▌A: 경수는 어디 가서 형이 전역을 했는데 **코빼기도 안 보이는** 거야? =*His brother just got discharged from the military and Gyeongsu is nowhere to be found?* B: 아까 친구들이랑 나갔어요. =*He went out earlier with his friends.*

NOTE: 코빼기는 코를 저속하게 이르는 말이다. 어떤 사람의 모습이 보이지 않는다는 의미로 코가 보이지 않는다고 말하는 이유는, 코가 사람의 얼굴을 측면에서 봤을 때 가장 튀어나와 있기 때문이 아닌가 싶다.
코빼기 is a more impolite word for nose. The reason the feature used in this expression is the nose is likely because it's the most prominent part of a person's face.

콧김이 세다 [Lit. to have strong steam coming from one's nostrils] IDIOM

영향력이 강하다 =to have strong influence (*equiv.* to have great sway (over people etc.) *syn.* 입김이 세다) ▌A: 사장님도 참 불쌍해요. 의사 결정을 마음대로 할 수 없으니. =*I really feel bad for the boss too. He just doesn't have that much decision-making authority.* B: 이사진의 **콧김이 세**니 어쩔 수 없겠지. =*The board of directors just has too much influence for anything to be done about it.*

콧대(가) 높다 [Lit. to have a bridge to one's nose] IDIOM 잘난 체하고 뽐내는 태도가 있다 = to brag and have a swagger about one (*equiv.* to put on airs / to be stuck up / to walk around with one's nose in the air *syn.* 코가 높다, 콧대(가) 세다) ▌A: 어디 좋은 여자 없어? = *Aren't there any OK women around?* B: 멀리서 찾을 거 있냐? 우리 과 지은이 어때? = *You don't have to look far. What about Jieun from our department?* A: 걔는 콧대가 너무 높아 부담스러워. = *She's too stuck up. I don't think I could handle it.*

콧대(가) 세다 IDIOM = 콧대(가) 높다

콧대를 꺾다 [Lit. to break the bridge of someone's nose] IDIOM 잘난 체하는 사람의 기를 죽이다 = to break the will of someone who had been acting arrogantly (*equiv.* to cut someone down to size / to put someone in their place) ▌A: 준비는 많이 하셨어요? = *Have you done a lot of preparation?* B: 네. 이번에야말로 녀석의 콧대를 꺾어 놓고 말겠어요. = *I sure have. This is my chance to finally put those jerks in their place.*

콧대(를) 세우다 [Lit. to raise up the bridge of one's nose] IDIOM 거만하게 굴다 = to act arrogantly (*equiv.* to keep one's head held high) ▌A: 너는 여자가 되어 가지고 좀 도도한 면도 있어야지. = *As a woman, you've got to hold your head a little higher than that.* B: 엄마, 콧대 세우면 뭐해요? 그러다 좋은 사람 놓치면 저만 손해죠. = *Mom, what's acting stuck up going to get me? What if I end up missing the perfect guy because I was acting that way?*

콧등이 시큰하다 [Lit. for the bridge of one's nose to be tingling] IDIOM 감동하거나 슬퍼서 눈물이 나오려 하다 = to be close to tears after being moved or saddened (*equiv.* to be brought to tears *syn.* 코끝이 찡하다) ▌A: 어제가 영수 졸업식이었죠? = *Yesterday was Yeongsu's graduation, right?* B: 응. 내 아들이 언제 저렇게 컸나 싶으니까 콧등이 시큰했어. = *Yep. Seeing him all grown up like that—it nearly brought me to tears.*

콧방귀도 안 뀌다 IDIOM = 콧방귀(를) 뀌다

콧방귀(를) 뀌다 [Lit. to make a nose fart] IDIOM 남의 말을 대수롭지 않게 여기거나 무시하다 = to disregard the words of another or consider them to be of little consequence (*equiv.* to scoff at / to snort at *syn.* 콧방귀도 안 뀌다) ▌A: 너무 덥다. 우리 에어컨 살까? = *It's just too hot. How about we get some air conditioning in this place.* B: 전에 내가 사자고 할 때는 **콧방귀를 뀌더니!** = *When I suggested that before, you just scoffed!*

NOTE: 콧방귀는 코와 방귀가 합쳐진 재미있는 단어이다. '콧방귀를 뀌다'와 '콧방귀도 안 뀌다'라는 두 표현이 모두 쓰이는데, 그 둘의 표면적 의미는 반대지만 실질적으로는 같은 의미이다.
This expression combines the words for nose and fart, to create the undeniably vivid "nose-fart." The meaning is a snort or scoff in a derisive way. It's used in the two forms, 콧방귀를 뀌다 and 콧방귀도 안 뀌다, which at first glance would appear to be opposites but are in fact of the same meaning.

콩가루가 되다 [Lit. to become bean dust] IDIOM 집안이나 어떤 조직이 망하다 = for a household or an organization etc. to fall apart ▌A: 전에 우리 동네 살던 명수네 있잖아. 명수 아빠 회사가 망해서 집안이 **콩가루가 됐대.** = *That's the house that our old neighbor Myeongsu and family used to live in. After his father's company went belly up, his whole family came unraveled.* B: 저런. 참 착실한 사람인데 어쩌다 그 지경이 되었을까. = *That's terrible. His father was such a kind person. It's a shame to see what become of him.*

NOTE: 콩가루는 뭉치려고 해도 잘 뭉쳐지지 않는다. 가족 간의 질서가 무너지고 제 역할을 하지 못하는 집안을 '콩가루 집안'이라고 한다.
Bean flour can not easily be clumped up together. A family that has descended into chaos or seems to lack definable familial roles is often referred to as a 콩가루 집안.

콩고물도 없다 [Lit. for there to not even be any bean powder] IDIOM 돌아오는 이익이 전혀 없다 = for there to be absolutely no benefit to doing something (*equiv.* to be left high and dry *syn.* 국물도 없다) ▌A: 어디 갔

다 와? = *Where are you just coming back from?* B: 요 앞 새로 생긴 마트에. 뭐 공짜 행사라도 하나 싶어 가 봤는데 **콩고물도 없더라고**. = *I went to the new mart in front of the house. I thought they might be having some special deals for the opening and all, but there was nothing at all to be had.*

콩고물이 떨어지다 [Lit. for bean powder to spill down] IDIOM 어떤 일에서 부수적인 이익을 얻다 = to be the beneficiary of secondary profits of some venture (*equiv.* to be eating table scraps *syn.* 떡고물이 떨어지다) ▌A: 이번에 우리 회사 주식이 크게 올랐다는 뉴스가 나간 뒤로 모르는 데서 연락이 엄청나게 와요. = *After the news broke about our stock price going way up, I've been getting calls from all over the place.* B: 어디 **콩고물이라도 떨어질까** 싶어 그런 거겠지. = *They're just sniffing around for something they can grab onto.*

콩밥(을) 먹다 [Lit. to eat (soy)bean rice] IDIOM 감옥살이를 하다 = to spend time in prison (*equiv.* to be in lock-up / to be in the big house / to be behind bars *syn.* 별(을) 달다) ▌A: 어제 뉴스 봤어요? 학생들 상대로 불량식품 판매하다 걸린 사람 얘기 말이에요. = *Did you see the news yesterday? I mean the story about the guy who was selling dangerously low quality food to students until he got busted.* B: 네, 봤어요. 그럼 놈들은 **콩밥을 먹어야** 정신을 차릴 거예요. = *Yeah, I saw that too. Those people might have to spend some time in jail before they'll wise up.*

NOTE: 과거 재소자들은 콩이 섞인 밥을 먹었다. 콩밥이 영양이 풍부하면서 값이 쌌기 때문이라고 한다. 이제는 더 이상 감옥에서 콩밥을 주지 않지만, '콩밥'은 감옥살이를 상징하는 것으로 여전히 쓰이고 있다.
Inmates were formerly fed rice mixed with beans during their time in the big house. The reason being that the mixture was a nutritious and low-cost meal. Despite that inmates are no longer feed this concoction, the phrase lives on as a euphemism for time spent behind bars.

콩 심은 데 콩 나고 팥 심은 데 팥 난다 [Lit. Where you plant soybeans, soy will grow and where you plant red bean, red bean will grow.]

PROVERB 원인에 따라서 결과가 생긴다는 말 = suggests that there is an effect that is in accordance with the cause (*equiv.* You reap what you sow. / the law of cause and effect *syn.* 뿌린 대로 거둔다) ▌A: 어디서 돈벼락이라도 맞았으면 좋겠네. = *I wish I could just strike it rich someday.* B: 콩 심은 데 콩 나고 팥 심은 데 팥 나는 거지, 뭐 그런 되지도 않는 요행을 바라니? = *You reap what you sow. Are you really just going to wait around for some fluke success that's never going to happen?*

콩으로 메주를 쑨다 해도

[Lit. even if you say that you make fermented soybeans clumps with soybeans] IDIOM 아무리 당연한 말을 해도 = no matter how obvious what you're saying is (*equiv.* You've already cried wolf too many times. / I'm not going to fall for it again.) ▌A: 내일 선생님이 몸이 안 좋으셔서 안 오신대. = *The teacher said he's not feeling well and won't be coming in tomorrow.* B: 이제 네 말은 **콩으로 메주를 쑨다 해도** 안 믿을 거야. = *Yeah, I've fallen for your tricks one too many times already.*

쿵짝이 맞다

IDIOM = 꿍짝이 맞다

*큰코다치다

[Lit. to injure one's large nose] IDIOM 크게 망신을 당하다 = to be deeply humiliated (*equiv.* to pay dearly) ▌A: 이번 상대는 누구예요? = *Who are you going up against this time?* B: 글쎄, 잘 모르는 친구야. 신인이라더라고. = *Some guy I don't know much about. I heard he's a newcomer.* A: 그래도 얕보면 안 돼. 그러다 **큰코다치는** 수가 있어. = *Even still, you'd better not underestimate him. That's a surefire way to be put to shame.*

키를 쥐다

IDIOM = 열쇠를 쥐다

타산지석 [Lit. 他other + 山mountain + 之of + 石stone → Even a bad stone from another mountain stone of poor quality can be used to cut a precious stone.] CHINESE-DERIVATION 다른 사람의 잘못된 말이나 행동도 자신에게 도움이 될 수 있다는 말 = describes how even the thoughtless words or misdeeds of another can be beneficial (*equiv.* (I'll) let this (the mistakes or failures of another) be a lesson. *cf.* 거울(로)삼다) ▌A: 죄송합니다. 저 때문에 일이 이렇게 돼서 ……. = *I'm so sorry. It's all my fault that things came to this.* B: 아니야. 이번 경험을 **타산지석**으로 삼아서 다음에 잘하면 되지. = *It's all right. Just let this be a lesson for you.*

탁상공론 [Lit. 卓table + 上over + 空empty + 論argue → an empty argument on the table] CHINESE-DERIVATION 현실성이 없는 논의 = an unrealistic discussion (*equiv.* a discussion that is disconnected from reality) ▌A: 지금 우리가 이렇게 앉아서 **탁상공론**만 하고 있을 때가 아니에요. 현장의 목소리를 들어야 합니다. = *This is not the time to be having some theoretical discussion. We have to hear what people are actually saying in the real world.* B: 맞습니다. 우리끼리 야기해 봤자 현실성이 떨어질 뿐이에요. = *You're right. Talking amongst ourselves here will only serve to make our discourse more disconnected.*

탄탄대로 [Lit. 坦flat + 坦flat + 大big + 路road → a wide, flat road] CHINESE-DERIVATION 어려움이 없이 순탄한 장래 = a carefree future (*equiv.* It's smooth sailing from here on out. / The road ahead is smooth.) ▌A: 이번에 회장님 아들이 신입사원으로 들어온다죠? = *The CEO's son was recently hired here, right?* B: 응. 밑에서부터 일을 배우는 거겠지. 좋은 대학에 아버지 배경에, 앞날이 **탄탄대로**겠구먼. = *Yeah, it looks* *like he's learning from the ground up. Graduating from a good school, with his father being who is on top of that, it looks like it'll be smooth sailing for him.*

탈을 쓰다 [Lit. to use a mask] IDIOM 속마음을 숨기기 위해 거짓으로 꾸미다 = to deceitfully conceal one's true self or true thoughts (*equiv.* to wear a mask / a wolf in sheep's clothing *syn.* 가면을 쓰다) ▌A: 저런 놈은 인간도 아니야. 어떻게 인간의 **탈을 쓰고** 저런 짓을 할 수가 있지? = *That guy isn't even human. How could he pretend to be normal and act like that?* B: 그러게. 저런 놈들 보면 세상 살기가 겁이 나. = *That's what I'm saying. Seeing that there are people out there like that makes me afraid to live in this world.*

NOTE: '인간의 탈을 쓰고', '양의 탈을 쓴 늑대'와 같은 표현을 흔히 쓴다. This phrase is often used in the forms, 인간의 탈을 쓰고 and 양의 탈을 쓴 늑대.

터무니(가)없다 [Lit. to have (left behind) no traces] IDIOM 근거가 없고 허황되다 = to be groundless and absurd (*equiv.* to be groundless / to be baseless) ▌A: 어때? 이제 내 말이 좀 믿어져? = *How about now? Are you starting to believe what I'm saying?* B: 야, 그렇게 **터무니없는** 말은 태어나서 처음 들어 본다! = *That's the most baseless thing I've ever heard in my life.*

NOTE: 터무니는 터를 잡은 흔적을 뜻하는 말이다. 터를 잡은 흔적이 없는데도 사람이 살았다고 주장한다면 그 말은 근거가 없어 허황되게 들릴 것이다. The word 터무니 from this phrase means the traces of a building's foundation. To say something is "터무니없다" is equivalent to saying "터를 잡았던 흔적이 없다," which in this case means that a statement is groundless.

털어서 먼지 안 나는 사람 없다 [Lit. Dust will fall off of everyone if you shake them.] PROVERB 누구나 약점이나 허점이 있다는 말 = points out that everyone has a weakness or blind spot (*equiv.* Everyone has a few skeletons in their closet.) █A: 왜 감사를 할 때마다 모든 팀에서 벌벌 떠는 걸까?= *Why do you think all the teams tremble in fear whenever it's time for inspections?* B: 털어서 먼지 안 나는 사람 있겠어?= *Everyone has a flaw if you just look hard enough.*

테이프(를) 끊다 [Lit. to cut the tape] IDIOM 처음 시작하다= to begin (*equiv.* to get the ball rolling) █A: 우리 이러지 말고 교수님한테 한 명씩 찾아가서 여쭤 보자.= *Come on, let's just go ask the professor individually.* B: 그래. 그럼 네가 첫 **테이프를 끊는** 게 좋겠다.= *OK. Then you can get the ball rolling.*

텐트(를) 치다 [Lit. to set up a tent] IDIOM (속된 말로) 발기하다= (slang) to have an erection (*equiv.* to raise the tent pole / to get a boner) █A: 영수야, 나 고민이 있어.= *Yeongsu, I've got something on my mind.* B: 뭔데?= *What is it?* A: 우리끼리 얘기지만, 나 요즘 아침에 일어나도 **텐트를 안 쳐.** 건강에 문제가 있는 거 아닐까?= *Let's just keep this between us, but when I wake up in the mornings the old tent pole isn't there anymore. Do you think it may be for health reasons?*

NOTE: 텐트의 모양에서 착안한 속된 표현이다.
As is true of the expression in English, this idiom comes from the similarities between a tent and this part of the male anatomy.

통이 작다 [Lit. for the container to be small] IDIOM 씀씀이가 작거나 대범하지 못하다= for one's spending habits to be cheap or to not be generous with money (*equiv.* to be cheap / to be stingy / to be a tightwad *ant.* 통이 크다) █A: 이번에 회사 보너스 나왔지? 얼마 나왔어?= *You got a bonus this time right? How much did you get?* B: 50만 원 주더라고.= *They gave me 500,000 won.* A: 에계? 고작? 회사가 너무 **통이 작은** 거 아니야?= *Huh? That's all? That's a little too cheap, don't you think?*

통이 크다 [Lit. for the container to be big] IDIOM 씀씀이가 크거나 대범하다= to spend a lot or be generous with money (*equiv.* to be a big spender *ant.* 통이 작다) █A: 이 세탁기는 혼수로 해 온 거야?= *Did your parents* *buy you two this washing machine for your wedding gift?* B: 아니, 대학 선배가 결혼 선물로 해 준 거야. = *No, a friend from college gave it to me as a wedding gift.* A: 우와, **통이 큰** 분인가 보네. = *Wow, that's some generous friend.*

퇴짜(를) 놓다 [Lit. to put the letter *toe* (on something)] IDIOM **1.** 물건이나 의견을 받아들이지 않고 거절하다 = to refuse an item or someone's opinion (*equiv.* to turn down a suitor / to reject (a marriage proposal) / to stamp "reject" on something *syn.* 딱지(를) 놓다 *ant.* 퇴짜(를) 맞다, 딱지(를) 맞다) ▌A: 팀장님은 왜 내가 내놓는 기획안마다 **퇴짜를 놓는지** 모르겠어. = *I don't know why our boss has to reject all of my plans like that.* B: 무슨 이유가 있겠지. = *I'm sure he has his reasons.* **2.** 선을 본 상대에게 사귈 의사가 없음을 밝히다 = to indicate that one has no intentions of further meeting a prospective mate (*syn.* 딱지(를) 놓다 *ant.* 퇴짜(를) 맞다, 딱지(를) 맞다) ▌A: 걔는 왜 선 보는 남자들마다 **퇴짜를 놓을까**? = *Why do you think she rejects all her suitors like that?* B: 눈이 높아서 그렇지 뭐. = *I guess she just has really high standards.*

NOTE: 조선 시대 때는 각 지방의 특산물을 정기적으로 임금에게 바쳐야 했다. 담당 부서에서 해당 물건의 품질이 부적합하다고 판단하면 그 물건에 퇴(退) 자가 새겨진 도장을 찍어 도로 가져가게 만들었다. 원래대로라면 '퇴 자를 놓다'라고 써야겠지만, 소리나는 대로 쓰이다 현재의 '퇴짜를 놓다'로 굳어진 것으로 보인다.
During the Joseon period, each region had to submit certain local goods to the king. If the offerings were not up to royal standards, an agent in charge would stamp the goods with the Chinese character 退(퇴), which means "withdraw" or "reject," and return them posthaste. Technically the phrase should be written 퇴 자를 놓다, but the written form followed the pronunciation and has now solidified this way.

***퇴짜(를) 맞다** [Lit. to be hit with the letter *toe*] IDIOM 물건이나 의견 등이 거절을 당하다 = for one's product or suggestion etc. to be refused (*equiv.* to get turned down / to be refused / to get shot down *syn.* 딱지(를) 맞다 *ant.* 퇴짜(를) 놓다, 딱지(를) 놓다) ▌A: 왜 그렇게 시무룩해? = *What's* *with the long face?* B: 미희 씨한테 주말에 영화 보러 가자고 했다가 **퇴짜 맞았어.** =*I asked Mihee out to a movie this weekend and she shot me down.*

NOTE: See the note on 퇴짜(를) 놓다.

*틈집(을) 잡다 [Lit. to grab a crack] IDIOM 조그마한 흠집을 들추어 남을 괴롭히다

=to point out a small fault and annoy someone about it (*equiv.* to nitpick / to find fault *syn.* 꼬투리(를) 잡다 *cf.* 트집(을) 잡히다) ▌A: 김 과장, 오늘 발표 아주 좋았어. **트집을 잡을래야** 잡을 데가 없이 완벽했어. =*Mr. Kim, the presentation today was excellent. I can't say a single bad thing about it.* B: 아, 그래요? 다행이네요. =*Oh, really? I'm glad to hear that.*

NOTE: 트집은 한 덩이가 되어야 할 물건의 벌어진 틈을 의미한다. 여기서 '잡다'는 손으로 잡는다는 의미보다는 '잡아내다', '찾아내다'의 의미로 볼 수 있다. 어떤 물건이나 일의 흠을 공연히 잡아낼 때 이 표현을 쓴다. A 트집 is the crack or niche in an item that should be a single clump. The verb 잡다 is, in this case, means something more along the lines of finding something than catching something. This is an expression that describes needlessly finding fault in an item or project.

트집(을) 잡히다 [Lit. for a crack to be caught] IDIOM 다른 사람에게 약점을 노출하거나 시비 거리를 제공하다

=to provide someone with grounds for a quarrel or expose one's own weaknesses (*equiv.* to provide someone with ammunition *syn.* 꼬투리(를) 잡히다 *cf.* 트집(을) 잡다) ▌A: 야, 여기 청소 다시 해. 괜히 **트집 잡히지** 말고. =*Hey, clean this part up again. Don't just give them something to use against us.* B: 네. 어디를 다시 하면 되나요? =*Yes, OK. Where exactly do you mean?*

NOTE: See the note on 트집(을) 잡다.

틈이 벌어지다 IDIOM =틈이 생기다

틈이 생기다 [Lit. for a crack to appear] IDIOM 사이가 나빠지거나 멀어지다 = for a relationship to grow distant (*equiv.* for cracks to appear (in the veneer of) a relationship *syn.* 금(이) 가다, 틈이 생기다) ▌A: 이번에 영희 엄마랑 별것도 아닌 일로 다툰 이후로 **틈이 생겼어요**. = *After bickering with Yeonghee's mom over some little thing, there's definitely been some cracks in our friendship.* B: 이웃끼리 그러면 불편하잖아요. 얼른 화해해요. = *It'll be awkward to be on bad terms with a neighbor. Hurry up and smooth things over.*

티끌 모아 태산 [Lit. (if you) gather up many specks of dust, it will make a great mountain] PROVERB 작은 것도 조금씩 쌓이면 큰 것이 된다는 말 = describes how gathering up small quantities of something will eventually lead to a large amount (*equiv.* Many drops make a shower.) ▌A: 돼지저금통에 돈은 많이 모였어? = *Have you saved up a lot in your piggy bank?* B: 어. 동전을 다 합치면 30만 원도 넘을걸? = *Yep. I bet it's more than 300,000 won now.* A: **티끌 모아 태산**이라더니, 너 대단하다! = *Drop by drop and pretty soon you have a flood. That's really amazing!*

ㅍ

파경 [Lit. 破break + 鏡mirror → a broken mirror] CHINESE-DERIVATION 이혼 = a divorce (*equiv.* a broken home) ▌A: 요즘 혼수 문제로 결혼한 지 얼마 안 되어 **파경**에 이르는 부부들이 많대요. = *I heard that a lot of couples are breaking up right after marriage over the issue of marriage expenses.* B: 저도 들었어요. 정말 안타까운 일이에요. = *I heard that too. It's a real shame.*

파김치가 되다 [Lit. to become green onion kimchi] IDIOM 몹시 지쳐서 몸이 축 늘어지다 = to be very worn out and drooping with fatigue (*equiv.* to be dead tired / to be exhausted) ▌A: 퇴근한 뒤에 운동하는 거 있으세요? = *Do you exercise after work?* B: 마음은 있는데, 몸이 **파김치가 되기** 일쑤라 엄두가 안 나요. = *Well, I'd like to but I'm dead tired. I can't even think about exercise right now.*

NOTE: 파로 김치를 담글때 파를 소금에 절이면 싱싱하던 파가 팍 오므라들어 물렁해진다. 사람이 피곤에 지쳐 축 늘어진 모습을 그러한 파의 모양에 비유한 표현이다.

When green onions are tossed into the kimchi mix, they quickly change from their former glory into shriveled and soft green strings. When a person looks wilted by the pressures and hardships of daily life, using this expression to refer to them as a wilted green onion will be just what they need to hear.

파란만장(하다) [Lit. 波wave + 瀾wave + 萬ten thousand + 丈unit of length → waves of ten thousand *jang* (unit of measure)] CHINESE-DERIVATION 인생이나 일에 시련이 많고 변화가 심하다 = for there to be many trials or changes in one's life or endeavors (*equiv.* to be full of ups and downs) ▌A:

우와, 일 년 동안 세계여행을 다녀오셨다고요? 어떠셨어요?＝ *Wow, so you traveled around the world for one whole year?* B: 한마디로 **파란만장했어요**. ＝*In a nutshell, it was full of ups and downs.*

파란불이 켜지다 [Lit. for the green light to turn on] IDIOM 앞일이 잘되어 나갈 것 같은 조짐이 보이다＝to get a sign that things will proceed well (*equiv.* to get the green light *syn.* 청신호가 켜지다 *ant.* 빨간불이 켜지다, 적신호가 켜지다) ▌A: 오늘 경기를 이김으로써 결승 진출에 **파란불이 켜졌습니다**. ＝*The win today is a green light for our trip to the finals.* B: 네. 다음 경기에서 큰 점수 차로 지지 않는다면 결승에 진출하게 됩니다. ＝*As long as we don't lose the next game by a huge margin, we're going to the finals.*

파리(를) 날리다 [Lit. to make flies fly] IDIOM 장사가 잘 안되다＝for business not to go well (*equiv.* for one's place of business to be like a ghost town / Customers are few and far between.) ▌A: 요즘 사업은 잘돼?＝ *How's business been recently?* B: 말도 마. 만날 **파리만 날려**. ＝*Don't ask. It's like a ghost town, day after day.*

NOTE: 이 표현은 파리를 날게 한다는 것이 아니라, 장사가 잘 안되어 사람이 아닌 파리만 꼬인다는 뜻이다.
This expression actually doesn't mean to make flies fly, but rather that because one's business is completely empty and flies—not people—are gathering.

파리 목숨 [Lit. the life of a fly] IDIOM 하찮은 목숨＝a trivial life (*equiv.* a nothing existence) ▌A: 들리는 소문으로는 회사에서 구조조정을 한다는데 걱정이에요. ＝*I heard a rumor that people are worried about a restructuring at work.* B: 정말 말단 직원들은 목숨이 **파리 목숨**인 것 같아요. ＝*Low-level employees really are treated about as well as flies.*

파문을 일으키다 IDIOM ＝파장을 일으키다

파장을 일으키다 [Lit. to make waves] IDIOM 커다란 논란을 불러오다＝

to instigate a major controversy (*equiv.* to kick up a firestorm / to make waves / to rock the boat *syn.* 파문을 일으키다) ▌A: 저 선수 이면계약으로 **파장을 일으켰던** 그 선수 아냐? 코트에 복귀했어? = *Isn't that the athlete who made waves by signing a dual contract? Is he back in the uniform again?* B: 응. 얼마 전에 다른 팀으로 옮겨서 뛰고 있어. = *Yeah, he moved to a new team a while ago and plays for them now.*

팔방미인 [Lit. 八 eight + 方 direction + 美 beautiful + 人 people] CHINESE-DERIVATION 모든 분야에서 뛰어난 사람 = someone who excels in all fields (*equiv.* a renaissance man / a well-rounded person) ▌A: 미희는 공부면 공부, 운동이면 운동, 외모면 외모 어느 하나 빠지는 게 없구나. = *Mihee really is tops in all categories: school, sports, and looks—she's got it all.* B: 걔 정말 **팔방미인**이에요. = *Yeah, she really is a renaissance woman.*

팔을 걷어붙이다 [Lit. to fold up one's sleeves] IDIOM 적극적으로 나서다 = to assume a proactive approach (*equiv.* to roll up one's sleeves *syn.* 소매를 걷고 나서다, 발 벗고 나서다, 맨발 벗고 나서다) ▌A: 역시 장정 둘이 **팔을 걷어붙이니** 일이 금세 끝나는구나. = *Just as I thought, once two strong young men rolled their sleeves up and started taking part, the work got finished in an instant.* B: 엄마, 아들 뒀다가 어디 쓰려고 그러세요? 힘든 일은 저희가 다 할게요. = *Mom, what do you think sons are for? We'll handle all the hard work.*

팔이 안으로 굽는다 [Lit. The arms fold inwards.] PROVERB 혈연관계에 있거나 자기와 가까운 사람에게 유리한 쪽으로 마음이 기울기 쉽다는 말 = describes the tendency of people to favor those related to them or those close to them (*equiv.* I've got to look out for my own. / Blood is thicker than water. *syn.* 가재는 게 편, 초록은 동색) ▌A: 역시 우리 팀 상현 씨가 일이나 운동이나 최고야. = *Naturally, my employee Sanghyeon is the best at work and at sports.* B: 김 부장, **팔이 안으로 굽는다고** 하더니 자기 팀원이라고 너무 펀드는 거 아니야? = *I know you've got to look out for your own, Mr. Kim, but aren't you just saying that because he's on your team?*

팔짝 뛰다 IDIOM = 펄펄 뛰다

팔짱(을) 끼고 구경만 하다 [Lit. to fold one's arms and just sightsee] IDIOM 적극적인 행동을 하지 않고 방관하고 있다 = to just watch without assuming an active posture (*equiv.* to just stand by with arms folded *syn.* 뒷짐만 지고 있다, 가만히 앉아 있다, 앉아서 보고만 있다) ▌ A: 시누이가 미워 죽겠어. = *I just despise my sister-in-law.* B: 왜? = *Why?* A: 명절 되면 나는 일하느라 바빠 죽겠는데 자기는 **팔짱 끼고 구경만 하면서** 이래라 저래라 참견만 해. = *On holidays, when I'm slaving away in the kitchen, she just stands there with her arms folded, barking out orders.*

패가망신(하다) [Lit. 敗 ruin + 家 family + 亡 fail + 身 body] CHINESE-DERIVATION 집안을 망가뜨리고 신세를 망치다 = to ruin a household and one's circumstances (*equiv.* (to gamble etc.) oneself out of house and home) ▌ A: 아빠, 나도 고스톱 치는 법 가르쳐 주면 안 돼? = *Dad, why don't you teach me how to play go-stop?* B: 아서라. 재미로 노름하다가 **패가망신하는** 사람도 많다. = *Knock it off with that talk. Many people started out just gambling a little for fun and ended up out on the streets because of that game.*

펄펄 뛰다 [Lit. to run around huffing and puffing] IDIOM **1.** 몹시 화를 내다 = to be extremely angry (*equiv.* to go ballistic / to go berserk / to go through the roof / to hit the ceiling *syn.* 팔짝 뛰다) ▌A: 방학 때 아프리카로 자원봉사 가겠다니까 아빠는 뭐라셔? = *How did your dad react when you told him you were going to do volunteer work in Africa over break?* B: **펄펄 뛰시지** 뭐. = *He went ballistic on me, of course.* **2.** 강하게 부인하다 = to adamantly refute (*syn.* 팔짝 뛰다) ▌A: 그렇게까지 **펄펄 뛰는** 걸 보니 아무래도 범인이 그 사람이 아닌가 봐요. = *Seeing the way that he's carrying on about how it wasn't him, I'm starting to think he didn't do it.* B: 아니야. 속지 마. = *No way. Don't fall for that.*

펜대(를) 굴리다 [Lit. to roll a penholder] IDIOM 사무직 노동에 종사하다 = to have an administrative position (*equiv.* to have a white-collar job / to have a desk job / a pencil pusher) ▌A: 새로 온 소장은 어떤 사람 같아요? = *What kind of a guy is the new manager?* B: 글쎄, **펜대 굴리다** 온 젊은 친구가 뭘 알겠어? = *Well, he seems like a know-nothing pencil pusher.*

평행선을 긋다 IDIOM = 평행선을 달리다

평행선을 달리다 [Lit. to run on parallel lines] IDIOM 의견이 대립되어 조정되지 않다 = to have opposing viewpoints and not make concessions (*equiv.* to be diametrically opposed to each other / to dig in one's heels *syn.* 평행선을 긋다) ▌A: 벌써 파업이 한 달째인데, 이거 큰일이네. = *It's already been a month since the strike began. This is becoming a major problem.* B: 노사 양측이 **평행선을 달리고** 있으니 파업이 언제 끝날지 지금으로서는 아무도 몰라. = *With labor and management diametrically opposed to each other, no one knows how long this will go on.*

포복절도(하다) [Lit. 抱carry in one's arms + 腹stomach + 絕extreme + 倒fall] CHINESE-DERIVATION 몹시 웃다 = to laugh hugely (*equiv.* to roll on the floor with laughter / gut-busting laughter / a knee-slapper) ▌A: 뭘 읽고 있길래 그렇게 **포복절도를** 해? = *What did you read that was so funny you're rolling on the floor with laughter like that?* B: 너도 이 만화 읽어봐. 정말 웃겨. = *Read this comic. It's hilarious.*

포석을 깔다 [Lit. to lay down the stones for a strategic play (in the game of go)] IDIOM 앞으로의 일에 대비해 미리 조치를 취하다 = to take measures against contingencies that may arise (*equiv.* to pave the way / to lay the groundwork *syn.* 포석을 놓다) ▌A: 오늘 사장님 말씀이 좀 의미심장하지 않아? 회사에 도움이 안 되는 사람은 있을 필요가 없다고 하셨잖아. = *Didn't you think what the boss said today was profound? That people who are not aiding the company have no reason to be here.* B: 사람 자르기 위한 **포석을 깐** 거 아닐까요? = *Don't you think he was laying the ground work for a round of layoffs?*

NOTE: 포석은 바둑에서 앞으로 본격적인 수를 진행하기 전에 돌을 벌여 놓는 것을 의미한다.

포석 is the word used to describe the preparatory moves in the game of go for a strategic attack.

포석을 놓다 IDIOM = 포석을 깔다

품 안의 자식 [Lit. a child in a hug] PROVERB 자식이 어렸을 때는 부모의 말을 잘 듣지만 크고 나면 자기 뜻을 내세운다는 말 = describes how young children listen to their parents when they are young but develop their own inclinations when they grow up ▌A: 수희는 전화 자주 해? = *Does Suhee call often?* B: 아니. 통 연락이 없어. 어쩌면 그렇게 무심한지 몰라. = *Nope, she never calls. I don't understand how she could care so little.* A: 그러게 **품 안의 자식**이라잖아. = *Once they grow up and move out, they've got other things to worry about, you know?*

풍비박산 [Lit. 風wind + 飛fly + 雹hail + 散disperse] CHINESE-DERIVATION 산산이 부서져 사방으로 흩어짐 = breaking into little bits and dispersing in all directions (*equiv.* to scatter in the wind) ▌A: 요 아랫집 참 안됐어요. 아들이 사기를 당해서 재산을 다 날렸다나 봐요. = *That family has really had a hard time of it. The son was the victim of fraud and it looks like he lost the family fortune.* B: 아, 그런 일이 있었어? 집이 **풍비박산** 났겠구먼. = *That really happened? That household is going to scatter in the wind.*

풍지박산 CHINESE-DERIVATION '풍비박산'의 잘못된 말 = an incorrect form of 풍비박산

피가 거꾸로 솟다 [Lit. for blood to spurt backwards] IDIOM 몹시 화가 나다 = to be very angry (*equiv.* for one's blood to boil) ▌A: 자, 어떻게 해서 싸우게 된 건지 얘기해 보세요. = *OK, tell me how you two ended up fighting.* B: 이 사람이 제 여자 친구한테 집적대더라고요. **피가 거꾸로 솟아서** 저도 모르게 주먹이 나갔습니다. = *This guy was hitting on my girlfriend. My blood started to boil and before I knew it, my fists were flying.*

피(가) 끓다 [Lit. for one's blood to boil] IDIOM **1.** 화가 치밀어 오르다＝for anger to rise within one (*equiv.* for one's blood to boil) ▌A: 내일 동창회에 전학 간 찬열이도 온대.＝*I hear that guy who transferred to another school, Chanyeol, is coming to the alumni meeting tomorrow.* B: 야, 걔 얘기는 하지도 마. 내가 걔한테 괴롭힘 당한 거 생각하면 지금도 **피가 끓어**.＝*Don't even speak his name. When I think about the way he bullied me, my blood boils even now.* **2.** 힘과 열정이 넘치다＝to overflow with passion or strength (*equiv.* to be a hot-blooded (youth, youngster etc.) *syn.* 피가 뜨겁다) ▌A: 이 추운 겨울날 저 젊은이들은 춥지도 않나 봐요. 찬 바다로 아무렇지도 않게 뛰어드네요.＝*It looks like those youngsters don't even feel the cold of a winter's day like today. They just prance around in the waves like it's nothing.* B: **피 끓는** 청춘들이잖아요.＝*That's because they've got the hot blood of youth coursing through their veins.*

피가 되고 살이 되다 [Lit. to become blood and flesh] IDIOM 큰 도움이 되다＝to be of great help ▌A: 어때? 사회 생활이라는 게 만만하지 않지?＝*How's life treating you? Living in the real world isn't that easy, huh?* B: 네. 일이며 사람이며 쉬운 게 없는 것 같아요.＝*Yeah, nothing is easy—work or personal relationships.* A: 그래도 그게 다 **피가 되고 살이 되는** 거야. 열심히 해.＝*Even so, that will all build character. Just stay strong.*

피가 뜨겁다 [Lit. for one's blood to be hot] IDIOM 열정이 있다＝to have passion (*equiv.* to be hot-blooded *syn.* 피(가) 끓다) ▌A: 아직도 **피가 이렇게 뜨거운데** 은퇴라니 믿기지가 않네요.＝*I've still got warm blood coursing through these veins and they tell me it's retirement? I just can't believe it.* B: 아직도 그렇게 열정이 넘치시는 걸 보니 젊은 제가 부끄럽네요.＝*Seeing how passionate you still are makes me feel a little ashamed of myself.*

피(가) 마르다 [Lit. for one's blood to dry] IDIOM 몹시 초조하다＝to be very nervous (*equiv.* for one's blood to run cold *cf.* 피(를) 말리다) ▌A: 내일이 합격자 발표지? 기분 어때?＝*Tomorrow they announce who they* *admitted, right? How do you feel?* B: **피가 마르는** 기분이에요. = *My blood is running cold.*

피눈물(을) 흘리다 [Lit. to shed tears of blood] IDIOM 몹시 슬퍼하거나 억울해하다 = to be very sad or indignant ▌A: 가슴 아픈 얘기입니다만, 작년에 아드님이 교통사고로 유명을 달리했다고 들었습니다. = *I'm so sorry to bring it up, but I heard that your son passed away in a car accident last year.* B: 네. 한동안은 매일 밤 **피눈물을 흘렸지요.** = *I wept for him every night for a long time.*

피는 물보다 진하다 [Lit. Blood is thicker than water.] PROVERB 혈육의 정은 다른 무엇보다 깊다는 말 = stresses that relationship among kin is stronger than all else (*equiv.* Blood is thicker than water.) ▌A: 이산가족들이 만나 우는 걸 보니 나도 눈물이 나려 하네. = *Watching the reunions of families split across the two Koreas always makes me tear up.* B: 역시 **피는 물보다 진한** 거군. = *Blood really is thicker than water.*

피도 눈물도 없다 [Lit. to have neither blood nor tears] IDIOM 인정이 없다 = to lack human compassion (*equiv.* to be coldblooded / to be coldhearted) ▌A: 기한을 며칠만 연기해 달라고 사정해 볼까? = *What about telling him about what happened and asking for an extension on the deadline for just a few days.* B: 소용없을걸. 그 사람은 **피도 눈물도 없는** 사람이야. = *There's no use. He's completely coldhearted.*

피땀(을) 흘리다 [Lit. to shed sweat of blood] IDIOM 온갖 정성을 쏟아 노력하다 = to pour one's greatest efforts into something (*equiv.* to put your blood, sweat and tears into something) ▌A: 평생 **피땀 흘려** 번 재산을 기부하시다니 대단하십니다. = *It's just astounding that you would donate the fortune that took a lifetime of blood, sweat and tears to build.* B: 아니에요. 저야 뭐 재산 물려줄 자식이 있는 것도 아니라서요. = *It's nothing really. I have no kids to hand it down to.*

피를 나누다 [Lit. to share blood] IDIOM 혈육의 관계가 있다 = to be of blood relation (*equiv.* to be kin / to be blood) ▌A: 자네와 자네 형은 **피를**

나눈 형제인데도 어쩌면 그렇게 다른가? = *You and your older brother are blood, but yet you're so different.* B: 형이랑 저는 어릴 때 떨어져 자랐거든요. = *We grew up apart. That's probably why.*

피(를) 말리다 [Lit. to dry blood] IDIOM 몹시 초조하게 만들다 = to make someone very nervous (*equiv.* to make someone's blood run cold *cf.* 피(가) 마르다) ▌A: 양 팀 모두 **피를 말리는** 승부군요. = *Both teams have their hopes pinned on victory here today.* B: 어느 팀이 지더라도 타격이 정말 크겠습니다. = *The losing team is going to take a major blow.*

피(를) 보다 [Lit. to see blood] IDIOM 1. 싸움으로 피를 흘리다 = to shed blood in a fight (*equiv.* to shed blood) ▌A: 오늘 너랑 나랑 남자답게 결판을 내자. = *Let's fight today like men: one on one.* B: 너는 꼭 **피를 봐야** 직성이 풀리겠냐? = *Is it the sight of blood that will finally satisfy you?* 2. 뜻밖에 망신을 당하거나 손해를 보다 = to endure an unexpected shaming or injury ▌A: 너 수업 시간에 까불다 반성문 써야 한다며? = *I heard you had to write an apology letter after talking back in class.* B: 어. 혀 한번 잘못 놀렸다가 **피 봤어.** = *Yep, I flapped my tongue a little too much and paid the price.*

피(를) 토하다 [Lit. to vomit blood] IDIOM 격렬하게 무엇이 잘못 되었다고 주장하다 = to vehemently denounce something one thinks is unjust (*equiv.* to be out for blood / to be on the war path) ▌A: 그나저나 이 일을 명호 씨가 알게 돼서 골치 아프게 생겼어. = *At any rate, Myeongho finding out about this complicates things immensely.* B: 자기는 이대로 넘어갈 수 없다면서 **피를 토하던데요.** = *He's on the war path.*

피부로 느끼다 [Lit. to feel something with one's skin] IDIOM 실제로 직접 느끼다 = to feel something directly (*equiv.* to experience something in the flesh / for something to hit home *cf.* 피부에 와 닿다) ▌A: 좀 있으면 추석인데 시장에 나가면 물가가 너무 비싸서 지갑을 열기가 두려워요. = *Chuseok is just around the corner but with the high prices of everything at the market, I'm afraid to even get out my wallet.* B: 물가가 얼마나 올랐는지 **피부로 느낄** 수가 있겠군요. = *Now your wallet is feeling just how* *much the prices have gone up.*

피부에 와 닿다 [Lit. for something to touch one's skin] IDIOM 실제로 직접 느껴지다 = for something to be felt directly (*cf.* 피부로 느끼다) ▌A: 뉴스를 보면 경제가 성장했다는데 저 같은 서민층은 그게 **피부에 와 닿지가** 않아요. = *On the news they say that the economy has grown, but for the common folk like me, it's hard to feel any difference.* B: 저는 오히려 전보다 살기가 더 힘들어진 느낌이에요. = *I feel like life has actually gotten a lot harder.*

***필름이 끊기다** [Lit. to have one's film cut off] IDIOM 술을 마시고 기억을 잃다 = to get drunk to the point of losing one's memory (*equiv.* to black out (from drinking too much) / pass out (drunk)) ▌A: 어제는 잘 들어가셨어요? = *Did you get home all right yesterday?* B: **필름이 끊겨서** 택시를 탄 것까지는 기억이 나는데, 그 다음부터는 기억이 안 나요. = *I blacked out. The last thing I remember is getting in the taxi. After that I don't remember anything.*

NOTE: 여기서 필름은 기억이나 의식을 의미한다.
"Film" in this case is a stand-in for memories or consciousness.

핑계 없는 무덤 없다 [Lit. There is no grave that doesn't have an excuse.] PROVERB 무슨 일이든지 핑계를 만들어 낼 수 있다는 말 = suggests that an excuse can be manufactured for anything (*equiv.* The path to hell is paved with good intentions.) ▌A: 당신 또 술이야? 제발 집에 있는 가족들 생각도 좀 해. = *Are you drinking again? Could you please think about the family that's waiting for you at home?* B: 다 우리 가족들 먹여살리려고 내가 마시는 거지, 내가 마시고 싶어 마시는 건 줄 알아? = *I'm out here drinking so I can keep a roof over your heads. Do you think I drink because I like it?* A: **핑계 없는 무덤 없다**더니 왜 가족 핑계를 대? = *The path to hell is paved with good intentions.*

NOTE: 사람은 누구나 죽고 죽음에 이르기까지의 과정에는 다 저마다의 사연이 있게 마련이다. 이처럼 누구에게나 사정이라는 게 있기 때문에 자칫 그것이 핑계가 될 수 있다. 구차한 핑계나 변명을 늘어놓는 사람에게 핀잔을 줄 때 쓰는 표현이다.

Everyone dies, and until the moment everyone dies they are have their reasons for living the way they did. Because everyone's life is a process, everyone has their own set of excuses. This expression depicts people who give flimsy excuses for their behavior.

ㅎ

하나를 보면 열을 안다 [Lit. Seeing one (means) knowing ten.] PROVERB
1. 어떤 대상의 일부만으로도 전체를 미루어 알 수 있다는 말 = describes how seeing just a bit of something is sometimes good enough to judge it all by (*equiv.* Seen one, you've seen 'em all.) ▌A: 너는 계집애가 빨래 개 놓은 모양이 이게 뭐니? 이래 가지고 시집이나 가겠니? = *Do you call this folding the laundry? How do you expect to find a husband if you do things like this?* B: 엄마, 빨래 개는 거랑 시집이랑 무슨 상관이야? = *Mom, what does folding the laundry have to do with me finding a husband?* A: **하나를 보면 열을 아는** 거야. = *It's obvious by just looking at you.* **2.** 학습 능력이 매우 뛰어나다 = to be a very astute learner ▌A: 우리 민정이 말이야, 천재 아닐까? 애가 **하나를 보면 열을 아는** 것 같아. = *Don't you think little Minjeong is a genius? If you teach her one thing, she figures the rest out herself.* B: 다 당신 착각이야. = *It's all just your imagination.*

하나만 알고 둘은 모른다 [Lit. to know one and not know two] PROVERB
사물을 전체적으로 두루 살피지 못하고 한쪽에서만 보는 어리석음을 가리키는 말 = describes the ignorance of only seeing one facet of a thing and not considering the whole (*equiv.* to not see the forest for the trees) ▌A: ➡ p.340 사흘이 멀다 하고 산을 깎고 강을 파내는 걸 보면 정말 걱정이야. = *It really concerns me how they are leveling the mountains and widening the rivers almost every day now.* B: 왜 아니겠어? 당장 눈앞의 이익에 눈이 멀어 ➡ p.149 **하나만 알고 둘은 모르는** 거지. = *Why wouldn't they? They only care about the benefits right in front of their noses and miss the forest for the trees.*

하나부터 열까지 [Lit. from one to ten] IDIOM 어떤 것이나 다 = whatever it is, all ▌A: 지수가 지금 나이가 몇인데 아직도 쫓아다니면서 뒤치다꺼리를 해? = *Jisoo is how old now? And you're still cleaning up after her like that?* B: 나이만 먹었지, 아직 애야. 내가 **하나부터 열까지** 챙기지 않으면 아무것도 못 해. = *Yeah, she's older, but she's still just a kid. If I don't get everything lined up for her, she can't do anything.*

***하늘과 땅 차이** [Lit. the difference between heaven and earth] IDIOM 매우 큰 차이 = an immense difference (*equiv.* (the difference between them is like) night and day) ▌A: 저 두 사람은 자매인데도 성격이 완전히 달라. = *Those two are sisters, but their personalities are completely different.* B: 맞아. 외모는 비슷한데 성격은 **하늘과 땅 차이야**. = *Yeah. They look similar, but their personalities are like night and day.*

하늘 높은 줄 모르다 [Lit. to not know that the sky is high] IDIOM **1.** 물가 따위가 매우 높이 올라가다 = for the price of things to rise greatly (*equiv.* for the price of things to go through the roof / to skyrocket) ▌A: 요즘 물가가 **하늘 높은 줄 모르고** 뛰어서 지갑 열기가 겁나. = *With the way the price of everything has been skyrocketing, I'm afraid to even get out my wallet.* B: 맞아. 만 원 가지고는 살 것도 없어. = *Yeah, 10,000 won doesn't buy a thing anymore.* **2.** 분수를 모르다 = to not know one's limitations (*equiv.* to not know one's place) ▌A: 저 친구, 아버지가 국회의원이라고 **하늘 높은 줄 모르고** 날뛰는 거 아냐? = *Don't you think that guy just wrecks havoc like that because his dad is in the National Assembly?* B: 안 그래도 목에 힘 주고 다닌다고 사람들이 수군수군대요. = *Yeah, now that you mention it, there have been murmurs about how he walks around with his nose in the air.*

하늘 보고 침 뱉기 [Lit. looking up at the sky and spitting] IDIOM 자기에게 해가 돌아올 짓 = acting in a self-injurious manner (*equiv.* to spit while lying down / to shoot yourself in the foot *syn.* 누워서 침 뱉기) ▌A: 저 녀석만 보면 속이 터져서 원. = *Whenever I look at that guy, I feel like I'm going to explode.* B: 그래 봤자 **하늘 보고 침 뱉기지**. = *What does that help? You're just hurting yourself.*

하늘에 맡기다 [Lit. to turn it over to the heavens] IDIOM 일의 결과를 운명에 맡기다 = to leave the results up to fate (*equiv.* to leave it up to the heavens / to place something in God's hands) ▌A: 이 작품이 성공할 수 있을까요? = *Do you think this work will be a success?* B: 우리는 최선을 다했으니 이제 나머지는 **하늘에 맡깁시다**. = *We've done our best. Now it's in God's hands.*

하늘에서 떨어지다 [Lit. to fall from the sky] IDIOM 노력 없이 저절로 생기다 = for something to appear with no efforts of one's own (*equiv.* (for something) to fall in one's lap) ▌A: 성공의 비결이 있으신가요? = *Is there a secret to success?* B: 성공은 **하늘에서 뚝 떨어지는** 게 아닙니다. 오랜 시간 묵묵히 최선을 다하는 것밖에 방법이 없습니다. = *Success doesn't just fall in your lap. There's no other way except keeping your mouth shut and putting in years of hard work.*

하늘은 스스로 돕는 자를 돕는다 [Lit. Heaven helps those who help themselves.] PROVERB 다른 사람에게 의지하지 않고 스스로 노력해야 한다는 말 = emphasizes the importance of self-reliance and hard work (*equiv.* Heaven helps those who help themselves.) ▌A: 쉽게 돈 벌 수 있는 방법 없을까? = *Isn't there an easy way to earn money?* B: **하늘은 스스로 돕는 자를 돕는다는** 말도 몰라? 열심히 일해서 돈 벌 생각이나 해. = *Don't you know heaven helps those who help themselves? Why don't you start by working hard?*

NOTE: 영어 격언인 'Heaven helps those who help themselves.'에서 온 표현이다. 사실 이 표현은 관용적으로 쓰이기는 하지만 상당히 어색한 번역인데, '하늘은 스스로 노력하는 자를 돕는다'가 정확한 의미라 하겠다. This expression comes from the saying "Heaven helps those who help themselves." This rather awkward translation is in wide use, but a more accurate translation might be 하늘은 스스로 노력하는 자를 돕는다.

하늘을 봐야 별을 딴다 [Lit. You have to look at the sky to pluck a star.] PROVERB 어떤 성과를 거두려면 노력과 준비가 있어야 한다는 말 = emphasizes the role of effort and preparation in success ▌A: 둘째는 가질

계획 없어? = *Do you have plans for a second child?* B: **하늘을 봐야 별을 따지.** 요즘 신랑이 회사에서 바빠서 얼굴 보기도 힘들어. = *We haven't yet had the time to get to work on that. I barely have the time to even see my husband he's so busy at work these days.*

NOTE: 한국에서는 아이가 없는 부부에게 아이를 갖지 않느냐고 묻는 것이 관례상 실례가 아니다. 이런 경우에 여자가 '남편과 잠자리를 할 시간이나 기회조차 없어서 아이가 생기지 않는다'라는 의미를 희화적으로 전달하고자 할 때 흔히 이 표현이 쓰인다.
Asking a couple without children if they're going to have children isn't conventionally considered rude in Korea. Fielding such a question, women often use this expression to mean that haven't even had time to sleep together yet, or for whatever reason, still haven't had the opportunity.

*****하늘의 별 따기** [Lit. plucking a star from the sky] PROVERB 매우 어려운 것 = something very difficult (*equiv.* (something that is) next to impossible *ant.* 식은 죽 먹기, 누워서 떡 먹기, 땅 짚고 헤엄치기) ▎A: 직장은 구했어? = *Have you been able to find a job?* B: 응, 다음 주부터 출근이야. = *Yeah, I start next week.* A: 와, 잘됐다! 요즘 직장 구하기가 **하늘의 별 따기**인데. = *Wow, that's great. It's next to impossible to find a job these days.*

하늘이 노랗다 [Lit. The sky is yellow.] IDIOM 1. 기운이 없다 = to have no energy ▎A: 왜 그렇게 힘도 없어 보이고, 얼굴색이 안 좋아? = *Why do you look so lethargic and pale?* B: 요즘에 다이어트 한다고 물만 먹었더니 **하늘이 노래**. = *I've been trying to lose weight and so I've only been drinking water and now I have no energy at all.* 2. 충격을 받아 어찌할 바를 모르다 = to be so shocked that one doesn't know what to do (*syn.* 눈앞이 캄캄하다, 눈앞이 깜깜하다) ▎A: 그동안 고생 많았어. 힘들었지? = *You've had a hard time, haven't you?* B: 응, 지금에서야 하는 얘기지만 처음에 공부를 1년 더 해야 한다고 생각하니 **하늘이 노랗더라**. = *Yeah. Now I can talk about it, but at first when I thought about having to study another year, I was utterly dumbstruck.*

하늘이 두 쪽(이) 나도 [Lit. even if the sky splits in half] IDIOM 어떤 일이 있어도 = no matter what happens (*equiv.* even if the sky falls / even if it's the last thing I do *syn.* 세상없어도, 죽었다 깨어나도) ▌A: 수진아, 이리 좀 와 봐라. = *Sujin, come here.* B: 엄마, 나 지금 바빠. = *Mom, I'm busy now.* A: 오늘은 하늘이 두 쪽이 나도 너랑 얘기 좀 해야겠다. = *I'm going to talk to you today even if it's the last thing I do.*

하늘이 무너져도 솟아날 구멍이 있다 [Lit. Even if the sky falls, there's a hole to poke through.] PROVERB 아주 어려운 상황에서도 살아 나갈 방법이 있다는 말 = describes how even in the most dire circumstances there is a means of escape (*equiv.* There's always a way out. *syn.* 죽으라는 법은 없다) ▌A: 정말 이제 모든 게 끝인가 봐. = *It looks like it's really all over now.* B: 하늘이 무너져도 솟아날 구멍이 있다잖아. 포기하지 마. = *Even when the world seems like it's collapsing all around you, there is always a way out. Don't give up.*

하늘이 무너지다 [Lit. for the sky to fall] IDIOM 극심한 슬픔이나 절망감을 느끼다 = to feel a profound sadness or despair (*equiv.* for things to go terribly wrong / (for it to be) the end of the world *syn.* 억장이 무너지다) ▌A: 어머님이 돌아가셨을 때 기분이 어땠어요? = *How do you feel when your mother died?* B: 하늘이 무너지는 것 같았어요. = *It was as if the world had come to an end.*

하던 짓도 멍석 펴놓으면 안 한다 [Lit. to not do even things one had done once the mat is spread out] PROVERB 보통 때는 시키지 않아도 잘하던 일을 막상 하라고 시키면 안 한다는 말 = describes how people suddenly are unable to do the things they normally do once someone has asked them to do it (*equiv.* not being able to do something when someone puts you on the spot / to have performance anxiety *cf.* 멍석(을) 펴다) ▌A: 예림아, 할머니 오셨는데 오랜만에 어린이집에서 배운 동요 한번 불러 봐. = *Yerim, since Grandma's finally here again, why don't you sing her a song that you learned at preschool.* B: 싫어. 부끄럽단 말이야. = *No. I'm too embarrassed.* A: 쟤는 평소에는 잘하다가 오늘따라 왜 이럴까. 하던 짓도 멍석 펴놓으면 안 한다니까. = *She normally sings all the* *time. I wonder why she's being like this today. I guess that's just what happens when you put her on the spot.*

NOTE: See the note on 멍석(을) 깔다.

하루가 멀다 하고 [Lit. as if one thinks that one day is far off] IDIOM 자주＝often (*syn.* 사흘이 멀다 하고, 하루에도 열두 번) ▌A: 또 왜 그래?＝*Now what's wrong?* B: 남편이랑 싸웠어.＝*I fought with my husband.* A: 어떻게 된 게 너희 부부는 **하루가 멀다 하고** 싸우니?＝*How is it that you two can't even go a day without fighting?*

하루라도 책을 읽지 않으면 입안에 가시가 돋는다 [Lit. Going even a day without reading will make thorns poke out of your mouth.] QUOTE 평소에 독서를 꾸준히 해야 한다는 말＝used to encourage regular reading ▌A: 경희야, 텔레비전 그만 보고 책 좀 읽어라.＝*Gyeonghee, turn off the TV and read for a change.* B: 엄마, 책 재미없어요.＝*Books are boring, Mom.* A: 너는 학교에서 **하루라도 책을 읽지 않으면 입안에 가시가 돋는다는** 말도 안 배웠니?＝*Didn't they teach you at school that you shouldn't even go a day without reading?*

NOTE: 안중근 의사가 한 말이다. 독서를 하지 않으면 마음이 거칠어져 남에게 상처를 주는 말을 쉽게 내뱉게 된다는 의미이다.
This is a quote from the patriot Ahn Junggeun. His words can be interpreted to mean that without books, one's heart hardens and it is easy to say things that hurt others.

하루에도 열두 번 [Lit. twelve times in even a day] IDIOM 매우 자주＝very often (*syn.* 하루가 멀다 하고, 사흘이 멀다 하고) ▌A: 아 이놈의 회사 때려치우고 싶은 생각이 **하루에도 열두 번씩** 들어요.＝*Ah, I swear I think of quitting this darn company 12 times a day.* B: 사람이 그렇게 우유부단해서 되겠어? 얼른 사직서 내.＝*Stop riding the fence then and write a letter of resignation.*
➡ p.438

하룻강아지 범 무서운 줄 모른다 [Lit. A day-old puppy doesn't know

to fear a tiger.] PROVERB 철없이 함부로 덤비는 경우를 이르는 말 = describes thoughtless attacks of the immature on more powerful foes ▌A: 하룻강아지 범 무서운 줄 모른다더니, 자네 지금 이 분이 누구인 줄 알고 그러는 건가? = *You're too dumb to know who you're messing with. Do you have any idea who that man is?* B: 왜요? 이 분이 사장이라도 됩니까? = *Who is he? Is he the new boss?* A: 바로 이 분이 새로 오신 사장님이네. = *Yes, this gentleman is your new boss.* B: 죄송합니다. = *I'm so very sorry.*

하룻밤에 만리장성을 쌓다 [Lit. to build the Great Wall of China in one night] IDIOM 성관계를 맺다 = to have sexual relations (*syn.* 살을 섞다, 몸을 섞다, 떡(을) 치다) ▌A: 소영이가 남자 친구랑 단둘이 여행을 가겠대요. = *Soyeong says she and her boyfriend are going to go on a trip by themselves.* B: 설마 무슨 일이야 있겠어요? = *Well, I'm sure nothing's going to happen.* A: 무슨 말이에요. **하룻밤에도 만리장성을 쌓는** 게 남녀 사이예요. = *What do you mean? Things always happen between men and women.*

NOTE: 이 표현의 유래에 대해 다음과 같은 설이 있다. 한 남자가 만리장성을 쌓는 공사에 강제로 차출되었다. 이 공사는 언제 끝이 날지 알 수 없는 데다가 아주 위험해서 목숨을 잃는 경우도 많았다. 이를 걱정한 그 남자의 아내는 평소 자신을 흠모하던 다른 남자와 하룻밤을 보내는 조건으로 남편을 대신해 노역에 참여하도록 했다. 한 번의 정사와 만리장성 쌓는 일을 맞바꾼 것이다.
The Great Wall of China is a 2,400-kilometer wall that was built by successive generations of Chinese kings to ensure the defense of the country. The story of the origin of this phrase is as follows. A certain man was forced to participate in the construction of the wall. Many men lost their lives while working on the wall and it was impossible to know how much longer it would take to complete. Not wanting to lose her husband, the woman spent a night with a man who had long adored her and forced him to go off to work on the wall in her husband's stead. A single night with her was paid for with years of toil at the wall. Ever since, the expression "to build the Great Wall" or 만리장성을 쌓다, has been used as a euphemism for sexual relations.

학수고대하다 [Lit. 鶴crane + 首head + 苦bitter + 待wait + 하다verbal suffix ⟶ to wait desperately with one's head sticking out like a crane] CHINESE-DERIVATION 몹시 기다리다 = to wait desperately (*syn.* 목을 길게 빼고 기다리다) ▌A: 아드님이 시험에 붙었다고요? 축하드립니다. = *I heard your son passed the test. Congratulations.* B: 네, 감사합니다. = *Yes, thank you.* A: **학수고대하던** 합격 소식을 들으셨으니 얼마나 기쁘세요. = *The news of his success must have been like music to your ears.*

한 ～ 하다 [Lit. to be one ...] IDIOM ～이 매우 뛰어나다 = to be a very amazing ... (*equiv.* to be quite the ...) ▌A: 사진 속 이 훤칠한 청년이 누구야? = *And who's this strapping lad in the picture?* B: 내 아들이야. = *That's my son.* A: 와, 아들이 **한 인물 하는구나**. = *He looks like he's quite the guy.*

NOTE: 여러 사람이 모여 일을 할 때 자신에게 주어진 역할을 충실히 해내면 '한몫했다'라고 얘기한다. '한 무엇무엇 하다'라는 표현은 이 말에서 발전한 어법이 아닌가 싶다. 무엇무엇 자리에는 어떤 명사도 쓰일 수 있지만, '한 인물 하다'라는 말이 가장 보편적으로 많이 쓰인다.

When a group handles a task and everyone does their job well, the phrase 한몫했다 (to do one's part), is often used. This pattern, 한 무엇무엇 하다, most likely stems from this method of expression. Any noun can be inserted in this phrase, but the most common form is 한 인물 하다.

한가닥 하다 IDIOM '한가락 하다'의 잘못된 말 = an incorrect form of 한가락 하다

한가락 하다 [Lit. to sing a tune] IDIOM (속된 말로) 어떤 방면에 솜씨가 있다 = (slang) to have talent in a certain area ▌A: 너 학교 끝나고 이번에 전학 온 애랑 싸우기로 했다며? 걔 주먹으로 **한가락 했다고** 하던데. = *I hear you're going to fight the new kid after school gets out today. That guy's supposedly a good fighter.* B: 야, 왕년에 주먹 좀 안 써 본 사람이 어디 있냐? = *Hey, who out there hasn't kicked some butt in their day?*

NOTE: 한가락의 본래 의미는 노래 한 곡이다. 그러나 앞에서 나온 '한 무 엇무엇 하다'의 용법과 연관지어 이해하면 '한가락 하다'는 '노래를 잘 하다'라는 의미로 이해할 수 있다. 지금은 노래뿐 아니라 어떤 방면에 뛰어난 사람에게 이 말을 쓴다.
한가락 originally means "a song." But applying the form from the previous expression, this phrase can be understood to mean "He sings quite a song." This phrase is not just used about singing, however, and can describe excellence in any category.

한 귀로 듣고 한 귀로 흘리다 [Lit. to listen with one ear, and spill with the other] PROVERB 주의 깊게 듣지 않다 = to not pay much attention (*equiv.* to go in one ear and out the other) ▌A: 인표야, 엄마 말 **한 귀로 듣고 한 귀로 흘리지** 마라. = *Inpyo, don't just let what I'm saying go in one ear and out the other.* B: 네, 알았어요. 엄마 시키는 대로 할게요. = *All right, I won't. I'll do what you asked me to do.*

한눈(을)팔다 [Lit. to sell one eye] IDIOM **1.** 해야 할 일이 아닌 다른 일에 몰두하다 = to be distracted by something other than what one is supposed to be doing (*equiv.* to let one's eyes wander) ▌A: 학원 끝나면 **한눈팔지** 말고 곧장 집으로 오너라. = *Don't get distracted on the way home from your after-school classes. Come straight home.* B: 네. 걱정 마세요, 아빠. 오락실 이제 안 갈게요. = *OK, Dad. Don't worry. I won't go to the arcade anymore.* **2.** 배우자나 사귀는 사람이 아닌 이성에 마음을 빼앗기다 = to fall for someone other than the person you're seeing or your spouse (*equiv.* to cheat / to have a wandering eye *syn.* 바람(을)피우다) ▌A: **한눈팔면** 죽어, 알지? = *You know you're dead if you cheat, right?* B: 알아. 너나 딴 남자한테 눈길 주지 마. = *Yep. And don't you dare look at another guy either.*

한 배를 타다 [Lit. to be taking the same boat] IDIOM 운명을 같이하다 = to have the same fate (*equiv.* to be in the same boat / to sink or swim together) ▌A: 자, 우리 한번 잘해 봅시다. = *All right everyone, let's do our best.* B: 네. 이제 양사는 **한 배를 탄** 거나 마찬가지니까요. = *Sounds good. Now both companies share the same fate, whatever that may be.*

NOTE: 배에 타고 있는 사람들은 저마다 목적지는 다를 수 있어도 무사히 육지에 도착하고자 하는 근본 목적은 같다. 또한 바다 위의 배는 늘 위험에 노출되어 있다는 점에서 이 표현은 생사의 운명을 같이한다는 의미로 자주 쓰인다.

Although passengers on a boat may all have different final destinations, their desire to arrive safely on land is the same. As a boat is always exposed to danger on the seas, this expression is also used to mean that two parties will live or die together.

한 번만 더 들으면 백 번이다 [Lit. If I hear it one more time, that will be 100 times.] IDIOM 어떤 얘기를 이미 여러 차례 들어 지겹다 = to hear something countless times and be sick of hearing it (*equiv.* You've already said that a million times. / I'm sick of hearing that. *cf.* 귀에 못이 박히다) █ A: 경수야, 자기 전에 이 닦는 거 알지? = *Gyeongsu, you know you have to brush your teeth before you go to bed, right?* B: 엄마, **한 번만 더 들으면 백 번째예요**. = *Mom, you've already told me that a hundred times.*

한 번 실수는 병가의 상사다 [Lit. One mistake is commonplace for commander] PROVERB 일을 하다 보면 실수를 할 수 있다는 말 = describes how after working at something for a while, it is only normal to make mistakes █ A: 왜 그리 풀이 죽은 얼굴을 하고 있어? = *Why do you look so defeated?* B: 내가 실수를 하는 바람에 우리 팀이 경기에서 졌어. = *My team lost the match because of my mistake.* A: **한 번 실수는 병가의 상사라잖아**. 기운 내. = *Everybody makes mistakes. Cheer up.*

NOTE: 병가(兵家)는 군대의 지휘관을 말하고 상사(常事)는 늘 있는 일이라는 뜻이다. 전투에서의 패배나 실패는 흔히 있을 수 있는 일이다. 일상에서도 누구나 실수를 할 수 있기 대문에 크게 낙담할 필요가 없다는 뜻이다.

병가 is a word for a commander in the military and the word 상사 means something that happens every day. There are victories and defeats in war. Just as even the greatest generals have at times been bested on the battlefield, everyone is allowed to make a mistake or two from time to time.

한솥밥(을) 먹다 [Lit. to eat rice from the same pot] IDIOM 동일한 조직이나 직종에 속하다 = to be part of the same organization or work in the same field (*equiv.* We drink from the same well.) ▮A: 소개해 드릴게요. 이쪽은 저랑 옛날에 같은 팀에서 **한솥밥 먹던** 고영민입니다. = *I'll introduce you. This is Go Yeongmin, a brother in arms from way back when we were on the same team.* B: 아, 말씀 많이 들었습니다. 안녕하세요? = *Ah, I've heard so much about you. How do you do?*

한술 더 뜨다 [Lit. to scoop up one more bite] IDIOM 이미 상황이 좋지 않은데 거기에 상황을 더 나쁘게 만드는 행동을 하다 = to do something that worsens an already bad situation (*equiv.* to make a bad situation worse / to take it (a bad situation) to a new level) ▮A: 요즘 보면 팀장보다 김 과장이 더 얄미워. = *Recently Mr. Kim has been getting under my skin even more than our team leader.* B: 맞아. 힘든 일은 다 우리한테 시키고. 팀장보다 **한술 더 뜬다니까**. = *Yeah. He always just gives us the hard work ... He's taking it to a whole new level.*

***한 우물(을) 파다** [Lit. to dig one well] IDIOM 한 가지 일에만 집중하다 = to focus on one pursuit (*equiv.* to not spread oneself to thin) ▮A: 지금 하는 일은 나랑은 안 맞는 거 같아. 아무래도 다른 일을 찾아봐야 할까 봐. = *The work I'm doing now isn't a good fit. I think I'll have to find another job.* B: 조금만 참아 봐. **한 우물을 파야** 물이 나오는 법이야. = *Just hold on a little longer. You've got to stick with one thing for a while if you want to see any kind of success.*

한줌(의) 재가 되다 IDIOM = 한줌(의) 흙이 되다

한줌(의) 흙이 되다 [Lit. to become a handful of dirt] IDIOM '죽다'를 완곡하게 이르는 말 = a euphemism for "to die" (*syn.* 한줌(의) 재가 되다) ▮A: 오늘은 불 속에서 수십 명의 생명을 구하고 자신은 **한줌 흙이 된** 소방관 고 김명철 씨의 1주기가 되는 날입니다. = *It has now been a year since the death of firefighter Kim Myeongcheol, who gave his own life to rescue scores of others from a blazing inferno.* B: 고인의 숭고한 정신을 되새겨 보는 시간을 갖겠습니다. = *Let's take this time to meditate on* *this great man's sacrifice.*

NOTE: See the note on 세상(을) 뜨다.

할 일이 태산이다 [Lit. to have too much to do] IDIOM 해야 할 일이 매우 많다 = to have an immense amount of things to do ▌A: 우리 주말에 놀러 갈까? = *Want to hang out this weekend?* B: 지금 **할 일이 태산인데** 놀러는 무슨. = *I'm completely maxed out with work right now. There's no way I can hang out.*

함흥차사 [Lit. 咸all + 興encourage + 差send + 使dispatch → a messenger sent to Hamheung] CHINESE-DERIVATION 심부름을 보낸 사람이 돌아오지 않거나 소식이 없을 때 쓰는 말 = describes someone who never returns after being sent on an errand (*equiv.* to never be heard from again) ▌A: 은행 간 김 대리는 아직 안 왔어? 벌써 두 시간이 넘었잖아. = *Mr. Kim's still not back from the bank yet? It's already been more than two hours.* B: 원래 김 대리가 어디 가면 **함흥차사**잖아요. = *That's kind of his M.O.*

NOTE: 조선을 세운 태조 이성계는 왕위 계승을 두고 다투는 아들들에게 실망하여 고향인 함흥으로 가 버렸다. 새로 왕이 된 태종은 함흥으로 신하를 보내 아버지를 모셔 오려 했지만, 화가 풀리지 않은 이성계는 그들을 모두 죽이거나 가두어 돌려보내지 않았다. 그때부터 어디론가 떠난 사람이 돌아오지 않을 때 함흥차사라는 말을 하게 되었다.
During the Joseon Dynasty, there was a quarrel over succession between princes. The king and founder of Joseon was disappointed in his sons for behaving this way and he installed one as king and returned to his hometown or Hamheung. The son wished to apologize to his father for what had happened and dispatched a messenger to bring him back to the capital. The father was still not ready to make nice with his disappointment of a son and instead killed or imprisoned the messengers. Ever since, someone who leaves on an errand never to be heard from again is called a 함흥차사.

해가 서쪽에서 뜨겠다 [Lit. The sun will rise in the west.] IDIOM 전혀 예상하지 못한 일이 일어났을 때 쓰는 말 = used when something completely unanticipated occurs (*equiv.* when pigs fly / when hell freezes over) ▌A: 오늘 우리 백화점에 쇼핑하러 갈까?=*How about going shopping at a department store today?* B: 당신이 백화점에 간다고? 우와, **해가 서쪽에서 뜨겠네!**=*You, at a department store? Wow, does this mean hell has frozen over?*

해괴망측하다 [Lit. 駭shock + 怪strange + 罔no + 測measure + 하다 adjectival suffix] CHINESE-DERIVATION 대단히 괴상하고 보기에 낯뜨겁다= to be queer and shocking ▌A: 옛날에는 남자와 여자가 길거리에서 손을 잡고 다니는 건 상상할 수도 없었어요.=*It was unimaginable for a man and woman to walk along holding hands in the old days.* B: 그때 기준으로 보면 **해괴망측한** 일이겠죠.=*In those days it must've been beyond belief.*

해괴망칙하다 CHINESE-DERIVATION '해괴망측하다'의 잘못된 말=an incorrect form of 해괴망측하다

햇빛을 보다 [Lit. to look at the sun's rays] IDIOM 그동안 잘 알려져 있지 않던 것이 세상에 알려지다=for something previously unknown to become well known to the world (*equiv.* to see the light of day *syn.* 빛을 보다) ▌A: 이번 영화가 촬영이 끝난 지 3년이 넘은 작품이라고 들었습니다. 소감이 어떠세요?=*I heard that this movie actually finished shooting more than three years ago. How did you think it was?* B: 뒤늦게 **햇빛을 보게** 되어서 말할 수 없이 기쁩니다.=*I'm just overjoyed that it finally saw the light of day.*

허리가 휘다 [Lit. for one's waist to be crooked] IDIOM 육체적으로나 금전적으로 몹시 어려운 일을 하느라 힘이 부치다=to exhaust all one's energy after undergoing financial or physical hardships (*equiv.* to break one's back (working hard) / to be hunched over from overwork *syn.* 등이 휘다) ▌A: 요즘 같은 세상에 아이를 넷씩이나 어떻게 키우세요?=*How do you manage to raise four kids in today's world?* B: 아이들 분유 값 대느라 **허리가 휠** 지경이에요.=*I'm breaking my back just to pay for their formula.*

허리띠(를) 졸라매다 [Lit. to tighten one's belt] IDIOM 검소한 생활을 하다 = to live frugally (*equiv.* to tighten one's belt) █ A: 요즘같이 힘들 때는 **허리띠를 졸라매지** 않으면 버틸 수가 없어요. = *In the hard economic times like these days, we can't survive unless we live frugally.* B: 맞아요. 저희 집도 지난 달부터 생활비를 줄였어요. = *You're right. We've cut down our living expenses over the last month.*

허심탄회하다 [Lit. 虛empty + 心heart + 坦generous + 懷mind + 하다 adjectival suffix] CHINESE-DERIVATION 솔직하게 마음속에 있는 생각을 표현하다 = to candidly express one's innermost feelings (*equiv.* to open up to someone) █ A: 우리 **허심탄회하게** 얘기 좀 하자. = *Let's just open up to each other about everything.* B: 그래. 나도 너한테 할 말 많아. = *All right. I've got a lot to say to you too.*

허파에 바람(이) 들다 [Lit. for wind to go in one's lungs] IDIOM **1.** 지나치게 웃어 대다 = to laugh too much █ A: 야가 **허파에 바람이 들었나**, 왜 이렇게 웃어 대? = *Hey Mr. Gigglebox, what's so funny?* B: 텔레비전의 코미디 프로가 너무 웃겨서요. = *This comedy show on TV is just so funny.* **2.** 마음이 들뜨다 = to be in high spirits (*syn.* 바람(이) 들다) █ A: 지선이 어디 갔어? = *Where did Jiseon go?* B: 놀러 나가서 아직 안 들어왔어. = *She went out to play and still isn't back.* A: 요 녀석, 방학 됐다고 **허파에 바람이 잔뜩 들어서** 맨날 늦게 들어오네. = *That little whippersnapper—ever since her vacation started, she's gotten home late every night.*

NOTE: 실제로 허파에 바람이 들어가는 병이 있는데 기흉이 그것이다. 그러나 기흉에 걸린다고 이유 없이 웃게 되는 것은 아니다. 단지, 허파가 호흡기관이므로 숨이 넘어갈 듯이 웃는 사람을 보며 호흡에 문제가 생긴 것 아니냐는 우스개소리가 관용 표현이 된 것이 아닌가 싶다.
Actually having air in the lung wall is a disease called pneumothorax. But this is not to say that if one contracts this disease they laugh without reason. This expression simply means that one is laughing to the point of collapse, and laughingly suggests that maybe one has caught this disease.

헛물(을)켜다 [Lit. to pretend to drink water] IDIOM 애쓴 보람이 없이 헛수고가 되다＝for one's great expectations and exertions to be for naught (*equiv.* to waste your time (pursuing something that will never happen)) █ A: 이번에 부산 내려 간 일은 잘됐어?＝*Did things go well out in Busan?* B: 아니요. 만나기로 한 사람한테 갑자기 딴 일이 생겨서 내려가자마자 **헛물만 켜고** 다시 올라왔어요.＝*No, the guy I was supposed to meet suddenly had something come up, so it was all a big waste of my time.*

혀를 내두르다 [Lit. to swing one's tongue around] IDIOM 몹시 놀라 말을 못하다＝to be astonished to the point of losing one's powers of speech (*equiv.* to be dumbstruck / to have one's jaw wide open) █ A: 범인이 정말 대담한 놈이군요.＝*The culprit is one daring fellow.* B: 범행의 대담성이 저희 경찰들도 **혀를 내두를** 정도였습니다.＝*The way he brazenly carried out his criminal activities was even enough to have us police dumbstruck.*

혀(를) 놀리다 IDIOM＝입(을) 놀리다

혀를 차다 [Lit. to slap one's tongue] IDIOM 마음에 들지 않는다는 표현을 하다＝to express one's dislike of something (*equiv.* to smack one's tongue (in disgust)) █ A: 지금은 대한민국 최고의 작곡가가 되었지만 어릴 때는 문제아였다고 들었는데요.＝*Now you've become Korea's greatest composer but I heard when you were young you were a real problem child.* B: 네. 동네 어른들이 다 저만 보면 **혀를 찰** 정도였지요.＝*Yeah, so much so that the adults in the neighborhood would say, "tsk, tsk" whenever I walked by.*

혈안이 되다 [Lit. for one's eyes to become bloodshot] IDIOM 이익을 챙기거나 무엇을 경계하느라 집중하고 있는 모습을 묘사한 말＝describes the image of someone intently guarding a place or out to get their share of profits (*syn.* 눈이 벌겋다) █ A: 범인은 언제쯤 잡힐까? 불안해서 못 살겠어.＝*When do you think they'll catch the criminal? I can't live on edge like this.* B: 글쎄. 경찰이 범인을 잡으려고 **혈안이 돼** 있다

고 하니까 곧 잡히겠지. = *Well, the police are burning the midnight oil working the case, so I'm sure he'll be apprehended soon.*

혈혈단신 [Lit. 孑lonely + 孑lonely + 單single + 身body] CHINESE-DERIVATION 의지할 데 없이 외로운 사람이나 그런 처지 = a person who has no one to turn to, or that circumstance itself ▌ A: 남들보다 한참 늦게 결혼하는 소감이 어때? = *How does it feel to be getting married so much later than everyone else?* B: 40 평생 **혈혈단신**으로 살아왔는데 이제 둘이서 알콩달콩 살아야죠. = *If spent my first 40 years without a soul I could rely on. Now I plan to live the rest of it in loving harmony with my wife.*

형만 한 아우 없다 [Lit. There is no younger brother as good as an older brother.] PROVERB 나이가 많은 형이 동생보다는 아무래도 모든 면에서 낫다는 말 = suggests that an older brother is better than a younger one in every way ▌ A: 지호야, 너는 왜 동생이 너한테 버릇 없이 대해도 다 참고 받아 주니? = *Jiho, why do you put up with your brother even though he is rude to you?* B: 지민이는 아직 어리잖아요. 마냥 귀여운 걸요. = *Jimin is still young. He just looks cute to me.* A: 역시 **형만 한 아우 없군**. = *That's why they say an older brother is always best.*

호랑이는 죽어서 가죽을 남기고 사람은 죽어서 이름을 남긴다 [Lit. When a tiger dies, it leaves behind its coat. When a person dies, they leave behind their name.] PROVERB 사람은 살아 있을 때 훌륭한 일을 하여 죽고 나서 사람들이 이름을 기억할 수 있도록 해야 한다는 말 = emphasizes the importance of living in a way that ensures people will know your name even after you're gone (*equiv.* Let your name echo throughout history.) ▌ A: 한국어 책을 쓰시는 이유가 뭔가요? = *Why is it that you write books about the Korean language?* B: **호랑이는 죽어서 가죽을 남기고 사람은 죽어서 이름을 남긴다**고 하잖아요. 뭔가 보람된 일을 하고 싶습니다. = *I hope to leave something behind, long after I'm dead and gone. I've always wanted to do something rewarding.*

호랑이 담배 피우던 시절 [Lit. the days when tigers smoked cigarettes] IDIOM 아주 오래 전 = a long time ago (*equiv.* once upon a time / a million years ago) ▌A: 내가 어렸을 때는 텔레비전이 있는 집이 마을에 한 두 집밖에 없었다. = *When I was a boy, only a couple of people in the neighborhood even had TVs.* B: 아빠, 그건 **호랑이 담배 피우던 시절** 얘기잖아요. = *Dad, that was like a million years ago.*

NOTE: 한국에 담배가 들어온 것은 17세기 초로 알려져 있다. 처음에는 나이와 신분에 관계없이 누구나 즐길 수 있었지만 시간이 갈수록 나이 어린 사람이나 신분이 낮은 사람은 제한을 받게 되었다. 호랑이는 전통적으로 서민들에게 가장 친숙하게 여겨지던 동물이었는데, 호랑이가 담배를 피운다는 것은 사실 일반 서민들이 자유롭게 담배를 피운다는 것을 의미한다. 자유로웠던 과거를 그리워하며 만든 표현이 아닌가 싶다. It is understood that cigarettes were first introduced to Korea in the early 17th century. At first, smoking was a privilige afforded to all classes, but in time, tobacco was restricted from use by the youth and those of low status. The tiger is traditionally the animal that is most familiar to the commoners, and this phrase, therefore, means the days when commonfolk could smoke. It most likely was born out of a longing for the era when not just the genteel classes could partake in the pleasures of tobacco.

호랑이도 제 말 하면 온다 [Lit. Even tigers come when people talk about them.] PROVERB 다른 사람에 관한 이야기를 하고 있는 도중에 그 사람이 나타났을 때 쓰는 말 = used when you are discussing someone and that person suddenly shows up (*equiv.* speak of the devil *syn.* 양반은 못 된다) ▌A: 다들 여기 모여서 뭐 해? = *What are you guys doing here all huddled up like that?* B: **호랑이도 제 말 하면 온다**더니 너 마침 잘 왔다. = *Wow, speak of the devil! You got here just in time.*

호랑이 새끼를 키우다 [Lit. to raise a tiger cub] IDIOM 장차 자신에게 해가 되거나 적수가 될 사람을 가르치고 보살피다 = to look after or teach someone who is likely to eventually pose a threat to you ▌A: 뉴스 봤어? 자기 양부모를 살해한 남자 얘기 말이야. = *Did you see the news about the guy who killed his adoptive parents?* B: **호랑이 새끼를 키운** 셈이네. = *Wow, talk about living under the same roof as your eventual killer.*

호랑이에게 물려 가도 정신만 차리면 산다 [Lit. Even if you are bitten and carried off by a tiger, you'll live if you just keep your wits' about you.] PROVERB 아무리 위급한 상황에 놓이더라도 정신을 차리면 위기를 벗어날 수 있다는 말 = suggests that no matter how grave the situation, one can evade danger if one just remains calm █ A: 갈수록 태산이라더니 날마다 새로운 문제가 터져서 정신이 없어요. = *My problems are just adding up by the day. I'm at my wits' end right now.* B: 이런 때일수록 정신 바짝 차려야 한다. 호랑이에게 물려 가도 정신만 차리면 산다 잖아. = *This is exactly the time when you need to keep your wits about you. If you just stay calm, you can think your way out of any disaster.*

호미로 막을 것을 가래로 막는다 [Lit. to block something with a shovel that should be blocked with a hoe] PROVERB 작은 힘을 들여서 해결할 수 있는 일을 방치했다가 나중에 큰 힘을 들여야 하는 경우를 가리키는 말 = describes a situation in which an easily remedied problem is left till it becomes almost insurmountable (*equiv.* A stitch in time saves nine.) █ A: 왜 그래? 이 아파? = *What's wrong? Do your teeth hurt?* B: 며칠 전부터 이가 시려요. = *My teeth have been aching for the last few days.* A: 얼른 병원 가 봐라. 호미로 막을 것을 가래로 막지 말고. = *You'd better get to the dentist's. If you just ignore it, it could get a lot worse.*

호박씨(를) 까다 IDIOM = 뒤로 호박씨(를) 까다

호박이 넝쿨째 굴러 들어오다 [Lit. for pumpkins still on the vine to come on in] PROVERB 뜻밖에 좋은 물건을 얻다 = to receive something good that one had not expected (*equiv.* to get a windfall *cf.* 굴러 온 호박) █ A: 어디서 저렇게 노래 잘하는 아이를 찾으셨습니까? = *Where did you find a kid that good at singing?* B: 오디션 공고를 보고 찾아왔더군요. = *He saw the ad for the open auditions and just came on in.* A: 호박이 넝쿨째 굴러 들어온 셈이군요. = *Wow, so he just fell right into you lap then!*

호시탐탐 [Lit. 虎tiger + 視see + 眈stare + 眈stare → A tiger stares at its prey.] CHINESE-DERIVATION 남의 것을 빼앗기 위해 기회를 노리는 모양 =

the image of someone stalking another for something they lust after (*equiv.* to eye something / to be on the lookout for something) ▌A: 지금 팀장 자리가 비어 있는데, 다음 팀장은 누가 될까? = *The post of chief is vacant. Who will be the next chief?* B: 글쎄 ……. **호시탐탐** 그 자리를 노리는 사람도 많을 텐데. = *Well, I'm sure there are many people with their eye on that post.*

호언장담(하다) [Lit. 豪giant + 言word + 壯grand + 談talk] CHINESE-DERIVATION 자신 있게 큰소리치다 = to speak loudly with confidence (*equiv.* to make a big noise) ▌A: 어? 여기가 아닌가? 오랜만에 왔더니 길이 헷갈리네. = *Huh? Wasn't this the place. Coming here after so long, I'm all confused.* B: 자기만 믿으라고 **호언장담하더니**! = *What? You made a big noise about how I should just trust you.*

호위호식(하다) CHINESE-DERIVATION '호의호식(하다)'의 잘못된 말 = an incorrect form of 호의호식(하다)

호의호식(하다) [Lit. 好good + 衣clothes + 好good + 食meal → to wear nice clothes and eat good food] CHINESE-DERIVATION 편하고 안락한 생활을 하다 = to live a comfortable and relaxed life ▌A: 세상은 불공평해. 나는 이렇게 열심히 일해도 가난을 못 벗어나는데 부모 잘 만난 사람은 평생 **호의호식하잖아**. = *The world is so unfair. I work this hard and can never break free of poverty, while people who were born into a rich household live in the lap of luxury.* B: 그래도 우리에게 로또가 있잖아. 로또나 사러 가자. = *Well, at least there's always the lottery for people like us. Let's go buy some lottery tickets.*

호적에 빨간 줄(이) 그이다 [Lit. for there to be a red line on one's family register] IDIOM 죄를 지어 감옥에 갔다 오다 = to serve time in prison for a crime (*syn.* 별(을) 달다) ▌A: 어제 운전하다가 하마터면 사람을 칠 뻔했어요. = *Yesterday while I was driving I almost crashed into someone.* B: 저런. **호적에 빨간 줄 그일** 뻔했네. = *How terrible! You almost brought shame on your family.*

NOTE: 호적은 가족의 이름이나 주소, 생일 따위를 기록하는 문서를 말한다. 2008년부터는 가족관계등록부라는 이름으로 바뀌었다. 죄를 지어 전과가 남았다고 해서 호적에 빨간 줄로 표시가 된 적은 없었다고 한다. 다만, 호적이 가족 전체의 신분을 증명하는 문서라는 점에서 보면, 전과 기록이 개인뿐 아니라 가족 전체에 불명예로 남게 될 것을 경계하는 뜻에서 생겨난 표현이 아닌가 싶다. The 호적 is a document that contains all the names, addresses, and birthdays of a family. In 2008 the name of this document was changed to 가족관계등록부. They say that if one commits a crime, they have a criminal record and therefore there was never any need to draw a red line in this record. Considering, however, that this document holds the identity of everyone in a family, it seems as though this expression evolved as a precautionary statement that if a member of the family committed a crime, it would besmirch the honor of the entire extended clan.

호주머니(를) 털다 IDIOM =주머니(를) 털다

혹 떼러 갔다 혹 붙여 온다 [Lit. to go out to have a cyst extracted and come back with one (more) attached] PROVERB 자기의 부담을 덜려고 하다가 다른 일까지도 맡게 되었을 때 쓰는 말=describes a situation in which one was trying to shirk a responsibility but ended up saddled with even more responsibility (*equiv.* to go out for wool and come home shorn) ▌A: 돈 있으면 빌려 달라고 하려고 희경이 집에 갔는데, 걔 집 사정이 말이 아니더라고.=*I went over to Heegyeong's house to see if she could lend me some money, but the situation over there is bad beyond words.* B: 그래서 어쨌어?=*So, what did you do?* A: 내가 갖고 있던 돈도 주고 왔지.=*I gave her all the money I had on me.* B: **혹 떼러 갔다 혹 붙여 온** 꼴이구나.=*Wow, that plan kind of backfired on you.*

혹(을) 달다 [Lit. to have a cyst attached to one] IDIOM 예전 배우자와의 사이에서 낳은 자식이 있다=to have a child from a previous marriage when one is getting remarried ▌A: 우리 민수도 이제 재혼을 해야 할 텐데.=*I think it's about time Minsu got remarried.* B: 마침 좋은 사람이

있는데 아이가 한 명 있어요. = *Well, I know a good woman, but she has a child from a previous marriage.* A: **혹을 달고** 있는 게 흠이군. = *Yes, already having a child could be a problem.*

혼비백산(하다) [Lit. 魂spirit + 飛fly + 魄spirit + 散disperse] CHINESE-DERIVATION **▶p.192** 몹시 놀라다 = to be extremely surprised ▌A: 어제 회사 땡땡 이치고 사우나 갔는데 글쎄 사장님이 들어오시는 거야. = *Yesterday I ditched work and went to the sauna. And who should I see but the boss himself.* B: 하하. 그래서 어떻게 했어? = *Ha ha. So, what did you do?* A: **혼비백산해서** **▶p.110** 꽁무니를 뺐지. = *I was so shocked I just hightailed it out of there.*

혼연일체 [Lit. 渾mixed + 然so + 一one + 體body] CHINESE-DERIVATION 생각 이나 행동이 완전히 하나가 된 상태 = one's words and actions being in perfect accord (*equiv.* to be as one) ▌A: 정말 멋진 연주였어. 그렇지? = *It was a beautiful performance. Don't you think?* B: 응. 연주자랑 악기가 **혼연일체**가 된 것 같더라니까. = *Yeah, It's like she was one with her instrument.*

홀홀단신 CHINESE-DERIVATION '혈혈단신'의 잘못된 말 = an incorrect form of 혈혈단신

홍당무가 되다 [Lit. to become a carrot] IDIOM 부끄럽거나 술에 취해 얼 굴이 빨개지다 = for one's face to be red with shame or due to drunkenness (*equiv.* to be flushed / to be red as a beet) ▌A: 너는 친구들 앞에서는 말 잘하면서 왜 여자 앞에만 가면 **홍당무가 돼서** 말도 못하냐? = *You are such a smooth talker in front of your friends. Why is it that you turn red as a beet in front of women?* B: 몰라. 그냥 부끄러운 걸 어떡해. = *I don't know. I just get really shy and there's nothing I can do about it.*

홍역을 치르다 [Lit. to get the measles] IDIOM 몹시 애를 먹거나 어려움 을 겪다 = to put a great amount of effort into something or undergo hardship (*equiv.* to go through hell / to be put through the wringer) ▌A: 이번 수능에 서 또 문제 오류가 발견됐대. 들었어? = *They found another error on*

this year's college entrance exam. Did you hear? B: 응. 교육계가 큰 **홍역을 치르겠군**. = *Yeah, the academic world is going through the wringer again.*

NOTE: 홍역은 과거 한국에서 자주 걸렸던 급성 전염병으로 영아 사망률이 매우 높았다. 대신 낫고 나면 면역이 되어 평생 다시 걸리지는 않는다. 한 번은 겪어야 하는 어려움이라는 의미로 쓰인다.
The measles often plagued the Korea of old and as a highly infectious disease, killed many infants. On the other hand, those that survive it, develop an immunity and never have to go though that experience again. This phrase is used to describe the kind of hardship that everyone has to go through at least once.

화살을 돌리다 [Lit. to turn the arrow around] IDIOM 비난이나 공격을 다른 쪽으로 돌리다 = to turn someone's attacks in another direction (*equiv.* to deflect someone's attack) ▌A: 너, 민수랑 싸웠다며? = *I heard you got in a fight with Minsu?* B: 어. 이게 다 너 때문이야. 네가 우리 둘 문제에 끼어드니까 이렇게 됐잖아. = *Yeah. It's all your fault. This is because you got involved in our problems.* A: 왜 갑자기 **화살을 나한테 돌리는** 거야? = *Why are you suddenly pointing the finger at me?*

화촉을 밝히다 [Lit. to light the wedding candles] IDIOM 결혼식을 올리다 = to have a wedding ceremony ▌A: 연예 뉴스를 전해 드리겠습니다. 탤런트 김영호 씨와 이정아 씨가 오늘 결혼식을 올렸습니다. = *Now it's time for some celebrity news. Kim Yeongho and Lee Jeongah were married today.* B: 신랑과 신부는 10년의 열애 끝에 오늘 드디어 **화촉을 밝히게** 되었습니다. = *They finally walked down the aisle today after a 10-year romance.*

화통(을) 삶아 먹다 [Lit. to boil and eat a funnel] IDIOM 목소리가 크다 = to have a very loud voice ▌A: 엄마, 밥 줘! = *Mom, give me some food!* B: 애가 **화통을 삶아 먹었나**, 오늘따라 왜 이렇게 목소리가 커? = *Did you swallow a bullhorn? Why's your voice so loud today?*

확고부동(하다) [Lit. 確certain + 固firm + 不no + 動move] CHINESE-DERIVATION 뜻이 분명하고 단단하다 = for one's intentions to be concrete ▌A: 좀 설득해 봤어? = *Did you try to persuade him?* B: 했는데 소용없어요. 뜻이 아주 **확고부동해요**. = *I tried, but it was no use. He's resolute.*

활개(를) 치다 [Lit. to flap one's wings] IDIOM 1. 부정적인 것이 성행하다 = for something undesirable to run rampant ▌A: 인터넷이 발달하면서 음란물이 **활개를 치고** 있어서 큰일이에요. = *Pornography running rampant after the rise of the Internet is a major problem.* B: 아이들 키우기도 점점 힘들어지는 것 같아요. = *It's getting harder and harder to raise children in this world.* 2. 새가 날개를 펼쳐서 퍼덕이다 = (for a bird) to beat its wings ▌A: 너 키우던 새 날려 보내줬다며? = *I heard you freed that bird you raised.* B: 어. 왠지 좀 불쌍해서. **활개 치면서** 뒤도 안 돌아보고 가 버리더라. = *Yeah, I just felt bad for it. It just flapped its wings and flew away without even looking back.*

활개(를) 펴다 [Lit. to spread one's wings] IDIOM 남의 눈치를 보지 않고 당당하게 행동하다 = to not consider what others think and act in a dignified manner (*equiv.* to let one's hair down) ▌A: 우리도 언젠가 남들처럼 **활개를 펴고** 살 수 있을까? = *Will we ever be able to just let our hair down?* B: 그럼. 지금 조금만 더 고생하면 돼. = *Of course. We're almost there. Just keep working hard for a little longer.*

획을 긋다 [Lit. to make a brush stroke] IDIOM 그 전과 후를 구분 지을 정도로 중요한 업적을 남기다 = to perform a deed so great that times are labeled before or after it ▌A: 제 은사이신 김 교수님은 한국어 분야에서 큰 **획을** 그으신 분입니다. = *My mentor in the Korean language field, Prof. Kim, left his mark on the academic world.* B: 훌륭한 분께 배우셨군요. = *Wow, you really learned from someone special.*

NOTE: 보통 '한 획을 긋다', '큰 획을 긋다'와 같은 형태로 쓰인다.
This phrase is most often used in the forms, 한 획을 긋다 and 큰 획을 긋다.

횡설수설(하다) [Lit. 橫horizontal + 說say + 竪vertical + 說say → calling something horizontal and then calling it vertical] CHINESE-DERIVATION 앞뒤가 맞지 않는 말을 지껄이다＝to prattle on nonsensically ▌A: 쟤 도대체 뭐라고 하는 거야?＝*Just what is that guy talking about?* B: 나도 모르겠어. 술 마시고 **횡설수설하는** 소리를 알아들을 수가 있어야지.＝*I don't know either. How am I supposed to understand the nonsense that guy speaks when he's drunk?*

흐르는 물은 썩지 않는다 [Lit. Flowing water doesn't putrefy.] PROVERB 늘 노력하고 활동을 해야 뒤처지지 않는다는 말＝used to suggest constant activity and effort to keep from falling behind (*cf.* 구르는 돌에는 이끼가 끼지 않는다) ▌A: 연기에 노래, 이제 코미디까지 이렇게 여러 분야에 도전하시는 특별한 이유가 있나요?＝*You started off with acting, then singing, and now comedy. Is there a special reason that you continue to challenge yourself in so many different fields?* B: 제 좌우명이 '흐르는 물은 썩지 않는다'거든요.＝*My motto is "flowing water stays fresh."*

흑백을 가리다 [Lit. to distinguish between black and white] IDIOM 옳고 그름을 따지다＝to delineate right and wrong ▌A: 엄마, 엄마가 말해 줘. 형이랑 나랑 누가 잘못한 거야?＝*Mom, Mom, tell me. Who's fault was it, mine or his?* B: 너희는 형제끼리 꼭 사사건건 **흑백을 가려야겠니**? 어서 들어가서 공부나 해.＝*Do you two always have to bicker about who was right and wrong? Hurry up and study.*

흙(을) 파서 장사하다 IDIOM＝땅(을) 파서 장사하다

희로애락 [Lit. 喜happy + 怒angry + 哀sad + 樂enjoy → happiness, anger, sadness, pleasure] CHINESE-DERIVATION 사람이 살아가면서 느끼게 되는 여러 가지 감정＝all the feelings people may feel as they go through life (*equiv.* the gamut of human emotion) ▌A: 너는 야구를 왜 좋아해?＝*Why do you like baseball?* B: 야구는 인생과 같거든. **희로애락**이 그대로 다 녹아 있어.＝*Because baseball is like life: it's infused with all human emotions.*

희비가 교차하다 IDIOM = 희비가 엇갈리다

희비가 엇갈리다 [Lit. for happiness and sadness to cross paths] IDIOM 기쁨과 슬픔이 동시에 나타나 극명하게 대조되다 = to experience bittersweet feelings (*syn.* 희비가 교차하다, 명암이 엇갈리다, 명암이 교차하다) ▌A: 참 승부라는 건 잔인한 거야. 아까 결과 발표될 때 두 선수 표정 봤어? = *Swim or sink—it's a cruel world out there. Did you see their expressions when the results were announced?* B: 응. 얼굴에 극명하게 **희비가 엇갈리더라**. = *Yeah, it was like immense joy and sorrow had met on the same stage.*

Index by Korean Keyword

계산기

계산기(를) 두드리다 53

고개

고개가 수그러지다 54
고개를 갸웃거리다 54
고개를 내밀다 54
고개를 들다 54
고개를 못 들다 55
고개(를) 숙이다 55
벼는 익을수록 **고개**를 숙인다 311

고기

고기는 씹어야 맛이고 말은 해야 맛
이다 55
고기도 먹어 본 사람이 많이 먹는다
56
그물에 든 **고기** 91
까마귀 **고기**를 먹었나 104
물 만난 **고기** 270
물이 너무 맑으면 **고기**가 없다 274

고래

고래(를) 잡다 56
고래 싸움에 새우 등 터진다 57

고무신

고무신(을) 거꾸로 신다 57

고배

고배를 들다 57
고배를 마시다 58

고삐

고삐가 풀리다 58
고삐를 늦추다 58

고사

고사(를) 지내다 59

고사리

고사리 같은 손 59

고생

고생 끝에 낙이 온다 60
고생을 사서 하다 60
사서 **고생**(을)하다 337
젊어서 **고생**은 사서도 한다 483

고스톱

짜고 치는 **고스톱** 513

고슴도치

고슴도치도 제 새끼는 예쁘다고 한
다 61

고양이

고양이 목에 방울 달기 61
고양이 세수 62
고양이 앞의 쥐 62
고양이에게 생선 가게 맡긴 격 63
고양이 쥐 생각 63
얌전한 **고양이** 부뚜막에 먼저 올라
간다 408
쥐도 궁지에 몰리면 **고양이**를 문다
502

고추

눈꼴(이)시다 136

눈높이

눈높이가 낮다 136
눈높이가 높다 136
눈높이를 낮추다 136
눈높이를 높이다 136
눈높이를 맞추다 136

눈독

눈독(을) 들이다 137

눈물

남의 눈에 눈물 내면 제 눈에는 피눈
　물이 난다 121
눈물이 앞을 가리다 139
병아리 눈물만큼 315
피눈물(을) 흘리다 550
피도 눈물도 없다 550

눈살

눈살(을) 찌푸리다 139

눈썹

눈썹도 까딱 안 하다 139
눈썹이 휘날리게 달려오다 139

눈앞

눈앞에 선하다 139
눈앞에 아른거리다 140
눈앞이 깜깜하다 140
눈앞이 캄캄하다 140

눈총

눈총(을) 맞다 151

눈총(을) 받다 151
눈총(을) 주다 151

눈치

눈칫밥(을) 먹다 151

능선

~ 부 능선을 넘다 318
~ 분 능선을 넘다 319

늪

늪에 빠지다 152

다람쥐

다람쥐 쳇바퀴 돌듯 153

다리[1]

다리야 날 살려라 154
두 다리(를) 쭉 뻗고 자다 175
상다리가 부러지다 345
상다리가 휘어지다 345
양다리(를) 걸치다 409

다리[2]

다리(를) 놓다 154
돌다리도 두드려 보고 건너라 169
원수는 외나무다리에서 만난다 442

다홍

기왕이면 다홍치마 101
이왕이면 다홍치마 451

단추

첫 단추를 끼우다 520

도둑

도둑이 제 발 저리다 163
바늘 도둑이 소도둑 된다 284

도둑질

늦게 배운 도둑질에 날 새는 줄 모른다 152
도둑질을 해도 손발이 맞아야 한다 164

도랑

도랑 치고 가재 잡기 164

도루묵

말짱 도루묵 226

도마

도마 위에 오르다 165

도매금

도매금으로 넘기다 165

도시락

도시락 싸 가지고 다니면서 말린다 165

도장

도장(을) 찍다 166

도토리

개밥에 도토리 44
도토리 키 재기 166

독

독 안에 든 쥐 167
밑 빠진 독에 물 붓기 279
쌀독에서 인심 난다 390

독(毒)

독을 품다 168
독(이) 오르다 168

돈

눈먼 돈 138
돈방석에 앉다 168
돈벼락(을) 맞다 168
돈을 물쓰듯 하다 168
돈이 나오냐 밥이 나오냐? 169
돈이 썩어 나다 169
일확천금 457
주머닛돈이 쌈짓돈 494
코 묻은 돈 531

돌

구르는 돌에는 이끼가 끼지 않는다 73
굴러 온 돌이 박힌 돌 뺀다 78
돌다리도 두드려 보고 건너라 169
돌(을) 던지다 169
모난 돌이 정 맞는다 245
일석이조 454
타산지석 537

동

동문서답(하다) 170
동분서주하다 171
동서고금 171
동에 번쩍 서에 번쩍 171
마이동풍 212

불난 집에 **부채**질한다 321

부처

뛰어 봤자 **부처**님 손바닥 201

북

뒷**북**치다 182
북 치고 장구 치고 319

분

분초를 다투다 320

불

강 건너 **불**구경 40
강 건너 **불** 보듯 40
급한 **불**을 끄다 96
눈에 **불**을 켜다 142
눈에(서) **불**이 나다 143
맞**불**(을) 놓다 230
물과 **불** 269
물**불**(을) 가리지 않다 270
발등에 **불**이 떨어지다 292
발등의 **불**을 끄다 292
발바닥에 **불**이 나다 293
발에 **불**이 나다 294
불(을) 보듯 뻔하다 322
불(을) 보듯 훤하다 322
빨간**불**이 켜지다 329
파란**불**이 켜지다 544

불꽃

불꽃(이) 튀다 320

불똥

불똥(이) 튀다 321

불씨

불씨가 꺼지지 않다 321
불씨가 남아 있다 321
불씨가 되다 322

붓

붓을 꺾다 323
붓을 놓다 323

비

가랑**비**에 옷 젖는 줄 모른다 20
가물에 단**비** 21
눈이 오나 **비**가 오나 150
비가 오나 눈이 오나 323
비 온 뒤에 땅이 굳어진다 324
우후죽순 439

비단

금상첨화 94
금수강산 94
금의환향(하다) 95

비행기

비행기(를) 태우다 324

빈대

빈대도 낯짝이 있다 325
빈대 붙다 325
빈대 잡으려다 초가삼간 다 태운다
   325

빙산

빙산의 일각 326

빛

말 한마디에 천 냥 **빚**도 갚는다　227

빛

빛을 발하다　327
빛을 보다　327
빛을 잃다　327
빛(이)바래다　327
빛 좋은 개살구　327

빨강

빨간불이 켜지다　329
적신호가 켜지다　479
호적에 빨간 줄(이) 그이다　572

뺨

종로에서 뺨 맞고 한강(에) 가서 눈
흘긴다　489

뼈

뼈(가) 빠지게 일하다　330
뼈(가) 있다　330
뼈도 못 추리다　331
뼈를 깎다　331
뼈를 묻다　331
뼈만 남다　331
뼈에 사무치다　332
뼈와 가죽뿐이다　332
뼈와 살이 되다　332
잔뼈가 굵다　476

뽕

임도 보고 뽕도 딴다　457

뿌리

기둥뿌리(가) 뽑히다　99
기둥뿌리(를) 뽑다　99
뿌리(가) 깊다　332
뿌리(를) 내리다　333
뿌리(를) 뽑다　333

뿔

못된 송아지 엉덩이에 뿔 난다　257
쇠뿔도 단김에 빼라　378

사

사면초가　336
사족을 못 쓰다　339
조삼모사　488

사공

사공이 많으면 배가 산으로 간다
334

사돈

사돈 남 말 한다　334
사돈의 팔촌　335

사람

고기도 먹어 본 사람이 많이 먹는다
56
떡 줄 사람은 생각도 없는데 김칫국
부터 마신다　197
법 없이도 살 사람　309
사람들 눈이 있다　335
사람(을) 잡다　335
사람(이)되다　336
생사람(을) 잡다　347
선무당이 사람 잡는다　350

설마가 **사람** 잡는다 351

안되는 **사람**은 뒤로 넘어져도 코가 깨진다 400

열 길 물속은 알아도 한 길 **사람** 속은 모른다 423

털어서 먼지 안 나는 **사람** 없다 538

호랑이는 죽어서 가죽을 남기고 **사람**은 죽어서 이름을 남긴다 569

사랑

며느리 **사랑**은 시아버지 242

사위 **사랑**은 장모 338

사위

사위는 백년손님이다 337

사위 사랑은 장모 338

사자

사자 없는 산에 토끼가 왕 노릇 한다 338

사촌

먼 **사촌**보다 가까운 이웃이 낫다 239

사촌이 땅을 사면 배가 아프다 339

사흘

사흘이 멀다 하고 340

산

금강**산**도 식후경 93

넘어야 할 **산**이 많다 128

사공이 많으면 배가 **산**으로 간다 334

사자 없는 **산**에 토끼가 왕 노릇 한다 338

산 넘어 산이다 340

산전수전 341

산해진미 342

첩첩**산**중 520

청**산**유수 522

타**산**지석 537

산통

산통(을) 깨다 341

산통(이) 깨지다 342

살

뼈와 **살**이 되다 332

살을 깎다 342

살을 붙이다 342

살을 섞다 343

제 **살** 깎아 먹기 487

피가 되고 **살**이 되다 549

삶

구사일**생** 74

기사회**생**(하다) 100

사**생**결단 337

삼

빈대 잡으려다 초가**삼**간 다 태운다 325

삼삼오오 343

삼척동자 343

서당개 **삼** 년이면 풍월을 읊는다 348

작심**삼**일 475

조삼모사 488

삼십육

삼십육계 343

삼천

척하면 삼천리 516

삼천포

삼천포로 빠지다 344

삽

삽질(을)하다 344
첫 삽을 뜨다 521

상

상다리가 부러지다 345
상다리가 휘어지다 345

새

낮말은 새가 듣고 밤말은 쥐가 듣는
　다 123
높이 나는 새가 멀리 본다 130
새 발의 피 345
일석이조 454
일찍 일어나는 새가 벌레를 잡는다
　455
쥐도 새도 모르게 502

새끼

개미새끼 하나(도) 얼씬 못하다 43
개미새끼 하나 볼 수 없다 43
고슴도치도 제 새끼는 예쁘다고 한
　다 61
미운 오리 새끼 278

호랑이 새끼를 키우다 570

새우

고래 싸움에 새우 등 터진다 57

생각

고양이 쥐 생각 63
과대망상 70
꿈에도 생각하지 못하다 113
떡 줄 사람은 생각도 없는데 김칫국
　부터 마신다 197
생각이 짧다 347

생선

고양이에게 생선 가게 맡긴 격 63

샴페인

샴페인을 너무 일찍 터뜨리다 348

서

동문서답(하다) 170
동분서주하다 171
동서고금 171
동에 번쩍 서에 번쩍 171
해가 서쪽에서 뜨겠다 565

서리

된서리를 맞다 173
설상가상 351
여자가 한을 품으면 오뉴월에도 서
　리가 내린다 422

서슬

서슬이 시퍼렇다 348

쌍심지

눈에 **쌍심지**를 켜다 143

쌍지팡이

쌍지팡이(를) 들고 나서다 390
쌍지팡이(를) 짚고 나서다 390

쐐기

쐐기(를) 박다 392

쑥대

쑥대밭을 만들다 392
쑥대밭이 되다 392

쓸개

간**담**이 서늘하다 32
간도 **쓸개**도 없다 32
간에 붙었다 **쓸개**에 붙었다 하다 33
쓸개(가) 빠지다 393

씨

말이 **씨**가 된다 226
씨가 마르다 393
씨를 말리다 394

아내

조강지**처** 488

아들

그 아버지에 그 **아들** 92
부전**자**전 318

아버지

그 **아버지**에 그 아들 92

부전**자**전 318

아우

형만 한 **아우** 없다 569

아이

미운 **아이** 떡 하나 더 준다 277
아이 브는 데는 찬물도 못 먹는다
 399
우는 **아이** 젖 준다 437

아저씨

까마귀가 **아저씨** 하겠다 104

아침

조삼모사 488

악

권선징**악** 81
극**악**무도하다 92

안개

안개 속 400
오리무중 430

안경

색**안경**(을) 끼다 347
색**안경**(을) 쓰다 347
제 눈에 **안경** 485

알

꿩 먹고 **알** 먹기 115
낙동강 오리**알** 119

암초

자충수를 두다 474

작살

작살(을)내다 475
작살(이)나다 475

잔

쓴잔을 들다 393
쓴잔을 마시다 393
잔을 기울이다 476

잔치

남의 잔치에 감 놓아라 배 놓아라 한
  다 122
소문난 잔치에 먹을 것 없다 358

장

구더기 무서워 장 못 담글까 72
뚝배기보다 장맛이다 200
손가락에 장(을) 지지다 365
손에 장(을) 지지다 372

장구

맞장구(를) 치다 230
북 치고 장구 치고 319
선무당이 장구 탓한다 350

장군

장군 멍군 477

장날

가는 날이 장날 17

장님

눈뜬장님 138

장님 코끼리 만지기 477

장단

어느 장단에 춤을 춰야 할지 모르겠
  다 412
장단(을) 맞추다 478
장단이 맞다 478

장모

사위 사랑은 장모 338

장사

땅(을) 파서 장사하다 190
밑지는 장사 280
흙(을) 파서 장사하다 577

장사(壯士)

세월 앞에 장사 없다 355

장수

엿장수 마음대로 425

재

재(를) 뿌리다 478
한줌(의) 재가 되다 564

재갈

입에 재갈(을) 물리다 464

재수

재수 없는 놈은 뒤로 자빠져도 코가
  깨진다 478

재주

굼벵이도 구르는 재주가 있다 80

한국어 관용어 사전

초판 3쇄 인쇄 2019년 8월 27일
초판 3쇄 발행 2019년 9월 6일

지은이 Kyubyong Park(박규병), Michael Elliott(마이클 엘리엇)
펴낸이 서덕일
펴낸곳 도서출판 문예림

출판등록 1962.7.12 (제406-1962-1호)
주소 경기도 파주시 회동길 366 3층 (10881)
전화 (02)499-1281~2 **팩스** (02)499-1283
대표전자우편 info@moonyelim.com **통합홈페이지** www.moonyelim.com
카카오톡 ("도서출판 문예림" 검색 후 추가)

디지털노마드의 시대, 문예림은 Remote work(원격근무)를 시행하고 있습니다.
우리는 세계 곳곳에 있는 집필진과 원하는 장소와 시간에 자유롭게 일합니다.
문의 사항은 카카오톡 또는 이메일로 말씀해주시면 답변드리겠습니다.

값 28,000원

ISBN 978-89-7482-712-0(13710)